A FREEplace to learn FINANCE

• The Math Practice Center

DON'T LET MATH STAND IN THE WAY OF A GOOD GRADE!

Created by Dr. Puneet Handa of the University of Iowa, FinCoach has been proven to improve students' grades by enabling them to learn and practice the math of finance on their own time and at their own speed.

• Career Center

EXPLORE THE WORKING WORLD OF FINANCE!

"A Day in the Life" profiles how finance professionals use the concepts that students are currently learning to improve personal interviewing skills, survey the job market, and more!

MODERN CORPORATE FINANCE

A Multidisciplinary Approach to Value Creation

Alan C. Shapiro

University of Southern California

Sheldon D. Balbirer

University of North Carolina at Greensboro

Prentice Hall
Upper Saddle River, New Jersey 07458

Acquisitions Editor: Paul Donnelly
Associate Editor: Gladys Soto
Editorial Director: James C. Boyd
Editor-in-Chief: PJ Boardman
Editorial Assistant: Cheryl Clayton
Marketing Manager: Lori Braumberger
Associate Managing Editor: Cynthia Regan
Manufacturing Buyer: Lisa DiMaulo
Senior Manufacturing Supervisor: Paul Smolenski
Manufacturing Manager: Vincent Scelta
Senior Designer: Kevin Kall
Design Manager: Patricia Smythe
Interior/Cover Design: Karen Quigley
Illustrator (Interior): Omegatype Typography, Inc.
Cover Illustration/Photo: Burstein Goldman/The Stock Rep., Inc.
Composition: Omegatype Typography, Inc.

Library of Congress Cataloging-in-Publication Data
Shapiro, Alan C.
    Modern corporate finance : a multidisciplinary approach to
value creation / Alan C. Shapiro, Sheldon D. Balbirer.
      p. cm.
    Includes bibliographical references and index.
    ISBN 0-13-080098-8
    1. Corporations—Finance.   I. Balbirer, Sheldon D.   II. Title.
HG4011.S445   2000
658.15—dc21   99-34674

                        CIP
                        Rev.

Prentice-Hall International (UK) Limited, London
Prentice-Hall of Australia Pty. Limited, Sydney
Prentice-Hall Canada, Inc., Toronto
Prentice-Hall Hispanoamericana, S.A., Mexico
Prentice-Hall of India Private Limited, New Delhi
Prentice-Hall of Japan, Inc., Tokyo
Prentice-Hall (Singapore) Pte. Ltd.
Editora Prentice-Hall do Brasil, Ltda., Rio de Janeiro

Printed in the United States of America

10 9 8 7 6 5 4 3 2

Calculator Guide for Financial Management

Note: See that the memory is cleared; you are in the correct mode for financial calculations; P/Y = 1.00 (if relevant); and you have adequate decimal places.

Compound Sum of $1: $FVIF_{i,n} = \$1(1+i)^n$

Texas Instruments BAII Plus

1 | +/– | PV | (No. of periods (Days, mths., or yrs.)) | N | (Interest rate per period) | I/Y | 0 | PMT | CPT | FV | → ANSWER

Texas Instruments BAII

1 | +/– | PV | (No. of periods (Days, mths., or yrs.)) | N | (Interest rate per period) | %i | 0 | PMT | 2nd | FV | → ANSWER

Texas Instruments BA-35

1 | +/– | PV | (No. of periods (Days, mths., or yrs.)) | N | (Interest rate per period) | %i | 0 | PMT | CPT | FV | → ANSWER

Hewlett-Packard HP-10B (%YR replaces I/YR for HP-17B II, HP-19B II)

1 | +/– | PV | (No. of periods (Days, mths., or yrs.)) | N | (Interest rate per period) | I/YR | 0 | PMT | FV | → ANSWER

Hewlett-Packard HP-12C

1 | CHS | PV | (No. of periods (Days, mths., or yrs.)) | N | (Interest rate per period) | i | 0 | PMT | FV | → ANSWER

Present Value of $1: $PVIF_{i,n} = \dfrac{\$1}{(1+i)^n}$

Texas Instruments BAII Plus

1 | +/– | FV | (No. of periods (Days, mths., or yrs.)) | N | (Interest rate per period) | I/Y | 0 | PMT | CPT | PV | → ANSWER

Texas Instruments BAII

1 | +/– | FV | (No. of periods (Days, mths., or yrs.)) | N | (Interest rate per period) | %i | 0 | PMT | 2nd | PV | → ANSWER

Texas Instruments BA-35

1 | +/– | FV | (No. of periods (Days, mths., or yrs.)) | N | (Interest rate per period) | %i | 0 | PMT | CPT | PV | → ANSWER

Hewlett-Packard HP-10B (%YR replaces I/YR for HP-17B II, HP-19B II)

1 | +/– | FV | (No. of periods (Days, mths., or yrs.)) | N | (Interest rate per period) | I/YR | 0 | PMT | PV | → ANSWER

Hewlett-Packard HP-12C

1 | CHS | FV | (No. of periods (Days, mths., or yrs.)) | N | (Interest rate per period) | i | 0 | PMT | PV | → ANSWER

Sum of an Annuity of $1:

$$FVIFA_{i,n} = \$1 \sum_{t=0}^{n-1} (1+i)^t = \$1 \left[\frac{(1+i)^n - 1}{i} \right]$$

Texas Instruments BAII Plus

1 [+/-] [PMT] (No. of periods (Days, mths., or yrs.)) [N] (Interest rate per period) [I/Y] 0 [PV] [CPT] [FV] → ANSWER

Texas Instruments BAII

1 [+/-] [PMT] (No. of periods (Days, mths., or yrs.)) [N] (Interest rate per period) [%i] 0 [PV] [2nd] [FV] → ANSWER

Texas Instruments BA-35

1 [+/-] [PMT] (No. of periods (Days, mths., or yrs.)) [N] (Interest rate per period) [%i] 0 [PV] [CPT] [FV] → ANSWER

Hewlett-Packard HP-10B ([I% YR] replaces [I/YR] for HP-17B II, HP-19B II)

1 [+/-] [PMT] (No. of periods (Days, mths., or yrs.)) [N] (Interest rate per period) [I/YR] 0 [PV] [FV] → ANSWER

Hewlett-Packard HP-12C

1 [CHS] [PMT] (No. of periods (Days, mths., or yrs.)) [N] (Interest rate per period) [i] 0 [PV] [FV] → ANSWER

Present Value of an Annuity of $1:

$$PVIFA_{i,n} = \left(\sum_{t=1}^{n} \frac{\$1}{(1+i)^t} \right) = \$1 \left[\frac{(1+i)^n - 1}{i(1+i)^n} \right]$$

Texas Instruments BAII Plus

1 [+/-] [PMT] (No. of periods (Days, mths., or yrs.)) [N] (Interest rate per period) [I/Y] 0 [FV] [CPT] [PV] → ANSWER

Texas Instruments BAII

1 [+/-] [PMT] (No. of periods (Days, mths., or yrs.)) [N] (Interest rate per period) [%i] 0 [FV] [2nd] [PV] → ANSWER

Texas Instruments BA-35

1 [+/-] [PMT] (No. of periods (Days, mths., or yrs.)) [N] (Interest rate per period) [%i] 0 [FV] [CPT] [PV] → ANSWER

Hewlett-Packard HP-10B ([I% YR] replaces [I/YR] for HP-17B II, HP-19B II)

1 [+/-] [PMT] (No. of periods (Days, mths., or yrs.)) [N] (Interest rate per period) [I/YR] 0 [FV] [PV] → ANSWER

Hewlett-Packard HP-12C

1 [CHS] [PMT] (No. of periods (Days, mths., or yrs.)) [N] (Interest rate per period) [i] 0 [FV] [PV] → ANSWER

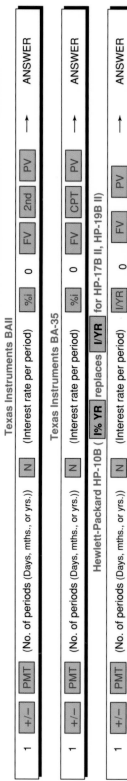

To Diane and Roslyn, our wives,
for their love and support.

Brief Contents*

The following additional topics have been prepared for *Modern Corporate Finance: A Multidisciplinary Approach to Value Creation.* Please check with your instructor to determine whether any of these topics are required reading. They may be copied from the text's homepage found at: *http://www.prenhall.com/financecenter.*

*Note: Answers to the end-of-chapter problems can be found on this text's homepage at: *http://www.prenhall.com/financecenter.*

Contents*

*Note: Answers to the end-of-chapter problems can be found on this text's homepage at: *http://www.prenhall.com/financecenter.*

Chapter 12

Preface

Money has a universal fascination, but few people seem to understand it very well. It is the subject of countless myths, false theories, and illogical beliefs. One of the few organized attempts to study the relationship between money—past, present, and future—and financial markets and financial decision making is provided by the discipline of financial economics. In the course of their work, financial economists have dispelled many of the myths and ad hoc reasoning surrounding traditional financial advice and substituted an insightful and subtle logic firmly grounded in economic analysis.

Our basic objective in writing *Modern Corporate Finance: A Multidisciplinary Approach to Value Creation* is to make accessible to students and practitioners alike the practical implications for mangers of the exciting new theoretical and empirical breakthroughs in financial economics. The book is written to help the reader understand how and why finance matters, regardless of whether the reader intends to pursue a career in finance. We have tried to motivate the non–finance major by illustrating the application of financial analysis and reasoning to problems faced by executives in marketing, operations, and personnel. It is intended for managers and other professionals enrolled in executive MBA and evening MBA programs as well as other executive education programs but is equally suitable for use by first-year MBA students taking their introductory corporate finance course.

Although the book relies on material covered in economics, accounting, and statistics courses, it is self-contained so that prior knowledge of those areas is useful but not essential. The only real prerequisites are algebra and an interest in understanding how the world works.

DISTINCTIVE FEATURES

Modern Corporate Finance identifies the discipline that the external financial market imposes on the financial affairs of the firm. It also attempts to decipher the messages the market sends about the proper objectives of corporate financial decision making and the appropriate tactics and strategies for achieving them. Throughout, the text emphasizes value creation and the role of corporate finance in facilitating this process.

To achieve these aims this book tells finance as a single coherent story, rather than as a collection of short stories. It also includes features that distinguish it from its competitors.

Practical Approach

There is nothing quite so practical as a theory that works. We have tried to reinforce this belief by taking a commonsense approach to finance. This involves showing students *why* the various theories discussed make sense and *how* to use these theories to solve problems. The book relates the subject matter to material students are already familiar with or have learned in previous chapters, making it less intimidating and more interesting. Basic intuition is emphasized throughout.

Numerous Applications of Finance Principles

In keeping with its down-to-earth approach, the textbook contains numerous real-world examples and vignettes that help illustrate the application of financial theories and demonstrate the use of financial analysis and reasoning to solve financial problems. These examples promote understanding of basic theory and add interest to finance.

Appeal to Non–finance Majors

Because so many of the issues dealt with by nonfinancial executives have financial implications, from determining advertising budgets and credit policies to investing in management training programs, it is clear that financial theory has broad application to general management as well. Persuading readers who are not interested in pursuing a career in finance of this is a different matter. We have attempted to motivate these doubting Thomases by using numerous illustrations, scattered throughout the text, of the application of financial analysis to nonfinancial problems. Moreover, we have attempted to concentrate on those aspects of corporate finance that are most important to financial and nonfinancial executives. In this way, we have tried to highlight why the reader should care about the topics covered.

Emphasis on Value Creation

The text emphasizes two related issues: how companies create value and how corporate finance can facilitate the process of value creation. Because this is a book on corporate finance, the focus is on how the financial manager can add value to the firm. The viewpoint taken in this text is that the comparative advantage of the financial manager lies in understanding the intricacies of the modern financial marketplace and using this knowledge to full advantage to manage the firm's financial affairs.

The text's guiding principle is that financial management is subordinate to the "real" business of the firm, which is to produce and sell goods and services. This does not, of course, preclude the financial manager from finding and exploiting profitable opportunities that may occasionally arise in financial markets. It does, however, require that the financial executive be able to recognize when these circumstances exist or are likely to exist. This necessitates a firm grounding in modern finance theory.

Having said all of this, we should recognize that the processes of creating value—particularly shareholder value—and running the "real" business are interrelated. Specifically, firms that are effective at running the real business (by creating value for customers and a productive work environment for employees) should also be in a position to create shareholder value. Thus, the strategic goal of creating competitive advantage and the financial goal of creating shareholder value are two sides of the same coin. This interdisciplinary approach to value creation permeates the text and is unique to this work.

Incorporation of the Human Factor in Finance

Although this text takes its basic driving principle to be the maximization of shareholder wealth, it recognizes that the separation between ownership and control can help explain the frequent discrepancy between observed corporate financial policy and neoclassical economic predictions. This is the topic known as agency theory, and it is utilized to analyze manager–owner and stockholder–bondholder conflicts in professionally managed firms. The material is also useful in helping to understand the wave of corporate restructuring that is now occurring.

By integrating agency theory and its companion, information asymmetry, and their applications throughout, we have tried to illustrate the human factor in financial decision making. The basic perspective taken is that seemingly irrational (from the standpoint of the shareholder) managerial actions can best be understood as the rational response of managers to uncertainty and specific evaluation criteria and mechanisms.

Coverage of International Topics

On a more personal note, we believe that managers must view business from a global perspective; *international* is not just another section of the domestic economy, like office machines or autos, that can be ignored at no cost. Instead, an international orientation has become a business necessity, not a luxury. Those American television manufacturers determined to remain purely domestic operations learned this lesson the hard way; their greatest competitive threat came from companies located 8,000 miles away, across the Pacific, not from other American producers. To facilitate the development of a global perspective, we have tried to integrate domestic and international financial management throughout the book. To the extent we have succeeded, this is one of the distinctive features of the text.

Focused Coverage

The subject matter of this book is focused on those subjects in corporate finance that are critical to an understanding of finance. Focused textbook coverage is a plus for programs that have reduced the amount of time devoted to finance and wish to have a relatively short book that concentrates on the key topics of corporate finance. At the same time, we have taken advantage of the new technology available via the Internet to develop a web site that contains additional topic coverage. The availability of a menu of additional topics on our web site allows instructors to customize a text based on their individual course needs. Students benefit because they can keep the text while having available a broader array of chapters in cyberspace. The combination of the two gives students a comprehensive reference after completing the course.

Numerous Questions and Problems

Another distinctive feature of *Modern Corporate Finance* is the large number of end-of-chapter questions and problems and their close relationship to the material in the chapters. Good conceptual questions are as important as computational problems in promoting understanding, and the ones presented in this text are consistently challenging, interesting, and extremely useful. They provide practical insights into the types of decisions faced by financial executives and offer practice in applying financial concepts and theories.

Additional Features

The textbook also includes a number of other distinguishing features that relate to the subject matter covered; it

- Includes the most comprehensive discussion and illustration of financial statement analysis available; shows students how to conduct a detailed financial analysis and points out the numerous pitfalls involved in such an analysis; provides a unique discussion of the qualitative aspects of corporate control; as well as showing how segmented financial statements can be used to evaluate the performance of individual units of a diversified firm (Chapter 2).
- Emphasizes the distinction between accounting and economic performance (Chapter 2).
- Links financial planning and working capital management to the strategic planning process (Chapter 3)
- Shows the linkages between corporate growth strategies and shareholder value creation, and indicates when such growth can actually dissipate value (Chapter 5).
- Demonstrates how to value a firm using the concept of free cash flow and presents several alternatives to estimate the terminal value using the real-life example of Warner Communications at the time of its acquisition by Time, Inc. (Appendix 5A).
- Indicates the circumstances under which corporate diversification can create value, and when it cannot (Chapter 6).
- Stresses the value of international, as opposed to domestic, diversification (Chapter 6).
- Contains a relatively early introduction to option pricing and contingent claims, which allows these concepts to be used for valuing growth options and

explaining stockholder–bondholder conflicts in later discussions of capital structure and financial strategy (Chapter 7).

■ Features a detailed discussion of estimating project cash flows, including incremental versus total cash flows, the effects of inflation on cash flows, the valuation of foreign projects, and the valuation of growth options. It gives students hands-on experience in estimating project cash flows and helps them gain an appreciation for the real-world difficulties in valuing projects (Chapter 9).

■ Provides a discussion of how the total risk of an investment project can be assessed (Appendix 9A) and how that risk can affect expected cash flows (Chapter 14).

■ Features a discussion of how investment decisions can help create competitive advantage and thereby enhance shareholder value (Chapter 9).

■ Contains a unique chapter on how companies create value—including value-based analysis and corporate restructuring—as well as the links between return on investment, required return on capital invested, and the pricing of stocks. It also deals with issues of executive compensation from a financial standpoint (Chapter 11).

■ Features a detailed presentation of financing patterns of companies around the world and discusses the evolution of these financing patterns, particularly the rise of securitization. This helps to put financing options and patterns into perspective (Chapter 12).

■ Addresses the qualitative factors that determine financial strategy, concentrating on the costs of financial distress and the value of financial flexibility, thereby putting the design of financial packages in perspective (Chapter 14).

ORGANIZATION

Although the ideas underlying financial economics are interrelated, by necessity they must be elaborated individually. Eventually, they must also be integrated because they are all part of a grand framework. To accomplish this objective, the book is arranged so that each chapter builds on the previous material.

To bring the full power of modern finance theory to bear on the subject matter of corporate financial management, we require a unified theory of how and why individuals behave in the presence of choice situations involving limited resources, current versus future consumption, and uncertainty. This is supplied by the general equilibrium framework of financial economics, which attempts to study how all the financial factors mentioned earlier interact simultaneously. We introduce this material in Chapter 1 by discussing a series of deceptively simple principles and then applying those principles to specific problems faced by the modern financial manager. By providing an overview of the basic concepts and principles applicable to the practice of corporate finance in the first chapter, readers have a clear road map of where we are headed and why. This discussion also helps set these ideas in perspective.

Chapters 2 and 3 discuss financial planning and the evaluation and control of operations. Topics include basic financial statements and how management, investors, lenders, and other interested parties can analyze these statements to check on a firm's financial well-being. These chapters also show how financial managers can forecast future financial statements and use these projections to develop an overall financial plan for the firm.

In Chapters 4 to 7, we provide students with a firm grounding in the essentials of modern corporate finance: the time value of money, the pricing of stocks and bonds, portfolio theory and the capital asset pricing model, market efficiency, the nature and pricing of options, and the crucial distinction between accounting profits and cash flow. This material supplies the foundation that enables students to see financial problems from a different frame of reference. Above all else, our aim is to get students to begin thinking in the distinctive way that characterizes the mindset of a financial economist.

Chapters 8 to 11 apply these basic financial principles to the capital-budgeting decision. In these chapters, we are concerned with the most important problem facing management—finding or creating investment projects worth more than they cost. Topics covered include the basics of capital budgeting, the estimation of project cash flows and the project cost of capital, risk analysis in capital budgeting, and corporate strategy and its relationship to the capital-budgeting decision. Throughout these chapters, we emphasize how management creates value for its shareholders.

Chapters 12 to 15 are concerned with developing a long-term financing strategy. They discuss the long-term financing options firms have, how firms go about raising long-term capital, the theory and practice surrounding capital structure, and dividend policy. Throughout these chapters, the emphasis is on how financing can add value.

The web site for this textbook contains coverage of special topics in financial management, including mergers and acquisitions, international finance, leasing, convertibles and warrants, management of working capital (cash management, accounts receivable, and inventory), bankruptcy and reorganization, and financial hedging techniques. These important subjects are treated as applications of concepts and principles developed in the body of the text.

FOR THE STUDENT

The Prentice Hall Finance Center CD

Contained in the inside back cover of this text is the *Prentice Hall Finance Center CD*. This robust learning tool contains the following features, all designed to increase student awareness of what finance professionals do, ensure comprehension and mastery of the financial mathematics contained in the text, and supply a direct link to PHLIP (Prentice Hall Learning on the Internet Partnership).

■ *Careers Center.* Introduces the student to a vast array of professional opportunities in finance through video interviews with professionals and insights into what they do on the job in an average day. Here the student will meet an options trader, a mutual fund manager, investment analysts, a CFO, and others. Also accessible are features for personal development, resume writing, interviewing techniques, and career planning information.

- *FINCOACH—The Financial Math Practice Center.* Contains more than 5 million problems and self-tests in virtually all math areas covered in this text and financial management. Save problems, review them, print them. This is a step-by-step guide to solve any corporate finance mathematics problem and allow the student to rapidly gain mastery in all mathematical challenges.
- *Student Lecture Notes.* Downloadable for printing out, this handy lecture aid for the student contains PowerPoint presentations with space for lecture note taking for each chapter in the text.

FOR THE INSTRUCTOR

- *Instructor's Resource Manual.* Prepared by the authors of the text, this manual contains concise chapter teaching strategies, detailed chapter outlines, additional problems and worked out solutions, and suggested cases from popular external sources. An Instructor's Guide to using PHLIP (Prentice Hall Learning on the Internet Partnership) and a Guide to Using the Prentice Hall Finance Center are also contained in this manual.
- *Solution's Manual.* Prepared by the authors of the text, this manual contains complete answers to end-of-chapter questions and worked out solutions to all problems in the text. This manual will be available for purchase by the student if the instructor so desires.
- *Test Item File.* This file contains over 800 true/false, multiple-choice, and short-answer questions.
- *PH Custom Tests.* Available for both Windows and Macintosh, PH Custom is the computerized version of the test item file. It permits the instructor to edit, add or delete questions from the test item file, and generate their own custom exams.
- *FINCOACH Test Manager and FINCOACH Instructor's Manual.* Test Manager software has been developed to allow instructors to generate tests based on FINCOACH—*The Financial Management Math Practice Program* contained within the Prentice Hall Finance Center CD available to all students using *Corporate Finance.* In addition, an Instructor's Manual for using FINCOACH Test Manager and FINCOACH in the course has been developed and is included with every copy of Test Manager.
- *PowerPoint Presentation.* To encourage more active learning, the slides include sample problems for students to solve in class. The presentations are available from the Prentice Hall PHLIP web site (http://www.prenhall.com/shapiro or http://www.prenhall.com/financecenter).
- Additional materials are available for instructors by clicking "faculty site" in the above referenced URLs for *Corporate Finance.* ID and Password designations are available from the local Prentice Hall representative. These faculty sites include:
  - Instructor's Manual downloadable per chapter.

- Downloadable Excel spreadsheet templates and solutions to all end-of-chapter problems, including solutions to Integrated Problems.

ACKNOWLEDGMENTS

We greatly appreciate the comments and suggestions of the following reviewers: Victor Abraham, Los Angeles Technical College; Anat Admati, Stanford University; Vickie L. Bajtelsmit, Colorado State University; John F. Boschen, College of William and Mary; Richard A. DeFusco, University of Nebraska at Lincoln; Joseph E. Finnerty, University of Illinois at Urbana-Champaign; Delvin D. Hawley, University of Mississippi; Marlin Jensen, Auburn University; Robert Kleiman, Oakland University; Thomas M. Krueger, University of Wisconsin–La Crosse; Surendra Mansinghka, San Francisco State University; William McDaniel, Florida Atlantic University; Joseph Messina, San Francisco State University; L. W. (Bill) Murray, University of San Francisco; Joe Ogden, University of Buffalo; Patricia A. Ryan, Drake University; Scott Smart, Indiana University; Robert Stretcher, Hampton University; Michael Toyne, Northeastern State University; David Volkman, University of Nebraska at Omaha; and Joe Walker, University of Alabama at Birmingham.

We'd like to thank all of the people at Prentice Hall who helped with the project, including Jodi Hirsh, Lori Braumberger, and Gladys Soto. A special thanks goes to our editor, Paul Donnelly, who kept us on task and helped pull the pieces of this project together.

During the development of *Corporate Finance* both Prentice Hall and ourselves benefited immensely from feedback we accumulated from many of our colleagues who teach in the area of corporate finance. This feedback came in the form of responses to a survey conducted in the fall of 1998 and personal conversations. We are most appreciative to all of these individuals for sharing their thoughts and their valuable time with regard to our text. They are Saul Adelman, Miami University; Kofi Amoateng, North Carolina Central University; Leslie Anderson, Portland State University; Thomas Anderson, Kennesaw State University; Tony Apap, University of West Florida; David Arnold, College of the Southwest; Leroy Ashorn, Sam Houston State University; Anthony Avallone, Point Loma Nazarene University; Yu-Jung Avis, College of St. Rose; Curtis Bacon, Southern Oregon University; Sung Bae, Bowling Green State University; Bruce Bagamary, Central Washington University; Dean Baim, Pepperdine University; Ray Baker, Rockford College; Mary Ballantyne, Passaic County Community College; Joel Barber, Florida International University; Marisa Baron, Isothermal Community College; Scottie Barty, Northern Kentucky University; Ron Bealer, Norwalk Community Technical College; Thomas Bear, Stetson University; Kenneth Beller, Washington State University–Tri Cities; Scott Below, East Carolina University; Yvette Bendeck, University of Houston–Clearlake; Gary Benesh, Florida State University; Art Berman, Chemeketa Community College; Robert Berry, University of Houston; Carol Billingham, Central Michigan University; John Bilson, Illinois

Institute of Technology; Michael Binder, Buena Vista University; Homer Bonitsis, New Jersey Institute of Technology; John Boos, Ohio Wesleyan University; Brian Boscaljon, Calvin College; Steve Bouchard, Goldey Beacom College; James Boyd, Kent State University; Michael Boyd, Stetson University; William Brent, Howard University; Billie Brotman, Kennesaw State University; William Brown, Claremont Mckenna College; Richard Brunell, Concordia University; Wayne Buchanan, Alice Lloyd College; Paul Bursik, Saint Norbert College; Alva Butcher, University of Puget Sound; Kirt Butler, Michigan State University; Robert Butler, Olivet College; Joseph Byers, Community College of Allegheny County; Ezra Byler, Millikin University; Tony Byrd, University of Central Florida; Julie Cagle, Xavier University; Alan Carper, Bob Jones University; David Carter, Abilene Christian University; Steven Carvell, Cornell University; Stephen Cassidy, Howard University; Jennifer Caudill, Auburn University; Karen Chambliss, Florida Institute of Technology; P Chandy, University of North Texas; Robert Chatfield, University of Nevada Las Vegas; Leo Cheatham, Northeast Louisiana University; Carl Chen, University of Dayton; Chao Chen, California State University–Northridge; Haiyang Chen, Youngstown State University; Yin-Wong Cheung, University of California Santa Cruz; Andreas Christofi, Monmouth University; Bert Connell, Loma Linda University; C. Mitchell Conover, University of North Carolina–Wilmington; Clyde Cooley, Weber State University; Thomas Corrigan, Sacred Heart University; John Cresson, Northeastern State University; Robert Cullen, Mercyhurst College; Tom Curry, Morningside College; Robbie Dail, Beaufort County Community College; Wallace Davidson, Southern Illinois University–Carbondale; Steve Davis, Northwestern College; Dennis Debrecht, Carroll College; Karen Denning, West Virginia University; Anand Desai, Kansas State University; Les Dlabay, Lake Forest College; David Dubofsky, Virginia Commonwealth University; Martine Duchatelet, Barry University; Mary Ducy, Texas Southern University; John Dunkelberg, Wake Forest University; Michael Dunn, California State University–Northridge; Dan Ebels, University of Michigan–Ann Arbor; David Echevarria, St. Joseph's University; Richard Edelman, American University; Al Eferstein, Lindsey Wilson College; Imad Elhaj, Colorado School of Mines; Barry Ellis, Southeastern Oklahoma State University; Ronel Elul, Brown University; Lisa Fairchild, Loyola College; Hsing Fang, California State University–Los Angeles; Greg Fink, Richard Stockton State College; Peggy Fletcher, Northeastern University; Jennifer Foo, Stetson University; Swint Friday, University of South Alabama; Mark Geiger, William Woods University; Richard Gendreau, Bemidji State University; Tommy Georgiades, Devry Institute of Technology; Bruno Gerard, University of Southern California; John Gerlach, Sacred Heart University; Erika Gilbert, Illinois State University; Preston Gilson, Fort Hays State University; Chris Gingrich, Eastern Mennonite University; Ruth Gitzendanner, Tri State University; David Gordon, Governors State University; Douglas Gordon, Arapahoe Community College; Ray Gorman, Miami University–Oxford; Diane Gregory, Bentley College; Deborah Griest, Lake Tahoe Community College; John Griffith, University of Minnesota–Duluth; Richard Gritta, University of Portland; Russell Grosjean, Erie Community College; Mahmoud Haddad, University of Tennessee–Martin; Richard Halberg, Houghton

College; Dan Hall, East Central College; Karen Hallows, George Mason University; Tom Hannen, College of Notre Dame; Robert Hanson, Eastern Michigan University; Eugene Harris, Hanover College; Rick Harvey, Fairmont State College; Ron Heisner, Kishwaukee College; Larry Heldreth, Danville Community College; Glenn Henderson, University of Cincinnati; Helmut Hergeth, North Carolina State University; Linda Herrington, Community College of Allegheny; George Hicks, Muskingum Area Technical College; Pat Hill, University of Alabama–Birmingham; Bob Hoerber, Westminster College; Marion Hoginboom, Elmhurst College; Leonard Hopkins, Central Carolina Technical College; James Horrell, University of Oklahoma; Ronald Horwitz, Oakland University; Sylvia Hudgins, Old Dominion University; Carl Hudson, Auburn University; Jerry Hunt, East Carolina University; Virginia Ingram, Kennesaw State University; Zahid Iqbal, Texas Southern University; Steven Isberg, University of Baltimore; Thomas Jackman, Nebraska Wesleyan University; Katherine Jackson, Indiana University; John Jahera, Auburn University; Terrance Jalbert, University of Hawaii at Hilo; William Jennings, California State University–Northridge; Jeff Jewell, Lipscomb University; Zhenhu Jin, Illinois Wesleyan University; Craig Johnson, California State University–Hayward; Steve Johnson, University of Texas–El Paso; Dick Johnston, Monmouth College; Alan Jung, San Francisco State University; Ashok Kapoor, Marist College; Janice Karlen, Laguardia Community College; James Kehr, Miami University–Oxford; Alfred Kelly, Northwest Missouri State University; David Ketcham, Bryant College; James Keys, Florida International University; Kashi Khazeh, Salisbury State University; Brian Kluger, University of Cincinnati; John Knight, University of the Pacific; Barbara Kouskoulas, Lawrence Technological University; Jim Krause, University of Tampa; Duncan Kretovich, Eastern Michigan University; Thomas Krueger, University of Wisconsin–La Crosse; Linda Kuechler, Daemen College; Craig Kuhlemeyer, University of Northern Colorado; George Kutner, Marquette University; Frank Laatsch, Bowling Green State University; Gene Lai, University of Rhode Island; John Lajaunie, Nicholls State University; Douglas Lamdin, University of Maryland–Baltimore; Howard Lanser, University of Notre Dame; Martin Laurence, William Paterson College; Joe Lavely, Longwood College; Rick LeCompte, Wichita State University; Kyoo-hwan Lee, Brooklyn College of CUNY; Youngho Lee, Howard University; Elaine Leff, Laguardia Community College; Steven Lifland, Eastern Connecticut State University; Ralph Lim, Sacred Heart University; J. Barry, Lin Husson College; Kenneth Locke, University of Missouri–St. Louis; Raymond Lopez, Pace University; Maria Lorusso, University of Texas–San Antonio; Lynne Luper, Ocean County College; Thomas Lynch, Hocking College; Paul Maloney, Providence College; George Mangiero, Iona College; Susan Mangiero, Sacred Heart University; Inayat Mangla, Western Michigan University; Surendra Mansinghka, San Francisco State University; Timothy Manuel, University of Montana; Jay Marchand, Westminster College; Paul Marshall, Widener University; Don Materniak, Franciscan University; Judy Matteson, Cleary College; Patricia Matthews, Mount Union College; Thomas Maynard, Converse College; Michael Mazzeo, Michigan State University; Anna Mcaleer, Beaver College; Roger McCallister, Touson General Agency; Joseph McCarthy, Keuka College; Gilbert McKee, Cal State Polytech University; Bruce

McManis, Nicholls State University; Kathy McNichol, La Salle University; Gillermo Melendez, Metropolitan University; David Merrifield, Christian Heritage College; Joseph Messina, San Francisco State University; Stuart Michelson, University of Central Florida; David Minars, Brooklyn College of CUNY; John Mitchell, Central Michigan University; Cheryl Mitteness, St. Cloud State University; Naval Modani, University of Central Florida; Timothy Moffitt, Kalamazoo College; Lynn Moller, Kansas Wesleyan University; Robert Monfort, Saint Josephs College; Scott Moore, John Carroll University; Dianne Morrison, University of Wisconsin–La Crosse; Saeed Mortazari, Humboldt State University; Jon Moulton, Oregon State University; David Mullis, University of South Carolina; Laurie Murphy, Flathead Valley Community College; L. William Murray, University of San Francisco; James Nelson, University of Arizona; Randy Nelson, Colby College; William Nelson, Indiana University Northwest; Jeffry Netter, University of Georgia; Chee Ng, Rowan University; Joan Nix, Queens College of CUNY; John Nofsinger, Marquette University; Gary Noreiko, University of Southern Colorado; Jamie O'Brien, South Dakota State University; Oris Odom, University of Texas at Tyler; Jim Owens, West Texas A&M University; R. Daniel, Pace University of West Florida; Therese Pactwa, Florida International University; Roger Palmer, University of St. Thomas; Chang Park, Clinch Valley College; Andrew Parkes, East Central University; Sam Penkar, University of Houston–Downtown; Jonathan Peters, Wagner College; Corey Pfaffe, Maranatha Baptist Bible College; Michael Phillips, Austin Peay State University; Jim Philpot, Ouachita Baptist University; Eugene Poindexter, State University of West Georgia; J. C. Poindexter, North Carolina State University; Thomas Potter, University of North Dakota; Annette Poulsen, University of Georgia; Cynthia Powell, Southern Nazarene University; Rose Prasad, Central Michigan University; John Primus, California State University–Hayward; Richard Proctor, Siena College; Dennis Proffitt, Grand Canyon University; Frances Quinn, Merrimack College; Ganas Rakes, Ohio University–Athens; Kumoli Ramakrishnan, University of South Dakota; Sanjay Ramchander, Minnesota State University Mankato; Ganga Ramdas, Lincoln University; Robert Rainish, University of New Haven; Linda Ravelle, Moravian College; David Rayome, Northern Michigan University; John Reik, University of Minnesota; Cecilia Ricci, Seton Hall University; Hong Rim, Shippensburg University; Kenneth Roberts, Southwestern University; Georges Rocourt, Barry University; Foster Roden, University of North Texas; Bernard Rose, Rocky Mountain College; Mike Rosen, Pepperdine University; Stan Rosenberg, La Roche College; Herbert Roth, Shippensburg University; Arlyn Rubash, Bradley University; Bruce Rubin, Old Dominion University; Chip Ruscher, James Madison University; Patricia Ryan, Drake University; Robert Saemann, Alverno College; Paul Sarmas, Cal State Polytech University; Vincent Scerbinski, Southampton College; Patricia Schaeff, Miami University–Oxford; Burton Schaffer, California State University–Sacramento; Michael Schellenger, University Wisconsin Oshkosh; Stephen Schepman, Central Washington University; Bill Schmidt, Shorter College; Jeffrey Schultz, Christian Brothers University; Robert Schweitzer, University of Delaware; James Seifert, Marquette University; Jimmy Senteza, Washington State University; Rodney Serizawa, San Francisco State University; Edward Shafer, University of

Maryland; Dianna Shallenburger, Central Methodist College; Peter Sharp, California State University–Sacramento; Allen Shin, Frostburg State University; Kilman Shin, Ferris State University; Julian Shlager, Plymouth State College; Joseph Shott, Westmoreland County Community College; Connie Shum, Pittsburgh State University; Debra Skaradzinski, Hollins University; Fred Siegel, University of Louisville; Julie Smith, Oral Roberts University; Patricia Smith, North Carolina Wesleyan College; Ronald Smith, St. Thomas Aquinas College; Stephanie Smith, Texas A&M International University; Ira Sohn, Montclair State University; Patricia Sommerville, St. Mary's University; Kean Song, Prairie View A&M University; Austin Spencer, Western Carolina University; Katherine Spiess, University of Notre Dame; Hubert Spraberry, Howard Payne University; Jan Squires, Southwest Missouri State University; Suresh Srivastava, University of Alaska–Anchorage; Marty St. John, Westmoreland County Community College; Richard Stackman, University of Washington–Tacoma; Edward Stendardi, St. John Fisher College; Glenn Stevens, Franklin Marshall College; Jerry Stevens, University of Richmond; Eric Stiles, Fordham University; Gabe Stoeppler, Limestone College; Steve Stover, California Maritime Academy; John Stowe, University of Missouri–Columbia; Charles Strang, Western New Mexico University; Robert Stretcher, Hampton University; Jan Strockis, Santa Clara University; Barbara Suleski, Cardinal Stritch College; Mark Sullivan, Wor Wic Community College; Michael Sullivan, University of Nevada Las Vegas; Janice Swain, Regis College; George Swales, Southwest Missouri State University; Wonhi Synn, Elon College; Harry Tamule, Providence College; Amir Tavakkol, Kansas State University; Janet Thatcher, University of Wisconsin–Whitewater; Madeline Thimmes, Utah State University; Bruce Toews, Walla Walla College; José Trinidad, Southwest Texas State University; George Trivoli, Jacksonville State University; C. Joe Ueng, University of St. Thomas; E. Upton, Virginia Commonwealth University; David Vang, University of St. Thomas; Dennis Varin, Southern Oregon University; Sue Visscher, University of Toledo; Ashok Vora, Baruch College of CUNY; Jean Walker, West Texas A&M University; Edward Waller, University of Houston–Clearlake; Stan Warren, Niagara University; Randi Waxman, Columbia Union College; Samuel Weaver, Lehigh University; Marsha Weber, Moorhead State University; Loren Weishaar, Texas Lutheran College; Charles Wellens, Fitchburg State College; Gary Wells, Idaho State University; Peng Wen, Fresno Pacific College; Mark Wencel, Piedmont Community College; John White, Georgia Southern University; Michael White, Bob Jones University; Howard Whitney, Franklin University; Marilyn Wiley, Florida Atlantic University; Gary Wishniewsky, California State University–Hayward; Edward Wolfe, Western Kentucky University; Bob Wood, Tennessee Technical University; David Wright, University of Wisconsin; Mark Wrolstad, Winona State University; Jerry Yang, University of Arizona; Richard Yanow, Massachusetts College of Liberal Arts; Philip Young, Southwest Missouri State University; Ken Yung, Old Dominion University; Richard Zock, California State University–Hayward; and Thomas Zwirlein, University of Colorado.

Finally, we'd like to acknowledge the patience and encouragement of our wives, Diane and Roslyn, and our children, Tom and Kathryn, and Rena and Amy.

They had to bear the brunt of countless hours spent over the computer looking for the right words and examples to bring *Modern Corporate Finance* to life.

A.C.S.
Pacific Palisades, CA

S.D.B.
Durham, NC

A SPECIAL ACKNOWLEDGMENT

From my perspective, this book owes its greatest debt to Alan's earlier work *Modern Corporate Finance* (MCF), published in 1989 by Macmillan. I fell in love with it the first time I saw it. The work's emphasis on value creation, the integration of domestic and international finance, its interdisciplinary flavor, and student-friendly writing style (among other things) set the book apart from other graduate texts. Had MCF gone to a second edition, I never would have gotten into the textbook writing "business."

However, life takes some curious bounces, and I found myself developing material for a concise finance text to fit executive education and/or evening MBA programs, in which there may be a limited amount of time to spend on corporate finance. Paul Donnelly quickly recognized that the themes permeating my proposed work were identical to Alan's earlier work and brought us together for this collaborative effort. In the process of getting together to write this book, Alan and I found that we both grew up in the same neighborhood—Coney Island in Brooklyn. We also share the same alma mater—I did my undergraduate engineering work at Carnegie Tech, whereas Alan did his doctoral work in finance at Carnegie-Mellon. More important, we both see corporate finance as a dynamic field of study and hope we can share some of that excitement with you.

S.D.B.
Durham, NC

Introduction

There are two things, science and opinion; the former
begets knowledge, the latter ignorance.
Hippocrates

KEY TERMS

agency conflict
arbitrage
arbitrage pricing theory
capital asset pricing
   model (CAPM)
corporation
efficient financial market
financial economics

future value
incremental cash flows
information asymmetries
limited liability
nominal interest rate
opportunity cost
opportunity cost of funds
partnership

present value
real interest rate
sole proprietorship
systematic or market risk
time value of money
unsystematic or
   diversifiable risk
value gap

CHAPTER LEARNING OBJECTIVES

Upon completion of this chapter, students should be able to:

■ Describe the activities of a firm's chief
financial officer in terms of the acquisition and allocation of funds.

■ Explain why managers should focus
on creating shareholder value.

■ Describe the different forms of business organizations in terms of their
owners' legal liability, the life of the
entity, and their ability to raise capital.

■ Explain how the fates of the firm's customers, employees, and shareholders
are interrelated.

■ Describe the nature of the agency
problem and the types of conflicts that
can arise between managers, shareholders, and creditors.

■ Explain finance's role in the strategic
management process and indicate
which corporate goals and objectives

are consistent with maximizing shareholder value.

■ Describe the importance of the global
marketplace to the operations of a
business.

■ Explain the difference between nominal and real values.

■ Distinguish between earnings and cash
flow.

■ Explain the meaning and importance
of the concepts of arbitrage, market
efficiency, and the capital asset pricing model.

■ Explain the meaning and importance
of options.

■ Explain the importance of distinguishing between anticipated and unanticipated events.

Corporate finance means different things to different people. A layperson might think that finance has to do with large Wall Street transactions such as the acquisition of MCI Communications by Worldcom, the breakup (again) of AT&T, or R. H. Macy's bankruptcy. These blockbuster transactions conjure up the idea that corporate finance involves huge amounts of money being made, lost, or transferred from one party to the next.

> Finance is concerned with the acquisition and allocation of funds among a firm's activities.

However, the public perception of corporate finance is only a small part of the story. Underlying these events are the activities of a firm's chief financial officer, who sees finance in terms of two interrelated functions: the *acquisition* and *allocation* of resources among a company's present and potential activities and projects. The first function, the *financing decision,* involves generating funds either internally or from external sources at the lowest possible cost. The second function, the *investment decision,* is concerned with allocating funds over time in such a way that shareholder wealth is increased. This latter task is accomplished by undertaking activities and purchasing or creating assets that are worth more than they cost.

Exhibit 1-1 shows some of the assets that companies invest in and how these assets are financed. Some of these assets—such as plant and equipment—are tangible, but others—a strong brand name or a dedicated, well-trained work force—

EXHIBIT 1-1
Key Functions of Corporate Finance

The Investment Decision: Assets	The Financing Decision: Liabilities and Equity
Current Assets Cash Marketable Securities Accounts Receivable Inventory	*Current Liabilities* Accounts Payable Short-Term Debt Product Warranties
Fixed Assets Buildings Equipment Land	*Long-Term Liabilities* Long-Term Debt Pension Obligations Deferred Taxes Leases
Intangible Assets Brand Names Trademarks and Patents Distribution Network Customer Loyalty Loyal and Skilled Work Force	*Intangible Liabilities* No-Layoff Policy Commitment to Quality Products and Services Need to Advertise and Promote
	Equity Proceeds from Stock Sales Retained Earnings Value Created by Investments

> The intangible assets of some firms are more important to their prosperity than their tangible assets.

are intangible yet very valuable. In fact, to some firms that rely on creative talent to generate a stream of new ideas, these intangible assets may be more critical to survival and prosperity than the tangible assets. Looking at the other side of the balance sheet, we see a series of intangible liabilities that help finance these assets. For example, a commitment to workers that they won't be laid off even if business turns down helps to create and maintain a dedicated work force.

Understanding the connection between intangible assets and intangible liabilities is crucial in designing mutually supportive marketing, operations, and financial policies. For instance, the value of intangible assets such as brand names and customer loyalty depends on the extent to which a firm has met its customers' needs. However, the acquisition costs of these intangible assets come in the form of intangible liabilities (e.g., a stream of advertising and promotion expenses and quality-assurance programs). If the value of the intangible assets associated with meeting customer needs exceeds the costs of their related intangible liabilities, customer and shareholder value is created simultaneously.[1]

> The financial goal of the firm is to maximize shareholder wealth.

The objective of both financial functions is to maximize the shareholders' wealth. This means financing and investment decisions must add as much value as possible to the firm. It also means that companies must manage their assets effectively. Because all corporate actions affect the value of the firm, understanding the nature of value—its creation, preservation, and destruction—is vital for all corporate executives, not just those designated as financial managers. Thus, although this book focuses on financial management, employees in all functional areas—such as marketing, human resources, and operations—can benefit from the concepts and techniques presented here. In addition, despite our concentration on private-sector firms, most of the financial principles developed here are equally applicable to public-sector organizations such as hospitals, schools, and government agencies.

The importance of finance is reflected in the evolution of the chief financial officer's (CFO) role in the modern corporation. Until recently, the CFO was often pigeonholed as the keeper of numbers, the head bean counter. But in today's global economy, the CFO has become a key player who designs corporate strategy and serves as the architect for acquisitions, takeover defenses, overseas expansion, and corporate restructuring. In line with this growth in responsibility, the CFO now often sits on the board of directors and ranks third in the company hierarchy, behind the chairman and the president.

1.1 OBJECTIVE

> The principles of financial economics can help managers understand how markets work.

The objective of this book is to help the reader make sound financial decisions, many of which involve marketing, production, and other functional areas. To do this, we require a conceptual framework that managers can use to analyze key

---

[1] Similarly, the value of a firm's human assets, which are vital to producing high-quality goods and services and creating patents and trademarks, reflects its success in creating a productive work environment.

financial decisions. Our effort benefits greatly from the insights of **financial economics**—a discipline that uses economic analysis to understand the workings of financial markets, particularly the measurement and pricing of risk and the intertemporal allocation of funds, which refers to the choice between investing money for future consumption and spending money today.

By focusing on the behavior of financial markets and their participants rather than on specific problems, we can derive fundamental principles of valuation. With this basic theory, we can develop superior courses of action, much as an engineer applies the basic laws of physics to design better products and processes. We can also gauge the validity of generally accepted financial practices by seeing whether their underlying assumptions are consistent with our current knowledge. Policies that are plausible on the surface often turn out to be based on assumptions that are unrealistic in light of our understanding of how financial markets work. Rules of thumb that worked under one set of conditions may no longer work if circumstances change.

> Insights from financial economics can help firms develop superior courses of action.

Properly applied, the modern theory of corporate finance can provide managers with a more sensible basis for setting corporate goals and answering the questions and problems they deal with on a daily basis. For example:

- Should we overhaul our equipment or replace it?
- Do we use staff people for this project or hire outside services?
- Should we lease or buy this asset?
- Should we pay a cash dividend to our stockholders? If so, how much? Or should we use the money to repurchase our stock?
- Should we fund this research and development project?
- Which loan gives us the most favorable financial terms?
- Should we borrow money from a bank or issue more bonds?
- Should we raise equity capital instead of borrowing more money?
- Which division(s) should be allocated more funds and which should be sold off or shut down?
- Should managers be paid higher salaries or be given bigger bonuses? How should managerial bonuses be structured?
- How should we communicate with Wall Street?
- Should we acquire this company?

> Firms raise capital by selling investors claims to future cash flows.

To answer these questions, we need to understand how financial markets work. The reason is simple. Firms raise capital in financial markets by selling investors claims—in the form of financial securities such as stocks and bonds—to certain future cash flows. The financial markets determine the price of those claims. To the extent that managers view (as they should) their role as providing the maximum returns to shareholders, all financial decisions must be grounded in a theory of how investors value financial securities and other capital assets. Unless managers know how the financial markets are likely to view particular transactions, they may make decisions that cost their shareholders money.

1.2   THE CORPORATE ENTITY

Over time, the modern corporation has emerged as the dominant global economic force. Because businesses can be organized as sole proprietorships, partnerships, or corporations, we'll want to look at how these forms differ in terms of (1) their owners' legal liability, (2) the life of the entity, and (3) their ability to raise capital. We now examine each of these forms of business organization in turn.

Sole proprietorships are businesses owned by a single individual.

A **sole proprietorship** is owned by a single individual. Getting into business as a sole proprietor is pretty simple—you just do it! Many cities will require a business license, but the fees are minimal. Depending on the nature of the business, you might need to hire personnel or borrow money from the bank before you begin operations. However, sole proprietorships require no formal charter and are subject to fewer governmental regulations than other types of businesses.

With a sole proprietorship, there's no legal distinction between the business and the owner. Thus, the enterprise pays no taxes; all of the profits accrue to the proprietor and are taxed as individual income. Further, the owner in a sole proprietorship has *unlimited personal liability* for the business' debt. If the business goes under, the proprietor may have to dip into personal assets in order to satisfy creditor claims. Because of unlimited liability, large business losses in sole proprietorships often translate into personal bankruptcies.

The inability to raise large amounts of money limits the growth of sole proprietorships.

A serious drawback of the sole proprietorship is the inability to raise large amounts of capital. Because the only money invested in the business is the owner's, the equity that can be raised is limited to the proprietor's personal wealth. True, the business can borrow from a financial institution like a bank. However, a bank's willingness to lend will depend on the owner's personal wealth because the owner's *total assets*—both business and personal—provide the basis for the business' borrowing capacity. Creditors are also reluctant to lend large amounts of money to a sole proprietorship because the life of the business is limited to the life of the individual who created it.

Partnerships involve two or more individuals getting together to conduct business.

Two or more people can get together to form a **partnership** to conduct their business. The individuals must agree on (1) who provides what share of the work, (2) who's going to come up with the start-up capital, and (3) how the profits or losses will be shared. These understandings can be as informal as an oral agreement and a handshake or may involve a formal document filed with the secretary of state of the state in which the partnership does business.

Like sole proprietorships, partnerships are generally inexpensive and easy to form and often require little more than a business license. Partners also have unlimited liability for all of the business' debts. Therefore, if any partner can't meet his or her pro rata claim in the event of bankruptcy, the remaining partners must make good on any unsatisfied claims. Transfer of ownership is also difficult; if one partner dies or decides to leave the business, the partnership often dissolves. Because there is more than one owner, partnerships can raise money somewhat more easily than sole proprietorships; however, the ability to raise large amounts of cash is still limited by the partners' personal wealth.

The primary merit of both the sole proprietorship and the partnership is ease of getting started. However, their shortcomings—(1) unlimited liability of the owners, (2) the difficulty in transferring ownership, and (3) the limited life of the organization—make it difficult for these organizations to raise large amounts of capital. This may not be a drawback for the slow-growing enterprise, but growth opportunities typically require a good bit of cash. Growth firms that can't raise cash easily will find themselves at a serious competitive disadvantage. For this reason, businesses in growing markets may start as sole proprietorships or partnerships but eventually switch to the corporate form.

> Corporations are legal entities and have the same rights as individuals.

In terms of sales revenues and assets managed, the **corporation** is by far the most important form of business enterprise. It is a distinct legal entity, separate and apart from its owners or managers. As a "legal being," corporations enjoy many of the same rights as people. These include: (1) the ability to buy and sell assets, (2) the ability to enter into contracts, and (3) the right to initiate and be the subject of legal action. In the United States, the laws under which a corporation operates are dictated by the state in which it incorporated.

> Corporations have three advantages over unincorporated businesses: limited liability, ease of ownership transfer, and unlimited life.

The corporate form offers three distinct advantages over the unincorporated business:

1. *Limited Liability:* Because the corporation is a separate legal entity, shareholders' liability is limited to the amount invested in the business. *This significantly reduces the downside risks borne by the owners.* Suppose, for instance, that you invest $100,000 in a partnership that goes bankrupt owing $2 million to creditors. As a part owner, you would be liable for a pro rata share of this debt. Worst yet, if your partners didn't have sufficient assets to assume their "fair share" of the debt, you'd be liable for the entire $2 million. In contrast, if you invested that $100,000 in the stock of a corporation that went bankrupt, losses would be limited to your initial investment.

2. *Easy Transfer of Ownership:* The ownership interest in a corporation is represented by shares of stock, which can be transferred to new owners far more readily than the equity interest in either a sole proprietorship or partnership. Thus, an investment in the stock of a corporation is far more *liquid* than a similar investment in an unincorporated business.

3. *Unlimited Life:* Because the corporation exists as a distinct legal entity, it can exist long after its owners and managers have withdrawn from the business.

The combination of **limited liability**, easy transfer of ownership, and unlimited liability enhances the ability of a corporation to raise large amounts of money. This access to cash allows corporations to exploit growth opportunities far more easily than either a sole proprietorship or a partnership could in similar markets.

Although their ability to attract capital is a competitive advantage, corporations have two disadvantages relative to partnerships and proprietorships. First, setting up shop as a corporation is far more complex and costly than starting up an unincorporated business. Before beginning operations, the owners must prepare a charter and a set of by-laws to guide its scope. The charter is filed with the secretary of state of the state in which the firm will be incorporated. Approval by the state is required before the corporation can formally come into existence.

Second, corporate earnings are subject to double taxation. At the business level, federal and state governments both tax corporate income. Further, when corporate profits are paid out as dividends, they are treated as income to shareholders and taxed again. Since dividends of U.S. corporations are paid out of after-tax dollars, shareholders are effectively taxed twice. With sole proprietorships and partnerships, business profits are only taxed at a personal level.

1.3   BASIC CONCEPTS

You will now examine a series of basic principles, which together form a simple yet elegant and powerful conceptual framework. You will see these concepts and ideas over and over again in many different guises and circumstances. We introduce them here, at the very beginning of the book, to get you started thinking in a special way. Although some of the concepts will appear self-evident, indeed trivial, be assured that many of their implications are not at all obvious; they certainly are not always accepted in financial circles. In fact, much of what passes for financial wisdom on Wall Street and in the boardrooms of corporate America goes counter to these basic principles. This conflict stems, in part, from the previous lack of focused research. But the logic underlying the principles presented here and, more important, the empirical evidence available to support them are nearly irresistible, resulting in major changes in the way executives think about business and the decisions they make.

Investors prefer more wealth to less.

Our theoretical foundation begins with the simple economic notion that people try to maximize their well-being. Part of this well-being stems from the consumption of goods and services. All else being equal, this means that people generally prefer more wealth to less, where wealth represents the ability to consume. One way that people acquire more wealth is to defer consumption and invest the freed-up money in a company. Those who are relatively risk averse become bondholders, lending money to the company in return for a promised interest rate and repayment of the loan at an agreed-upon date. Those who are willing to bear more risk will become shareholders, providing equity capital to the company in return for partial ownership of it. As partial owners of the firm, stockholders receive a proportional share of the firm's profits and losses. However, stockholders have only a *residual* interest in the company's earnings; bondholders and other creditors must be paid off before stockholders can claim any of the firm's earnings. If the firm fails to make its interest and principal payments on time, it is said to be in *default*, and the bondholders can force it into bankruptcy to recover their money.

Investors who have a low toleration for risk become bondholders; those willing to bear more risk become stockholders.

The Importance of Shareholder Value

The relevance of this discussion to financial management is that the shareholders are the legal owners of the firm, and management has a fiduciary obligation to act

Shareholders are the firm's most important stakeholder; management has a fiduciary responsibility to act in their best interests.

in the shareholders' best interests. Other stakeholders in the company do have rights, but these aren't coequal with the rights of shareholders. Shareholders provide the risk capital that acts as a shock absorber to cushion the claims of other stakeholders. The value of the firm could drop by as much as the value of equity capital, and the company would still have enough assets to honor the claims of bondholders and noninvestor stakeholders. Allowing alternative stakeholders coequal control over capital supplied by others is equivalent to allowing one group to risk someone else's capital. This would undoubtedly impair future equity formation and produce numerous other inefficiencies. Without shareholders and their equity capital, for example, companies would be all-debt financed and would continually face the prospect of financial distress or bankruptcy.

By forcing managers to evaluate business strategies based on prospective cash flows, the shareholder value approach favors strategies that enhance a company's cash-flow-generating ability—which is good for everyone, not just shareholders. Politicians and other commentators should reflect on the fact that you have to create wealth before you can distribute it. That is, shareholders aren't the only beneficiaries of corporate success. Companies with lots of cash have more money to distribute to all of their stakeholders, not just shareholders. They also create more opportunities for employee advancement.

Firms should be managed to minimize value gaps.

A more compelling reason for focusing on creating shareholder wealth is that those companies who don't are likely to wind up with a **value gap**—the difference between the value of the company if it were optimally managed and the actual value of the company. Companies with large value gaps are prime takeover targets and candidates for a forced corporate restructuring. Conversely, maximizing shareholder value provides the best defense against a hostile takeover: a high stock price. In 1984, for example, Walt Disney Co. was a takeover target when its stock price was at $55. By 1998, when new management had lifted its stock to over $1,600 (adjusting for stock splits), Walt Disney was no longer a target. No one could afford to pay a higher price for Disney and still expect to earn a competitive return.

Boards of directors are also becoming more active in looking out for shareholders' interests and are demanding that CEOs do the same and be held accountable for their companies' performance. In recent years, activist boards of companies with large value gaps forced out the heads of IBM, General Motors, Apple, Digital Equipment, Goodyear, Borden, Allied-Signal, American Express, Westinghouse, Compaq, Kodak, and Tenneco and forced major restructurings at all these firms as well as at Sears.

At the same time, the historical evidence tells us that the longer restructuring to close a value gap is delayed, the greater the cost, trauma, and extent of the restructuring that must ultimately occur (e.g., the more employees that must eventually be let go) and the less the certainty of success (e.g., IBM).

There is no inherent conflict between shareholders and stakeholders.

Simply put, this is not a zero-sum game—where gains to shareholders come at the expense of other stakeholders; there is no inherent economic conflict between the two. Indeed, maximizing shareholder value is not merely the best way, it is the *only* way to maximize the economic interests of *all* stakeholders over time.

Companies that
create shareholder
value find it easier
to attract equity
capital.

For example, companies with the best record of value creation—Coca-Cola, Southwest Airlines, Disney, GE, and Wal-Mart—are also among the best at human resource management and taking care of their customers.

Companies that build shareholder value also find it easier to attract equity capital. Equity capital is especially critical for companies that operate in a riskier environment and for companies that are seeking to grow. Both these characteristics describe most companies today.

The import of this discussion is that the primary objective of financial management is to maximize the shareholders' well-being. Because shareholders have invested their money with the expectation of becoming better off financially, this objective translates into maximizing shareholder wealth. We shall see later on in this chapter that maximizing shareholder wealth is tantamount to maximizing the firm's share price.

Although an institution as complex as the modern corporation does not have a single, unambiguous will, the principle of shareholder wealth maximization provides a rational guide to financial decision making. However, we also examine other financial goals that reflect the relative autonomy of management and external pressures. These include maximizing earnings or earnings per share, boosting the size and degree of corporate diversification by acquiring other firms, and increasing financial flexibility by maintaining large levels of liquid assets and borrowing power.

Nominal versus Real Quantities

Inflation is equiva-
lent to a decline
in the value of
money.

Wealth is usually measured in terms of money, because money can be exchanged for goods and services. Indeed, when money is not accepted as a medium of exchange (e.g., Confederate dollars), it is not really money. For money is what money does. And what money does is buy goods and services. The rate at which this exchange takes place is called the *nominal* or money price of the specific good or service bought. As nominal prices change, the *purchasing power,* and hence the value, of money changes. The value of money, therefore, is determined by the level of nominal prices. Thus, inflation, a general rise in the nominal price level, is equivalent to a decline in the value of money.

To take account of changes in the purchasing power of money over time, we distinguish between the *nominal* or face value of money and its *real* or inflation-adjusted value. For example, if inflation is 5 percent per annum, the real value of a nominal dollar declines by 5 percent annually. In other words, a dollar next year will be worth only $.95 in real terms, that is, relative to the purchasing power of a dollar today. Thus, although past, present, and future dollars all have the same nominal value, what really matters for purposes of economic evaluation are their real values, the differing quantities of goods and services that each can buy. Exhibit 1-2 shows the dramatic erosion in the purchasing power of the U.S. dollar between 1946 and 1998. In effect, a dollar at the end of 1998 was worth only $.12 in 1946 dollars. This distinction between nominal and real magnitudes is crucial to understanding the relationship among prices, inflation, and interest rates.

EXHIBIT 1-2
The Purchasing Power of the U.S. Dollar Plunged between 1946 and 1998

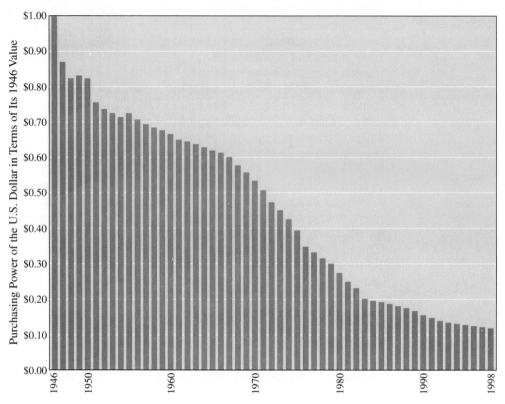

The real value of money is its nominal, or current, value adjusted for inflation.

In particular, the **nominal interest rate** is the price quoted on lending and borrowing transactions in financial markets. It is generally expressed as the premium that must be paid when current dollars are exchanged for future dollars. For example, an interest rate of 10 percent on a one-year loan means that 1 dollar today is being exchanged for 1.1 dollars a year from now. What really matters, however, is the exchange rate between current and future purchasing power as measured by the **real interest rate.** Put another way, the real interest rate is the nominal interest rate adjusted for inflation.

An increase in the real interest rate means that the cost of consuming goods today has risen in terms of future goods. In other words, the *opportunity cost* of today's consumption has risen relative to future consumption. As we shall see, changes in real interest rates have enormous implications for savings and investment decisions.

People expect the real rate of interest on their investments to be positive.

The real rate of interest that people expect to receive on their investments is always positive. There are two basic reasons for this expectation. First, people generally prefer present consumption over consumption in the future. This *positive time preference* means that people value the current use of resources (goods) more highly than they do their future use. Those who have strong preferences for immediate consumption will borrow from those who are less impatient and willing to delay their satisfaction. Because the second group also has a positive time preference, the first group must pay it a positive rate of interest to gain its acquiescence in the transaction.

Even without a positive time preference, however, we would still see a positive real rate, because resources can be used productively over time. Some goods, like trees and cattle, physically grow over time, whereas other goods, like wine and cheese, may improve in quality with age. Most important, resources can be converted into capital goods—for example, machinery and trucks—that produce more goods and services. Because in our world more is preferred to less, the present use of resources must have a positive price; competition among potential users will ensure that this is so.

The notion that a dollar today is worth more than a dollar in the future is known as the time value of money.

The existence of a positive rate of interest results in what is known as the **time value of money,** the notion that a dollar today is worth more than a dollar in the future. The difference in the values of current and future dollars is determined by the rate of interest. Thus, if the interest rate is 10 percent per annum, the **present value,** or value in terms of today's dollars, of one dollar a year from now is $.91. This is because $.91 invested today at 10 percent will be worth $.91 \times 1.10 = \$1$ one year from now. Alternatively, the **future value** of one dollar today is $1.10 a year from now.

Earnings versus Cash Flow

Cash flow, not accounting profits, is what matters to investors.

The emphasis on money is not misplaced. In most economies of the world, including our own, people consume by spending money to buy goods and services. The more money one has, the more one can consume. Firms benefit their shareholders, therefore, by providing them with cash, either by paying current dividends or by reinvesting the money to pay future dividends. This statement, simple as it sounds, has a profound and controversial implication: Accounting profits not associated with cash flows are of no value to investors. It means, for example, that switching depreciation methods for reporting—but not tax—purposes so as to boost reported profits does not benefit shareholders because it does not affect cash flow.

If financial markets are efficient, debates as to which accounting method to use will be irrelevant to shareholders except insofar as they may be misled concerning the firm's true cash flow. Moreover, because the value of the cash received is based on its purchasing power, the measure of a firm's performance depends on how much it increases its shareholders' purchasing power. A higher cash flow not associated with greater purchasing power does not increase the shareholders' wealth. Thus a firm generating 10 percent more cash when inflation is running at a rate of 12 percent is actually suffering a diminution in its performance.

Arbitrage, Market Efficiency, and Capital Asset Pricing

Three concepts of financial economics have proved especially valuable in developing a theoretical foundation for the study and practice of corporate finance:

arbitrage, market efficiency, and the distinction between systematic and unsystematic risk as reflected in the capital asset pricing model. Because we will use these concepts throughout this book, it is worthwhile to briefly describe them.

Arbitrage promotes product and financial market efficiency.

Arbitrage.   **Arbitrage** has traditionally been defined as the purchase of securities or commodities on one market for immediate resale on another to profit from a price discrepancy. Under this definition, the positions being taken are close to riskless. More recently, the term has been used to describe a broader range of financial activities. *Tax arbitrage,* for example, is the shifting of gains or losses from one tax jurisdiction to another or from one category of income to another to profit from differences in tax rates. Until the Tax Reform Act of 1986, a standard means of saving taxes was to convert ordinary income, then taxed at rates of up to 50 percent, to capital gains, whose top rate was 20 percent. Similarly, to the extent that multinational firms can shift export income to their operations in, say, Ireland, they can receive that income tax free because of a 15-year tax holiday provided by the Irish government. Even more important from our standpoint is the extension of arbitrage to include trading activities that involve risk. *Risk arbitrage,* sometimes termed *speculation,* has been used to describe the process that ensures that, in equilibrium, risk-adjusted returns on different assets are equal, unless market imperfections that hinder this adjustment process exist. In fact, it is the process of risk arbitrage, fueled by new information or differences of opinion, that ensures market efficiency.

In an efficient market, prices reflect all relevant and available information.

Market Efficiency.   An **efficient financial market** is composed of numerous well-informed individuals and institutions whose trading activities cause prices to adjust rapidly to reflect all relevant and available information. Thus, price changes at any moment must be due solely to the arrival of new information. Because new information useful for profitable trading activities arrives randomly (otherwise it would be neither new nor useful), price changes must follow a random walk.[2] In other words, in an efficient market, price changes from one period to the next are independent of past price changes and are no more predictable than is new information. Consistent with this implication, numerous studies of U.S. and overseas financial markets have shown that prices of domestic and foreign securities follow random walks. A number of studies also indicate that securities are correctly priced in that trading rules based on past prices or publicly available information do not consistently lead to profits net of transaction costs in excess of those due solely to risk taking.

The basic idea underlying market efficiency is that when Exxon announces that it's just discovered a billion-barrel oil field in the Beaufort Sea off the northern coast of Alaska, all the smart types who had figured out that Exxon stock was worth $38 will go back to their computers and decide that it's now worth $41.25. If you do the same and attempt to profit from this knowledge by buying Exxon

---

[2]In reality, asset prices follow a submartingale, which is a random walk with a drift. The drift equals the expected return on the asset.

stock, the odds are that by the time you placed an order with your broker, the price would have already risen to $41.25.

The idea that securities and other assets are fairly priced, given their anticipated risks and returns, is intuitively appealing. In a world in which hundreds of thousands of investors, including numerous professional *arbitrageurs* on exchange floors, are endlessly searching for marginally higher returns, it would be difficult to explain how over- or undervalued securities *could* exist for more than a few seconds or so. This is especially true today with computers and high-speed telecommunications giving investors worldwide access to nearly instantaneous price quotes and other relevant information.

Capital Asset Pricing. It is generally agreed that investors require higher returns on riskier investments, whose return can come in the form of either a cash payment (e.g., interest or dividends) or appreciation in the value of the investment (e.g., a higher stock or bond price). The difficulty for the financial manager lies in quantifying the riskiness of an investment and establishing the tradeoff between risk and expected return (i.e., the price of risk). Probably financial economists have devoted more effort to this issue than to any other and have posited a specific relationship among diversification, risk, and required return, which is now formalized in the **capital asset pricing model** (CAPM).[3] Risk itself is assumed to depend on the variability of returns; the more highly variable the return is, the riskier the asset will be.

The CAPM is based on the idea that the total variability of an asset's returns can be attributed to two sources: (1) marketwide influences that affect all assets to some extent (the level of interest rates or growth in GNP) and (2) other risks specific to a given firm (a strike or a new patentable invention). The former type of risk is usually termed **systematic** or **market risk,** and the latter, **unsystematic** or **diversifiable risk.** Unsystematic risk is largely irrelevant to the investor holding a well-diversified portfolio, because the effects of such disturbances can be expected to cancel out, on average, in the portfolio. On the other hand, no matter how well diversified the investment portfolio is, systematic risk, by definition, cannot be eliminated.

The distinction between systematic and unsystematic risks underlies the pricing of risk in the CAPM, as well as in the more general (in some respects) **arbitrage pricing theory** (APT).[4] According to both the CAPM and the APT, intelligent, risk-averse investors seek to diversify their asset holdings to eliminate the unsystematic component of risk. As a result, only the systematic component will be rewarded with a risk premium. Arbitrage among securities will ensure that investors will not be paid for bearing unsystematic risks, because they can avoid

> **The capital asset pricing model (CAPM) defines the market tradeoff between diversification, risk, and expected returns.**

> **The market does not reward investors for bearing risk that can be eliminated through diversification.**

---

[3]The bases of the CAPM were provided by Markowitz (1959), Sharpe (1964), and Lintner (1965). Jack Treynor also pioneered in the development of the CAPM but his paper was never published.

[4]The formal theory of arbitrage pricing was first developed in Ross (1976). It is discussed in detail in Chapter 6. Unlike the capital asset pricing model, which assumes that only one factor is priced (the market factor), the APT permits the pricing of a number of factors.

these risks at no cost simply by diversifying their portfolios. In other words, the CAPM and APT assume that enough people will follow the adage "don't put all your eggs in one basket" to ensure that investors will be compensated only for bearing market risk. This illustrates one of the most important rules in finance: You don't get paid for doing something that is unnecessary or irrelevant. It is the equivalent of the economist's dictum that there is no free lunch.

Recognizing and Valuing Options

Options represent an opportunity to defer decisions into the future.

The recognition and valuation of options are becoming an increasingly important part of corporate finance. An option gives the holder the right—but not the obligation—to do something in the future. That something can be the right to buy or sell assets such as stocks or bonds, foreign currencies or gold, or wheat or corn at a set price and date. Options are also present in the opportunity to undertake future investments or to expand, shut down, or abandon projects already undertaken. For example, investments in research and development often yield a variety of new investment opportunities, depending on the outcome of the research. Similarly, the owner of an oil well always has the option of shutting down production if the price of oil drops too low. More financial securities are being created with explicit options built right into them. For example, convertible bonds grant holders the right to exchange them for shares of the issuing company. Even when explicit options are not present, many corporate securities contain implicit options. For example, the right to file for bankruptcy gives companies the implicit option to default on the bonds they have issued.

Options are valuable because they allow the holder to defer a decision until a later date, by which time more information will have been acquired. The more uncertain the future, the more valuable the ability to delay decisions will be. This implies, for example, that all else being equal, research and development (R&D) funds should be directed to projects with the widest range of possible outcomes.

Despite their importance, however, options have historically been very difficult to value because they are so complex. Then in 1973, Fischer Black and Myron Scholes pioneered a new approach to option pricing that greatly expanded our ability to value even highly complex and unusual options.[5] The Black-Scholes option pricing model is one of the great advances of modern finance.

1.4   BASIC LESSONS

Despite widespread evidence of market efficiency, many companies persist in expending real resources in attempts to provide shareholders with something, like corporate diversification, that is probably unnecessary or to fool them by manipulating accounting profits in one way or another. For instance, during the decade of rapid inflation that began in late 1973, many American companies decided to

---

[5]See Black and Scholes (1973).

remain on the FIFO (first-in, first-out) method of inventory valuation, which results in a lower reported cost of goods sold (and hence higher reported profits), in order to "dress up" their financial statements. Switching to the alternative method of inventory valuation, LIFO (last-in, first-out), during a period of rising prices decreases reported earnings (by showing a higher cost of goods sold) but increases corporate cash flow owing to the reduction in taxes paid. Those firms that stuck with FIFO reported higher income but suffered a decline in cash flow because of the higher taxes they had to pay. Thus, this financial "window dressing" came at the expense of shareholders. As was stressed earlier, according to the "economic" model of the firm, what matters is cash, not accounting profits. Certainly in filling out their own tax returns, corporate executives understand well enough that minimizing their reported income (the equivalent of a firm's accounting income) will maximize their share of its purchasing power. We will see the influence of taxes on corporate financial decisions throughout the text.

The basic issue is whether investors respond mechanically and unthinkingly to earnings reports or whether they exercise their collective judgment and seek to determine the underlying cash flows. The available evidence suggests that investors pay attention to accounting profits only insofar as they believe reported profits reflect real cash flows.[6] When reported earnings differ significantly from cash flows, investors disregard those reported earnings. Hence, the basic rule to follow whenever there is a conflict between the two is to "take the money and run." Not surprisingly, the stock market isn't fooled by the tricks accountants can play with inventory valuations. After all, this information is part of the public domain. To underscore this fact, when inflation was rampant in the United States, publications like *Business Week* regularly presented LIFO-adjusted earnings of those firms clinging to FIFO.

The Irrelevance of Financial Manipulations

The markets are not fooled by financial manipulations.

There are two fundamental insights into financial management to be gained from evidence on the effects of financial window dressing. First, attempts to increase the value of a firm by purely financial measures or accounting manipulations are unlikely to succeed except under certain specific circumstances such as when capital market imperfections don't allow prices to fully reflect all available information or asymmetries in tax regulations exist (like our current system of levying taxes on nominal income rather than on true economic earnings). Neither of these circumstances was present when Rapid-American Corporation replaced its low-coupon debt with higher-coupon debt and recorded a taxable gain of $30 million. Similarly, Aetna Life & Casualty improved its financial appearance by recording over $73 million in taxable income, nearly 40 percent of its operating income, by an accounting gimmick known as "selling loss reserves." Without getting into the technical details of these transactions, the point is that both firms created taxable income without generating any additional cash. In fact, these deals, which looked

---

[6]The classic studies providing evidence on the ability of investors to see through accounting numbers are Ball and Brown (1968) and Kaplan and Roll (1972).

so good on the income statements, actually cost the firms cash in the form of higher taxes and transaction costs.

Incentives and Management Behavior

The second lesson is that people typically act on their own behalf and respond rationally to incentives and disincentives. Managers who sacrifice cash flow for higher reported profits are often judged and rewarded on the basis of those profits. This is just one example among many of an evaluation system that rewards behavior that is detrimental to the best interests of the firm's shareholders. Because corporate executives are at best only partial owners of the firms they manage, they don't bear all the harmful consequences of their behavior, but they do receive all the benefits (in the form of higher incomes, added perquisites, or less effort). The theme of the separation between ownership and control and the consequences of that separation is one we shall return to many times. It is known formally as the **agency conflict,** a reference to the fact that managers act as agents for absentee owners.[7] The threat of being fired or suffering a hostile takeover limits the extent to which managers can abuse their shareholders. There is still, however, a good deal of room for harmful managerial behavior.

An illustration of the potentially huge gap between management actions and shareholder preferences is the embarrassing run-up of 47 percent in the price of Gulf & Western's stock following the sudden death of its chairman, Charles Bluhdorn, in 1983. One interpretation of the stock market's reaction is that G&W shareholders felt that Bluhdorn was pursuing inappropriate policies but that his position was secure as long as he was alive. A similar embarrassment occurred in 1966 after Walt Disney died. Disney stock rose by about 25 percent in the following week.

The agency conflict also extends to the relations between stockholders and creditors. The potential for conflict between the two classes of investors arises because managers may make dividend, financing, and investment decisions that transfer wealth from creditors to stockholders. We frequently see this behavior in firms that are in financial difficulty and borrow to take on high-risk, high-return investments. If the project is successful, then the company can get itself out of trouble quickly. On the other hand, if the investment fails, limited liability means that stockholders are no worst off than they were before; creditors simply get stuck holding another worthless project.

We saw these risk incentives at work in the savings and loan (S&L) industry during the 1980s. Many S&Ls with low, fixed-rate mortgages saw their net worth evaporate when market interest rates skyrocketed in the early 1980s. These S&Ls thought they could get themselves out of their financial difficulties by taking on high-risk, high-return real estate development loans. Normally, creditors would completely cut off funds to a firm adopting a high-risk strategy with virtually no equity. However, because the main creditors were depositors whose funds were protected by deposit insurance, S&Ls were not shut off from the financial markets.

---

[7]The formal theory and implications of agency in corporate finance were first presented in Jensen and Meckling (1976).

Instead, depositors continued to pour money into crippled thrifts because they knew that if these loans went sour (and many did), the federal government would end up covering losses. The result was far greater losses than if the troubled S&Ls had stuck to their traditional mortgage lending. The cost to the U.S. taxpayer of this high-risk strategy financed by insured deposits was over $150 billion.[8]

Similarly, in 1986 Colt Industries announced that it would borrow $1.4 billion to pay shareholders an $85-a-share dividend. Colt shares, which were then trading at $66.75, soared on the news, but some long-term Colt bonds tumbled as much as $200 for each $1,000 face amount. The bond price drop reflected the combination of a greater risk of default—Colt's interest and principal payments rose substantially—and a smaller payoff to bondholders if default occurred—fewer assets remained to satisfy the increased bondholder claims.

Information Asymmetry

The financial markets have designed mechanisms for dealing with information asymmetries.

Related to the agency problem is the fact that one party to an exchange often knows something relevant to the transaction that the other party does not. The lesson for the financial manager is that such **information asymmetries** are pervasive, for example, in the relationship between the stockholders and the managers of a firm, between the issuer and the purchaser of a security, between the insurer and the insured, and between lender and borrower. To counter the problem of information asymmetry that, if allowed to go unchecked, could cause financial markets to cease to function, a variety of mechanisms and institutions have arisen. These include the use of investment bankers to certify the quality of the securities they issue, incentive contracts structured so that all parties to the transaction will find it in their own interest to be honest, and the use of various financial instruments and structures that reduce the costs of duplicity to the ignorant party and raise them for the knowledgeable party. An important aspect of many of these solutions is the development of reputations that would be destroyed if the knowlegeable party in a transaction used inside information to exploit the ignorant party.

Anticipated versus Unanticipated Events

Prices in the financial markets react to *unanticipated* events.

Another important lesson in corporate finance is also simple to describe but has wide-ranging, though at times subtle, implications for financial decision making. As we have seen previously, in an efficient market, asset prices already incorporate expectations of factors likely to affect their values. This means that investors often react not to what actually happens but to the *difference* between what happens and what was expected to happen. Thus, for example, on the day Gap Inc. announced an 11 percent increase in 1992 first-quarter earnings per share, its share price fell by 9 percent (a loss in market value—the number of shares times the price drop—of over $500 million), not because investors didn't care about its earnings but because the increase was less than expected. Conversely, Digital Equipment's stock price *rose* by 21 percent (a gain in market value of over $850

---

[8]For a short, readable article on the costs of the S&L crisis, see Meredith (1994).

million) on the day it announced a *loss* of $74 million in its fiscal 1993 second quarter, because the loss was less than investors had expected.

This distinction between *anticipated* and *unanticipated* phenomena plays an important role in describing the market's reaction to such events as dividend and inflation announcements as well as providing some clues as to the proper objectives of management. Here is an illustration of the latter: A common piece of financial advice is to borrow during times of inflation and profit at the lender's expense by paying back the loan with cheaper money. But if nominal interest rates already reflect anticipated inflation (as we would expect them to and which seems to be the case), such a policy can be successful only if actual inflation consistently exceeds the amount predicted. This is highly unlikely in a market with numerous well-informed participants. In fact, one would have to expect the unexpected—a logical impossibility—to anticipate profiting from such a situation. An alternative rationale for borrowing during inflation, which is to protect the firm against *unexpected* inflation, may be more sensible.

The basic financial principles we have touched upon briefly so far can be summarized easily: More wealth is preferred to less wealth; sooner is better than later; less risk is preferred to more risk; and options are valuable. All the other concepts presented (including market efficiency, arbitrage, capital asset pricing, the time value of money, and the distinction between nominal and real interest rates) and conclusions reached (what matters is not the quantity of money per se but the purchasing power represented by that money; investors will pay only for value received; one can't expect to profit from or successfully protect against expected changes; the more uncertain the environment, the more valuable the opportunity to make decisions contingent on future information; and managers and investors respond in a rational manner, on average, to economic incentives, opportunities, and information) are logically derived consequences of the rational pursuit of economic self-interest, based on the preceding four principles.

Insights from Microeconomics

The financial manager must also pay heed to three fundamental rules of microeconomic theory. First, and perhaps most important, is the following maxim: *Profit-making activities should be undertaken up to the point at which marginal revenue equals marginal cost.* Specifically, money should be invested in long-term assets, like new plant and equipment, and working capital items, like inventory and accounts receivable, up to the point at which the additional returns from these assets just equal the cost of the capital invested.

For financial decision making, only **incremental cash flows** matter.

Related to the idea of equating marginal costs and benefits is the notion that only **incremental cash flows** are relevant. This means, for example, that sunk costs are sunk. In other words, costs that have already been incurred and cannot be recovered are irrelevant in deciding what to do in the future. This advice is contrary to the common wisdom, expressed in such statements as, "If we don't invest another million dollars, we'll lose the million dollars we already have tied up in the project." But investing more money to protect a poor investment is just throwing good money after bad.

Returns from investments should exceed the opportunity cost of funds.

Similarly, it will not pay to invest more money in expanding a good project if new returns are less than the opportunity cost of the capital employed. This rule introduces the third key concept from microeconomics, **opportunity cost.** The opportunity cost of an asset is the maximum return the asset could generate for the firm if it were sold or put to some other productive use. Financial decision making is most concerned with the **opportunity cost of funds,** the yield forgone on the best available investment alternative. As such, it becomes the basic criterion of financial success. This opportunity cost will vary with the riskiness of the project; the higher the risk, the greater the opportunity cost. An investment that earns less than its opportunity cost of capital reduces shareholder wealth. For example, money invested in drilling new oil wells will be misspent if the returns on the funds are 12 percent and the cost of the funds is 16 percent.

Other resources used by firms also have opportunity costs that must be included when evaluating projects. For example, a software development project requiring extensive computer time should be charged the opportunity cost of that time even if the firm owns the computer. This opportunity cost could equal the profits the firm forgoes by not having extra time to lease out to others or the cost of additional computer time that must be bought by another department because the new project used up all the available time. But if the computer system has excess capacity, with no other plans for its use, then the opportunity cost will be zero.

These basic concepts and principles are used throughout this text to point out how managers, financial and otherwise, can add value to their firms. The focus is on those areas and circumstances in which financial decisions can measurably increase value as well as on the characteristics of those investment and financing decisions most likely to benefit shareholders. The value of good financial management is enhanced in today's world because of the greater complexity of the decisions that must be made, the increase in the available financing options, and the added competition and opportunities provided by an integrated global economy.

1.5   CORPORATE OBJECTIVES

Thus far, we have talked about shareholder wealth maximization without spelling out what this means in practice. Investors have a diverse set of preferences for risk and for current versus future consumption. If corporate management attempted to satisfy all these contradictory demands simultaneously, this could result in paralysis. Fortunately, this problem is more apparent than real as indicated by the following statement: *In well-functioning capital markets, where investors are able to freely buy and sell financial securities with minimal transaction costs, the goal of shareholder wealth maximization translates into maximizing the current share price.*

The goal of shareholder wealth maximization translates into maximizing share price.

Maximizing Share Price

Regardless of individual shareholders' preferences, they will be able to increase their perceived welfare by owning more valuable shares. Those who prefer increased consumption today can either sell some of their higher-priced shares or borrow against them. Shareholders who wish to save for consumption later can either hold their more valuable shares or, if they are risk averse, convert some of their increased wealth into less risky assets. What actions contribute to higher share prices? As we will see in Chapter 5, share prices are based on the present value of the future cash distributions, in the form of dividends and share repurchases, to shareholders. Hence, corporate actions that increase the present value of these cash distributions will increase share prices.

Although other objectives are often pursued by corporate management, none is as encompassing as share price maximization. No other objective so fully accounts for differences in the amounts, timing, and riskiness of future cash flows. Maximizing corporate profits or earnings per share has serious defects as a corporate goal.

Maximizing Earnings or Earnings per Share

Maximizing earnings or earnings per share ignores the distinction between earnings and cash flow, timing of returns, and risk.

Total corporate profits can always be increased by issuing additional shares of common stock and investing the proceeds in safe Treasury bills. But investors are more interested in earnings per share (EPS), assuming there is no divergence between earnings and cash flow, and these could decline if the company sold more shares. Consider, for example, a company with 1 million shares outstanding that has $5 million in annual earnings or $5 per share. Suppose the firm issues an additional million shares and uses the proceeds to acquire assets that produce $3 million in income. As Exhibit 1-3 shows, although total earnings are now $8 million, earnings per share have declined from $5 to $4. Focusing on earnings per share can avoid such earnings dilution, but the objective of maximizing earnings per share also has serious shortcomings. It ignores the crucial distinction between earnings and cash flow, the timing of the earnings, and the riskiness of these earnings.

As discussed earlier, in the example of LIFO versus FIFO inventory valuation, managers can sometimes increase earnings at the expense of corporate cash flows. Other methods, which we will explore later, can increase earnings without having any impact on cash flows. What really matters to shareholders, of course, is an earnings increase that results in more cash flow.

EXHIBIT 1-3
Effects of Issuing New Shares on Earnings per Share

	Before	**After**
Number of Shares Outstanding	1,000,000	2,000,000
Earnings	$5,000,000	$8,000,000
Earnings per Share	$\dfrac{\$5,000,000}{\$1,000,000} = \$5.00$	$\dfrac{\$8,000,000}{\$2,000,000} = \$4.00$

Another problem with focusing on earnings or earnings per share to the exclusion of other considerations is that it pays no attention to the timing of the earnings. Often the firm must sacrifice current earnings for greater future earnings. Suppose, for example, that a project that costs $1 million will return $300,000 for each of the next five years. Is the tradeoff worthwhile? Then, consider two mutually exclusive investments, one of which will pay out $.25 per share for the next five years, or $1.25 in total, and the other of which will pay out nothing for the first four years and $1.50 per share in the fifth year. Which investment is preferable? The answer depends on the time value of money to investors, a consideration conspicuously absent from the goal of EPS maximization.

Yet another shortcoming of EPS maximization is its disregard of the riskiness of these earnings streams. One way to boost expected returns is to invest in riskier projects. Suppose two mutually exclusive projects cost the same, but one is expected to yield an increase in EPS of $1.00 whereas the other, which is riskier, is expected to increase earnings by an average of $1.15 per share. Which project, if either, should be selected? Another way to increase projected EPS, which also involves assuming added risk, is to raise the proportion of debt in the firm's capital structure, thereby increasing the chance of bankruptcy. The correct project to select and the appropriate capital structure depends on the price of risk, which, in turn, hinges on how risk averse the shareholders are. The basic message is that shareholders don't value growth in earnings or even growth in cash flow. They value financial policies that increase the present value of future cash flow, taking into account the cost of generating that growth.

Of course, if capital markets did not rationally price corporate securities, managers would be hard pressed to design strategies to maximize firm values. Fortunately, as we have already seen, there is strong evidence that capital markets are relatively sophisticated in responding to publicly available information. For example, announcements of major earnings write-downs by Lockheed and Texas Instruments led to significant increases in their share prices because they resulted from decisions by the managements of both companies to cut their losses and abandon unprofitable lines of business (Lockheed's L-1011 and TI's home computers).

1.6   THE INTERNATIONALIZATION OF BUSINESS AND FINANCE

The new global economic environment is characterized by brutal price and service competition.

A key theme of this book is that companies today operate within a global marketplace and can ignore this fact only at their peril. The internationalization of finance and commerce has been brought about by the great advances in transportation, communications, travel, and technology. This introduces a dramatic new commercial reality—the global market for standardized consumer and industrial products on a previously unimagined scale. It places primary emphasis on the one great thing all markets have in common—the overwhelming desire for dependable, world-class products at aggressively low prices. The international integration of markets also introduces the global competitor, making firms insecure even in their home markets. Tandon Corp., a major California-based supplier of disk drives for microcomputers, cut its U.S. work force by 39 percent and transferred production overseas in an effort to achieve "cost effectiveness in an extremely competitive marketplace."[9] As the president of Tandon put it, "We can wait for the Japanese to put us out of business or we can be cost-effective."[10]

The transformation of the world economy has dramatic implications for business. American management is learning that the United States can no longer be viewed as a huge economy that does a bit of business with secondary economies around the world. Rather, the United States is merely one, albeit very large, economy in an extremely competitive, integrated world economic system. To succeed, U.S. companies need great flexibility; they must be able to change corporate policies quickly as the world market creates new opportunities and challenges. Big Steel, which was virtually the antithesis of this modern model of business practice, paid the price for failing to adjust to the transformation of the world economy.

Today's financial reality is that money knows no national boundary. The dollar has become the world's central currency, with billions switched at the flick of an electronic blip from one global corporation to another, from one central bank to another. The international mobility of capital has given firms more financial options, while complicating the job of the CFO by increasing its complexity.

Because we operate in an integrated world economy, all students of corporate finance should have an international orientation. Thus, a key aim of this book is to help you bring to bear on key business decisions a global perspective, manifested by questions like "where in the *world* should we locate our plants?"; "which *global* market segments should we seek to penetrate?"; and "where in the *world* should we raise our financing?" This international perspective is best captured in the following quotation from an ad for J. P. Morgan, the large and successful New York bank: "J. P. Morgan is an international firm with a very important American business."

1.7   OUTLINE OF THE BOOK

The remainder of this book elaborates on and applies the ideas set forth here. Although these ideas are interrelated, by necessity they must be discussed individually. Eventually, they must also be integrated because they are all part of a grand framework. Thus, each chapter in the book builds on the previous material. The text begins with two chapters on financial analysis and planning. Because accounting is the language of finance, Chapter 2 provides an overview of the firm's financial statements and how these statements can be used to assess the organization's financial health. The tools of analysis in this chapter represent a useful way to focus management's attention on the *financial strengths* that can be a source of *competitive advantage* or on *financial weaknesses* that must be corrected. Utiliz-

---

[9]"Tandon to Reduce U.S. Work Force, Concentrate Abroad," *Wall Street Journal,* March 1984, 22.
[10]Ibid.

ing these tools, we'll deal with the financial aspects of strategy implementation by looking at the interrelated areas of working capital management, financial planning, and funds forecasting in Chapter 3.

To create shareholder value, managers have to understand how markets value securities. We'll develop these valuation principles by looking at the concept of the time value of money in Chapter 4 and applying this framework to the pricing of stocks and bonds in Chapter 5. As we'll see in Chapter 5, share prices are based on the present value of future cash distributions. Hence, corporate strategies that increase the present value of these distributions will tend to enhance shareholder wealth.

We continue the development of valuation principles in Chapter 6 by examining the links between risk, return, and value. In this chapter, we'll see how diversification reduces portfolio risk and assess the degree to which corporate diversification strategies can create value. Chapter 7 explains the basic concepts of option pricing and shows how options are embedded in many corporate operating and financial decisions.

The valuation principles developed in Chapters 4 through 7 will be extended to the investment or capital budgeting decision in Chapters 8 through 11. Because a company's projects are a direct reflection of its corporate strategy, identifying projects that enhance shareholder wealth is tantamount to identifying strategic options that are consistent with maximizing shareholder value. Chapters 12 through 15 investigate the degree to which financing and dividend policies can influence stock price.

> For many companies, developing and exploiting competitive advantage and creating shareholder value are two sides of the same coin.

This text looks at the strategic decisions of a firm from the perspective of its common stockholders and, as such, is concerned with how to create shareholder value. A message that will appear frequently in many aspects of financial decision making is that *companies cannot create value by doing things that stockholders can do for themselves at the same or lower costs.* How to create value is the managerial challenge. In some cases, this may be done by taking advantage of imperfections in the financial markets that are not available to individuals. For other companies, *value creation* is linked to *developing* and *exploiting a competitive advantage* in the product/ service markets. After all, *firms that can do useful and valuable things for customers that their competition can't* should be able to generate returns that are higher than those investors can generate themselves. In these instances, *shareholder value creation* will be a *by-product* of a *well-conceived* and *competently executed corporate strategy.* The analytical tools discussed in this text will prove useful in supporting a company's strategy and measuring its impact on the common stockholder.

SUMMARY

Financial management is concerned with the efficient allocation of resources. As such, it lies at the heart of the decision-making process, whether in a private- or public-sector organization. This chapter provides an overview of the basic concepts and principles of corporate finance. It began by establishing the key objective as maximizing shareholder wealth. We saw that this objective can best be pursued with corporate strategies and financial policies that maximize price per share. The chapter then discussed many relevant considerations that lie behind the achievement of this goal, including the time value of money, the tradeoff between risk and return, the distinction between nominal or money values and real or inflation-adjusted values, and the value of delaying decisions until more information becomes available. We saw that growth in corporate sales, earnings, or assets will not necessarily enhance stock price. This decoupling of growth from shareholder-wealth maximization as well as its continuous focus on decision making from the standpoint of the common stockholder is finance's primary contribution to the development of corporate strategy.

The companion to value maximization is market efficiency, the notion that, on average, investors rationally incorporate all available information in forming judgments as to the values of different assets. To the extent that markets are efficient, managers can concentrate on developing strategies to maximize corporate value without having to worry about whether investors will misinterpret their decisions. The idea of market efficiency provides a series of fundamental insights into financial management that are of enormous value in deciding on appropriate financial actions.

QUESTIONS

1. What are the principal functions of financial managers? How do these roles support the strategic management process?
2. What is the distinguishing characteristic of the following assets?
   a. IBM's trademark
   b. A patent on a new wrinkle cream
   c. The Tropicana brand name
   d. Avon's sales force
3. Compare and contrast the forms of business organization with respect to: (a) the legal liability of their owners, (b) the life of the entity, and (c) their ability to raise capital.
4. Comment on the following: "It's really impossible to satisfy all corporate stakeholders simultaneously; strategies designed to attract and retain customers will invariably reduce profits and hence stockholder returns."
5. How would the agency problems in a corporation differ from those in a sole proprietorship? A partnership?
6. Why do people usually prefer to receive $1 today instead of $1 next year?
7. What is the distinction between nominal and real interest rates? Why is this distinction important?
8. Why might 150 percent be considered a low interest rate in Brazil at the same time that 15 percent is a high interest rate in the United States?
9. What is the difference between earnings and cash flow?
10. What is the problem with the stock market advice to "buy low and sell high"?

11. What is the distinction between systematic and unsystematic risk? How does this distinction affect the premium that investors demand for bearing risk?
12. What is an option? Why is it valuable?
13. What option does debt give stockholders?
14. Define the agency conflict. How does it help explain the price run up in Gulf & Western's stock when its chairman died?
15. How do informational asymmetries contribute to agency problems?
16. Why did Colt Industries' bond prices drop and its stock price soar after management announced that it would borrow $1.4 billion to pay a huge dividend to shareholders?
17. Comment on the following statement: "It makes sense to borrow during times of high inflation because you can repay the loan in cheaper dollars."
18. What is an opportunity cost? Give some examples of opportunity costs.
19. Why is shareholder wealth maximization a better objective than maximizing earnings or earnings per share?
20. a. In 1988, Hewlett-Packard announced a 30 percent increase in second-quarter earnings per share. What do you think happened to H-P's stock price? Why?
    b. In 1983 when Analog Devices announced a 76 percent increase in earnings per share, from $.55 in 1982 to $.97, its share price dropped by almost 4 percent. Explain what might have triggered this decline. Is this explanation consistent with market efficiency?

REFERENCES

Ball, R., and P. Brown. "An Empirical Evaluation of Accounting Income Numbers." *Journal of Accounting Research,* Autumn 1968, 159–178.

Black, Fischer, and Myron Scholes. "The Pricing of Options and Corporate Liabilities." *Journal of Political Economy,* May–June 1973, 637–654.

Jensen, Michael C., and William H. Meckling. "Theory of the Firm: Managerial Behavior, Agency Costs, and Ownership Structure." *Journal of Financial Economics,* October 1976, 305–360.

Kaplan, Robert, and Richard Roll. "Investor Evaluation of Accounting Information: Some Empirical Evidence." *Journal of Business,* April 1972, 225–227.

Lintner, John. "The Valuation of Risk Assets and the Selection of Risky Investments in Stock Portfolios and Capital Budgets." *Review of Economics and Statistics,* February 1965, 13–37.

Markowitz, Harry. *Portfolio Selection: Efficient Diversification of Investments.* New York: Wiley, 1959.

Meredith, Robyn. "Ultimate Tab for the S&L Crisis Pegged at $150 Billion," *American Banker,* August 8, 1994, p. 6.

Ross, Stephen A. "The Arbitrage Theory of Capital Asset Pricing." *Journal of Economic Theory,* December 1976, 341–360.

Sharpe, William F. "Capital Asset Prices: A Theory of Market Equilibrium Under Conditions of Risk." *Journal of Finance,* September 1964, 425–442.

2

Evaluating a Firm's Financial Condition

Enthusiasm is the greatest asset in the world. It beats money and power and influence.
Henry Chester

We developed statistics correctly reflecting the relation between net return and invested capital for each operating division—the true measure of efficiency.
Alfred P. Sloan

KEY TERMS

accounts receivable
    turnover
activity ratios
aging of accounts
    receivable
amortization
average collection period
balance sheet
brand-name capital
cash flow coverage
cross-sectional analysis
current assets
current liabilities
current ratio
debt-equity ratio

debt ratio
depreciation
DuPont analysis
economic value
equity multiplier
financial leverage ratios
first-in, first-out (FIFO)
free cash flows
gearing
gross profit margin
income statement
intangible assets
inventory turnover
last-in, first-out (LIFO)
leverage ratios

liquidity ratios
matching principle
net profit margin
net working capital
operating profit margin
profitability ratios
quick or acid-test ratio
return on assets (ROA)
return on equity (ROE)
return on investment
    (ROI)
statement of cash flows
times interest earned
total asset turnover
trend analysis

CHAPTER LEARNING OBJECTIVES

Upon completion of this chapter, students should be able to:

- Identify the basic elements of a company's balance sheet, income statement, and statement of cash flows.
- Explain why a firm's financial statements based on historical cost may

not reflect either economic value or economic profits.
- Describe the differences between a firm's accounting income and its cash flows.

- Use financial ratio analysis to evaluate a firm's financial position.
- Indicate how nonfinancial measures of operating effectiveness can be valuable in assessing a firm's ability to remain competitive.

- Explain how segmented financial statements can be used to evaluate the performance of diversified firms.
- Describe the differences between the financial statements of U.S.- and foreign-based companies.

As we noted in Chapter 1, strategy formulation and implementation involve matching market opportunities with a company's skills. The idea is to identify customer needs and then to focus the organization's resources on those needs. A key element in this process is figuring out what the firm *excels* at doing. A reality of the global marketplace is that just being good is not good enough; *competitive advantage requires excellence.* More often than not, firms that can *create competitive advantage* have little difficulty in *creating shareholder wealth.*

A firm's financial position is critical to the design and execution of corporate strategy. Even if they don't have the appropriate skills or resources at present, firms with enough financial firepower can acquire the human and production resources needed to implement just about any strategy. In contrast, a financially weak company will have difficulty surviving, let alone trying to grow.

In this chapter, we'll develop some tools for determining the financial health of a company. To get our blood circulating, we'll begin with an overview of a firm's balance sheet, income statement, and statement of cash flows. We don't intend to provide a comprehensive treatment of accounting principles but will point out differences in perspective between accounting and finance. Next, we will take up financial ratio analysis—an important tool for gauging a firm's financial condition. Two themes will emerge from our discussion. First, trying to reach conclusions from a limited set of numbers can be dangerous. Typically, policy implications can only be drawn by looking at ratios as a package. Second, a firm's financial results may be heavily influenced by its corporate strategy. Wal-Mart and Neiman-Marcus are both retailers; however, they serve two very different market niches and shouldn't be compared directly.

2.1   THE BASIC ACCOUNTING STATEMENTS

In order to assess a firm's financial status, you must be a financial detective. You have to sift and organize the mass of available data for clues to the company's health. The most important clues are usually contained in the firm's three basic financial statements: the balance sheet, the income statement, and the cash flow statement. For publicly traded companies, these statements appear in the annual report issued to stockholders and the Form 10-K filed each year with the Securities and Exchange Commission (SEC). The firm's financial statements are also important means of communicating with outside stakeholders as well as serving as important tools as a company plans its financing needs over time.

The Balance Sheet

The balance sheet is a snapshot of a firm's financial position at a given point in time.

A **balance sheet** is a tabulation of what a firm owns (its assets), and what it owes (its liabilities) at a *specific point in time.* Exhibit 2-1 indicates how the balance sheet is organized for the typical American company. The asset side of the balance sheet is listed in decreasing order of the time it takes for an ongoing firm to convert the assets to cash. Current assets are likely to be converted into cash in a year; fixed assets include land, plant, and equipment investments; other assets normally represent ownership in other companies and goodwill.[1] On the liabilities and shareholder's equity side, current liabilities are debts that are payable within one year. Long-term liabilities include not only bonds and mortgages but also items like employee postretirement benefits and deferred taxes.[2] Shareholders' equity is the difference between total assets and all of the liabilities. By accounting convention, shareholders' equity is a measure of the firm's value to the owners. However, this "book value"—usually termed net worth or owners' equity—may be very different from what we'd get after we liquidated all of the assets and paid off the creditors.[3] **Net working capital,** which is **current assets** less **current liabilities,** is rarely highlighted on the balance sheet of an American firm, but it is an important measure of liquidity.[4]

Assets are listed in order of decreasing liquidity. Liabilities and equities are listed in terms of increasing order of when they come due.

EXHIBIT 2-1
The Balance Sheet

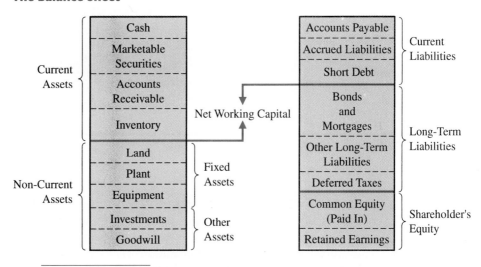

[1]Goodwill arises when a company pays more than the "fair market value" for an asset. We typically see goodwill when a company acquires all or part of another company.

[2]Deferred taxes reconcile the differences in tax versus financial reporting of certain income and expense items.

[3]We'd also expect differences between book value and the aggregate market value of a company's common stock. Discrepancies like this mean that the balance sheet has some serious limitations as an indicator of value.

[4]Working capital is shown directly on the balance sheet of many European companies. The balance sheet of Glaxo Wellcome in the Appendix to this chapter shows this and provides other examples of differences in the financial statements of U.S.- and foreign-based companies.

EXHIBIT 2-2
Anheuser-Busch Companies, Inc.
Consolidated Balance Sheet (in million $)

December 31	1997	1996
ASSETS		
Current Assets		
Cash and Marketable Securities	$ 147.3	$ 93.6
Accounts Receivable	713.4	632.7
Inventories	550.2	531.1
Other Current Assets	173.0	208.4
Total Current Assets	$ 1,583.9	$ 1,465.8
Investments and Other Assets	2,392.6	1,789.6
Net Plant and Equipment	7,750.6	7,208.2
Total Assets	$11,727.1	$10,463.6
LIABILITIES AND SHAREHOLDER'S EQUITY		
Current Liabilities		
Accounts Payable	$ 791.8	$ 726.8
Accrued Salaries, Wages, and Benefits	224.3	227.6
Accrued Taxes	183.9	233.0
Other Current Liabilities	300.7	243.5
Total Current Liabilities	$ 1,500.7	$ 1,430.9
Postretirement Benefits	525.4	524.6
Long-Term Debt	4,365.6	3,270.9
Deferred Income Taxes	1,293.6	1,208.1
Shareholders' Equity	4,041.8	4,029.1
Total Liabilities and Equity	$11,727.1	$10,463.6

Source: Anheuser-Busch Companies, Inc., *1997 Annual Report,* p. 50.

Exhibit 2-2 gives the 1996 and 1997 balance sheets for Anheuser-Busch (BUD[5]). Like that of a typical U.S. firm, the asset side of BUD's balance sheet begins with its most liquid assets—cash and marketable securities—and works its way down to net plant and equipment. *Net plant and equipment* is the cost of BUD's fixed assets less any accumulated depreciation. In the liabilities and shareholders' equity portion, current liabilities like payables and accruals are listed first, followed by the firm's long-term liabilities. Shareholders' equity, which in BUD's case consists entirely of common stock, is last in line.

In an ideal world, there should be no differences between accounting and economic values. However, the accounting conventions don't permit such a reconciliation. There are three main problem areas.

---

[5]Anheuser-Busch's common stock is traded on the New York Stock Exchange. BUD is the firm's trading, or ticker, symbol and is derived from its most important product—Budweiser beer.

The accountant's reliance on historical cost means that accounting and economic balance sheet values may differ.

1. *Asset and Liability Accounts Do Not Represent Current Values:* Accountants have adopted historical cost as the basis for valuation. The virtue of historical cost is objectivity; 2 (or 20 or 200) accountants with the same set of data can generally agree on the cost of a piece of equipment. However, historical cost reflects the prices that were in effect at the time the asset was acquired or when the liability was incurred. For example, suppose BUD bought land for its St. Louis brewery in 1878 for $100,000. Even though the land might be worth $20 million today, it would still appear on the balance sheet at $100,000. Further, from the perspective of finance, economic value is based on the *expected future cash flows from an asset* and has nothing to do with historical costs.

Important intangible assets are often omitted from a company's balance sheet.

2. *Intangible Assets Are Excluded from the Balance Sheet:* Because they cannot be valued "objectively," intangible assets, such as management skill, reputation, and strategic positioning never appear on the balance sheet. Yet for many companies, these are the most important assets of the enterprise. In the case of BUD, for instance, the Budweiser brand's reputation as the "King of Beers" would be a thing of value, paid for by millions of dollars in advertising and promotion over generations. Since accountants have difficulty valuing this thing called "reputation" objectively, it gets left off the balance sheet completely.

3. *Important Liabilities May Be Understated or Omitted:* Important progress over the past 20 years has ensured that the divergence between book and market values of a firm's liabilities are minimized. For example, until the late 1980s, the value of future pension and health care benefits was not included on the balance sheet. Today it is, and the cost of these benefits to BUD are more than $500 million. However, some companies may have contingent liabilities that are seriously understated. For instance, a company like Philip Morris may find it impossible to assess the extent of the damage claims filed against it by nonsmokers who claim that they have been harmed by secondhand smoke.

The Income Statement

The firm's income statement summarizes revenues, expenses, and profits over some time period.

The balance sheet is a snapshot of a business at a point in time; the **income statement** records transaction flow *over a specific time period.* Exhibit 2-3 shows BUD's consolidated income statement—the revenues that are recognized for a specific period, the costs and expenses associated with these revenues, taxes, and gains and losses on special items (e.g., sale of the St. Louis Cardinals baseball team, effects of accounting changes). Net income is just the difference between sales and the various costs and taxes.

Because accountants use the matching principle, accounting profits and the generation of cash flows by a firm may be different.

It's important not to confuse accounting income with the generation of cash—they are two very different things. In coming up with net income, the accountant employs the **matching principle,** in which costs are "matched" against revenue recognized. In most instances, revenue is recognized when goods are shipped or when the service is provided. For a firm that sells on credit, there's a time lag between the recognition of revenues and the date that the company collects from its customers. This time lag is reflected in an increase in accounts receivable. In the

EXHIBIT 2-3
Anheuser-Busch Companies, Inc.
Consolidated Statement of Income (in million $)

Year Ended December 31	1997	1996
Net Sales	$11,066.2	$10,883.7
Cost of Goods Sold	7,096.9	6,964.6
Gross Profit	$ 3,969.3	$ 3,919.1
Marketing and Administrative Expenses	1,916.3	1,890.0
Gain of Sale of St. Louis Cardinals	—	54.7
Operating Income	$ 2,053.0	$ 2,083.8
Interest Expense Less Interest Income	220.5	190.9
Income Before Taxes	$ 1,832.5	$ 1,892.9
Provision for Taxes	703.6	736.8
Equity Income	50.3	—
Income from Continuing Operations	$ 1,179.2	$ 1,156.1
Effect of Accounting Change	(10.0)	—
Income (Loss) from Discontinued Operations	—	33.8
NET INCOME	$ 1,169.2	$1,189.9

Source: Anheuser-Busch Companies, Inc., *1997 Annual Report,* p. 50.

case of BUD, net sales in 1997 were $11,066.2 million, but accounts receivable increased by $80.7 million. Therefore, collections on sales would be $10,985.5 million ($11,066.2 − $80.7).

There are similar problems associated with many expense categories. For instance, a firm may get extended credit terms from suppliers and not have to pay for goods until six months after shipment. However, the materials used are a relevant cost if they can be associated with revenues generated during the accounting period. The fact that the company may not have to lay out cash for another three months doesn't come into play; these costs are still *accrued* in an accountant's calculation of net income.

As we will soon see, the gap between reported net income and cash flows can be closed by a cash flow statement. However, an accountant would have to reconcile one or more of the following problems in order to ascertain a firm's "true" earnings:

1. *Depreciation Expense May Not Measure the Consumption of Long-Lived Assets:* When a company like BUD builds a new plant, it trades in one asset—cash—for this new fixed asset. But over time, as this plant wears out or becomes technologically obsolete, its economic value will decline. This decline in **economic value** is a cost of production that should be reflected in the income statement.

   Practical problems in trying to measure this periodic decline in economic value have led accountants to adopt some straightforward methods for allocating the cost of fixed assets over their useful lives. Either the asset is written off on a straight-line basis, thereby allocating costs evenly over the life of the asset, or the firm can use one of the accelerated methods of depreciation that allocate a larger part of costs to earlier periods. Further, to come up with depreciation expense, the firm must estimate the asset's useful life as well as its salvage value at the end of that period. Even if a firm tries to use data from its engineers to make its assessment, the differences between accounting depreciation and the "true" decline in economic value may be significant. These gaps can be particularly large if a company operates in an area in which technology is changing rapidly.

2. ***Treatment of R&D and Advertising Expenditures:*** Most firms consider R&D and advertising expenditures as expenses in the period in which they are incurred. Yet these expenditures are really more like investments than operating expenses. A company like BUD uses advertising to develop a stock of **brand-name capital** (e.g., Budweiser, Michelob) to enhance future sales in much the same way as a company like Lucent Technologies uses R&D to enhance the firm's future stock of new products and process technologies.

> Many expenditures, such as R&D and advertising, are more like investments than operating expenses.

Treating advertising and R&D as expenses rather than investments goes beyond the accounting issue of labeling. Firms that are having a difficult year may be tempted to cut deeply into either R&D or advertising (or both). This will make their short-term results look good. However, well-managed firms like BUD know that consumers can be forgetful, and if Anheuser-Busch doesn't trot out the Clydesdales every Christmas, future sales will suffer. Similarly, technology-driven firms like Motorola can't really reduce R&D significantly without jeopardizing their competitive position.

3. ***Issue of Inflation in Measuring Income and Valuing Assets:*** Inflation increases the market value of the firm's assets. Under historical cost accounting, assets consumed in the business are valued at their historical costs, not their replacement costs. This makes it difficult to apply the matching principle in an inflationary environment because you may be matching today's higher revenues with yesterday's lower costs. By underreporting the true costs of replacing the assets consumed in its operations, the firm will overstate its actual earnings for that period.

> Inflation can distort both the measurement of income and the valuation of assets.

The problem of overstating income in a period of inflation is particularly acute with regard to depreciation and cost of goods sold. Accounting depreciation charges are not adjusted to reflect the higher replacement costs of new plant and equipment. Similarly, the charges for inventory reported in cost of goods sold will understate the replacement cost of inventory when prices are rising. If a company uses the **first-in, first out (FIFO)** method of valuing inventories, the cost of goods sold will reflect the prices paid for the oldest—and usually the cheapest—items in inventory. With rising prices, FIFO produces "phantom" inventory profits equal to the difference between replacement goods and their original cost. These illusory "profits" evaporate, of course, the minute stocks are replenished. The **last-in, first-out (LIFO)** method of inventory valuation corrects some of these problems by matching current revenues with the most recent prices for goods. However, LIFO still can distort the balance sheet by valuing inventory at costs that may have existed years ago.

Statement of Cash Flows

Statements of
cash flows recon-
cile differences
between account-
ing revenues
and costs, and
between cash
receipts and
disbursements.

A **statement of cash flows** attempts to reconcile the differences between the accrual basis of financial accounting and the cash transactions within a business. It enables an analyst to answer three important questions: (1) How much cash did a firm generate during the accounting period? (2) Where did the cash come from? and (3) What did the company do with the cash?[6]

Exhibit 2-4 presents a condensed version of BUD's cash flow statement for 1996 and 1997. Structurally, the statement of cash flows is divided into three sections: operating, investing, and financing activities. Mathematically, cash flow from operations (*OCF*) is:

$$OCF = NI + (DEP + AMOR) - \Delta WC \qquad [2\text{-}1]$$

where *NI* is net income, (*DEP* + *AMOR*) depreciation and amortization expense, and ΔWC the change in working capital. The section on cash flow from operating activities is essentially an effort to recognize that net income calculated on an accrual basis may be quite different than a firm's cash flow. For instance, as **depreciation** and **amortization** are *noncash expenses,* they're added to net income. Moreover, decreases (increases) in working capital are designed to reflect (among other things) the distinctions between sales and collections and cost of goods sold and cost of goods produced. The net effect of these adjustments is the item labeled "cash flow from operating activities."

Free cash flows,
not accounting
profits, are critical
to valuing an
entity.

The segment on investing activities shows transactions associated with the purchase of long-term assets and allows us to identify a company's **free cash flows,** that is, the cash flows generated by the entity after it takes on all profitable investment projects. As we'll see in later chapters, identification of free cash flows is critical to valuing an entity. In terms of the cash flow statement, a firm's free cash flow (*FCF*) is given by:

$$FCF = OCF - INVEST \qquad [2\text{-}2]$$

where *INVEST* is the cash used by investing activities. As you can see from BUD's cash flow statement, these investment transactions included the sale of an operating unit, acquisitions, and the purchase of plant and equipment. Financing activities include those cash flows associated with the sale (or retirement) of long-term debt, the sale (or repurchase) of common stock, and the payment of dividends.

BUD's statement of cash flow indicates that the firm generated about $1.9 billion in cash flow from operations in 1997. These cash flows reflected: (1) solid profits, and (2) a large amount of funds from depreciation and amortization. BUD's investment activities included about $1.2 billion in new plant and equipment. In

---

[6]Despite their strengths, cash flow statements have their weaknesses. For example, important noncash activities, such as capital leases and asset exchanges, are not included. Further, the practice of treating interest and dividends received as an operating activity yet classifying dividends paid as a financing activity is a bit inconsistent.

EXHIBIT 2-4
Anheuser-Busch Companies, Inc.
Consolidated Statement of Cash Flows (in million $)

Year Ended December 31	1997	1996
CASH FLOW FROM OPERATING ACTIVITIES		
Income from Continuing Operations	$1,179.2	$1,156.1
Adjustments:		
Depreciation and Amortization	683.7	611.5
Decrease (Increase) in Working Capital	5.4	233.7
Other Adjustments	(51.7)	19.6
Total Cash Flow from Operations	$1,816.6	$2,020.9
CASH FLOW FROM INVESTING ACTIVITIES		
Capital Expenditures	(1,199.3)	(1,084.6)
Proceeds from Sale of St. Louis Cardinals	—	116.6
Acquisitions	(683.3)	(135.7)
Cash Used by Investing Activities	(1,882.6)	(1,103.7)
CASH FLOW FROM FINANCING ACTIVITIES		
Increase in Long-Term Debt	1,104.3	198.5
Dividends Paid to Shareholders	(492.6)	(458.9)
Stock Repurchases	(587.1)	(770.2)
Shares Issued under Employee Stock Plans	95.1	113.4
Cash Used in Financing Activities	119.7	(917.2)
Change in Cash + Marketable Securities during Year	53.7	—
Cash + Marketable Securities at Beginning of Year	93.6	93.6
Cash + Marketable Securities at End of Year	$ 147.3	$ 93.6

Source: Anheuser-Busch Companies, Inc., *1997 Annual Report,* p. 53.

addition to its capital expenditures, acquisitions consumed another $683.3 million. According to the notes to BUD's financial statements, the new business acquisitions reflect the company's global expansion: It took a minority position in a Mexican brewery and purchased the balance of a Scottish brewery. After this aggressive investment program, BUD's free cash flow in 1997 was negative:

$$(FCF)_{1997} = \$1,816.6 - \$1,882.6 = -\$66.0$$

The financing activities section indicates that the company raised $1.1 billion through new long-term debt offerings. In addition to filling the $66 million free cash flow gap, the debt issue facilitated BUD's dividend and stock repurchase programs.

2.2   FINANCIAL RATIO ANALYSIS

Ratio analysis is a tool for organizing information in order to allow an analyst to diagnose a firm's financial condition and assess performance.

Ratio analysis is a relatively simple yet powerful tool in diagnosing the financial condition of a firm and enables the analyst to relate one piece of financial data to another. A ratio by itself has little meaning: Ratio analysis is useful only as a comparative tool. Two types of comparisons can be made. First, we can use **trend analysis** to detect a significant improvement or deterioration in a firm's financial or competitive position. Second, an analyst can use **cross-sectional analysis** to compare a firm with others in its industry. In this context, a successful firm is one that continually outperforms its competitors' norms.

The principal sources of data on industry averages are Robert Morris Associates (an association of credit managers), Dun and Bradstreet, and the Federal Trade Commission. Most of these organizations classify ratio norms by asset size. This avoids the difficulty of trying to compare the ratios of a company with $1 million in assets with one having over $1 billion. One must still use judgment in making cross-sectional comparisons. A company's ratios can differ from industry averages for a variety of reasons, not the least of which is that its corporate strategy may be different from that of the "average" firm in the industry. Further, it may be impossible to place a diversified firm like General Electric within any specific industry.

Ratio Categories

Different stakeholders may be concerned with different ratio categories.

The various stakeholders in a company will have different concerns about a firm's performance. For example, a supplier extending trade credit is primarily interested in the company's ability to pay its bills on time. Stockholders and bondholders, on the other hand, will probably be far more concerned about a company's long-term profitability and how well it's being run. Management is concerned with both the short- and long-run aspects of the company's operations as it is responsible for running the firm on a day-to-day basis and charting its long-term course.

No single ratio or small set of ratios can begin to meet the burdens imposed by these different needs. Thus, four ratio categories have been developed to address important aspects of a firm's financial condition:

1. **Liquidity ratios** measure the quality and adequacy of current assets to meet current liabilities as they come due.
2. **Activity ratios** measure the efficiency with which a firm uses its resources.
3. **Financial leverage ratios** measure a company's ability to handle its debt.
4. **Profitability ratios** measure management's effectiveness at generating net income in relation to sales, total assets, and shareholder equity.

To illustrate the types of questions that might arise from ratio analysis, let's turn to the 1997 through 1999 financial statements of Spectrum Manufacturing Company, shown in Exhibits 2-5 and 2-6. To simplify our lives, we'll assume that the industry averages used as a basis of comparison remain constant over the three-year period covered by our analysis. As a practical matter, we should match the trend of the company's ratios with the industry's trend. It is entirely possible that the decline in the ratios for a firm simply mirrors the decline for the industry.

EXHIBIT 2-5
Spectrum Manufacturing Company
Balance Sheets as of December 31, 1997 to 1999 (in thousand $)

Assets	1999	1998	1997
Current Assets			
Cash	$ 45	$ 355	$ 210
Accounts Receivable	4,545	4,403	3,150
Inventories	3,932	4,089	2,025
Prepaid Expenses	234	291	134
Total Current Assets	$ 8,756	$ 9,138	$5,519
Plant and Equipment, Net Depreciation	4,640	2,979	2,275
Total Assets	$13,396	$12,117	$7,794
Liabilities and Equity			
Current Liabilities			
Accounts Payable	$ 3,360	$ 2,783	$ 806
Taxes Payable	465	735	855
Accrued Expenses	720	789	255
Bank Loan	225	-0-	-0-
Total Current Liabilities	$ 4,770	$ 4,307	$1,916
Long-Term Debt	3,686	3,302	1,779
Total Liabilities	$ 8,456	$ 7,609	$3,695
Shareholders' Equity	4,940	4,508	4,099
Total Liabilities + Equity	$13,396	$12,117	$7,794

EXHIBIT 2-6
Spectrum Manufacturing Company
Income Statements
Fiscal Years 1997–1999 (in thousand $)

	1999	1998	1997
Sales	$21,015	$27,450	$21,900
Cost of Goods Sold			
Materials	10,785	16,695	13,395
Direct Labor	2,880	3,075	2,220
Manufacturing Overhead	1,455	1,455	960
Gross Profits	$ 5,895	$ 6,225	$ 5,325
Operating Expenses			
Selling Expenses	1,593	1,676	1,440
Depreciation	470	327	108
General and Administrative Expenses	2,567	2,447	1,862
Net Operating Income	$ 1,265	$ 1,775	$ 1,915
Interest Expense	389	363	142
Earnings before Taxes	$ 876	$ 1,412	$ 1,773
Taxes	324	576	829
Net Income	$ 552	$ 836	$ 944

Liquidity Ratios

Liquidity refers to a company's ability to meet its short-term obligations and is closely related to the size and composition of the firm's working capital position (current assets minus current liabilities). Other things being equal, a higher working capital position implies a more liquid position. This is because a firm's current assets are the easiest to convert to cash, making them the main source of cash to meet maturing obligations.

An evaluation of the *quality* of a firm's receivable and inventory accounts is critical to any assessment of liquidity.

Several measures can be used to assess a company's liquidity position. Although very useful, they are no substitute for a careful examination of the *quality* of the firm's current assets. When looking at liquidity ratios, the financial analyst must examine carefully the receivable and inventory accounts. A firm's liquidity position might appear to be favorable only because it has neglected to write off bad debts, allowed accounts to become overdue, or accumulated excess inventory. The two main measures of liquidity are the current ratio and the quick ratio.

The **current ratio** equals current assets divided by current liabilities, or

$$\text{Current Ratio} = \text{Current Assets}/\text{Current Liabilities} \qquad [2\text{-}3]$$

This ratio indicates the amount of current assets available to meet all of the maturing obligations listed under current liabilities. Creditors look at this ratio carefully as it measures the "cushion" between current obligations and the firm's most liquid assets. The current ratios for Spectrum are computed as follows:

	1999	**1998**	**1997**
Total Current Assets	$8,756	$9,138	$5,519
Total Current Liabilities	4,770	4,307	1,916
Current Ratio	1.84	2.12	2.88
Industry Average = 2.16			

High current ratios may not be accurate indicators of a firm's ability to pay its bills on time.

The sharp decline in Spectrum's current ratio from 1997 to 1999 represents a serious drop in the firm's liquidity position. Moreover, in 1997, Spectrum's current ratio was far above the industry average; in 1999, it's significantly below. From a lender's standpoint, a higher current ratio is more desirable since it provides a bigger cushion against erosion in value of the current assets in the event of bankruptcy and liquidation. However, viewed from a managerial perspective, a high current ratio could also mean poor operating practices such as excess cash balances, slow-paying receivables, or obsolete inventory that should be written off.

Since inventories are generally the least liquid of a company's current assets, they may not be available to readily settle claims. Therefore, a more conservative measure of liquidity is the **quick** or **acid-test ratio,** which excludes inventory from the denominator of a liquidity measure:

$$\text{Quick Ratio} = (\text{Current Assets} - \text{Inventories})/\text{Current Liabilities} \qquad [2\text{-}4]$$

The quick ratios for Spectrum are as follows:

	1999	1998	1997
Total Current Assets Less Inventory	$4,824	$5,049	$3,494
Total Current Liabilities	4,770	4,307	1,916
Quick Ratio	1.01	1.17	1.82
Industry Average = 1.52			

The decline in Spectrum's quick ratio shouldn't surprise us in light of the decline in the company's current ratio. This decline should worry both current and potential short-term creditors, particularly if an analyst suspects that some of the receivables may be uncollectable. The warning flag is up because the dollar amount of Spectrum's receivables is rising in the face of declining sales.

Finally, the ratio of cash to total assets has declined from 2.7 percent ($210/$7,794) in 1997 to 0.3 percent ($45/$13,396) in 1999.[7] This is troublesome. After all, bills are paid with cash, and a decline of this magnitude signals a deterioration in Spectrum's liquidity position.

Activity Ratios

Activity or asset utilization **ratios** are concerned with how well a company uses its productive resources and are related to the amount of sales generated per dollar invested in particular assets. We'll look at activity ratios relating to accounts receivable, inventory, and total assets. Although many analysts calculate these ratios based on an average of beginning and ending assets, we'll use the actual year-end values of the assets in our computations. This not only simplifies calculations but makes the resulting numbers comparable with published industry averages.

For starters, let's look at the **accounts receivable turnover,** which equals net credit sales divided by receivables, or

$$\text{Accounts Receivable Turnover} = \text{Net Credit Sales}/\text{Receivables} \qquad [2\text{-}5]$$

This ratio measures the number of times that accounts receivable turn over during the year. The higher the receivables turnover, the shorter the time between the sales and collection period. Thus, the ratio indicates how well the firm is managing its credit and collection policies. If a company has a lower turnover rate than the industry does, its receivables policy and the *quality* of its receivables should be looked at more closely. The company could be pursuing an overly lenient credit policy or failing to collect its receivables on time.

Carelessness in the management of accounts receivable may lead to credit losses, increases in collection expenses, and an increased amount of assets tied up

---

[7]The ratio of cash to assets is sometimes referred to as the *cash ratio.* An alternative measure of liquidity focusing exclusively on cash is the ratio of cash to sales.

in receivables. Although lenient credit policy typically generates more sales, it also produces more bad debts and involves a significant opportunity cost—the cost of funds invested in receivables.

If all of Spectrum's sales are on credit, its receivables turnover ratios are as follows:

	1999	1998	1997
Net Credit Sales	$21,015	$27,450	$21,900
Accounts Receivable	4,545	4,403	3,150
Receivables Turnover	4.62 times	6.23 times	6.95 times
Industry Average = 6.79 times			

The figures indicate that one dollar of receivables supported $4.62 in sales in 1999, as compared to $6.95 in annual sales in 1997. This is not the direction you'd like to be taking. However, before analyzing Spectrum's situation further, it's worthwhile to introduce another measure of receivables management—the **average collection period.** This ratio is given by:

$$\text{Average Collection Period} = (365)(\text{Receivables})/\text{Net Credit Sales} \quad [2\text{-}6]$$

and represents the time it takes for an "average" customer to pay its bills.[8] In most instances, a lengthening of the average collection period means higher delinquencies and higher potential bad debt losses. A longer collection period also means that a company will have more money tied up in accounts receivable.

Assuming all of Spectrum's sales are on credit, the average collection period is as follows:

	1999	1998	1997
Accounts Receivable	$4,545	$4,403	$3,150
Credit Sales	21,015	27,450	21,900
Average Collection Period (Days)	78.9	58.5	52.5
Industry Average = 53.8 days			

Additional information is needed to evaluate the importance of the 26.4-day increase in the collection period from 1997 to 1999. This usually requires an **aging of accounts receivable.** Aging involves categorizing receivables according

---

[8]The average collection period is sometimes referred to as *days sales outstanding (DSO)*.

to the length of time they are outstanding.[9] This should be done for at least two different time periods to permit an analysis of trends. An aging analysis covering 1999 and 1998 is presented as follows:

	1999		1998	
	Amount Outstanding	**Percentage of Total**	**Amount Outstanding**	**Percentage of Total**
Receivables:				
0–30 Days Old	$2,545	56%	$2,994	68%
31–60 Days Old	1,153	25	793	18
61–90 Days Old	445	10	352	8
Over 91 Days	402	9	264	6
	$4,545	100%	$4,403	100%

The aging analysis indicates a worsening trend in receivables collection within the standard 30-day collection period. In 1998, 32 percent of the receivables were past due compared to 44 percent a year later. Moreover, a higher percentage of the accounts was at least 60 days old. This raises many questions about the liquidity and the value of the receivables, because the more delinquent an account is, the harder it is to collect it.

The sharp increase in the collection period from 1997 to 1999, coupled with the increased delinquency data from the aging analysis, should have someone knocking on the door of the credit manager and asking some pointed questions about whether credit policy is too lenient or whether Spectrum is making enough of an effort to collect overdue accounts. However, before Spectrum begins using its credit manager as a punching bag, it needs to understand the critical relationship between credit policy and sales. Specifically, when a company like Spectrum sells on credit, it's providing its customers with a product (or service) *plus* financing for a short amount of time. It does so in the belief that allowing customers to pay within 30 or 60 days will lead to higher sales than if it insisted on cash. From this perspective, *credit terms can be viewed as a competitive weapon for stimulating sales.* Thus, the 26-day increase in the collection period might reflect a conscious attempt by Spectrum to increase sales in a market in which price cuts—a very visible act—will be sure to draw a competitive response. Relaxing credit terms, on the other hand, can be done quietly, on a customer-by-customer basis.

Many firms use credit policy as a dynamic tool for stimulating sales.

If Spectrum were using credit terms rather than price to compete, we'd expect account profitability to be higher. To look at this issue in more detail, let's

---

[9]Although an outside analyst would not have the information to do an aging analysis, these data would be available to the company's managers as well as to lenders who might be financing these receivables.

jump ahead a bit and introduce one of the profitability ratios, the **gross profit margin** on sales where

$$\text{Gross Profit Margin} = \text{Gross Profits/Net Sales} \qquad [2\text{-}7]$$

Spectrum's gross profit margins are as follows:

	1999	**1998**	**1997**
Gross Profits	$5,895	$6,225	$5,325
Net Sales	21,015	27,450	21,900
Gross Profit Margin	28.0%	22.7%	24.3%
Industry Average = 23.1%			

Taken by itself, the increased gross profit margin in 1999 relative to 1998 is commendable. However, this improved profitability must be considered in light of a much longer collection period and higher delinquencies. The 5 percent higher profit margin on 1999 sales is $1,050,750 (5% of $21,015,000), but this increase in gross profits may be illusory. After all, Spectrum's investment in accounts receivable is higher, and financing these increases isn't costless. Further, the company is probably taking on marginal customers to boost sales, and some of these customers may show up as bad-debt losses. The fundamental question is whether the $1 million or so in higher gross profits will be wiped out by the combination of increased bad-debt losses and higher financing costs.

After accounts receivable, the most liquid asset is inventory. **Inventory turnover** is an index of how fast goods flow through inventory, either from purchase to sale in a retail or wholesale business or from raw material to sale in a manufacturing firm. It is computed by dividing cost of goods sold by inventory,[10] or

$$\text{Inventory Turnover} = \text{Cost of Goods Sold/Inventory} \qquad [2\text{-}8]$$

Using year-end values as a basis for calculations, Spectrum's inventory turnover is as follows:

	1999	**1998**	**1997**
Cost of Goods Sold	$15,120	$21,225	$16,575
Inventory	3,932	4,089	2,025
Inventory Turnover	3.8 times	5.2 times	8.2 times
Industry Average = 6.3 times			

---

[10]Another way to look at inventory activity is the *days inventory on hand,* which is equal to 365 divided by the inventory turnover. This measures the average time, in days, that a firm could meet customer demand with its existing stock of inventory.

Managing inventories is a balancing act; low inventory turnover could mean losses due to obsolescence whereas rapid turnover could mean lost sales due to stockouts.

The figures reflect a *significant* decline in the firm's inventory turnover over a two-year period. Slow inventory turnover is potentially dangerous if a company's products are subject to obsolescence because of either style changes (e.g., designer clothing) or a competitor's technological breakthrough. In either instance, excess inventory can turn into losses very quickly. On the other hand, if the company manufactures household products such as pots, pans, and other cooking utensils, obsolescence might not be a concern. Instead, the company will have to do a better job of adjusting production to sales.

Finally, we can examine the **total asset turnover,** which encompasses all of the activity ratios we've looked at up to this point and is defined as

$$\text{Total Asset Turnover} = \text{Net Sales}/\text{Total Assets} \qquad [2\text{-}9]$$

Ideally, high asset turnovers are preferred to lower ones because rising values imply that a firm will need fewer assets to generate a dollar of sales. This also translates into lower financing needs because any asset increases must be matched with subsequent increases in liabilities and equity. The total asset turnover for Spectrum is as follows:

	1999	1998	1997
Net Sales	$21,015	$27,450	$21,900
Total Assets	13,396	12,117	7,794
Total Asset Turnover	1.6 times	2.3 times	2.8 times
Industry Average = 2.6 times			

As with all of the other activity ratios we've examined, this one also shows significant deterioration. The trends in these activity ratios should also raise questions about the real values of the assets listed on Spectrum's balance sheet. Combined with Spectrum's liquidity position, the activity ratios give us a sense that this firm is in brittle condition. If you're a short-term creditor, you should be reaching for the Tums or Maalox bottle just about now.

Financial Leverage Ratios

Financial leverage ratios measure a firm's risk by focusing on its financing mix. Analysts typically use two approaches to measuring leverage.[11] One is to examine the various balance sheet ratios to determine the extent to which a firm uses debt to finance total assets. The presumption is that the more debt is used to finance operations, the greater risk. The other approach is to use income statement data to develop *coverage ratios,* which measure the company's ability to service that debt.

---

[11]In the United Kingdom and countries on the European continent, leverage is referred to as **gearing.**

Two of the most widely used balance sheet ratios are the debt ratio and the debt-equity ratio. As used here, debt includes *all of the firm's liabilities*—current liabilities as well as long-term debt. The **debt ratio** is defined as

$$\text{Debt Ratio} = \text{Total Liabilities}/\text{Total Assets} \qquad [2\text{-}10]$$

and the **debt-equity ratio** is

$$\text{Debt-Equity Ratio} = \text{Total Liabilities}/\text{Equity} \qquad [2\text{-}11]$$

The debt-to-equity ratio can be derived from the debt ratio by noting that total assets equals total liabilities plus equity. Equation [2-11] then becomes

$$\text{Debt-Equity Ratio} = \text{Debt Ratio}/(1 - \text{Debt Ratio}) \qquad [2\text{-}11a]$$

The debt ratios and debt-equity ratios for Spectrum are calculated as follows:

	1999	1998	1997
Total Liabilities	$8,456	$7,609	$3,695
Total Assets	13,396	12,117	7,794
Stockholder's Equity	4,940	4,508	4,099
Debt Ratio	0.63	0.63	0.47
Debt-Equity Ratio	1.71	1.69	0.90

Industry Average (Debt Ratio) = 0.55
Industry Average (Debt-Equity Ratio) = 1.22

Both ratios have increased over time, indicating that creditors are being exposed to more risk. Most of the deterioration occurred between 1997 and 1998. In addition, the increases in these ratios will impair Spectrum's ability to borrow in the future, thereby reducing the firm's flexibility in meeting competitive and other threats.

More important than the level of debt is a company's ability to handle that debt. **Times interest earned,** a commonly used ratio, measures the firm's ability to meet its interest payments out of annual earnings before interest and taxes (EBIT) and is defined as

> A firm's ability to handle its debt is far more important than the level of debt per se.

$$\text{Times Interest Earned} = \text{EBIT}/\text{Interest} \qquad [2\text{-}12]$$

This ratio indicates how many times the firm's operating earnings (EBIT) can "cover" its interest expense. The times interest earned for Spectrum is as follows:

	1999	1998	1997
Net Operating Income (EBIT)	$1,265	$1,775	$1,915
Interest Expense	389	363	142
Times Interest Earned	3.3 times	4.9 times	13.5 times

Industry Average = 5.4 times

Although this ratio has deteriorated over time and is now lower than the industry norm, it still appears to be high enough to provide good security to creditors. Further, the problem with the decline in interest coverage also appears to have as much to do with the erosion of operating income as it does with increases in debt. If, for example, EBIT in 1999 had been the same as it was in 1997, times interest earned would be $1,915/$389 or 4.92.

> **A company's ability to generate cash is critical to its being able to service its contractual obligations.**

Times interest earned has some weaknesses as a measure of a firm's ability to meet its debt obligations. What matters is the amount of *cash,* not *accounting earnings,* that's available to service that debt. Therefore, the numerator of Equation [2-12] should be increased by depreciation (a noncash charge to earnings) and reduced by necessary working capital investments. The denominator in Equation [2-12] should also be adjusted to include all of the firm's fixed financial charges—including debt repayment, leases and other rental payments as well as preferred stock dividends.

One way to deal with some of these issues is to calculate a firm's **cash flow coverage**, which is given by

$$\text{Cash Flow Coverage} = \frac{\text{EBIT} + \text{Lease/Rental Payments} + \text{Depreciation}}{\text{Interest} + \text{Lease/Rental Payments} + \text{Principal Repayment}/(1 - T)} \quad [2\text{-}13]$$

where T is the firm's tax rate. Principal payments are divided by $(1 - T)$ because they are not tax deductible and so must be paid with after-tax dollars. Therefore, the firm must generate more pre-tax dollars (EBIT) so there's enough income to repay debt.

Spectrum's balance sheet doesn't show any lease obligations. Although a balance sheet doesn't specify debt repayment, you can get this information from the notes to a firm's financial statements. For our purposes, let's assume that annual principal repayment is $680,000 a year. With depreciation of $470,000 in 1999 and a tax rate of 40 percent, Spectrum's cash flow coverage is

$$\text{Cash Flow Coverage} = \frac{\$1,265 + \$470}{\$389 + \$680/0.60} = 1.14 \text{ times}$$

Spectrum's cash flow coverage is marginal in terms of any cushion in meeting its financial commitments. Considering the possibility of losses from uncollectable receivables and worthless inventories, there is a strong possibility of a financial crisis next year. Moreover, the calculation doesn't take into account the increases in working capital that will be required if the company is to improve its liquidity position.

Profitability Ratios

> **Profitability ratios are vital in assessing managerial performance.**

Profitability or operating ratios are designed to help evaluate management's performance. Two types of operating ratios are used: profit margins on sales and returns on assets employed. Profit margins attempt to measure the firm's ability to control expenses in relation to sales. They include the gross profit margin, the operating profit margin, and the net profit margin. The gross profit margin was defined earlier as

$$\text{Gross Profit Margin} = \text{Gross Profits}/\text{Net Sales}$$

The **operating profit margin** is

$$\text{Operating Profit Margin} = \text{EBIT}/\text{Net Sales} \qquad [2\text{-}14]$$

while the **net profit margin** is

$$\text{Net Profit Margin} = \text{Net Income}/\text{Net Sales} \qquad [2\text{-}15]$$

Let's see how these ratios work as a "package" for Spectrum:

	1999	1998	1997
Gross Profits	$5,895	$6,225	$5,325
Net Operating Income (EBIT)	1,265	1,775	1,915
Net Income	552	836	944
Net Sales	21,015	27,450	21,900
Gross Profit Margins	28.0%	22.7%	24.3%
Operating Profit Margins	6.0%	6.5%	8.7%
Net Profit Margins	2.6%	3.0%	4.3%

Industry Average (Gross Profit Margin) = 23.1%
Industry Average (Operating Profit Margin) = 7.3%
Industry Average (Net Profit Margin) = 3.4%

The gross profit margin measures the relative profitability of sales in relation to cost of goods sold. As we eluded to earlier, gross profit margins say something about a firm's pricing policy; management can opt for low margin and higher volume or vice versa. Spectrum's strategy appears to be geared around higher margins even if that means declining sales.

The decline in operating profit margins, combined with the increase in gross profit margins, may indicate a decline in management's operating efficiency. Examining the income statement data more closely, we see that part of the reason for the decline in operating profits is the much higher depreciation expense associated with the added investment in fixed assets. Also contributing to the decline is the fact that Spectrum's general and administrative expenses have risen in the face of declining sales.

The profitability of firms with high fixed expenses can suffer if sales fall unexpectedly.

Spectrum's net profit margins have also declined, reflecting the higher interest expenses associated with higher levels of debt. The deterioration of the firm's operating and net margins reflects, in part, the difficulties that any growing firm experiences when sales fail to meet expectations. We may be seeing a company at which sales increased rapidly from 1997 to 1998. Anticipating another sales increase in 1999, Spectrum not only added to plant and equipment (hence the higher depreciation) but also increased its general and administrative staff to service the (anticipated) higher customer base. Unfortunately, the forecasted sales increase didn't materialize; instead, it declined sharply. Since some expenses, such as general and administrative expenses, tend to be fixed in the short run, profit margins suffer when sales fall unexpectedly. If the decline in sales is due to an unexpected recession, there may be little management can do but try to ride out the storm. However, Spectrum's problems may be far more serious if it has lost sales because of poor product quality or a competitor who supplied customers with a superior product at a lower price.

In addition to looking at profits in relation to sales, we can relate returns to assets and shareholder's equity. The two most frequently used measures are **return on assets (ROA),** commonly referred to as **return on investment (ROI),** and **return on equity (ROE).** ROA focuses on the earning power of on going operations and is defined as

$$\text{Return on Assets (ROA)} = \text{Net Income}/\text{Total Assets} \qquad [2\text{-}16]$$

ROE measures returns solely in relation to the shareholders' investment in the business and is

$$\text{Return on Equity (ROE)} = \text{Net Income}/\text{Shareholders' Equity} \qquad [2\text{-}17]$$

Spectrum's ROA and ROE for 1997 through 1999 are as follows:

	1999	1998	1997
Net Income	$ 552	$ 836	$ 944
Total Assets	13,396	12,117	7,794
Shareholders' Equity	4,940	4,508	4,099
Return on Assets	4.1%	6.9%	12.1%
Return on Equity	11.2%	18.5%	23.0%
Industry Average (Return on Assets) = 7.3%			
Industry Average (Return on Equity) = 16.7%			

Not surprisingly, both ROA and ROE exhibit declining trends. Spectrum's performance on both of these return measures has deteriorated both in absolute terms and relative to the rest of the industry. Creditors may not be particularly concerned with these trends, but they are of vital importance to shareholders. Although ROA and ROE are accounting-based measures of returns, firms that consistently generate high ROAs and ROEs will see this performance translated into higher stock prices.

Putting It Together: The DuPont Analysis

A manager's understanding of ratios as a system is vital to improving a firm's performance.

Financial ratios are interrelated because all ratios are derived from the same income statement and balance sheet. In trying to assess a company's financial strengths and weaknesses, managers must understand ratios as a system rather than as a set of independent measures. It's not unusual for a company to have the same ratio in successive years or for two companies to have identical numbers for a given ratio. But these numbers may have quite different implications when viewed in concert with other numbers. What we need is a way of seeing how ratios interrelate with one another to produce a given result.

Return on equity is a function of profitability, efficient asset utilization, and leverage.

Perhaps the most widely used method of looking at the relationships among ratios is the **DuPont analysis.** Developed by this large chemical firm in the 1930s, the DuPont analysis dissects a firm's return on equity through the following equation:

$$\text{ROE} = (\text{Net Profit Margin})(\text{Total Asset Turnover})(\text{Equity Multiplier}) \qquad [2\text{-}18]$$

$$= \frac{\text{Net Income}}{\text{Sales}} \times \frac{\text{Sales}}{\text{Assets}} \times \frac{\text{Assets}}{\text{Equity}}$$

The ratio "Assets/Equity" is called the **equity multiplier** and indicates the amount of debt supported by each dollar of equity. We can see this more clearly by recognizing that total assets equals total liabilities (debt) plus equity, so the equity multiplier can be written as [1 + (Debt/Equity)]. Thus, an increase in the equity multiplier means that proportionately more debt is being used to finance the firm's assets. The DuPont analysis for Spectrum Manufacturing covering 1997 through 1999 is presented in Exhibit 2-7.

The resulting ROEs are the same ones we calculated directly in the previous sections, but now we can see how the profit margin, total asset turnover, and financing mix combine to produce Spectrum's return on equity. Using the DuPont framework, it becomes clear that the sharp declines in both the net profit margin and in asset utilization, as reflected in the lower total asset turnover, are equally to blame for Spectrum's significantly lower ROE. The return on equity would have dropped even further but for an increase in financial leverage. However, while increasing the debt ratio "improves" returns to equity, it also increases risk. In the 1997–1999 period, Spectrum's financial risk has increased while returns to equity have decreased. This is not the path any company should be going down.

EXHIBIT 2-7
Spectrum Manufacturing Company
DuPont Analysis
Fiscal Years 1997–1999

Year	Net Profit Margin (%)	×	Total Asset Turnover	×	Equity Multiplier	=	ROE (%)
1997	4.3		2.8		1.9		23.0
1998	3.0		2.3		2.7		18.5
1999	2.6		1.6		2.7		11.2

The DuPont analysis is a good starting point for assessing the firm's financial health because it focuses attention on those areas with the greatest impact on owner returns. Beyond simplifying the financial analysis, the DuPont framework can also provide some useful insights into linkage between corporate strategy and finance. Consider, for instance, the situation faced by discount retailers like Wal-Mart or Kmart. Both of these firms are (or should be) executing a *low-cost provider strategy* with price as their major competitive weapon. Purchasing prowess and cost containment will be important elements of how these companies conduct business. However, despite their best efforts, net profit margins are likely to be far lower than those of, say, a pharmaceutical company. The challenge for the Wal-Marts and Kmarts of this world is how to generate respectable ROEs in this environment.

Holding profit margins constant, the DuPont analysis tells us that we have two policy variables to "play with." First, we can improve ROE by increasing the equity multiplier, which is the same as saying that we should increase debt. However, using debt to finance asset growth will increase interest expense and lower profit margins. Besides, increasing leverage adds to financial risk, and it is already tough enough to maintain a competitive advantage in retailing without adding to our list of worries.

> For many highly competitive industries, high asset utilization is the key to high ROEs.

A more useful approach would be to focus on increasing total asset turnover. For a Wal-Mart, this might mean: (1) dealing on a cash basis and avoiding in-house credit cards (which means no receivables),[12] (2) maintaining an inventory control system that produces high turnover with a maximum of customer service, (3) allocating shelf space to items that are selling rapidly, and (4) leasing, rather than owning, its facilities. In order to efficiently allocate shelf space, Wal-Mart must have a "real-time" information system that tells the company what's selling where, supported by a state-of-the-art distribution system. This "things-to-do" list might be easier said than done, but at least the company will be pointed in the appropriate direction.[13,14]

Southwest Airlines (LUV[15]) is another company that creatively uses high asset turnover and cost control to generate superior returns. Like all airlines, LUV

---

[12]This doesn't mean a firm like Wal-Mart shouldn't accept any credit cards. When it takes VISA or MasterCard, it can turn the receipts in and get cash immediately.

[13]Dell Computer is another company that's turned a low-margin mail-order operation into a high ROE business through superior asset utilization. By tapping into credit cards and electronic payments, Dell has been able to convert orders into cash within a day. Further, using state-of-the-art inventory management techniques, inventory turnover is about 24 times a year. More details on how Dell generates some of the best returns among computer manufacturers can be found in "Whirlwind Among Computer Manufacturers," *Business Week,* April 7, 1997, pp. 132–136.

[14]The challenges of a retail jeweler are different from those of a Wal-Mart or Kmart. Inventory is made up of high-ticket items, with selection being the key to making the sale. Many jewelers also have in-house payment plans that allow the purchaser to finance large purchases over time. In this setting, total asset turnover will be quite low—perhaps as little as once a year. To generate good ROEs, a retail jeweler must pay attention to profit margins.

[15]Southwest Airline's common stock is traded on the New York Stock exchange under the ticker symbol *LUV.*

EXHIBIT 2-8
Operating Expenses per Seat Mile (in cents) 1993–1997

Carrier	1993	1994	1995	1996	1997
Southwest Airlines	7.25	7.08	7.07	7.50	7.40
American Airlines	8.25	8.34	8.43	8.91	9.27
United Airlines	8.67	8.82	8.86	9.36	9.53
Delta	9.25	9.49	8.83	9.17	8.63
Northwest Airlines	8.00	8.08	8.66	8.78	8.63

wants to keep its planes full and flying, the key dimensions to asset turnover. The firm's marketing strategy is keyed around low price and reliable, no-frills service. Southwest's operating strategy complements its marketing approach by focusing on short-haul routes that service high-traffic destinations (e.g., Phoenix to LA). It also emphasizes rapid turnaround, which keeps planes in the air longer. Rapid turnaround is facilitated by operating out of secondary airports, such as Love in Dallas, Hobby in Houston, Oakland in the San Francisco Bay area, Midway in Chicago, and BWI in the Washington, D.C., area. The fleet consists *exclusively* of Boeing 737s, which are fuel efficient and ideally suited for short-distance flights. Sticking to one aircraft also minimizes the firm's inventory of spare parts as well as controlling maintenance and training costs. Through its route selection strategy, Southwest has made the Boeing 737 an *extremely valuable asset.*

Flexible work rules contribute to Southwest's profitability. It is not unusual for LUV's flight attendants to serve at the check-in counter when they are not in the air. The combination of *route selection, equipment choice, and personnel practices* has made LUV one of the lowest-cost providers in the industry. Exhibit 2-8, drawn from financial data from the Web sites of major airlines, indicates that Southwest's operating expenses per *available seat mile*—a measure of both cost control and equipment utilization—are far lower than its competitors'. For example, LUV's costs per seat mile in 1997 were 20 and 22.4 percent lower than American's and United Airlines', respectively. That's a huge competitive advantage!

2.3   NONFINANCIAL MEASURES OF OPERATING EFFECTIVENESS

Because generating returns to shareholders is the corporate *raison d'être,* this chapter has emphasized financial measures of performance. However, the focus on the bottom line shouldn't blind managers of well-run companies to what it takes to get there. Many of the most important determinants of future corporate profitability are more difficult to quantify: innovation, customer service, and product quality. Yet these and similar indicators, hard as they may be to quantify, are leading signs of a company's ability to remain competitive and create shareholder value.

For many firms, nonfinancial measures of operating performance may be more important to creating shareholder value than those things that are easily quantified.

The appropriate measures to use in controlling operations depend on the performance desired from a business unit, which, in turn, is driven by the overall corporate strategy. For the marketing-oriented firm, market share, the rate of new product introductions, timeliness of deliveries, or sales cost per dollar of revenues may be the most relevant yardsticks. In contrast, a firm such as 3M, which thrives on product innovation, would pay close attention to the fraction of sales accounted for by products developed within the past five years. When this ratio begins slipping, the company knows that its future sales and profitability will suffer. In recognition of its increasing global competition, 3M recently raised the required ratio from 25 percent to 30 percent.

Moreover, there's no rule that says that each unit within a company should be judged in the same way. Even a marketing-oriented firm's production unit will likely be judged on the basis of production costs and product quality, whereas the research and development group may be evaluated, in part, on the time between the inception of an innovation and its introduction as a successful product in the marketplace.

Some companies' traditional accounting data are inadequate. For example, although quality is a byword among firms these days, many companies find that they don't know what it would cost to make a product of requisite quality or what it might be worth to do so. These companies have never figured out what it costs to do things wrong—sending back things that aren't up to standard, pulling defective parts off an assembly line, employing quality inspectors to check other workers' mistakes, and smoothing the ruffled feathers of angry customers. If more things are done right the first time, these costs shrink.

Some key performance measures are more nebulous but no less important. Customer satisfaction, a company's reputation as an innovator, good employee relations—all of these translate into profits down the line by building intangible assets such as brand names and loyal customers and employees. The fact that we can't measure these things precisely doesn't mean that we should ignore these aspects of a company's operations completely. For many firms, the **intangible assets** are more important to creating competitive advantage and shareholder value than the tangible assets. For example, Texas Instruments helped create the technologies behind such products as hand-held calculators, digital watches, and personal computers, but despite some initial success, TI ultimately took a beating in its markets. Others had a better understanding of the marketplace and customers' needs. Earlier emphasis on customer satisfaction—and what was needed to ensure it—might have enabled TI to capitalize on its innovative research and development.

2.4 SEGMENTED FINANCIAL STATEMENTS

One of the challenges of performing a cross-sectional analysis is finding an appropriate industry norm to use as a basis of comparison. This problem is particularly acute for diversified firms like Philip Morris or General Electric that can't be conveniently placed in any specific industry. Fortunately, the notes to the financial statements of these firms contain data on their business segments. While the data may not be as detailed as we'd like, the notes can provide us with a greater understanding of the firm being reviewed.

For example, BUD has two principal business segments: beer/beer-related units and entertainment. The beer/beer-related segment produces and markets the company's beer products. Included in this segment are BUD's manufacturing, recycling, and transportation operations. Major U.S. competitors are Miller Brewing (part of Philip Morris) and Coors. The entertainment segment includes the company's Sea World, Busch Gardens, and other theme parks as well as real estate development operations. In terms of market share, BUD's entertainment segment is second to Disney. Until late 1995, BUD also had a food products segment, which included the company's bakery products and Eagle Brand snack foods operations. In 1995, the company sold its snack foods plants and divested its bakery products operation through a 100 percent spin-off to its shareholders. The notes to BUD's financial statements provide some clues as to why the company divested these and other assets.

In these notes you will find the sales, operating income, and identifiable assets associated with each line of business. These data were used to generate Exhibit 2-9, which looks at the pre-tax return on assets (ROA) for each current and past segment as well as for the company as a whole from 1985 through 1997. The graph indicates that the beer/beer-related segment is far and away BUD's most profitable line of business. The consistently low profitability of the food products unit explains why the company finally abandoned this business in 1995. Further, the weak operating performance of the entertainment segment helps us to understand why BUD sold an asset—the St. Louis Cardinals baseball team—that it had owned for over 100 years. The poor performance of its entertainment business suggests that BUD may also decide to sell off the rest of this unit to focus on its profitable beer business.

EXHIBIT 2-9
Anheuser-Busch Companies, Inc.
Pretax Return on Assets by Business Segment 1985–1997

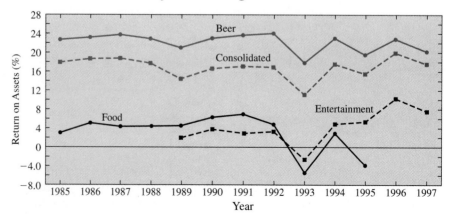

> Use of seg-
> mented financial
> statements can
> help managers
> identify the
> value-destroying
> effects of cross-
> subsidization.

At a strategic level, the use of segmented statements illustrates *cross-subsi-dization*—a situation where good results in one unit can cover up poor results in another. We'll say much more about cross-subsidization in Chapter 11, where we deal with creating shareholder value. At this juncture, we will simply note that in the case of BUD, the "OK" results *on a consolidated basis* were the results of a high ROA for the beer unit and weak results in both the food and entertainment segments. The segmented statements allowed management to identify the wealth-dissipating units and take corrective behavior.

SUMMARY

This chapter introduced some tools to assess the financial health of a company. We began by looking at the three basic financial statements essential to analyzing a firm's financial position: the balance sheet, the income statement, and the cash flow statement. The balance sheet is a snapshot of a company's assets, liabilities, and shareholders' equity at a specific point in time, whereas the income statement looks at the results of operations over a particular period of time. Combining data from both the balance sheet and income statement, the cash flow statement describes the origin and destination of cash over a specific period.

We saw that there are often significant differences between the accounting and economic values of assets and liabilities. These differences arise because of the use of historical cost as a basis for statement preparation and the omission of important intangible assets and liabilities from the balance sheet. Similarly, reported income, calculated according to generally accepted accounting principles, does not measure true economic income, which is the change in shareholders' wealth during the period. Revenues and costs are usually measured on an accrual basis rather than a cash basis. Thus, there's no necessary relationship between a firm's accounting income and cash flow. Further, the use of historical costs can misstate the true costs of production and true incremental revenues.

With this background, we moved to a consideration of ratio analysis, an important tool for financial analysis. Although they can provide insights into a firm's health and its competitive position, ratios themselves must be put in perspective. Any ratio is likely to have little meaning by itself, rather, the usefulness is derived from the analyst's ability to compare ratios over time or against the ratios of comparable companies and to understand the relationships among ratios. By combining ratios from different categories, we can often get a better picture of the firm's condition. The DuPont analysis, which focuses on return on equity (ROE), is one approach to analyzing ratios collectively and shows how ROE relates to profit margins, the efficiency with which a firm manages its assets to generate sales, and the firm's financing mix. Properly used, the DuPont system can be an important tool in linking corporate strategy and financial performance.

APPENDIX 2A   FINANCIAL STATEMENTS OF FOREIGN-BASED COMPANIES

With the globalization of the product and financial markets, American investors *and* managers will increasingly find themselves having to review financial statements of foreign-based companies. To become familiar with the differences in terminology and the structure of financial statements, let's take a look at the income statement and balance sheet of Glaxo Wellcome (GLX [16]), a U.K.-based pharmaceutical company. This company is the product of a merger between Glaxo Holdings and Burroughs Wellcome. The firm is best known for Zantac (an anti-ulcer drug) and AZT

---

[16]Glaxo Wellcome's stock is traded on the London Stock Exchange. The firm's American Depository Receipts (ADRs)—which are dollar-denominated certificates representing a foreign company's common stock—are traded on the New York Stock Exchange. *GLX* is the company's ticker symbol.

EXHIBIT 2A-1
Glaxo Wellcome
Condensed Profit and Loss Accounts (in million £)

Year Ended December 31	1997	1996
Turnover (*Sales*)	7,980	8,341
Costs and Overheads	(5,158)	(5,209)
Trading (*Operating*) Profits	2,822	3,132
Interest Expense Less Interest Income	(136)	(168)
Profit on Ordinary Activities (*Profit before Taxes*)	2,686	2,964
Taxation	(819)	(933)
Profit for Year	1,867	2,031

Source: Glaxo Wellcome, *Annual Review,* p. 18. Reproduced with permission of the Glaxo Wellcome Group of Companies.

(the AIDS drug). GLX has a huge research facility in North Carolina's Research Triangle Park.

Exhibit 2A-1 presents GLX's income statement for 1996 and 1997. Structurally, the income statement—the statement of profit and loss—looks very much like that of a U.S.-based company. True enough, our British cousins label some items differently (e.g., sales are referred to as turnover); however, the statement begins with sales and ends with a calculation of profits for the year as it would in the United States.

The balance sheet is another matter. As Exhibit 2A-2 indicates, not only are there some strange-looking labels but the balance sheet is organized differently from that of a U.S.-based company. First, like that of its counterparts on the European continent, GLX's balance

sheet *begins with fixed assets,* followed by current assets. (In contrast, U.S. balance sheets begin with cash and work their way down to the most illiquid assets—fixed assets.) Next, current liabilities are subtracted from current assets to obtain net current assets, equivalent to our working capital. The account labeled "provisions for liabilities and charges" contains: (1) employee post-retirement benefits, (2) costs of integrating Glaxo Holdings and Burroughs Wellcome, and (3) deferred taxes. Everything balances to "Capital Employed," which is equivalent to shareholders' equity.

There are numerous differences between generally accepted accounting principles (GAAP) in the United States and the United Kingdom, so it is difficult to compare financial results across "the pond" without the help

EXHIBIT 2A-2
Glaxo Wellcome
Condensed Balance Sheet (in million £)

As of December 31	1997	1996
Fixed Assets*	3,635	3,946
Current Assets	4,802	4,368
Creditor: Due within One Year (*Current Liabilities*)	(3,886)	(4,154)
Net Current Assets (*Working Capital*)	916	214
Total Assets Less Current Liabilities	4,551	4,160
Creditors: Amounts Due after One Year	(1,964)	(1,846)
Provisions for Liabilities and Charges	(697)	(1,047)
Capital Employed (*Shareholders' Equity*)	1,890	1,225

*Includes investments in other firms.

Source: Glaxo Wellcome, *Annual Review 1997,* p. 18. Reproduced with permission of the Glaxo Wellcome Group of Companies.

of professionals who have specific expertise in the area. However, the differences in accounting standards between the United States, United Kingdom, Canada, and Australia are small when compared to those between the United States and, say, Mexico, Argentina, and Brazil. The International Accounting Standards Committee (IASC) has attempted to narrow differences in global accounting practices. While the efforts of the IASC haven't resulted in a common set of accounting standards, we do have more disclosure of the principles being used.

QUESTIONS

1. For many years, the cost of a retiree's health benefits was not included on the balance sheet as a liability. Over the protests of both organized labor and business, the Financial Accounting Standards Board (FASB) now requires that firms recognize this obligation. Companies opposed the change because it would reduce the annual profits of big industrial firms by about 25 percent and wipe out about one-third of the net worth of corporate America.
   a. Evaluate business's argument against the FASB rule to include the cost of retiree health benefits as a liability. Why do you think business was so opposed to the rule?
   b. According to one critic of the rule, "No one's been right in guessing health care costs even one year out, let alone decades. So why slam it into the balance sheet?" Evaluate this argument.
   c. Why do you think organized labor opposed this rule?
   d. Many companies said that if the FASB proposal is implemented, they would be forced to reduce or eliminate retiree health benefits or to raise prices for their products to cover these costs. Evaluate this argument.
   e. How do you think the stock market would react to a trillion-dollar increase in reported liabilities for retiree health benefits?
2. Some financial analysts have suggested that firms operating in a highly inflationary environment should use NIFO (next-in, first-out) rather than LIFO accounting to value inventory. Comment on this suggestion.
3. A company switching from LIFO to FIFO accounting during 1980, when inflation was 13.5 percent, reported that the switch would increase its after-tax profit for the year by over $30 million. However, the firm's stock price fell upon the announcement of the switch. Explain why the announcement might have triggered the stock price decline.
4. Cable TV companies must spend many millions of dollars to put their cables in place. Once in place,

however, a cable is unlikely to need replacement for many years. Thus, high depreciation charges will continue to depress reported earnings in the cable TV industry long after there is a need to lay new cable.
   a. How will these high depreciation charges affect the reported earnings and free cash flow of a mature cable TV company?
   b. What will be the likely effect of these high depreciation charges on the P/E ratios of cable TV companies?
5. In 1988 financial analysts stated that Philip Morris overpaid for its acquisition of Kraft. Similar comments were made about Procter & Gamble's 1997 purchase of Tambrands, which made a single consumer product—Tampax tampons. Corporate strategists have argued that the prices paid for companies like Kraft and Tambrands with recognized brand names were fair and reflect the: (1) value of the cash flows these "megabrands" are expected to generate over a long period of time, and (2) the premium a competitor would have to spend to create an equivalent brand. Evaluate this argument.
6. Distinguish among economic income, accounting income, and cash flow.
7. Suppose Silver Star has reported a profit of $10 million during the year. Its net worth is $90 million and its cost of equity capital is estimated at 14 percent. Will Silver Star's shareholders be pleased at the company's performance? Explain.
8. What is likely to happen to the income of a bank holding a large amount of 30-year, fixed-rate mortgages when inflation rises?
9. Management of Superior Metals claims that it is unable to meet its debt payments despite having a current ratio of 3:1 and record earnings last year.
   a. Is this possible? Explain.
   b. What financial ratios could be used to determine the cause of this situation?

10. What factors would you attempt to change if you wanted to increase a firm's rate of return on
    a. Total assets?
    b. Equity?
11. A firm's EBIT is less than its interest expense. Does this mean that the firm did not generate enough cash to service its debt? Explain.
12. After completing a ratio analysis of Arden Co. based on its 1998 financial statements, you learn that several relevant events occurred in early 1999: The company sold its headquarters building to Sumitomo Inc. Sale proceeds were used to pay off mortgage bonds secured by the building. Arden then entered into a long-term lease with Sumitomo.
    a. Predict the impact of these events on your calculation of the following ratios: current ratio, return on assets, interest coverage, and debt-equity ratio.
    b. How comparable are your new ratios with the historical ones?
13. Financial analysis can be applied to a company's business units as well as to the company overall.
    a. What adjustments should be made to the standard return on investment figures to ensure comparability among business units and to aid in the capital allocation process?
    b. What are some strategic considerations that result in a difference between business unit performance measured on a stand-alone basis and unit performance measured from the standpoint of its contribution to the overall corporation?
14. In a retail establishment, one of the most important considerations in employee performance is "customer satisfaction." As a manager, what objective measures would you use to measure this quality in regard to your employees?
15. As the head of the R&D department for Byotek, a biotechnology company, you want to encourage your employees to propose ideas that are both innovative and of some practical significance.
    a. Given the usually long lead time and development process between research proposals and salable products, what measures can you use to gauge your employees' performance with regard to these two qualities?
    b. What sort of compensation do you think would best motivate your employees to achieve these two goals?

PROBLEMS

⌨—Excel templates may be downloaded from **www.prenhall.com/financecenter.**

1. The following are the equity accounts for McDoonan's Co. for 1998 and 1999 as well as the year-end prices for McDoonan's stock.
    a. Calculate the return on equity for McDoonan's in 1998 and 1999 based on accounting values and on the year-end market values.
    b. Is either one an accurate measure of the return to McDoonan's shareholders? Why or why not?

	1999		1998	
Common stock*				
(no par value)	$	10,251	$	10,241
Paid-in capital*		134,620		122,619
Retained earnings*		2,499,448		2,146,736
Net income*		433,039		389,089
Number of shares				
outstanding		85,630,063		87,362,169
Share price		80 5/8		53 5/8

*000 omited

2. The following is the income statement for Many-Corp., a conglomerate formed through the merger of several forest-products, energy, and fast-food concerns. Given the information in the income statement, recalculate the net income to reflect actual cash flow. Include as part of your calculation the purchase of a headquarters building for $20.5 million.

Income Statement (in thousands $)	
Sales	$430,000
Cost of goods sold	305,500
Gross profit	$124,500
Expenses:	
Selling	50,250
Interest	15,000
Depreciation	12,500
Depletion allowance	17,500
Goodwill	20,300
Total	115,550

EBT	8,950
Taxes (35% rate)	3,133
Net income	$ 5,817

3. DataCalc is considering the purchase of a computer link between its mainframe and the office PCs. The finance officer would like to formulate a depreciation method that would truly reflect the machine's depreciation. She has collected estimates of the probable economic life of the equipment and has found that replacement times varied from as short as three to as long as five years. Also, experts indicated that either: (1) the equipment will depreciate evenly over its life, or (2) fully half of its value will be lost in the first year; the decline will be relatively even after that point. In either case, the equipment will have no salvage value. The purchase price of the machine is $l00,000; DataCalc's tax rate is 40 percent; and the shares outstanding are expected to remain at 250,000. Given the expected revenue and other expenses for the next four years described below, calculate the distribution of probable earnings, EPS, and taxes of DataCalc using the following estimates: ✖

Income Statement (in thousand $)	Year 1	Year 2	Year 3	Year 4
Sales	$450.0	$475.0	$525.0	$425.0
Cost of goods sold	375.0	425.0	435.0	375.0
Selling/ administrative expenses	18.5	19.5	19.5	15.5
Interest expense	10.0	10.0	10.0	10.0

4. Cal-Tex Refining purchases oil in the spot market (cash and carry) and refines the oil into heating oil and distillates. Cal-Tex had in its inventory 3 million barrels purchased at $29/barrel and 1.5 million barrels purchased (after a massive oil price cut) at $10/barrel. The company used 3.5 million barrels of oil last year.
   a. Given the following revenue and other expenses, calculate the net income for this year under LIFO and FIFO. Assume a 35 percent tax rate.
   b. Which would you recommend as being nearer to "economic value"? Does the method of accounting make a difference to shareholders?

   c. Recalculate the net income at a 50 percent tax rate. Does this make a difference in your answer to (b)?

Revenue	$145 million
Other expenses	12 million
Interest	3.5 million

5. Because of fluctuations in the value of the Hungarian currency, Spicy Foods, Inc. (SFI) had to purchase its Hungarian paprika, a raw material in its packaged dehydrated sauces, at widely differing prices throughout the year. The following table lists its purchases. SFI used 2,250,000 lb of paprika during the year. The company has a 40 percent tax rate. ✖
   a. Given the other accounting data, calculate the company's net income under the LIFO and FIFO methods. Assume an initial inventory of zero.
   b. Calculate net income if SFI used an average price for its cost of goods sold.
   c. Calculate the net income if SFI used only replacement cost ($5/lb) in valuing its inventory for cost of goods sold.

Purchase Date	Amount per Pound	No. of Pounds Purchased
Jan. 10	$1.50	750,000
Mar. 5	2.10	1,000,000
June 7	3.75	1,000,000
Oct. 11	5.00	750,000

Revenue	$30 million
CGS (other)	7.5 million
Other expenses	10 million

6. Selected Information for the PUD Corporation is given in the following table. Compute the current ratio, the acid-test ratio, the collection period, and the inventory turnover and use this information to assess the firm's liquidity position.

	1996	1997	1998
Cash	$ 34,000	$ 74,000	$ 90,000
Marketable securities	60,000	48,000	99,000
Accounts receivable	96,000	103,000	111,000

(continued)

	1996	1997	1998
Notes receivable	20,000	16,000	12,000
Inventory	270,000	125,000	155,000
Total current assets	$480,000	$366,000	$467,000
Current liabilities	$165,000	$210,000	$260,000
Annual credit sales	460,000	534,000	585,000
Cost of goods sold	450,000	572,000	600,000

7. The following information (in thousand $) taken from the financial statements of the Whing Ding Company. Calculate those ratios dealing with asset management, and indicate what problems (if any) you see. ✍

	1996	1997	1998
Total sales	$750	$850	$860
Credit sales	420	520	550
Cost of goods sold	450	595	645
Cash	50	60	55
Accounts receivable	150	165	180
Inventory	130	160	170
Fixed assets net of depreciation	120	260	250

8. Designer Dinnerware has completed its second year of selling gourmet cooking utensils. The following are its balance sheets for the past two years. It pays no dividends.
   a. Construct a sources and uses of funds statement for DD.
   b. What would you suggest to DD concerning its financial condition?

Year 1 (in thousand $)

Cash	$105.0
Securities	64.0
Accounts receivable	123.5
Inventory	104.3
Plant and equipment	544.0
Accumulated depreciation	(18.5)
Notes payable	113.0
Accounts payable	64.0
Accrued wages	17.0
Accrued taxes	4.0
Long-term debt	518.0
Common stock	44.0
Retained earnings	162.3

Year 2 (in thousand $)

Cash	$175.0
Securities	43.0
Accounts receivable	210.3
Inventory	75.0
Plant and equipment	623.0
Accumulated depreciation	(20.7)
Notes payable	$175.0
Accounts payable	188.0
Accrued wages	5.0
Accrued taxes	2.5
Long-term debt	509.2
Common stock	48.5
Retained earnings	177.4

9. The following are the changes in working capital and sources and uses of funds statements for the Earthtone Interiors furniture company along with last year's balance sheet. Working from these three financial statements, reconstruct the balance sheet for this year. ✍

Sources and Uses of Funds (in thousand $)

Sources:	
Net income	$450
Depreciation	95
Sales of common stock	10
Uses:	
Dividends	15
Plant and equipment	320
Retirement of bonds	45

Changes in Working Capital Accounts (in thousand $)

Cash	+ 22
Securities	+ 10
Accounts receivable	+ 180
Inventory	+ 45
Accounts payable	+ 25
Accruals	+ 47
Taxes payable	+ 10
Increase in working capital	+ 175

Balance Sheet at Start of Year (in thousand $)

Cash	$100
Securities	14
Accounts receivable	88
Inventory	144
Plant and equipment	675
Depreciation	45
Notes	125
Accounts payable	10
Accruals	24
Taxes payable	5
Long-term debt	185
Common stock	425
Retained earnings	202

10. As the fast-food analyst for a major brokerage firm, you have collected the following information on McDonald's, Wendy's, and Church's Fried Chicken for the last three years. Use the DuPont system to compare the three companies. What can you say about their relative standing and activity through time? ✍

Wendy's (in thousand $)

	Year 3	Year 2	Year 1
Sales	$944,768	$720,383	$606,964
Net income	68,707	55,220	44,102
Assets	613,636	506,713	453,561

Church's (in thousand $)

	Year 3	Year 2	Year 1
Sales	$533,208	$454,490	$413,144
Net income	42,595	31,552	41,598
Assets	334,068	302,155	277,562

McDonald's (in thousand $)

	Year 3	Year 2	Year 1
Sales	$3,414,798	$3,062,822	$2,770,000
Net income	389,089	342,640	301,000
Assets	4,229,638	3,727,307	3,263,000

11. As a money market manager, you must decide whether to buy a rather large amount of commercial paper from either of two companies, Scylla and Charybdis. The following are selected items from their balance sheets and income statements. All figures are in millions of dollars. The tax rate is 35%. ✍

a. Calculate the liquidity ratios, the activity ratios, the times interest earned, and the cash flow coverage for both companies. Which company is in a better short-term position?

b. What other information, if any, would you like to see before making your decision?

Company	Scylla	Charybdis
Cash	$ 143.3	$ 351.2
Accounts receivable	1,598.7	1,591.3
Inventory	253.5	159.3
Notes payable	227.4	178.3
Accounts payable	1,244.0	1,237.9
Accrued expenses	595.7	443.1
Sales	9,012.1	8,436.7
Credit sales	85.0%	75.0%
Cost of goods sold	1,602.7	1,437.3
Depreciation	242.0	135.0
Interest	412.9	463.6
Lease payments	124.9	117.5
Preferred dividends	13.5	45.7

12. Hatari Fashions is a family-owned manufacturer of high-quality casual clothing. Three years ago, its founder and the driving force behind the company died unexpectedly in a plane crash. Now, the family has decided to hire a professional manager to arrest the company's apparent decline. The financial statements are given below. ✍

a. Calculate the liquidity, leverage, activity, and profitability ratios for Hatari.

b. Using the ratios from three years ago as a standard, what do you suggest the company do to bring itself back to these levels?

Hatari Balance Sheet and Income Statement (in thousand $)

	Year 1	Year 2	Year 3
Balance Sheet			
Cash	$2,123	$24,841	$17,811
Marketable securities	35,650	2,845	1,125
Accounts receivable	13,309	30,079	35,129

(continued)

	Year 1	Year 2	Year 3
Inventory	1,557	3,585	7,679
Gross plant	52,268	49,997	44,665
Depreciation	(1,894)	(335)	(475)
Accounts payable	9,951	6,446	2,125
Notes payable	2,715	1,715	849
Accruals	5,056	1,722	4,095
Long-term debt	26,751	27,443	32,741
Common stock	17,222	23,447	21,653
Retained earnings	1,228	7,012	4,471
Income Statement			
Revenue	$182,631	$102,618	$57,311
Cost of goods sold	83,966	46,665	12,942
Selling expense	21,458	14,000	7,302
General and administrative expense	10,000	4,494	1,409
Lease payments	17,000	289	0
Interest expense	23,210	29,162	38,199
Dividends	12,213	222	0

13. Here are the financial statements for the Beta Company. ✍

Balance Sheet (in thousand $)		
Assets	**12/31/99**	**12/31/98**
Cash	$ 150	$ 200
Accounts receivable	425	450
Inventory	625	550
Net plant and equipment	1,400	1,200
Total assets	$2,600	$2,400
Liabilities and equity		
Accounts payable	$ 150	$ 200
Other current liabilities	150	0
Bonds	600	600
Net worth	1,700	1,600
Total liabilities plus equity	$2,600	$2,400

Income Statement		
	1999	**1998**
Sales	$1,450	$1,200
EBIT	360	250
Interest	60	50
Taxes	120	80
Net income	$ 180	$ 120

a. What was Beta's total return on total assets in 1999 (that is, net income plus interest)?

b. What was Beta's average receivables collection period in 1999? Use a 360-day year. Assume all sales are on credit.

c. What was Beta's interest coverage ratio for 1999?

d. Based on these and other relevant data, how would you describe Beta's financial position?

14. Reconstruct the balance sheet for Blank Paper Co. Sales for the year were $125 million.

Sales/total assets	2.75
Total debt/total assets	55%
Current ratio	3.75
Inventory turnover	10
Average collection period	25 days
Fixed-assets turnover	7.5

15. Mystic Supply Co.'s management was surprised to learn that the return on equity of the company had declined from 24 percent in 1998 to 18 percent in 1999. Upon further examination of Mystic's financial records, the owner found that this decrease had occurred even though company sales had increased from $15 million in 1998 to $18 million in 1999. In the course of her investigation, three additional facts came to light. First, Mystic's fixed assets had increased from $24 million in 1998 to $28.8 million in 1999. Second, net income as a percentage of fixed assets had remained constant at 15 percent between 1998 and 1999. Third, the 1998 debt ratio was 50 percent and ROI in 1999 was 9 percent. However, even with this additional information, the owner was still not positive that she knew what had caused the decrease in ROE. She has therefore asked you to complete the analysis and to prepare a report that analyzes the decrease. What will you report to her?

Financial Planning and Funds Forecasting

Forewarned, forearmed; to be prepared is half the victory.
Miguel de Cervantes Saavedra

KEY TERMS

aggressive financing
  strategy
asset-based financing
bankers' acceptances
cash budget
cash conversion cycle
cleanup clause
commercial paper
commitment fee
compensating balances
conservative financing
  strategy
countertrade
Euronote

floating lien
inventory conversion
  period
just-in-time technique (JIT)
letter of credit (L/C)
line of credit
matching strategy
operating cycle
outsourcing
payables period
percent of sales method
permanent current assets
pledging accounts
  receivable

prime rate
pro forma
revolving credit
  agreement
spontaneous source
  of funds
sustainable growth
temporary current assets
transaction loan
trust receipt plan
universal commercial
  paper (UCP)
warehouseman

CHAPTER LEARNING OBJECTIVES

Upon completion of this chapter, students should be able to:

- Explain the role of financial planning in the strategic planning process.
- Describe the working capital flows within a company and how shortening the cash conversion cycle can minimize external financing needs.
- Prepare pro forma financial statements and use them to identify a firm's external financing requirements.
- Explain the relationship between a company's financing needs and its working capital policy.
- Understand the concept of sustainable growth and how it is related to a firm's

profitability, asset utilization, leverage, and dividend policy.
- Prepare a cash budget and use it to identify the amounts and timing of a firm's short-term needs.
- Discuss the risk–return tradeoffs of the strategies that can be used to finance a firm's working capital requirements.
- Explain the vehicles that can be used to finance a company's short-term needs.
- Understand why the proper handling of inflation is critical in identifying a company's financing needs.

In a business environment characterized by changing global markets and accelerating competition, strategic planning is critical for *survival* as well as growth. The planning process involves four interrelated steps: (1) the establishment of a corporate mission, (2) the definition of goals and objectives, (3) strategy formulation, and, finally, (4) strategy implementation. Resources are central to the process; you can't execute the best of strategies if you don't have the human, physical, and financial resources to implement the plan. If these resources aren't currently available, then a company has to figure out how to get them.

An important role of the chief financial officer in the strategic planning process is to construct the long-range financial plan and the operating budget. The long-range plan's primary objectives are to identify (1) how much capital will be needed to meet the firm's goals and (2) how much of this capital must come from outside sources. The operating budget, which should be developed within the framework of the long-term plan, has three functions: (1) it's the operating manager's short-run road map, (2) it is an instrument in the accomplishment of the long-range plan, and (3) it provides a basis for short-term cash budgeting.

This chapter deals with the financial planning process. The chapter begins with an overview of the financial planning process. It then examines the key elements of working capital management and how the interactions between these current accounts influence the need for funds. Next, we will present some techniques a company can use to identify its financing needs. As part of our discussion, we'll see how changes in working capital policy can influence financing requirements. We'll then approach planning from another direction by examining the concept of sustainable growth—the growth that a firm can sustain without issuing new common stock. The chapter concludes with a look at how cash budgets fit into the planning process.

3.1   THE PURPOSES OF FINANCIAL PLANNING

Once a company has formulated its objectives, it faces the problem of getting from here to there. This is the realm of strategy formulation. It includes forecasting likely business scenarios and devising various courses of action consistent with these scenarios. From among the alternative courses of action, the company must select those that have a high probability of achieving the company's objectives; provide major competitive advantages; and closely conform to the company's resources, capabilities, opportunities, and strengths. Based on this assessment, management must then formulate a strategic plan that defines the company's strategy in explicit terms of budgeting and resource requirements and the action plans of each corporate unit.

Making the assumptions of a strategic plan visible increases the likelihood that corporate goals will be achieved.

An important benefit of the strategic planning process is that by making explicit—and therefore subject to scrutiny—many of the implicit assumptions underlying company policies, it increases the odds that these assumptions are sound and relevant and that the plan is feasible. The company can also anticipate and thereby avoid difficulties before they arise. Many firms develop contingency plans to deal with potential problems pointed out by the planning process. For example, a firm can line up additional funds on a standby basis if a large increase in sales is possible and its analysis shows that the working capital requirements necessitated by such a sales increase cannot be financed through currently available sources.

The financial plan is also one of the most important means whereby a firm communicates, with external stakeholders such as customers, suppliers, distributors, creditors, and investors. Effective communication is vital to firms with substantial organizational assets, the value of which depends on stakeholder trust.

A financial plan also sets the standards by which to measure performance. Before the plans are put into effect, top management must assign responsibilities and establish tolerance points. These tolerance points specify the minimally acceptable levels of performance (e.g., sales volume, ROI) and the maximum levels of expenditures for each action plan. When these tolerance points are exceeded, management must step in and take corrective action.

An intangible benefit is that the planning process makes operating managers knowledgeable about long-term corporate goals and the way in which they contribute to them. Perhaps most importantly, by involving the entire management team, not just top management, the plan has the commitment of those who will be responsible for carrying it out.

To maximize their joint effectiveness, the operating budget and the long-range financial plan should be closely linked. Where operating budgets are not a specific part of the long-term plan, managers find it hard to relate their performance to the firm's long-term goals and objectives and tend to emphasize short-run objectives. One way to counter this tendency is to weigh long-term goals more heavily in measuring managerial performance.

> The financial plan serves as a vehicle for communicating with corporate stakeholders as well as setting standards to measure performance.

3.2   OVERVIEW OF WORKING CAPITAL MANAGEMENT

For many companies, current assets—cash and marketable securities, accounts receivable, and inventories—represent a large portion of their asset base, and current liabilities represent a substantial portion of total corporate financing. It's not surprising then that the operating plan focuses on working capital transactions. Managers need a good understanding of the nature of working capital and the way that their management of working capital influences financing needs.

Some Basics

Exhibit 3-1 presents a (very) condensed accounting representation of the balance sheet of a company that's not a bank or some other financial institution. Assets are categorized as current or noncurrent. As we indicated in Chapter 2, current assets are likely to be converted into cash within one year. On the liabilities and equity side, we have current and noncurrent liabilities along with equity. Current liabilities are those debts that are due and payable within one year.

Unfortunately, describing current assets as those that can be turned into cash within one year communicates the idea that current assets are short-term assets. This can be misleading because the *ongoing firm* needs a certain level of receivables

> For the ongoing firm, current assets are not short-term assets.

EXHIBIT 3-1
Condensed Balance Sheet
Accounting View

Assets	Liabilities + Equity
Current Assets	Current Liabilities
Noncurrent Assets	Noncurrent Liabilities
	Equity

and inventories to support sales. The following example will hammer home this point: Suppose that a company has sales of $360 million a year, offers credit terms to its customers of net 30 days, *and* has customers that pay (on average) in 30 days. To simplify matters, let's also suppose that a year has 360 days made up of twelve 30-day months. With sales of $1 million a day, the average level of accounts receivable for this company would be $30 million.

Whether you believe that this $30 million ever entirely converts into cash depends on your frame of reference. If you're the bookkeeper, you are likely to see accounts receivable as a short-term asset. After all, every day you: (1) receive an average of $1 million in customer checks, (2) credit the appropriate customer accounts, (3) fill out a deposit slip, and (4) take the checks to the bank. Once the checks are processed through your bank's clearing system, these customer checks are converted into cash. A given customer invoice is thus converted into cash within 30 days.

However, the perspective of the firm's chief financial officer (CFO) is likely to be different. While the CFO is quite aware that a *given set of customer invoices* converts into cash quickly, he/she also recognizes that the *level of receivables won't change* because the $1 million collected every day will be replaced by $1 million in receivables arising from new sales. Thus, accounts receivable, as a category, won't go away and will have to be financed on a permanent basis. Why? For the firm that offers credit to its customers, accounts receivable are as critical to the selling effort as the plant and equipment required to manufacture products or deliver services. The same could be said for inventories, which are essential for a smooth-running production operation and for servicing customers. Instead of looking at receivables and inventories as short-term assets, it's more useful to think about these accounts as **permanent current assets** to highlight their ongoing role in supporting sales. **Temporary** or short-term **current assets** only come into play when a company builds inventories and/or receivables in response to seasonal or other transitory sales patterns.

What we've said about current assets also holds for some current liabilities. Accounts payable, for instance, is an ongoing process. True enough, a given invoice must be paid within the terms of sale. However, this reduction in payables is likely to be offset by additional purchases; thus, the overall level of payables will not change. Moreover, if a company's sales increase and greater numbers of purchases are needed to support the production and/or selling effort, payables will increase automatically to produce a **spontaneous source of funds.**

Current liabilities, such as payables and accruals, represent an ongoing source of financing.

EXHIBIT 3-2
Condensed Balance Sheet
Financial Planning View

Assets	Liabilities + Equity
Permanent Assets	Permanent Current Liabilities
Temporary Assets	Short-Term Liabilities
	Long-Term Capital

> **It is useful to think of assets and liabilities as being temporary or permanent.**

For planning purposes, the balance sheet in Exhibit 3-2 is a more helpful framework for thinking about the nature of a company's assets as well as its sources of financing. Assets are characterized as being permanent or temporary, a permanent asset being *any* asset—receivables, or inventory, or plant and equipment—that's needed to support a firm's core sales. In contrast, temporary assets come into play to accommodate seasonal needs or when a company accumulates cash over time for a specific purpose. On the liabilities and equity side, we have permanent current liabilities such as payables and accruals, whose levels will be determined by the level of production. Short-term liabilities are such debts as bank loans that actually have to be repaid (or refinanced) within a year. Finally, we have long-term capital, which includes not only preferred and common stock but long-term debt as well.

The Cash Conversion Cycle

A useful way of seeing how the management of individual working capital accounts impacts financing needs is through the **cash conversion cycle.** As illustrated in Exhibit 3-3, the cash conversion cycle focuses on the length of time between the payment of cash for inventory purchased and the collection of accounts receivable.

EXHIBIT 3-3
The Cash Conversion Cycle

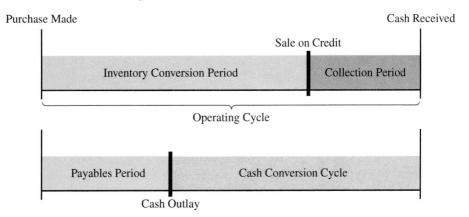

To illustrate, we'll look at the case of Deep-Discount Building Supply (DDBS), which has just bought $500,000 worth of bricks to satisfy builder demand during the spring residential construction period. To entice DDBS to purchase this large amount of material, the company's supplier was willing to defer payment for 60 days rather than its usual terms of net 30 days. Let's examine each element of the cash conversion cycle:

1. ***Inventory Conversion Period:*** For DDBS, the $500,000 brick purchase represents a six-month supply. Some of the bricks will be sold immediately; some won't be sold for another six months. Therefore, the *average* length of time between DDBS's receipt of the bricks and their sale would be three months or 91 days. The **inventory conversion period** (91 days here) can also be interpreted as the average number of days of inventory on hand and is related to a firm's inventory turnover as follows.

> The cash conversion cycle measures the time between the payment for inventory and the collection of accounts receivable.

$$\text{Inventory Conversion Period} = \frac{\text{Inventory}}{\text{Cost of Goods Sold}/365} = \frac{365}{\text{Inventory Turnover}} \qquad [3\text{-}1]$$

2. ***Collection Period:*** DDBS sells to customers on a variety of terms depending on their past payment record. "Dead beats" pay cash, but solid credit risks can purchase on open account with payment due in 30 days. Given its mix of customers, let's assume that DDBS's collection period is 23 days. As we saw in Chapter 2, the collection period for any company is

$$\text{Collection Period} = \frac{\text{Accounts Receivable}}{\text{Sales}/365} \qquad [3\text{-}2]$$

3. ***Operating Cycle:*** The **operating cycle** is the sum of the inventory conversion period and the collection period. It represents the time, on average, from the receipt of inventory to the collection of accounts receivable. For DDBS, the operating cycle is $91 + 23 = 114$ days.

4. ***Payables Period:*** This is the average time between the purchase of goods and the date that the company has to pay for them. In our example, we were told that DDBS's supplier will allow 60 days to pay for the brick shipment. For any company, the **payables period** is given as:

$$\text{Payables Period} = \frac{\text{Accounts Payable}}{\text{Annual Purchases}/365} \qquad [3\text{-}3]$$

5. ***Cash Conversion Cycle:*** As Exhibit 3-3 indicates, the cash conversion cycle (C^*) is the difference between the operating cycle and the payables period or

$$C^* = \text{Inventory Conversion Period} + \text{Collection Period} - \text{Payables Period}$$
$$[3\text{-}4]$$

In the case of DDBS's brick order, the cash conversion cycle would be:

$$C^* = 91 + 23 - 60 = 54 \text{ days}$$

The cash conversion cycle of 54 days represents the time between the date DDBS has to pay for the bricks and the date the firm can expect payment from customers. It also represents a gap, in terms of days of sales, that must be financed. If DDBS could somehow talk its supplier into deferring payment for 114 days—the average time it takes to sell the bricks and collect from its customers—sales would be self-financing. Otherwise, DDBS will have to cover this gap.

The cash conversion cycle represents a financing gap; minimizing the gap minimizes financing needs.

To minimize their financing needs, firms should try to *shorten their cash conversion cycle* by: (1) speeding up collections, (2) increasing inventory turnover, and/or (3) lengthening the payables period. Identifying the "buttons to push" is the easy part; the trick is to shorten the cash conversion cycle without either jeopardizing sales or destroying supplier relationships.

Many companies have been able to increase inventory turnover dramatically by changing over to the **just-in-time (JIT) technique.** Called *kanban* by the Japanese, JIT works under the assumption that raw materials and work-in-progress should flow from start to finish without stopping. They arrive where needed "just in time" rather than sitting around as inventory. U.S. auto manufacturers such as GM and Ford saw multibillion-dollar reductions in their inventory when they installed JIT programs in the early 1980s. The retailers Wal-Mart and Kmart have also used JIT inventory management techniques effectively.[1]

3.3   FINANCIAL FORECASTING

The heart of the financial plan is contained in the **pro forma** (forecasted) balance sheet and income statements. Based on these pro forma financial statements, the firm puts together the operating and cash budgets. An important planning decision is the determination of the appropriate level of accounting and financial data. For example, the operating budget is usually broken down on a monthly basis for measuring performance and insuring control. For effective control, financial reports must provide the detail needed to measure key performance areas such as profitability, market position, productivity, innovation, and asset utilization. To manage cash effectively, the monthly periods may have to be divided into smaller time segments, usually one week or less.

---

[1]The smaller inventories associated with JIT systems also lower warehousing and financing costs, ensure fast identification of poor-quality parts, and permit manufacturers to change over to new products without being stuck with thousands of obsolete components. However, these systems are not without their problems. Without a buffer of inventory on site, a strike at either a supplier's plant or a company's own parts operation can shut assembly plants down very quickly.

Sales Forecasting

For a nonfinancial company, the planning process begins with a forecast of sales. Formal sales projections are done in increments of one year, up to five years ahead. These annual forecasts are often broken into quarterly or monthly forecasts during the first year. As a general rule, more specific and accurate information is available for the early years of the planning period. Sales forecasts should be stated in dollars or physical units. Having both a physical unit and dollar sales forecast allows management to consider the effects of price, volume, and inflation changes on financing needs.

Most companies forecast sales by combining estimates from salespeople, customer surveys, time-series models, and econometric models. *Sales-force estimates* can be a valuable source of customer information. To guard against the subjectivity that often creeps into such estimates, they should be compared with results from other forecasting methods in order to flag potential discrepancies. Holding salespeople accountable for their forecasts is one way to guard against overoptimism.

In some industries, firms use *customer surveys* to gauge customer purchase plans over the forecast period. Although unforeseen events can disrupt the forecast, a well-designed survey can provide valuable insights. Surveys work best for industrial firms whose customers plan purchases well in advance or whose product lines aren't undergoing rapid technological change.

Time-series analysis is a good statistical method for forecasting sales in companies that have strong time trends. Time patterns can be divided into three types: trend, cyclical, and seasonal. The *trend* reflects the general trend in sales over time; the *cyclical* varies with the business cycle; and the *seasonal* pattern varies with the time of year. Because history is an important element in a time-series analysis, this approach works well if good databases are available.

Econometric models relate sales to macroeconomic variables such as interest rates, growth in GNP, or industry data such as plant capacity, building starts, and so on. If a company is large enough, these data can be generated using in-house models developed by its own economists. However, many firms use outside forecasting services such as Chase Econometrics and Data Resources.

With four alternative sets of forecasts, there are bound to be conflicts; therefore, management still has the task of uncovering (and understanding) the assumptions underlying each of the forecasts and determining which is most reasonable. We also need to recognize that sales forecasting for many companies is as much of an art as it is a science. This is particularly true of firms in industries in which technological change has dramatically shortened product life cycles. Taking a more realistic view of their ability to gaze into a crystal ball and predict the future, many companies not only develop a "most likely" forecast but also "optimistic" and "pessimistic" ones as well.

Financial Forecasting: The Percent of Sales Method

After sales have been forecast, the next step is to identify financing needs based on these forecasts. Typically, this is done by the **percent of sales method.** This approach assumes that each expense, asset, and liability item can be estimated as some percentage of sales. The percentage used can reflect either past performance or some other benchmark if management believes it will better reflect the future. However the percentages are arrived at, the percent of sales method assumes a direct linear relationship between projected sales and specific assets and liabilities.

The percent of sales method assumes a linear relationship between sales and various expense, asset, and liability categories.

Regardless of how a company formally puts the data together, all approaches to financial forecasting are based on the idea that in any period, sources and uses of funds must equal each other, that is,

$$\text{USES OF FUNDS} = \text{SOURCES OF FUNDS}$$

Needed Investment in Assets to = Internal Sources + External Sources
Support Sales Change   of Funds   of Funds

All approaches to financial forecasting assume that in any period, sources and uses of funds must equal each other.

The difference between the projected uses of funds and the internal funds generated through the business equals the external financing requirements. Identifying each of these pieces using the percent of sales method involves three steps:

A firm's asset needs are related to the level of sales and its asset utilization.

1. *Forecast the net assets needed to support the increased level of sales.* This amount equals the difference between the increase in assets and the increase in current liabilities associated with any increase in sales. Assuming a linear relationship between assets and current liabilities and sales, the increase in *net assets required* can be expressed as

Increase in Net Assets =
$$\text{Increase in Total Assets} - \text{Increase in Current Liabilities}$$

$$= (\Delta S)(A/S) - (\Delta S)(CL/S) \qquad [3\text{-}5]$$

where ΔS is the expected change in sales, (A/S) the expected number of dollars in assets needed to support a dollar of sales, and (CL/S) the expected ratio of current liabilities—excluding borrowings—per dollar of sales. The current liabilities in Equation [3-5] typically include items like accounts payable and accrued wages that tend to vary with sales. Equation [3-5] also assumes that the firm has no excess plant capacity; thus, any increase in sales will require a corresponding increase in fixed assets. If the company has enough productive capacity to meet the projected increase in sales, the plant and equipment should not be included in the asset-to-sales ratio.

2. *Calculate the internal financing provided by retained earnings.* Retained earnings is the amount of money a company plows back into a business after paying dividends. Net income is the product of a firm's after-tax profit margin on sales and the forecasted level of sales. This relationship can be expressed as

Internally generated funds are a function of the level of sales, profit margins, and the proportion of earnings paid out in dividends.

$$\text{Internal Financing Provided} = (1 - a)(NPM)(S + \Delta S) \qquad [3\text{-}6]$$

where a is the proportion of earnings paid out in dividends, NPM the after-tax profit margin on sales, and $S + \Delta S$ the forecasted level of sales.

3. **Finally, calculate the amount of external financing required.** This can be done by subtracting Equation [3-6] from Equation [3-5] to obtain

External Financing Needed (*EFN*) =
$$(\Delta S)(A/S) - (\Delta S)(CL/S) - (1 - a)\,(NPM)(S + \Delta S) \qquad [3\text{-}7]$$

Let's see how Equation [3-7] works for the Specialty Steel Products Company (SSP), which wants to assess its financing needs for the coming year. The firm's current sales are $200 million and are expected to rise by 10 percent to $220 million in 2000. Because making steel is a capital-intensive business, $0.90 in assets is needed to generate a dollar of sales; historically, current liabilities are 20 percent of sales. After-tax profit margins on sales are 5.1 percent, and SSP typically pays out 40 percent of its earnings in dividends.

These numbers yield the following values for the parameters of Equation [3-7]: ΔS = $20 million, (A/S) = 0.90, (CL/S) = 0.20, NPM = 0.051, $a = 0.40$, and S = $200 million. Substituting these values into Equation [3-7], we find that SSP's external financing needs (*EFN*) are:

EFN = $20,000,000(0.90) − $20,000,000(0.20) − (1 − 0.40)(0.051)($220,000,000)

   = $7,268,000

Since the steel business is highly cyclical, the $7,268,000 in estimated financing needs should be taken with a grain of salt. Sales could be significantly higher or lower than the $220 million depending on the strength of the economy. It's therefore useful to perform a sensitivity analysis, such as shown in Exhibit 3-4 to determine how the external financing needs might change with sales. Note that flat or negative sales growth generates surplus funds because retained earnings exceed the required increase in net assets. As a matter of fact, with negative sales growth, net assets become a *source of funds* because fewer assets are needed to maintain the lower levels of sales. The result is *negative net financing,* which simply means that the company is *generating cash.*

EXHIBIT 3-4
Specialty Steel Company
Relationship between Sales Growth and Financing Requirements

Sales Growth Rate (%)	Change in Sales	Forecasted Sales	External Financing Needs
30	$60,000,000	$260,000,000	$34,044,000
20	40,000,000	240,000,000	20,656,000
10	20,000,000	220,000,000	7,268,000
0	-0-	200,000,000	−6,120,000
−10	−20,000,000	180,000,000	−19,508,000
−20	−40,000,000	160,000,000	−32,896,000
−30	−60,000,000	140,000,000	−46,284,000

Rapidly growing firms tend to be "cash hogs."

The SSP example illustrates a point that is not always obvious—companies that experience rapid increases in sales are more likely to be strapped for cash than those with more moderate sales growth. Even though profits rise with sales volume, cash flow is generally negative because the assets needed to support a dollar of sales typically exceed the return on these assets. Product lines, divisions, or entire firms that are "stars" because of their strong market position and rapid sales growth also tend to be "cash hogs." A product line, division, or company typically becomes a "cash cow," generating lots of free cash flow, only when its business matures, its sales growth moderates, *and* it's in a secure market position to ensure profitability.[2]

Financial Forecasting Using Pro Forma Financial Statements

The primary virtue of using Equation [3-7] to estimate financing needs is its simplicity. In less than five minutes, you can estimate external needs with no more computational firepower than an eight-function calculator. Generating Exhibit 3-4 may take another ten minutes. Moreover, the insights provided are significant. For example, SSP's financial manager has learned quickly that: (1) external financing needs are in the order of $7.3 million, and (2) these needs are subject to very wide fluctuations based on what sales actually turn out to be. Given the market uncertainties, a line of credit from a financial institution for about $40 million might just be a safe financing vehicle because SSP would only pay interest on the amount actually borrowed plus a small commitment fee on the unborrowed balance.

Pro forma statements may be needed if expense, asset, and liability categories are not linearly related to sale.

However, SSP may not feel particularly comfortable going to its bank for a $40 million credit line based on a set of "back-of-the-envelope" estimates. Besides, the percent of sales approach may work well for some of SSP's expenses, assets, and liabilities but not for others. For instance, SSP is planning a major modernization of its manufacturing facilities this year that will add significantly to the company's fixed asset base. Therefore, SSP needs to modify the percentage of sales method by putting together a set of pro forma financial statements.

Exhibit 3-5 illustrates the pro forma financial statement approach for identifying SSP's 2000 financing needs. It uses many of the same elements of the percentage of sales method, but there are a number of differences. Let's examine Exhibit 3-5 to see how a firm might put together a set of financial statement forecasts.

Starting with the sales forecast of $220 million, cost of goods sold and operating expenses are calculated as a percentage of sales to get at operating profits (EBIT). These expense accounts can be broken down in greater detail depending how each of their components varies with sales in a given year. For instance, operating expenses typically include items such as marketing, general, and administrative expenses. While most of these categories tend to increase with sales over the long run, some may be fixed on a year-to-year basis. Interest expense is assumed to be unchanged. With interest set at $3 million, we can complete the rest of the income statement rather easily.

---

[2]The fact that a firm is in a low-growth market does not mean that it will be a cash cow. Unprofitable companies in mature markets are likely to need funds in the short run to revitalize the business.

EXHIBIT 3-5
Specialty Steel Products Company
Pro Forma Financial Statements
(in thousand $)

I. Income Statement	1999 Actual	Percent of Sales		2000 Forecast
Sales	$200,000	100%		$220,000
Cost of Goods Sold	140,000	70%	0.7 × $220,000 =	154,000
Gross Profits	$ 60,000			$ 66,000
Operating Expenses	40,000	20%	0.2 × $220,000 =	44,000
Operating Profits (EBIT)	$ 20,000			$ 22,000
Interest	3,000			3,000*
Profit before Taxes	$ 17,000			$ 19,000
Taxes @ 40%	6,800			7,600
Net Income	$ 10,200			$ 11,400
Dividends @ 40% of Net Income	4,080			4,560
Additions to Retained Earnings	$ 6,120			$ 6,840

II. Balance Sheet	1999 Actual	Percent of Sales		2000 Forecast
Assets				
Current Assets	$ 80,000	40%	0.4 × $220,000 =	$ 88,000
Net Fixed Assets	100,000			112,000
Total Assets	$180,000			$200,000
Liabilities				
Current Liabilities	$ 40,000	20%	0.2 × $220,000 =	$ 44,000
Long-Term Debt	30,000			30,000
Common Stock	20,000			20,000
Retained Earnings	90,000		$90,000 + $6,840 =	96,840
Total Liabilities + Equity	$180,000		Total Internal Sources	$190,840
			Additional Financing Required	9,160
			Total Liabilities + Equity	$200,000

*Assumes that no new debt is issued. If new debt is issued: (1) interest will be understated, (2) profits overstated, and (3) financing needs understated.

Now let's move to the balance sheet. Current assets are estimated as a percentage of sales, but net fixed assets[3] are increased by 12 percent—a greater percentage than the sales increase—to reflect the modernization program. Adding these two items together gives us total assets. SSP may wish to break current assets into its component parts if some of the accounts do not have a linear relationship with sales.

---

[3]Net fixed assets are defined as fixed assets at cost *less* accumulated depreciation.

Estimating current liabilities (as a percentage of sales), long-term debt (the same as last year), and common stock (no new stock issues planned) is relatively straightforward. Adding the retained earnings from the 2000 pro forma income statement to 1999's retained earnings gives us the retained earnings by year-end 2000. Totaling all of these items gives us the total liabilities plus equity in the absence of external financing. The external financing of $9.16 million is just the "plug" number that makes the balance sheet balance.

In all likelihood, SSP would use a computer-generated spreadsheet to estimate its external financing needs. The calculations we've just performed can readily be programmed, and pro forma statements for different sales scenarios can be generated easily. Armed with these projections, SSP can now go to its bank to seek credit.

Financing Needs and Working Capital Policy

Whenever we forecast a specific current asset or current liability using the percent of sales approach, we should keep in mind that there's a set of operating practices behind these percentages. Any shift in these policies will implicitly change the relationship between sales and specific working capital accounts and ultimately change external financing requirements.

Working capital policies designed to promote rapid sales growth can increase financing needs.

To illustrate, let's consider the case of Gale Supply Company (GSC), a distributor of upscale bathroom fixtures. The firm's main customers are home remodeling contractors and builders. Credit terms are net 30 days; however, the company's owner, Martin Gale, allows customers an extra 30 days to pay their bills. In addition, Gale tries to keep most items on hand at all times. The company's inventory turnover is low—only 3.7 times a year compared to an industry average of 6.1 times—but customer service levels are high. Liberal credit terms and an inventory policy that minimizes stock-outs have allowed GSC to grow rapidly without price cutting. Sales are expected to increase by 20 percent from a current level of $3.2 million to $3.84 million in 2000. In addition, even though suppliers offer a discount of 2 percent for payment within 10 days, GSC passes up these discounts and pays within the 30 days allowed.

Gale's pro forma income statement and balance sheet for 2000 are presented in Exhibit 3-6. As in the earlier examples, the income statement was prepared by the percent of sales method. On the balance sheet, the current accounts—receivables, inventory, and payables—reflect GSC's operating practices on a direct basis. Let's look at some of the details.

The projected sales of $3,840,000 for the year 2000 translate into daily sales of $10,520.55 ($3,840,000/365). If the average collection period is 60 days (the listed terms of 30 days plus the "extra" 30 days Martin allows), accounts receivable should reflect 60 days' worth of sales, or $631,233. Inventories can be calculated by recalling that inventory turnover is:

$$\text{Inventory Turnover} = \frac{\text{Cost of Goods Sold}}{\text{Inventory}}$$

so that

$$\text{Inventory} = \frac{\text{Cost of Goods Sold}}{\text{Inventory Turnover}}$$

EXHIBIT 3-6
Gale Supply Company
Pro Forma Financial Statements
(in thousand $)

I. Income Statement	1999 Actual	2000 Forecast
Sales	$3,200	$3,840
Cost of Goods Sold @ 60% of Sales	1,920	2,304
Gross Profits	$1,280	$1,536
Operating Expenses @ 30% of Sales	960	1,152
Profit before Taxes	$ 320	$ 384
Taxes @ 30%	96	115
Net Income	$ 224	$ 269

II. Balance Sheet	1999 Actual	2000 Forecast
Assets		
Cash	$ 12	$ 18
Accounts Receivable (60-day Collection Period)	526	631
Inventory (Turnover = 3.7 Times)	519	623
Current Assets	$1,057	$1,272
Net Fixed Assets	240	300
Total Assets	$1,297	$1,572
Liabilities		
Accounts Payable (30-day Payables Period)	$ 165	$ 198
Accruals (Assumed Increase with Sales)	12	15
Bank Loans	-0-	-0-
Current Liabilities	$ 177	$ 213
Long-Term Debt	340	310
Net Worth	780	1,049*
Total Liabilities + Net Worth	$1,297	$1,572

*Net worth of $780 in 1999 plus 2000's net income.

With a cost of goods sold of $2,304,000, and an inventory turnover of 3.7, the level of inventory would be $622,703 ($2,304,000/3.7). Rounding to the nearest thousand gives us the $623,000 figure shown in Exhibit 3-6.

Estimating accounts payable is a bit tricky since we don't have a forecast of purchases for 2000. However, we can get at purchases using the following accounting relationship:

$$(INV)_b + \text{Purchases} - \text{Cost of Goods Sold} = (INV)_e \qquad [3\text{-}8]$$

where $(INV)_b$ and $(INV)_e$ are the inventory levels at the beginning and end of the accounting period, respectively. From the data in Exhibit 3-6, $(INV)_b =$

$519,000, cost of goods sold is $2,304,000, and $(INV)_e = \$623,000$, so that purchases are

$$\$519,000 + \text{Purchases} - \$2,304,000 = \$623,000$$
$$\text{Purchases} = \$2,408,000$$

Average daily purchases would, therefore, be $6,597 ($2,408,000/365). If GSC pays suppliers in 30 days, there will be 30 days in purchases, for a total of $197,910, sitting in accounts payable. Rounding to the nearest thousand gives us the $198,000 figure in Exhibit 3-6.

Although it allows the company to avoid bank borrowing, Gale's policy of passing up cash discounts and paying within 30 days is extremely costly. On an order of $1,000, GSC's cost would be $980 if the bill were paid in 10 days. By taking an extra 20 days, Gale is effectively paying $20/$980 or 2.04 percent more for the goods. Since there are 365/20 = 18.25 20-day periods in a year, this works out to an implied interest rate of (2.04)(18.25) = 37.23 percent a year.[4] That's expensive![5]

> **Forgoing cash discounts is typically an expensive way to raise funds.**

Exhibit 3-7 illustrates the difference between forgoing and taking discounts by reducing the payables period to 10 days. Since the level of payables by taking discounts is one-third what it is when discounts are passed up, bank borrowing of $103,000 would be required to fill the gap. However, if GSC can borrow at 10 percent, the $10,300 in interest ($103,000 in borrowings times a 10 percent rate) is far less than the $48,000 in savings on purchases that the company could earn by taking discounts. Armed with its pro formas, a company like Gale should be in a position to go to its bank and get the needed credit.

Pro formas such as the ones we've just prepared give GSC a framework for thinking about other aspects of the firm's working capital policy. For example, the company could shorten its cash conversion cycle and perhaps eliminate the need for borrowing altogether by either reducing the average collection period and/or reducing the days inventory outstanding by increasing turnover. For example, a 25 percent reduction in the average collection period from 60 to 45 days will lower the level of receivables by 25 percent, from $631,233 to $473,425. This $157,808 decrease in receivables should be more than enough to avoid bank borrowing. For a small business, the $10,000 savings in interest expense is nothing to sneeze at.

However, before we go ahead and recommend that GSC "tighten up" collections, it's important to carefully consider the impact that such a policy change

---

[4]In general, the cost of passing up a cash discount (r^*) is

$$r^* = \frac{DIS}{100 - DIS} \times \frac{365}{PAY - DP}$$

where DIS is the cash discount as a percent, PAY the number of days before invoices are paid, and DP the number of days invoices must be paid in order to qualify for discounts.

[5]Beyond its high cost, forgoing cash discounts sends a chilling message to creditors. Since it's generally so expensive, only risky or naive buyers would choose to finance their operations by not taking discounts when they're available. Because of its cost, passing up cash discounts should be viewed as a financing method of last resort.

EXHIBIT 3-7
Gale Supply Company
2000 Pro Forma Financial Statements for Different Trade Credit Strategies
(in thousand $)

I. Income Statement	Forgo Discounts	Take Discounts
Sales	$3,840	$3,840
Cost of Goods Sold @ 60% of Sales	2,304	2,304
Gross Profits before Cash Discount	$1,536	$1,536
Plus: Cash Discounts Taken*	-0-	48
Gross Profits	$1,536	$1,584
Operating Expenses @ 30% of Sales	1,152	1,152
Operating Profits	$ 384	$ 432
Interest	-0-	10
Profit before Taxes	$ 384	$ 422
Taxes @ 30%	115	127
Net Income	$ 269	$ 295

II. Balance Sheet	Forgo Discounts	Take Discounts
Assets		
Cash	$ 18	$ 15†
Accounts Receivable (60-day Collection Period)	631	631
Inventory (Turnover = 3.7 Times)	623	623
Current Assets	$1,272	$1,269
Net Fixed Assets	300	300
Total Assets	$1,572	$1,569
Liabilities		
Accounts Payable	$ 198	$ 66‡
Accruals	15	15
Bank Loans	-0-	103
Current Liabilities	$ 213	$ 184
Long-Term Debt	310	310
Net Worth	1,049	1,075
Total Liabilities + Net Worth	$1,572	$1,569

*2 percent of Gale's annual purchases of $2,408.
†Assumed minimum cash balance.
‡By taking discounts, GSC will be reducing the payables period from 30 to 10 days. Therefore, the level of payables will be one-third that of passing up discounts.

might have on sales. Let's keep in mind that Martin instituted his liberal credit policy to stimulate sales; thus, any effort to monitor collections more closely might result in lost sales. How many? That's difficult to say ahead of time. What we know is that gross profit margins average 30 percent; therefore, a sales loss of about $32,000 would result in a reduction in gross profits of $9,600 ($32,000 times the gross profit margin of 30 percent). That would wipe out the entire interest savings.

Exploring ways to reduce the number of days of inventory on hand might be more profitable. GSC's current inventory turnover is 3.7 times a year—well below the industry average of six times annually. If turnover could be improved to just five times, inventory could be reduced from the projected level of $623,000 to $461,000 (the cost of goods sold of $2,304,000 divided by a five-time inventory turnover). The $162,000 in lower inventories is more than enough to avoid bank borrowing. Working with his suppliers on a JIT inventory management program might allow Gale to reduce inventory without affecting service.

3.4   THE CONCEPT OF SUSTAINABLE GROWTH

Sustainable growth measures a company's ability to expand without issuing new common stock.

Up to this point, we've focused our attention on the factors influencing a firm's external financing needs. Implicit in our approach is that a company is willing (and able) to take on new debt, as well as perhaps to issue new common stock, to finance profitable growth. This assumption essentially removes all financial constraints on growth. However, for some firms, new equity may not be an option. In a publicly traded company, managers may be unwilling to issue common stock as a matter of policy. In a closely held corporation whose stock isn't publicly traded, a new common stock issue is simply not feasible. For these companies, the funds for growth come from two sources: internally generated funds and new borrowing. Even the new debt may be limited by policy or by restrictions imposed by creditors. In these instances, the question is not how much money is needed to support a firm's desired level of growth but how fast it's capable of growing.

A company's **sustainable growth** is one aspect of a firm's ability to expand without a new common stock issue. The sustainable growth rate (g^*) of a firm was first popularized by R. C. Higgins more than twenty years ago and is approximately equal to:

$$g^* = \frac{RE}{NI} \times ROE \qquad [3\text{-}9]$$

where RE is earnings retained in the business, NI the firm's net income, and ROE the company's return on equity. The term RE/NI represents the proportion of a firm's earnings that is not paid out in dividends. We should recall from Chapter 2 that according to the DuPont analysis, ROE is the product of a company's net profit margin, total asset turnover, and the equity multiplier. Therefore, Equation [3-9] can be written as

$$g^* = \frac{\text{Retained Earnings}}{\text{Net Income}} \times \frac{\text{Net Income}}{\text{Sales}} \times \frac{\text{Sales}}{\text{Assets}} \times \frac{\text{Assets}}{\text{Equity}} \qquad [3\text{-}10]$$

Equation [3-10] indicates that a company's ability to grow depends on its: (1) dividend policy, (2) net profit margins, (3) ability to utilize assets to generate sales,

EXHIBIT 3-8
Sustainable Growth Rate

Factor Increases	Change in Sustainable Growth Rate
Dividend Payout	Decrease
Net Profit Margin	Increase
Asset Utilization	Increase
Leverage	Increase

A firm's sustainable growth is a function of its dividend policy, profitability, asset utilization, and leverage.

and (4) leverage.[6] The relationship between these variables and the sustainable growth rate is summarized in Exhibit 3-8.

Calculating the Sustainable Growth Rate: An Example

To see how the idea of a sustainable growth rate can be used in the planning process, let's return to the example of Specialty Steel Products Company (SSP). To refresh our memory, a condensed version of SSP's income statement and balance sheet for 1999 is presented in Exhibit 3-9.

EXHIBIT 3-9
Specialty Steel Products Company
Condensed Balance Sheet and Income Statements—1999
(in million $ except ratios)

Sales	$200.0
Profit after Tax @ 5.1% Sales	10.2
Current Assets @ 40% Sales	80.0
Fixed Assets	100.0
Total Assets	$180.0
Current Liabilities @ 20% Sales	$ 40.0
Long-Term Debt	30.0
Equity	110.0
Total Liabilities + Equity	$180.0

Dividends as Proportion of Earnings = 0.40
Retained Earnings as Proportion of Net Income = 0.60
Net Profit Margin = $10.2/$200.0 = 0.051
Asset Turnover = Sales/Assets = $200.0/$180.0 = 1.11
Equity Multiplier = Assets/Equity = $180.0/$110 = 1.64

---

[6]Equation [3-8] is an approximation. More elegant (and less intuitively appealing) formulations may be found in Higgins (1977; 1981) and Van Horne (1988).

The variables influencing sustainable growth are included in the exhibit. Based on its current (1999) operating and financial characteristics, the sustainable growth is

$$g^* = [RE/NI] \, [\text{Net Income}/\text{Sales}] \, [\text{Sales}/\text{Assets}] \, [\text{Assets}/\text{Equity}]$$

$$= (0.6)(0.051)(1.11)(1.64) = 0.056 \text{ or } 5.6 \text{ percent}$$

That's well below the 10 percent unit sales growth that the company expects in the next year. If SSP wants to increase sales faster than its sustainable growth rate, then it has to be prepared to make changes in its operating and financial characteristics.

Increasing the Sustainable Growth Rate

According to Equation [3-9], SSP can increase its sustainable growth rate by (1) increasing net profit margins, (2) improving asset turnover, (3) increasing leverage, or (4) increasing the proportion of earnings retained in the business. Let's look at each of these policy choices in turn.

Seeking ways to improve operational efficiency will increase net profit margins and/or asset turnover. As it looks at its operations, SSP should be asking such questions as: Can we further reduce our manufacturing costs, perhaps by outsourcing? Is it possible to service additional customers without increasing marketing or distribution expenses? Can we reduce our average collection period without losing customers? Should we reduce inventories by reducing the number of grades of steel that we offer or by investing in a JIT inventory system? The answers to all these questions may be "no," but the questions still need to be asked.

One way to increase sustainable growth is through **outsourcing**. Outsourcing involves shifting an in-house activity to some outside supplier. We're currently seeing a great deal of outsourcing by corporate America to reduce costs and improve net profit margins. What's less obvious—but no less important—is that outsourcing frees assets that would have been tied up, thereby increasing the company's asset turnover. Both of these factors increase sustainable growth.

> Outsourcing can be an effective way to reduce costs and increase sustainable growth.

Firms can increase sustainable growth by increasing leverage. In essence, increasing leverage involves borrowing more for every dollar of equity retained in the business. Using debt as the sole source of external financing has its challenges. Even if SSP can borrow the amount it needs, provisions in the debt agreement might just prevent the company from meeting its growth targets.

And finally, SSP's sustainable growth can be increased by increasing the proportion of earnings retained by reducing dividends. If SSP is a publicly traded firm, any change in dividend policy that isn't properly communicated to the market could adversely affect share price.

3.5   DEVELOPING THE CASH BUDGET

The cash budget is an integral part of corporate financial planning. It details forecasted cash inflows and outflows over some future time period. To demonstrate the construction of the cash budget, consider the case of Ambex, Inc. Ambex's

<table>
<tr><td>

Cash budgets are a good way of identifying financing needs for a seasonal business.

</td></tr>
</table>

products are standard equipment in many new car models. Its sales move in line with new car sales production, which, in turn, leads new car sales by about one month. Since auto sales are seasonal, Ambex's sales will also be seasonal: The most important months are September through December when new car sales are at their peak. Sales in the summer months are slow because auto manufacturers are retooling for the introduction of new models in early fall.

To simplify our example, the cash budget will be prepared on a quarterly basis. In practice, Ambex would prepare its cash budget on a monthly, if not a weekly basis, with the actual cash management done on a daily basis.

Ambex purchases materials based on sales forecasts. These purchases are made one quarter in advance of sales and are 40 percent of sales. Labor is budgeted at 30 percent of sales, and depreciation and other expenses, such as electricity, selling, and administrative costs, are 20 percent of sales. However, labor expenses and expenses other than materials don't vary over the year. Rather than hire and lay off according to seasonal needs, Ambex determines the size of the work force needed at the beginning of the year and maintains this number over the year. Based on forecasted annual sales of $22 million for 2000, other expenses would be $4,400,000 a year or $1,100,000 each quarter. Of this quarterly amount, $600,000 is depreciation expense. Quarterly interest payments are $150,000 and taxes are 50 percent of profits. Ambex receives tax refunds when losses occur.

Exhibit 3-10 is the pro forma income statement for Ambex for 2000. Such a statement is driven by the sales forecast, which is presented in the first line. Based on the pro forma income statement, we can go ahead and put together the cash budget for 2000. In preparing the cash budget, shown in Exhibit 3-11, we've assumed that 70 percent of the sales generated in a particular quarter are collected in that quarter, with the remaining 30 percent being collected in the next quarter. Thus, if S_t is the sales in period t, then the collections in period t would be

EXHIBIT 3-10
Ambex, Inc.
Pro Forma Income Statement—2000
(in thousand $)

	First Quarter	Second Quarter	Third Quarter	Fourth Quarter	Total for the Year
Sales	$6,000	$4,000	$3,000	$9,000	$22,000
Materials	2,400	1,600	1,200	3,600	8,800
Labor	1,650	1,650	1,650	1,650	6,600
Depreciation	600	600	600	600	2,400
Other Expenses	500	500	500	500	2,000
Interest	150	150	150	150	600
Profit before Taxes	$ 700	−$ 500	−$1,100	$2,500	$ 1,600
Taxes@50%	350	−250	−550	1,250	800
Profit after Taxes	$ 700	−$ 250	−$ 550	$1,250	$ 800

$0.7S_t + 0.3S_{t-1}$. For example, given the first- and second-quarter sales of $6 million and $4 million, respectively, second quarter collections would be:

$$\text{Collections} = (0.7)\ \$4\ \text{million} + 0.3\ (\$6\ \text{million}) = \$4.6\ \text{million}$$

Payments for materials, labor, and other expenses are made at the end of the quarter in which they are incurred. Interest expenses and taxes are also paid at the end of each quarter. The proportion of earnings paid out in dividends is set at 75 percent of estimated yearly income. This high dividend payout is in line with companies operating in mature industries in which sales growth is very slow.

The difference between the cash flows and reported income is striking. For one thing, materials are purchased and paid for in the period prior to the sale of goods even though their cost—from an accounting standpoint—is recorded at the time of sale one quarter later. To further increase the gap between the cash outflows for materials, 30 percent of sales recorded are not collected until the following period. In addition, depreciation, a noncash expense on the income

EXHIBIT 3-11
Ambex, Inc.
Cash Budget for 2000
(in thousand $)

	First Quarter	Second Quarter	Third Quarter	Fourth Quarter
Sales	$6,000	$4,000	$3,000	$9,000
Sources of Cash				
Collections	6,300‖	4,600	3,300	7,200
Tax Refund*	-0-	250	550	-0-
A. Total Sources of Cash	$6,300	$4,850	$3,850	$7,200
Uses of Cash				
Payment of Materials	1,600	1,200	3,600	2,800
Labor and Other Expenses	2,150	2,150	2,150	2,150
Interest	150	150	150	150
Taxes	350	0	0	1,250
Capital Expenditures	0	1,000	2,000	0
Dividends†	150	150	150	150
B. Total Uses of Cash	$4,400	$4,650	$8,050	$6,500
C. Net Cash Flow (A − B)	1,900	200	−4,200	700
D. Beginning Cash Balance	500	2,400	2,600	−1,600
E. Ending Cash Balance (C + D)‡	$2,400	$2,600	−$1,600	−$ 900
F. Minimum Cash Balance	1,000	1,000	1,000	1,000
G. Financing Required (F − E)§	−$1,400	−$1,600	$2,600	$1,900

*Tax losses are assumed to be carried back and a tax refund received for taxes paid previously.
†Dividends are 75 percent of estimated annual profits and are made in equal quarterly payments.
‡A negative cash balance implies that Ambex will be borrowing money during this time period.
§A negative financing requirement implies that Ambex will have surplus cash for short-term investment.
‖Fourth-quarter sales for the previous year were $7 million.

statement, never shows up on the cash budget. Moreover, Ambex plans to buy some capital equipment in the second and third quarters to accommodate the large influx of orders in the fourth quarter.

The pro forma cash budget indicates that Ambex will have surplus funds for the first two quarters, followed by cash deficits for the next two quarters despite a profitable fourth quarter. It would appear that Ambex will need $2.6 million in financing in the third quarter. The financing needs will drop to $1.9 million in the fourth quarter because of cash flows from operations of $700,000 during the quarter. These figures reflect year 2000 fourth-quarter sales of $9 million and projected first quarter sales in 2001 of $7 million.

Flexible Budgeting

Flexible budgets are most useful when sales or profit margins are unpredictable.

The cash budget for Ambex illustrates the traditional fixed budget. It's based on a single-best-estimate approach in which only the most likely sales forecast is used. Based on this forecast, estimates are made of all related items. Fixed budgets work well when business volume is relatively constant or fluctuates in an expected and predictable way such as with seasonal highs and lows. If no significant deviations from the sales forecast are expected, then the additional time and expense of developing alternative budgets aren't really necessary.

With the single-best-estimate approach, deviations from the expected are not totally ignored; they're just not considered important enough to worry about. However, for many firms, deviations from some most-likely scenario is the rule, not the exception. These companies really can't adopt the fixed budget because sales volume and/or profit margins may be highly unpredictable even on a month-to-month basis. These firms must project all reasonable levels of sales—and the level of each item related to sales—for the period under review.

The key to developing a flexible budget is to determine which costs "flex" with business activity and which will be fixed—at least in the short run. Every cost will either be fixed (not dependent on the level of business activity), variable (changing directly with activity), or mixed. Mixed or semivariable costs have two components—a fixed minimum or base cost and an additional cost that varies with business activity. Flexible budgets recognize that the future can't be captured by a single set of numbers. By analyzing alternative forecasts of business activity, a company can determine the extent to which its financing needs vary. Such an analysis can help establish the amount of cash, marketable securities, and credit lines the company should maintain in case things turn out differently than expected.

Cash Budgeting and Financial Planning

Like the pro forma income statement and balance sheet, the cash budget indicates the total amount of financing required and the timing of these needs. These estimates, in turn, depend on the firm's strategic objectives and the policies adopted to achieve these goals. However, the objectives of the plan must fall within a firm's financial capacity. The cash budget identifies how much money is required to carry out the action plan and how much will come from external rather than internal sources. The analysis should be performed well in advance to warn of any mismatch between the company's strategic plan and its ability to finance that plan.

In line with our earlier discussion, a cash budget should be a flexible instrument that allows management to see how a change in its operating policies can affect the rest of the forecast. For example, suppose a catalogue firm such as L.L. Bean wants to gain additional market share by telling customers that it will guarantee shipment on the day an order is placed. However, improving service levels in the face of uncertain demand will require higher inventories. Unless suppliers are willing to expand the payables period, additional financing will be needed. If L.L. Bean doesn't have the financing capacity to support these higher inventories, it may not be able to raise the level of customer service.

> Properly prepared, cash budgets allow managers to see how changes in operating policies can affect financing needs.

A cash budget can predict potential cash shortfalls months and even years in advance. That's what financial planning is all about. A financial manager's worst nightmare is to wake up one morning and find that the company can't pay its bills or make strategically important investments. The cash budget buys senior management the time they need to raise capital. At a somewhat different level, a cash budget enhances a firm's credibility with lenders and other stakeholders by demonstrating that the company has its act together.

SUMMARY

Financial planning plays an important part in the strategic management process by identifying the capital requirements needed to carry out the plan. By developing a set of pro forma financial statements, a company can create a vehicle for measuring and controlling key performance areas such as profitability, market position, and costs. Included in this process is the development of a long-range financial plan, operating budgets, and cash flow statements.

Key to the financial planning process are the sales forecast and the relationship between sales and other income and balance sheet items. The principal approach to forecasting is the percent of sales method in which various expense and asset and liability categories are directly related to sales. Historical relationships typically form the basis for linking sales and net asset requirements. The percent of sales approach is very amenable to spreadsheet modeling, thereby making it easy to test the changes in financing needs and changes in assumptions relating to sales growth rates, asset utilization, and the like.

We also took a look at the sustainable growth rate—the steady-state growth in sales/assets that a firm might achieve without a new common stock issue. This is a useful planning tool for the closely held company or the firm that wants to avoid the adverse signs of new common stock issues, as it allows managers to test their sales growth goals against their ability to meet these objectives.

APPENDIX 3A   FINANCING CURRENT ASSETS

In addition to determining its funding needs, a company has to decide on the proportion of short-term debt and long-term capital to use in financing its working capital. This is part of a more general problem faced by companies in deciding on the maturity structure of their liabilities, which, in turn, will depend on the maturity structure of their assets. Three generic strategies can be used in the financing of working capital: a matching strategy, a conservative strategy, and an aggressive strategy. Let's look at each of these approaches in detail.

The Matching Strategy

As a time-honored guide to setting financial policy, the **matching strategy** is based on the idea that firms should match the maturity of the fund source with the maturity of the asset being financed. As Exhibit 3A-1 indicates, this means that fixed assets and the permanent portion of current assets are financed with long-term sources of capital, and the temporary assets normally associated with seasonal businesses are financed with short-term debt. Once seasonal needs pass, the short-term loans will be repaid.

Suppose that a company bought a piece of equipment with a life of ten years. Proponents of the matching strategy would argue that the best way to finance this asset would be with a combination of equity and a ten-year loan: The maturity of the source of funds would exactly match the maturity of the asset. If the company prefers to use only debt, the loan's amortization schedule should be set to coincide with the equipment's depreciation—in this way, the source of cash (depreciation) would match the use of cash (repayment of the equipment loan).

The company might also be able to finance this equipment with a six-month loan. However, in six months, the cash flows associated with the equipment (depreciation plus profit after taxes) probably won't be sufficient to repay the loan when it comes due. This might not present much of a problem—the company could repay whatever it could and refinance the balance. As a matter of fact, the lender might be willing to refinance continuously over the life of the asset. But perhaps the lender will be reluctant to renew its loan, leaving the company to scramble for money at the last minute. That's not much fun. The matching approach, which insists that a firm finance the equipment with long-term sources, avoids problems like this because investors are committed over the entire life of the asset.

The Conservative Financing Strategy

For financial managers seeking peace of mind, there's the conservative strategy. As Exhibit 3A-2 indicates, the **conservative financing strategy** involves the firm's use of long-term capital to finance all of its long-term assets (fixed assets plus permanent current assets) plus a portion of its temporary assets. As you can see, short-term financing is used only at or near seasonal peaks. Most other times, no short-term financing is

EXHIBIT 3A-1
The Matching Strategy

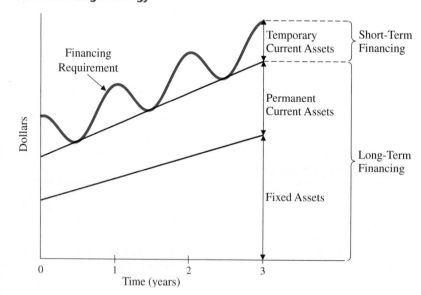

EXHIBIT 3A-2
The Conservative Financing Strategy

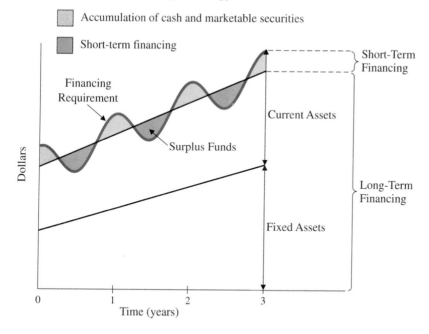

needed. Surplus liquidity will accumulate when sales are at their lowest point of the year.

By relying heavily on long-term capital, firms don't have to worry about the availability of short-term financing for their seasonal needs, nor do they have to be concerned about the cost of that borrowing. If long-term debt is used, you can usually get creditors to commit to fixed-rate financing for up to thirty years. In short, if managers want to use long-term capital to finance *all of the firm's permanent assets,* and *all of its temporary assets,* there should be no uncertainty about the availability or cost of funds over time. That's a pretty safe world. However, in a company with a lot of intangible assets—such as organizational capital—this excess liquidity allows the firm to ride out difficult financial times without losing human capital.

The Aggressive Financing Strategy

For chief financial officers with a spirit of adventure, there's the **aggressive financing strategy.** As we can see in Exhibit 3A-3, this approach relies on short-term funds to finance not only the firm's temporary assets but also a portion of its permanent assets. Since short-term funds cost less, *on average,* than long-term funds,

the aggressive approach tends to increase profitability over the long haul by reducing interest expense.

However, using short-term sources of funds to finance long-term assets is not without risks. As we've indicated earlier, creditors may not agree to continuously refinance these short-term liabilities. Also, short-term interest rates aren't always lower than long-term rates. When inflation is high, the Federal Reserve will push up short-term rates as a means of restricting credit in the economy. Thus, a company using the aggressive strategy will have to contend with high interest rates in an economy in which credit is restricted.

Risk–Return Characteristics of Financing Strategies

The choice of strategies to finance current assets is a classic tradeoff between risk and return. One extreme is the conservative strategy, which represents a low-risk, low-return approach. By using long-term sources of capital to finance all of its permanent assets and a portion of its temporary assets, a company is assured of having the money to meet its needs at a known cost. However, this security comes at a price: Long-term capital is typically more expensive than short-term

EXHIBIT 3A-3
The Aggressive Financing Strategy

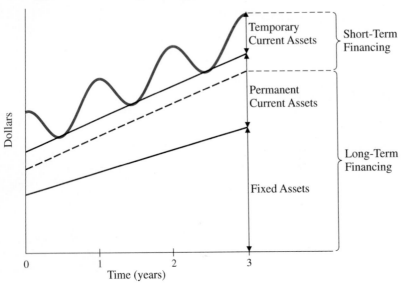

borrowings. All other things being equal, firms adopting a conservative strategy should be less profitable than those using either the aggressive or matching approach.

In contrast, the aggressive strategy will produce the highest profits *over the long haul*. However, a firm will have to refinance debt more frequently. Lower-quality firms may not be able to do so under reasonable terms and conditions. Even if the firm has no difficulty renewing the short-term loan used to finance permanent assets, it still faces the risk that interest rates may rise sharply in the interim and that its return on investment will be insufficient to service the loan, putting the company's survival at stake.

The matching strategy represents a compromise between the other two approaches and is sometimes referred to as the *hedging strategy*. By limiting the short-term funds to the financing of temporary assets, it minimizes the risk that loans won't be renewed. Why? Lenders tend to be more receptive to financing seasonal needs because they know that cash will become available once the company is "out-of-season." By matching permanent assets with long-term sources of capital, a firm can make rational investment decisions by comparing returns on projects with a known cost of funds that can be "locked-in" at the time the investment is made.

APPENDIX 3B   SHORT-TERM FINANCING VEHICLES

Firms focusing the matching strategy prefer to finance the temporary portion of their current assets with short-term funds. In selecting from among the various short-term instruments available, the financial manager is apt to focus first on their relative costs. However, other aspects of a funding source—including reliability, restrictions, and flexibility—are likely to come into play as well. For example, firms may be willing to pay extra for greater certainty that funds will be available when needed. Similarly, lenders who impose fewer restrictions are favored over those who insist on very restrictive conditions. Beyond this, many short-term financing arrangements can be renewed continuously; therefore, sources that are temporary in a technical sense can have some of the same characteristics as longer-term borrowing.

Short-Term Bank Loans

Although a number of financial firms lend to businesses, commercial bank loans are the dominant form of interest-bearing financing in the United States and other developed countries. These loans are often described as *self-liquidating* because they're frequently used to finance seasonal increases in accounts receivable and inventory. Once the firm's seasonal peak is past, these increases in working capital are converted into cash, which can then be used to repay the loan.

Short-term bank loans are generally unsecured. The borrower signs a note evidencing an obligation to repay the loan when due, along with accrued interest. Most loans must be repaid or renewed every 90 days. The need to roll over these loans periodically gives the bank a good bit of control over the funds, thereby reducing the need for a restrictive loan agreement. To ensure that this temporary financing is not used for the acquisition of permanent assets, a bank usually insists on a **cleanup clause** requiring the company to be completely out of debt to the bank for at least 30 days during the year.

Bank credit has the advantage of flexibility as its terms and conditions can be tailored to meet the needs of the borrower. One form of accommodation is the **transaction loan.** This type of loan is negotiated and administered for a specific purpose, with specific conditions, and is repaid in a single lump-sum payment. Transaction loans are used most often by borrowers who have an infrequent need for bank credit.

Arranging separate loans for frequent borrowers is a relatively expensive way of doing business. Transaction costs can be reduced by setting up a **line of credit,** which is an informal agreement permitting a company to borrow up to a stated maximum amount from the bank. The firm can draw down its line of credit when it requires funds and pays back the loan balance when it has excess cash. Although the bank is not legally obligated to honor the line of credit, it always does so unless the firm runs into financial difficulty. A line of credit is good for one year, with renewals renegotiated every year.

A **revolving credit agreement** is similar to a line of credit except that now the bank (or group of banks) is legally committed to extend credit up to a stated maximum. The firm pays interest on the outstanding borrowing plus a **commitment fee.** The commitment fee can range from one-eighth to a half of 1 percent per annum on the unused portion of the credit line. Revolving credit agreements are usually renegotiated every two to three years. Since there's typically no cleanup period, revolving credit agreements with renewal provisions have the characteristics of a longer-term source of funds.

Like most other terms of the loan agreement, the interest rates on bank borrowing are negotiated by the banker and the borrower. The borrower's prior relationship with the institution plays a role in loan pricing, but bank interest rates are determined by the same factors as interest rates in the financial markets: the risk-free rate plus a risk premium based on credit risk, maturity, and the provisions of the loan agreement. We'd expect nothing less in competitive markets where the pricing of a commodity—money—cannot be out of line with the prices that others are willing to charge.

Historically, bank interest rates have scaled upward from the **prime rate,** the rate of interest a bank charges its most creditworthy customer. Loans for higher-credit-risk customers are set at some premium, say 1 or 2 percent, above prime. In recent years, prime has played a less important role as a benchmark for the pricing of business loans. In order to compete with market rates, many banks are willing to lend to "prime" credit risks at less than prime. Moreover, with the globalization of the financial markets, prime is not the only base rate in use. For example, revolving credit agreements routinely offer a choice between the prime rate, LIBOR (the London Interbank Offer Rate), or the rates on domestic CDs.

Determining the interest rate on bank loans is sometimes tricky because interest can be paid at maturity or in advance. Each payment method gives a different effective rate even though the quoted rate may be the same. When the bank deducts interest in advance, the loan is said to be quoted on a *discount* basis. Regardless of whether interest is paid in advance or at maturity, the effective interest rate is:

$$\text{Effective Interest Rate} = \frac{\text{Annual Interest Paid}}{\text{Usable Funds Available}}$$

To calculate the difference between the quoted and effective interest rates on loans that are priced on a discounted basis, suppose a company borrows $100,000 for one year at 10 percent interest. If interest is paid at maturity, the company will owe the bank $110,000 at the end of the year. This yields an effective rate that is the same as the nominal rate:

$$\text{Effective Interest Rate} = \frac{\$10,000}{\$100,000} = 0.10 \text{ or } 10 \text{ percent}$$

On the other hand, if the loan is quoted on a discount basis, the $10,000 in interest will be paid in advance, leaving the company with $90,000 now and $100,000 to be repaid in one year. The effective rate exceeds the nominal rate as the company pays interest on $100,000 but only has the use of $90,000:

$$\text{Effective Interest Rate} = \frac{\$10,000}{\$90,000}$$
$$= 0.111 \text{ or } 11.1 \text{ percent}$$

The higher the quoted interest rate, the greater the difference between paying interest at maturity and paying interest on a discount basis. An extreme illustration is provided by the level of interest rates in Mexico in 1985. At this time, the nominal interest rate on a peso bank loan was 70 percent; about 15 percent higher than Mexico's annual inflation rate. By collecting interest in advance, Mexican banks boosted the effective interest rate dramatically. For example, if a customer borrowed 100,000 pesos, 70,000 pesos in interest would be paid in advance. Thus, the bank would be lending 30,000 pesos but collecting 100,000 pesos at maturity. The effective rate on the loan would be 233 percent:

$$\text{Effective Interest Rate} = \frac{70,000 \text{ pesos}}{30,000 \text{ pesos}}$$
$$= 2.33 \text{ or } 233 \text{ percent}$$

Further complicating the process of determining the effective cost of bank borrowing is the existence of **compensating balances**, when a bank sometimes requires a borrower to keep between 10 to 20 percent of the loan balance on deposit in non-interest-bearing demand deposit accounts. These compensating balances raise the cost of bank credit to the extent that a company must hold more cash on deposit than normal. By reducing the amount of usable funds available, the effective cost of borrowing is increased.

To see this in quantitative terms, let's return to our earlier example in which a company wanted to borrow $100,000 at a 10 percent nominal rate with interest paid at maturity and a 20 percent compensating balance requirement of $20,000. If the firm already has $5,000 on deposit, it will only need to keep an additional $15,000 on deposit. However, this $100,000 loan only provides usable funds of $85,000, thereby raising the effective rate to 11.76 percent:

$$\text{Effective Interest Rate} = \frac{\$10,000}{\$85,000}$$
$$= 0.1176 \text{ or } 11.76 \text{ percent}$$

A bank's ability to impose compensating balance requirements on borrowers has weakened in recent years. With increased competition from other financial intermediaries, the commercial banks' share of the loan market has declined. In addition, more and more companies now have the ability to access the financial markets directly. To deal with these competitive pressures, many banks are now making loans without compensating balance requirements. Further, the ability of borrowers to analyze loan costs has gotten banks to move toward pricing based on interest rates and fees rather than on hidden factors such as compensating balances.

Commercial Paper

Companies with relatively large needs can sometimes borrow by issuing commercial paper. **Commercial paper** is an unsecured[7] short-term promissory note sold in the financial market on a discount basis. The major purchasers of commercial paper are financial intermediaries and other corporations. Because commercial paper is typically unsecured and bears only the name of the issuer, the market is dominated by the largest, most creditworthy companies.

Firms can issue commercial paper directly through their own marketing organizations or through dealers. Industrial firms, public utilities, and some financial intermediaries sell their commercial paper through dealers. These dealers buy an entire issue from a company and, in turn, sell it to investors. Dealers generally charge one-eighth of a percent commission on the face value of the paper. Therefore, placing $100 million dollars in commercial paper with a dealer would cost $125,000. Large finance companies, like General Motors Acceptance Corporation (GMAC), normally bypass the dealer organization in favor of selling paper through their own sales force. Such issuers can tailor both the maturity and amount of the note to the needs of investors.

The principal virtue of commercial paper is that it is generally cheaper than a bank loan. Depending on the borrower, commercial paper may be a full percentage point or more below the prime rate. However, the "market" is unforgiving to companies who cannot

---

[7]Most commercial paper is unsecured, but beginning in the mid-1980s, we began to see *asset-backed commercial paper* being issued by some financial institutions. Commercial banks, for instance, have issued commercial paper secured by auto loans, leases, and credit-card receivables.

meet their obligations on time. Creditors expect to be repaid on time; if a firm gets itself in a bind, a credit extension is simply unacceptable. For many years, the commercial paper market was restricted to very high-quality borrowers for just this reason. Today, lower-quality companies do issue commercial paper but only if they have backup lines of credit with a bank to ensure repayment. Commitment fees to banks for these backup lines, coupled with the need to maintain compensating balances, are part of the noninterest costs of commercial paper for the low-quality issuer.

Commercial paper was an American innovation: The first issues date back to the early 1900s. The mid-1980s saw the development of a nonbank short-term credit instrument called the **Euronote.** Euronotes bear a strong resemblance to commercial paper in that they are short-term notes, usually denominated in dollars, which are issued by corporations and governments outside the United States. In a variation on the theme, some corporations have issued **universal commercial paper (UCP),** the commercial paper of United States corporations that is both denominated and payable in some currency other than the U.S. dollar. To appeal to a larger group of holders, an individual issue may be denominated in a number of currencies. Because UCP is not dollar-denominated, it gives foreign investors a high-quality, short-term instrument with which they don't have to worry about exchange rate risk.

Commercial paper issued in the United States has a maturity of 270 days or less. What's so magical about a 270-day maturity? Under the Securities Act of 1933, all notes with proceeds used to finance current transactions and maturities of less than nine months are exempt from SEC registration requirements. Thus, commercial paper could be issued without registration, thereby reducing issuance costs dramatically if maturities are kept short. Since the Euronote is issued outside the United States and isn't subject to SEC regulation, its maturities tend to be longer than those of either "garden-variety" commercial paper or UCP.

Asset-Based Financing

All of the financing arrangements that we've discussed up to this point are unsecured. Many small and medium-sized companies do not have a good enough credit standing to permit unsecured borrowing and will turn to **asset-based financing,** whereby a bank or a commercial finance company lends money secured by some pledged asset, usually accounts receivable or inventory.

Pledging Accounts Receivable.   Accounts receivable are one of the firm's most liquid assets and are frequently used as collateral against loans. When **pledging accounts receivable,** a firm assigns these assets to the lender; the borrowing firm is still liable for the collection of the receivable should the customer default. Normally, the borrower's customers are not informed that their accounts have been assigned. In evaluating an arrangement in which receivables are used as collateral, the lender will evaluate a company's customers. All other things being equal, the higher the quality of a firm's customers, the higher the percentage a lender might be willing to lend against the face amount of the receivables.

In terms of mechanics, the pledging of accounts receivable is continuous in nature. Let's take a look at how it might work. Suppose that a bank decides to lend up to 80 percent against the face value of the accounts receivable assigned. The firm then sends the bank details of the specific accounts, which include the name of the customer, the date of the billings and the amount owed; typically, evidence of shipment is sent as part of this initial package. The firm then gets 80 percent of the amount on the schedule of accounts. When the company receives payment from a customer, it forwards this payment to the bank. The bank checks the record against its record of receivables outstanding and reduces the amount the borrower owes by 80 percent. The other 20 percent is credited to the borrower's account. At the same time, the company will be generating new receivables. These receivables are assigned and add to the security base against which a company can borrow. As the security base rises and falls with the amount of receivables generated, a company has a spontaneous form of financing.

The pledging of accounts receivable can be an expensive form of financing, with added expenses coming from two quarters. First, the companies that must pledge their receivables to get credit accommodation are typically weaker firms with above-average risks of default. Interest rates may be as high as 3 to 4 percent above prime to compensate the lender for these higher risks. Second, there's a good bit of paperwork associated with this type of arrangement, so that it's not unusual for lenders to add additional fees to cover bookkeeping and other administrative costs. On the plus side, receivables loans are not subject to compensating balances nor are there any commitment fees. Therefore, the company only pays interest on the amount of the credit line actually used.

Factoring.   When it pledges its receivables, a company retains legal title to the asset. When it *factors* its receivables, it actually sells the receivables to a financial intermediary known as a *factor* at a discount. Most factoring is done on a *nonrecourse* basis, which means that the factor bears the credit risk. By contrast, pledging is done with *recourse*. Thus, if pledged receivables cannot be collected, the lender can ask the firm to make good on the loan.

A factor provides three services: bearing credit risk, collecting the receivables, and lending. Fees on the order of 1 percent of the face amount of the receivable are charged for bearing credit risk and servicing the accounts. The receivables sold to the factor will not be collected from the accounts for some period of time; however, the factor will make advances against these receivables if the company needs cash now. Interest is, of course, charged on these advances.

To get a better feel for the costs of factoring, let's suppose that a small textile company generates $1 million a month in receivables. Because the sale is on a nonrecourse basis, the factor will charge a one-time commission of 3 percent, or $30,000, on these receivables and credit the company's account for $970,000. If the company wants to draw against its balance, it will have to pay 9 percent annually, or three-quarters of a percent a month. This comes to $7,275 monthly ($0.0075 \times $970,000). Suppose the receivables remain open for 60 days. On the surface, this looks like very expensive borrowing because the company is paying $44,550 (the factoring commission of $30,000 plus interest of $7,275 \times 2 = $14,550) to borrow $970,000 for two months. This works out to be 4.59 percent ($44,550/$970,000) or about 28 percent annually.

However, comparing this 28 percent to the cost of borrowing secured by receivables is very misleading. Remember, a factor not only provides a lending function but also relieves a company of its credit and collection expenses. The question is whether a factor can perform these functions at a lower cost than the firm. For many small companies operating in industries in which customer default rates are high (e.g., retailing, garment manufacturers), factors may have significant economies of scale in administering receivables.

Inventory Financing.   The use of inventory to secure loans is similar to the use of receivables in that the lender must decide what type of security arrangement to use and what fraction of the value of different inventory components to lend against. A **floating lien** is a widely used arrangement in which the lender ends up with a general claim against all of the borrower's inventory without specifying the items involved. It is the simplest type of arrangement and the least expensive to police. It's also the least secure form of inventory collateral. The borrower maintains control over the inventory and can sell and replace items at will. In the event of liquidation, there's no telling what will be in inventory.

A lender has far more security with a **trust receipt plan,** which is a security arrangement under which a firm pledges to hold "in trust" for the lender proceeds from the sale of identified inventory. Sales proceeds are then forwarded to the lender and used to reduce the outstanding loan balance. Trust receipt plans work best for items like automobiles, appliances, and other types of durable goods that can be clearly identified by serial number. Inventory that can be identified by make, model, and serial number lends itself to easy periodic inspection by the lender.

As long as goods remain with the borrower, the lender is always vulnerable to fraud or misrepresentation. To gain greater control over the inventory held as collateral, the goods may be placed under the control of a third party, referred to as a **warehouseman.** The warehouseman retains physical control over the pledged goods and only releases it when the lender gives permission. Since inventory must be controlled item by item, warehousing tends to be an expensive source of financing.

There are two principal forms of warehousing arrangements. A *terminal warehouse* is a public warehouse where goods are stored until released on the lender's orders. When the goods are delivered to the public warehouse, the warehouse company issues a *terminal warehouse receipt* listing the specific items received. This receipt is sent to the lender, who then advances funds against the collateral. As the borrower repays the loan, the lender authorizes the warehouse company to release inventory to the borrower.[8]

The need to physically move inventory to and from the warehouse makes terminal warehousing a relatively expensive arrangement. This problem is eased by using a *field warehouse,* which is a warehouse on the

---

[8]A field warehouse is not a foolproof arrangement. In the Allied Salad Oil Scandal of 1963, a financing subsidiary of American Express lost over $100 million when tanks that were supposed to contain salad oil were found to contain water with a thin coating of oil on the top as "dressing."

borrower's premises. A warehouse company physically separates the pledged inventory from the borrower's other inventory with a fence or by some other means, and lender permission is still needed to release inventory. However, the fact that storage is on the borrower's premises makes this arrangement less cumbersome (and less expensive) than a terminal warehouse.

International Short-Term Financing Vehicles

The **letter of credit (L/C)** is perhaps the most widely used vehicle for facilitating international trade. If the importer is not well known to the exporter or if currency restrictions exist or are possible in the importer's country, then an exporter selling on credit may wish to have the importer's promise of payment backed up by a bank. On the other hand, the importer may not wish to pay the exporter until the merchandise is received in good condition. Properly structured, an L/C can address both of these concerns.

The letter of credit is a letter addressed to a seller, written and signed by a bank acting on the seller's behalf. In it, the bank promises that it will honor *drafts* (checks) drawn upon it if the seller meets the conditions set forth in the L/C. Through an L/C, the bank substitutes its own commitment to pay for that of its customer (the importer). Therefore, the exporter only needs to check on the reputation of the issuing bank.

Let's see how the L/C might work. Suppose that a small auto producer in the Czech Republic orders a piece of automated equipment from an American tool and die manufacturer. The Czech firm is not particularly well known to the American company. Thus, there are some concerns about payment. The American company can insist on payment in advance, but our Czech automaker is probably not going to be thrilled about paying for a piece of expensive equipment until it been delivered, installed, and found to perform up to specs.

To deal with this mutual dilemma, the Czech auto firm would go to a bank that (presumably) regards it as a good credit risk and is willing to issue an L/C guaranteeing payment for the equipment once it's delivered *and* found to work properly. In this way, the bank substitutes its credit for that of the Czech automaker. Once the equipment is shipped and installed, the American tool and die maker will draw a draft in accordance with the terms of the L/C. The bank will then pay the amount designated, assuming all of the conditions of equipment performance are met. The Ameri-

can tool and die maker gets its money, and the bank will turn to the Czech automaker for payment.

Bankers' acceptances have also played a major role in financing international trade. A banker's acceptance (B/A) is a time draft drawn on a bank that has been accepted by the bank. By "accepting" the draft, the bank makes an unconditional promise to pay the draft's holder a stated amount on a specified day. Thus, like the L/C, the bank effectively substitutes its own credit for that of a borrower and in the process creates a negotiable instrument.

Exhibit 3B-1 shows a typical set of transactions that can lead to the creation of an acceptance as a U.S. importer seeks to finance the purchase of foreign goods until they can be resold. First, an importer requests its bank to issue an L/C on its behalf authorizing the foreign exporter to draw a time draft on the bank for payment for the goods. Based on this authorization, the exporter ships the goods on an order bill of lading made out to itself and presents a time draft along with endorsed shipping documents to its bank. The foreign bank then forwards the draft along with appropriate shipping documents to the importer's bank, which accepts and thus creates the B/A. The exporter discounts the draft with the accepting bank and receives payment for the shipment. The shipping documents are delivered to the importer, who may now claim the shipment. The accepting bank may now buy the acceptance and hold it in its portfolio or sell (rediscount) the B/A in the money market. In Exhibit 3B-1, we've assumed that the bank sells the B/A in the money markets.

The demand for acceptance financing has fallen off over time. One factor in this decline has been the increased availability of funding from nonbanks in the U.S. commercial paper market. Prime commercial paper usually trades at rates near those on acceptance liabilities of prime banks. For firms with access to the commercial paper market, the overall cost, including placement fees, is usually below the all-in cost of acceptance financing.

In recent years, a number of multinational companies have had to engage in **countertrade** in order to do business. While not a financing vehicle in the traditional sense, countertrade covers a wide range of barter-like transactions in which the sale of goods to one country is linked to the purchase or exchange of goods from the same country. These transactions typically take place between a firm in an industrialized country and a firm in a country whose currency cannot be exchanged into a widely accepted one like U.S. dollars, Japanese yen, or the Swiss franc. For example,

EXHIBIT 3B-1
Example of Bankers' Acceptance Financing

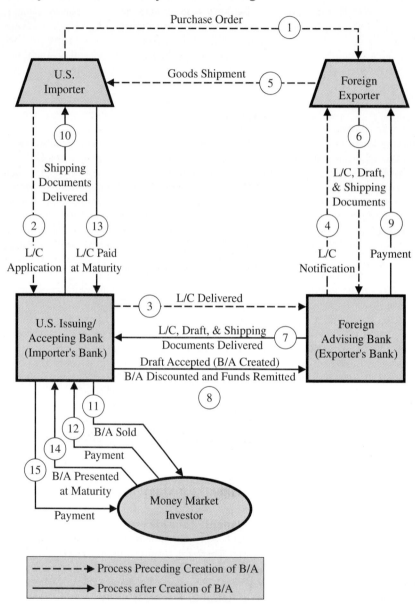

with the Asian crisis and shortage of liquidity throughout the region, countertrade has become a more frequent way of doing business.

Countertrade can take a variety of forms. *Barter,* which is thousands of years old, involves the direct exchange of goods between two parties. A U.S. oil drilling equipment company might exchange drill bits for Russian furs. A variation of bartering is a *counterpurchase,* where one exchange contract is conditional on the fulfillment of another contract. We are also seeing a significant number of *buyback arrangements* in which there is an agreement to build a plant in exchange for buying a specific portion of the plant's output over a period of time.

Countertrade transactions typically take place between a multinational and a less developed country, but that's not always the case. For example, in order to sell its military jets to Japan, McDonnell Douglas had to teach Japanese manufacturers how to produce military aircraft in order to offset the cost to Japan in currency and jobs. Closer to home, the state of Alabama agreed to purchase 1,500 sports-utility vehicles as part of an incentive package to get Mercedes Benz to locate a plant in Huntsville.

APPENDIX 3C   FORECASTING FUNDS NEEDS IN AN INFLATIONARY ENVIRONMENT

It is essential for companies to take inflation into account when forecasting their funds needs. "Constant dollar" forecasts, i.e., projections that ignore inflation, typically *understate* long-term financing requirements. It's virtually impossible for a company to minimize its financing costs over time when it continuously underestimates its needs.

To see how constant dollar forecasts can be misleading, let's look at the case of the Sunshine Solar System Company (SSSC), a firm that manufactures and installs residential solar heating panels. Condensed pro forma income statements and balance sheets for the 2000–2004 planning horizon are presented in Exhibit 3C-1. SSSC prepared the statements using the percent of sales approach and assumed that external financing needs would be met by issuing new debt. By keeping profit margins at 4 percent of sales, SSSC is implicitly assuming that the increased interest expense that comes with new debt will be offset by operating economies elsewhere in the business. The statements

EXHIBIT 3C-1
Sunshine Solar System Company
Condensed Pro Forma Balance Sheet and Income Statements
(in million $ except ratios)

	Actual	Forecast				
	1999	2000	2001	2002	2003	2004
Sales (10% Annual Growth)	$200.0	$220.0	$242.0	$266.2	$292.8	$322.1
Profit after Tax @ 4% Sales	$ 8.0	$ 8.8	$ 9.7	$ 10.6	$ 11.7	$ 12.9
Current Assets @ 60% Sales	$120.0	$132.0	$145.2	$159.7	$175.7	$193.3
Fixed Assets	60.0	65.0	70.0	75.0	80.0	85.0
Total Assets	$180.0	$197.0	$215.2	$234.7	$255.7	$278.3
Current Liabilities @ 20% Sales	$ 40.0	$ 44.0	$ 48.4	$ 53.2	$ 58.6	$ 64.4
Long-Term Debt (Plug)	18.0	22.2	26.3	30.4	34.3	38.2
Equity*	122.0	130.8	140.5	151.1	162.8	175.7
Total Liabilities + Equity	$180.0	$197.0	$215.2	$234.7	$255.7	$278.3
Debt-to-Equity Ratio	0.15	0.17	0.19	0.20	0.21	0.22

*SSSC pays no dividends. Thus, equity in a given year is equal to equity at the beginning of the year plus net income in that year.

in Exhibit 3C-1 reflect a 10 percent annual *unit sales growth* but assume no increases in prices or costs of solar panels. Ignoring the potential for price increases tends to understate sales in nominal terms.

Let's see how this works. Suppose that 1999's $200 million in sales revenues represents the sale and installation of 100,000 solar panel units at $2,000 each. A 10 percent increase in units sold with no increase in prices means that sales in 2000 would be $220 million—110,000 units sold at $2,000 each. However, if SSSC were able to increase prices by 5 percent to offset increases in costs, then sales for 2000 would be $231 million—110,000 units sold at an increased selling price of $2,100 each. Thus, ignoring inflation and the ability to raise prices tends to understate (1) sales, (2) the asset needs to support these sales, and, ultimately, (3) the company's financing requirements. The longer the planning horizon, the more dramatic the differences between forecasts prepared in nominal versus constant dollar terms.

A revised estimate of SSSC's financing needs assuming a series of 5 percent price increases superimposed on a 10 percent annual increase in unit sales over the 2000–2004 planning horizon is presented in Exhibit 3C-2. As we can see, sales and asset needs in Exhibit 3C-2 are far greater than those in Exhibit 3C-1. External financing needs, as reflected by the increases in the debt plug number, are dramatically higher. Further, the sharp increase in the debt-to-equity ratio is an indication of the financial risk of SSSC's strategy of relying exclusively on retained earnings and debt to support what is effectively a 15 percent annual sales growth rate.

Despite the increases in leverage, the financial plan in Exhibit 3C-2 may be entirely feasible. After all, the company doesn't have much debt right now and is expected to be profitable through 2004. With a more realistic picture of its financing needs, the firm's financial manager might be able to line up the required funds well ahead of time. However, if SSSC ignores the impact of price increases and plans around a constant dollar forecast, it may find itself short of borrowing capacity. At this point, the chief financial officer could be placed in the position of recommending: (1) a reevaluation of the firm's growth plans, or (2) a costly common stock issue. Neither of these suggestions is likely to be a career builder.

EXHIBIT 3C-2
Sunshine Solar System Company
Condensed Pro Forma Balance Sheet and Income Statements
5 Percent Inflation Superimposed on 10 Percent Unit Sales Growth
(in million $ except ratios)

	Actual	Forecast				
	1999	2000	2001	2002	2003	2004
Sales	$200.0	$231.0	$266.8	$308.2	$355.9	$411.1
Profit after Tax @ 4% Sales	$ 8.0	$ 9.2	$ 10.7	$ 12.3	$ 14.2	$ 16.4
Current Assets @ 60% Sales	$120.0	$138.6	$160.1	$184.9	$213.5	$246.7
Fixed Assets	60.0	65.0	70.0	75.0	80.0	85.0
Total Assets	$180.0	$203.6	$230.1	$259.9	$293.5	$331.7
Current Liabilities @ 20% Sales	$ 40.0	$ 46.2	$ 53.4	$ 61.6	$ 71.2	$ 82.2
Long-Term Debt (Plug)	18.0	26.2	34.8	44.1	53.9	64.7
Equity	122.0	131.2	141.9	154.2	168.4	184.8
Total Liabilities + Equity	$180.0	$203.6	$230.1	$259.9	$293.5	$331.7
Debt-to-Equity Ratio	0.15	0.20	0.25	0.29	0.32	0.35

QUESTIONS

1. In a brief statement, convince the company president that strategic planning is a necessity in today's business environment. Be sure to explain the main elements of strategic planning.
2. Discuss at least three methods of sales forecasting and the importance of sales forecasting in the firm's financial plan.
3. Explain how each of the following might affect the firm's funding requirements as developed through the percent of sales method of financial forecasting:
   a. A change in the firm's dividend payout ratio.
   b. A change in the firm's profit margin.
   c. Increased competition has necessitated increased advertising.
   d. The firm has decided to relax its collection policies to stimulate sales.
   e. Increased tensions in labor relations have caused fluctuations in the firm's supply of raw materials used in production.
4. Firm A is in a period of projected high growth. Firm B is a more mature, slower-growing firm. Which firm is more likely to require external financing? Explain.
5. Explain what is meant by a firm's "sustainable growth rate." Why are so many firms concerned with this concept?
6. Compare fixed and flexible cash budgeting. When is each appropriate?
7. Explain the intimate relationship of the firm's strategic plan and its cash budget. Why are they connected? Should they be?
8. What method would you use to estimate the amount of permanent short-term assets to be funded with long-term debt?
9. What would you expect to see happen to the pre-interest profit margins of firms in industries that commonly operate with negative working capital?
10. One of the first moves of a company acquired in a leveraged buyout is to dramatically reduce its working capital.
    a. What is the purpose of reducing working capital?
    b. How might an LBO reduce its working capital requirements?
    c. What costs might an LBO that reduces its working capital be subject to?

PROBLEMS

✎—Excel templates may be downloaded from **www.prenhall.com/financecenter.**

1. In attempting to determine its working capital policy, XNL Corp., an electronics manufacturer, has two policies to choose from. Under the first plan, XNL would finance its long-term assets, permanent short-term assets, and one-quarter of its temporary current assets through long-term debt. Under the second plan, XNL would finance only its long-term assets with long-term debt. The current rate on long-term debt is 12 percent and the short-term rate is 7.5 percent. EBIT for XNL is expected to be $550,000 under either plan. Total assets of the firm are $1.5 million, with current assets of $650,000, half of which are considered permanent. ✎
   a. Calculate XNL's net income under each plan, using a tax rate of 35 percent.
   b. What would happen to the figures if short-term rates suddenly rose to 15 percent?
   c. Which plan do you think is better for XNL? Why?
2. Pacific Paper (PP), a paper products company, is considering altering its inventory policy. Specifically, under the new policy, PP would decrease its inventory by half, to $750,000. The company estimates it might lose as much as $450,000 in sales owing to unmet demand, on which it earns a pretax profit margin of 10 percent. However, PP estimates that storage and financing costs currently amount to 12 percent of inventory. PP has a tax rate of 40 percent. Based on these facts, should PP reduce its inventory?
3. A firm with annual sales of $1.3 million and a cost of goods sold of $820,000 has an average collection period of 45 days. The firm pays its accounts payable, on average, in 40 days. It takes about 65

days to transform inventory into finished goods, and another 10 days to sell those finished goods.

   a. What is the length of the firm's operating cycle?

   b. What is the company's average investment in accounts receivable? In inventory?

   c. What fraction of the operating cycle is financed with supplier credits?

   d. What is the average company-financed (i.e., net of supplier credits) investment in working capital?

4. Current sales for IGG Telecommunications are $375 million and sales for next year are forecast to be $425 million. The following is IGG's current balance sheet: ✍

Balance Sheet (in million $)	
Cash	11.25
Accounts receivable	71.25
Inventory	61.875
Plant and equipment	140.625
Accounts payable	56.25
Accruals	37.50
Bank loan	85.50
Long-term debt	25.00
Common stock	35.00
Retained earnings	45.75

   a. Using the percent of sales method, calculate IGG's total and external financing requirement for next year. Retained earnings are expected to increase by $12.5 million. The bank loan and the other long-term financing accounts are assumed to remain at their current levels.

   b. Suppose that plant and equipment are expected to be unchanged next year. How will this affect your estimate of next year's financing requirement in (a)?

5. Sun Corp., a manufacturer of solar generators, forecasts a 15 percent growth in sales for next year. The company has calculated that its current total of $750,000 in assets will increase in line with sales; current liabilities equal $285,000, all of which vary directly with sales. Sun's net income is forecast to be $100,000, and its dividend payout will remain at 50 percent. ✍

   a. Calculate the dollar amount of Sun Corp.'s expected total and external financing needs.

   b. Calculate the company's external financing requirement if sales increase by 25 percent and the profit margin is expected to remain the same as before.

   c. If sales increase by 20 percent but Sun decreases its dividend payout to 25 percent, what will be the company's external financing requirement?

6. Mason Lumber projects next year's sales to be $6 million and expects a net profit margin of 8 percent. Equity is presently $1.2 million, there is no debt, and Mason pays out half its after-tax earnings in dividends. Mason also projects that current assets will equal 20 percent of sales, current liabilities will equal 10 percent of sales, and fixed assets will remain at their current level of $1.5 million.

   a. How much money will Mason have to borrow to achieve its projected sales goal?

   b. What are Mason's total borrowing requirements for the coming year if it can increase its total asset turnover to 3.0 times?

7. Sandia Manufacturing projects next year's sales will increase to $40 million from sales this year of $30 million. Current assets are $10 million, fixed assets are $10 million, and the net profit margin is 5 percent after taxes. At present, Sandia has $3 million in accounts payable, $4 million in long-term debt, and equity of $13 million. Sandia forecasts that current assets and accounts payable will rise in direct proportion to the increase in sales but that fixed assets will increase by only $200,000. Sandia plans to pay dividends of $1 million next year.

   a. Based on Sandia's projections and dividend payment plans, how much additional money must it borrow to meet its financial projections?

   b. Based on the projections given (with respect to dividends and the proportional increases in current assets and accounts payable) and assuming the $200,000 expansion in fixed assets will occur, what is the largest increase in sales Sandia can support without having to resort to additional borrowing?

   c. What are Sandia's total asset requirements for the coming year if it can increase its total asset turnover to 2.5 times?

8. Autrex Electronics projects next year sales will increase to $18 million from sales this year of $13.5 million. Current assets are $4.5 million, fixed assets are $4.5 million, and the net profit margin is 5% after taxes. At present, Autrex has $1.35 mil-

lion in accounts payable, $1.8 million in long-term debt, and equity of $5.5 million. Autrex forecasts that current assets and accounts payable will rise in direct proportion to the increase in sales, but fixed assets will increase by only $200,000. Autrex plans to pay dividends of $500,000 next year.

a. What are Autrex's total financing needs (i.e., total assets) for the coming year?
b. Based on Autrex's projections and dividend payment plans, how much additional money must it borrow to meet its financial projections?
c. Based on the projections given (with respect to dividends and the proportional increases in current assets and accounts payable) and assuming the $200,000 expansion in fixed assets will occur, what is the largest increase in sales Autrex can support without having to resort to additional borrowing?

9. Earth Dish (ED), a manufacturer of stoneware dinnerware and glasses, has forecast sales for the next six months (July through December). Credit sales account for 75 percent of Earth Dish's sales; the remaining 25 percent of sales are cash. ED has found that 60 percent of its credit sales will be collected in the next month after purchase, 25 percent within two months, and 12.5 percent within three months (2.5 percent of credit sales are never collected). Calculate ED's expected collections for the last six months of the year (include collections from sales made in previous months as well).

Month	Mar.	Apr.	May	June	July	Aug.	Sept.	Oct.	Nov.	Dec.
Sales (in hundred $)	10	12.5	11	11	12	13.5	14.75	15	16.5	20

10. The Day Company, a regional retailer, has developed the following four-month sales forecast:

Month	Oct.	Nov.	Dec.	Jan.
Sales (in hundred $)	400	650	1,250	525

Credit sales account for 75 percent of Day's sales; of these credit sales, 25 percent are collected within one month and 70 percent within two months (5 percent of credit sales are generally bad debts). Purchases are 40 percent of next month's forecast sales but are paid for one month after purchase. Labor and other overhead expenses are budgeted at $250,000, except for December when an additional $200,000 will be paid to Christmas help. Day must make a $125,000 interest payment in October and a $50,000 dividend payment in December. Day forecasts no other expenses. Day expects to begin in October with $40,000 in cash on hand but would like to keep a cash balance on hand equal to one-quarter of the current month's sales. Sales for August were $250,000 and $350,000 for September. Calculate Day's cash budget, including any financing required.

11. Ambex must revise its assumptions concerning its credit collections. The company has found that it collects 80 percent of its sales in the current quarter, and 15 percent in the next (with 5 percent uncollectible). What are Ambex's new forecast financing requirements?

12. Ambiance, a paint and furniture supplier, has forecast its sales for the next four quarters:

Quarter	1	2	3	4
Sales	$100,000	$125,000	$135,000	$165,000

Sales for the current quarter are $160,000. Credit sales are collected in the same quarter as the sale is made. The payments for half of the purchases made, however, lag a quarter. Purchases are 25 percent of sales. Labor is assumed to be $50,000 per quarter regardless of sales. Capital expenditures are expected to be as follows:

Quarter	1	2	3	4
Budgeted	$30,000	$45,000	$20,000	$25,000

Interest and dividends are expected to average $25,000 per quarter.

a. Calculate the company's cash budget and financing needs. Ignore taxes.
b. In deciding on financing, Ambiance has several sources from which to choose. The company has a $12,500 line of credit against which to borrow and can also sell up to $25,000 of commercial paper (CP). Include these two sources of funds in the cash budget. How much outside financing does Ambiance need now?

c. Ambiance must pay 10 percent interest on the funds borrowed through the line of credit and sale of CP. Include interest payments in the quarterly estimate of cash flow when the borrowing occurs. How much does Ambiance need now?

13. Ergo Corporation has a profit margin of 10 percent, dividend payout of 50 percent, debt-equity ratio of 2:1, and a total asset turnover of 0.75.
   a. What is its current sustainable growth rate?
   b. Ergo would like to double the growth rate in (a). By how much would the dividend have to be adjusted to accomplish this? By how much would the profit margin have to change?

14. Here are 1998 financial data for Coca-Cola. All figures are in millions. What was Coca-Cola's sustainable growth rate in 1998? ✖

Income	$1,045
Net sales	8,500
Total assets	7,038
Dividends	438
Equity	3,350
Liabilities	3,688

15. Express, Inc. has no definite working capital management policy. Two of the firm's whiz kids have offered the following two policies for consideration:
   a. Current assets held at 50 percent of sales. Any debt financing must be 50 percent long term.
   b. Current assets held at 65 percent of sales. Any debt financing must be at a ratio of 70 percent long term and 30 percent short term.

Under both policies, fixed assets are projected to remain at 60 percent of sales. Although policy 1 requires fewer assets than policy 2, expected profit margins are also lower because of higher operating costs.

Forecast sales for next year	$25 million
Average operating profit margin (EBIT/Sales)	18% (policy 1)
	22% (policy 2)
Current (target) debt-equity ratio	1.0
Cost of short-term borrowing	9%
Cost of long-term borrowing (issuing bonds)	12%

If the corporate tax rate is 40 percent, what are the respective returns on equity for the firm under the two plans?

REFERENCES

Higgins, R. C. "How Much Growth Can a Firm Afford?" *Financial Management,* Fall 1977: 7–16.

Higgins, R. C. "Sustainable Growth Under Inflation." *Financial Management,* Autumn 1981: 36–40.

Van Horne, J. C. "Sustainable Growth Modeling." *Journal of Corporate Finance,* Winter 1988: 19–25.

Foundations of Valuation: Time Value of Money

When one has had to work so hard to get money, why should he impose on himself the further hardship of trying to save it?
Don Herold

If you would know the value of money, go and try to borrow some.
Benjamin Franklin

KEY TERMS

annual percentage rate (APR)
annuity
annuity due
compound interest
discount rate
effective interest rate
Fisher effect
future value (FV)

future value interest factor
future value of an annuity
net present value (NPV)
nominal interest rate
opportunity cost of capital
ordinary annuity
perpetuity
present value (PV)

present value interest factor
present value of an annuity
real interest rate
simple interest
term structure of interest rates
zero-coupon bond

CHAPTER LEARNING OBJECTIVES

Upon completion of this chapter, students should be able to:

- Explain why money has time value and the importance of the interest rate in the valuation process.
- Use the concepts of compound interest to determine the future value of both individual amounts as well as streams of payments.

- Use discounting to determine the present value of both individual amounts as well as streams of payments.
- Describe how the concept of present value can be used to value assets ranging from plant and equipment to marketable securities.

- Understand the difference between the stated and annual percentage rate (APR) and how this difference influences the present and future values of a stream of payments.

- Understand the concept of an investment's net present value (NPV) and how it relates to the building of shareholder value.

Almost all financial decisions involve exchanges of money over time. Because money is valued not for its own sake but rather for what it will buy—its *purchasing power*—the exchange of current for future dollars is really an exchange of consumption today for consumption in the future. The rate of exchange depends on the *time value of money*.

This concept—that the value of money varies according to when it is to be received and when it is to be paid out—is probably the single most important idea in all of finance. Yet it rests on the simple notion that a dollar today is worth more than a dollar tomorrow. How much more is determined by the time preference of individuals, their investment opportunities, and the amount of expected inflation. The more that individuals prefer current over future consumption and the more lucrative the available investments are, the more valuable will be current dollars relative to future dollars. In addition, because inflation erodes the purchasing power of money, the higher the expected rate of inflation is, the less valuable future dollars will be relative to current dollars.

> The time value of money is based on the idea that a dollar received today is worth more than a dollar received tomorrow.

Understanding the time value of money is essential to shareholder wealth maximization because a host of key corporate activities—valuing securities and other assets, pricing potential acquisitions, and making credit extension decisions—involve an exchange between current dollars and future dollars. To know whether it is worthwhile to engage in these activities, you must be able to compare dollars today with dollars in the future.

In this chapter, we'll examine the basic techniques for comparing cash flows over time by first looking at the principles of future value (i.e., compound interest). We can then take up the *discounting* of future cash flows to determine their present value. Our ability to determine how much future receipts are worth today is fundamental to valuing assets ranging from marketable securities to potential acquisition candidates. We then show how to value an annuity, a stream of equal cash payments received at regular intervals, and follow this with a discussion of valuing a stream of uneven cash flows. The chapter ends with a consideration of the major determinants of the opportunity cost of money.

4.1   FUTURE VALUE

Principles of Compound Interest

Suppose that you have $1,000 to invest and decide to put this money into a bank account paying 6 percent interest a year. You will want to know how much money you'll have at the end of five years. For simplicity, let's assume that the bank pays interest once a year based on the amount on deposit at the beginning of the year.

EXHIBIT 4-1
Account Balances for $1,000 Investment
Five Years at 6 Percent Interest

Year	Beginning-of-Year Balance	Interest Earned during Year	End-of-Year Balance
1	$1,000.00	$60.00	$1,060.00
2	1,060.00	63.60	1,123.60
3	1,123.60	67.42	1,191.02
4	1,191.02	71.46	1,262.48
5	1,262.48	75.75	1,338.23

Exibit 4-1 illustrates how we might go about finding out how much would be in the account after five years.

> Compound interest involves the ability to earn interest on interest.

In Exhibit 4-1, we've assumed that the bank compounds interest. The idea behind **compound interest** is that interest earned is added to the end-of-year balance and then becomes the basis for calculating interest in the next period. As a result, interest is paid on interest, thereby increasing the amount on hand at the end of five years. **Simple interest,** on the other hand, implies that you would receive interest only on the $1,000 originally invested, or $60.00 a year. With simple interest, you would only have $1,300 at the end of five years—your original investment of $1,000 plus five annual interest payments of $60.00 each.

> Simple interest is paid only on the amount originally invested.

In general, the **future value (FV)** of a principal amount, also known as the *present value (PV)*, can be calculated using the following equation:

$$FV = PV[(1 + k)^n] \qquad [4\text{-}1]$$

where k is the periodic interest rate, and n is the number of periods over which interest is compounded. Rather than running calculations in table form, we can get the same answer using Equation [4-1] for the future value in the bank account by setting $PV = \$1,000$, $k = 6$ percent, and $n = 5$ as follows:

$$FV = \$1,000(1.06)^5 = \$1,000(1.3382) = \$1,338.20$$

This is almost identical to the answer we got in Exhibit 4-1.

The term $[(1 + k)^n]$ is often referred to as the **future value interest factor (FVIF).**[1] Equation [4-1] can therefore be written as

$$FV = PV(FVIF_{k,n}) \qquad [4\text{-}1a]$$

---

[1]Tables such as Appendix B have been constructed as an alternative to Equation [4-1]. This table provides the $FVIF_{k,n}$ for different interest rates (k) and time periods (n). For our example, the $FVIF$ for 6 percent over five years is 1.3382. Assuming an initial investment of $1,000, the future value using Equation [4-1a] is the same as we got earlier:

$$FV = \$1,000(1.3382) = \$1,338.20$$

The future value
interest factor is
the amount to
which $1 will
grow during a
specified period
when invested at
a particular com-
pound interest
rate.

The difference in the account balances between simple and compound interest in our example is only $38.20 over five years—not enough to get very excited about. However, the power of compounding can best be appreciated over a long time horizon. Assume, for example, that you want your great-grandchild to inherit at least $1 million. This is really long-term planning because your oldest son is only ten years old. Suppose also that you've got $1,000 to invest right now. A banker friend of yours tells you that it's possible to place money in a trust account from which the accumulated value could be paid to your oldest surviving heir in 100 years. The quoted rate on the trust account is 8 percent.

Your goal of accumulating $1 million would depend greatly on whether the bank intended to compound interest. If you earn simple interest, the account would only grow by $80 a year since you'd receive just the 8 percent interest on the original $1,000 invested. Therefore, with simple interest, the account would only have $9,000 at the end of 100 years—your original investment of $1,000 plus 100 payments of $80 each. In contrast, if interest was compounded annually, the ending account balance using Equation [4-1] would be

$$FV_{100} = \$1,000\,[(1.08)^{100}] = \$2,199,761.26$$

The difference between an ending account balance of $9,000 on a simple interest basis and $2 million-plus with compounding is dramatic. While you probably won't be around to enjoy the difference, your great-grandchild should have a big smile on his/her face.

Illustration

An even more dramatic example of the value of compound interest involves the purchase of Manhattan Island in 1626. In what's often considered one of the great bargains in history, Peter Minuit bought Manhattan Island from the Indians for $24 in trinkets. Suppose that the Indians had taken cash instead and invested the $24 at an annual rate of 6 percent. At the end of 1998, 372 years later, the initial $24 would have grown to

$$FV_{372} = \$24(1.06)^{372} = \$62.229 \text{ billion}$$

This represents a price of about $64.20 per square foot for all of Manhattan.

The higher the in-
terest rate and the
longer the time
period, the higher
the future value.

The higher the interest rate and the greater the number of compounding periods, the larger will be the future value of a given investment. Moreover, the future value of an initial amount grows more rapidly over time because, with compounding, the principal amount on which interest must be paid becomes

EXHIBIT 4-2
Future Value of $1

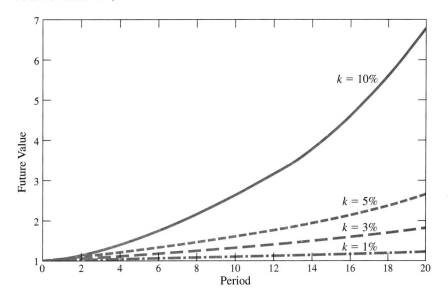

progressively larger over time. These points are illustrated in Exhibit 4-2, which plots the future value of $1 over time, compounded at different interest rates.

Equation [4-1] or [4-1a] is typically used to compute how much we would have at the end of some time horizon after investing a specific amount of money at some interest rate. However, the equation contains four variables—*FV, PV, k,* and *n*. Knowing any three of these four variables can allow us to calculate the missing piece.

Frequency of Compounding

For our little investment problem in Exhibit 4-1, we assumed that the bank paid interest once a year. This was unrealistic because most financial instruments pay interest more than once a year. We must adjust our future value formula to permit compounding more often than once a year. The future value in *n* years, when interest is paid *m* times a year is

$$F_{n,m} = PV(1 + k/m)^{n \times m} \qquad [4-2]$$

More frequent compounding leads to higher future values.

In our example of money invested at 6 percent, if compounding occurred semiannually rather than annually, the future value of $1,000 in five years would be

$$F_{5,2} = \$1,000[1 + (0.06/2)]^{5 \times 2} = \$1,000[1.3439] = \$1,343.90$$

This compares with \$1,338.20 in the case of annual compounding. With quarterly compounding, we would get \$1,000(1.015)^{20}, or \$1,346.86. In general, *more frequent compounding of interest leads to higher future values of present amounts.*

The Annual Percentage Rate

Because of different compounding intervals, it is often difficult to compare financial securities. For example, is it better to receive 9 percent compounded annually on a Eurobond,[2] or 8.8 percent on an equivalent-risk U.S. corporate bond that pays interest semiannually? To deal with this confusing situation, a convention puts all interest quotes on a comparable basis by distinguishing between the *stated* or *quoted rate* and the **annual percentage rate (APR)**. The *APR*, also known as the **effective interest rate**, is the rate that would produce the same return under annual compounding using the quoted rate.

In general, we can convert a stated rate *k*, compounded *m* times a year into an *APR* using the following formula:

$$APR = FVIF_{k/m,m} = [1 + (k/m)]^m - 1 \qquad [4\text{-}3]$$

We can now use Equation [4-3] to answer the question of which investment is best: the Eurobond paying interest at 9 percent annually or a risk-equivalent U.S. corporate bond with a quoted rate of 8.8 percent. Because the Eurobond pays interest annually, its *APR* is its stated rate of 9 percent. The *APR* for the 8.8 percent corporate bond paying interest semiannually is

> Where opportunities for compounding exist, the annual percentage rate (APR) is higher than the quoted interest rate.

$$APR = FVIF_{8.8/2,2} = (1.044)^2 - 1 = 8.99 \text{ percent}$$

Because the returns for the Eurobond and the U.S. corporate bond are virtually identical, an investor would probably be indifferent about choosing between the two instruments. These results are what we'd expect in global financial markets in which two risk-equivalent instruments denominated in the same currency should provide the same effective rate of return.

Financial Calculator Solutions

Financial calculators and spreadsheets have made formulas obsolete for virtually all time value of money computations. Appendix A reviews how to find the time value of money using one of the more popular brands of calculators. Regardless of the calculator used, all build on the following most frequently used keystrokes:

N or n = the number of periods interest is compounded
I or I/Y = the periodic interest rate

---

[2]A Eurobond is a dollar-denominated instrument sold outside the United States. We'll say more about Eurobonds in Chapter 5.

FV = the future value of a current or present amount
PV = the current or present value of a future amount
PMT = the periodic payment or receipt. Used when dealing with a stream of payments, which are the same in each period.
CPT = the "compute" button. Some calculators require that you hit this key prior to running a calculation.

The calculator solution for the problem in which we put $1,000 in an account earning 6 percent for five years is[3]

Inputs	5	6	1,000		
	N	I	PV	PMT	FV
Answer:					1,338.23

In addition to using the time value of money formulas, financial calculator solutions will be provided for most of the problems from this point forward.

4.2 PRESENT VALUE

The process of converting future dollars into present dollars is known as discounting.

Most financial decisions require a tradeoff between money today and money in the future. To properly evaluate these tradeoffs, we need to determine the value today or the **present value** of future cash flows. We want to know how much a dollar in the future is worth in terms of today's dollar. This requires that we find the amount of money that would leave us indifferent as to whether we receive that amount today or one dollar in the future. The process of converting future dollars into present dollars is known as *discounting*. The interest rate used to calculate the present value is known as the **discount rate.**

Some Basics

Suppose that you can purchase a piece of land today for $10,000 and believe you can sell it in eight years for $20,000. Sounds good on the surface. However, by giving up $10,000 today, you forego the opportunity to put this money into an investment of equivalent risk paying 10 percent compounded annually.

[3]The resulting future value may carry a negative sign because some calculators require that you identify the amounts as either inflows or outflows. In the case of our savings example, the $1,000 placed on deposit would be a cash outflow at the point of deposit and an inflow five years from now. If you don't like seeing negative answers, you should enter the deposit *PV* as −$1,000.

Therefore, you can't simply look at this "land deal" in isolation; it has to be evaluated in relation to your alternative investment opportunities.

One way to approach this investment problem is to determine how much you would have at the end of eight years if you put $10,000 into the alternative investment earning 10 percent interest. Using Equation [4-1],[4] the future value of your investment would be

$$FV = \$10,000[(1.10)^8] = \$21,435.89$$

We can arrive at the same answer with a financial calculator:

Inputs	8	10	10,000		
	N	I	PV	PMT	FV
Answer:					21,435.89

Regardless of how we do the computations, the real estate venture doesn't seem to be a particularly good choice in light of your alternative investment opportunities.

Another way to evaluate this land deal is to determine the present value of the $20,000 you expect to receive at the end of eight years. We can get at the present value of a future amount by rearranging Equation [4-1] as follows:

$$PV = FV\left[\frac{1}{(1+k)^n}\right] \qquad [4\text{-}4]$$

Substituting $FV = \$20,000$, $k = 10$ percent, and $n = 8$ years into Equation [4-4], we get

$$PV = FV\left[\frac{1}{(1+k)^n}\right] = \$20,000[1/(1.10)^8] = \$9,330.15$$

Using a calculator with the following keystrokes gets us to the same place:

Inputs	8	10	20,000		
	N	I	FV	PMT	PV
Answer:					9,330.15

---

[4]We could also use Appendix B to solve the problem as follows:

$$FV = PV(FVIF_{k,n}) = \$10,000(FVIF_{10,8})$$
$$= \$10,000(2.1436) = \$21,436$$

The present value is the amount today that is equivalent to a cash payment to be received in the future.

This $9,330.15 present value is the *maximum* amount that we should be willing to give up today in exchange for $20,000 received at the end of eight years. Why? Because if we put $9,330.15 into an account earning 10 percent, we should end up with (you guessed it!) $20,000 at the end of eight years. Any investment that asks us to give up more than $9,330 for a promised receipt of $20,000 after eight years is a "bad deal." Therefore, the real estate venture, with its purchase price of $10,000 should be passed up.

The present value interest factor is the present value of a dollar to be received at a specified point in the future given a particular discount rate.

The term $[1/(1 + k)^n]$ is known as the **present value interest factor** $(PVIF_{k,n})$, and k is referred to as the **discount rate.**[5] Equation [4-4] can be written more compactly as

$$PV = FV(PVIF_{k,n}) \qquad\qquad [4\text{-}4a]$$

The opportunity cost of money represents what we can earn on equivalent investments.

Looking at present values as *the maximum amount that we should be willing to pay for future cash flows* gives us a powerful tool for valuing *any asset.* Unlike the accountants who value assets based on their historical cost, a financial perspective suggests that asset values should be determined by the magnitude and timing of future cash flows, discounted to their present value at some opportunity cost of money. We'll apply this concept throughout the text to value assets ranging from stocks and bonds to new product introductions and acquisitions. The discount rate, often referred to as the **opportunity cost of capital,** is central to the valuation process and should reflect what we can earn on equivalent risk investments over time.

To illustrate how these ideas can be used to value assets, let's consider the case of the zero-coupon bond. As the name suggests, a **zero-coupon bond** pays no periodic interest. Instead, it pays a fixed amount—known as the *maturity* or *face value*—at some point in the future. An investor's return comes from the difference between the amount paid and the bond's face value. The U.S. Treasury is by far the largest issuer of zero-coupon bonds.

Suppose that a zero-coupon bond will mature in 20 years at a face value of $10,000. What should an investor be willing to pay for this bond? Because an asset's value is tied exclusively to its ability to generate future cash flows, the value of the "zero" is the present value of the $10,000 received in 20 years discounted at a rate that reflects the investor's opportunity cost of money. As we indicated in the introduction to this chapter, the opportunity cost of capital represents what we could earn on alternate investments of equivalent risk. If the investor's opportunity cost of money is 8 percent, the value of the bond, from Equation [4-4a], would be

$$PV = FV(PVIF_{8,20}) = \$10,000(0.2145) = \$2,145.00$$

---

[5]Like its first cousin the $(FVIF_{k,n})$, the $(PVIF_{k,n})$ is available in tables such as Appendix C for different combinations of k and n. The $(PVIF_{k,n})$ for $k = 10$ and $n = 8$ is 0.4665. Substituting this into Equation [4-4a], the present value of the $20,000 expected selling price would be

$$PV = \$20,000(0.4665) = \$9,330$$

The calculator solution for valuing the "zero" is as follows:

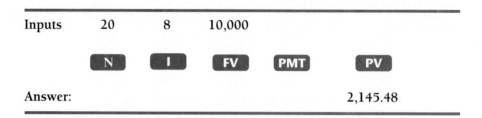

Inputs	20	8	10,000		
	N	I	FV	PMT	PV

Answer: 2,145.48

The higher the discount rate and the longer the time period, the lower the present value of a future amount.

As the discount rate increases, the opportunity cost of receiving future dollars goes up and the present value goes down. Similarly, the farther into the future that money is received, the less valuable it is today. These aspects are illustrated in Exhibit 4-3. For relatively high discount rates or for money received far into the future, the present value is likely to be minimal. For instance, $1 due in 10 years will be worth $0.74 if discounted at 3 percent, but its present value will drop to less than $0.25 if the discount rate is 15 percent. Similarly, $1 to be received in five years discounted at 4 percent is worth $0.82 today, but the same dollar due in 50 years is only worth $0.14 today. When discounted at 15 percent, a dollar to be received in 50 years is essentially worthless today.

EXHIBIT 4-3
Present Value of $1

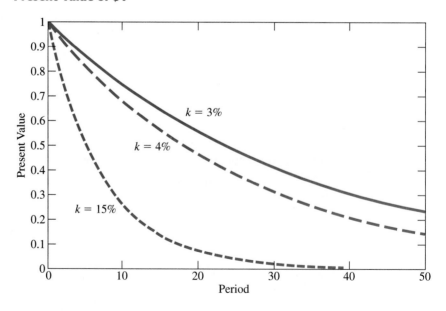

The Discounting Period

The present value formula must be modified when interest can be earned more often than once a year. This can be done along the same lines as with the calculation of future values, with Equation [4-4] becoming

$$PV = FV\left[\frac{1}{(1 + k/m)^{n \times m}}\right] \qquad [4\text{-}5]$$

More frequent compounding leads to lower present values of future amounts.

To illustrate the impact of the discounting interval on present values, let's go back to the zero-coupon bond that we valued in the last section. With an 8 percent rate, discounted annually, the present value of a zero maturing in 20 years at a face amount of $10,000 was $2,145.00. If interest could be earned semiannually, the periodic discount rate would be 4 percent for 40 periods. Under these conditions, the value of the zero would be

$$PV = \$10,000\left[\frac{1}{(1 + .08/2)^{20 \times 2}}\right] = \$10,000\left[\frac{1}{(1 + .04)^{40}}\right] = \$2,083.00$$

Using a financial calculator, the value of the zero would be

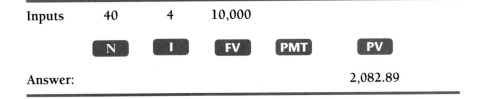

Inputs	40	4	10,000		
	N	I	FV	PMT	PV
Answer:					2,082.89

The fact that the zero's value with semiannual discounting is lower than with annual discounting shouldn't surprise us. Present values and future values are inversely related. If *more frequent compounding* leads to *higher future values of present amounts,* it should also result *in lower present values of future amounts.*

4.3 VALUING PERPETUITIES AND ANNUITIES

So far, we have examined the present and future values of individual cash flows. Most financial problems, however, involve calculations of multiple cash flows at different points in time. Although these calculations tend to be more time-consuming, there are shortcuts for two classes of cash flow problems: perpetuities and annuities.

An annuity is a series of equal cash flows. Annuities that go on forever are perpetuities.

Perpetuities

An **annuity** is a series of equal cash flows per period for a specific number of periods. Most annuities have payments over some finite time period. For instance, life insurance companies sell annuities for retirement purposes that promise to pay a set amount for 10-, 15-, or 20-year periods. However, some annuities go on forever, generating an infinite series of equal payments. Such annuities are referred to as **perpetuities.** The present value of a constant perpetuity of CF dollars per period is given by

$$PV \text{ (Constant Perpetuity)} = \frac{CF}{k} \qquad\qquad [4\text{-}6]$$

where k is the opportunity cost of money as a decimal.

We see constant perpetuities most often in financial instruments. For instance, during the Napoleonic Wars, the Bank of England sold a large bond issue with no maturity date and used the proceeds to repay a number of smaller issues that had financed past wars. Because the bonds were used to consolidate past debts, they were called *consols.* These bonds are still traded today.

Suppose a consol pays £50 per year and the investor's required yield (i.e., the opportunity cost of money) is 10 percent. Using Equation [4-6], we can calculate its price as

$$\text{Price} = \frac{£50}{0.10} = £500$$

Alternately if we were quoted a price of £500 for a consol paying £50 annually, we could easily solve for the required yield of 10 percent. In general, a perpetuity valued at PVA^* paying CF dollars, yen, pounds sterling, etc., annually has a yield (k^*) of

$$k^* = \frac{CF}{PVA^*} \qquad\qquad [4\text{-}7]$$

Preferred stock dividends are constant annuities.

The dividends on preferred stock are another example of a constant perpetuity. For most issues, the dividends remain the same from one year to the next. Therefore, valuing preferred stock boils down to valuing an infinite stream of constant cash flows. As an example, if an investor had a 10 percent required yield, a preferred stock issue that paid an annual dividend of $6 a share would be worth $6/0.10 = $60 a share. We'll say more about preferred stock valuation in Chapter 5.

Firms with constant dividend growth can be valued as growing perpetuities.

Frequently, we run into perpetuities that grow over time. The cash flows from profitable long-lived consumer products or the dividend streams from companies that have a history of continuously increasing dividends are examples of growing perpetuities. Algebraically, we can represent a growing perpetuity as

$$P \text{ (Growing Perpetuity)} = \frac{CF}{(1+k)} + \frac{CF(1+g)}{(1+k)^2} + \frac{CF(1+g)^2}{(1+k)^3} + \cdots [4\text{-}8]$$

where g is the growth rate per period. Equation [4-8] is a geometric progression in which each term differs from the next by a factor of $[(1+g)/(1+k)]$.

Fortunately, as long as $g < k$, this progression simplifies to

$$P \text{ (Growing Perpetuity)} = \frac{CF}{k - g} \qquad \text{[4-8a]}$$

Equation [4-8a] is a convenient way to value just about any cash flow stream that is expected to grow at (approximately) some constant rate over time. For instance, let's assume that the average customer of Tinker Bell—a regional telephone company—is expected to spend $480 on phone service next year. With deregulation, Tinker Bell can now get into long-distance service, cable television, or just about any other service that can be delivered through a telephone line. Suppose that the company believes that it can increase revenues by an average of 8 percent a year indefinitely by aggressively marketing new services to its existing customers. If 12 percent is the appropriate discount rate, then the value of the revenue stream, per subscriber, would be

$$\text{Value (per Subscriber)} = \frac{CF}{k - g} = \frac{\$480}{(.12 - .08)} = \$12{,}000$$

If Tinker Bell had 5 million subscribers, a relatively small number even for a regional phone company, the value of the revenue stream would be $60 billion! Moreover, with a revenue stream valued at $12,000, each subscriber would be worth his or her weight in gold. Perhaps you can now understand why you get so many annoying calls from phone companies to either sell you new services or ask you to switch carriers.

Equation [4-8a] can also be used to value a *declining* cash flow stream by assigning a *negative value* to g. Suppose that you are considering the purchase of a business that is expected to generate a cash flow of $100,000 next year. However, because the business is in a mature, labor-intensive industry that is likely to face increased foreign competition, you believe that the cash flows from this business will decline by 8 percent a year. If your opportunity cost of money is 12 percent, the maximum amount you should be willing to pay is

$$P = \frac{\$100{,}000}{[.12 - (-.08)]} = \frac{\$100{,}000}{.20} = \$500{,}000$$

For Equation [4-8a] to make economic sense, the growth rate g must be lower than the opportunity cost of money (k). As the growth rate approaches the interest rate, the denominator gets very small, making the present value of this growing perpetuity very large. A g greater than or equal to k produces nonsensical answers because the formula doesn't apply. In practice, Equation [4-8a] should not lead to "off-the-wall" valuations as long as we keep in mind that g represents a *long-term* growth rate that is sustainable into the indefinite future.

Present Value of Annuities

There are two basic types of annuities. If the payments occur at the beginning of each period, for example, lease payments, we have an **annuity due.** Far more common in finance is the **ordinary** (or *deferred*) **annuity,** which involves payments made at the end of each period. All annuities referred to in this text will be ordinary annuities. That is, cash flows are assumed to occur at the end of each period, with today being time zero. Examples of ordinary annuities include the periodic interest paid on bonds and mortgage payments.

> The present value of an annuity is the sum of the present values for each cash flow.

Since present values are additive, the **present value of an annuity** is just the sum of the present values of each individual cash flow. The present value of an annuity (PVA_n) lasting n years is given by

$$PVA_n = \begin{array}{c}\text{Present Value}\\\text{of Payment}\\\text{in Period 1}\end{array} + \begin{array}{c}\text{Present Value}\\\text{of Payment}\\\text{in Period 2}\end{array} + \cdots + \begin{array}{c}\text{Present Value}\\\text{of Payment}\\\text{in Period } n\end{array} \qquad [4\text{-}9]$$

$$= PMT(PVIF_{k,1}) + PMT(PVIF_{k,2}) + \cdots + PMT(PVIF_{k,n})$$

where PMT is the periodic payment. Equation [4-9] can be written as

$$PVA_n = PMT[(PVIF_{k,1}) + (PVIF_{k,2}) + \cdots + (PVIF_{k,n})]$$

or

$$PVA_n = PMT[(PVIFA_{k,n})] \qquad [4\text{-}9a]$$

> The present value interest factor for an annuity is the present value of a dollar received each year for a given number of years discounted at a specific rate.

where $PVIFA_{k,n}$ is the *present value interest factor* of an annuity. As the name suggests, the $PVIFA_{k,n}$ is simply the present value of a dollar received (or paid) each period, for n periods, discounted at k percent. The $PVIFA_{k,n}$ can be calculated using the following formula:

$$PVIFA_{k,n} = \frac{(1+k)^n - 1}{k(1+k)^n} \qquad [4\text{-}10]$$

Equation [4-10] is used in most financial calculations as a basis for computing the present value of an annuity.[6]

Let's look at annuity valuation in an investment setting. Suppose your company is negotiating with a supplier to purchase a piece of equipment that's expected to reduce production costs. A manufacturing engineer working with your financial staff estimates that after-tax cash flows associated with these savings will be $50,000 a year over the equipment's six-year economic life. For simplicity, we'll assume that the equipment will be worthless at the end of six years and will

---

[6]In the absence of a financial calculator, tables like those in Appendix D are available for determining the $PVIFA_{k,n}$ for different combinations of interest rates and time periods.

have no salvage value. As a starting point for negotiations, you want to determine how much this piece of equipment is worth based on your company's 10 percent opportunity cost of money.

As suggested earlier, the maximum price we should be willing to pay for this cost-saving equipment should be the present value of $50,000 a year for six years discounted at 10 percent. Based on Equation [4-9], the $PVIFA_{10,6}$ would be[7]

$$PVIFA_{k,n} = \frac{(1.10)^6 - 1}{0.10(1.10)^6} = \frac{0.771561}{0.177156} = 4.35526$$

Substituting this value into Equation [4-9a] we get

$$\$50,000\,[4.35526] = \$217,763$$

We get essentially the same answer using a financial calculator:

Inputs	6	10		50,000	
	N	I	FV	PMT	PV
Answer:					217,763.03

If the equipment supplier is willing to sell this equipment at an installed cost of *no more* than $217,763, we could probably cut a deal. Actually, we should really insist on a lower price; after all, exchanging $217,763 today for an annuity of $50,000 for six years that's only worth $217,763 is just trading dollars. Stockholders don't pay managers big bucks just to trade dollars.

Illustration

On a lighter side, most of us recognize that the odds of winning a lottery are remote. However, on July 30, 1998, 13 Ohio machine shop workers found out that they held the single winning Powerball lottery ticket worth a record $295.7 million. The workers had the choice of receiving a $161.5 million lump-sum payment at once or receiving $11.83 million a year ($295.7/25) for 25 years, with the first payment to be received immediately.

The choice between the lump-sum amount and a stream of payments over time would depend heavily on the discount rate used to value the annuity. As the calculator solution below indicates, the present value of $11.83

---

[7]The $PVIFA_{k,n}$ using Appendix E is 4.3553. The difference between this number and the calculated value is due to rounding.

million a year beginning next year, lasting for 24 years, would be $163.21 million if discounted at 5 percent.

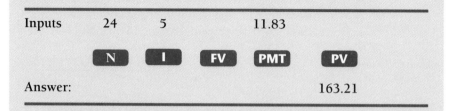

Inputs	24	5		11.83	
	N	I	FV	PMT	PV
Answer:					163.21

Coupled with the $11.83 million to be received immediately, the value of the stream of payments would be $175.04 ($163.21 + $11.83)—far greater than the lump sum being offered. On the other hand, discounting at 6 percent gives a value of the future payments of $148.47. Adding the $11.83 immediate payment, we get a total value of $160.30—below that of the lump-sum payment. Therefore, the "Lucky 13"—as the Ohio workers referred to themselves—should choose the lump-sum payment if they can earn 6 percent on some equally safe alternative investment.

> A loan amortization schedule is one that breaks down each loan payment into its principal and interest components.

In addition to valuing equipment and sweepstakes, Equation [4-8a] can be used to *amortize loans.* For example, suppose that a small business borrows $200,000 from a bank for three years at an interest rate of 12 percent, compounded annually. The loan, including interest, is to be repaid in equal installments starting next year. Using a modified version of Equation [4-8a], the annual payments would be

$$PMT = \frac{\$200,000}{PVIFA_{12,3}} = \frac{\$200,000}{2.4018} = \$83,269.80$$

Because interest on borrowing is deductible for corporate tax purposes and principal payments are not, it is useful to put together a *loan amortization schedule* such as the one in Exhibit 4-4 that breaks the yearly payment into interest and principal repayment components. The interest component is calculated by multiplying

EXHIBIT 4-4
Loan Amortization Schedule
$200,000 Loan @ 12 Percent Interest

Year	Payment	Interest Portion	Principal Repayment	Year-End Balance
1	$83,269.80	$24,000.00	$59,269.80	$140,730.20
2	83,269.80	16,887.62	66,382.18	74,348.02
3	83,269.80	8,921.76	74,348.00	-0-

the interest rate (12 percent) times the unpaid balance; the amortization of principal is simply the payment less the interest. Subject to rounding error, the remaining principal after the last payment should be zero. Many types of installment loans, such as mortgages or automobile loans, are amortized in the same way.

Alternately, knowing that the yearly loan amount is $83,269.80, we can use a calculator to compute the interest on the loan employing the following keystrokes:

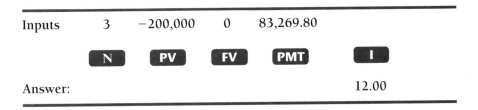

Inputs	3	−200,000	0	83,269.80
	N	PV	FV	PMT	I
Answer:				12.00

A rate of 12 percent should show up, which is, of course, the same interest rate we used in solving for the annual loan payments.

Future Value of an Annuity

> The future value of an annuity is the amount to which an annuity will grow at the end of the period when each payment is reinvested.

Frequently, individuals would like to know the future value of a stream of deposits into an interest-paying account. For instance, suppose you were to receive $1,000 annually for three years and then deposit each receipt in an account paying 8 percent, compounded annually. If you wanted to know how much would be in the account at the end of three years, you might put together a set of calculations such as those illustrated in Exhibit 4-5. The first $1,000 payment is invested at the end of year 1 and, therefore, earns interest for two years; the $1,000 received at the end of year 2 only earns interest for one year; the third payment of $1,000 earns no interest. The sum of the future value of these payments—the **future value of an annuity**—is $3,246.40.

In general, the future value of an annuity (FVA_n) lasting n periods, with payments of *PMT* dollars received at the end of each period, compounded at a rate k, is

$$FVA_n = \begin{array}{c}\text{Future Value}\\\text{of Payment}\\\text{in Period 1}\end{array} + \begin{array}{c}\text{Future Value}\\\text{of Payment}\\\text{in Period 2}\end{array} + \cdots + \begin{array}{c}\text{Future Value}\\\text{of Payment in}\\\text{Period } n-1\end{array} + \begin{array}{c}\text{Future Value}\\\text{of Payment}\\\text{in Period } n\end{array}$$

$$FVA_n = PMT(1+k)^{n-1} + PMT(1+k)^{n-2} + \cdots + PMT(1+k)^1 + PMT$$

[4-11]

Equation [4-11] is an extension of the formula for the future value of an individual payment, summed over a series of payments. Because the first payment is received at the end of the first period, it is compounded for $(n-1)$ rather than n

EXHIBIT 4-5
Calculating the Future Value of a 3-Year Annuity

Period	Cash Flow		Future Value
1	$1,000 \times (1.08)^2$	=	$1,166.40
2	$1,000 \times (1.08)^1$	=	1,080.00
3	$1,000 \times (1.08)$	=	1,000.00
			$3,246.40

periods. The final term in the sum is *PMT:* There's no interest earned on the last payment. The equation may be simplified as

$$FVA_n = PMT\,[(1 + k)^{n-1} + (1 + k)^{n-2} + \cdots + (1 + k)^1 + 1] \qquad [4\text{-}11a]$$

> The future value interest factor of an annuity is the future value of one dollar invested each year for a given number of years at a specific interest rate.

The terms in the bracket represent the future value of an annuity of one dollar a period for *n* periods, invested at some periodic rate *k*. The sum of these future values, known as the **future value interest factor** of an annuity ($FVIFA_{k,n}$), can be written as

$$FVIFA_{k,n} = \frac{(1 + k)^n - 1}{k} \qquad [4\text{-}12]$$

Rather than using the method of brute force illustrated in Exhibit 4-5, we can find the factor for a three-period annuity at 8 percent using Equation [4-12] as follows:

$$FVIFA_{8,3} = \frac{(1.08)^3 - 1}{0.08} = 3.2464$$

Multiplying this factor by $1,000 gives us $3,246.40—the same value as in Exhibit 4-5.[8] Or if we want to solve our annuity problem using a calculator, we get

Inputs	3	8		−1,000	
	N	I	PV	PMT	FV
Answer:					3,246.40

---

[8]The sum of future value interest factors for annuities ($FVIFA_{k,n}$) for various interest rates and time periods is also summarized in Appendix E. Looking at $k = 8\%$, and $n = 3$ periods, we get the factor of 3.2464 as calculated above.

Future values of annuities have a number of important applications in personal financial planning. Suppose, for example, that you want to know how much money you'd have to set aside each year in an account earning 6 percent interest in order to accumulate $1 million in 30 years. We can solve this problem by representing Equation [4-11a] as

$$FVA_n = PMT\,[FVIFA_{k,n}] \qquad\qquad [4\text{-}13]$$

and rearranging it as follows

$$PMT = \frac{FVA_n}{[FVIFA_{k,n}]} \qquad\qquad [4\text{-}13a]$$

The FVA_n is our investment goal of $1 million in 30 years; using Equation [4-12] to calculate $FVIFA_{k,n}$, we obtain 79.058. Substituting these values in Equation [4-13a], we get

$$PMT = \frac{\$1,000,000}{79.058} = \$12,648$$

Using the following keystrokes, we get (approximately) the same answer using a calculator

Inputs	30	6			1,000,000		
	N	I	PV	FV			PMT
Answer:							−12,648.91

The Annuity Period

If annuity payments are received or paid more than once a year, then the present and future value formulas must be revised to reflect compounding opportunities within a year. Let FVA_{nm} be the future value of an n-year annuity in which payments are received m times a year, and $FVIFA_{k/m,nm}$ the future value interest factor of an annuity, where k is the stated interest rate. Similarly, let PVA_{nm} be the present value of this annuity and $PVIFA_{k/m,nm}$ the present value interest factor. The revised versions of Equations [4-13] and [4-8a], respectively, are

$$FVA_{nm} = PMT\,[FVIFA_{k/m,nm}] \qquad\qquad [4\text{-}14]$$

and

$$PVA_{nm} = PMT\,[PVIFA_{k/m,nm}] \qquad\qquad [4\text{-}15]$$

Let's look at a specific example. Suppose a company has signed a three-year agreement to lease 10,000 square feet of warehouse space for $60,000, paid annually. If the relevant discount rate is 6 percent, the value of the lease would be

$$PVA = \$60,000\,[PVIFA_{6,3}]$$

$$= \$60,000\,[2.6730] = \$160,380$$

Solving this problem using a calculator we get

Inputs	3	6		−60,000	
	N	I	FV	PMT	PV
Answer:					160,380.72

On the other hand, if the lease specified monthly payments, the company would have to pay $5,000 a month for 36 months. With a *monthly* discount rate of 0.5 percent, the value of the lease would be

$$PVA = \$5,000\,[PVIFA_{0.50,36}]$$

$$= \$5,000\,[32.8710] = \$164,355$$

or $3,975 higher. We get virtually identical results using a calculator:

Inputs	36	0.5		−5,000	
	N	I	FV	PMT	PV
Answer:					164,355.08

Illustration

We can also make use of the future and present values of monthly annuities to explore public policy issues. For instance, there's been a great deal of discussion on Social Security reform. One of the ideas being floated is to privatize Social Security by allowing individuals to put all or a portion of their contributions into their own retirement account. These payments, coupled with employers' contributions, would be used to acquire earning assets, which would be used, in turn, to generate a stream of monthly benefits at retirement.

To see how this would work, suppose that you're twenty-five years old and have just graduated with an engineering degree. You begin work for a company in the aerospace/defense business that's offered you a lifetime contract. However, there's a small condition: Your salary will remain at $30,000 a year until retirement at age sixty-five. Given the employment risks in the industry, you're willing to forgo expected annual salary increases in exchange for job security.

Suppose Social Security has been privatized so that your 6.2 percent payment, plus the employers' matching contribution, can be put in a personal retirement account. Given a salary of $30,000 a year or $2,500 a month, your contribution will be $155 ($2,500 times 6.2 percent); in addition, another $155 would be added by your employer for a total of $310 a month. This money will be placed in an account earning 6.0 percent annually for the next 480 months (40 years until retirement times 12). You can also continue with the existing Social Security program, in which $310 a month would be sent to the government and credited to your account. Which of these two approaches to retirement would be best for you? Let's look at the private program first.

With the private retirement program, you'd be placing $310 for 480 months into an account earning 0.5 percent *monthly.* By the time you retire at age sixty-five, the value of this account would be

$$FVA = PMT[FVIFA_{0.50,480}] = \$310\,[1,991.49] = \$617,361.90$$

At retirement, you can begin making withdrawals from this account. The trick is not to outlive your resources. Forty years from now, you'll have $617,362 to work with, and that money has to be managed carefully. High monthly withdrawals, coupled with a long life, could result in you running out of money eventually.

Under the current Social Security program, estimated monthly benefits are approximately $1,232 for a person who is expected to make $30,000 a year over a 40-year working career.[9] Social Security payments end when an individual dies; the value of the benefits depends on a person's life expectancy. If an individual lives only five years beyond retirement, the value *at the time of retirement* of $1,232 a month for 60 months discounted at 0.5 percent a month (6 percent annually) would be

$$PVA = PMT[PVIFA_{0.50,\,60}] = \$1,232\,[51.7256] = \$63,725.89$$

Values of other life expectancies are presented below in Exhibit 4-6. Our results indicate that the present value of the annuity represented by your Social Security benefits, even if you live 40 years after retirement (*to age 105!*), is much less than the $617,362 available at retirement if you self-insure. The issues surrounding the reform of Social Security are highly complex, and it's not our intent to resolve these questions through this admittedly simplified numerical example. What the calculations suggest is that under the current payment formula individuals contributing to the system right now will never see the full value of the money that they've contributed.

---

[9]*Source:* Social Security's Web site. The estimate ignores inflation adjustments.

EXHIBIT 4-6
Value of $1,232-a-Month Social Security Payment

Life Expectancy Beyond Age 65 Years (Months)	Present Value of Social Security Benefits Discounted @ 0.5 Percent
5 (60)	$ 63,725.89
10 (120)	110,970.50
15 (180)	145,996.33
20 (240)	171,963.51
25 (300)	191,214.85
30 (360)	205,487.27
40 (480)	223,913.02

Another application involving payments within a period is the evaluation of low-interest auto loans. In the summer of 1998, strikes at two General Motors (GM) parts plants virtually shut down GM's North American production. GM decided to keep producing 1998 models through September 1998. Incentives were offered in order to clear out 1998 models while competitors were introducing their 1999s.

Suppose that the loan amount is $20,000 to be repaid in 48 installments. Customers will have a choice between financing at an annual rate of 1.9 percent or receiving a rebate of $2,700. If market interest rates on auto loans are 8.75 percent, should customers accept the rebate or GM's special financing package?

The customer savings on GM's low-cost financing can be found by first calculating the monthly payment based on a 1.9 percent annual rate and then valuing that stream based on an 8.75 percent annual interest rate. The difference between the $20,000 loan amount and the cost of repaying (the market value of the annuity) equals the value of the financing package to customers. If this amount exceeds the rebate, then a customer should go ahead with the low-interest loan.

Using a financial calculator, the monthly payments on the low-interest rate loan are $433.03.

Inputs	48	$\frac{1.9}{12} = 0.1583$	20,000		
	N	I	PV	FV	PMT
Answer:					−433.03

The market value of the monthly annuity of $433.03 for 48 months, when discounted at 0.7292 (8.75 annual rate divided by 12) is $17,484.50.

Inputs	48	$\frac{8.75}{12} = 0.7292$		−433.03	
	[N]	[I]	[FV]	[PMT]	[PV]

Answer: 17,484.50

Therefore, the true cost to GM customers of repaying the $20,000 loan at 1.9 percent when the rates on auto loans are 8.75 percent annually is $17,484.50. The savings of $2,515.50 is less than the $2,700 rebate, so GM customers should pass up the special financing arrangement and take the rebate.

The Present Value of Uneven Cash Flow Streams

Computation of annuities and perpetuities (both constant and growing) is relatively straightforward. Unfortunately, financial decisions involving well-behaved cash flow patterns are rare in practice. For example, let's go back to our earlier attempt to value a piece of equipment that was expected to generate $50,000 a year in savings for six years. To illustrate how to calculate the present value of an annuity, we assumed that the (1) cash benefits were the same in each year, and (2) the equipment had no salvage value.

This example was unrealistic in two respects; first, as time goes on, any piece of equipment is likely to require more and more maintenance in order to keep it productive. Therefore, the cash benefits that it generates should decrease over time. Second, most pieces of equipment have some salvage value at the end of their economic life. If a company cannot sell it in the used-equipment market, then it may be able to extract some value as scrap.

A representative set of cash flows that tries to capture these real-world considerations as well as to illustrate the methodology for calculating their present value is presented in Exhibit 4-7. As Exhibit 4-7 indicates, all we need to do is multiply each year's cash flow by the appropriate *PVIF* and then sum over all years to get a present value of $190,562.20. Underlying this computation is that *present values are additive*, i.e., that the present value of a stream of cash flows equals the sum of the present values of the individual components.

The valuation of uneven cash flow streams can often put a more realistic perspective on so-called "blockbuster" professional sports contracts. For instance, shortly after the 1996 World Series, the Atlanta Braves re-signed National League Cy Young Award winner John Smoltz to a four-year deal reportedly worth $31 million. The details of the arrangement called for Smoltz to receive $7 million in 1997, $7.75 million in 1998 and 1999, and $8.5 million in the year 2000.

Exhibit 4-8 illustrates the value of Smoltz's contract, assuming that he could have invested money at the 8 percent interest rate that prevailed at the time the contract was signed. As we can see, the value of the deal is far less than the $31 million quoted in the media; however, over $25 million is not exactly pocket change either.

EXHIBIT 4-7
Valuing an Uneven Cash Flow Stream
Cost-Saving Equipment

Year	After-Tax Cash Flow	×	PVIF @ 10%*	=	Present Value
1	$50,000		0.9091		$45,455.00
2	48,000		0.8264		39,667.20
3	45,000		0.7513		33,808.50
4	40,000		0.6830		27,320.00
5	35,000		0.6209		21,731.50
6	40,000*		0.5645		22,580.00
			Total Present Value =		$190,562.20

*Includes an estimated $10,000 salvage value.

EXHIBIT 4-8
Valuing John Smoltz's New Contract

Year	Payment	×	PVIF @ 8%	=	Present Value*
1997	$7,000,000		0.9259		$6,481,481
1998	7,750,000		0.8573		6,644,376
1999	7,750,000		0.7938		6,152,200
2000	8,500,000		0.7350		6,247,754
			Total Contract Value =		$25,525,811

*Figures are rounded to nearest dollar.

Net Present Values

<table>
<tr><td>

Net present value tells us how much better off we are by taking on an investment.

</td><td>

In the example illustrated in Exhibit 4-7, we found that the labor-saving equipment was worth $190,562.20. However, this doesn't mean that we would be $190,562.20 better off; after all, equipment suppliers are not charitable organizations and will insist that we pay something for the equipment. If that "something" is $150,000, then we'd be better off since we would be paying $150,000 today for an asset that we believe is worth $190,562.20. The $40,562.20 *difference* between the investment's value (i.e., the present value of estimated cash flows) and its cost is called the **net present value (NPV)** and represents how much *better off* we'd be if we purchased the equipment.

</td></tr>
</table>

NPVs are important tools for evaluating investment projects, and we'll say more about them in our discussion of capital budgeting in Chapter 8. Our motivation in introducing them at this stage is to get at the heart of what wealth creation is all about. *If* the 10 percent discount rate used to calculate the equipment's present value represented the *stockholders'* opportunity cost of money, then its NPV measures how much better (or worse) off *stockholders* would be if an investment were undertaken. Calculating a project's NPV is fairly simple; the managerial challenge is to identify these opportunities and properly assess their cash flows.

4.4 DETERMINANTS OF THE OPPORTUNITY COST OF MONEY

Interest underlies the exchange of cash between savers and borrowers.

Up to this point, we've taken the interest rate used in various formulas and examples as given. Yet it should be clear from reading the financial press or watching the news that interest rates can change on a day-to-day basis. Therefore, it's important that we get a handle on what determines the level of interest rates.

To understand what drives interest rates, we have to understand the economic function of interest. The primary role of the financial markets is to facilitate the flow of cash between savers and borrowers. But savers aren't likely to give up cash, which represents the means of consuming goods and services today, unless they get something in return. Interest, or more generally, some rate of return, is their compensation for deferring the current consumption of frozen pizzas, cars, and alike to some point in the future. The idea is to give up consumption today in exchange for more consumption in the future. Borrowers, on the other hand, want to consume more than their current income allows. As a result, they agree to give up some of their future consumption in exchange for more buying power today. The market interest rate represents the amount of future income (and consumption) that will change hands between borrowers and lenders.

Four basic factors determine the opportunity cost of money: (1) risk, (2) inflation, (3) taxes, and (4) maturity. Let's take a look at each one of these aspects in turn.

Risk

This element of the opportunity cost of money is so important that all of Chapter 6 will discuss the relationship between risk and return in detail. However, it may be useful to sketch out some of the risks in holding financial assets at this time.

Default risk relates to a borrower's ability to repay debt.

First, it's important to remember that interest is an element in the exchange between borrower and saver; who the borrower is can have a dramatic effect on rates. For instance, if we are lending to the U.S. Treasury, we'd charge it a lower interest rate than a Russian real estate project because U.S. Treasury securities have no *default risk*. Default risk is a critical factor in determining interest on debt instruments and relates to the risk that a borrower won't be able to pay interest and principal as promised.

Price, or variability risk, relates to the changes in prices of financial assets due to changes in market interest rates.

Second, even in the absence of default risk, all financial assets are subject to *price,* or *variability risk*. Price risk refers to the fact that prices on all financial assets can change due to changes in (among other things) market conditions. U.S. Treasury securities are free from default risk; however, their prices can change in response to changes in the general level of interest rates. As we'll see in Chapter 5, when we take up bond valuation, price risk tends to be greatest with longer-term bonds.

The type of claim (e.g., debt versus equity) has an important bearing on the opportunity cost of capital.

Finally, differences among the types of claims influence the opportunity cost of money. With a debt instrument, the borrower promises to make interest and principal payments to the lender. Failure to meet these obligations is an act of default. Common stockholders aren't promised anything, so if management decides to suspend cash dividends, there's really not much an individual shareholder can do except write nasty letters to the company's president or sell stock. Therefore, we'd expect the holders of common stock to have a higher opportunity cost of capital than the firm's creditors.

Expected Inflation

The interest rates quoted in the financial press are **nominal** or **actual rates.** However, what matters is the **real rate**—the rate at which current goods can be exchanged for future goods. A lender would be concerned with how many more goods can be consumed in the future by forgoing consumption today. If the nominal rate is 6 percent and prices go up by 6 percent, lenders get no compensation for deferring consumption. Therefore, we'd expect lenders to adjust this nominal rate—the rate at which they are willing to give up present for future dollars—to account for this loss in purchasing power.

The American economist Irving Fisher proposed the following relationship among the nominal interest rate r, the real or inflation-adjusted interest rate a, and the expected rate of inflation i:

$$1 + r = (1 + a)(1 + i)   \qquad [4\text{-}16]$$

The term $(1 + a)$ represents the real required loan repayment, and $(1 + i)$ adjusts for expected inflation. Multiplying through and subtracting 1 from Equation [4-16] yields

$$r = a + i + ai   \qquad [4\text{-}16a]$$

A commonly used version of Equation [4-16a] simply drops the interest-inflation cross-product term to become $r = a + i$, an approximation that works quite well when expected inflation is relatively low.

According to the **Fisher effect,** as the relationship in Equation [4-16a] is called, borrowers and lenders alike factor expected inflation into the nominal interest rate. The operative phrase is *expected inflation.* For instance, suppose that inflation is expected to be 3 percent and that the real rate is 4 percent, giving us a nominal rate of 7 percent. If the inflation rate turns out to be 5 percent, firms or individuals that borrowed at 7 percent will effectively be getting money at a real rate of 2 percent—a bargain on an after-the-fact basis.

> The Fisher effect says that borrowers and lenders factor expected inflation into interest rates.

The historical evidence suggests that the Fisher effect is a close approximation to reality and that changes in nominal rates are related to inflationary expectations. Exhibit 4-9 illustrates the relationship between inflation—as measured by the year-to-year changes in the Consumer Price Index—and the 91-day Treasury bill rate from 1955 to 1997. Except for the 1970s, when inflation was unexpectedly high, the real rate of interest has been positive.

The Fisher message for the investor or borrower is that the nominal interest rate already incorporates expected inflation, and hence, no further adjustment is necessary or warranted. After the fact, of course, inflation can be more or less than expected, leading to a lower or higher real rate than originally anticipated. How-

EXHIBIT 4-9
Treasury Bill Rates versus Inflation
1955–1997

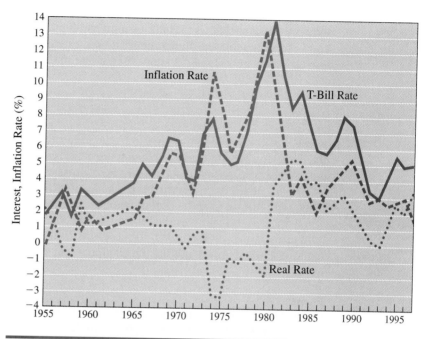

Source: The Annual Report of the Council of Economic Advisors, February 1998.

ever, it is difficult to anticipate this rate at the point of decision. After all, unexpected changes in inflation or other financial variables are unpredictable by definition and, therefore, cannot influence our current decisions. The Fisher effect does not take uncertainty into account, and the market is sometimes fooled. However, Exhibit 4-9 indicates that the market can be taken by surprise, but it also adjusts quickly to expectations, as interest rates adjust to new information.

Two other aspects of the Fisher effect are worth noting: First, a piece of advice that often passes for financial wisdom is that you should be a borrower during times of inflation. The idea here is that you get to repay your debts in "cheap" dollars. But the Fisher effect tells us that expected inflation is already built into the cost of borrowing. Therefore, borrowers will only win if inflation is *higher* than expected; they will lose if inflation is *lower* than expected.

Second, the *expected* real interest rate exerts a powerful influence on financial decisions. An increase in the real interest rate reduces the present value of claims to future income streams, even though these future amounts remain constant. This means that the owners of such claims will find that their wealth declines as interest rates rise. Conversely, when the real interest rates fall, the present value of future dollars rise, and this leads to an increase in wealth for owners of bonds, stocks, and other assets.

The Fisher effect also has some important implications in a global setting. A generalized version of the Fisher effect asserts that real interest rates should be equal across national boundaries. If that were not true, then capital would flow into currencies with higher real returns. With no government interference, we'd expect these capital flows to continue until real capital flows were equalized. Once equilibrium is achieved, the nominal interest rate differentials across currencies will approximately equal the anticipated inflation differential, or

$$\frac{1 + r_h}{1 + r_f} = \frac{1 + i_h}{1 + i_f} \qquad [4\text{-}17]$$

where r_h and r_f are the home and foreign currency interest rates, and i_h and i_f are the home and foreign-country inflation rates. Equation [4-17], known as the *generalized Fisher effect,* says that *currencies in countries with high rates of inflation should have higher interest rates than currencies with lower rates of inflation.* This is an important insight that we'll exploit later in a number of investment and financing settings.

Exhibit 4-10 illustrates the relationship between interest rates and inflation rates as measured by changes in the consumer price index for 20 countries during June 1998. It is evident from the graph that, on average, countries with higher

EXHIBIT 4-10
Fisher Effect: Interest Rates and Inflation Rates
for 20 Developed and Developing Countries
June 1998

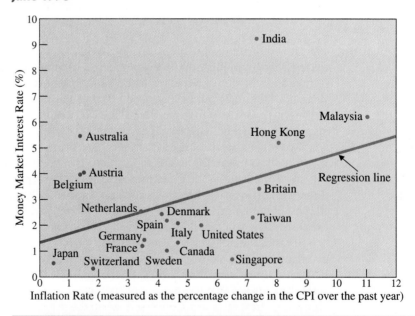

Source: Data on interest rates and inflation rates are from *The Economist,* June 12, 1998, 100–102.

inflation rates have higher interest rates. This empirical evidence is consistent with the idea that variations in nominal interest rates across countries can be attributed largely to differences in inflationary expectations.

Taxes

Changes in tax rates influence interest rate differentials between taxable and tax-exempt bonds.

Taxes impact the opportunity cost of money in the same way as inflation. If interest is tax deductible, borrowers know that this will reduce their future tax bill. Since the after-tax cost of borrowing declines as tax rates increase, borrowers would be willing to pay a higher interest rate because the after-tax rate stays the same. For example, if a borrower is in the 20 percent tax bracket, then the after-tax cost of a 10 percent loan would be 8 percent. If tax rates rise to 50 percent, the borrower could afford to pay up to 16 percent without the after-tax cost of borrowing being greater. In general, if r_B and r_A are the before- and after-tax interest rates, respectively, and t_b the borrower's tax rate, then

$$r_A = r_B(1 - t_b)$$

[4-18]

Lenders reason along similar lines. If tax rates rise, they need a higher pre-tax rate to get the same after-tax income. Because both borrowers and lenders are amenable to interest rate increases when taxes rise, market interest rates will also rise. Some evidence on the effect of taxes on market interest rates is provided by the spreads (i.e., interest rate differentials) between taxable and tax-exempt bonds. A drop in tax rates tends to narrow this spread, whereas a rise in rates tends to widen it.

Maturity

Interest rates tend to vary with maturity, with each maturity having its own interest rate.

In calculating the present value of future cash flows, we have implicitly assumed that the same interest rate held for each period in the future, regardless of how near or distant in time the cash flow is. This is a simplification, because interest rates tend to vary with the maturity of the cash flow, each period having its own interest rate. For example, money received in one year may be discounted at 5.4 percent, whereas money to be received in two years might be discounted at an annual rate of 6.0 percent. The differences in the discount rate reflect the market opportunities available to investors based on how long they are willing to tie up their money. The general formula for the present value (*PV*) of a stream of future cash flows, where interest rates may vary by the maturity of the cash flow, is

$$PV = \sum_{t=1}^{N} \frac{CF_t}{(1 + k_t)^t}$$

[4-19]

where CF_t is the cash flow in period t, and k_t the discount rate for the cash flows received in time period t.

The relationship between interest rates on cash flows of different maturities is called the **term structure of interest rates.** We'll examine the term structure in greater detail in Appendix 5B. In this chapter and in most applications, however, we assume that the term structure is "flat"—that is, that $k_1 = k_2 = \cdots = k_t = \cdots = k_n = k$, where k is a constant.

SUMMARY

In this chapter, we saw that money has time value because we can earn some return (interest) on the cash we have in hand today. The greater our expected return, the more valuable current dollars will be relative to future dollars and the less valuable future dollars will be relative to present dollars. The process of going from today's dollars to future values is known as *compounding*; going from future values to present values is referred to as *discounting*.

At a purely mechanical level, formulas were developed to convert present (current) dollars to future dollars and future dollars into present values. The most important of these formulas, which form the basis for the mathematics of finance, are summarized as follows:

Future Value
$FV = PV(1 + k)^n$, where FV is the future value of a present amount PV compounded at a rate k for n periods. The term $(1 + k)^n$ is known as the *future value interest factor* or $FVIF_{k,n}$.

Present Value
$PV = FV/(1 + k)^n$, where the terms are the same as those of the previous formula. All we are doing here is transforming a future amount to a present value. The term $1/(1 + k)^n$ is known as the *present value interest factor,* or $PVIF_{k,n}$, and is the reciprocal of $FVIF_{k,n}$.

Future Value of an Annuity
An annuity is a payment or receipt of PMT dollars per period for a specific number of periods. The future value of an annuity lasting n periods and compounded at a rate of k per period is

$$FVA_n = PMT\,[FVIFA_{k,n}]$$

The term $FVIFA_{k,n}$ is referred to as the *future value interest factor for an annuity* and represents the amount you'd have at the end of n years by investing a dollar a year at some interest rate k.

Present Value of an Annuity
The present value of an annuity of PMT dollars lasting n periods and compounded at a rate of k per period is

$$PVA_n = PMT\,[PVIFA_{k,n}]$$

The term $PVIFA_{k,n}$ is referred to as the *present value interest factor for an annuity* and represents the value today of one dollar received (or paid) for n years discounted at some interest rate k.

We spend most of our time talking about present values. Central to interpreting present values is the idea of *exchange;* i.e., the present value of future amounts represents what we would be willing to exchange (i.e., pay) today for future cash flows *given* our ability to earn a return equal to the discount rate. Using this principle, we can value *any asset* based on its expected stream of future cash flows. Further, if we know the asset's cost, we can calculate its **net present value (NPV),** which tells us how much better off we'd be if we purchased the asset. This *NPV* can serve as a basis for investment decision-making.

Finally, we have seen that the opportunity cost of money relates to the rate of exchange between current and future consumption. The primary determinants of this rate of exchange were found to be risk, inflationary expectations, taxes, and maturity.

 FINCOACH PRACTICE EXERCISES

To help you master the mathematics discussed in the chapter, open **FinCoach** on the *Prentice Hall Finance Center* CD-ROM and practice the problems in the following categories: *1. Valuation of Single Cash Flows, 2. Valuation of Multiple Cash Flows,* and *3. Valuation of Infinitely Many Cash Flows.*

QUESTIONS

1. What effect will an interest rate increase have on the value today of a loan repayment to be made in one year?
   a. Will the percentage change in value brought about by a rise in the interest rate be greater for a payment due in one year or one due in five years? Explain.
   b. Will an increase in the interest rate make the borrower better off or worse off? How about the lender? Explain.
2. Suppose the compounding interval is shortened.
   a. Will this increase or decrease the present value of a future payment? Explain.
   b. What will happen to the future value of money invested today? Explain.
3. Because of overbuilding, commercial office towers are offering a year of free rent to tenants who sign a five-year lease. Would you expect the "free" year to be the first year or the fifth year? Why?
4. Two side-by-side office towers are identical. However, one is fully leased at rates fixed for the next 20 years, whereas the other is also fully leased but its rates are renegotiated at the end of each year. At a time of rising office rents, explain which is likely to be the more valuable property.
5. Professional football teams often require season ticket holders to pay for their tickets by June 1 even though the football season doesn't start until September 1. Why might this policy exist?
6. A typical piece of advice is to be a borrower during a time of inflation. Comment on this advice.
7. Suppose borrowers, but not lenders, factor inflation into their financial decisions. Will the Fisher effect hold? Explain.
8. As the chief financial officer, you are responsible for funding your company's pensions. Because your company is fairly new, none of the employees has retired yet. You have invested primarily in fixed-rate, long-term bonds. Employee pensions are based on their earnings at the time they retire.
   a. What does a rise in interest rates do to the value of your bond portfolio?
   b. What will the interest rate increase do to your expected cost of funding these pensions? Consider the different effects of a nominal interest rate rise due to an increase in the real interest rate and one due to an increase in the anticipated rate of inflation.
9. Communist countries did not charge interest on the capital they supplied to their industries.
   a. Explain how this policy will introduce distortions in the capital allocation process.
   b. Are the distortions likely to be greater for projects with short-term payoffs or those with longer-term payoffs? Explain.
10. Usury laws in many states prohibit the charging of interest rates in excess of a set amount (say, 18 percent). What is rapid inflation likely to do to loan-sharking activity (supplying money at rates in excess of the usury rate)? Explain.

PROBLEMS

✒—Excel templates may be downloaded from **www.prenhall.com/financecenter.**

1. The parents of a newborn girl decide to put aside $5,000 today for her college education. ✒
   a. If the rate on the savings account is 6 percent, how much will she have in her college fund when she's ten years old?
   b. How much will she have in the fund at age eighteen?
   c. Do you think this will be enough for her education? Explain.
2. How long will it take your money to double if you invest it at 5 percent? At 15 percent?
3. Suppose you invest $500,000 in a five-year certificate of deposit that pays 12 percent compounded annually.
   a. How much will the CD be worth at its maturity?
   b. How much will the CD be worth if interest is compounded quarterly? Monthly? Continuously?
4. A $10,000 investment in Merck stock on January 1, 1988 would have grown to $54,984 by

December 31, 1997. What was the compound annual return on Merck over that 10-year period?

5. Sterling Character decides to put aside a sum of money to pay for his grandmother's operation. She needs $10,000. ✍

   a. If the operation is scheduled for five years in the future, how much should Sterling set aside today (assume an 8 percent rate of return on his investment)?

   b. If Sterling could get a 12 percent return on his investment, how much should he set aside?

   c. If the rate were 12 percent and the operation is rescheduled for ten years in the future, how much should he set aside today?

6. In comparing money market funds, you decide to invest in either the Morrell Lunch fund paying 8 percent compounded daily or the Don Wetter fund paying 8.5 percent compounded quarterly. Which fund pays the higher return?

7. On March 15, 1979, a Manhattan executive bought a three-story penthouse apartment overlooking Central Park for $750,000. Six years later, in 1985, the executive sold the apartment for $3 million, a record amount for a real estate transaction of its kind. What was the annual rate of return on this investment?

8. In 1989, Time, Inc., turned down an offer to be acquired by Paramount Communications for $200 per share in order to pursue its own acquisition of Warner Communications. At the time, Time was selling for about $125 per share. Time management argued that its proposed acquisition of Warner would benefit shareholders in the long run more than would selling out to Paramount. ✍

   a. Assuming that Time shareholders could earn 12 percent on their money, and that Time pays no dividends, how much would Time stock have to sell for in 1999 (ten years later) to justify turning down Paramount's offer of $200?

   b. Given its $125 price in 1989, what annual rate of return does Time stock have to compound at to equal this future price?

9. The Perpetual Care Memorial Garden will maintain a garden plot in perpetuity for a customer for $50 a year. If the payments are indeed perpetual, with the first one due immediately, what is the value of this maintenance agreement as of today? (Use an annual interest rate of 8 percent.)

10. As winner of a lottery, you can choose one of the following prizes: ✍

    a. $1,000,000 now

    b. $1,700,000 at the end of five years

    c. $135,000 a year forever, starting at year end

    d. $200,000 for each of the next ten years, starting at year end

    e. $75,000 at year end and increasing by 6 percent a year forever

    If the interest rate is 9 percent, which prize should you select?

11. In 1985, the New York State lottery awarded a prize of $40 million to be received in 20 annual payments of $2 million each, with the first payment due at year end. If interest rates in 1985 were 10 percent, how much was the lottery worth to the winner? ✍

12. The pension plan at your new company will set aside 25 percent of your annual salary of $32,000 every year until you retire in 25 years. Interest rates are currently 8 percent. ✍

    a. How much can you expect to have at retirement?

    b. If your company's plan begins setting aside this amount for you after five years of employment, how much can you expect to have at retirement?

13. The usual legal settlement for an industrial accident is the present value of the employee's lifetime earnings. If you make $50,000 a year, and expect to work for 30 more years, what would your settlement be? Assume a discount rate of 10 percent and no change in your salary.

14. The Early Saver invests $1,000 a year for ten years, at 9 percent compounded annually, and then stops. The Late Saver starts saving $1,000 a year ten years from now, also at 9 percent. ✍

    a. How many years will it take the Late Saver, depositing $1,000 a year, to catch up with the Early Saver?

    b. How would your answer to (a) change if the interest rate were 7 percent instead of 8 percent?

15. During a late-night television commercial, the Kwan-tzu Metalcraft Company offers its hardware set for the unbelievably low price of $200 or at its easy payment plan of $9 down and $9.50 a month for 25 months. What is the finance rate charged by Kwan-tzu on its easy payment plan? ✍

16. You are considering taking out a student loan of $10,000 at 4 percent interest. Repayment will commence one year from now and will consist of six equal yearly installments. Prepare an amortization schedule for this loan.

17. Metropolitan Life will sell you a 20-year annuity, paying $45,300 annually in regular monthly checks, for $500,000. ✍
    a. At what effective annual interest rate is this a fair deal?
    b. Alternatively, for $500,000, you can buy a package of 40 zero-coupon Treasury bonds paying $25,000 every six months. What is the annualized return on your money in this case?

18. Tom has invested his lump sum retirement pension of $300,000 in an account that guarantees him a 9 percent return. He wishes to make annual withdrawals of $40,000 beginning at the end of this year. ✍
    a. How long will it be until Tom exhausts his account?
    b. Suppose Tom waits ten years until he starts making withdrawals. How long will it be until he exhausts his account?

19. In 1992, a newly hired executive for AT&T opened a tax-exempt Individual Retirement Account (IRA) to which she plans to contribute at year-end $2,000 a year from now until she retires at the age of seventy in 2038. From this fund, the retired executive plans to draw an annual income of $65,000 for 20 years, from 2038 through 2058. Assuming that she leaves nothing to her estate, will the IRA fund be sufficient to cover her retirement plans? (Use an annual interest rate of 12 percent.) ✍

20. An individual graduates from college and begins work at age twenty-two. If she has an annual income of $35,000, pays 12.4 percent of this income into Social Security (including her employer's matching 6.2 percent contribution), and retires at age sixty-five with Social Security benefits of $8,300 annually, how long must she live before the present value of these benefits equals the value of her contributions? Assume a discount rate of 8 percent per year and that all payments and benefits occur at the end of the year. ✍

21. The Security Atlantic Bancorp. is buying an office building for its staff in downtown Manhattan for $45,000,000. The terms of the sale offered by Olympic Real Estate Co., the seller of the property, call for four annual payments of $7.8 million each, with the first payment occurring at the end of year 1, and one "balloon" payment of $45,000,000 at the end of year 5. ✍
    a. What is the annual mortgage rate charged by Olympic?
    b. Suppose, instead, that the terms offered by Olympic Real Estate Co. call for annual payments of $7.8 million for four years and a "balloon" payment of $13.8 million in year 5. If the annual mortgage rate on comparable properties is 9 percent, what is the true price of the building?

22. In March 1991, Exxon agreed to pay a total of $1 billion to settle state and federal legal claims related to the huge March 1989 *Exxon Valdez* oil spill off the Alaskan coast. Under the settlement, Exxon would pay $190 million immediately, $150 million in 1992, and $100 million in 1993. It would then pay $70 million a year for eight years through 2001. Assuming that each yearly payment will take place in March of the year it is due, what is the present value of this settlement? Use the 7.5 percent return required in March 1991 on ten-year Treasury bonds. ✍

23. Chrysler has just announced that to spur sales it will offer free financing on selected models. How much will a zero-interest $15,000 loan, to be repaid in 30 equal monthly installments, be worth to customers if the market rate on loans of this type is 12 percent (1 percent monthly)? ✍

24. Susan is retiring this year at age sixty-five, with a life expectancy of 20 years. Suppose she has saved $300,000. ✍
    a. Assume Susan can earn a 10 percent annual return on her money. How much capital can she withdraw each year so that her money holds out for at least 20 years?
    b. Suppose that inflation is projected at 3 percent annually. Assuming that Susan can still earn a 10 percent nominal return on her money, how much capital can she withdraw each year in equal *real* amounts so that her money holds out for at least 20 years?
    c. Redo (a) and (b) assuming an 8 percent nominal return on Susan's savings.

d. How long will Susan's savings last if she withdraws $45,000 annually, assuming she earns a 7 percent rate of return?

25. Suppose you are quoted a rate (not an APR) of 8.75 percent on a 15-year, fixed-rate, $150,000 mortgage. The loan will be repaid in 180 monthly installments, with the first payment due one month from now (assuming that the loan is approved and granted today). ✄

a. What is the monthly payment for the loan?
b. Suppose two years from now 15-year mortgages plummet to 5 percent and you want to refinance the loan. If there is no penalty for early repayment, how much will you have to pay the mortgage company to settle the loan?
c. What happens to the monthly payment in (a) if you can repay the mortgage in 360 equal installments over a period of 30 years?

Bond and Stock Valuation

We should all be concerned about the future because we
will spend the rest of our lives there.
Charles F. Kettering

KEY TERMS

book value per share
call premium
call provision
competitive equilibrium
constant dividend growth
   model
coupon interest rate
current yield
debentures
duration
efficient markets
   hypothesis (EMH)

Eurobonds
event studies
expectations theory
face value
indenture
junk, or high-yield bonds
liquidity premium theory
modified duration
notes
par value
perfectly competitive
   capital markets

preferred stock
present value of growth
   opportunities (PVGO)
price-earnings (*P/E*)
   multiple
required rate of return
segmented markets
   theory
sinking fund
true value
yield curve
yield to maturity

CHAPTER LEARNING OBJECTIVES

Upon completion of this chapter, students should be able to:

- Explain the concept of market efficiency and how it influences the market prices of securities.
- Describe the features of bonds, preferred stock, and common stock.
- Understand the concept of an investment's required rate of return and its importance in the valuation of marketable securities.
- Use valuation principles to calculate a bond's value and/or its yield to maturity.
- Calculate prices and required rates of return for common stock using the constant dividend growth model.

- Use stock valuation models to describe when corporate growth strategies can create shareholder value.
- Use stock valuation principles to value the acquisition of a company.
- List and describe the various theories for explaining the term structure of interest rates.
- Use the concept of duration to evaluate the interest sensitivity of individual bonds and bond portfolios.

Academicians and practitioners generally agree that the financial goal of a company should be to increase its owners' wealth over time by maximizing the market price of the firm's common stock. A senior manager's ability to accomplish this requires an understanding of how the financial markets value the corporation's securities. Without some sense of how the financial markets translate corporate actions into prices, it's impossible for managers to design decision rules that can serve the stockholders' interests.

As a first step in understanding the valuation process, we'll examine discounted cash flow (DCF) models. These models are based on the idea that the value of *any asset* is the present value of future cash flows that the holder expects to receive from owning the asset. We'll begin by examining asset valuation, in general, with particular emphasis on the role information plays in the valuation process. Then, we will look at bonds and their pricing, followed by a brief discussion of preferred stock valuation. With this background, we can examine the principles underlying the valuation of a company's common stock and explore the linkages between corporate growth strategies and shareholder wealth creation.

5.1   VALUATION OF ASSETS

The value of any asset is determined by the present value of its future cash flows. In the case of financial assets, these cash flows take the form of future interest or dividend payments plus the amount you get on the sale of the security. Ultimately, of course, investors are really concerned with the quantity of goods or services they can buy with that stream of future cash. In effect, the people who buy stocks and bonds are trading off *consumption today* for (they hope) *higher future consumption*.

As we saw in Chapter 4, the terms of that tradeoff are dictated by the investor's opportunity cost of capital. For financial assets, such as stocks or bonds, the investor's opportunity cost of capital is referred to as the **required rate of return,** which reflects what an investor can expect to earn on investments of equivalent risk. Thus, investors who want to maximize their wealth shouldn't accept any investment in which the risk-adjusted return is lower than that which can be obtained elsewhere. *If each investor faces virtually identical investment opportunities in the capital markets, then all investors will have the same minimum risk-adjusted required return.* The ability of investors to get the best risk-adjusted returns possible depends on the existence of capital markets that are both *competitive* and *efficient.* We'll examine both of these ideas in turn.

> The required return on an asset equals what investors expect to earn on investments of equivalent risk.

Competitive Capital Markets and Asset Valuation

The fundamental role of the financial markets is to bring suppliers and users of funds together. Countries with well-developed capital markets present opportunities to invest in a wide array of financial assets with different risk characteristics. At the same time, these markets also allow companies to raise long-term capital by allocating investors' funds to their best possible risk-adjusted return. Because investors are risk averse (i.e., all other things being equal, they prefer less risk to more), we'd expect them to demand higher expected returns for greater perceived risk.

The assumption that every investor has essentially the same investment opportunities in the capital markets has some important implications for corporate finance. Specifically, *any two individuals, no matter how different their consumption preferences or wealth, will always use the same discount rate to value the cash flows associated with a specific asset.* Managers don't have to worry about different shareholders assigning different present values to the same investment; the market establishes a single discount rate to be used for all investments having the same risk. Therefore, two individuals who can agree on the future cash flows and risk characteristics of a specific stock or bond will always assign it the same value.

The proposition that all investors will assign the same discount rate in valuing assets depends on the existence of a **perfectly competitive capital market.** This is a capital market in which buyers and sellers can enter and leave the market freely. Further, the idea of a perfectly competitive market also means that market participants can buy and sell securities with no transaction costs and have costless access to economically relevant information.[1] Clearly, no market meets this standard of "perfection." However, there's a good bit of evidence that the financial markets in developed countries closely approximate this ideal. What's important is that asset prices behave *as if* they were being traded in a perfectly competitive market. Because this assumption closely describes reality, most financial market models in this and subsequent chapters assume that securities are priced in perfectly competitive markets.

Market Efficiency and Asset Valuation

The global financial markets are highly competitive. This means that any security that is clearly identified as a superior investment will have its price bid up by alert investors. This process will continue until its expected return is equivalent to other investments with similar risks. Conversely, investments expected to provide below-average returns will be sold until their prices decline enough to again yield acceptable returns. The adjustment of security prices to their perceived worth takes place quickly; as long as investors believe that they can earn above-average returns by buying underpriced securities and selling overpriced ones, they will execute trades as quickly as they see opportunities. The rapid response of investors to perceived profit opportunities ensures the competitive nature of the markets.

The competitive nature of markets is at the heart of the **efficient markets hypothesis (EMH)**—the idea that current security prices reflect everything that is known about the prospects of an individual security. What other result would we expect when we have literally tens of thousands of bright security analysts rummaging around for information in order to identify over- or undervalued securities?

> In well-developed capital markets, any two investors should have the same required return for the same asset.

> The efficient markets hypothesis states that asset prices reflect all that is currently known about these assets.

---

[1]If these conditions are violated—either because there are significant transactions costs or because not all investors have access to the same financial assets—then investors face different risk–return tradeoffs and may value risk and the opportunity cost of their funds differently.

In such a market, prices are informationally driven and should adjust instantaneously to each and every new piece of information as it becomes available.

It's useful to talk about three levels of market efficiency:[2] (1) a *weak-form efficient* market in which prices reflect all past price changes, (2) a *semistrong efficient* market in which prices reflect all publicly available information, and (3) a *strong-form efficient* market in which the present prices embody *all* information about a security, whether it is publicly available or privately held. Each level is nested within the other. For example, a semistrong efficient market is also weak-form efficient because past price history is also part of the public record.

There's a good bit of empirical evidence to support the idea that the markets are weak-form efficient and that no useful information can be gleaned from examining past changes in stock price. In one of the earliest studies, Maurice Kendall (1953), a British statistician, examined weekly stock prices on the London Exchange and tried to find a pattern in the price movement. To his surprise, Kendall found that his chart of prices looked "almost as if the Demon of Chance drew a random number . . . and added it to the current price to get the next price."

Further, a number of academic studies—known as **event studies** because they examine the stock market's reaction to specific events—show that the market reacts quickly to *announcements* of earnings or dividends changes or unexpected mergers. In other cases, the event announcement may have a negligible effect on the price of a stock because the market has already anticipated the news from other sources. As we'll see, the market's reaction to changes in a firm's financing and dividend decisions will depend, in large measure, on whether the news is truly new and how the market interprets the data.

The idea that the market is strong-form efficient has not been warmly welcomed by investment professionals. Why? If market prices reflect all information, both *public* and *private,* then efforts to find inside information in order to beat the market would be a waste of time; after all, this information is already imbedded in security prices. Proponents of strong-form market efficiency would, therefore, contend that no one can beat the market on a consistent basis over time. Money managers, of course, make a good living by convincing investors that they can beat the market through superior security selection.

The claims of superior performance by professional money managers are not borne out by the historical record. In some early studies, both Sharpe (1966) and Jensen (1968) presented evidence that mutual fund managers as a group couldn't beat the market on a risk-adjusted basis. Even more discouraging is the fact that those managers who beat the market in one year couldn't seem to repeat this performance in the next. In a pioneering study, Michael Jensen (1968) examined the performance of 115 mutual funds over the ten-year period 1945–1964. He found that a mutual fund that had a better-than-average year had only a 50 percent chance of repeating that performance next year. That is exactly what you'd expect if mutual fund investing were a random process. The most important factor in determining rankings seemed to be that patron saint of investors—Lady Luck.

Empirical evidence supports the weak and semistrong forms of market efficiency.

There's no evidence to support the idea that professional money managers can outperform the market on a risk-adjusted basis.

---

[2]For a comprehensive review of market efficiency, see Fama (1970). While this work is very quantitative, it can still be read by nonmathematicians with a little patience.

Jensen's results have been replicated many times since using different markets and time periods but with similar results. However, recent evidence has suggested that a few superior investors—such as Peter Lynch, formerly the head of Fidelity's Magellan Fund, and Warren Buffet, chairman of Berkshire Hathaway—systematically beat the market. Although this could be blind luck, it seems unlikely. Indeed, it would be surprising if among the millions of people who try their hand at beating the market, none would succeed. Some investors must be able to perceive patterns where others see only chaos or to forecast trends although others see nothing.

Price and Value in an Efficient Market

With prices in competitive markets reacting quickly to information, there's sometimes a tendency to see price and value as being equivalent. They are not! The *price* of a security is nothing more than the amount a buyer is willing to pay a willing seller at a given point in time. If the markets are efficient at a semistrong level, we would expect this exchange price to reflect all publicly available information and this information to be equally available to both parties. Prices, then, are very precise and well-defined quantities.

Value is another matter. Publicly-traded corporations acquire assets and issue claims against them. These claims can take the form of bonds or preferred and/or common stock. The *value* of these *claims* should reflect the *value* of the *underlying assets* whose value, in turn, should be related to their ability to generate cash. In the long run, there ought to be a connection between the value of securities issued and the value of the firm's assets; otherwise the financial markets cannot efficiently allocate capital to its best use.

> Prices and value are not necessarily the same for all securities at every point in time.

However, because value and prices are equal over the *long run,* this does not mean that they are equal for all securities *at each point in time.* To say that the financial markets are efficient is not to say that they are always right; they can't be because prices are based on future events, which can only be guessed at today. Put another way, prices reflect current information plus a set of beliefs about the future based on that information. As the future unfolds and new information regarding asset values is revealed, expectations regarding security returns will change and prices will be adjusted accordingly. Thus, prices in an efficient market represent an *estimate* of value. There is some "intrinsic value" out there, but we can also see a good bit of randomness as new (and sometimes irrelevant) information is absorbed by the market.[3] Proponents of efficient markets can only claim that market prices are informationally driven and respond quickly to new information. Few, if any, supporters of efficient markets equate price with value for all securities at each instant in time.

One more point must be clarified before discussing bond and stock pricing in an efficient market: To say that securities are correctly priced does not mean

---

[3]There's also a question about how the market interprets that information. De Bondt and Thaler (1985; 1987) present some compelling evidence that the prices of individual stocks overreact to information and then undergo "corrections."

Poor managment will lead to a value gap.	that the securities reflect the maximum possible value—often called the **true value**—of the corporate assets that underlie them. Corporate assets and, therefore, the financial claims against them will attain their maximum value only if the firm turns out products efficiently, safely, and in keeping with its customers' desires. Indeed, as we will see in Chapter 11, when corporate managers are viewed—rightly or wrongly—as bunglers or wastrels, corporate raiders perceive an opportunity for creating value by taking over the company and restructuring it. However, only in an ideal world would bad management be instantly and costlessly replaced before assets are squandered. The time lag and the costs associated with corporate takeovers permit a gap between a company's potential value and its current market value. The more efficient the market is for corporate control, the smaller this *value gap* will be.

5.2 CHARACTERISTICS AND PRICING OF CORPORATE BONDS

When a company borrows money through a bond issue, it promises to pay some principal amount plus interest to the holder according to a schedule contained in the bond contract. These principal and interest payments must be met before dividends can be paid to either preferred or common stockholders. If payments aren't met on time or in the amounts specified in the bond's **indenture**,[4] debtholders can take action to press their claims. These steps include (but are not limited to) forcing the company into bankruptcy and, perhaps, liquidation. If the company is forced out of business, creditors will have first claim on the proceeds from the sale of assets.

Features of Corporate Debt

A bond's par value, coupon interest rate, and maturity date define the amounts and timing of cash flows to investors.	The cash flows from a bond are defined by its **par value, coupon interest rate,** and *maturity date.* The par value is the stated **face value** of the bond, which is usually set at $1,000 per bond although multiples of $1,000 exist. The par (or face) value generally represents the amount of money the issuer borrowed (per bond) and promised to repay at some future date. The coupon interest rate is the stated interest rate on the bond and is the percentage of the par value the issuer promises to pay each year in interest.[5] For example, a 10-year bond with a $1,000 par value and a coupon rate of 8 percent, paying interest annually, promises to pay the investor $80 a year (8% of $1,000) for 10 years. In 10 years, the firm will pay the bondholder the $1,000 par value, after which interest payments stop.

On the issue date, companies usually try to set the coupon interest rate on the new bond equal to the prevailing rate on other bonds of similar maturity and credit quality. This will ensure that the initial market price of the bond will be ap-

---

[4]An indenture is a legal term used to describe the debt contract and may contain provisions that go beyond simply describing the amounts and dates of principal and interest payments.

[5]Typically, the coupon rate is set at the time of issue and will not change over the life of the bond. Some bonds, however, have "floating" rates that change with market conditions.

proximately equal to its par value. After issue, the market price of the bond can differ significantly from its par value based on changes in market interest rates. We'll have much more to say about the response of bond prices to changes in prevailing interest rates in the next section.

Most bond issues make provisions for the orderly repayment of debt over time. This can be done with either a **sinking fund** or with *serial maturities*. With a sinking fund, the issuer makes regular payments into a fund managed by a trustee. The payments can be in the form of cash or bonds that the company has bought in the marketplace. If the payment is made in cash, the trustee will select the bonds to be retired by lottery and use the cash to redeem the bonds at par. If the bonds are selling in the market for less than par, the issuing company can satisfy the sinking fund requirement by buying its own bonds in the market. A *serial bond* differs from a bond containing a sinking-fund provision in that bondholders know in advance which bonds will be repurchased and when. Both sinking funds and serial maturities allow the issuer to avoid a large final payment known as a *balloon payment*. Because bonds with sinking funds or with serial maturities are less risky, they typically carry lower interest rates than those bonds without any retirement provision.

| A call provision can be valuable to issuers in periods of declining interest rates. | Most corporate bonds contain a **call provision,** which gives the firm the ability to retire an entire issue prior to maturity. The call provision is valuable in periods of declining interest rates because it gives a firm the option of replacing its high-interest debt with less expensive debt. The firm's gain in a refinancing, or *refunding,* comes at the expense of investors who lose a high-yielding bond. Creditors, therefore, require compensation for extending this call privilege. This is done by charging a higher interest rate on callable debt compared to issues that don't have a call option. The company may also be required to pay a **call premium**— some amount greater than par—as a penalty for early retirement. In some cases, the bond may have a *delayed call provision,* meaning that the issue can't be called until it's been outstanding for some period of time. |

Corporate debt comes in many forms. Almost all debt issues of industrial and financial companies are general unsecured obligations. Longer-term unsecured issues are called **debentures**[6]; shorter-term issues are usually referred to as **notes.** The vast majority of secured debt is in the form of *mortgage bonds.* As the name suggests, these bonds are secured by real property and are used frequently by public utilities as a means of raising large amounts of capital. *Collateral trust bonds* resemble mortgage bonds except that the claim is secured by securities held by the firm. Generally, these bonds are issued by holding companies—that is, firms whose main assets consist of the common stock in a number of subsidiaries. Railroads frequently use *equipment trust certificates* to finance new rolling stock. Under this arrangement, a trustee obtains formal ownership of the equipment. The railroad makes a down payment of 10 to 25 percent of the cost, and the balance is provided by a package of trust certificates. Only when the debt has been paid off does the railroad take legal title to the equipment. Finally, there are *subordinated debentures*

---

[6]There are international differences in terminology. In the United Kingdom, for example, the term *debenture* usually refers to a bond that has a prior claim on the firm's assets.

that rank behind *senior debt* with respect to their claim on assets. If a firm defaults, the subordinated claims are only paid off after all of the senior claims are met. Most bonds are senior unless they are specifically labeled as subordinated.

About 25 percent of the corporate debt issued in the United States has a *convertible* feature. This provision gives an investor the option to exchange the bond for a predetermined number of common shares. Investors buy convertibles in the hope that the issuing company's stock price will rise so that the bond can be converted at a profit. Because of the potential for participating in the upside movement of the firm's common stock, convertible issues typically pay lower coupon interest rates than comparable straight-debt issues.

Finally, we should note that corporations can issue either *fixed-* or *floating-rate* bonds. A fixed-rate bond's coupon interest rate is set at the time of issue and does not change over the life of the bond. As we will see shortly, the prices of fixed-rate securities, in general, change in response to changes in market interest rates. With floating-rate debt, the coupon interest rate is changed periodically when some benchmark rate changes. For instance, a particular issue might have a rate that was "pegged" at 2.00 percent above the 10-year Treasury bond rate with the coupon rate changing if the 10-year Treasury bond yield changed. These bonds would have far less price volatility than their fixed-rate counterparts.

Domestic Bonds, Foreign Bonds, and Eurobonds: Some Comparisons

Well-known U.S. firms can issue debt in the domestic markets or raise money overseas. One way of borrowing outside the U.S. market is through the use of *foreign bonds.* When a multinational corporation issues foreign bonds, it functions just like a local firm. The bond is denominated in the local currency, and the terms must conform to local custom and regulation. For American borrowers, the most important markets for foreign bonds have been Switzerland and Japan.

The existence of the Eurobond market allows multinational firms greater flexibility in raising funds globally.

There is also an international market for long-term debt known as the **Eurobond** market. The Eurobond market is not a specific place but a network of international securities dealers who sell and create a global market for these bonds. Although Eurobonds may be sold throughout the world, underwriters and dealers are mainly located in London and include the London branches of U.S., European, and Japanese commercial and investment banks.

Eurobond issues are generally made in currencies that are actively traded, fully convertible into other currencies, and relatively stable. The U.S. dollar is the most popular choice, followed by the Japanese yen, the Deutsche mark, and the British pound sterling. The advent of the euro will result in fewer bonds being issued in the European national currencies and more in the euro. The development of the Eurocurrency market—a Eurocurrency is any currency held outside its country of origin (as distinguished from the euro, which is an actual currency)—means that the currency to be borrowed can be different from the country in which the borrowing takes place. This means that IBM can borrow dollars in both New York and London and that Novartis can borrow Swiss francs in either Zurich or Frankfurt.

There are a number of important differences between the U.S. domestic and the Eurobond markets. First, virtually all bond issues in the United States, whether corporate or government bond issues, pay interest semiannually. In the case of the 8 percent, $1,000 par-value bond we discussed earlier, the issuer would make two semiannual payments of $40 each, thereby allowing the investor to earn interest on interest over the year. The typical practice in any of the Eurocurrency markets is to pay interest annually. Investors must use effective, rather than nominal yields, when comparing yields in markets that differ in terms of how frequently interest is paid.

Second, all bonds issued in the U.S. domestic markets are in *registered form,* which means that the issuing company will record the ownership of the bonds and write checks directly for principal and interest to these registered owners. In contrast, most Eurobonds are issued in *bearer form,* which means that physical possession of the certificate is the primary evidence of ownership. To receive interest payments, the bondholder must detach a coupon from the certificate and send it to the issuing firm to receive payment. Principal payments are received by turning in the bond certificate at maturity. The ownership of bearer bonds can't be traced, so investors can collect interest without reporting it for tax purposes. Needless to say, the IRS takes a dim view of this and has tried to discourage U.S. citizens from purchasing bearer bonds. As we might expect, investors find the nonregistered characteristic attractive and are willing to accept a lower interest rate on bearer bonds than on registered bonds of equivalent risk. Many U.S. multinational corporations with excellent credit ratings have taken advantage of this opportunity to reduce borrowing costs by issuing Eurobonds in bearer form.

> The Eurobond market thrives because it enables issuers and investors to avoid regulation and taxes.

Bond Credit Ratings

> A bond's credit rating tries to capture its relative risk of default.

In the United States, bond issues are rated by investment advisory services according to their relative degree of default risk. The main rating agencies are Moody's and Standard & Poor's.[7] In coming up with their ratings, agencies consider many factors including earnings stability, leverage, interest and fixed-charge coverage, and asset protection. Management's ability to compete within the relevant business sectors is also an important intangible aspect of the rating process.

Exhibit 5-1 summarizes the bond-rating definitions for Moody's and Standard & Poor's (S&P). Bonds can also have a 1, 2, 3 rating with Moody's (e.g., Aa2), with the higher number representing lower credit quality within that category. Standard & Poor's denotes differences within a grade by assigning a plus or minus. Bonds rated *Baa* or better by Moody's, or *BBB* or better by S&P are considered *investment grade.* Because banks and other institutional investors can hold only investment-grade bonds, this rating is important for companies that want to

---

[7]A number of smaller agencies also rate corporate debt. These include Fitch Investors Service, Duff and Phelps, and McCarthy, Crisanti, and Maffei.

EXHIBIT 5-1
Key to Bond Ratings

Moody's Investors Service		Standard & Poor's	
Aaa	Judged to be the best quality with a small degree of risk.	AAA	Highest debt rating assigned. Borrower's capacity to repay is strong.
Aa	High quality; rated lower than Aaa because the margin of protection is not as great.	Aa	Capacity to repay is strong and differs only slightly from the highest quality.
A	Bonds possess favorable investment attributes but may be susceptible to risk in the future.	A	Strong capacity to repay; however, borrower is vulnerable to changes in circumstances and economic conditions.
Baa	Neither highly protected nor poorly secured; adequate repayment capacity.	BBB	Has adequate capacity to repay, but adverse economic conditions or circumstances may lead to risk.
Ba	Judged to have speculative elements.	BB,B,	Regarded on balance as primarily
B	Lacks characteristics of a desirable investment; assurance of repayment small.	CCC, CC,C, D	speculative, BB indicating the lowest and CC the highest risk. C ratings are reserved for bonds on which no interest is being paid, and D ratings
Caa, Ca, C	Poor standing and perhaps in default. Level of danger increases as rating moves from Caa to C.		are bonds in default or with payment in arrears.

broaden the market for their debt. Bonds not considered investment grade are often called **junk,** or **high-yield bonds.**[8]

Bond ratings are assigned at the time of issue and don't change unless the firm's ability to repay improves or deteriorates.[9] Since risk and required returns are related, lower credit ratings translate into higher interest costs for issuing firms. The interest rate differentials or *quality* spread between higher- and lower-rated bonds will also vary with market conditions. For example, in 1982, a recession year that also had high inflation, the spread between Moody's Aaa and Baa bonds was on the order of 2.30 percent. By contrast, 1997 saw low inflation and good economic conditions with Aaa-Baa quality spreads narrowing to 0.60 percent.

---

[8]The term *junk bond* is an unduly pejorative term embracing any corporate bond rated Ba or lower by Moody's, or BB or lower by S&P. Junk bonds, to be sure, carry higher risks than investment grade bonds. However, associating junk bonds with junky companies is unfair and misses the point. Many start-up companies in the early 1980s issued low-rated debt because they couldn't get accommodation from their commercial bank.

[9]Issuers pay the investment advisory services to have their bonds rated as a means of improving their marketability. In a world of asymmetrical information, the reputation of an outside firm can reduce agency costs between the firm and its creditors.

Bond Pricing

Once issued, bonds are traded in a *secondary market* by securities dealers. Prices of bonds traded on the New York Stock Exchange are published weekdays in the *Wall Street Journal*. Exhibit 5-2 contains an excerpt from the "New York Exchange Bonds" section of the *Journal* for September 16, 1998.

The first column shows the issuer (e.g., Bell South) as well as the coupon rate and year of maturity for the issue. Thus, the 8¼ 32 for Bell South has a coupon

EXHIBIT 5-2

New York Exchange Bond Quotations: September 16, 1998

NEW YORK EXCHANGE BONDS

Quotations as of 4 p.m. Eastern Time
Wednesday, September 16, 1998

Volume $17,815,000

SALES SINCE JANUARY 1
(000 omitted)

1998	1997	1996
$2,718,494	$3,861,302	$4,110,855

	Domestic Wed.	Domestic Tue	All Issues Wed.	All Issues Tue.
Issues Traded	233	215	242	224
Advances	122	102	126	107
Declines	73	80	75	82
Unchanged	38	33	41	35
New highs	26	12	26	12
New lows	12	9	12	10

Dow Jones Bond Averages

–1997– High	–1997– Low	–1998– High	–1998– Low		---1998--- Close	---1998--- Chg.	---1998--- %Yld	--1997-- Close	--1997-- Chg.
105.13	101.09	105.82	104.42	20 Bonds	105.71	+0.13	6.69	104.26	+ 0.23
102.89	97.64	103.27	102.02	10 Utilities	103.22	–0.03	6.83	102.16	+ 0.47
107.49	104.54	108.59	106.48	10 Industrials	108.21	+0.30	6.54	106.35	– 0.01

CORPORATION BONDS
Volume, $17,145,000

Bonds	Cur Yld.	Vol.	Close	Net Chg.
AMR 9s16	7.4	35	122	+ 1½
ATT 6s00	6.0	223	100⅜	+ ⅛
ATT 5⅛01	5.2	50	99½	...
ATT 7⅛02	6.8	30	104⅝	– ⅛
ATT 6¾04	6.4	5	106⅛	+ ¼
ATT 7s05	6.5	25	107¼	+ ¼
ATT 7½06	6.8	48	110¼	+ ¼
ATT 8⅛22	7.6	7	107½	– ¼
ATT 8⅝31	7.7	35	112¼	...
Aames 10½02	10.5	50	100	– ¼
AcmeM 12½02	12.9	31	97¼	– 3½
AlldC zr2000	...	60	90⅛	...
AlldC zr03	...	25	74½	+ ½
AlldC zr05	...	165	65¾	+ ¼
AlldC zr07	...	30	59⅞	+ 2⅜
AlldC zr09	...	20	49½	– ⅛
Alza 5s06	cv	16	118	– 2
AForP 5s30	7.1	10	70	...
ARetire 5¾02	cv	50	86	+ 4
Amresco 8¾99	9.0	25	97¼	– ¼
Amresco 10s03	12.7	95	79	– 8
Amresco 10s04	12.7	60	79	– 3
Anhr 8⅝16	8.4	30	102⅝	– ¼
AnnTaylr 8¾00	8.6	50	101½	– ½
Argosy 12s01	cv	55	92	...
Argosy 13¼04	12.7	32	104½	+ 1
BkrHgh zr08	...	21	67⅜	+ ⅜
BellsoT 6¼03	6.0	36	104	+ ⅜
BellsoT 5⅞09	5.7	74	102⅝	– ¼
BellsoT 8¼32	7.4	10	110⅞	+ ⅛
BellsoT 7⅞32	7.4	85	106⅞	– ⅛
BellsoT 7½33	7.0	40	107⅜	+ ⅛
BellsoT 6¾33	6.6	62	101¾	+ 1⅛
BstBuy 8⅝00	8.4	40	102 11/32	– 1/32
BethSt 8⅜01	8.4	7	99⅝	– ⅜
BethSt 8.45s05	8.5	92	99⅝	+ ¼
Bevrly 9s06	9.1	243	99	+ ½
Bordn 8⅜16	8.4	4	100⅛	– ¾
BosCelts 6s38	10.1	83	59⅝	+ ¼
BoydGm 9¼03	9.2	55	100¾	+ 1½
BrnGp 9½06	9.1	5	104½	...
CalEgy 10¼04	9.7	135	106	+ ½
CaterpInc 9s06	7.7	9	116¼	– ⅜
ChaseM 8s99	8.0	10	100½	– ½
ChaseM 6¾08	6.6	25	102⅛	+ ⅛
ChaseM 6⅛08	6.1	85	100¾	+ ½
ChespkE 9⅛06	10.2	5	89⅜	+ 6⅝
ChryF 13¼99	12.5	75	106¼	– ¾
Clardge 11¾02f	...	2	79½	...
ClrkOil 9½04	9.4	30	101½	+ ¾
ClevEl 8⅜11	8.2	50	102¼	...
CoeurDA 7¼05	11.5	65	63	...
Coeur 6⅜04	cv	17	65½	– ¼
CmwE 8s03	7.9	20	101⅝	+ ¼
CmwE 7⅝03F	7.5	10	101¼	+ ¼
CmwE 7⅝03J	7.6	4	100⅝	– ½
CmwE 8⅛07J	8.0	26	102⅛	...
CompUSA 9½00	9.4	10	101⅜	– ¼
CompMgt 8s03	cv	39	26	– 3
CompMgt 8s03	cv	39	24	– 3½
Convrse 7s04	cv	24	47⅜	– ⅝
DR Hrtn 10s06	9.7	30	103	+ ½
Dole 7s03	6.8	5	103⅛	...
Dow 6.85s13	6.5	35	105¾	+ ¼
DukeEn 5⅞01	5.7	37	102½	+ ¾
DukeEn 6¼04	6.2	10	101⅝	+ 1¼
DukeEn 7s05	6.6	205	106⅜	– ⅛
DukeEn 7⅞24	7.6	40	103⅜	+ ¼
DukeEn 6¾25	6.8	5	99¾	+ ⅛
DukeEn 7s33	6.9	17	102⅛	+ ⅝

interest rate of 8¼ percent and matures in the year 2032. The second column gives the bond's **current yield.** The current yield is simply the coupon interest rate divided by the latest market price of the bond. With a price of 110.875 and a coupon rate of 8¼ percent, Bell South's bond's current yield is 8¼ divided by 110.875 or 7.44 percent. The third column gives the trading volume in thousands of dollars. The last two columns give the closing price of the bond along with the change in price from the previous day. Bonds are quoted as a percentage of face value. Each percentage of face is called a *point*. Thus, Bell South's 8¼ coupon bonds closed at $110.875 per $100 of face, up ⅛ point, or $.125 from the previous trading day's closing price.

> A bond's value is the present value of its cash flows discounted at the holder's required rate of return.

The price or value of a bond is just the present value of the coupon interest payments plus the face value at maturity:

$$P = \frac{C}{(1 + k_d)} + \frac{C}{(1 + k_d)^2} + \cdots + \frac{C}{(1 + k_d)^N} + \frac{M}{(1 + k_d)^N} \qquad [5\text{-}1]$$

where P is the price (or value) of the bond, C the periodic interest payments in dollars, N the number of years to maturity, M the maturity (par) value of the bond, and k_d the required rate of return. Traders refer to a bond's required rate of return as its yield to maturity (YTM).

> The bondholder's required rate of return is known as the yield to maturity (YTM).

To illustrate the mechanics of bond pricing, let's consider the AT&T bond with a 7 percent coupon maturing in 2005 listed in Exhibit 5-2. If interest were paid annually and the bond had a face value of $1,000, an investor buying these bonds would receive a seven-year annuity of $70 a year (0.07 times the $1,000 face) plus the $1,000 at the end of 2005. To calculate the bond's market value, we need to determine its yield to maturity. For computational purposes, let's assume that investors can get a 7.5 percent return on bonds of equivalent risk. Using a 7.5 percent rate for discounting the coupon interest payments plus principal at maturity, the present value of the bond's cash flows is presented in Exhibit 5-3.

If 7.5 percent is the correct rate of return required by investors who hold the bond, then the price of the AT&T bond should be $973.56. In the jargon of Wall Street, AT&T's bond has been *priced to yield 7.5 percent to maturity.* This yield is not the same as the current yield discussed earlier. The current yield only captures

EXHIBIT 5-3
Valuation of ATT 7 2005
Assuming a 7.5 Percent Yield to Maturity

Period	Cash Flows	Present Value Factor @ 7.5%	Present Value
1–7	$70	5.2966	$370.76
7	$1,000	.6028	602.80
		Value of Bond =	$973.56

the interest income portion of the return, but the YTM incorporates both interest income plus any capital gains or losses. In the case of the AT&T bond, an investor holding until maturity not only gets interest income but would also see a gain of $26.44 by purchasing the bond today at $973.56 and having it retired seven years later at $1,000 face.

Bond YTMs, Coupon Interest Rates, and Bond Prices

Bonds trading below face are said to be selling at a discount; those trading above face are selling at a premium.

The AT&T bond example illustrates an important aspect of bond pricing; namely, that if the coupon interest rate is below the yield to maturity, a bond will sell at less than its face value. In our illustration, the AT&T bond is said to be selling at a 2.64 percent *discount* from face. Alternately, as Exhibit 5-4 indicates, if the yield to maturity on the AT&T bond is less than its coupon interest rate, the bond will sell at a *premium* from its face. A bond will *only* sell at face if its coupon rate and yield to maturity are the same.

These results should come as no surprise. Equation [5-1] indicates that as k_d increases, bond prices decline. Conversely, a fall in interest rates will lead to a rise in prices. The rationale for these price movements goes something like this: If a bond were priced at face, it would yield exactly the coupon rate of 7 percent. But if market interest rates were to rise above 7 percent to, say, 8 percent, investors in the secondary markets will not want to pay full price for bonds yielding 7 percent when they can buy new ones paying 8 percent. They'll only be interested in buying existing bonds if they can earn a return comparable to that available on new issues. Because the coupon payments and the face value are fixed at the time of issue, the only way to increase the bond's yield to maturity is for the price to decline below face value. In this way, the lower coupon rate will be offset by the capital gain when the bond is redeemed at face. Similarly, a decrease in the required yield will lead to a rise in market price. In this case, the higher coupon rate will be offset by the capital loss.

Prices and interest rates are inversely related.

The point is that bond prices—*and, indeed, security prices in general*—fluctuate inversely with market interest rates. After all, a bond's yield to maturity represents little more than the "going" market interest rate for bonds of similar risk, and we'd expect the prices of these fixed-income securities to change in response

EXHIBIT 5-4
Valuation of ATT 7 2005
Assuming a 6.5 Percent Yield to Maturity

Period	Cash Flows	Present Value Factor @ 6.5%	Present Value
1–7	$70	5.4845	$383.92
7	$1,000	.6435	643.50
		Value of Bond =	$1,027.42

to changes in market conditions. Beyond the inverse relationship between its price and YTM, a bond's price sensitivity to changes in market interest rates is related to both its maturity and coupon rate. Let's look at both of these aspects.

First, the prices of long-term bonds are more sensitive to changes in YTMs than are shorter-term bonds. To clarify this, suppose that we have two 8 percent coupon bonds issued by the same firm. One bond has a maturity of 10 years, the other matures in 20 years. For simplicity, let's assume that the YTM of both bonds is also 8 percent, so the bonds should be trading at par.

Exhibit 5-5 summarizes what would happen to the price of each bond should the YTM (1) drop to 6 percent or (2) rise to 10 percent. Note that with a decline in market rates, the price of the 10-year bond goes from $1,000.00 to $1,147.20—an increase of 14.7 percent. With a similar decline in market rates, the price of the 20-year bond increased by 22.9 percent. Conversely, an increase in YTM from 8 to 10 percent results in a smaller percentage decline in price for the 10-year bond.

Our example suggests that investors who anticipate *increases* in market rates should *shorten* the maturity of their bond portfolios in order to minimize the impact of price declines. Conversely, the maturities of bond portfolios should be lengthened if you expect a decline in rates. Further, the prices of high-coupon bonds are *less* sensitive to a given change in YTM than lower-coupon bonds. Suppose, for example, that a firm had two bond issues outstanding; one with a 6 percent coupon rate, the other with an 8 percent coupon. The 8 percent bond is newly issued, and the 6 percent bond was issued 10 years ago when market rates were lower. If the maturities of these bonds were identical, their YTMs should be approximately the same. Under these conditions, the price change of the 6 percent coupon bond—in percentage terms—would be greater than the 8 percent bond for a given change in YTM.[10]

> **Long-term bond prices are more sensitive to changes in interest rates than are shorter-term bonds.**

EXHIBIT 5-5
Prices of 10- and 20-Year Bonds
8 Percent Coupon
$1,000 Face
Interest Paid Annually

YTM	10-Year Bond	20-Year Bonds
6 Percent	$1,147.20	$1,229.40
8 Percent	$1,000.00	$1,000.00
10 Percent	$877.11	$829.73

---

[10]Compared to lower-coupon bonds, higher-coupon bonds derive a greater proportion of their value from the stream-of-interest payments. In contrast, a greater proportion of the value of lower-coupon bonds is tied up in the return of principal. The reason for the increased price sensitivity of the lower-coupon bonds is that small changes in interest rates can have a relatively large effect on the value of the more distant return of principal.

Finally, it may be important for a company to know the YTM on its existing debt because this yield provides the firm with information on what it could offer investors on new debt issues. For example, on September 16, 1998, the AT&T 7 percent bonds traded at $1,072.50 per $1,000 face. Although the current yield on this issue is 6.5 percent (70/1072.50), an investor who bought the AT&T bond today at the current market price and holds it to maturity would see a *capital loss* of $72.50. Clearly, the investor's total return would be less than the 6.5 percent current yield.

According to Equation [5-1], a bond's YTM is simply the discount rate that equates the present value of the coupon interest payments plus principal at maturity with the bond's current price. Financial calculators that have a variety of bond-pricing functions are the simplest way to compute the YTM.[11] In the absence of this "technology," Equation [5-2] can be used to approximate a bond's YTM:

> The yield to maturity is the discount rate that equates the present value of a bond's interest and principal payments with its price.

$$YTM = \frac{[C + (M - P)/N]}{(M + P)/2} \qquad [5\text{-}2]$$

where C is the annual interest payments (in dollars), M the maturity (face) value of the bond, P the current market price of the bond, and N the number of years to maturity. The numerator of Equation [5-2] is the average annual dollar return per year—both interest income and average gain or loss per year—over the life of the bond, and the denominator is a simple average of purchase and maturity price, representing the investor's average investment in the bond over its expected life. In the case of the ATT 7s, the estimated YTM would be

$$YTM = \frac{[\$70.00 + (\$1,000 - \$1072.50)/7]}{(\$1,000 + \$1,072.50)/2}$$

$$= 0.0576 \text{ or } 5.76 \text{ percent}$$

This is very close to the 5.71 percent YTM we'd get using a financial calculator. Regardless of the computational procedure, the results tell us that if AT&T wanted to raise funds through a new debt issue with a 7-year maturity, it would have to provide a coupon rate of about 5¾ percent in order for the issue to be sold at close to face.

Semiannual Interest Payments

In calculating the value of the ATT 7 2005 bonds earlier, we assumed that interest was paid annually. Although Eurobonds typically pay interest annually, most bonds in the U.S. market pay interest every six months. Thus, instead of receiving interest of $70 annually for seven years, the holder of the AT&T bond would receive $35.00 every six months for 14 "periods," plus principal at maturity. We

---

[11]Appendix A at the end of the book on page 537 indicates how to compute a bond's YTM using the Texas Instruments BAII Plus financial calculator.

EXHIBIT 5-6
Valuation of ATT 7 2005
Assuming Semiannual Interest Payments

Period	Cash Flows	Present Value Factor @ 3.75%	Present Value
1–14	$35.00	10.7396	$375.89
14	$1,000	.5973	597.30
		Value of Bond =	$973.19

also assumed that the 7½ percent rate of return in Exhibit 5-3 was an annual compound rate; however, where interest is paid semiannually, the required return would be 3.75 percent every six months.

A sample calculation of the value of the ATT 7 2005 with semiannual payments is presented in Exhibit 5-6. The value of 973.19 is slightly lower than the value of $973.56 we got in Exhibit 5-3 with annual payments. The $.37 difference occurs because a 3.75 percent required return every six months represents a higher effective rate than 7½ percent annually, thereby discounting the $1,000 maturity value more heavily.

5.3   CHARACTERISTICS AND PRICING OF PREFERRED STOCK

A preferred stock issue's dividend rate and par value determine dividends per share.

Preferred stock is a hybrid security with characteristics of both debt and common stock. Preferred stock dividends are similar to interest payments in that they are generally fixed in amount and must be paid before common stockholders can receive any dividends. However, interest on debt (both short and long term) must be paid before preferred stockholders can receive anything; therefore, creditors look at preferred stock as equity. Further, if the preferred dividend is not earned, the firm's directors can choose to omit it without throwing the firm into bankruptcy. In contrast, not paying interest on borrowed money is an act of default. If the company goes bankrupt, preferred stock has priority over common stock in terms of claim on assets in liquidation. Once creditors have been paid in full, any money left over from the sale of assets can be used to settle preferred stockholder claims.

Features of Preferred Stock Issues

Preferred stock has a number of distinguishing features common to virtually all issues. We'll review these features with the help of Exhibit 5-7, which presents the preferred stock section of DuPont's (DD[12]) balance sheet as of December 31,

---

[12]DuPont stock is traded on the New York Stock Exchange. DD is the firm's trading or ticker symbol.

EXHIBIT 5-7
Preferred Stock of DuPont de Nemours & Company
December 31, 1997

Cumulative Preferred Stock, without Par Value—23 million shares authorized
Issued at December 31:

$4.50 Series—1,672,594 shares issued (callable at $120)
Aggregate Book Value $167,259,400

$3.50 Series—700,000 shares issued (callable at $102)
Aggregate Book Value $70,000,000

Source: DuPont de Nemours & Company, *1997 Annual Report.* Extracted from company's web site.

1997. Unlike bonds, which always have a par value, preferred stock may be is-sued with or without a par value. If an issue does not have a par value, the divi-dend rate is set in terms of dollars per share. When a preferred stock has a par value, it's frequently the initial offering price. For issues with a par value, the div-idend *rate* and the **par value** determine the dividends per share. For example, a preferred issue with a $50 par value and a 3.60 percent dividend rate would pay annual dividends of $1.80 a share. Since DD's preferred stock issues have no par value, there's a need to indicate the dividends per share for each issue.

> Unpaid preferred dividends are car-ried forward from year to year.

Virtually all preferred stock issues contain a cumulative feature. If the firm's board of directors skips its normal dividend, these unpaid dividends are carried forward from year to year. Until this obligation is cleaned up, the company can-not pay any dividends on common stock. For instance, suppose that DD skipped dividends for two years on the $4.50 preferred stock issue. Before it could legally pay any common stock dividends, it would have to pay preferred stockholders $9.00 a share for each share held. In the absence of a cumulative feature, the firm could pay large irregular dividends to common stockholders while paying no pre-ferred dividends.[13]

Under normal conditions, preferred stockholders don't enjoy voting rights unless the firm violates the provisions of the agreement with them. For example, the New York Stock Exchange only lists preferred stock issues that provide con-tingent voting rights after the firm has skipped the equivalent of six quarterly div-idend payments. In such an event, the preferred stockholders may have the right to elect one-third of the members of the board of directors.

Although preferred stock has no fixed maturity date, firms generally make provisions for its retirement. As with most bond issues, almost all preferred stock issues have a call provision giving the company the right to buy back the issue at a price specified when it first came to market. For instance, DuPont has the op-tion of redeeming its $3.50 series issue at $102 a share. This option is valuable in a declining interest rate environment because it allows the issuing company to replace an existing issue with a less expensive one. Some preferred stock issues

---

[13]From an agency perspective, the cumulative feature represents a contractual mechanism used to resolve potential conflicts of interest between preferred and common stockholders.

also have a sinking fund requiring the company to set aside money to retire a certain number of shares annually.

Finally, we should note that unlike interest payments on debt, preferred and common stock dividends are not deductible as expenses for tax purposes. However, dividends received from domestic corporations are 70 percent tax free to corporate investors, whereas interest income is fully taxed. Therefore, an insurance company receiving a dividend of $100 would only be required to pay taxes on $30. If the insurance company were in the 35 percent tax bracket, the taxes on the $100 dividend would be just $10.50 ($30 times the 35 percent tax rate). Because of this tax advantage, most preferred stock issues are held by corporations; these same companies tend to avoid debt securities on which interest income is fully taxable.

Valuation of Preferred Stock

The value of a share of preferred stock is the present value of its stream of dividends plus the redemption price, if callable, discounted at the holder's required rate of return.

The market value of a share of preferred stock is the present value of the promised dividend payments plus the redemption price if the issue is called or retired. In mathematical terms, the value of a share of preferred stock is given by

$$P = \frac{D}{(1 + k_p)} + \frac{D}{(1 + k_p)^2} + \cdots + \frac{D}{(1 + k_p)^N} + \frac{M}{(1 + k_p)^N} \qquad [5\text{-}3]$$

where P is the value of a share of preferred stock, D the stated dividend per share of preferred stock, k_p the required rate of return on preferred stock, and M the issue's per-share redemption value in year N.

Since the preferred stock of a firm is riskier than its bonds, you'd think that the required rate of return (k_p) on preferred stock would invariably be higher than the yield to maturity on a company's bonds. However, this is not always the case. Because of the tax advantage of preferred stock to corporate investors, the required rate of return on preferred stock is often lower than bond yields, particularly for those companies whose preferred stock is considered safe.

If there is no maturity date, preferred stock dividends can be treated as a perpetuity and Equation [5-3] will reduce to

$$P = \frac{D}{k_p} \qquad [5\text{-}3a]$$

Illustration

Equation [5-3a] has some applications from the standpoint of both investors and issuing corporations. For instance, suppose that an investor is considering the purchase of a preferred stock that is expected to pay $5 a year in perpetuity. If the investor has assigned a required return of 10 percent to the issue, the maximum amount he/she should be willing to pay for a share would be

$$P = \frac{D}{k_p} = \frac{\$5}{0.10} = \$50$$

From the perspective of the issuing firm, Equation [5-3a] can also be used to "design" new security issues. To illustrate, on September 16, 1998, DuPont's $4.50 series preferred stock finished the trading day on the New York Stock Exchange at $90.00 a share. Using Equation [5-3a], we can estimate the required return on DuPont's preferred stock as follows:

$$\$90.00 = \frac{\$4.50}{k_p}$$

or

$$k_p = \frac{\$4.50}{\$90.00} = 0.050 \text{ or } 5.0 \text{ percent}$$

The calculated required rate of return suggests that if DuPont planned on issuing a new preferred stock issue soon, the combination of offering price and dividend would have to produce a yield of 5.0 percent. After all, investors wouldn't buy a new DuPont issue that was priced to yield *less than* 5.0 percent because they can get this return by purchasing an existing issue. Therefore, if DuPont wanted to come out with a new issue priced at $50 a share, the dividend would have to be set at $50.00 × 0.050 = $2.50 a share.

Floating-rate preferred is less volatile than fixed-rate preferred.

Compared to bonds, preferred stock issues have greater price volatility with changes in market interest rates. This should come as no surprise; preferred stock is conceptually similar to bonds with very long maturities. During the volatile interest-rate environment of the early 1980s, a number of U.S. companies began issuing *floating-rate preferreds*. Unlike the "plain vanilla" preferreds with fixed dividends, the returns on these securities changed with short-term interest rates. The prices of these securities tend to be less volatile than fixed-rate issues, making them attractive havens for excess corporate cash.

5.4 CHARACTERISTICS AND PRICING OF COMMON STOCK

The common stockholders of a corporation are its owners. They are *residual claimholders* who get what's left over from income and assets once the demands of creditors and preferred stockholders are satisfied. If the company does well, this residual income can be substantial; on the other hand, if the firm does poorly, stockholders are the chief losers. Because of limited liability, however, shareholder losses can be no more than their initial investment.

The Accounting for Common Stock

The common equity section of a firm's balance sheet is sometimes confusing to the nonaccountant. To make sure that we have a working understanding of terminology, let's take a look at Exhibit 5-8, which shows an abbreviated version of Coca-Cola's (KO[14]) equity section as of year-end 1997. The exhibit indicates that KO had issued about 3.443 billion shares of common stock out of a possible 5.6 billion authorized by its shareholders. Authorized shares are the maximum amount that Coke can issue without amending its charter. Although amending a corporate charter isn't difficult, it requires the approval of stockholders and that takes time. Therefore, management generally likes the flexibility of having a certain amount of shares authorized but not issued. When these authorized shares are sold, they become issued stock. Outstanding stock is the number of shares actually held by the public; the firm can buy back part of its issued stock and hold it in the form of Treasury stock. The 972,812,721 difference between issued and outstanding shares for KO is due to the effects of stock repurchases over time. The $11.582 billion entry for Treasury stock in Exhibit 5-8 reflects the dollar cost of these repurchases.

> Treasury stock is issued stock that has been repurchased.

    A share of common stock can be authorized with or without par value. In the case of Coke, the par value is $.25 a share. Par value has little (if any) economic significance aside from the fact that a purchaser who paid less than par value would be liable for the difference between par value and the price paid. For this reason, the par value of most common stocks is set fairly low relative to market value.

    The difference between the price at which new stock is issued and par value is entered on the balance sheet in an account called *capital in excess of par* or something similar. KO has chosen to use the description *capital surplus* on its balance sheet. The $1,527,000,000 entry means that KO has sold stock to the public at

EXHIBIT 5-8
Shareholders' Equity for Coca-Cola
December 31, 1997
(in million $ except share data)

Common Stock $.25 Par Value	$ 861
Capital Surplus	1,527
Reinvested Earnings	17,869
Adjustments	(1,364)
Treasury Stock at Cost	(11,582)
Total Shareholders' Equity	$7,311
Shares Authorized	5,600,000,000
Shares Issued	3,443,441,902
Shares Outstanding	2,470,629,181

Source: The Coca-Cola Company, *1997 Annual Report*, p. 45.

---

[14]Coca-Cola common stock is traded on the New York Stock Exchange. KO is the firm's trading or ticker symbol.

prices well in excess of its par value. If KO were to sell an additional 10 million shares at $75 a share, the common stock account would increase by $2.5 million (the $.25 par value times the 10 million new shares), and the capital surplus account would rise by $747.5 million—the difference between the $750 million raised and the $2.5 million par value.

The most important component of the common equity section for KO (and for most profitable businesses that have been around for ages) is *reinvested* or *retained earnings*. Reinvested earnings are not equivalent to cash! This category sits on the liability and equity side of a firm's balance sheet and represents the accounting earnings of the company, from the time of incorporation to the present, that have not been paid out in dividends.

Some financial analysts pay attention to a firm's **book value per share**, which is simply the total shareholder's equity divided by the number of shares outstanding. For KO, the book value per share at the end of the year was about $2.96 a share, compared to a year-end market price of $66.66 a share. A gap between book and market value isn't unusual; book value is an accounting measure based on an accumulation of what the firm has done in the past. *At best,* book value might reflect the stock's value if all of the assets could be liquidated at book value, creditors paid off, and the rest given to stockholders on a pro rata basis. Market values reflect expectations of the firm as an ongoing entity. Having book values higher than common stock prices isn't exactly a vote of confidence for management and may suggest that the market believes that the firm's value in liquidation would be greater than its value as an ongoing business.

> The book value per share of a firm's common stock reflects its past history; market values measure investor expectations.

Return on Investment in Common Stock

> Shareholders get direct returns from dividends and stock price appreciation.

When investors buy common stock, their return comes from two sources: (1) dividends over some investment horizon, and (2) possible share price appreciation. If the current price of the stock was P_0, the price expected at the end of the year was P_1, and the dividends expected over the coming year were D_1, then an investor's expected rate of return would be

$$\text{Expected Return} = \frac{D_1 + P_1 - P_0}{P_0} \qquad [5\text{-}4]$$

Let's see how Equation [5-4] might work for KO. At the end of 1997, Coke's common stock was selling at $66.66 a share ($P_0 = \$66.66$). Let's assume that you believe that KO will pay a $.60 cash dividend during 1998 ($D_1 = \$.60$), and will sell for $80.00 by the end of 1998. Based on these expectations, the anticipated return on Coke stock for 1998 would be

$$\frac{\$.60 + (\$80.00 - \$66.66)}{\$66.66} = 0.209 \text{ or } 20.9 \text{ percent}$$

If your required return for KO was 16 percent, you should buy the common stock at $66.66. Why? Recall that the required return reflects what investors can expect to earn on assets of equivalent risk. As such, it represents the *minimum acceptable* rate of return on an investment. Logic suggests that we should go ahead with *any* investment as long as the *expected* return *exceeds* the **required return.** This basic investment principle should hold regardless of what type of asset we are thinking about acquiring.

Alternatively, we could *value* what we believe KO stock is worth today using the following:

$$P_0 = \frac{D_1 + P_1}{(1 + k_e)}$$ [5-5]

where k_e is the required rate of return.

> The value of a share today is based on its expected price next year, the expected dividend over the coming year, and the required return.

Equation [5-5] is consistent with the idea that the value of any asset is the present value of future cash flows discounted at some appropriate opportunity cost of money. Given our forecast for dividends (D_1 = $.60), the future stock price (P_1 = $80.00), and the required return (k_e = 16%), the value we should assign to a share of KO's common stock would be

$$P_0 = \frac{\$.60 + \$80.00}{1.16} = \$69.48$$

Given a current market price of $66.66 a share, KO's common stock would appear to be "undervalued" and should be purchased. This is essentially the same decision we reached when we compared our expected return to our required return.

This simple example points up the distinction between price and value that we talked about at the beginning of the chapter. Based on our forecast of dividends and stock price one year from now, we came up with a *value* of $69.48 a share. With a current *price* of $66.66, the market disagrees with this assessment. The difference of opinion could be due to any combination of a (1) lower expected dividend (Coke paid $.56 a share in 1997), or (2) lower forecasted stock price in one year, or perhaps (3) the market assigned a higher-than-justified required rate of return. Who is right? Probably neither, but that's not the point. If we really believe in our forecasts, we should buy Coke stock today at $66.66 and hope that over the next year the market will see the "error" of *its* ways and bid up the price of the stock accordingly. In a real sense, we are relying on *market efficiency* over the next year to correct what we believe is mispricing today.

Valuation of Common Stock: The Dividend Discount Model

Through Equation [5-5], we can explain the value of a share of common stock today in terms of the expected dividend over the next year (D_1), the expected price next year (P_1), and the required rate of return (k_e). However, this formula begs the question as to what will determine next year's stock price. In fact, if our valuation formula—Equation [5-5]—holds today, then it should serve as a basis for valuing the stock in one year as well:

$$P_1 = \frac{D_2 + P_2}{(1 + k_e)} \qquad\qquad [5\text{-}5a]$$

What Equation [5-5a] is telling us is that any investor looking to buy the stock next year will be looking for dividends during year 2 and the stock price at the end of year 2. By substituting Equation [5-5a] into [5-5], we can express stock values today in terms of D_1, D_2, and P_2.

$$P_0 = \frac{D_1}{(1 + k_e)} + \frac{D_2}{(1 + k_e)^2} + \frac{P_2}{(1 + k_e)^2} \qquad\qquad [5\text{-}5b]$$

You'll probably not be shocked to know that we could go on to replace P_2 by $(D_3 + P_3)/(1 + k_e)$, which would result in relating the value of the stock today to forecasted dividends for three years plus the forecasted price at the end of three years. In fact, if we look out into the indefinite future—common stock, after all, has no maturity—then we will end up with the following general stock valuation model:

$$P_0 = \frac{D_1}{(1 + k_e)} + \frac{D_2}{(1 + k_e)^2} + \cdots + \frac{D_N}{(1 + k_e)^N} + \cdots \qquad [5\text{-}6]$$

Cash distributions are the foundation of common stock valuation.

Equation [5-6] suggests that dividends or, more accurately, cash distributions should be the foundation of common stock valuation. These distributions can be in the form of periodic cash dividends, a liquidating dividend if the firm is sold, or cash if the company repurchases some of its own stock. Although the return to an individual investor may consist of dividends plus a final selling price, the returns to investors *in the aggregate* are comprised solely of cash distributions. Equation [5-6] is, therefore, consistent with the idea that the value of any asset is the present value of the future cash flows generated by that asset.

One implication of Equation [5-6] is that a stock that is never expected to pay a dividend or some other form of cash distribution is worthless. The logical question to ask is why do the stocks of firms like Microsoft that pay no dividends have positive, and often very high, values. Actually, there is no contradiction once we recognize that the current price of the stock is based on future expected dividends. The *ultimate expectation* is that the company will eventually pay dividends and that future investors will receive a cash return on their investment. In the short run, investors are content with the belief that the company is reinvesting earnings in assets that will enhance its future earning power and ultimate dividends. If this is done, they will be able to sell their stock because there'll be a good market for it.

The constant dividend growth model assumes steady increases in dividends into the indefinite future.

Constant Dividend Growth Model

From a management perspective, Equation [5-6] tells us that the value of a share of common stock in a rational market is based on the ability of the firm to generate and distribute cash to its shareholders. This is an important insight: It

suggests that managers should be more concerned with the cash-flow characteristics of the firm's investment and financing decisions than with their accounting
consequences.

We can develop a simplified version of Equation [5-6] by assuming that
dividends will be growing at some constant rate g; that is, $D_2 = D_1(1 + g)$,
$D_3 = D_1(1 + g)^2$, etc. Substituting these relationships in Equation [5-6], we get

$$P_0 = \frac{D_1}{(1 + k_e)} + \frac{D_1(1 + g)}{(1 + k_e)^2} + \frac{D_1(1 + g)^2}{(1 + k_e)^3} + \cdots \qquad [5\text{-}7]$$

As we saw in Chapter 4, Equation [5-7] is a growing perpetuity in which one term
differs from the next by a factor of $(1 + g)/(1 + k_e)$. If $k_e > g$, then the series reduces to:[15]

$$P_0 = \frac{D_1}{(k_e - g)} \qquad [5\text{-}8]$$

Equation [5-8] is known as the **constant dividend growth model.** The critical
assumption in this valuation model is that dividends per share will grow at some
constant compound annual rate into the indefinite future. While this assumption
isn't true for all companies, it's actually a pretty good approximation of the dividend growth patterns for electric utilities and consumer products firms. To illustrate the use of Equation [5-8], suppose that the A&G company's dividends per
share are expected to be $4.00 a share next year and that the market expects these
dividends to grow at a 6 percent compound annual rate into the indefinite future.
If the required rate of return on A&G's common stock were 14 percent, its expected market value would be

$$P_0 = \frac{D_1}{(k_e - g)} = \frac{\$4.00}{(.14 - .06)} = \$50.00$$

The constant dividend growth model has been around for a long time and is
widely used by security analysts to identify over- and undervalued common
stocks. It also has a number of important applications to corporate finance. First,
Equation [5-8] can be rearranged as follows:

$$k_e = \frac{D_1}{P_0} + g \qquad [5\text{-}9]$$

This relationship allows managers of firms whose dividend growth is "well-
behaved" to estimate their shareholders' required return based on the current
market price of the common stock (P_0), the near-term dividend (D_1), and the es-

---

[15]The formula for the constant dividend growth model was first developed by Williams (1938)
and later rediscovered by Gordon and Shapiro (1956). This model is an interesting example of
some very old "technology" kept alive by solid applications.

timated dividend growth rate. For instance, in mid-September of 1998, Procter & Gamble's (PG[16]) common stock was selling for about $66 a share and had a current dividend (D_0) of $1.14. Over the past ten years, dividends had grown by an average of 13 percent a year, and this growth was expected to continue into the indefinite future. On this basis, PG's required return would be

$$k_e = \frac{D_1}{P_0} + g = \frac{D_0(1 + g)}{P_0} + g = \frac{\$1.14(1.13)}{\$66} + 0.13$$

$$= 0.020 + 0.13 = 0.150 \text{ or } 15 \text{ percent}$$

The *P/E* multiple represents what investors are willing to pay for a dollar of reported earnings.

Second, Equation [5-8] can give us some understanding of the things that influence a firm's price-earnings multiple (or ratio)—a number that investment analysts typically pay a good bit of attention to. The **P/E multiple** is defined as the ratio of today's stock price to the firm's earnings per share (EPS) and says something about what the market is willing to pay for a dollar of reported accounting earnings. Financial analysts use the anticipated earnings per share in calculating the P/E multiple; however, the financial press, for example, the *Wall Street Journal,* generally uses the most recent earnings. If we divide both sides of Equation [5-8] by E_1, we get

$$P_0/E_1 = \frac{D_1/E_1}{(k_e - g)} \qquad [5\text{-}10]$$

Equation [5-10] tells us that a firm's *P/E* multiple is related to its: (1) *dividend payout ratio,* that is, the proportion of earnings paid out in dividends, (2) required rate of return, which reflects investors' perceptions of the firm's risk, and (3) expected growth in earnings and dividends. Studies have shown that investors' growth expectations are perhaps the most important determinant of price-earnings multiples.

Should a firm celebrate if it has a high *P/E* multiple? The answer depends on why the *P/E* is so high. According to Equation [5-10], a high *P/E* can be due to low current earnings, which would generally be bad, or to a high payout ratio, which could be good (if it indicates that the company is generating lots of cash), bad (if it is due to a lack of good investment opportunities), or neutral (if it is caused by a firm's raising outside capital instead of using retained earnings). In most instances, high *P/E*s are associated with high expected growth in earnings or a low required return on equity capital. Either of these would be a good sign.

P/E multiples are heavily influenced by investor growth expectations.

These factors, in turn, are influenced by a company's investment prospects and their associated risks and rewards. Firms having good investment opportunities are likely to retain a greater proportion of their earnings. The combination of high retentions and high returns on these retentions will tend to produce high growth in earnings per share. This growth in earnings will make a firm's stock very attractive. The high *P/E*s of technology-based companies such as Dell Computer and

---

[16]PG is the ticker symbol for Procter & Gamble. The firm's shares trade on the New York Stock Exchange.

Microsoft, and pharmaceutical firms like Warner-Lambert and Pfizer are due, in large measure, to the market's belief that these companies can deliver high growth in earnings into the foreseeable future.

But market expectations can change quickly. For instance, through July 1998, Coca-Cola (KO) had a *P/E* of close to 60—a very high multiple for a consumer products company. The high multiple reflected investor optimism about the company's ability to grow sales, earnings, and dividends in a highly competitive global soft-drink market. This optimism went up in smoke with a weaker-than-expected second quarter earnings report, which saw KO's stock plummet from $88.00 a share at the end of June to under $60 a share in early October.

Growth Strategies and Wealth Creation

In Chapter 1, we suggested that growth in profits or earnings per share may not necessarily result in an increase in share price. To see the conditions under which growth can be value creating, let's think about the price of a share of common stock in terms of the following equation:

$$P_0 = \frac{E_1}{k_e} + PVGO \qquad [5\text{-}11]$$

The present value of growth opportunities (PVGO) is the value created by future investment opportunities.

Equation [5-11] can be interpreted as follows: the first term represents the value of a no-growth firm that pays out all of its earnings, E_1, in dividends. It is essentially the value of the assets in place. The second term is the increase in value that arises from *reinvesting* earnings in the firm's operations to support future growth. The finance literature refers to this as the **present value of growth opportunities (PVGO)**;[17] it is a significant component of value for many high-technology companies with strong growth prospects.

Illustration
The initial public offering of Netscape, the Internet software firm, is a good example of what the PVGO means to a technologically driven company. In August 1995, Netscape sold 5 million shares at $28 a share, thereby making the value of the shares *before* the start of trading *$1.4 billion!* Netscape opened trading at $72 a share, went to $72¾, and eventually closed the first day of trading at about $58 a share. All this for a company in which *revenues* for the first half of 1995 were less than $20 million and which was not expected to earn a profit for two years. Clearly, the aggregate stock value of *$2.9 billion* at the close of Netscape's first day of trading was being driven by investor expectations of future growth.

---

[17]The present value of growth opportunities was first identified by Myers (1977).

A firm's growth depends on the proportion of earnings plowed back in the business and the amount that the firm can earn on reinvested funds. Mathematically, earnings growth is linked to the reinvestment rate by the following equation:

$$g = (1 - b)r^* \qquad\qquad [5\text{-}12]$$

where r^* is the rate of return on new investments, and b the proportion of earnings paid out in dividends. If a company reinvested half of its earnings in projects that were expected to earn 14 percent, then the expected growth rate would be 7 percent (0.5 times 14 percent).

To get a handle on what this all means in terms of value creation, consider the Stonier Systems Company, which is expected to have earnings per share of $4.00 next year. The company will retain 60 percent of its earnings to support continuing operations and future growth. These investment projects are expected to earn a 20 percent rate of return. If the required rate of return on equity is 16 percent, then (1) what is the market price of the common stock, and (2) what part of this value is associated with growth?

The stock price calculation is pretty straightforward. We know the next period's earnings, E_1, is $4.00 a share. The proportion of earnings retained is 60 percent, so the proportion of earnings paid out, b, is 40 percent. The next period dividend, D_1, is therefore (0.4)(4.00) or $1.60 a share. If the company is going to invest 60 percent of its earnings in projects which are expected to earn 20 percent a year, then the growth in earnings/dividends will be

$$g = (1 - b)(r^*) = (.6)(.20) = 0.12 = 12 \text{ percent}$$

Now we can plug directly into the constant dividend growth model to obtain

$$P_0 = \frac{D_1}{(k_e - g)} = \frac{\$1.60}{(.16 - .12)} = \$40$$

The value of the assets in place is E_1/k_e; for Stonier, $E_1/k_e = \$4.00/.16 = \$25$. With an estimated stock price of $40 a share, the PVGO, the wealth created through the reinvestment process, must be $40 − $25 = $15 a share.

Now let's take a look at what happens to the market value of Stonier's common stock and the PVGO, if the firm can only earn 16 percent on new investment projects. Reducing the rate of return on reinvested funds will directly impact the future growth in earnings and hence dividends, that is,

$$g = (1 - b)(r^*) = 0.096$$

Substituting this value of g into the constant dividend growth model, we get

$$P_0 = \frac{D_1}{(k_e - g)} = \frac{\$1.60}{(.16 - .096)} = \$25$$

With a theoretical value of $25 a share, the PVGO is zero. Thus, there is no value created by reinvestment.

This result is not an accident. The assumed rate of return in our second example was 16 percent—exactly equal to the shareholders' required rate of return! If the best that Stonier can do is reinvest 60 percent of its earnings in projects that just earn the required return, then the stockholders would be just as well off by getting *all of the earnings in dividends,* and investing the dividends themselves at 16 percent. From the stockholders' standpoint, the 9.6 percent growth in earnings and dividends is not important. What matters to them is the return on their earnings that are retained in the firm.

> **Corporate growth and shareholder wealth creation are not necessarily the same thing.**

Our two numerical examples suggest that *growth, per se, will not necessarily translate into an increase in market values.* As we indicated in Chapter 1, *to create value, managers have to do something for shareholders that they cannot do for themselves.* In the case of the investment decision, this means that managers need to *find investment projects that offer returns that are greater than the shareholders' required rate of return.* This intuitively appealing result seemed to be lost on many corporate managers of the 1960s, 70s, and early 80s, who appeared to be far more concerned with growing the firm than in the profitability of that growth. Some of these excesses underlie the large number of corporate "restructurings" that began in the mid-1980s and continue today.

Above-Average Growth

In the long run, no company can grow more rapidly than the economy in which it operates, whether this be domestic or international. This means that the real, or inflation-adjusted, sustainable-dividend growth rate for a company will probably be in the order of 3 to 4 percent. Therefore, a 15 percent annual dividend growth rate should be regarded as a temporary deviation from the long-run path.

> **Using the constant growth model will overvalue firms with high short-term growth.**

Trying to use the constant-dividend growth formula to value the stock of a rapidly growing company without allowing for the temporary nature of this rapid growth will lead to overvaluation. For instance, suppose that over the past 10 years a company's dividend growth rate was 10 percent in real terms. If the rate of inflation during this period averaged, say, 5 percent, then the nominal growth rate would have been about 15 percent. Suppose that the company is expected to pay a $3.00 dividend, in nominal terms, next year, and its required rate of return is 17 percent. If we assume that this rapid growth rate will continue in perpetuity, then the stock value would be

$$P_0 = \frac{D_1}{(k_e - g)} = \frac{\$3.00}{(.17 - .15)} = \$150$$

On the other hand, if the past nominal growth rate was 17 percent, and we substituted this blindly in the constant dividend growth formula, the estimated stock value would be infinitely large. This answer would be nonsensical because it's based on a dividend growth rate that would be impossible to sustain forever.

Bottom line: All high-flying firms are eventually brought back to earth, and this must be explicitly taken into account when estimating stock values. For example, suppose that Logicon Semiconductor has recently developed a line of specialty microchips that's been well received by the market. Logicon just paid a dividend of $1.50, and this dividend is expected to grow at a rate of 20 percent over the next five years. Beginning in year 6, Logicon's long-run dividend growth rate will settle down to 4 percent annually. How much would you pay for Logicon if your required return were 13 percent?

The general approach is to first calculate the present value of the dividends during the period of high growth, then calculate the stock price at the end of this period, take its present value, and, finally, add together the two present value components. That is,

$$
\text{Current Stock Price} = \begin{array}{c} \textit{Present Value of Dividends} \\ \textit{during Period of} \\ \textit{Above-Average Growth} \end{array} + \begin{array}{c} \textit{Present Value of Stock Price} \\ \textit{at End of Above-Average} \\ \textit{Growth Period} \end{array}
$$

We can implement this approach by using the following four-step procedure:

1. *Calculate the Present Value of Dividends Received during the Period of Rapid Growth.* With a constant-dividend growth rate for the next five years, the expected dividend (D_t) for any of the next five years will equal $D_t(1 + g)^t$. Discounting this dividend at the required return on equity capital yields a present value of D_t, call it $PV(D_t)$, of

$$
PV(D_t) = \frac{D_0(1 + g)^t}{(1 + k)^t} = \frac{\$1.50(1.2)^t}{(1.13)^t} \text{ , for } t = 1, \ldots, 5
$$

As shown in Exhibit 5-9, the present value of this dividend stream is $9.01.

EXHIBIT 5-9
Present Value of Dividends; Rapid Growth Period

Year	Dividend	×	Present Value Factor @ 13%	=	Present Value
1	$1.80		0.8850		$1.59
2	2.16		0.7832		1.69
3	2.59		0.6931		1.80
4	3.11		0.6133		1.91
5	3.73		0.5428		2.02
					Total $9.01

2. **Calculate the Price of the Stock at the End of the Rapid Growth Period.** At the end of the fifth year, dividends are expected to grow at a more normal rate of 4 percent. This allows us to calculate the price, P_5, at this time by applying the constant-dividend growth formula:

$$P_5 = \frac{D_5(1 + g)}{k - g} = \frac{\$3.73 \times 1.04}{(.13 - .04)} = \$43.10$$

3. **Find the Present Value of the Stock Price Calculated in Step 2.** This requires calculating

$$PV(P_5) = \frac{P_5}{(1 + k)^5} = \frac{\$43.10}{(1.13)^5} = \$23.39$$

4. **Sum the Two Present Values.**

$$P_0 = \$9.01 + \$23.39 = \$32.40$$

Based on this analysis, you should be willing to pay $32.40 a share for Logicon's stock, the same as the present value of all of the dividends.

SUMMARY

In this chapter, we've looked at the pricing of corporate securities based on the idea that their worth in competitive markets depends on investor expectations of future cash flows. For fixed-income securities such as bonds and preferred stock, the cash flows are generally well defined. The only question is the certainty with which investors believe that the interest, principal payments, or preferred stock dividends will be met. In the case of common stock, estimating their expected stream of dividends is more of an adventure because companies don't make the same kind of contractual arrangements on dividends that they do when debt or preferred stock is issued.

A couple of general points should be kept in mind as we move forward. The first is that the prices and yields of all securities are inversely related. In the case of bonds, long-term issues with low coupons tend to be more price sensitive to changes in market yields than equivalent short-term, high-coupon issues. The prices of preferred and common stock, which are very long-maturity financial assets, are highly sensitive to changes in market interest rates.

Second, the discount rate used to value securities should reflect what investors can earn on alternative financial assets of equivalent risk. Whether we call this rate an opportunity cost of money, an opportunity cost of capital, or a required rate of return, this rate should *always* reflect some market reinvestment rate.

Finally, it is useful to think about the value of a company's common stock as having two components: the value of the assets currently in place plus the present value of growth opportunities. From the *market's perspective,* the investment (and reinvestment) process can only increase the stock price if the company can identify and properly implement projects whose returns exceed the required rate of return on common stock. Reinvestment at rates below the required rate of return can grow earnings and/or dividends, but such growth will destroy value; the profitability of that growth is what is important.

APPENDIX 5A   THE ROLE OF FREE CASH FLOW AND THE PRESENT VALUE OF GROWTH OPPORTUNITIES IN VALUING A BUSINESS

Because securities are just claims on the cash flows generated by a business, the same discounted cash flow (DCF) techniques used to value stocks and bonds can be used to value the business itself. Specifically, the value of a firm equals the present value of the free cash flows (FCF) generated by the business, discounted at the appropriate required rate of return, or

$$P = \frac{FCF_1}{(1+k)} + \frac{FCF_2}{(1+k)^2} + \cdots + \frac{FCF_N}{(1+k)^N} \cdots$$

[5A-1]

Rather than estimate an infinite series of period-by-period cash flows, the usual practice is to estimate individual cash flows for a limited number of periods (say, N) and then summarize the present value of the cash flows beyond the initial evaluation period with a terminal value (*TERM*):

$$P = \frac{FCF_1}{(1+k)} + \frac{FCF_2}{(1+k)^2} + \cdots + \frac{FCF_N}{(1+k)^N} + \frac{TERM}{(1+k)^N}$$

[5A-2]

The trickiest part of business valuation is estimating the terminal value because this number embodies a projection of growth and the present value of these growth opportunities (PVGO). The PVGO, in turn, reflects the competitive pressures in the product/service markets in which a firm operates. After all, a firm's cash flows are a reflection of how well a company can design operating strategies to deal with its environment. If you're trying to establish the value of a business for the purpose of acquiring it, thinking through your strategy in a competitive context is critical to coming up with meaningful terminal values.

To illustrate this process, we will look at material prepared in connection with Time, Inc.'s purchase of Warner Communications, Inc., in 1989. This merger was one of the first combinations of print and film/broadcasting media firms. The idea was that by putting together two companies dealing with different aspects of communications, the combined entity would have a competitive advantage over other firms operating in the individual parts of the industry. As we will see, assumptions about the competitive environment and the degree to which above-average returns are possible can have a dramatic effect on the PVGO and the price Time paid for Warner.

Valuing Warner Communications

Exhibit 5A-1 contains Warner's projected free cash flows for 1989 through 1994. These estimates were developed by Warner's financial advisor, the investment banking firm of Lazard Freres & Company. Lazard's approach was to use the free cash flows to establish the value of Warner's assets and then subtract the value of its debt—$970 million at the time—to get the value of the equity. This approach is known as the weighted average cost of capital method, and we'll say more about this approach in Chapter 11 when we discuss how to value businesses in greater detail.

To get at free cash flows, Lazard started with Warner's operating earnings, subtracted taxes and added back noncash items like depreciation and deferred taxes. Then, much like a statement of cash flows, the cash costs of capital expenditures were subtracted, and working capital and acquisitions net of any asset sales were added. Because interest on borrowed money was ignored in the calculation, the resulting *free cash flows* were available to *compensate all sources of capital.* By discounting these 6 years' worth of free cash flows at 11.5 percent—determined to be the appropriate discount rate—Lazard came up with a value of $3.072 billion. To get at the value of Warner, we must now add the present value of the terminal value.

Estimating the Terminal Value

There are a number of ways to arrive at a terminal value for Warner Communications.

1. *Use a Multiple of Cash Flows.* One approach used by Lazard was to multiply Warner's operating cash flow in 1994 (the last year of the initial evaluation period) by a factor that represented a likely multiple for comparable companies. The operating cash flow for 1994 is just the net income plus noncash charges like depreciation and deferred taxes, $1.514 billion ($993 + $273 + $248). At a 12 times multiple, the terminal value as of 1994 is $18.168 billion. Discounted at 11.5 percent, this

TABLE 5A-1
Free Cash Flow Analysis of Warner Communications
1989 through 1994
(in millions $)

	1989	1990	1991	1992	1993	1994
Operating Income (EBIT)	$770	$893	$1,145	$1,320	$1,482	$1,655
Taxes*	(193)	(246)	(458)	(528)	(593)	(662)
After-Tax Operating Income	$577	$647	$ 687	$ 792	$ 889	$ 993
Depreciation	228	245	270	271	271	273
Deferred Taxes	(7)	-0-	172	198	222	248
Capital Expenditures	(336)	(225)	(180)	(177)	(183)	(188)
Change in Working Capital	5	(80)	(80)	(80)	(80)	(80)
Acquisitions Net of Asset Sales	(416)	(15)	(5)	(3)	(3)	(3)
Free Cash Flow	$ 52	$572	$ 863	$1,001	$1,117	$1,243

*Assumes a tax rate of 25 percent in 1989 and 1990 and 40 percent thereafter.
Source: Samuel C. Thompson, "A Lawyer's Guide to Modern Valuation Techniques in Mergers and Acquisitions," *Journal of Corporation Law,* vol. 21, 1996, p. D-5. Reprinted with permission of the *Journal of Corporation Law,* © 1996.

terminal value has a present value of $9.455 billion. Therefore, the value of Warner is

PV (Business)
= PV (Free Cash Flows) + PV (Terminal Value)
= $3.072 billion + $9.455 billion = $12.527 billion

Subtracting Warner's debt of $.97 billion leaves an equity value of $11.557 billion. Dividing this equity value by the 190.5 million shares outstanding yields a per-share value of $60.67.

2. *Use a Multiple of Earnings in the Terminal Year.* A related though conceptually different approach is to estimate the terminal value by applying a price-earnings multiple based on the *P/E* of comparable companies to the earnings in the terminal period. For example, Lazard estimated that comparable firms sold at a *P/E* multiple of 18. With projected net income of $993 million in 1994, this implies a terminal value of $17.874 billion. The present value of this terminal value, discounted at 11.5 percent, is $9.302 billion. Based on this terminal value, Warner is worth $12.372 billion:

PV (Business) = $3.072 billion + $9.302 billion
= $12.374 billion

Subtracting Warner's debt of $970 million leaves an equity value of $11.474 billion. Dividing this

by the 190.5 million shares outstanding yields a value per share of $59.86.

3. *Use the Constant Growth Model.* A third approach to estimating the terminal value is to use the constant growth model. Suppose that after 1994, Warner's free cash flows are expected to grow at 5 percent annually. With free cash flows for 1995 of $1.305 billion (1.05 × $1.243 billion), this yields a present value for the 1994 terminal value of $10.45 billion:

$$PV \text{ (Terminal Value} = \frac{1}{(1.115)^6} \times \frac{\$1,305}{(.115 - .05)}$$
$$= \$10.45 \text{ billion}$$

Given this terminal value, Warner is worth $13.594 billion:

PV (Business) = $3.072 billion + $10.450 billion
= $13.522 billion

or $65.89 a share after subtracting its $970 million in debt and dividing by the number of shares outstanding.

4. *Assume the PVGO Is Zero.* A somewhat more conservative approach to estimating Warner's terminal value is to assume that profitable approaches to doing business in an industry will attract competitors who will try to mimic the behavior of market leaders. These competitive pressures will

ultimately reduce the likelihood of earning returns on new projects that exceed shareholder's required rate of return. This situation in which competitors catch up with market leaders is known in economics as a **competitive equilibrium.** Since the present value of growth opportunities (PVGO) is only positive when a firm is expected to earn more than the required rate of return, *a competitive equilibrium means that the PVGO equals zero.* Recall that the PVGO equaling zero does not mean that there's no growth in earnings or cash flow; it simply means that this growth does not create shareholder value because the return on additional assets just equals the required rate of return.

Applying this idea to the proposed Time-Warner combination, let's suppose that there is some initial competitive advantage to combining a company whose primary business is delivering entertainment (Time) with one that's involved with the creation of entertainment (Warner). In the absence of government interference, we'd expect other combinations like this to follow; after all, there are some very large firms in the media–entertainment field that will begin looking around for global partners.

If a competitive equilibrium is reached in 1994, so that the PVGO as of 1995 is zero, then the value of Warner at the end of 1994 would simply be the value of the assets in place, which is

$$P = \frac{E_{1994}}{k} = \frac{\$993 \text{ million}}{0.115} = \$8.635 \text{ billion}$$

The present value of this terminal value is $4.494 billion, yielding a value of $7.566 billion for Warner:

$$PV(\text{Business}) = \$3.072 \text{ billion} + \$4.494 \text{ billion}$$
$$= \$7.566 \text{ billion}$$

Although Lazard didn't employ this method, it yields a $34.62 a share value for Warner after subtracting its $970 million in debt.

5. *Use a Market-to-Book Ratio.* A fifth method that could be used to estimate the terminal value is to multiply the expected book value in the terminal period by the market-to-book ratio—the ratio of the stock price to the book value per share—at which comparable companies trade. In the case of Warner, an examination of six comparable companies at the start of 1989 found an average market-to-book of 2.79. Based on a projected

$5.055 billion in book value for the Warner at the end of 1994, this approach yields an estimated terminal value of $14.104 billion. Discounted at 11.5 percent, this terminal value is now $7.340 billion. Based on this terminal value, Warner is worth $10.412 billion:

$$PV(\text{Business}) = \$3.072 \text{ billion} + \$7.340 \text{ billion}$$
$$= \$10.412 \text{ billion}$$

After subtracting off the $970 million in debt, Warner's per-share value is estimated at $49.56.

The difference in values for Warner using these different approaches to estimating the terminal value is pretty dramatic and indicates how an assessment of the competitive environment can affect the "numbers." Which method gives the "correct" answer? That's tough to say because each is based on a grab bag of assumptions that can only be verified after the fact. What should be clear is that regardless of the methodology used, the value was far lower than the $70 a share that Time actually offered for Warner. Even if we were to concede that Time's management can create and sustain a competitive advantage, Time's shareholders could suffer heavy losses because of overpaying.

Conclusion

Time's stock plummeted when it announced that it planned to purchase Warner for $70 a share. Even though it is impossible to estimate the "true value" of Warner precisely, the decline in price appears to reflect the market's opinion that Time had overpaid for Warner. Subsequent events appear to have borne out the market's initial assessment. Following the acquisition, there were a large number of mergers in the media field. These included (but are not limited to) Disney's acquisition of ABC and Viacom's acquisition of both Paramount and Blockbuster Video. Paramount, the movie studio, was in publishing as well. In short, the competitive equilibrium that we speculated about actually developed. Whether management should have seen this coming at the time of acquisition is open to debate since Time was itself the subject of a hostile takeover by Paramount. Therefore, from the perspective of Time's shareholders, the purchase of Warner seems to have been a very expensive antitakeover defense, since the company paid $70 a share for a company worth only about $35 a share in a competitive environment. With 190.5 million shares outstanding, this overpayment comes to $6.67 billion!

APPENDIX 5B   THE TERM STRUCTURE OF INTEREST RATES

Up to now, we've talked about "the" interest rate as if there were only one rate applicable to debt in a particular risk class. Yet a casual glance at the financial page of any newspaper indicates that there are many such interest rates. As we can see from Exhibit 5B-1, even restricting our discussion to U.S. Treasury securities, we can verify that interest rates vary based on their term to maturity.

The yield curve for Treasury securities for August 20, 1997, is presented in Exhibit 5B-2. A **yield curve** is little more than a graphical representation of the relationship between the **yield to maturity (YTM)** of bonds of the same credit quality and their maturity. The yield curve shown in Exhibit 5B-2 slopes upward, indicating that long-term rates are higher than short-term rates. Historically, this is the "normal" shape of the yield curve. However, we have also seen *inverted yield curves* in which short-term rates are actually higher than long-term rates. We've typically seen inverted yield curves in a high-inflation environment, such as 1979 through 1981, when the Federal Reserve was attempting to restrict credit by pushing up short-term interest rates.[18]

EXHIBIT 5B-1
Yields to Maturity for Select Treasury Securities
August 20, 1997

Maturity Date	Maturity (Years)	Yield to Maturity
November 1997	0.25	5.40%
February 1998	0.50	5.56
August 1998	1.00	5.71
August 1999	2.00	5.88
August 2000	3.00	5.98
August 2002	5.00	6.12
August 2007	10.00	6.22
August 2017	20.00	6.61

Source: Wall Street Journal, August 21, 1997.

---

[18]The yield curve has also been flat or had a humped shape. These shapes have never been persistent and appear to occur when the yield curve is moving from a normal to an inverted shape and vice versa.

Three theories have been put forth to explain the shape of the yield curve: (1) the expectations theory, (2) the liquidity premium theory, and (3) the segmented markets theory. In this appendix, we'll take a brief look at each of these theories and their implications for the corporate manager.

The Expectations Theory

Like most economic models, the **expectations theory** is built around a number of assumptions about the markets and the nature of investors. For one, investors are presumed to be interested in nothing more than maximizing returns over a particular planning horizon and have no preferences for shorter versus longer maturities or vice versa. Second, the market is assumed to be efficient, with prices adjusting immediately to new information. Finally, there are no taxes, information-gathering costs, or other transactions costs, so investors can trade securities quickly and costlessly. In this setting the expectations theory finds that observed long-term rates will be a geometric average of current and expected short-term rates.

To see how this works in numerical terms, let's suppose that it's August 20, 1997, and that you have a three-year investment horizon. The current YTM on a one-year Treasury is 5.71 percent. As you gaze into your crystal ball, you forecast that one-year interest rates a year from now will rise to 6.05 percent. You also expect one-year rates to further increase to 6.18 percent in two years. Given these expectations, you want to know whether it would be better to buy a three-year Treasury with a yield of 5.98 percent or a series of one-year Treasuries.

If you purchase the three-year Treasury, the future value per dollar invested will be

$$(1.0598)^3 = 1.1903$$

On the other hand, if you bought a series of one-year Treasuries, reinvesting the proceeds from one issue to the next as you go along, the future value would be related to the current rate of one-year Treasuries, coupled with your forecasts of future rates:

$$(1.0571)(1.0605)(1.0618) = 1.1903$$

Because we've rigged the numbers to get these results, you'd also find that there's no advantage to buying a two-year Treasury at the current market yield of 5.88

EXHIBIT 5B-2
Treasury Yield Curve—August 20, 1997

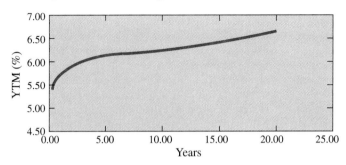

percent, followed by a one-year Treasury at the forecasted yield of 6.18 percent in two years. It would appear that your expectations match those of the market as reflected in the yields in Exhibit 5B-1. Otherwise, there might be an opportunity to trade profitably across the yield curve. For example, if you didn't expect one-year rates to rise much above their current level of 5.71 percent, then you could earn a higher return by purchasing a three-year Treasury maturing in the year 2000.

Like our example, the expectations theory maintains that the yield curve is determined solely by expectations of future interest rates. If rates were not expected to rise, then the yield curve would be flat. However, if short-term rates were expected to rise, the yield curve would be upward sloping; long-term rates would exceed short-term rates by just enough to equate the return from investing in long-term securities to the expected return from investing in short-term securities and rolling them over at the higher expected short-term rates. Conversely, the inverted yield curve reflects an expectation of falling short-term rates. In short, the shape of the yield curve reflects the "market's" consensus of the future course of short-term rates.

The expectations theory also suggests that, *for a given investment horizon, the average expected returns on all maturity combinations will be the same.* If you're a bond portfolio manager, this is important because it tells us that we shouldn't waste our time trying to profitably trade across the yield curve *unless* we believe that our forecasting ability is superior to that of the market as a whole. In an efficient market, that's generally not a good long-term assumption. On the financing end, the expectations theory tells corporate managers that *they cannot lower interest expense in the*

long run by the way they structure the maturity of a firm's debt. This means that if you've got a piece of equipment with an economic life of 10 years, it will make no difference whether you finance it with a 10-year bond or issue a one-year security and continuously refinance for another nine years.

The Liquidity Premium Theory

The implications of the pure expectations theory flow from some very restrictive assumptions about the nature of markets and investor preferences. Unfortunately, it doesn't do a particularly good job of explaining the historical bias towards upward-sloping yield curves. If the shape of the yield curve is determined strictly by expectations of future rate movements, then the "normal" upward-sloping yield curve means that investors believe that rates will be rising "most" of the time. Or is there some factor other than expectations that gives the yield curve its normal shape? The existence of liquidity or risk premiums provides an explanation for what we observe.

At the heart of the liquidity premium argument is the view that investors have a built-in preference for buying short-term, rather than long-term bonds. Why? As we've already seen, the prices of long-term bonds tend to fluctuate more than short-term bonds for a given change in the YTM. Since long-term bonds are riskier than short-term bonds, issuers must provide investors with some extra return to compensate for risk. This extra return, or liquidity premium, gives the yield curve its upward bias. The existence of liquidity premiums doesn't rule out the possibility of an inverted yield curve; what it does say is that declining rate expectations, coupled with other factors, simply overcome the liquidity premium effect.

If the **liquidity premium theory** is correct, an upward-sloping yield curve might not mean that short-term rates will be increasing in the future. Therefore, investors with a long-term horizon could earn a higher rate over time by purchasing long-term bonds. True, there's additional risk in buying these bonds because their prices fluctuate more than those of shorter-term bonds. However, if you have a 20-year investment horizon and plan to buy and hold until maturity, you really shouldn't care about the day-to-day price fluctuations. For you, the purchase of a 20-year Treasury provides a more certain return than buying a series of one-year Treasuries and having to deal with the changes in short-term yields. On the financing end, the existence of risk premiums that increase with maturity means that firms with good access to the financial markets could minimize their cost of borrowing by continuously refinancing short-term debt rather than taking on long-term debt.

The Segmented Markets Theory

The idea behind the **segmented markets theory** is that the debt markets are not really a single large market; instead, they consist of a set of submarkets based on maturity, with the supply and demand for bonds of a specific maturity determining yield. The different preferences arise from an attempt by borrowers and lenders to match the maturities of their assets and liabilities in order to reduce their vulnerability to changes in market interest rates.

For example, pension funds have predictable long-term liabilities. They owe known amounts of money to pensioners in the distant future and have the incentive to lend (or invest) long term to ensure that they will have sufficient funds to meet these obligations. Given the nature of their liabilities, these financial intermediaries place a high priority on the certainty of return and really can't expose themselves to the fluctuating returns by continuously investing and reinvesting in short-term bonds. Commercial banks, on the other hand, get most of their money from deposits and other short-term sources. Because their cost of borrowing fluctuates with changes in short-term rate, they prefer to buy either buy short-term securities or make short-term loans.

If each maturity range represents a separate market, the pattern of supply and demand within each segment can produce many possible shapes of the yield curve. The segmented markets approach states that shifts in the term structure are caused by changes in supply and demand for bonds of different maturities. For this theory to be correct, market participants have to be quite risk averse in the sense that they are unwilling to shift from one maturity to another in their borrowing and lending activities.[19] This follows from the assumption that investors strongly prefer to invest in assets with maturities matching their liabilities, and borrowers prefer to issue liabilities that match the maturity of their assets.

---

[19]A less rigid form of the segmented markets theory argues that market participants will seek out their *preferred habitat* along a scale of varying maturities matching their risk preferences. Under normal conditions, they will stay within these limits in their borrowing and lending activities. However, they will move from their preferred habitat if the right yield incentives present themselves.

APPENDIX 5C   DURATION AND INTEREST RATE SENSITIVITY

In this chapter, we saw that bond prices and bond yields are inversely related. Moreover, this price sensitivity was found to be related to a bond's maturity and coupon rate: (1) the longer a bond's maturity, the greater its sensitivity to changes in yields, and (2) the lower the bond's coupon rate, the more its price will change with a given change in market rates. Therefore, if you truly believed that overall market yields were going to decline, you could maximize your return by purchasing very long-term zero-coupon bonds. Of course, if you are wrong and interest rates rise instead of fall, your losses would be large.

The guidelines on price sensitivity to interest rate changes as outlined above are broad in nature. A more precise measure of interest sensitivity is a bond's **duration.** Developed by Frederick Macaulay in the 1930s as a way to better represent a bond's maturity,[20] duration seeks to measure the average timing of the cash

---

[20]Macaulay's work on duration (1938) was developed in *Some Theoretical Problems Suggested by the Movement of Interest Rates, Bond Yields, and Stock Price Movements in the U.S. Since 1856.* A review of the early history of duration may be found in Weil (1973).

flows from a bond. Mathematically, a bond's duration (D) is given by

$$D = \frac{[1 \times PV(C)]}{P} + \frac{[2 \times PV(C)]}{P} + \cdots$$
$$+ \frac{[N \times PV(C + M)]}{P}$$

$$[5C\text{-}1]$$

where C is the coupon interest payment in dollars, N the bond's maturity, M the par or maturity value, and P the bond's price. The numerator of Equation [5C-1] is the present value (PV) of each cash flow weighted by the period in which it is received. Therefore, each term in the equation represents the proportion of a bond's value received each year, weighted by the time it's received.

To see how Equation [5C-1] works in numerical terms, Exhibit 5C-1 shows the duration calculations for two five-year bonds. The 12 percent coupon bond has a current market value of $1,044.96 per $1,000 face and a yield to maturity of 10.79 percent, and the 8 percent bond has a market value of $892.89 and a

yield to maturity of 10.89 percent. As we can see, the cash flows in the last year account for 64.2 percent of the 12 percent bond's higher coupon payments, and 72.1 percent of the 8 percent bond's value. As we might expect, the duration of the 12 percent bond is shorter than that of the 8 percent bond.

A bond's interest rate sensitivity, often referred to as its **modified duration,** is tied to its duration as follows:[21]

$$\text{Interest Rate Sensitivity} = \frac{D}{(1 + YTM)} \quad [5C\text{-}2]$$

where YTM is the bond's yield to maturity as a decimal. The interest rate sensitivities for the 12 and 8 percent bonds are

Volatility (12 percent) = 4.06/(1.1079) = 3.66

Volatility (8 percent) = 4.267/(1.1089) = 3.85

---

[21]Equation [5C-2] is an approximation that works well for relatively small changes in YTMs. Once rate changes get above 1 percent, actual price changes will differ somewhat from that calculated using Equation [5C-2].

TABLE 5C-1
Calculation of a Bond's Duration

	12 Percent Coupon Bond			
Year	Cash Flow	Present Value @ 10.79%	Proportion of Bond Price	Proportion of Bond Price × Time
1	$120	$108.31	0.104	0.104
2	120	97.76	0.094	0.187
3	120	88.24	0.084	0.253
4	120	79.65	0.076	0.305
5	1,120	671.00	0.642	3.211
		Value = $1,044.96	1.000	Duration = 4.06 years

	8 Percent Coupon Bond			
Year	Cash Flow	Present Value @ 10.89%	Proportion of Bond Price	Proportion of Bond Price × Time
1	$80	$72.14	0.081	0.081
2	80	65.06	0.073	0.146
3	80	58.67	0.066	0.197
4	80	52.91	0.059	0.237
5	1,080	644.11	0.721	3.606
		Value = $892.89	1.000	Duration = 4.267 years

The interpretation of these numbers is that a 1 percent increase (or decrease) in the YTM will lead to a 3.66 percent drop (rise) in the price of the 12 percent coupon bond, and a 3.85 percent drop (rise) in that of the 8 percent coupon bond. The higher volatility of the 8 percent bond is due to its longer duration.

Properties of Duration

Some of the more important properties of duration are

1. *The duration of a zero-coupon bond is equal to its maturity.* If the only cash flow associated with a bond is its maturity, or par value, the duration and maturity must be the same.
2. *All other things being equal, a bond's duration and its maturity are directly related.*
3. *All other things being equal, a bond's duration declines with increases in the coupon rate.* This is why higher-coupon bonds are less sensitive to changes in market yields than lower-coupon bonds.
4. *Durations are additive.* The duration of a portfolio (D_p) is equal to a weighted average of the duration of the individual components, i.e.,

$$D_p = \sum_{i=1}^{N} w_i D_i \qquad [5C\text{-}3]$$

where D_i is the duration of the individual securities, w_i the proportion invested in each bond, and N the number of bonds in the portfolio.

Duration concepts have become important to individual investors, bond portfolio managers, and financial institution managers as a means of dealing with the risks of changing interest rates. In a 1970s article, Fisher and Weil[22] showed how bond portfolios could be immunized against interest rate risks by setting bond durations equal to the investment planning horizons. The growth in the market for zero-coupon bonds since they were first introduced in 1982 is a direct manifestation of this principle. Since the duration of zeros is equal to their maturity, individuals planning

for their child's education or for retirement could "lock-in" a specified return by purchasing maturities that exactly match their need for cash. Duration-based techniques have also been applied to the management of financial institutions in which the time-honored principle of minimizing interest rate risk by matching maturities of assets and liabilities has been replaced by the idea of matching durations.[23]

Applying Duration Concepts: The Orange County Disaster

On December 1, 1994, Orange County announced that its investment fund (known as the Orange County Investment Pool) had lost approximately $1.5 billion. Several days later Orange County filed for bankruptcy protection and began liquidating the assets held in the Investment Pool. Total losses in the Pool were ultimately estimated to be about $1.6 billion.

The history of financial markets indicates that the only sure way to earn higher returns is to take higher risks. Rather than stick with safe investments, which earned relatively low returns, Robert Citron (the county treasurer) sought to increase the returns on the County Pool by "playing the yield curve." Entering 1994, the yield curve was upward sloping with about a 2.00 percent spread between 90-day Treasury bills, which yielded about 3 percent, and five-year Treasury notes, which were yielding about 5 percent. By increasing the maturity of the County Pool, Citron was able to earn a positive spread between short- and longer-term rates. However, we know that lengthening the maturity of any securities portfolio increases risk because it subjects the portfolio to greater price declines if rates go up.

Citron magnified this risk by using borrowed short-term funds to buy additional longer-term securities. By borrowing at the low rates associated with short-term securities and lending at the higher longer-term rates, Citron could add to the spread already being earned on the pool of funds. If this were not enough, interest rate risk was increased still further through the use of *structured notes*. These are securities whose in-

---

[22]See Fisher and Weil (1971).

[23]A very readable discussion of how duration techniques can be applied to financial institutions can be found in Kaufman (1984).

terest rates are not fixed but rather are reset periodically by reference to a formula tied to some prespecified interest rate index. Many of the structured notes were *inverse floaters,* for which yields rose as interest rates fell and vice versa. Overall, the Orange County investment portfolio was filled with securities whose returns varied inversely with interest rates and were financed by borrowed money. The result was a portfolio that was exposed to significant interest rate risk, with a big payoff if rates held steady or declined and huge losses if they rose. Simply put, Citron bet that rates would not rise, and he used financial leverage (borrowing) to increase the size of that bet.

Up until early 1994, Citron's bet on stable or declining interest rates paid off handsomely, with the Investment Pool yielding investors returns that were several percentage points higher than those of other money market funds. However, beginning in February 1994, the Federal Reserve began a series of six interest rate increases that altogether boosted the Fed funds rate—a key short-term rate—by 2.50 percent. Longer-term rates rose by about the same amount during 1994. This rise in rates caused significant losses in market value of the County Pool. This loss translated into a much bigger percentage loss in the value of the Pool's invested funds because of the significant amount of leverage being employed. Let's look at some of the specifics.

The dollar gain or loss on a bond portfolio for a particular interest rate change is

$$\begin{aligned}\text{Gain(Loss)} = \ &\text{Modified Duration}\\ &\times \text{Dollar Value of the Portfolio}\\ &\times \text{Rate Decrease (Increase)}\end{aligned}$$

[5C-4]

where the modified duration is defined by Equation [5C-2]. In December 1994 when the fund went bankrupt, the California state auditor estimated that the County Pool had a duration of 7.4 years *once you properly accounted for the leverage applied to the pool.* Given a yield of 6 percent, the modified duration (or interest-rate sensitivity) of the Pool was about 7.0 (7.4/1.06). With a rise in the yield on three-year Treasury bonds of 2.83 percent by the end of November, and deposits of $7.6 billion in the County Pool, Equation [5C-4] predicts that the Orange County Investment Pool's losses would be

$$\begin{aligned}\text{Loss} &= (7.0)(\$7.6 \text{ billion})(0.0283)\\ &= \$1.506 \text{ billion}\end{aligned}$$

This amount closely approximates the fund's actual losses, particularly when we recognize that the realized losses take into account the transaction costs associated with the rapid liquidation of the portfolio's securities.

 FINCOACH PRACTICE EXERCISES

To help you master the mathematics discussed in the chapter, open **FinCoach** on the *Prentice Hall Finance Center* CD-ROM and practice the problems in the following categories: *1. Valuation of Multiple Cash Flows, 2. Valuation of Infinitely Many Cash Flows, 3. Bond Valuation, and 4. Stock Valuation.*

QUESTIONS

1. According to a story in *Fortune* (June 23, 1986, p. 27), the strategy for investing in the stock market is "Draw up a checklist for telling good managements from bad, and buy accordingly." Will picking stocks of well-managed companies be more rewarding than picking stocks of poorly managed companies? Comment.

2. Thirty-year, fixed-rate mortgages were common in the past for small homeowners. During the 1980s, variable-rate or short-term mortgages became more common. What can explain this change?

3. Some money management companies tout asset-allocation funds as a low-risk way to improve your investment returns. These funds try to boost prof-

its by periodically adjusting their portfolio mix between different asset classes—stocks, bonds, and money market instruments. The idea is to always be in those assets with the highest prospective return by, for example, shifting from stocks to bonds when the stock market is expected to fall.

a. How well do you think asset-allocation funds have done relative to equity funds?

b. A newer product is the global asset-allocation fund, which not only shifts money from asset class to asset class but from country to country. How well do you think global asset-allocation funds have done relative to equity funds and relative to domestic asset-allocation funds?

4. The Central Bank recently issued the following securities:

Day of Issue	Face	Terms
1 Oct 1999	$100	7¼s 2014
1 Oct 1999	$100	10¾s 2014

Both bonds trade freely in an organized market. In which bond would you prefer to invest $100,000?

5. Although the market-determined yield on 20-year corporate bonds is 11 percent, the treasurer of XYZ Corporation has been advised by the corporation's investment banker that it would be easy to sell a bond issue with a coupon at only 10 percent. The treasurer reasons that he will save the company interest expense by floating debt at only 10 percent. Do you agree? Why or why not?

6. How is the value of a share of common equity determined? Why do stocks that pay no dividends sell at positive prices and often at high price/earnings ratios?

7. Comment on the following statement: Northern Telecom has a high *P/E* ratio while Gaz Metropolitan has a low *P/E*. Therefore, we should buy more Northern Tel and dump all our Gaz Metropolitan.

8. On October 19, 1987, the price of IBM stock dropped from $135 to $102. Because IBM's assets had not changed from one day to the next, this drop is prima facie evidence that the stock market is not efficient. Comment on this statement.

9. On January 2, a steel company's common equity sold for $50 a share. Over the course of the year, a $5 dividend was paid. On January 2, a pharmaceutical company's common equity sold for $100 a share, and a $1 dividend was paid over the course of the year. Which company has a higher rate of return for the year?

10. When is it valid to use the following stock valuation models?
   a. $P_0 = D_1/(k - g)$
   b. $P_0 = D_1/k$
   c. $P_0 = D_1/(1 + k)$

11. The executives of an oil company recently announced a large new investment in foreign oil fields. Although currently underdeveloped, the executives know the fields will be very profitable in 10 to 15 years. Despite this, the oil company's stock price dropped after the announcement. Can you explain this puzzle with a simple stock valuation model?

12. On May 18, 1988, Hewlett-Packard announced gains of 30 percent in fiscal second-quarter profit, but its stock price fell about 8 percent. How do you account for this seemingly paradoxical stock price change?
   a. On July 17, 1992, IBM's shares fell by 5.2 percent despite reporting a more than 500 percent jump in quarterly earnings. What might account for this fall in IBM's stock price given such good news?
   b. On October 15, 1990, Polaroid was awarded damages of $909.5 million in its patent infringement suit against Kodak. Upon announcement of the award, its stock price plunged 22 percent. What might explain the market's reaction to Polaroid's gain of almost $1 billion?

13. When a firm repurchases its own shares, it pays out cash and receives treasury stock that is of no productive value to the firm. How might shareholders gain from such a transaction?

14. An investor is considering placing $100,000 in the stock of either Corporation A or Corporation B. Although each sells for $52 per share, A's common stock has a par value of $2, whereas B's common stock has a par value of zero. Given that the prices are equal, which share is the better investment?

15. A company issues $1 million of floating-rate perpetuities. The bonds are sold at face value, and the coupon rate is adjusted instantaneously to reflect interest rate changes. Demonstrate that the bond will always sell at face value.

16. According to an article in *Business Week* (June 29, 1992, p. 98), "The only way to win the drug-stock game is to find those with the best product pipelines." *Business Week* then singled out Merck

and Pfizer as companies with particularly strong product pipelines and went on to say that "their price-earnings ratios are the highest and their yields the lowest in their industry." Are these two statements in *Business Week* consistent? Explain. What is the relationship between strong product pipelines and high *P/Es*?

17. MacroCorp. has had a string of product successes, and analysts are forecasting profitable growth in the future. By contrast, MicroCorp. has had a series of product failures, and analysts are saying that the company's future is dismal. Which company should you invest in? Does it matter?

18. On October 13, 1989, the stock market fell 7 percent. On that same day, the Senate blocked President Bush's proposal to cut the capital gains tax rate by 30 percent. How might these two events be related?

19. According to some market analysts, a bill by New York Senator Alfonse D'Amato to restrict interest rates on credit cards, which passed the Senate by a 74–19 vote, triggered the steep decline in the stock market on November 15, 1991. Comment on the possible links between these two events.

20. The S&P 500 rose 30 percent during 1991 even though the United States was in the midst of a recession, with unemployment over 7 percent and major corporations going bankrupt. How could the economy be doing so poorly and the stock market be doing so well?

21. Show that the present value of growth opportunities for Stonier will be negative if its ROE on new equity investments is less than its 16 percent cost of equity capital.

PROBLEMS

📳 —Excel templates may be downloaded from **www.prenhall.com/financecenter.**

1. Suppose the market interest rate is 10 percent. You buy a Treasury bill that will pay you $1,000 in one year.
   a. What is the maximum amount you would pay for the bill?
   b. If you bought the bill for $892.86, what interest rate will you earn for the year?

2. Two bonds have a face value of $1,000 and a maturity of two years. One pays a yearly coupon of $200, whereas the other pays a yearly coupon of $50. 📳
   a. If the market rate of interest is 8 percent, what will be the prices of the two bonds?
   b. If inflation suddenly causes the interest rate to rise to 20 percent, what will be the new prices for the two bonds?
   c. Which bond suffers a greater percentage decrease in its price when the interest rate rises? Why?
   d. Suppose interest rates suddenly decline to 5 percent. What will be the new prices of the two bonds?
   e. With returns at 8 percent, what are the future values of the cash flows from the two bonds? That is, how much money will you have in two years from each of the bonds, taking into account the reinvestment of your coupon income at 8 percent for two years plus your final principal repayment at maturity?
   f. Suppose the maturities of the two bonds are extended to 10 years. What will be the prices of the two bonds given a required yield of 8 percent? Of 5 percent? Of 10 percent?

3. Three bonds have a "10 percent" coupon rate. One pays 10 percent annually, one pays 10 percent semiannually (5 percent every six months), and one pays 10 percent monthly (10/12 percent each month). What are the effective annual yields of the three bonds?

4. The principal value of each of the following bonds is $1,000. The current yield on Treasury securities (of all maturities) is 7 percent compounded semiannually. All coupons are paid semiannually. 📳

   U.S. Treasury bond, 10 percent coupon, 10-year maturity
   U.S. Treasury note, 5 percent coupon, 10-year maturity
   U.S. Treasury bond, 10 percent coupon, 20-year maturity
   U.S. Treasury zero-coupon bond, 10-year maturity
   U.S. Treasury zero-coupon bond, 20-year maturity

a. What are the current prices of the bonds?

b. If interest rates rise to 10 percent, what will be the change in the value of each bond?

c. Which bond suffers the greatest percentage price decline from the rise in interest rates? Why? Which suffers the least percentage price decline? Why?

5. In early 1988, the Mexican government sought to swap about $15 billion of its outstanding bank debt for $10 billion in bonds. The principal amount of the Mexican bonds would be secured by 20-year, zero-coupon U.S. Treasury bonds having a face value of $10 billion. Because of doubts about Mexico's creditworthiness, Mexican bank debt was then valued by the market at about 50 cents on the dollar. ✖

a. What is the value of the U.S. Treasury bonds securing Mexico's $10 billion of principal repayments? Assume that the market yield on the zero-coupon U.S. Treasury bonds is 8.25 percent.

b. What will the $10 billion in Mexican bonds be worth if Mexico's creditworthiness is unchanged by the swap?

c. What is the value of the $15 billion in bank loans to Mexico before the swap?

d. Based on your analysis, how eager were banks likely to be to swap their bank loans for Mexican bonds?

e. As noted previously, the Mexican promise to pay $1 in bank debt is worth about 50 cents. Suppose the bond interest payments are less risky than bank debt payments. How much must a Mexican promise to pay $1 in bond interest be worth for the bond swap to be worthwhile (e.g., 32 cents, 47 cents)?

6. On December 15, 1987, Southland Corporation issued $1,000 par value bonds due December 15, 2002, in conjunction with its leveraged buyout. These bonds would pay no interest until December 15, 1992, but would pay an 18 percent annual coupon semiannually afterward (the first coupon was to be paid on June 15, 1993). If these bonds were priced to yield 16 percent, compounded semiannually, what was their price at issue? ✖

7. An investor is considering the purchase of a preferred share, which will pay a dividend of $3 per year in perpetuity.

a. If the current market rate of interest is 8 percent, what is the maximum price the investor should pay for the share?

b. Suppose there is a call provision, and the issuing company has the right to repurchase the issue at a price of $20 in five years. Does this change your estimate of the maximum price an investor should pay for the share? Explain. (*Hint:* Under what circumstances is the firm most likely to call the preferred stock?)

8. Commonwealth Edison $2.75 preferred stock is currently selling for $25. ✖

a. What is the required rate of return on the stock?

b. Calculate the price of the Commonwealth preferred if expected inflation suddenly increased the required yield by 2 percent.

c. Calculate the price of the Commonwealth preferred if Commonwealth announces it will redeem its preferred stock for $44.95 in 10 years.

9. Apex Products has an issue of 6 percent cumulative preferred stock on which it has paid no dividends for the past three years. This year's net income after tax is $900,000. If there are 20,000 shares ($100 par value) of the preferred outstanding and 200,000 shares of common, what will be the largest common dividend that Apex can pay this year?

10. A railroad has outstanding 400,000 shares of $3.50 cumulative preferred with a $50 par value. A participation feature requires that one half of any dividend in excess of $.50 paid to common stockholders must also be paid to preferred. For example, if common receives a $1 dividend, preferred will receive an extra 25 cents participation dividend. Suppose there are 2 million common shares outstanding. What would the maximum dividends per share for common and preferred equal, given the following levels of after-tax earnings?

a. $1,200,000

b. $2,200,000

c. $4,000,000

11. Suppose Atlantic Bank's $2.80 convertible preferred is selling for $123 a share and its $3.00 convertible preferred is selling for $349.

a. At what stock price will it be worthwhile for the preferred holders to convert their preferred shares?

b. On the same day, Atlantic Bank's common is selling for $51.75. Will preferred shareholders convert their shares? Why or why not? If holders of Atlantic Bank knew that the firm would go bankrupt in five years, what would be the market price of the preferred shares today? Assume the preferred dividends are paid as scheduled until bankruptcy, and the rate of return required is 11 percent higher.

12. A new office services firm has issued its first shares of common stock. The shares have a par value of $.50 a share and an issue price of $37.50; 100,000 shares were issued.

    a. Show the balance sheet accounts for the stock after the offering.
    b. If a buyer eventually obtained 250 shares of the stock for $.25, what will be her liability in the event of bankruptcy?

13. A stock sells for $50 on January 1 and pays $2 in cash dividends over the course of the year.

    a. If the stock closes at $60 on December 31, what was the rate of return for the year?
    b. If the stock closed at $40, what was the rate of return for the year?
    c. If the expected rate of return is 8 percent, what is the expected price of the stock at the end of a year?

14. A stock with an expected rate of return of 15 percent will pay a dividend of $2 this year. ✎

    a. If this dividend is paid in perpetuity, what will be the value of the stock?
    b. If this dividend grows by 10 percent a year in perpetuity, what will be the value of the stock?
    c. If the dividend grows by 10 percent a year for five years, 5 percent a year thereafter for 20 years, and then ceases to grow, what will be the value of the stock?

15. SBC Communications is expected to pay a dividend of about $3 during the upcoming year, and this dividend is forecast to grow at a rate of about 6.1 percent annually. ✎

    a. If the return required by shareholders is 11 percent annually, what is a reasonable estimate for SBC's stock price?
    b. SBC has an estimated population figure in its cellular system of 27.61 million. In the vernacular of the cellular business, SBC has 27.61 million *pops*. It also has 300.5 million shares outstanding. Suppose SBC's cellular phone system has a market penetration rate of 2.3 percent (that is, 2.3 percent of the population are subscribers), produces average monthly revenues of $105 per subscriber, and has a 61 percent after-tax profit margin (earnings divided by sales revenue). If the discount rate applied to

these earnings is 12 percent, and earnings per pop are expected to grow about 4.3 percent per annum, what would the cellular system be worth to SBC?

    c. Based on your answers to parts a) and b), what fraction of SBC's value is accounted for by its cellular operations?

16. Stock A has a current price of $28, a projected dividend for the upcoming year of $1.91, and a current and projected return on equity of 15 percent. ✎

    a. If 60 percent of earnings are paid out as dividends, what will be the growth rate of earnings?
    b. If the book value of equity is currently $20, what will it be in two years?
    c. What is the stock's required rate of return?
    d. What is the expected price of the stock in one year?

17. Hotshot Enterprises is enjoying a period of very rapid growth in sales, earnings, and dividends. Hotshot is expected to pay a dividend of $10 per share next year (year 1), and dividends are expected to grow at a 20 percent rate during the following two years (years 2 and 3). However, such rapid growth cannot be sustained. Beginning with the dividend in year 4, Hotshot's dividends are expected to grow steadily at a 5 percent rate forever. The required return on Hotshot stock is 10 percent. ✎

    a. What is the current price of a share of Hotshot?
    b. What is the expected price per share in year 1?
    c. What is the total expected rate of return in year 1?
    d. What are the expected prices and rates of return in years 2–4?

18. The management of Unioil is interested in calculating the value of the company's stock under four possible scenarios. Under the first, Unioil will experience declining oil revenue as old wells are depleted and substitute wells are not found; the second forecasts a steady state for the company; under the third, the company will grow with the economy; and under the fourth, the company will strike an extremely profitable but short-lived well and then resume growing along with the rest of the economy. In all cases, the company is expected to pay a dividend of $2.10 per share next year out of projected earnings of $3.85 per share. The required rate of return for a stock like Unioil is 11 percent and is expected to remain so under all four scenarios. Find the price, dividend yield, and *P/E* ratio

under each of the four growth scenarios, given the following projected dividend growth rates associated with each of these growth scenarios. ✍

Scenario:	1	2	3	4
$g =$	−3.5%	0.0%	4.0%	15% for 6 years, then 4% thereafter

19. Xenophobia, Inc., is expected to earn $6.00 a share next year. The firm's shareholders have a required rate of return of 15 percent.
    a. What would Xenophobia's stock price be if it retained 50 percent of its earnings and invested them in projects earning 15 percent? What would the stock price be if the retention rate was increased to 70 percent and the ROE stayed at 15 percent?
    b. Suppose that Xenophobia can earn 18 percent on all new investments. What would the stock price be if it retained 50 percent of its earnings?

What would the stock price be if the earnings retention rate was increased to 70 percent?

20. Suppose that Paradise Corp. has assets that generate perpetual (cash) earnings per share of $5 annually. Since Paradise has no reinvestment opportunities, it will pay out all its earnings as dividends; the level of assets will be maintained over time. ✍
    a. If investors require a 12 percent rate of return, what is the price of this no-growth firm?
    b. Now suppose that because of an unexpected increase in consumer demand the management estimates that Paradise can increase its sales by expanding its capacity. Management concludes that the firm can reinvest 40 percent of its earnings annually for the next 20 years (i.e., at $t = 1, \ldots, 20$). These reinvested earnings are expected to generate a permanent 20 percent return. After the growth period, there will be no new growth opportunities. If investors require a 12 percent rate of return, what will be the share price of Paradise Corp. with its new growth opportunities?

REFERENCES

De Bondt, W. F. M., and R. H. Thaler. "Does the Stock Market Overreact?" *Journal of Finance,* July 1985, 793–805.

De Bondt, W. F. M., and R. H. Thaler. "Further Evidence on Investor Overreaction and Stock Market Seasonality." *Journal of Finance,* July 1987, 557–581.

Fama, E. F. "Efficient Markets: A Review of Theory and Empirical Work." *Journal of Finance,* May 1970, 383–417.

Fisher, L., and R. L. Weil. "Coping with Risk of Interest Rate Fluctuations: Returns to Bondholders from Naive and Optimal Strategies." *Journal of Business,* October 1971, 408–431.

Gordon, M. J., and E. Shapiro. "Capital Equipment Analysis: The Required Rate of Profit." *Management Science,* October 1956, 102–110.

Haugen, R. A. *The Inefficient Stock Market: What Pays Off and Why?* Upper Saddle River, NJ: Prentice Hall, 1999.

Jensen, M. C. "The Performance of Mutual Funds in the Period 1945–1964." *Journal of Finance,* May 1968, 389–416.

Jensen, M. C. "Risks, the Pricing of Capital Assets, and the Evaluation of Investment Performance." *Journal of Business,* April 1969, 167–247.

Kaufman, G. G. "Measuring and Managinig Interest Rate Risk: A Primer." *Economic Perpectives,* Federal Reserve Bank of Chicago (January/February 1984), 16–29.

Kendall, M. C. "The Analysis of Economic Time Series, Part I, Prices." *Journal of the Royal Statistical Society,* 96 (1953), 11–25.

Macaulay, F. *Some Theoretical Problems Suggested by the Movement of Interest Rates, Bonds, Yields, and Stock Price Movements in the U.S. since 1956.* New York: National Bureau of Economic Research, 1938.

Myers, S. "Determinants of Corporate Borrowing." *Journal of Financial Economics,* January 1977, 147–175.

Sharpe, W. F. "Mutual Fund Performance." *Journal of Business,* January 1966, 119–138.

Sharpe, W. F., G. L. Alexander, and J. V. Bailey. *Investments.* Upper Saddle River, NJ: Prentice Hall, 1999.

Weil, R. L. "Macaulay's Duration: An Application." *Journal of Business,* October 1973, 589–592.

Williams, J. B. *The Theory of Investment Value.* Cambridge, MA: Harvard University Press, 1938.

Risk and Return

6

The earth is just too small and fragile a basket for the human race to keep all its eggs in.
Robert A. Heinlein

KEY TERMS

aggressive stock
American Depository
  Receipt (ADR)
arbitrage pricing theory
  (APT)
beta
capital asset pricing
  model (CAPM)
capital market line (CML)
characteristic line
correlation coefficient
countercyclical stock
cyclical stock

defensive stock
diversifiable or
  unsystematic risk
efficient frontier
expected return
home bias
market or systematic
  risk
market price of risk
market risk premium
Morgan Stanley Capital
  International World
  Index

opportunity set
related diversification
security market line
  (SML)
standard deviation
synergies
unrelated or
  conglomerate
  diversification
variance
zero-beta portfolio

CHAPTER LEARNING OBJECTIVES

Upon completion of this chapter, students should be able to:

- Describe the pattern of historical returns in the capital markets.
- Understand how to measure the risk and expected return for individual securities as well as for portfolios.
- Explain how diversification can reduce the risk of an investment portfolio.
- Identify the linkages between risk and expected return for securities and use this relationship to calculate the required rate of return for a firm's common stock.

- Explain how the capital asset pricing model (CAPM) and the arbitrage pricing theory (APT) measure risks and how these models relate that risk to expected return.
- Indicate how the insights from capital market theory can be used to design corporate diversification strategies that can enhance shareholder value.
- Explain why globally diversifying a securities portfolio can reduce risk.

Risk is the common denominator of virtually all financial decisions. Investors deciding which securities to purchase, marketing managers deciding whether to launch a new product, plant managers deciding on the installation of a new production line, and financial executives deciding how to finance the firm's operations and investments all face choices that involve uncertain future cash flows. Evaluating these risks and factoring them into decisions are thus essential aspects of financial decision making.

The objective is not to avoid risk—that is impossible—but to recognize its existence and to ensure that expected compensation is adequate for the risks borne. Compensation is required because investors are generally risk averse; that is, all other things being equal, investors prefer less risk to more risk. Of course, all other things are usually not equal, and so managers and investors must constantly select among choices entailing different amounts of risk and promised returns. To compare the various alternatives, it is necessary to convert the uncertain future cash flows associated with each into present values by discounting the future cash flows for both the time value of money and the degree of risk involved.

But to estimate the risk-adjusted discount rate—a task that we have ignored up to now—we must be able to measure and price financial risk. Perhaps the most important development in finance in the past 40 years is the ability to quantify what we mean by risk. The ability to measure risk has led, in turn, to new theoretical and empirical work relating risk and return. The result has been a vastly improved understanding of the way that risky assets and projects are valued in a competitive market.

This chapter covers four major aspects of risk and return. Its purpose is to define risk and establish the link between risk and the required rate of return of various risky assets. The chapter begins by examining the historical record to see how returns on securities of differing riskiness have varied over time, discusses the nature of risk in a portfolio context, and demonstrates how, for the same level of expected return, risk can be reduced through portfolio diversification. Next, we explore the implications of modern portfolio theory for the pricing of risky assets in a competitive market. In the following two sections, we'll examine the capital asset pricing model (CAPM) and the arbitrage pricing theory (APT). Both the CAPM and the APT enable us to estimate the risk-adjusted discount rate for choices involving uncertainty. The final section examines the effects of international diversification.

The subject matter of this chapter provides the theoretical foundation for the study of risk in all financial decisions. Despite the technical nature of this material, the emphasis is on the basic insights into the tradeoff between risk and return implied by modern capital market theory rather than on the methodology.

6.1   HISTORICAL RETURNS IN THE CAPITAL MARKET

Much of our theory depends on the notion that over long periods of time individuals figure out what is going on in financial markets and respond rationally to this information. It is worthwhile, therefore, to examine the historical evidence regarding the rates of return realized by investors holding different types of securities.

Our intuition tells us that stocks are riskier than corporate bonds, which, in turn, are riskier than default-free government bonds. Within these categories, the common stock of smaller firms should be riskier than that of larger companies. Similarly, a long-term government bond, whose price fluctuates with interest rate movements, should be riskier than a Treasury bill, whose short maturity largely insulates it from price variations. Therefore, we would expect that, over time, small-company stocks would yield the highest average returns, followed in descending order by large-company stocks, corporate bonds, government bonds, and Treasury bills.

Exhibit 6-1 shows that empirical evidence supports our expectations. The data indicate that over the 72-year period from 1926 through 1997, common stock—the riskiest investment—earned the highest rate of return, with small-company stocks outperforming their larger cousins. Corporate bonds earned a lower return, in line with their lower risk, and long-term government bonds earned even less. The worst performance was turned in by the safest investment, Treasury bills, which yielded about 3.8 percent annually in nominal terms and 0.6 percent in real terms. Investors in common stock earned a return that averaged 9.2 percent annually more than the return on Treasury bills and 6.8 percent more than long-term government bonds.

Exhibit 6-2 depicts the relationship between investment risk and return for the period 1926 through 1997. The y-axis shows the annualized investment return of the major asset classes, whereas the x-axis presents the standard deviations of these returns. The **standard deviation** is a measure of the dispersion or variability around the expected outcome. The higher the standard deviation, the less predictable the outcome and so the riskier the investment. It is evident from Exhibit 6-2 that riskier assets have, over long periods of time, earned higher returns than less risky assets. This result is consistent with the commonsense notion that

EXHIBIT 6-1
Average Annual Security Returns
1926–1997
(in percent)

Security Type	Average Nominal Rate of Return	Average Real Rate of Return*	Premium over Treasury Bills
Small-Firm Common Stocks	17.7	14.5	13.9
Large-Firm Common Stocks	13.0	9.8	9.2
Corporate Bonds	6.1	2.9	2.3
Treasury Bonds	5.6	2.4	1.8
Treasury Bills	3.8	0.6	-0-

*Inflation averaged 3.2 percent over this period.
Source: Ibbotson Associates, *Stocks, Bonds, Bills and Inflation: 1998 Yearbook,* p. 33. Used with permission. © 1999 Ibbotson Associates, Inc. All rights reserved. [Certain portions of this work were derived from copyrighted works of Roger G. Ibbotson and Rex Sinquefield.]

EXHIBIT 6-2
Historical Relationship between Risk and Return
for Different Asset Classes: 1926–1997

Risk–Return

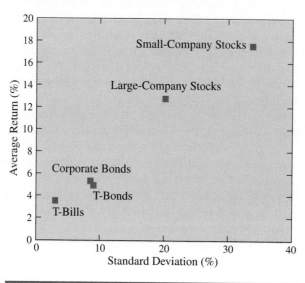

investors demand—and over time get—higher returns from riskier assets. In effect, investors discount the prices they are willing to pay for riskier assets so that the returns they receive are earned on a smaller investment base, thereby raising their return on investment.

> Because of year-to-year fluctuations, looking at actual returns over a long time period provides the best comparisons across security types.

The rationale for computing average returns with more than 70 years of data is that prices and, hence, returns fluctuate so much that return comparisons based on averages taken over short periods of time are pointless. This is especially true for stock prices, which are highly volatile. Exhibit 6-3 shows how variable an investment the stock market has been historically. These returns vary from a gain of 53.9 percent in 1933, following the stock market crash of 1929–1932, to a loss of 43.3 percent in 1931. Even in periods of low volatility (e.g., the 1960s), there were dramatic year-to-year price fluctuations.

6.2   PORTFOLIO RISK AND RETURN

Because the future is always uncertain, the cash flows associated with possible projects and activities are also uncertain. As the future unfolds, actual cash flows are revealed, and, to the extent that they diverge from those that were expected,

EXHIBIT 6-3
Year-by-Year Total Stock Market Returns: 1926–1997

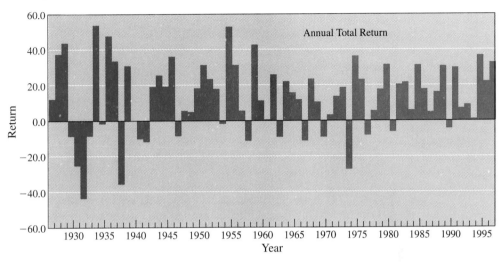

security values adjust to reflect the new information. Thus, for example, few people forecast the decline in oil prices in the early 1980s or again in the late 1990s, so when it happened, oil stocks tumbled in both periods.

It is this uncertainty, the inability to forecast the future accurately and reliably, that we intuitively understand as risk. Intuition takes us only so far, however. We need a more precise definition of risk that will enable us to compare alternative ventures in terms of both risk and return. This is possible with probability theory.

Probability Distributions

Probabilities measure the likelihood that events will occur.

The *probability* of an event is defined as the likelihood that the event will occur. For example, the chances of drilling successfully for oil in west Texas may be one out of ten. This is equivalent to saying that the probability of finding oil is 0.10 or 10 percent. In general, the probability of a particular outcome must lie between zero and one. Impossible events have a zero probability; if an event is certain (a sure thing), its probability is one. Most event probabilities, like the odds of heads on the flip of a coin, fall somewhere in between.

A complete description of all possible outcomes, along with their associated probabilities, is known as a *probability distribution*. The probabilities represented by a probability distribution must sum to 1; otherwise, some possible event has been omitted. This means that if the probability of finding oil is .10, the probability of drilling a dry hole must be .90, not .89 or .91.

From the data supplied by these probability distributions, we can compute two statistical parameters that are crucial to financial analysis: (1) the *expected return,* which describes the average of all possible outcomes, and (2) the *standard deviation,* which is a measure of the dispersion or variability around the expected outcome.

Expected Rate of Return.   Because the actual return is unknown when an investment is made, investors usually focus on the "likely return." The most common measure of "likely return" is the **expected return,** a weighted average of all possible returns multiplied by the associated probabilities. More precisely,

> An expected return is a weighted average of possible returns in which the weights equal the probability of occurrence.

$$E(R) = \sum_{i=1}^{n} p_i R_i \qquad\qquad [6\text{-}1]$$

where $E(R)$ is the expected return; R_i is the return for the ith possible outcome; p_i is the probability of earning that return; and n is the number of different possible returns.

Expected returns are not the same as actual returns, however. Despite a high expected return, the stock market is considered very risky because of the wide range of year-to-year returns. A standard statistical measure of dispersion is the *standard deviation.* Another is the *variance.* Definitions for these terms follow.

Variance.   The **variance,** denoted by σ_R^2 and pronounced "sigma squared," is the sum of the squared deviations $[R_i - E(R)]$ between the actual returns, R_i, and the expected return, $E(R)$, weighted by the associated probabilities p_i:

> The variance and standard deviation are measures of risk.

$$\sigma_R^2 = \sum_{i=1}^{n} p_i [R_i - E(R)]^2 \qquad\qquad [6\text{-}2]$$

Standard Deviation.   The standard deviation of the return, or σ_R (sigma), is simply the square root of the variance; that is, $\sigma_R = (\sigma_R^2)^{1/2}$, where σ (sigma) is the symbol for the standard deviation.

Most investors, however, do not put all their eggs in one basket. Their portfolios usually contain a variety of assets, including different stocks, bonds, real estate, and precious metals. What matters to well-diversified investors, therefore, is not the riskiness of individual securities held in isolation but the risk of their portfolios.[1] Thus, the relevant risk and return of a security to such investors is the contribution of that security to the variability and return of the entire portfolio. A consideration of the concept of contribution to portfolio risk requires a theory of portfolio risk and return. Before getting into all the technical details of portfolio

---

[1]Bondholders, managers, employees, customers, and other parties may well be concerned about the total risk of a company, and this will affect the company's future cash flows, but only the systematic component of risk should affect the discount rate. The effects of total risk on future cash flows are examined in Chapter 14.

theory, however, it is worthwhile to examine a concrete example of this somewhat abstract concept. The auto insurance business provides a good illustration.

An insurance company like State Farm holds a portfolio of auto insurance contracts. The net return on any one of these contracts, equal to the difference between the insurance premium and the claims paid out, is essentially unpredictable. It could be either positive (if no claim is filed) or significantly negative (if the insured gets into an expensive accident). Thus, any single insurance contract held by State Farm is highly risky.

> The financial markets don't reward investors for risk that can be eliminated through diversification.

But State Farm insures millions of cars and can predict with a great deal of certainty just how many accidents it will have to pay for on the average. Therefore, the unpredictability of individual driving records contributes very little to the riskiness of State Farm's insurance portfolio. Most of the risk associated with the uncertainty of a specific individual's accident experience can be diversified away. Competition among insurance firms ensures that this individual risk is not priced in an automobile insurance contract. Insurance companies will charge a fee based on an individual's expected driving record; they will not charge an additional fee for bearing the risk associated with driver unpredictability. This is a basic principle of risk in finance: *Risk that can be eliminated through diversification does not command a risk premium.*

Auto insurance portfolios do contain elements of risk that cannot be diversified away, however. Consider the effect of a shock such as the quadrupling of oil prices in 1973. The jump in oil prices induced people to drive significantly less, which meant fewer accidents per capita. In addition, the introduction of the 55-mile-per-hour speed limit further reduced the amount and severity of auto accidents. These factors systematically lowered claims costs, thereby raising the returns to State Farm on all its auto insurance contracts. On the other hand, because insurance premiums are set ahead of time, unexpectedly high inflation during the late 1970s led to unexpectedly high repair costs (because the cost of parts and labor rose in line with inflation) and, therefore, to unexpected losses on even the best-diversified insurance portfolio. From the standpoint of an insurance company, these risks are systematic; no matter how well diversified its portfolio of insurance contracts, returns on the portfolio are affected by oil-price shocks and inflation. These risks affect all assets to a greater or lesser extent and, therefore, will influence their required returns. This brings us to the second fundamental principle of risk in finance: *The market demands a return premium from an asset according to the asset's contribution to the risk of a fully diversified portfolio.*

> An asset's contribution to the risk of a fully diversified portfolio determines its risk premium.

Modern portfolio theory states that the motive for holding a diversified portfolio of risky securities is to reduce the variability of overall returns. *Diversification works because stock prices don't move perfectly in phase with one another.* As some stocks are moving up, others are moving down, and still others are not moving at all. The result is that some of the fluctuations in individual stocks cancel out. In general, therefore, the variability of portfolio returns is less than the average variability of returns on its component assets. This is reflected in the following important rule: *The risk of a portfolio depends not only on the inherent riskiness of its component assets but also on how returns on those assets relate to one another.*

> Diversification can reduce risk because stock prices don't move in lockstep with one another.

Exhibit 6-4 shows how diversification can almost halve the standard deviation of returns on a stock portfolio. According to recent data, the standard deviation of the average stock listed on the New York Stock Exchange (NYSE) is approximately 28 percent. This contrasts with a standard deviation of about 15 percent for the "market portfolio," the fully diversified portfolio consisting of all the stocks listed on the NYSE. Fortunately for the average investor, it is not necessary to hold all NYSE-listed stocks to benefit substantially from diversification. Exhibit 6-4 reveals that most of the benefits of diversification can be achieved with as few as ten different stocks. As additional securities are added to the portfolio, its standard deviation decreases but at a decreasing rate.

Systematic versus Unsystematic Risk

Exhibit 6-4 also shows that the part of risk that is eliminated through diversification is unique to the stock or group of stocks in the portfolio. Market risk, which affects all stocks to a greater or lesser extent, cannot be diversified away. This division of risk summarizes the basic insight of modern portfolio theory:

$$\text{Total Risk} = \text{Market Risk} + \text{Unique Risk}$$

> Unique or unsystematic risk can be eliminated through diversification.

Unique risk is known as **diversifiable** or **unsystematic risk.** It is an important component of total risk because many of the uncertainties confronting the typical firm are unique to that firm and perhaps some of its competitors. Diver-

EXHIBIT 6-4
Market Risk and Unique Risk

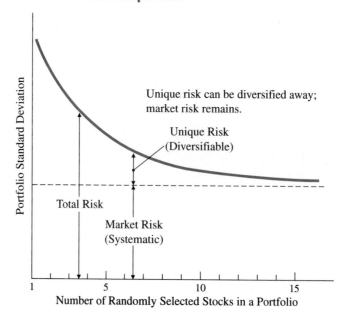

sifiable risks include changing consumer tastes, labor strikes, new product developments or marketing campaigns that affect a firm's competitive position, and fluctuations in raw materials prices. For example, major risks affecting Maxwell House, Kraft's' coffee division, include unpredictable changes in its market share, fluctuations in the price of green coffee beans, and the uncertain number of people switching among coffee, tea, and soft drinks. Depending on what happens to the Brazilian coffee bean crop and, therefore, to the price of coffee beans and how many people shift from drinking coffee to, say, Coca-Cola or from Maxwell House to Nestlé's Taster's Choice, Maxwell House could do better or worse than expected. Because these risk factors are limited to the small number of firms competing in the beverage industry, they can be diversified away.

No matter how well diversified you are, however, there is some risk you just can't avoid. This unavoidable component of risk is known as **market** or **systematic risk.** It exists because certain risk factors—such as variations in the GNP growth rate, changes in the level of real interest rates, or oil price shocks—systematically affect all firms in the economy to a greater or lesser extent. The existence of common risk factors explains why stocks tend to move together. No matter how many different stocks investors hold, they are still exposed to the vagaries of the market.

This was vividly demonstrated on October 19, 1987, when 1,973 of the 2,081 stocks traded on the New York Stock Exchange (95 percent) dropped in price. Even the most well-diversified investor would have suffered. However, even on Black Monday, although NYSE stocks dropped an average of 19.2 percent, some stocks dropped far more, and others actually gained.

Stocks can be categorized as cyclical, countercyclical, or acyclical. A **cyclical stock's** returns move in line with the state of the economy. It does well when the economy does well and poorly when the economy does poorly. Auto stocks are generally cyclical. A **countercyclical stock,** on the other hand, does well when the economy suffers and poorly when the economy prospers. For example, an auto replacement parts manufacturer's stock would be countercyclical because consumers tend to hold onto their cars longer during hard times, fixing them up as they break down rather than replacing them. A third group of stocks seems to be *acyclical.* Their returns may vary but not with the business cycle. Acyclical stocks would include the shares of medical supply companies like Johnson & Johnson and Baxter International. Demand for their products (sold to hospitals and doctors) is strong in good times and holds up in economic slumps. Most stocks are cyclical, moving in step with general economic conditions and, therefore, in line with one another. Hence, the countercyclical and acyclical stocks supply the greatest degree of diversification.

To illustrate the benefits and the limits of diversification, let's suppose that we are thinking about investing in General Motors stock. GM is a cyclical stock that tends to do well in an expanding economy and very poorly in a recession. Therefore, our estimates of returns will be closely linked to general economic conditions, which could range from rapid economic expansion to a recession triggered by global economic turmoil. The return characteristics of GM are described in Exhibit 6-5.

Market or systematic risk is unavoidable.

EXHIBIT 6-5
Probability Distribution for GM Common Stock

State of the Economy	Probability or Likelihood	Forecasted Return (in percent)
Economic Boom	0.50	40
"Normal Year"	0.30	15
Recession	0.20	−30

Based on these forecasts, the expected return on GM stock would be

$$E(R_{GM}) = 0.50(40\%) + 0.30(15\%) + 0.20(-30\%) = 18.5\%$$

and GM's standard deviation of returns would be

$$\sigma_{GM} = [0.50(40.0 - 18.5)^2 + 0.30(15.0 - 18.5)^2 + 0.20(-30.0 - 18.5)^2]^{1/2}$$

$$= [0.50(21.5)^2 + 0.30(-3.5)^2 + 0.20(-48.5)^2]^{1/2}$$

$$= (231.1 + 3.7 + 470.5)^{1/2} = 26.6\%$$

Like any expected value, the 18.5 percent return calculated here is a measure of central tendency for our probability distribution. Statistically, the standard deviation measures the dispersion or "spread" between the measure of central tendency and the forecasted returns under specific economic scenarios. One way to view the standard deviation is that it captures the "fuzziness" in the estimating process. If the probability distribution of GM's returns were *normal* (i.e., followed the bell-shaped curve that we see in statistics), then the chances would be approximately 2 out of 3 that the *realized* return would be between $(R_{GM} - \sigma_{GM})$ and $(R_{GM} + \sigma_{GM})$. With an expected return (R_{GM}) of 18.5 percent, and a standard deviation (σ_{GM}) of 26.6 percent, there is a two-thirds chance that GM common stock will produce returns somewhere between −8.1 percent and 45.1 percent.

Risk and Return in a Portfolio Context

The calculation of expected value and standard deviation for GM common stock confirms our intuition that buying a stock whose returns vary dramatically with the business cycle is a risky proposition. Our biggest concern with putting all of our wealth in GM is that forecasted economic booms have a nasty habit of not materializing. Therefore, if we invested heavily in GM, anticipating rapid economic growth, financial losses could be substantial if a recession should occur instead.

One way to mitigate these risks would be to create a portfolio by putting half of our wealth into GM stock and the other half in a stock such as Echlin (ECH[2]). ECH produces automobile and truck replacement parts as well as parts for lawnmowers, boats, and snowmobiles. Since replacement parts make up 75 percent of

---

[2]Echlin's common stock trades on the New York Stock Exchange under the symbol ECH.

its revenues, ECH might do well in an economic downturn because many consumers might opt to repair their existing cars and trucks rather than buy new ones.

Exhibit 6-6 presents the risk-return characteristics of a hypothetical portfolio split equally between GM and ECH. Combining GM with a stock like ECH significantly reduces overall risk because ECH common stock is expected to do well during recessions, thereby providing you with some downside protection. This risk reduction is not a free ride because ECH tends to do relatively poorly during economic booms; hence, the *expected return* on your portfolio is lower than if you were to invest solely in GM common stock. Given the data in Exhibit 6-6, individual investors would have to make a choice based on their own risk preferences and decide whether they wanted to: (1) invest their money in a low-risk, low-return stock like ECH, (2) invest in a high-risk, high-return stock like GM, or (3) combine GM and ECH in a portfolio for significant risk reduction at some sacrifice in return.

Portfolio Expected Return. Reducing risk through diversification depends on the relationship of return patterns for each security in the portfolio. To examine this linkage more closely, let's take a quick look at the mathematics of portfolio-building. First, the expected return on a portfolio of two or more securities is just a weighted average of the expected returns of the individual components; the weights are equal to the proportion of an investor's wealth placed in each security. In mathematical terms, this means that

$$E(R_p) = \sum_{i=1}^{n} w_i E(R_i) \qquad [6\text{-}3]$$

and

$$w_i = \frac{V_i}{I}$$

where $E(R_p)$ is the expected return on the portfolio; $E(R_i)$ is the expected return on asset i; n is the number of assets in the portfolio; and w_i is the value of the investment in asset i, V_i, as a fraction of the total investment I in the portfolio.

EXHIBIT 6-6
Portfolio Probability Distribution
50% General Motors–50% Echlin

State of the Economy	Probability or Likelihood	Forecasted Return— GM (in percent)	Forecasted Return— ECH (in percent)	Portfolio Return (in percent)
Economic Boom	0.50	40	4	22.0*
"Normal Year"	0.30	15	14	14.5
Recession	0.20	−30	18	−6.0
Expected Return		18.5	9.8	14.2
Standard Deviation		26.6	6.0	9.9

*The portfolio return for each state of the economy is a simple average of the forecasted returns for GM and ECH.

The correlation coefficient measures the degree to which security returns tend to move with one another.

Portfolio Risk and Correlation.   As mentioned, the contribution of an individual asset to a portfolio's risk is apt to be less than the asset's own standard deviation, owing to the diversification effect. In other words, the risk of a portfolio is not a simple weighted average of the standard deviations of the individual securities but depends on the relationship between returns among those securities. This relationship, based on the extent to which security returns tend to move together, can be measured by the **correlation coefficient**. The correlation coefficient between two securities i and j, r_{ij}, takes on values between -1 and $+1$. A positive correlation, such as exists between Ford and General Motors stock, indicates that the security returns tend to move in the same direction; securities that are negatively correlated tend to move in opposite directions. A zero correlation means that the security returns vary independently of each other. A related statistical measure of the tendency of two variables to move together that is often used in place of or in addition to the correlation coefficient is the *covariance*. The covariance between variables i and j, σ_{ij}, is $r_{ij}\sigma_i\sigma_j$.

The lower the correlation coefficient between two stocks, the greater the benefits from diversification.

The less positive or more negative the correlation or covariance among securities, the greater the risk-reducing benefits of portfolio diversification; conversely, combining securities that are highly positively correlated into a portfolio provides little in the way of risk reduction. For example, a portfolio containing Ford and GM stock provides less diversification than one that contains Ford and IBM stock. Although most asset returns tend to move together, they don't do so in lockstep. Thus, despite the generally positive correlation among asset returns, the risk-reducing benefits from diversification are enormous. As we saw in Exhibit 6-4, diversification can remove almost half the variation in the average stock.

For the two-asset case, the general formula for the standard deviation of a portfolio (σ_P) is

$$\sigma_p = [w_1^2\sigma_1^2 + w_2^2\sigma_2^2 + 2w_1w_2r_{12}\sigma_1\sigma_2]^{1/2} \qquad [6\text{-}4]$$

where w_1 and w_2 are the proportion of an investor's wealth placed in assets 1 and 2 ($w_1 + w_2 = 1$); σ_1 and σ_2 are the standard deviation of returns for securities 1 and 2; and r_{12} is the correlation coefficient.

Illustration

For example, suppose the standard deviations of the returns on Exxon and 3M stock are 31 percent and 44 percent, respectively, and the correlation between their returns is 0.14. According to Equation [6-4], a portfolio invested 60 percent in Exxon stock and 40 percent in 3M stock will have a standard deviation of

$$\sigma_p = [(0.6 \times 31)^2 + (0.4 \times 44)^2 + 2 \times 0.6 \times 0.4 \times 0.14 \times 31 \times 44]^{1/2}$$
$$= (747.38)^{1/2}$$
$$= 27.3\%$$

The portfolio standard deviation of 27.3 percent is less than the standard deviation of either Exxon or 3M. By contrast, the weighted average of the individual standard deviations is

$$0.6 \times 31\% + 0.4 \times 44\% = 36.2\%$$

Thus, diversification reduces the portfolio's standard deviation, in absolute terms, by 8.9 percent (36.2% − 27.3%) or, in relative terms, by a fraction equal to 24.6 percent (8.9%/36.2%). In other words, the standard deviation of the portfolio is only about 75 percent of the average standard deviation of its component stocks. As we vary the weights attached to the stocks, the expected return and standard deviation of the portfolio will change in line with Equation [6-4].

Similarly, the value of diversification will vary with the correlation between the stocks. For example, if the correlation between Exxon and 3M were zero, the portfolio standard deviation would fall to 25.6 percent:

$$\begin{aligned}
\sigma_p &= [(0.6 \times 31)^2 + (0.4 \times 44)^2]^{1/2} \\
&= (655.72)^{1/2} \\
&= 25.6\%
\end{aligned}$$

Conversely, if the correlation between the two stocks were 1, the standard deviation of the portfolio would rise to 36.2 percent:

$$\begin{aligned}
\sigma_p &= [(0.6 \times 31)^2 + (0.4 \times 44)^2 + 2 \times 0.6 \times 0.4 \times 1 \times 31 \times 44]^{1/2} \\
&= (1{,}310.44)^{1/2} \\
&= 36.2\%
\end{aligned}$$

In the purely hypothetical case of a perfectly negative correlation ($r_{12} = -1$), the standard deviation of the portfolio would fall to 1.0 percent, less than 3 percent of the weighted average standard deviation:

$$\begin{aligned}
\sigma_p &= [(0.6 \times 31)^2 + (0.4 \times 44)^2 + 2 \times 0.6 \times 0.4 \times -1 \times 31 \times 44]^{1/2} \\
&= (1.00)^{1/2} \\
&= 1.00\%
\end{aligned}$$

6.3 MODERN PORTFOLIO THEORY AND THE PRICING OF CAPITAL ASSETS

It has long been recognized that diversification reduces risk, but that was the extent of knowledge about portfolios until 1952. In that year, Harry Markowitz, the "father of modern portfolio theory," published an article describing the exact relationship between stock return correlations and risk reduction.[3] But Markowitz

---

[3]Harry Markowitz (1952).

was concerned with more than diversification per se; he was most interested in the basic principles of portfolio construction. These principles became the foundation for the study of the relationship between risk and return.

Markowitz recognized that a set of securities can be combined into an infinite number of portfolios by varying the weights assigned to the different securities. This is illustrated in Exhibit 6-7. Each "x" represents the expected return and standard deviation associated with an individual security. By combining these securities into portfolios and varying the weights on the stocks, you can attain a much wider range of risk–return combinations. The shaded area, known as the **opportunity set,** shows all the possible combinations of expected return and standard deviation associated with the set of feasible portfolios.

But investors, despite varying investment criteria, will be interested only in a particular subset of these feasible portfolios, the subset of efficient portfolios. An *efficient portfolio* has the smallest possible standard deviation for its level of expected return *and* has the maximum expected return for a given level of risk. Only this subset is consistent with the two objectives common to all rational, risk-averse investors: *higher return* and *lower risk.* These portfolios, which lie along the solid dark line at the top of the feasible set, comprise the *efficient set,* more commonly termed the **efficient frontier.** The efficient set of portfolios can be computed with a technique known as *quadratic programming.*

> Only efficient portfolios provide investors with the lowest risk for a given expected return and have the highest return for a given level of risk.

EXHIBIT 6-7
Portfolio Creation with Different Combinations of Stocks

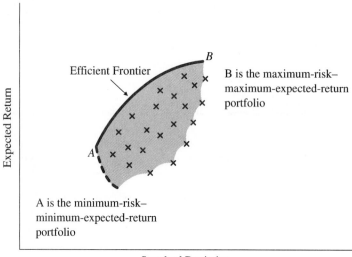

Optimal Portfolio Selection

Even the efficient frontier contains an infinite number of possible portfolio combinations, ranging from the minimum-risk–minimum-return portfolio (portfolio A) to the maximum-risk–maximum-return portfolio (portfolio B). Each represents a different risk–return tradeoff: The higher the expected return, the more risk must be assumed. No one portfolio is inherently better than any other. The optimal portfolio choice will vary from investor to investor and depend on the investor's degree of risk aversion. Those investors willing to take on added risk in the hope of earning a higher return will select a portfolio closer to B; those more risk averse will prefer a portfolio closer to A.

Optimal Portfolio Selection with a Risk-Free Security. The opportunity to borrow or lend at a risk-free rate r_f has a powerful implication for optimal portfolio selection. If you invest part of your money in a riskless security like a Treasury bill and the remainder in an efficient portfolio—like C in Exhibit 6-8—you can obtain any combination of expected return and risk lying along the line connecting the points r_f and C. For example, if you invest half your funds in the Treasury bill and the other half in portfolio C, your risk–return combination will be point D, halfway between r_f and C. It is evident from Exhibit 6-8, however, that you can do better than point D. For example, point E has a higher expected return but no added risk, whereas point F has the same expected return as D but less risk. Points E and F both lie on the line connecting points r_f and M. This line contains all possible combinations of the risk-free security and portfolio M.[4] Investors will always prefer to hold combinations of the risk-free security and portfolio M because they offer a superior risk–return tradeoff.

In fact, the points on line r_fMG, which is just tangent to the efficient frontier of risky portfolios, represent the best attainable combinations of risk and return. Thus, this line, the **capital market line (CML)**, dominates all other lines. No matter which point on another line you select, you can earn a higher return with the same amount of risk or less risk for the same return by selecting combinations of the risk-free security and the tangency portfolio M. If you lend money at the risk-free rate r_f, you will wind up at a point on the line segment r_fM; if you borrow money to leverage your investment in portfolio M, you will be at a point on the line segment MG. Therefore, when riskless borrowing and lending are available, the set of efficient portfolios is represented by the CML; it is no longer the curved portion of the set of feasible risky portfolios connecting points A and B. Thus, *portfolio M is now the only efficient portfolio of risky assets.*

> The capital market line (CML) represents the best combination of risk and expected return for portfolios.

---

[4]If w is the fraction of funds invested in the risk-free asset (with $1 - w$ being the fraction invested in portfolio M), then the expected return on the newly formed portfolio will be $wr_f + (1 - w)r_m$ and the standard deviation will be $(1 - w)\sigma_m$ (because $\sigma_{r_f} = 0$) where r_m and σ_m are the expected return and standard deviation of portfolio M. Thus, both risk and expected return are linear in w. This means that the risk and expected return of all portfolios involving possible combinations of the risk-free asset and portfolio M lie on line r_fMG.

EXHIBIT 6-8
**Selection of an Optimal Portfolio When
a Riskless Investment Is Available**

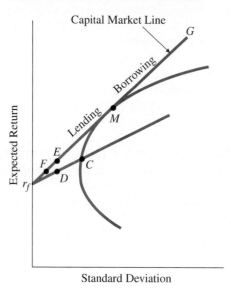

| The market port-folio contains each asset in proportion to its share of total market value. | If all investors share the same probability beliefs, they all will hold only efficient portfolios that are linear combinations of the risk-free asset and portfolio M. For the market to be in equilibrium, M must be the *market portfolio;* that is, M must contain each asset in proportion to that asset's share of the total market value of all assets. This means that if IBM comprises 5 percent of the market value of all securities, then 5 percent of portfolio M must consist of IBM stock. |

If all investors hold the market portfolio (or a reasonably well-diversified facsimile), which, by definition, contains no unsystematic risk, then only market risk will matter. This leads to one of the most important insights of modern finance theory: *Because the risk of a well-diversified portfolio depends only on the market risk of its component securities, the relevant risk of any security is its sensitivity to general market movements.*

| The market price of risk represents the premium over the risk-free rate per unit of risk. | The idea that only market or systematic risk matters underlies the pricing of risk. This can be seen by focusing attention on the capital market line. The CML has an intercept of r_f and a slope equal to $(r_m - r_f)/\sigma_m$, where r_m is the required return on the market portfolio and σ_m is the standard deviation of M. The term $r_m - r_f$ is the **market risk premium.** It depends on the average degree of investor risk aversion and the amount of market risk. Dividing the market risk premium through by σ_m yields the **market price of risk:** |

$$\text{Market price of risk} = \frac{r_m - r_f}{\sigma_m}$$

Illustration

The market price of risk is so called because it describes the risk premium expected by investors per unit of market risk as measured by the standard deviation of the market return. For example, we saw that historically, r_m = 13.0 percent; r_f = 3.8 percent, and σ_m = 15 percent, where the returns are in nominal terms. Thus, based on the historical data,

$$\text{Market price of risk} = \frac{13.0 - 3.8}{15} = 0.61\%$$

This number means that historically, investors have received about 0.61 percent in added return for each additional unit of risk that they were willing to bear when holding an efficient portfolio.

Because any efficient portfolio P must lie on the CML, the relationship between risk and return for such a portfolio is linear:

$$\begin{array}{ccccc} \text{Required return} & = & \text{Risk-free} & + & \text{Market price} & \times & \text{Standard deviation} \\ \text{on portfolio P} & & \text{return} & & \text{of risk} & & \text{of portfolio P} \end{array}$$

$$r_p = r_f + \frac{(r_m - r_f)}{\sigma_m} \sigma_p \qquad\qquad [6\text{-}5]$$

Equation [6-5] says that the required return on an efficient portfolio P, r_p, equals the risk-free rate of interest plus a risk premium equal to the market price of risk multiplied by the standard deviation of the portfolio σ_p. An important implication of Equation [6-5] is that the risk premium on the efficient portfolio $r_p - r_f$ varies directly in proportion to its standard deviation. For example, doubling σ_p doubles the required risk premium.

It is always possible that investors will have access to different information, and so each will hold a different risky portfolio. This is highly unlikely, however, in an efficient market in which information is widely disseminated and available at nominal cost. In such a world, investors will wind up with similar beliefs and information. We have already seen that this means that everybody will hold the market portfolio M. In that case, the relevant risk of a security is its contribution to the risk of the market portfolio. As noted earlier, this is the security's *systematic* or *market* risk.

Beta, the volatility of a security's return with respect to the market, measures systematic risk.

Market Risk and Beta

The market risk of a security, in turn, depends on its sensitivity to movements in the market portfolio. The sensitivity of an asset's return to market movements is called **beta** (β); beta measures the systematic risk of a security. Because the market portfolio's volatility relative to itself is 1, the market portfolio has a beta of 1.0.

A stock with a beta of 1.5 will be one and a half times as volatile as the market. When the market goes up 1 percent, the stock will go up, on average, 1.5 percent. Similarly, a stock with a beta of .5 will tend to move only about half as much as the market will. If the market goes up by 1 percent, the stock will generally rise only .5 percent. Conversely, a 1 percent drop in the market will cause the stock to drop by about .5 percent on average.

Technically, the beta of a risky asset i is the covariance of returns on that asset with returns on the market, σ_{im}, divided by the variance of the market return:

$$\beta \text{ for asset } i = \frac{\text{Covariance between Returns on Asset } i}{\text{and the Return on the Market Portfolio}} \frac{}{\text{Variance of the Market Portfolio}} \qquad [6\text{-}6]$$

$$\beta_i = \frac{\sigma_{im}}{\sigma_m^2}$$

As defined earlier, $\sigma_{im} = r_{im}\sigma_i\sigma_m$. Making the substitution yields

$$\beta_i = \frac{r_{im}\sigma_i\sigma_m}{\sigma_m^2} = \frac{r_{im}\sigma_i}{\sigma_m} \qquad [6\text{-}7]$$

As Equation [6-7] shows, another interpretation of beta is that it measures the fraction $r_{im}\sigma_i$ of the asset's standard deviation that contributes to the market portfolio's risk. Thus, if w_i is the weight of asset i in the market portfolio, $w_i\beta_i$ will be its relative contribution to the risk of the market portfolio. A stock with a beta exceeding 1.0 contributes a more than proportionate share of risk to the market portfolio. For example, Nike has a beta of 1.50, meaning that it contributes 50 percent more to portfolio risk than the average stock in the market portfolio (because the average beta must be 1.0). By contrast, AT&T, with a beta of 0.85, contributes less than its proportionate share of risk. Because the total proportion of risk contributed by all stocks in the market portfolio must equal 1.0, we must have

$$\sum_{i=1}^{n} w_i\beta_i = 1.0 \qquad [6\text{-}8]$$

Betas are additive; the beta of a portfolio is a simple average of the component securities.

In general, *the beta of a portfolio equals the weighted average of the betas of the component securities.* This makes the market risk of any given portfolio easy to calculate.

Exhibit 6-9 lists the betas of individual stocks in four different industries. Stocks with betas greater than 1.0, such as those of retailers, are often referred to as **aggressive stocks** because they go up faster than the market in a "bull" (rising) market but fall faster in a "bear" (declining) market. Gold and silver mining stocks, with betas of less than 1.0, that tend to fluctuate less than the market are called **defensive stocks.**

The stocks with the highest standard deviations are not necessarily those with the highest betas; there is no necessary relationship between a stock's individual risk and its contribution to market risk.

EXHIBIT 6-9
Betas of Stocks in Four Different Industries

Textile Companies		Retailers	
Burlington Industries	0.70	Dayton Hudson	1.05
Cone Mills	0.70	Federated Department Stores	1.15
Guilford Mills	0.60	JC Penney	0.95
Unifi	0.65	Sears, Roebuck	1.10
Westpoint Stevens	0.60	Wal-Mart	0.95
Foreign Electronics Firms		**Gold/Silver Mining Companies**	
Hitachi	0.75	Barrick Gold	0.70
NEC Corporation	0.70	Coeur D'Alene Mines	0.75
Pioneer Electronics	0.80	Homestake	0.65
Sony Corporation	0.95	Newmont Mining	0.70
Philips Electronics	1.25	Placer Dome, Inc.	0.90

Source: Value Line Investment Survey, various issues; July–September 1998.

> Beta is the slope of the *characteristic line*—a statistical construct relating returns on a security to those in the market.

Estimating Beta.   Stock betas are usually estimated from historical data, even though they are based on expectations about *future* performance relative to the market. The technique used is called *regression analysis,* and it involves fitting a straight line through the points representing past combinations of returns on the market and the stock as is shown in Exhibit 6-10. The line that fits the data best—in the sense of minimizing the sum of the squared deviations between the line and the data points—is the **characteristic line** for the stock. The estimated beta equals the slope of the characteristic line and is the regression coefficient on market returns.[5]

Each of the points on the graph in Exhibit 6-10 represents the return for a specific time period. Data point A, for example, might represent the return on the stock in relation to the market for March 1999 (if, as is often done, monthly data are being used). Analytically, it's useful to think about the individual data point and the characteristic line in terms of the following equation:

$$r_{it} = \alpha_i + \beta_i r_{mt} + \varepsilon_{it} \qquad [6\text{-}9]$$

where r_{it} is the return on an individual stock during time period t; r_{mt}, the return on the market in the same time period; and ε_{it} is an "error term" representing the difference between an individual data point and the regression line. The constant α is the y-intercept of the regression line, and β_i its slope. The slope of the characteristic line, β_i, is the volatility of an individual stock's returns with respect to the market.

Equation [6-9] provides us with a useful way of thinking about the returns and risks in holding individual common stocks. The first two terms of Equation

---

[5]Rather than calculating beta directly, you could use the services of investment advisory firms like Merrill Lynch or Value Line, which regularly provide updated estimates of the betas of actively traded stocks. Estimates vary from one service to another because of different time periods or estimation techniques used, but they should be similar.

EXHIBIT 6-10
Estimating Beta from Stock Return Data:
The Characteristic Line

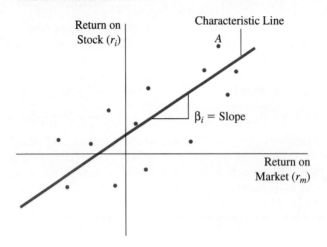

[6-9], $\alpha_i + \beta_i r_{mt}$, form the regression line and represent that component of a stock's return that is tied to the movements in the market. As we noted earlier, this *market* or *systematic risk* cannot be eliminated through diversification. In contrast, ε_{it}, the error term, can be interpreted as that portion of an individual stock's return that is unrelated to market movements. These movements represent *diversifiable* or *unsystematic risk* because they are unique to an individual security and can be eliminated through portfolio diversification. For an individual firm, unsystematic risk—which can arise from such events as the development of a new product or the discovery of toxic waste underneath the company's new state-of-the-art manufacturing plant—can influence the returns for that firm but would have only a minor effect on a well-diversified portfolio.

6.4   THE CAPITAL ASSET PRICING MODEL

The basic premise of all financial models is that investors are risk averse and, therefore, demand a premium for bearing risk. This means that higher-risk assets are priced to yield higher expected returns than lower-risk assets. An implication is that the expected return on an asset can be decomposed into the risk-free return plus a risk premium:

Expected Return on a Risky Asset = Risk-Free Return + Risk Premium

The risk-free rate compensates for the time value of money and is measured as the return on a riskless instrument like a Treasury bill.[6] The important issue now

---

[6]In reality, Treasury bills are free only of *default risk*. Because they are stated in nominal terms, investors in T-bills must still bear inflation risk. The CAPM can be modified to incorporate inflation risk.

is what determines the risk premium for a given security or other asset. We have already seen that fully diversified investors holding the market portfolio care only about an asset's systematic risk as measured by its beta. But what is the expected risk premium for an individual security given its beta, that is, what is the relationship between a stock's beta and its required return? To begin with the simplest cases first, a stock which has a beta of 1.0, the same as the market portfolio, should yield a risk premium of $r_m - r_f$, whereas a riskless asset, with a beta of 0, should provide a return equal to r_f. Otherwise, it would be possible to earn arbitrage profits. But what about all the other assets with betas unequal to 0 or 1?

The CAPM relates required returns on individual assets to their risk.

The answer to this question is contained in the **capital asset pricing model** (CAPM). Developed simultaneously in the early 1960s by John Lintner, William Sharpe (who won the Nobel prize in economics in 1990 for his work on the CAPM), and Jack Treynor, the CAPM provides the following key result: *The risk premium on any asset is proportional to its beta.*[7] This means that the expected risk premium on asset i with a beta of β_i must be

$$r_i - r_f = \beta_i(r_m - r_f) \qquad [6\text{-}10]$$

where r_i is the required return on asset i. Rearranging the terms of Equation [6-10] yields the more familiar form of the CAPM:

$$r_i = r_f + \beta_i(r_m - r_f) \qquad [6\text{-}11]$$

According to Equation [6-11], the required return on asset i equals the risk-free return plus a risk premium equal to the asset's beta multiplied by the market risk premium $r_m - r_f$. The linear relationship between an asset's expected return and its beta coefficient is known as the **security market line** (**SML**) and is depicted in Exhibit 6-11. The slope of this line is the market risk premium $r_m - r_f$.

Illustration

Using the CAPM

The market has an expected rate of return of 15 percent, the riskless rate of interest is 5 percent, and a common stock has a beta of 2. Using the CAPM, what is the expected rate of return of the stock?

Solution
Apply the CAPM as follows:

$$\text{Expected return on the stock} = r_f + \beta(r_m - r_f)$$
$$= 5\% + 2\,(15\% - 5\%)$$
$$= 25\%$$

---

[7]Treynor's article on capital asset pricing was never published. The other referenced papers are Sharpe (1964) and Lintner (1964).

EXHIBIT 6-11
Capital Market Relationship between Risk and Return

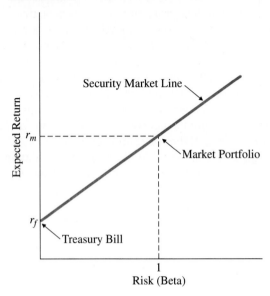

The more risk averse investors are, the higher the required return for bearing risk. Less risk aversion leads to a smaller risk premium and a lower required return. The result is higher stock prices because the same cash flows will be capitalized at a lower discount rate, thereby increasing the present value of those cash flows. Conversely, an increase in risk aversion causes stock prices to decline.

> An increase (decrease) in risk aversion causes stock prices to decline (rise).

Assumptions Underlying the CAPM

Modern financial theory rests on two key assumptions:

1. Securities markets are highly competitive and populated by highly sophisticated, well-informed buyers and sellers.
2. Securities markets are dominated by rational, risk-averse investors who seek to maximize the risk-adjusted returns from their investments.

The first assumption implies that markets are efficient; that is, relevant information is readily and universally available and quickly reflected in security prices. The consequences of the second assumption are that investors prefer more wealth to less and demand a premium in the form of higher expected returns for bearing risk.

The formal development of the CAPM requires additional specialized assumptions:

1. Financial markets are frictionless: There are no taxes, transaction costs, or restrictions on borrowing, lending, and short selling (selling stock that one

doesn't own in the hope of buying it back later at a lower price). Otherwise, expected returns would be affected by an individual's tax position, cost of trading, or access to information, and there might not be a definite relationship between risk and expected return in the market.

2. Either security returns follow specific probability distributions, or there are restrictions on what investors' preferences can be.[8] If these conditions fail to hold, investors may be interested in other measures of risk besides standard deviation (like the skewness of returns—the degree to which returns are not symmetrical around the expected return), and the relationship between these measures of risk and expected return will generally not be linear.

3. Investors share common beliefs as to the probability distributions of returns. If individuals disagree on the expected returns and risks associated with different assets, it becomes more difficult to imagine a common pricing mechanism that all can agree on.

> **In general, empirical testing appears to support the CAPM.**

Although these assumptions are clearly unrealistic, some simplification of reality is always necessary in order to develop usable models. Much research has gone into examining the implications of relaxing these restrictive assumptions. The result has been more complex models but ones that are generally consistent with the simple version of the CAPM contained here. The basic insight of the CAPM—that only the systematic component of total risk is priced—still holds. Ultimately, of course, what matters is not how fancy or "realistic" a model is but how well it fits the facts.

Empirical Tests of the CAPM

There have been numerous tests of the CAPM, the best known being the studies by Fischer Black, Michael Jensen, and Myron Scholes and by Eugene Fama and James MacBeth.[9] Most of these studies, including the two aforementioned, examined returns on portfolios rather than individual securities to avoid some measurement problems. With few exceptions, these studies have reached similar conclusions:

1. Security returns appear to be linearly related to beta as predicted by the CAPM. Inclusion of a factor representing unsystematic risk does not explain past returns any better.

2. There is a positive relationship between beta and past returns; that is, higher betas tend to lead to higher returns.

3. The empirical SML appears to be less steeply sloped than the theoretical SML. This means that low-beta stocks earn a somewhat higher return than the CAPM predicts, whereas high-beta stocks earn less than predicted. This could be due to measurement problems.

4. The intercept term is somewhat greater than its theoretically predicted value of r_f.

---

[8]Specifically, either investors have quadratic utility functions in wealth, or portfolio returns are normally distributed. The latter assumption is less questionable than the former.

[9]See Black, Jensen, and Scholes (1972) and Fama and MacBeth (1973).

Although these tests don't provide unequivocal support of the CAPM, they are consistent with its major implications. Beta, the measure of systematic risk, is linearly and positively related to past returns. However, this conclusion has been brought into question by two studies.

The Roll Critique.   According to Richard Roll, all empirical tests of the CAPM suffer from a basic flaw: Although systematic risk must be measured relative to the market portfolio, all tests to date of the CAPM use a proxy for the market.[10] Moreover, the distortion associated with using an index of stocks listed on the New York Stock Exchange as a proxy for the true market portfolio has become more severe over time. About 60 percent of the world's stock market capitalization is in non-U.S. companies, and this fraction has generally increased over time.

It is important to realize that Roll's critique does not invalidate the CAPM; it calls into question the results of previous tests of the model. The arbitrage pricing theory, introduced in the next section, does not have the problem of being unable to identify the correct market portfolio although it does have its own empirical problems.

Roll and Fama and French have presented serious challenges to the CAPM.

The Fama and French Study.   An even more serious challenge to the CAPM has been presented by the recent work of Eugene Fama and Kenneth French.[11] Fama and French studied the performance of more than 2,000 stocks from 1941 to 1990. Their conclusion: Beta cannot explain stocks' relative performance over time. Instead of beta, Fama and French found the best predictors of future returns to be firm size and the ratio of book value to market value—especially the latter. These latter variables are probably proxies for some underlying fundamental risk factors.

For someone who buys Roll's critique, beta's lack of empirical significance is not surprising because the Fama-French test, like all the others, fails to use the correct market index. An alternative response is that the Fama-French results stem from data mining. Yet another argument is that beta estimates based on historical data may be suspect because such estimates implicitly assume that the past is representative of the future. That is, these findings simply suggest that a stock's historical risk cannot be used to predict its future return. Louis Chan and Josef Lakonishok argue that beta's lack of statistical significance is due to the noisy environment generating stock returns, suggesting that the case for discarding beta is not clear-cut.[12] Regardless of whether the CAPM is theoretically correct or not, however, the results of Fama and French seriously question its current empirical implementation, that is, by estimating beta using a market proxy like the S&P 500 and historical data. Despite these blows to CAPM, its strong intuitive appeal and its widespread use among corporations mean that it is reasonable to demonstrate

---

[10]See Roll (1977).
[11]See Fama and French (1992).
[12]See Chan and Lakonishok (1992).

how the CAPM can be and is currently being used in corporate financial decision making.

Support for the use of CAPM also comes from the empirical research of Robert Harris and Felicia Marston.[13] Using the dividend discount model combined with analysts' growth forecasts to estimate the cost of equity capital, they find that required returns for individual stocks—and, therefore, their expected risk premia—vary directly with their estimated betas.

Illustration

Applying the CAPM

Suppose you want to find the required return on a stock like Wal-Mart (ticker symbol WMT). The CAPM tells you that you need three numbers to do this: r_f, β_{WMT}, and $r_m - r_f$. In September 1998 the return on 30-year Treasury bonds, a proxy for the long-term risk-free rate, was 4.7 percent. Based on the historical record, shown in Exhibit 6-1, a reasonable estimate of the market risk premium relative to Treasury bonds is about 7.4 percent. In Exhibit 6-9 the beta of WMT is given as 0.95. Thus, the CAPM-based estimate of the required return on Wal-Mart stock is 11.16 percent:

$$r_{WMT} = 0.047 + 0.95 \times 0.074 = 11.73\%$$

The Basic Message of the CAPM

According to the CAPM, higher expected returns go hand-in-hand with higher risk.

The basic message of the CAPM is that if you want to earn a higher return, you must be prepared to bear greater risk. There is no "free lunch" in an efficient market. Moreover, according to the CAPM, if you are holding a less than fully diversified portfolio, you are bearing risk (diversifiable risk) for which you will not be compensated. It should be stressed that these basic insights from the CAPM—that risk has its reward and that unsystematic risk is not priced—are not in dispute. The disagreement among financial economists is over how to incorporate these insights in a model.

6.5   THE ARBITRAGE PRICING THEORY

In the early 1970s, Stephen Ross developed the **arbitrage pricing theory** or **APT**, a generalized version (in some respects) of the CAPM.[14] Although it is a much more complex model than the CAPM, the Fama and French critique of the

---

[13]See Harris and Marston (1992).
[14]See Ross (1976).

CAPM will likely increase the use of APT to estimate discount rates. According to the APT, the expected return on security or asset i is

$$\begin{matrix} \text{Expected} \\ \text{Return on} \\ \text{Asset } i \end{matrix} = \begin{matrix} \text{Riskless} \\ \text{Return} \end{matrix} + \begin{matrix} \text{Sensitivity} \\ \text{of Asset } i \\ \text{to Factor} \end{matrix} \times \begin{matrix} \text{Factor} \\ \text{Risk} \\ \text{Premium} \end{matrix}$$

$$E(r_i) = r_f + \beta_i \lambda \qquad \text{[6-12]}$$

The APT includes multiple risk factors.

where r_f is the risk-free interest rate; β_i is security i's systematic risk; and λ is the market price of risk.[15] A security's systematic risk is due to a random risk factor, like changes in gross national product (GNP), that is shared by all securities to a greater or lesser extent. Arbitrage across the common factor ensures that only systematic risk is priced. If this sounds similar to the logic underlying the CAPM, it should. The main difference between the CAPM and the APT is that the CAPM specifies that the common risk factor is the random return on the market portfolio, whereas the APT does not prespecify the common risk factor(s).

One advantage of the APT is that it can be expanded to encompass several risk factors. The CAPM is limited to one common risk factor. The general multifactor APT can be expressed as

$$E(r_i) = r_f + \beta_{i1}\lambda_1 + \beta_{i2}\lambda_2 + \cdots + \beta_{\varepsilon}\lambda_n \qquad \text{[6-13]}$$

where β_{ij} is security i's systematic risk associated with the jth risk factor $(j = 1, \ldots, n)$; λ_j is the market price of risk for the jth risk factor; and n is the number of common factors. Empirical research based on Equation [6-13] seems to indicate that there are no more than three to five common factors affecting stock returns. The four factors identified by Chen, Roll, and Ross include unexpected changes in industrial output, in inflation, in the difference between the yield on a long-term and a short-term Treasury bond, and in bond risk premiums.[16]

The APT does not prespecify the common risk factors

These variables make intuitive sense as risk factors because unanticipated changes in them systematically affect the values of all assets. Thus investors who hold securities that are more exposed to these factors will find that their securities' market values fluctuate more over time. Investors will purchase these riskier securities, therefore, only if they expect to be compensated by a higher total return in the long run.

---

[15]When a risk-free asset doesn't exist, an alternative approach is to substitute the return on a **zero-beta portfolio,** one whose weights are set so that the portfolio has a beta of zero.

[16]See, for example, Chen, Roll, and Ross (1986).

Illustration

Using the APT

Suppose that a firm has the following factor sensitivities: .7 to the factor relating to industrial production, .3 to the factor relating to unanticipated inflation, .9 to the factor relating to the term structure of interest rates, and .4 to bond risk premiums. Further, suppose that the risk premiums for the factor sensitivities are 10 percent for industrial production, 6 percent for inflation, 4 percent for the term structure, and 3 percent for the bond risk premium. These risk premiums mean, for example, that an asset with a factor sensitivity of 1.0 to inflation risk will have an expected return that is 6 percent greater than the expected return of an otherwise identical asset that has a factor sensitivity of 0 to inflation. The risk-free interest rate is 7.5 percent. What is the expected return on this stock according to the APT?

Solution
Applying the APT yields

$$
\begin{aligned}
E(r) &= E(r_f) + \beta_1\lambda_1 + \beta_2\lambda_2 + \beta_3\lambda_3 + \beta_4\lambda_4 \\
&= 7.5\% + .7 \times 10\% + .3 \times 6\% + .9 \times 4\% + .4 \times 3\% \\
&= 21.1\%
\end{aligned}
$$

The most careful implementation of APT has been the collaboration between the financial consulting company Alcar and Ibbotson, Roll, and Ross. They employed the following four-step procedure implicit in Equation [6-12]:

1. *Identify the macroeconomic risk factors.* Alcar identified five macroeconomic factors, the fifth one (in addition to the four found by Chen, Roll, and Ross) being the separation of inflation into unexpected short-term changes and unexpected long-term changes.
2. *Estimate the risk premiums that investors demand for bearing these factor risks.* Using historical data, Alcar estimated the λ_js, the market price of risk for each of the five risk factors.
3. *Estimate the factor sensitivities for each stock.* Again using historical data, Alcar determined how sensitive each stock has been to these risk factors in the past. This gave Alcar the β_{ij}s for each security i.
4. *Calculate the expected return for each stock.* The final and easiest step was to substitute these factor risk premiums and price sensitivities into Equation [6-12] and estimate the expected returns for each stock.

Their study shows that both the CAPM and APT give very similar estimates for some industries, such as banking and oil and gas. For other industries, such as machinery and electrical equipment, the differences are substantial.

There is a great deal of research activity in the area of arbitrage pricing. Unfortunately, one outcome of this research is to call into question the testability of the APT. Although the issues raised are highly technical, as the sample of securities used to extract common factors increases, the number of estimated factors increases as well. Hence, if you find that the price of a factor varies from one portfolio to another—ordinarily, a prima facie case for rejecting the APT—the possibility always remains that your sample of securities is too small and the APT was wrongly rejected. This is analogous to the problem confronting tests of the CAPM. Another problem is the inability to identify clearly the economic forces that underlie the factors affecting security returns, particularly when these forces affect security returns in complex ways.[17] Each factor may be a construct representing the movements of several economic variables. For example, one factor may represent the interaction of inflation and changes in the difference between long-term and short-term interest rates on asset values. The jury is still out on the APT as it is on the CAPM.

Capital Market Theory and Corporate Diversification Strategies

Both the CAPM and the APT tell us that unless we have a fully diversified portfolio, we're probably bearing unsystematic risk for which we're not being compensated by the market. Therefore, from the perspective of an individual investor, diversification as a means of reducing risk makes sense.

However, at the corporate level, diversification is unlikely to pay. Why? The CAPM indicates that the appropriate measure of risk for an individual security is its volatility with respect to the market. In a portfolio context, all other risks associated with an individual stock are irrelevant because they can be diversified away. Corporate diversification efforts, such as mergers and acquisitions, which are undertaken for the *sole purpose of risk reduction do not enhance shareholder wealth because investors can eliminate unsystematic risk themselves by building diversified portfolios.* To be beneficial to shareholders, diversification, in general, and mergers and acquisitions, in particular, have to do things for stockholders that they cannot do for themselves through their own portfolio activities.

> Corporate diversification strategies for the sole purpose of risk reduction do nothing to create shareholder value.

This is an important insight and suggests that corporate mergers or acquisitions should be focused on **synergies** rather than risk reduction per se. The term synergy is used to describe a situation in which the combined entity can do things from a marketing, production, or financial standpoint that can't be accomplished by the individual firms. Synergies arise most often when a company pursues a strategy of **related diversification.** With related diversification, the lines of business a firm might profitably choose to enter would: (1) serve similar markets or utilize similar channels of distribution, (2) employ similar production technologies, and/or (3) exploit science-based skills similar to those used in its current businesses. In contrast, **unrelated** or **conglomerate diversification** involves get-

---

[17]See Shanken (1982).

ting into lines of business that may have little relationship to those currently being pursued. Typically, few synergies arise from conglomerate diversification.

For decades, many firms ignored the implications of financial theory and engaged in many unrelated acquisitions. Not surprisingly, most of these acquisitions were unsuccessful and destroyed value. Their lack of success attracted corporate raiders, who argued that the diversified conglomerates should be split into several smaller, more tightly focused companies. The idea was to eliminate the "negative synergy" that afflicts organizations when operations become too complicated and diverse to be easily manageable. In response to threats of hostile takeovers and activist shareholders, the 1980s and 1990s have seen the undoing of the diversified conglomerates of the 1960s and 1970s. For instance, in 1993, US Steel undid its 1981 acquisition of Marathon Oil by splitting itself into two publicly-traded firms—USX-Steel and USX-Marathon. In Europe, Hanson Industries, a large U.K.-based conglomerate with units in chemicals, tobacco, electric power, and cement (among others), also split itself into four separate operating companies. These splits are almost always seen as "good news" by investors, as evidenced by the stock price jumps on the date of the announcement. We predict that economic logic (and financial disaster) will force the breakup of the giant South Korean and Japanese conglomerates as well with similarly beneficial results.

> *The "negative synergies" of many conglomerate combinations are being undone by corporate restructuring.*

Illustration

Beatrice Foods aggressively acquired other companies from the early 1960s through the early 1980s. Over that 20-year period, Beatrice had acquired an array of brand names, which included Tropicana, Avis, Hunt-Wesson, Swift Meats, Max Factor, Samsonite Luggage, and Playtex among others. This stable of well-known names is impressive, but there are no significant operating (production) and marketing synergies here because the production technologies, channels of distribution, and even the brand names are very different. Sensing an opportunity to create value, the buyout firm of Kohlberg, Kravis, and Roberts (KKR) acquired Beatrice in 1986 and took it private. KKR began to sell off business units immediately and within two years had more than recouped its $6.2 billion purchase price while still retaining a number of very profitable units. The dismantling of Beatrice demonstrated what unrelated diversification can cost shareholders: The value of the firm in liquidation was far greater than its worth as an ongoing entity.

Corporate Diversification and Owner–Manager Conflicts

> *Agency conflicts between owners and managers help explain conglomerate diversification.*

As we've just noted, capital market theory provides corporate managers with some very clear guidelines on formulating diversification strategies to benefit shareholders. Specifically, related diversification can benefit stockholders *if* the acquiring company doesn't overpay for the target. On the other hand, unrelated (or conglomerate) diversification is questionable because shareholders can achieve pure risk reduction through their own portfolio. The Beatrice story was a dramatic case of ill-conceived unrelated diversification that made headlines during the mid-1980s. However, it is but one of literally dozens of instances when a firm's management engaged in diversification that didn't benefit shareholders. Agency conflicts between owners and managers are at the core of this unnecessary diversification. Let's look at a couple of dimensions of this issue.

First, from the investor's perspective, the unsystematic risk associated with an individual firm is largely irrelevant because firm-specific risk can be eliminated through diversification. However, managers who have a good deal of their human capital tied up in an individual firm can't be as cavalier about unsystematic risk as an investor can. From their perspective, any diversification—whether it's accomplished internally or through acquisition—that reduces the firm's risk also reduces their personal risk.

Coming at acquisitions from another direction, Jensen (1986) argues that managers have an incentive to increase the size of the firm beyond the point at which shareholder wealth is maximized. According to Jensen, growth increases managerial power by putting greater resources (free cash flow) at their command. It also tends to increase compensation because firm size and compensation appear to be related. Acquisitions are a way to increase a firm's size and management compensation very quickly.

There are a couple of ways to discourage non-value-producing diversification. First, some firms are willing to engage in hostile takeovers as a means of disciplining self-serving management. In the case of Beatrice, KKR acquired the company and then dismantled it. For other firms, the *threat* of a hostile takeover may be enough to "encourage" managers to serve the shareholders. In still other instances, the design of incentive contracts linking compensation to shareholder-value creation can effectively align the interests of owners and managers.[18]

6.6   THE BENEFITS OF INTERNATIONAL DIVERSIFICATION

Global diversification allows investors to achieve a better risk–return tradeoff than they could by investing solely in domestic securities.

The expanded universe of securities available internationally suggests the possibility of achieving a better risk–return tradeoff than by investing solely in U.S. securities. This follows from the basic rule of portfolio diversification: *The broader the diversification, the more stable the returns and the more diffuse the risks.*

Prudent investors know that diversifying across industries leads to a lower level of risk for a given level of expected return. Ultimately, though, the advantages of such diversification are limited because all companies in a country are more or less subject to the same cyclical economic fluctuations. By diversifying across nations whose economic cycles are not perfectly in phase, investors should be able to reduce still further the variability of their returns. In other words, risk that is systematic in the context of the U.S. economy may be unsystematic in the context of

---

[18]Jensen (1986) has suggested high levels of debt as a means of reducing owner-manager agency problems. We'll examine this argument more closely in Chapter 14 when we discuss a firm's target capital structure.

the global economy. For example, an oil price shock that hurts the U.S. economy helps the economies of oil-exporting nations and vice versa. Thus, just as movements in different stocks partially offset one another in an all-U.S. portfolio, so also movements in U.S. and non-U.S. stock portfolios cancel out each other somewhat.

The value of international equity diversification appears to be significant. Donald Lessard and Bruno Solnik, among others, have presented evidence that national factors have a strong impact on security returns relative to that of any common world factor.[19] They also found that returns from the different national equity markets have relatively low correlations with one another.

Exhibit 6-12 contains some data on correlations between U.S. and non-U.S. markets. The betas for the foreign markets relative to the U.S. market are calculated in the same way that individual asset betas are calculated:

$$\text{Foreign Market Beta} = \frac{\text{Correlation with U.S. Market} \times \text{Standard Deviation of Foreign Market}}{\text{Standard Deviation of U.S. Market}} \qquad [6\text{-}14]$$

For example, the Spanish market beta is $0.28 \times 82.44/49.52 = 0.47$.

Low correlations across markets are the key to international diversification.

Measured for the 27-year period 1970–1996, foreign markets in developed countries were correlated with the U.S. market from a high of 0.70 for Canada to a low of 0.12 for Austria. The relatively high correlation for Canada reveals that this market tracked the U.S. market's ups and downs. Austria's low correlation, on the other hand, indicates that the Austrian and U.S. markets have tended to move largely independently of each other.

Notice also that the investment risks associated with these different markets can be quite different—with the Hong Kong market showing the highest level and the Dutch market the lowest. Indeed, all the markets had a higher level of risk, as measured by the standard deviation of returns, than the U.S. market. Yet the internationally diversified **Morgan Stanley Capital International World Index** had the lowest level of risk—lower even than the U.S. market. The reason, of course, is that much of the risk associated with markets in individual countries is unsystematic and so can be eliminated by diversification as indicated by the relatively low betas of these markets. These results imply that international diversification may significantly reduce the risk of portfolio returns.

The obvious conclusion is that international diversification pushes out the *efficient frontier*—the set of portfolios that has the smallest possible standard deviation for its level of expected return and the maximum expected return for a given level of risk—allowing investors simultaneously to reduce their risk and increase their expected return. Exhibit 6-13 illustrates the effect of international diversification on the efficient frontier.

One way to estimate the benefits of international diversification is to consider the expected return and standard deviation of return for a portfolio consisting of a fraction a invested in U.S. stocks and the remaining fraction, $1 - a$, invested in foreign stocks. Define r_{us} and r_{rw} to be the expected returns on the U.S. and

---

[19]See Lessard (1974) and Solnik (1974).

EXHIBIT 6-12
Correlations of U.S. and Foreign Markets
1970–1996

Country	Correlation with U.S. Market	Standard Deviation of Returns (in percent)	Market Risk (Beta) from U.S. Perspective
United States	1.00	49.52	1.00
Canada	0.70	60.65	0.86
Australia	0.46	86.46	0.81
Hong Kong	0.30	110.87	0.68
Japan	0.25	86.37	0.44
Singapore	0.45	85.29	0.77
Austria	0.12	86.16	0.22
Belgium	0.42	68.25	0.57
Denmark	0.31	66.99	0.42
France	0.43	77.00	0.67
Germany	0.34	73.76	0.51
Italy	0.21	92.58	0.40
Netherlands	0.57	58.56	0.67
Norway	0.43	88.51	0.78
Spain	0.28	82.44	0.47
Sweden	0.41	83.02	0.68
Switzerland	0.49	63.22	0.62
United Kingdom	0.50	69.88	0.71
EAFE Index*	0.47	61.27	0.58
World Index†	0.82	48.75	0.81

*The Morgan Stanley Capital International Europe, Australia, Far East (EAFE) Index is a non–North American part of the world index and consists of 20 major stock markets from these parts of the world.
†The Morgan Stanley Capital International World Index has a combined market value of $8.6 trillion, covers 22 countries including the United States, and includes 1,500 companies worldwide.
Source: Based on data appearing in *Morgan Stanley Capital International,* various issues.

rest-of-world stock portfolios, respectively. Similarly, let σ_{us} and σ_{rw} be the standard deviations of the U.S. and rest-of-world portfolios. The expected return r_p can be calculated as

$$r_p = ar_{us} + (1 - a)r_{rw} \qquad [6\text{-}15]$$

To calculate the standard deviation of this portfolio, we repeat Equation [6-4], which is the general formula for the standard deviation of a two-asset portfolio with weights w_1 and w_2 ($w_1 + w_2 = 1$):

$$\text{Portfolio Standard Deviation} = [w_1^2\sigma_1^2 + w_2^2\sigma_2^2 + 2w_1w_2r_{12}\sigma_1\sigma_2]^{1/2} \qquad [6\text{-}4]$$

where σ_1^2 and σ_2^2 are the respective variances of the two assets; σ_1 and σ_2 are their standard deviations; and r_{12} is their correlation. We can apply Equation [6-4] to

EXHIBIT 6-13
International Diversification Pushes Out the Efficient Frontier

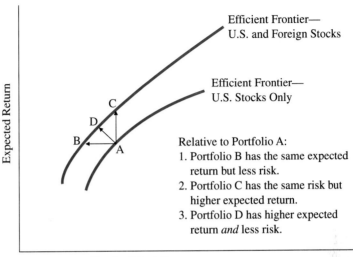

our internationally diversified portfolio by treating the domestic and foreign portfolios as separate assets. This operation yields a portfolio standard deviation σ_p equal to

$$\sigma_p = [a^2\sigma_{us}^2 + (1-a)^2\sigma_{rw}^2 + 2a(1-a)\sigma_{us}\sigma_{rw}\sigma_{us,rw}]^{1/2} \qquad [6\text{-}16]$$

where $\sigma_{us,rw}$ is the correlation between the returns on the U.S. and foreign stock portfolios.

To see the benefits of international diversification, assume that the portfolio is equally invested in U.S. and foreign stocks, where the EAFE Index represents the foreign stock portfolio. Using data from Exhibit 16-12, we see that $\sigma_{us} = 49.5\%$, $\sigma_{rw} = 61.3\%$, and $\sigma_{us,rw} = 0.47$. According to Equation [6-4], these figures imply that the standard deviation of the internationally diversified portfolio is

$$\sigma_p = [0.5^2(49.5)^2 + 0.5^2(61.3)^2 + 0.5^2 \times 2 \times 49.5 \times 61.3 \times 0.47]^{1/2}$$

$$= (2,265)^{1/2}$$

$$= 47.6\%$$

With barriers
to international
diversification
coming down,
U.S. investors
have many ways
to invest in foreign securities.

Here the risk of the internationally diversified portfolio is below the risk of the U.S. portfolio. Moreover, the expected return is higher as well.

Although there are barriers to international diversification by investors, many of them are being eroded. Money invested abroad by both large institutions and individuals is growing dramatically. Nonetheless, foreign investments still represent a relatively minor degree of international diversification. For example, in 1993, Americans held 94% of their equity investments in domestic stocks. This so-called **home bias**—the tendency to hold domestic assets in one's investment portfolio—is also apparent in other countries as well, with domestic residents holding a disproportionate share of the nation's stock market wealth.[20]

Several explanations for the home bias in portfolio investments have been put forth.[21] These include the existence of political and currency risks and the natural tendency to invest in the familiar and avoid the unknown. Whether these preferences are rational is another issue.

There are several ways in which U.S. investors can diversify into foreign securities. A number of foreign firms have listed their securities on the New York Stock Exchange (NYSE) or the American Stock Exchange. Historically, a major barrier to foreign listing has been the NYSE requirements for substantial disclosure and audited financial statements. For firms that wished to sell securities in the United States, the U.S. Securities and Exchange Commission's (SEC) disclosure regulations also have been a major obstruction. However, the gap between acceptable NYSE and SEC accounting and disclosure standards and those acceptable to European multinationals has narrowed substantially. Moreover, Japanese and European multinationals that raise funds in international capital markets have been forced to conform to stricter standards. This change may encourage other foreign firms to list their securities and gain access to the U.S. capital market.

Investors can always buy foreign securities in their home markets. However, buying stocks listed on foreign exchanges can be expensive, primarily because of steep brokerage commissions. Owners of foreign stocks also face the complications of foreign tax laws and the nuisance of converting dividend payments into dollars.

Instead of buying foreign stocks overseas, investors can buy foreign equities traded in the United States in the form of **American Depository Receipts** (ADRs). ADRs are certificates of ownership issued by a U.S. bank as a convenience to investors in lieu of the underlying shares it holds in custody. Investors in ADRs absorb the handling costs through transfer and handling charges. ADRs for about 1,000 companies from 33 foreign countries are currently traded on U.S. exchanges.

The easiest way to invest abroad is to buy shares in an internationally diversified mutual fund, of which a growing number are available. Four basic categories of mutual funds invest abroad:

1. *Global funds* can invest anywhere in the world, including the United States.
2. *International funds* invest only outside the United States.
3. *Regional funds* focus on specific geographical areas overseas, such as Asia or Europe.
4. *Single-country funds* invest in individual countries, such as Germany or Taiwan.

---

[20]The home bias has been documented by French and Poterba (1991); Cooper and Kaplanis (1994); and Tesar and Werner (1995).

[21]See, for example, Kang and Stulz (1997).

Investors can also create their own international fund "on-the-cheap" by putting together a portfolio of multinational American firms, such as Coca-Cola, Procter & Gamble, and 3M, that derive more than half their revenues from outside the United States.

Global Diversification and Foreign-Exchange Risk

Global diversification can expose investors to foreign exchange risk.

Although the benefits of global diversification are numerous, expanding our universe to include international investments can expose us to foreign exchange risk. Whenever we hold a foreign security, whether that security is a stock, a bond, or a mutual fund, we run the risk that its returns may be eroded if the foreign currency declines in value against the dollar. This risk can be seen by expressing the return on a foreign security in terms of dollars:

$$\text{Dollar Return} = \text{Foreign Currency Return} \times \text{Currency Gain (Loss)}$$

$$[6\text{-}17]$$

$$1 + R_{\$} = (1 + R_f)(1 + g)$$

where R_f is the foreign currency rate of return, and g is the change in the value of the foreign currency relative to the U.S. dollar. Ignoring the cross-product term, $R_f g$, which should be quite small relative to the other terms (because R_f and g are usually much less than 1) we can approximate Equation [6-17] by the following:

$$R_{\$} = R_f + g \qquad [6\text{-}18]$$

Equation [6-18] says that the dollar rate of return is approximately equal to the sum of the foreign currency return plus the change in the dollar value of the foreign currency. Foreign currency fluctuations introduce exchange risk. As mentioned above, the prospect of exchange risk is one of the reasons that investors have a preference for home country securities.

Using Equation [6-18], we can see how exchange rate changes affect the risk of investing in a foreign security (or a foreign market index). Specifically, we can write the standard deviation of the dollar return, $\sigma_{\$}$, as

$$\sigma_{\$} = [\sigma_f^2 + \sigma_g^2 + 2\sigma_f \sigma_g r_{fg}]^{1/2} \qquad [6\text{-}19]$$

where σ_f^2 = the variance (the standard deviation squared) of the foreign currency return

σ_g^2 = the variance of the change in the exchange rate

r_{fg} = the correlation between the foreign currency return and the exchange rate change

Equation [6-19] shows that the foreign exchange risk associated with a foreign security depends on both the standard deviation of the foreign exchange rate change and the covariance between the exchange rate change and the foreign currency return on the security.

For example, suppose that the standard deviation of the return on Mat-sushita, a Japanese firm, in terms of yen is 23 percent and the standard deviation of the rate of change in the dollar:yen exchange rate is 17 percent. In addition, the estimated correlation between the yen return on Matsushita and the rate of change in the exchange rate is 0.31. Then, according to Equation [6-19], the standard deviation of the dollar rate of return on investing in Matsushita stock is 32.56 percent:

$$\sigma_\$(\text{Matsushita}) = (0.23^2 + 0.17^2 + 2 \times .23 \times .17 \times .31)^{1/2} = 0.3256$$

Clearly, foreign exchange risk increases risk in this case. However, the foreign exchange risk is not additive; that is, the standard deviation of the dollar return—32.56 percent—is less than the sum of the individual standard deviations—23 percent + 17 percent, or 40 percent. It is also conceivable that exchange risk could lower the risk of investing overseas. Lowering risk would require a sufficiently large negative correlation between the rate of exchange rate change and the foreign currency return.

In a portfolio context, the correlation of the dollar returns of Matsushita with those of a portfolio comprised of U.S.-based firms is also important in assessing risk. According to data in Exhibit [6-12], the correlation between the Japanese and U.S. markets is only 0.25, a very low figure, indicating the potential benefits for investors of diversifying across both countries even in the presence of exchange risk.

SUMMARY

The primary objectives of this chapter were to (1) define risk, (2) show how it can be measured, and (3) explain how it affects expected asset returns. We began by examining one of the fundamental premises of modern financial theory: that on average, financial markets are dominated by people who are risk averse. The corollary is that to induce investors to bear the risk that is naturally present in all financial decisions, they must be compensated with a higher expected rate of return. The historical data support the view that risk hath its reward. Over the past 72 years, the riskiest investment, common stocks, has yielded an average annual return of 13.0 percent, approximately 9.2 percent more than the 3.8 percent annual return on the safest investment, short-term Treasury bills.

We then used the intuitive notion that risk is related to the unpredictability of future returns to show that a quantitative measure of this uncertainty is provided by the standard deviation of the probability distribution of returns. We saw that the riskiness of an indi-

vidual stock can be divided into two components—diversifiable or unsystematic risk, which is eliminated in a well-diversified portfolio, and systematic or market risk, which remains even in the best-diversified portfolio. Because investors hold diversified portfolios of stocks, thereby eliminating unsystematic risk, they are primarily concerned with the market risk of the individual stocks they hold. Only this latter risk, measured by the beta coefficient, contributes to the riskiness of their portfolios.

Beta measures the tendency of a stock to move up or down with the market. The market portfolio has a beta of 1.0, as does a stock of average riskiness. A stock with a beta greater than 1.0 tends to be more volatile than the overall stock market, whereas a stock with a beta less than 1.0 is more stable than the market.

The insight that systematic risk is the relevant risk in financial markets provides the basis for the capital asset pricing model (CAPM). According to the CAPM, the expected or required return on asset i, r_i, is equal to the risk-free interest rate, r_f, plus a risk premium. This risk premium equals the difference between the expected return on the market, r_m, and the risk-free rate multiplied by the stock's beta coefficient. Formally,

$$r_i = r_f + \beta_i(r_m - r_f)$$

This formula is also known as the security market line (SML).

An alternative approach to risk and return is provided by the arbitrage pricing theory (APT). According to the APT, security returns are affected by a number of common factors, instead of the CAPM's single-factor approach. Arbitrage across the common factors results in a market price of risk for each common factor and a required return for each security based on the security's sensitivity to these factors.

We also saw that the benefits of diversification extend to international investing. Holding an internationally diversified portfolio can lead to significant risk reduction even in the presence of foreign exchange risk.

FINCOACH PRACTICE EXERCISES

To help you master the mathematics discussed in the chapter, open **FinCoach** on the *Prentice Hall Finance Center* CD-ROM and practice the problems in the following categories: *1. Portfolio Diversification, and 2. CAPM.*

QUESTIONS

1. List four common stocks likely to have a high standard deviation of return and four stocks likely to have a low standard deviation of return. Then list two pairs of stocks likely to be highly correlated and two pairs likely to be relatively uncorrelated.

2. Comment on the following statement: "Risky stocks offer the investor a good shot at very high profits, and so these stocks should sell at a premium."

3. True or false?
   a. Because investors like to hold diversified portfolios, a conglomerate's shares are more prized than are shares of a company with only one business.
   b. The CAPM implies that an asset with a negative beta has an expected rate of return lower than the risk-free interest rate.
   c. A stock with a beta of .5 has a required return one-half as high as the market.
   d. Diversification will have no value if the returns of all risky assets are perfectly correlated.
   e. If an asset lies above the security market line, it is overvalued.
   f. If an asset lies inside the mean-variance frontier, it is overvalued.
   g. An undiversified portfolio with a beta of 2 is twice as risky as the market portfolio.

4. What factors could increase the diversifiable risk of a stock? What factors could increase the nondiversifiable risk of a stock?

5. Which situation would offer the best chance to reduce risk by forming a portfolio from two stocks? Explain.
   a. Perfect correlation between the stocks.
   b. No correlation between the stocks.
   c. Perfect negative correlation between the stocks.

6. Comment on the following statements:
   a. If I buy several hundred "penny" mining shares, I don't care about risk. The stocks can go up very high in price or, at worst, I can lose just a few dollars.
   b. Although our company has a very low beta, we feel it is misleading to our shareholders because our company is subject to very wide fluctuations in sales and profits.

7. If the market portfolio actually yields a rate of return different from the expected return predicted by the CAPM, does this mean the CAPM is a bad model?

8. What is the definition of covariance? What is the definition of correlation? What is an intuitive explanation of the difference between the two?

9. Given what you know about the benefits of diversification, what advice would you have for an

assembly-line worker in an auto plant who puts most of his savings into shares of auto companies?

10. Gold pays no dividends, is costly to store, and has often undergone long periods of price decreases. Why would investors ever want to hold this asset?

11. Many insurance companies sell auto insurance at competitive rates, yet none will offer earthquake insurance at any price. Can you explain this puzzle?

12. Sketch the efficient set of risky assets in a diagram with expected return on the vertical axis and standard deviation on the horizontal axis. Show how an investor's opportunity set will change if she can borrow and lend at the same interest rate. Now, show how the investor's opportunity set will change if the rate of interest at which she can borrow exceeds the rate of interest at which she may lend.

13. As seen in Exhibit 6-12, Hong Kong stocks are more than twice as volatile as U.S. stocks. Does that mean that risk-averse American investors should avoid Hong Kong equities? Explain.

14. What characteristics of foreign securities lead to diversification benefits for American investors?

15. Comment on the following statement: On October 19, 1987, the U.S. stock market crashed. As the globe turned the following day, the devastation spread from New York to Tokyo, Hong Kong, Sydney, and Singapore, and on to Frankfurt, Paris, and London, then back to New York. The domino-style spread of the crash from one market to the next accelerated as international investors attempted to outrun the wave of panic selling from Tokyo to London and back to New York. It is difficult to imagine that some investors thought they had been able to diversify their investment risks by spreading their money across different stock markets around the world, when, in fact, their downside risks were actually multiplying as one market followed another into decline.

PROBLEMS

✖—Excel templates may be downloaded from **www.prenhall.com/financecenter.**

1. Mary Smith has invested two thirds of her money in GM stock and the remainder in Ford. On past evidence, the standard deviation is 22 percent for GM and 44 percent for Ford. Suppose the correlation between GM and Ford is −1.0. What is the standard deviation of Mary Smith's portfolio?

2. An investor is considering forming a portfolio from two stocks, Atlantic Telesis and Valley Bell. They have a correlation coefficient of .50. ✖

	Atlantic Telesis (%)	Valley Bell (%)
Expected return	10	12.5
Standard deviation	5	6.0

a. What is the expected return and standard deviation of return of a portfolio with 50 percent invested in AT, 50 percent invested in VB?

b. What is the expected return, standard deviation of return of a portfolio with 25 percent invested in AT, 75 percent in VB?

c. What is the expected return, standard deviation of return of a portfolio with 75 percent invested in AT, 25 percent in VB?

d. Trace the efficient frontier composed of the two securities, Valley Bell and Atlantic Telesis.

3. Assume that you have $50,000 of your own funds to invest. You may borrow and lend at a risk-free rate of 6 percent and/or invest in a well-diversified mutual fund whose performance matches the market as a whole. The expected annual return of the fund is 16 percent, and the standard deviation of its annual returns is 20 percent. On a percentage basis, calculate the risk and the expected return of your investment if you:

a. Invest $50,000 in the risk-free asset

b. Invest $50,000 in the market portfolio

c. Invest $25,000 in the risk-free asset and $25,000 in the market portfolio

d. Borrow $10,000 at the risk-free rate and invest $60,000 in the market portfolio

e. Borrow $50,000 at the risk-free rate and invest $100,000 in the market portfolio

f. Graph your results.

g. Which of these portfolios (if any) is optimal in the Markowitz sense?

4. The common stocks of Smith Industries and Weston Products have expected returns and standard deviation of returns as given below. The correlation between the two stocks (*r*) is 0.80. ✄

	r	sd
Smith Industries	0.18	0.20
Weston Products	0.08	0.06

   a. Compute the risk (*sd*) and expected returns (*R*) for the following portfolios:
   (1) 100 percent A
   (2) 100 percent B
   (3) 80 percent A, 20 percent B
   (4) 80 percent B, 20 percent A
   (5) 60 percent A, 40 percent B
   (6) 60 percent B, 40 percent A
   (7) 50 percent A, 50 percent B
   b. Which portfolio (if any) is superior in terms of risk and return?

5. As part of your analysis of the Klunker Kar Company, you collected historical data on annual total returns of Klunker's common stock as well as returns on the market portfolio. Performing a simple linear regression, you find the firm's characteristic line to be as follows:

$$R_k = 3.25 + 1.60\,R_m$$

   where R_k is the average return on Klunker's common stock (as a percent), and R_m the average return on the market portfolio (as a percent). You also find the correlation of Klunker's returns with that of the market is 0.30.
   a. What is Klunker's beta?
   b. Suppose the return on the market for the coming year is expected to be 10 percent. According to the characteristic line, what would be the expected return on Klunker's common stock? How confident would you be that this expected return you have computed would be realized?
   c. Currently, the risk-free rate is 10 percent, and the required return on the market is 15 percent. If you believe that the security market line fairly represents the relationship between risk and required returns for individual stocks, what is Klunker's required rate of return?
   d. If dividends are expected to be $2.50 a share in the coming year (i.e., $D_1 = \$2.50$) and are expected to grow at a 13 percent rate into the in-

definite future, what price should Klunker's common stock sell for?

6. Suppose the beta for an oil company is 1.5, the expected return on the market is 20 percent, and the riskless rate of return is 10 percent. ✄
   a. Calculate the oil company's required rate of return using the CAPM.
   b. If the expected rate of return on the oil company's stock is 22 percent, should an investor buy the stock? Should an investor buy if the stock's expected rate of return is 28 percent?

7. A toy company has an expected return of 25 percent and a beta of 1.5, whereas a bank has an expected return of 17.5 percent and a beta of .75. What is the expected return on the market and the riskless rate of interest?

8. The risk-free rate of return is 7.5 percent and the market risk premium is 4 percent.
   a. The beta of ZBT stock has been estimated at 1.00. Given its current price of $10, what is its expected price one year from now (assume all returns to the stock are in the form of capital gains)?
   b. If Martin Metals stock has a beta of $-.2$, and its price is expected to be $45 next year, how much would you be willing to pay for the stock today?

9. You have some money that you want to invest and are considering two stocks; Mark Twain Cruise Lines and Nickels Mining. Mark Twain has a beta of 0.70, and Nickels has a beta of 0.80. You can earn 6 percent risk free, and the market risk premium is 7 percent. ✄
   a. Calculate the required rate of return for each stock.
   b. Suppose that you invest half of your money in Mark Twain and half in Nickels. What is the beta of the portfolio? What is the portfolio's expected return?
   c. What will be the beta of a portfolio made up of 30 percent Mark Twain and 70 percent Nickels? What is the portfolio's expected return?
   d. If you were risk averse, would you prefer the portfolio described in (b) or (c)?

10. The beta of Golf and Eastern Corp. is 1.35. The risk-free rate is 10 percent, and the market risk premium is 8 percent.
   a. Calculate the expected return of G&E.
   b. Assume G&E has a constant growth of dividends of 10 percent. If dividends are expected

to be $1.05 next year, what is the current price of the stock?

11. The risk-free rate is 7.5 percent, and the market return is 10.5 percent. ✖
    a. With a beta of 2.00, what is the expected return of the stock of Amp Electronics?
    b. If Amp Electronics has been growing at 5 percent, and dividends are expected to be $2.10 next year, what is the price of the stock?
    c. Suppose that management institutes changes that decrease AE's beta to 0.65. Assuming the same growth in dividends as before, what will happen to the price of its stock?

12. Agricorp has just paid its annual dividend of $1.75. At the same time, the president of the company announced that the goal of management was to double the dividend in each of the next five years and then to have the annual dividend double every five years thereafter. The risk-free interest rate is 8 percent, and the expected return on the market is 17 percent. The market applies a 14 percent discount rate to Agricorp's stock.
    a. What is Agricorp's stock worth, assuming the market believes the president will be able to fulfill her dividend intentions?
    b. What is the stock's beta?

13. Three factors have been found to influence the return of Unioil stock: an index summarizing energy costs (I1), changes in the level of the stock market (I2), and changes in the dollar in relation to a weighted average of exchange rates (I3). The betas associated with each risk factor are .7, .3, and 1.1, respectively. The risk premium for I1 is 3 percent; for I2, 5 percent; and for I3, 7.5 percent. The risk-free rate is 5.5 percent. ✖
    a. What is the expected return for Unioil according to the APT?
    b. What is the expected return according to the CAPM?

14. A portfolio manager is considering the benefits of increasing his diversification by investing overseas. He can purchase shares in individual country funds with the following characteristics: ✖

	United States (%)	United Kingdom (%)	Spain (%)
Expected return	15	12	5
Standard deviation of returns	10	9	4
Correlation with the United States	1.0	.33	.06

a. What is the expected return and standard deviation of return of a portfolio with 25 percent invested in the United Kingdom and 75 percent in the United States? With 50 percent invested in the United States and 50 percent in the United Kingdom? With 25 percent invested in the United States and 75 percent in the United Kingdom?
b. What is the expected return and standard deviation of return of a portfolio with 25 percent invested in Spain and 75 percent in the United States? With 50 percent invested in the United States and 50 percent invested in Spain? With 25 percent invested in the United States and 75 percent invested in Spain?
c. Plot these two sets of risk-return combinations, (a) and (b). Which leads to a better set of risk-return choices, Spain or the United Kingdom?

15. Suppose that the standard deviation of the return on Nestlé, a Swiss firm, in terms of Swiss francs is 19 percent, and the standard deviation of the rate of change in the dollar-franc exchange rate is 15 percent. In addition, the estimated correlation between the Swiss franc return on Nestlé and the rate of change in the exchange rate is 0.17. Given these figures, what is the standard deviation of the dollar rate of return on investing in Nestlé stock? ✖

REFERENCES

Black, F. "Capital Market Equilibrium with Restricted Borrowing." *Journal of Business,* July 1972, 444–455.

Black, F. "Beta and Return." *Journal of Portfolio Management,* Fall 1993, 8–18.

Black, F., M. C. Jensen, and M. Scholes. "The Capital Asset Pricing Model: Some Empirical Tests." In Michael C. Jensen, ed., *Studies in the Theory of Capital Markets.* New York: Prager, 1972.

Chan, L., and J. Lakonishok. "Are the Reports of Beta's Death Premature?" Faculty Working Paper No. 92-0168, College of Commerce and Business Administration, University of Illinois, September 1992.

Chen, N., R. Roll, and S. A. Ross. "Economic Forces and the Stock Market." *Journal of Business,* July 1986, 383–403.

Cooper, I. A., and E. Kaplanis. "What Explains the Home Bias in Portfolio Investment." *Review of Financial Studies,* 7, 1994, 45–60.

Dhrymes, P. J., I. Friend, and N. B. Gultekin. "A Critical Reexamination of the Empirical Evidence on Arbitrage Pricing Theory." *Journal of Finance,* June 1984, 323–350.

Fama, E. F., and K. R. French. "The Cross-Section of Expected Stock Returns." *Journal of Finance,* June 1992, 3–56.

Fama, E. F., and J. D. MacBeth. "Risk, Return, and Equilibrium: Empirical Tests." *Journal of Political Economy,* May 1973, 607–636.

French, K. R., and J. M. Poterba. "Investor Diversification and International Equity Markets." *American Economic Review, Papers and Proceedings,* 1991, 222–226.

Grundy, K., and B. G. Malkiel. "Reports of Beta's Death Have Been Greatly Exaggerated." *Journal of Portfolio Management,* Spring 1996, 36–44.

Harris, R. S., and F. C. Marston. "Estimating Shareholder Risk Premia Using Analysts' Growth Forecasts." *Financial Management,* Summer 1992, 63–70.

Ibbotson, R. G., and R. A. Sinquefield. *Stocks, Bonds, Bills and Inflation: 1998 Yearbook.* Chicago: Ibbotson Associates, 1998.

Jensen, M. C. "Agency Costs of Free Cash Flow, Corporate Finance, and Takeovers." *American Economic Review,* May 1986, 323–329.

Kang, J-K., and R. M. Stulz. "Why Is There a Home Bias? An Analysis of Foreign Portfolio Equity Ownership in Japan." *Journal of Financial Economics,* October 1997, 3–28.

Lessard, D. R. "World, National, and Industry Factors in Equity Returns." *Journal of Finance,* May 1974, 379–391.

Lintner, J. "The Valuation of Risk Assets and the Selection of Risky Investments in Stock Portfolios and Capital Budgets." *Review of Economics and Statistics,* February 1964, 13–37.

Markowitz, H. M. "Portfolio Selection." *Journal of Finance,* March 1952, 77–91.

Markowitz, H. M. *Portfolio Selection: Efficient Diversification of Investments.* New York: Wiley, 1959.

Roll, R. "A Critique of Asset Pricing Theory's Tests: Part I: On Past and Potential Testability of the Theory." *Journal of Financial Economics,* March 1977, 129–176.

Roll, R., and S. A. Ross. "An Empirical Investigation of the Arbitrage Pricing Theory." *Journal of Finance,* December 1980, 1073–1103.

Ross, S. A. "The Arbitrage Theory of Capital Asset Pricing." *Journal of Economic Theory,* December 1976, 341–360.

Shanken, J. "The Arbitrage Pricing Theory: Is It Testable?" *Journal of Finance,* December 1982, 1129–1140.

Sharpe, W. F. "Capital Asset Prices: A Theory of Market Equilibrium Under Conditions of Risk." *Journal of Finance,* September 1964, 277–293.

Solnik, B. H. "Why Not Diversify Internationally?" *Financial Analyst's Journal,* August 1974, 48–54.

Tesar, L., and I. M. Werner. "Home Bias and High Turnover." *Journal of International Money and Finance,* 14, 1995, 467–493.

Options and Corporate Finance

If chance would have me king, why, chance may crown me.
Shakespeare, Macbeth

KEY TERMS

American option
at-the-money option
Black–Scholes option-
   pricing model
call option

conversion price
conversion ratio
convertible bond
European option
exercise or strike price

in-the-money option
out-of-the-money option
premium
put option

CHAPTER LEARNING OBJECTIVES

Upon completion of this chapter, students should be able to:

- Explain the distinction between different types of options.
- Identify the factors that influence an option's value and describe how changes in these factors can influence the value of the option.
- Indicate how options may be embedded in investment decisions and why managerial flexibility may be considered an option.

- Describe the ways in which a company's common stock and a call option are similar.
- Indicate how the insights from option-pricing theory can help us understand the nature of complex securities such as convertible debt.
- Use option pricing theory to describe the agency conflicts between stockholders and creditors.

In 1973, the trading of stock options started on the Chicago Board of Options Exchange (CBOE). Since 1973, we've seen an enormous growth in the kinds of options available to investors. Options on stock indexes, commodities, foreign currencies, and government securities now exist and are listed on more than a dozen exchanges globally. There has also been a virtual explosion in investor interest, with the number of contracts traded increasing yearly.

Traded options are fascinating investment instruments. However, options were around long before their public trading on the CBOE. Options on real estate have existed for hundreds of years; beyond this, we see options in many other arenas. For instance, John Smoltz's contract, which we valued in Chapter 4, has a provision that gives the Atlanta Braves the option to sign Smoltz for $8 million in 2001. This clause could be valuable to the Braves if Smoltz has a great season in 2000 because the team then would have to pay far more than $8 million to keep him off the free-agent market without this option.

> Options convey the right, but not the obligation, to do something in the future.

Our reason for discussing options in a text on corporate finance is not to teach you how to value the contracts of professional athletes. Rather, it is because many corporate investment and financing decisions contain options in disguise. For example, an investment in new technology or a new distribution system can allow a company to expand into new products or new geographic markets at a later date. In each case, the firm is investing today for the *right* to exploit future opportunities *if* they appear to be profitable. Should these future opportunities not materialize or turn out to be less exciting once we learn more about them, then we're not obligated to throw good money after bad. However, not making these investments in the first place means that the company isn't positioned to take advantage of growth opportunities if they arise.

The main purpose of this chapter is to show you how the concepts and techniques developed in valuing options can be applied to issues in corporate finance. We want to get you thinking about the world as a collection of options. This perspective is useful not only in the valuation of financial instruments but in seeing *strategic choices* and *management flexibility* as a series of options. We'll begin by looking at some of the basic characteristics of options and option pricing and then quickly introduce a number of situations in corporate finance in which the option-pricing perspective is useful. This will set the stage for a more detailed study of options in corporate finance later in the book.

7.1   THE BASICS OF STOCK OPTIONS

Options come in many forms, but they all give their holder the right—*but not the obligation*—to buy or sell any asset at a set price at some future date. The right to buy is known as a **call option,** and the right to sell is called a **put option.** The seller of a call or put must fulfill the contract if the buyer so desires. The option or choice not to buy or sell has value; therefore, the buyer pays a **premium** for this privilege. An option that would be profitable to exercise at the asset's current price is said to be **in the money.** Conversely, an **out-of-the-money option** is one that would not be profitable at the asset's current price. The price at which the option can be exercised is called the **exercise or strike price.** Options that can only be exercised at expiration are known as **European options;** in contrast, **American options** can be exercised at any time before the expiration date.

Call Options

An in-the-money option will show a profit only if the gain is greater than the option premium.

The relationship between the stock price at expiration, the strike price, and the payoffs on the purchase of a European option is shown in Exibit 7-1. The figure illustrates the payoffs on a call option with an exercise price of $25 a share and a call premium of $3. At a price of $25 or lower, it wouldn't make sense for the holder to exercise the option; after all, why would anyone pay $25 a share when they could go out into the market and buy the stock for less. There would be a loss of the $3 option premium, but you'd lose no more than this amount regardless of how far the price of the underlying stock drops. At a price above $28 a share, the option is sufficiently deep in the money to cover the option premium and net a profit. For example, if the stock price were $32 a share at expiration, the option would be worth $7 ($32 − $25), and the profit after subtracting the option premium of $3 would be $4.

Between $25 and $28, the option would be exercised, but the gain wouldn't cover the option premium. For instance, if the expiration price were $27 a share, then the option would be worth $2 ($27 − $25), but overall the payoff is a loss of $1 net of the $3 premium.

In general, the value C of a call option at expiration with a stock price S at that price and an exercise price of X is

$$C = \max[0, (S - X)] \qquad [7\text{-}1]$$

where *max* refers to the maximum of $(S - X)$ and 0. The call is worth the difference between the current stock price and the exercise price. When the stock price is lower than the exercise price, that is, $S < X$, then the option is worthless. If the stock price just happens to be equal to the exercise price, the option is said to be

EXHIBIT 7-1
Payoffs from a European Call Option

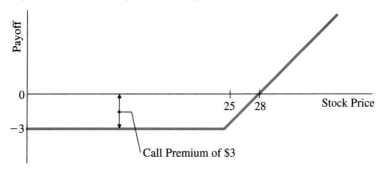

at the money, and the investor would be indifferent about exercising it for a zero gain or letting it expire unexercised.

The payoff to the buyer of a call is $C - a$, where a is the call premium. The payoff to the seller of the call is the mirror image to that of the buyer. If the stock price is lower than the exercise price, the option would go unexercised and the seller gets to keep the premium, but the buyer loses the premium. Once the stock price goes higher than the exercise price *plus* the premium, the seller would incur losses. For instance, in our earlier example, a rise in the stock price to $32 resulted in a $4 net gain to the buyer. This gain would come directly out of the hide of the seller. Why? The seller of the contract would have to deliver stock worth $32 a share for the exercise price of $25; the loss on this transaction would be $7. This loss would be partially offset by the $3 option premium, making the net loss $4.

> The payoff from buying a call option is the mirror image of selling a call option.

Put Options

Exhibit 7-2 illustrates the payoffs from buying a put option with an exercise price of $25 and a premium of $2. As the stock price declines, the option's payoff goes up by $1 for each dollar decline in the price of the stock. Suppose, for example, that the price of the stock dropped to $10 a share at expiration. The value of this option would be $15 because the holder could buy the stock in the market at $10 and exercise the option to sell at $25 a share. The profit on the transaction would be $13—the $15 value of the option less the $2 premium.

In general, the value of a put option would be

$$P = \max\,[0,\ (X - S)] \qquad\qquad [7\text{-}2]$$

If the premium on the put option is b, then the buyer's profit on the put would be $P - b$. Just as with a call, the seller of the put option would realize profits that are the mirror image of the buyer. After all, puts are bought to speculate on or

EXHIBIT 7-2
Payoffs from a European Put

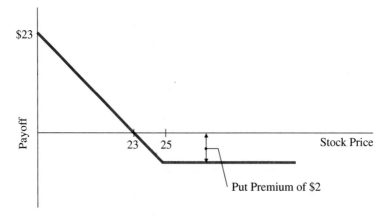

hedge against a decline in the price of a stock. An investor willing to sell a put must believe that the price will not decline or that it will not decline enough to wipe out the premium received. As with calls, both the buyer and seller can't be right simultaneously.

7.2   OPTION VALUATION

The valuation of options is one of the most complex tasks in corporate finance. Until fairly recently, only very simple options could be valued. But in 1973, Fisher Black and Myron Scholes developed a formula to value European options.[1] In this section, we'll look at the Black–Scholes model and some of its important properties.[2] As we have noted, many investment and financing decisions have option-like characteristics. Therefore, the more we understand how options are valued, the more insights we can get into the nature of important problems facing a company's management.

The Black–Scholes Option-Pricing Model

The Black–Scholes option pricing is one of the great achievments of modern finance

The **Black–Scholes option-pricing model** is based on the idea that investors can replicate the payoffs from a call option by holding an investment in the underlying asset and financing this investment (at least in part) with borrowed money. In equilibrium, the value of the option must equal the cost of creating the option equivalent. If it doesn't, then alert investors will be able to exploit this situation.

The model is set in continuous time and is based on the assumption that stock prices will move slightly up or slightly down during the next microsecond. However, once you assume short time intervals, the degree of borrowing will have to be updated continuously as the stock price and time to option expiration change. The mathematics of modeling option values when the stock prices, time to expiration, and leverage are constantly changing is not trivial. Despite these complexities, Black and Scholes derived Equation [7-3] for valuing European call options prior to their expiration date:

$$C(t) = SN(d_1) - Xe^{-rt}N(d_2) \qquad\qquad [7\text{-}3]$$

where

$C(t)$ = the value of a call option with an amount of time t remaining before expiration

t = the time until the option expires

---

[1]See Black and Scholes (1973).

[2]An alternative derivation of the Black–Scholes model was reported by Merton (1973). In 1997, Merton and Scholes shared the Nobel prize in economics for their contribution to option pricing. Unfortunately, Fisher Black had died and was unable to share in the honors because of a Nobel policy prohibiting posthumous awards.

S = the current price of the stock (or any underlying asset for that matter)

X = the exercise (or strike) price of the option

e = 2.71828—the base of the natural system of logarithms

r = the continuously compounded risk-free rate of interest

$N(d)$ = the value of the cumulative normal density function[3]

$$d_1 = \frac{\ln(S/X) + (r + .5\sigma^2)t}{\sigma\sqrt{t}}$$

$$d_2 = \frac{\ln(S/X) + (r - .5\sigma^2)t}{\sigma\sqrt{t}} = d_1 - \sigma\sqrt{t}$$

$\ln$ = natural logarithm

σ = standard deviation, per period, of the rate of return on the stock

As formulas go, Equation [7-3] is truly ugly. However, it's really just a more complex form of Equation [7-1] with the first term being the *expected stock price* at time period t, and the second term the *expected present value of the exercise price* at time period t. The value of the call option is the difference between the two terms. This formula has several important implications for valuing options. The relationship between the variables in Equation [7-3] and the value of a call option is summarized in Exhibit 7-3.

> **Options have both intrinsic value and time value.**

An option's time to expiration is an important factor in determining its value. The relationship between the value of a call option prior to expiration and the value of the underlying stock for different expiration dates is shown in Exhibit 7-4. The heavy solid line XZ is a graphical representation of Equation [7-1] and is referred to as the option's *intrinsic value*. It equals the amount by which the option is in the money. In other words, it represents the immediate exercise value of the option. The intrinsic value, which is also the option's value at expiration, is a lower bound on the value of the call. As we'd expect, an out-of-the-money option has no intrinsic value. Any excess of the option value over the intrinsic value is called the *time value* or *time premium* of the contract.

Before expiration, an out-of-the-money option has only time value, and an in-the-money option has both time and intrinsic value. At expiration, an option can have only intrinsic value.

EXHIBIT 7-3
Call-Option Valuation

Variable Increases	Option Value
Stock Price Volatility	Increases
Time to Expiration	Increases
Exercise Price	Decreases
Current Stock Price	Increases
Risk-Free Interest Rate	Increases

---

[3]$N(d)$ represents the probability that a normally distributed random variable will take on a value that is less than d.

EXHIBIT 7-4
Call-Option Values and Stock Prices for Various Expiration Times

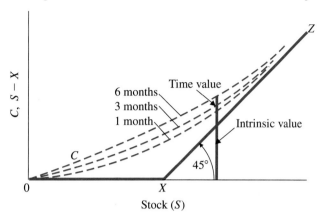

As Exhibit 7-4 indicates, option values—as represented by the dashed lines—increase with the time to expiration. The time premium also tends to increase with the option's time to expiration because there's more time for the contract to pick up additional value. The fact that an option has positive time value prior to expiration suggests that an option on a nondividend-paying stock should never be exercised early. Exercising the option yields the holder $S - X$ dollars. However, at any time before expiration, the option will have some time value; thus, the holder should be able to get something more than $S - X$ in the marketplace. Therefore, selling an option prior to expiration makes more sense than exercising it.

> **Increasing the variability of the underlying asset increases the value of an option.**

Perhaps the most important factor in deciding an option's value is the volatility of the underlying asset. The idea that option values go up as the standard deviation of the stock price increases may seem a bit strange; after all, in our discussion of risk and value in Chapter 6, we suggested that asset values tend to go *down*, not *up*, as risk increases. To see what's driving these seemingly contradictory results, suppose that you are a security analyst who regularly follows the stock of Frick Industries and Frack Products. Exhibit 7-5 represents your probability distribution of Frick and Frack's stock prices six months from now.

The stock of both companies is selling for the same price, but Frick Industries would be a superior investment to Frack Products. It has a higher expected price and lower risk as measured by the standard deviation of stock returns. Further, the likelihood of a price decline is minimized if you buy Frick rather than Frack.

However, let's assume that call options are available for both companies six months from now with a strike price of $76. Given the probability distribution in Exhibit 7-5, the expected value of the option for Frick Industries at expiration would be

Value of Frick Option

$$= .15(0) + .20(0) + .30(\$80 - \$76) + .20(\$84 - \$76) + .15(\$92 - \$76)$$

$$= \$5.20$$

EXHIBIT 7-5
Per-Share Stock Price Probability Distributions
Frick Industries and Frack Products

Probability	Frick Industries	Frack Products
0.15	$68.00	$ 44.00
0.20	76.00	56.00
0.30	80.00	72.00
0.20	84.00	88.00
0.15	92.00	100.00
Current Stock Price	75.00	75.00
Expected Stock Price in 6 Months	80.00	72.00
Standard Deviation of Stock Price	7.04	18.37

and the value of Frack Products' option would be:

Value of Frack Option

$$= .15(0) + .20(0) + .30(0) + .20(\$88 - \$76) + .15(\$100 - \$76)$$

$$= \$6.00$$

> The ability to walk away from poor outcomes while enjoying all of the upside potential makes options on high-risk ventures valuable.

The greater value of its option is due to the greater variability of Frack's stock price outcomes, coupled with the nature of the option contract. Specifically, the call option will be worthless if the stock price at expiration doesn't exceed the strike price of $76. Thus, if the stock price is at or below $76, the holder doesn't really care *how far below* because the option's value will be zero, and the worst an investor can do is lose the premium. On the other hand, the holder of Frack's option does benefit from the greater dispersion of its stock price because it increases the magnitude of favorable outcomes. This ability to "walk away" from unfavorable results and take advantage of favorable outcomes makes options on high-risk ventures valuable.

7.3   OPTION VALUATION AND INVESTMENT DECISIONS

The corporation must value the set of available investment projects in order to decide which ones to accept. As we'll see in Chapter 8, the recommended approach is identical to that used in valuing any asset—namely, to estimate the project's cash flows and discount them at an appropriate risk-adjusted required rate of return. The mechanics of valuing a project using discounted cash-flow techniques are pretty straightforward; the trick is getting good cash-flow estimates in a world where investment payoffs may be very uncertain. Further, many strategic investments may open up the potential for making additional profitable investments over time. Such investment opportunities are best valued with an options approach. In this section, we'll look at a few examples of how viewing investments as options can provide valuable insights.

Potential Plant Expansions and Real-Estate Options

The ability to expand or not expand future production capacity is a call option.

Consider a company that may need to expand production capacity within the next few years. We say *may* because if the economy continues to grow, demand for the firm's products will continue to be strong and new manufacturing capacity will be needed. However, the current production base should be more than sufficient to meet customer demand if there's a weakness in economic activity. Economists seem to be evenly split on whether the current expansion will continue or whether we are likely to see a recession within the next six months.

One way that the company might deal with these market uncertainties would be to make a down payment of $50,000 on a piece of undeveloped land suitable for a new plant. The down payment would permit the company to purchase the property within the next six months for an additional $500,000. If the company fails to come up with the additional money, it will forfeit the $50,000 down payment.

This arrangement is essentially a call option with the $50,000 down payment being equivalent to the option premium and the extra $500,000 needed to complete the deal the strike price. The decision to "exercise the option" and pay the $500,000 would depend on the state of the economy and the need for additional capacity. This company could, of course, decide not to take an option on that property, and if the economy turns sour, it will save the $50,000 down payment. On the other hand, if the economy continues to expand, the company may have to pay far more than $500,000 for the land in six months if the seller senses that the firm is desperate for capacity and needs a suitable plant location quickly.

Research and Development as an Option

R&D investments can be viewed as call options.

Many firms invest heavily in research and development (R&D). Evaluating these expenditures is often difficult because the outcome of a successful R&D project might be another set of projects. For example, Procter & Gamble's (PG's[4]) research into synthetic fats led to the development of a specific product—Olestra. This led to additional "projects," which were attempts to integrate Olestra into specific products like potato chips. Once the new consumer product was formulated, PG had to make additional marketing tests before it introduced products on a national basis. After all, a fat-free potato chip is worthless if consumers don't like the taste. The $500 million PG spent in the development and testing of Olestra indicates that new product development can be very expensive.

PG's initial investment in R&D for Olestra was very similar to a call option. At each stage in the process, PG had the choice of pushing further (and spending more money) if the research looked promising or terminating the project if it

---

[4]PG is Procter & Gamble's trading symbol on the New York Stock Exchange.

appeared as if the research were going nowhere. At each of these steps, there was no guarantee of commercial success; perhaps the only thing that was certain to PG was that not engaging in R&D would put it at a serious competitive disadvantage if someone else came up with a fat-free product first.

> **R&D has its greatest value in high-risk environments.**

Viewing R&D as an option has a number of interesting strategic implications. First, because the value of a call option increases with the volatility of the underlying asset, *R&D would be of greatest value to companies operating in risky environments.* Technology-driven firms such as Intel, Amgen, or Hewlett-Packard get greater value from their R&D efforts than a firm in the oatmeal or cornflakes business. Second, *we'd expect that the value and amount a firm spends on R&D should decline over time as its mix of businesses changes from a growth to a mature stage.* After all, firms in mature industries tend to face less uncertainty than those operating in high-growth markets; hence, there are likely to be lower payoffs from large R&D expenditures.

A firm's entry into new markets has many of the same characteristics as R&D investments. In this environment, the new product gives the company a foothold in markets where there may be the potential for add-ons or product line extensions. We'll take a closer look at this type of option in Chapter 9.

Abandoning a Project as a Put Option

> **The ability to abandon a project is a put option.**

As mentioned earlier, formal investment analysis involves a process of estimating the cash flows from the project and then valuing these cash flows by discounting them back to the present at some appropriate required rate of return. Unfortunately, the cash flows that we actually get from an investment project may be quite different from our estimates. If we're lucky, the realized cash flows will be better than we forecasted. However, sometimes a company can be as unpleasantly surprised as Ford was when it introduced the Edsel.

Fortunately, a company doesn't have to continue with a project that produces disappointing results; it can simply abandon it. In some instances, this "abandonment" option may consist of liquidating the project by selling the assets associated with it. In other cases, abandonment value might be realized by simply redeploying the assets to some other part of the business. Regardless of how you proceed, any project that allows you to extract value from it when things don't go as planned has an embedded put option. Explicit recognition of these forms of *management flexibility* is often an important aspect of valuing projects. Even if we can't quantify these options precisely, *we should recognize that ignoring them completely systematically undervalues projects.*[5]

---

[5]A variation on the abandonment theme is that management can choose to operate a facility when prices exceed variable costs and shut the production unit down when prices plunge. Widely fluctuating selling prices are a fact of life in natural resource industries such as oil and gas. In Chapter 9, we'll look at a numerical example involving a gold mine to show how an options approach differs from traditional investment analysis.

7.4 CORPORATE FINANCING DECISIONS AS OPTIONS

An important aspect of a company's financial policy is the way it approaches the capital markets to raise funds for investment projects. The range of possible securities to issue in a global setting are vast and must be ranked according to their relative costs and benefits. A crucial insight by Black and Scholes was their recognition that all corporate securities can be looked at as special types of options and valued accordingly. In this section, we'll take a look at how the concepts of option-pricing theory can be applied to a number of financing instruments.

Common Stock as a Call Option

For firms that use debt, common stock can be viewed as a call option.

In their paper on option pricing, Black and Scholes also pointed out that the common stock of companies that use debt can be thought of as a call option on the *firm's assets.* Let's see how this works with a simple numerical example.

Suppose that Greene Products, Inc., has borrowed $2 million that must be repaid next year. Because the corporation is a *limited liability entity,* Greene's owners can't lose more than the money that they have already invested in the business. Thus, the owners can choose to make the payment so that the firm can stay in business, or they can do nothing. There is a clear legal distinction between the company and its owners, so Greene's shareholders aren't obligated to come up with any more money next year. If they don't repay the money, control of the firm and its assets passes to the creditors.

The owners' decision to make additional equity infusions in one year is simple and can be explained in terms of Exhibit 7-6. Specifically, the owners will repay the debt if the *market value* of Greene's assets exceeds $2 million. Why? They get to keep the difference dollar for dollar. Conversely, if the value of the assets is

EXHIBIT 7-6
Payoffs to Greene Products' Stockholders

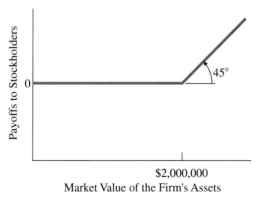

$2,000,000
Market Value of the Firm's Assets

less than the $2 million debt payment needed to keep Greene going, the owners will allow the firm to default on the loan.

The payoffs in Exhibit 7-6 look just like the call-option graph in Exhibit 7-1, and the decision here would be exactly analogous to the decision faced by the owner of a call option: If the stock price exceeds the strike price, the holder of a call will exercise the option and gain the difference. On the other hand, it makes no sense to exercise a call if the stock price is lower than the strike price.

If stockholders (theoretically) hold a call option on the market value of Greene's assets, then what's the position of the creditors? Well . . . if the market value of the assets is greater than $2 million, then the stockholders will "exercise" their option by coming up with $2 million, which will be paid to the creditors. Greene's creditors get no more than $2 million regardless of how much the assets are worth in one year. On the other hand, if the value of the assets is less than $2 million, Greene's stockholders will simply walk away, leaving the creditors with only the firm's assets to satisfy their claims. Once Greene's assets are worth less than $2 million, every additional dollar decline in value comes directly out of the hide of the creditors. This payoff schedule is shown directly in Exhibit 7-7.

The payoffs in Exhibit 7-7 look like those of the seller of a call. This shouldn't surprise us; after all, if the stockholders hold a call option on the firm, then someone has to have sold the option to them and it would appear that the writers of that option are the creditors. The strike price of that option is $2 million, the amount owed, and the term to expiration is the one-year maturity of the debt. What's important to recall from our earlier discussion is that the buyers and sellers of call options are not involved in "cooperative games" and *that the gains of one party often come out of the hide of the other.* We'll say more about common stock as a call option and how it plays into stockholder–creditor relationships in the next section. As we will see, the option-like nature of the common stock of a company that uses debt creates incentives for managers and stockholders to select investment and financing strategies that would differ from those of a company that finances its assets entirely with common stock.

EXHIBIT 7-7
Payoffs to Greene Products' Bondholders

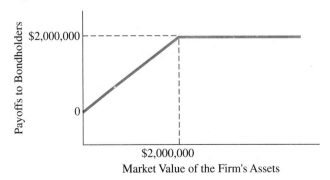

Market Value of the Firm's Assets

Valuing Complex Securities: A Look at Convertible Debt

Option pricing concepts can be used to understand complex securities.

As we noted in Chapter 5, about 25 percent of the corporate debt issued in the United States has a convertible feature. This provision allows an investor to exchange the bond for a specific number of shares of the same company. Convertibles have a dual personality: They offer investors some of the benefits of a fixed-income security plus the possibility of capital gains if the stock price appreciates. Because they can be converted into common stock, the price of convertible bonds usually rises and falls in response to price movements of the underlying stock.

The conditions of the exchange can be stated in terms of either a **conversion price** or a **conversion ratio.** Potomac Electric issued a 7 percent convertible debenture ($1,000 face value) that has a conversion price of $27.00 a share, implying a conversion ratio of 37.04 shares per bond. We get from conversion prices to conversion ratios by dividing the face value by the conversion price; in the case of Potomac Electric, $1,000/$27.00/share = 37.04 shares. At the time of issue, the $27 conversion price was $3 a share higher than the $24.00 market price of Potomac's common stock. Further, the 7 percent coupon rate was significantly below that of comparable nonconvertible (straight) debt issues. These pricing relationships are not unusual; **convertible bonds** have coupon interest rates below those of comparable straight-debt issues, and conversion prices are typically 10–20 percent higher than the stock price at the time of issue.

Convertible debt is often considered to be a "cheap" source of funds compared to both straight-debt or common stock. First, the convertible's lower coupon rate makes it superior to straight debt. Second, because conversion prices are set above the current market price of the common stock, the firm has the opportunity for a deferred sale of common stock at relatively high prices. In short, here is a means of financing that is "clearly" superior to all others.

This rationale for convertibles sounds like a "free lunch," and at this stage of our study we ought to be very skeptical of any story that tells us that we can get something for nothing in a well-functioning capital market. Besides, it doesn't make sense even if we believed that there was systematic mispricing. For instance, if management truly believed that the firm's common stock is undervalued and would rise in the future, then it should issue debt and retire it with the proceeds from a common stock issue when prices rise. Option-pricing theory provides us with some insights into the nature of convertible debt and, in doing so, gives us some direction as to how it might fit in a company's financing mix.

The value of convertible debt is the sum of its value as a bond plus an embedded call option.

An option approach would view the valuation of a convertible bond as the sum of its value as a bond plus the value of the call option embedded in the convertible. This conceptualization is useful because the investor has the *right* but not the *obligation* to exchange the bond at any time at the predetermined exchange rate. Analytically then, the value of a convertible bond is given by

$$V = BV + CV \qquad [7\text{-}4]$$

where V is the value of the convertible; BV, its bond value; and CV, the value of the conversion option. The convertible's value as a bond would be the present value of the coupon interest payments plus the principal at maturity, discounted at a yield the company would have to pay on straight debt.

Let's see how this model of convertible debt valuation might work. Suppose that a firm making equipment for wireless data transmission needs funds to grow. The company has been in business for only three years. Although sales growth has been excellent, this company might have to pay a high interest rate if it issued straight debt. After all, the credit analysts who rate bonds don't have enough operating history to see if the firm can compete in a high-tech environment against the likes of Lucent Technologies, Nokia, or Motorola.

However, if the firm issued convertible debt, the lack of historical data and risky operating environment might not mean higher interest costs. Why? Firms that face more business risk tend to have more volatile stock prices, which would make the option component (*CV*) of any convertible debt issued more valuable. Therefore, if a credit analyst made a mistake (perhaps) in overstating the firm's risk, any declines in the value of the bond component (*BV*) would be offset by increases in the value of the conversion option. The tendency of these risk factors to balance one another out means that a relatively high-risk company could issue convertible debt at close to the same coupon rate as a lower-risk firm.

> Option pricing theory suggests that convertible debt may play a useful role in financing firms whose risk may be difficult to access.

This case for convertibles was first articulated by Brennan and Schwartz (1988) and is known as the risk-synergy argument. It's appealing on theoretical grounds as it gives us a sound rationale for the use of convertible debt that doesn't assume that issuers of securities can somehow get something for nothing. Instead, it suggests that the market may perceive some firms as being risky or having a risk that is difficult to assess. The technology firms on the "information superhighway" fall into such categories. These firms might prefer convertibles because the lower interest costs would allow them to take on more investment projects than might otherwise be the case. However, they should recognize that the lower interest rate is not a "free ride," because they are giving creditors something of value—a call option on the firm's common stock.

7.5   AGENCY PROBLEMS: AN OPTION-VALUATION APPROACH

As we have already seen, the interests of stockholders, bondholders, and corporate managers do not always coincide. When conflicts arise, someone bears direct costs; further, the existence of asymmetric information among stakeholders often results in hidden costs. Solutions consist of identifying the problem and designing more precise contracts between the parties involved. Option-pricing concepts can help managers understand these problems and create solutions.

Conflicts between Stockholders and Bondholders

Let's return to the idea that the equity of a leveraged company can be thought of as a call option on the value of a firm's assets. An important implication of the Black–Scholes option-pricing model is that call-option values increase as the volatility of the returns from the underlying asset increases. Intuition tells us that higher volatility increases the chance of very high returns. Moreover, the call-option holder doesn't care about very low returns because the option will be worthless at any price below the strike price.

This option-like characteristic of equity suggests an obvious conflict of interest between stockholders and bondholders. Specifically, managers who act in the stockholders best interests have the *incentive* to increase the value of the equity by switching the firm's assets into projects or lines of business with a higher standard deviation of return. The stockholders benefit from the increased chance of very high returns. Conversely, the chance of *very low* returns does not concern them because the limited liability afforded common stockholders mitigates downside risk.

To see this in numerical terms, let's go back to the example of Greene Products. Recall that the company owed $2 million that had to be paid in a year and that the willingness of stockholders to come up with the money to pay off creditors would depend on the value of Greene's assets at that time. Column 1 in Exhibit 7-8 gives a probability distribution for the company's assets one year from now.

With its present asset base, the expected value of Greene's equity as a call option with a strike price of $2 million would be

Value of Equity (Existing Assets)

$$= .05(0) + .1(\$2,100,000 - \$2,000,000) + .2(\$2,300,000 - \$2,000,000)$$
$$+ .3(\$2,500,000 - \$2,000,000) + .2(\$2,700,000 - \$2,000,000)$$
$$+ .1(\$2,900,000 - \$2,000,000) + .05(\$3,100,000 - \$2,000,000)$$
$$= \$505,000$$

Suppose now that the managers, acting on behalf of the stockholders, are able to switch the company's assets into riskier projects so as to produce the outcomes

> *Managers acting in the shareholders' best interest have an incentive to increase asset risk.*

EXHIBIT 7-8
Probability Distributions for the Value of Greene Products' Assets before and after the Asset Switch

Probability	Column 1 Existing Assets	Column 2 After Switch
0.05	$1,900,000	$ 500,000
0.10	2,100,000	1,000,000
0.20	2,300,000	1,500,000
0.30	2,500,000	2,000,000
0.20	2,700,000	3,000,000
0.10	2,900,000	4,000,000
0.05	3,100,000	5,000,000
Expected Value of Assets	$2,500,000	$2,275,000

shown in Column 2 in Exhibit 7-8. Although this riskier set of projects lowers the expected value of the assets, as well as increases the probability of default, it also increases the chance of an extremely high payoff. These high potential asset values increase the value of the equity as a call option:

Value of Equity (After Asset Switch)

$$= .05(0) + .1(0) + .2(0) + .3(0) + .2(\$3,000,000 - \$2,000,000)$$
$$+ .1(\$4,000,000 - \$2,000,000) + .05(\$5,000,000 - \$2,000,000)$$
$$= \$550,000$$

Creditors can protect against risky asset shifts by writing restrictive loan agreements.

Creditors are not stupid, and they recognize the incentives for these types of asset switches. To protect their position, they may write a bond contract that constrains the stockholders' ability to move the firm into riskier lines of business. A carefully designed bond contract that prohibits the firm from switching assets into riskier businesses reduces the potential conflicts between bondholders and stockholders (and the costs of these conflicts). It also lowers the interest rate demanded by bondholders, saving the company money. The insight that equity can be viewed as a call option permits us to identify a potential problem and search for a solution.

Provisions that prohibit a company like Greene from increasing the risk of its assets are not without challenges and costs. Do creditors want to approve *all* new investment projects? If so, monitoring costs are likely to be high because creditors will be making management decisions in addition to supplying capital. Or are creditors willing to give managers the ability to implement small projects as they see fit while retaining final approval on *large* projects? There are some trade-offs here; tightly written bond contracts are expensive to keep track of, but letting managers make decisions without interference may lead to increases in risk, which work to the creditors' disadvantage.[6]

Convertible debt reduces the incentives of managers to engage in risky asset shifts.

Fortunately, option-valuation concepts provide us with some alternative approaches—for example, the simple inclusion of a convertible feature in the debt contract. Remember that a convertible bond can be viewed as part bond, part call option on the company's common stock. Increasing the riskiness of the firm's assets would lower the value of the debt component; however, increased volatility will increase the value of the option component. By giving the bondholder a "piece of the action" through the conversion option, a firm can eliminate a situation in which the creditor bears all of the downside risk but receives none of the upside potential. Therefore, although the conversion feature will not *prevent* firms from taking on risky projects, it will *reduce incentives* for risky asset shifts, because

---

[6]Beyond writing restrictive bond contracts, rational creditors may also demand a correspondingly higher coupon rate to compensate for this anticipated future risk as well as the higher costs of monitoring contracts. Therefore, regardless of which route is taken, the firm can incur high explicit or implicit costs of borrowing.

the existing stockholders will have to share the benefits of such projects with creditors.[7]

Risk Incentives, Deposit Insurance, and the S&L Debacle

The risk incentives just described, coupled with the structure of deposit insurance at the time, contributed to the S&L mess of the 1980s. Specifically, the U.S. government through the now-defunct Federal Savings and Loan Insurance Corporation (FSLIC) guaranteed the safety of depositor money up to $100,000 per account. In return, S&Ls paid the FSLIC a fixed insurance rate based on the dollar amount of deposits, regardless of the risks in the loan portfolio. These conditions created huge incentives for S&L operators to engage in risky lending practices. Let's look at the dynamics in an option-pricing setting.

From the standpoint of the owners, deposit insurance can be viewed as a put option written on the S&L's assets.[8] The exercise price is the face amount of the institution's deposits. When the value of the assets ($A_{S\&L}$) is less than the face value of the deposits (D), that is, $A_{S\&L} < D$, this put option is in the money. The S&L can exercise its option by closing its doors, thereby forcing the FSLIC to pay off the depositors. The deposit insurance put option is valuable, however, only if there is little equity in the S&L. This was the situation confronting the S&L industry in the early 1980s following the dramatic rise in interest rates and consequent decline in the value of the fixed-rate mortgages they were holding on their balance sheets.

Because insurance premiums are fixed, S&L managers could increase the value of the equity by taking on more and riskier loans. (In a risk-based deposit insurance system, shareholders would bear the cost of these riskier loans through higher premiums.) Depositors had little incentive to monitor these risky activities; from their perspective, deposit insurance meant that they had an option to sell (put) deposits to the FSLIC at face. Indeed, depositors had an incentive to deposit more money in risky S&Ls because these institutions paid higher interest rates. These structural problems, coupled with weak regulatory oversight, cost the U.S. taxpayer dearly.

Conflicts between Owners and Managers

Consider a firm in which the managers own a relatively small portion of the equity. As we have suggested, the owners will want the company to engage in investment projects that maximize the value of their shares even if that means high-risk activities. In contrast, managers will tend to look to low-risk projects

---

[7]Using convertibles to mitigate conflicts of interest between bondholders and stockholders was discussed early on in the agency literature by both Jensen and Meckling (1976) and Smith and Warner (1979).

[8]The idea that deposit insurance can be viewed as a put option was first put forth by Robert Merton (1977).

that minimize the possibility of bankruptcy. After all, if the company goes bankrupt, the managers might suffer a loss of reputation, making it tough to find another job. There is nothing inherently wrong with low-risk, low-return projects, but companies in some industries may not have the luxury of focusing on these types of investments. A low-risk strategy for firms such as Nokia, Amgen, or Intel would be a formula for disaster.

> The use of stock options can help align the interests of managers with those of stockholders.

One possible solution to owner–manager conflicts is to alter the form of compensation given to managers to ensure that their interests are aligned with those of the stockholders. Consider, for example, the impact of a stock-option plan that gives managers packages of out-of-the-money options in addition to their fixed salary and bonuses. The value of the options will tend to increase if managers direct the company away from low-risk projects to those that have higher risks along with higher returns. Thus, options will encourage managers to invest in those projects that the investors find desirable. At the same time, owners should recognize that options are valuable and that they ultimately bear the cost of transferring an increased share of ownership to managers.[9]

SUMMARY

In this chapter, we examined some of the characteristics of stock options, their valuation, and the manner in which options are imbedded in financing and investment decisions. The key feature of stock options may be stated as follows: put and call options are contracts between two parties. In return for an initial investment—the option premium—the buyer has the right to buy or sell securities to the other party. The owner of the contract must determine whether to exercise the option or to allow it to expire unused. It's important to remember that the option premium is a sunk cost that can only be recouped if the option is exercised at a profit.

We looked at the Black–Scholes option-pricing model for valuing European call options. This model is based on the ability of the investor to replicate the payoffs from a call option by holding an investment in the underlying stock that is financed, in part, with borrowed money. Looking at the properties of the Black–Scholes model, we found that call-option prices increase with the price of the underlying stock, the volatility of stock returns, the risk-free rate, and the time to expiration; option prices decline with increases in the exercise price.

With this background, we took a look at how options come into play with corporate financing and investment decisions. On the investment side, we identified how real-estate options might come into play in a potential plant expansion, research and development projects as call options, and the right to abandon a project as a put option. On the financing side, we saw how the firm's common stock could be viewed as a call option as well as how complex securities such as convertible bonds can be better understood as a combination of straight debt and a call option. The common theme is that options exist in many places and that a failure to recognize them omits an important dimension of the decision problem. Option-pricing theory was then extended to identifying potential conflicts of interest among corporate stakeholders and designing solutions to these problems.

---

[9]In practice, few executive stock-option plans are issued out of the money. Further, there has been a tendency for managers to try to lower the exercise price on options that are far out of the money. This is becoming an increasing source of friction between executives and shareholders.

APPENDIX 7A VALUING OPTIONS: THE TWO-STATE ARBITRAGE MODEL

To get a feel for how the Black–Scholes arbitrage technique works in a simple setting, let's consider the following example: Suppose the current stock price of Meridian, Inc., is $100 a share and that this is also the exercise price of a one-year call option. To keep matters simple, we'll also assume that Meridian's future stock price can take on only two values—it can either rise to $110 or fall to $90. Given a one-year interest rate of 5 percent, we will show that the value of the option must be worth $7.143.

If the stock price at the expiration of the call is $110 a share, the call will be in the money, and its value will be $10—the difference between the stock price and the strike price of $100. On the other hand, if the stock price a year from now is $90, the call option will expire as worthless. The possible payoffs from owning the option are therefore:

Stock Price	$90	$110
Value of the call option	0	10

The payoffs from *two* of these options can be replicated by purchasing *one* share of Meridian's stock financed, in part, with $85.714 of borrowed money.[10] This portfolio would have a current equity value of $14.286—the $100-per-share current price of the common stock less the amount borrowed. The payoffs in one year from this portfolio are as follows:

Stock Price	$90	$110
Value of one share	90	110
Repayment of loan plus interest @ 5%	90	90
Total payoff	$ 0	$20

Because the portfolio payoffs exactly duplicate the payoffs from *two* call options, their values must be identical. Therefore, given a current value of the portfolio equal to $14.286, the call option must be worth half that amount or $7.143. If the market price of the call option should differ from this amount, riskless arbitrage profits could be earned. However, such a situation could not last for long. In the process of trying to cash in on this profitable opportunity, arbitrageurs would drive the price of the call back to its equilibrium value of $7.143.

QUESTIONS

1. Insurance can be considered a put option from the policyholder's point of view. What is the exercise price and maturity of your car insurance? Do you think it is valued fairly?

2. As part of its month-long grand opening celebration, Rocky Burgers gives its customers a coupon entitling the holder to purchase two Rockyburgers for the price of one. Is this an option? How would you value it?

3. Imagine that the price of copper rises to the point that the copper value of a penny is worth more than $.01. As a result, pennies disappear from circulation. Your firm uses copper in its production process, and you can melt pennies down and retrieve their copper content at zero cost. At present, you have a six-month supply of copper reserves, and you have also managed to collect 1 million pennies. Should you melt the pennies down and add the copper to your stockpile? Why or why not?

4. A new accounting firm has agreed to rent its office furniture and equipment for a year with an option to purchase all of it at the end of the lease for $500,000 extra. What is the strike price of the option? What is the price of the option?

5. According to the Black–Scholes option-pricing model, shareholders *prefer* a riskier firm, other things being equal. Explain.

6. As interest rates rise, stock prices should fall, because the price of equity is the discounted value of

---

[10]To construct a levered position in the underlying stock that gives the same payoff as the call option, it is necessary to borrow an amount equal to $(S_L - C_L)/(1 + r)$, where S_L is the worst-case value for the end-of-period stock price, C_L the end-of-period option value associated with S_L, and r the borrowing rate. Substituting in the numbers in the text yields a borrowing amount equal to

$$(90 - 0)/1.05 = \$85.714$$

expected future cash flows. Would this statement be true under the option-pricing model?

7. Under the option-pricing model, what are the key determinants of a convertible bond's value?

8. Equity is considered an option on the firm's value after the bondholders are paid off.
   a. Are bondholders "paid off" in most firms? What does this say about the value of equity?
   b. From a stockholder's point of view, what is the optimal amount of debt for a firm?

9. A multidivisional corporation is planning to split into two companies. All the corporate debt would be placed in one of the new companies. The other company would be wholly owned by the shareholders (100 percent equity). Will the bondholders approve of this spinoff? Will the shareholders?

10. Will a gold mine ever be shut permanently? Why or why not?

11. Should the coupon interest rate on convertible debt be greater or less than the coupon rate on a regular issue of debt from the same company if both are issued simultaneously at par? Why?

12. At present, the U.S. Forest Service auctions off timber parcels to the high bidder, who then has to make a low down payment. What problems might this system present for the Forest Service?

13. A well-known money manager claims that he can achieve two-thirds of the stock market's return with only half the market's risk by selling at-the-money call options on his stock holdings for a premium that averages about 15 percent annually. According to the money manager, "Stocks have gone up an average of 10 percent a year since 1929. If we can sell their potential profits for 15 percent a year and keep the dividends besides, aren't we going to come out ahead in the long run?" Has the money manager figured out a way to use options to get a free lunch? Explain.

14. Many companies maintain defined-benefit pension plans for their employees. These plans promise to pay retirees a guaranteed amount of money each year. Companies fund these plans by setting aside money to be invested. If the investment returns are insufficient to finance the promised benefits, the company must make up the difference. Conversely, if the investment returns exceed the cost of the pension benefits, the company can recover for their own use the excess funds. Many of these plans are now overfunded because of the unexpectedly good performance of the stock market during the 1980s. Recent legislation would have the effect of forcing companies to pay out any excess funds in their defined-benefit pension plans to their retirees. What is the likely impact of such legislation on the desirability to corporations of maintaining defined-benefit plans?

15. The pension reform act, passed in 1974, was so uncontroversial that only two members of Congress opposed it. A key element of this legislation was the establishment of the Pension Benefit Guarantee Corporation (PBGC), a federal agency that now guarantees the pension benefits of over 40 million U.S. workers. Initially, PBGC was financed by charging most companies a flat insurance premium of $1 per employee annually. That premium is now $19 per employee.
   a. In what sense can PBGC insurance be considered an option?
   b. Who is likely to benefit from this insurance scheme?
   c. Who is likely to be hurt by this insurance scheme? How will they likely respond?
   d. How can companies take advantage of the PBGC? Which companies are most likely to do so?
   e. Why might premiums have risen so dramatically?

PROBLEMS

—Excel templates may be downloaded from **www. prenhall.com/financecenter.**

1. You have purchased a call option on AC stock for $5. The option has an exercise price of $15.

   a. Calculate the profit on the option if the final price of AC stock is expected to be $35, $30, $25, $10, and $5.
   b. Graph the profit on the option as in Exhibit 7-1.

2. A put option on Unioil stock is selling for $2.35. The put exercise price is $10.
   a. Calculate the profit on the put option if the final price of Unioil is expected to be $20, $15, $10, $5, $2.50.
   b. Graph the profit on the option as in Exhibit 7-2.
3. A call option on the stock of Q Mart has an exercise price of $50 and expires in one year. ☒
   a. If Q Mart rises to $55 from its current value of $50, how much will the option be worth at expiration?
   b. If Q Mart falls to $45 from $50, how much will the option be worth at expiration?
   c. You can duplicate the payoff on this option by taking a long position in one share of the stock and borrowing the amount $($45 − 0$)/1.10 = 40.91 at 10 percent interest toward the purchase price. What is the payoff from this position?
   d. How much should the option be worth?
4. Suppose that you want to write a six-month call option on Piper Precision Products common stock. The strike price of the option would be the same as Piper's current market price of $30 a share. If the option premium were $3 a share, at what stock price would you still make money?
5. Call options are currently traded on CD Audio Systems stock. The exercise price of one of the call options is $30. The current price of CD is 27½; the option maturity is in two months. The risk-free rate is 5 percent, and the stock's standard deviation of return is 10 percent. ☒
   a. Calculate the price of the CD option.
   b. Assume the stock is more volatile and has a standard deviation of 15 percent. Calculate the price of the CD option.
   c. If the maturity of the option declines to one month from two, calculate the price of the CD option (assume a standard deviation of 10 percent).
6. GE options are traded on the Chicago Board Options Exchange. The current risk-free rate is 6.5 percent, and the standard deviation of GE's rate of return is 12 percent. The current price of GE is 46¼. ☒
   a. Calculate the price of GE 45 calls if the expiration of the option is in eight months.
   b. Calculate the price of GE 45 calls if the expiration is in two months.

   c. Calculate the value of the option in (b) if it is expiring now.
   d. Will this option ever be exercised before maturity? Why or why not?
7. Suppose that you are interested in buying a three-month call option on Klein Electronics common stock at $4.50. The option's exercise price is $45, while Klein's present market price per share is $40. Your probability distribution for the firm's stock price in three months is as follows.

Probability	Stock Price
0.15	$38.00
0.20	40.00
0.30	45.00
0.20	50.00
0.15	55.00

   a. What's the expected value of the stock price three months from now?
   b. What's the expected value of the call option at expiration?
   c. Does the option appear to be fairly priced based on expected values?
8. You are attempting to assess the performance of Simon Semiconductor and Schuster Electronics and come up with the following probability distribution of their per-share stock price a year from now. Both are currently selling for $75 a share. ☒

Probability	Simon Semiconductor	Schuster Electronics
0.15	$68.00	$ 44.00
0.20	76.00	56.00
0.30	80.00	72.00
0.20	84.00	88.00
0.15	92.00	100.00

   a. Calculate the expected market price per share in a year for each company. Which firm's common stock appears to be the best buy?
   b. Suppose both firms have call options with a strike price of $78 a share, which trade on the CBOE. Calculate the expected value of both Simon and Schuster's call options. Which firm's call option should trade at a higher price?
9. The managers of a firm are asked to consider two possible new product lines for the firm. Project 1 is quite risky and may result in a market value for the

firm of $50 million in two years or nothing. Project 2 is much more certain in outcome and may result in a firm market value as high as $25 million or as low as $15 million. The face value of the company's debt, payable in two years, is $20 million.

a. What are the possible payoffs to the bondholders under projects 1 and 2?

b. What are the possible payoffs to the shareholders under projects 1 and 2?

c. Which will the shareholders favor? The bondholders?

10. A farmer has a two-year lease on a plot of land that will produce 1,000 bushels if the harvest is good or 640 bushels if the harvest is poor. The fixed cost of production is $400 per year, and the risk-free rate is 6 percent annually. The current price of the crop is $5 per bushel; this falls by 20 percent in a good year and rises by 25 percent in a bad year. This year's crop has just been harvested, and so only two more harvests remain during the life of the lease. The crop may be freely purchased or sold at the prevailing market price and may be stored free. The farmer wishes to sell his interest in the lease. What is the market value of the lease? (*Hint:* Diagram the possible crop price sequences, and calculate the cash flow at each point in time under each possible sequence of price outcomes.)

11. Suppose the price of Atlas Co. is currently $40 a share. A call option on Atlas stock that will expire in one year has an exercise price of $42.50. The risk-free interest rate is 10 percent per annum. Suppose that one year from now, Atlas stock will either go up to $50 a share or fall to $35 a share. What can you say about the price of the Atlas call option?

REFERENCES

Billingsley, R. S., R. E. Lamy, and G. R. Thompson. "Valuation of Primary Issue Convertible Bonds." *Journal of Financial Research,* Fall 1986, 251–259.

Black, F., and M. Scholes. "The Pricing of Options and Corporate Liabilities." *Journal of Political Economy,* May–June 1973, 637–659.

Brennan, M. J., and E. S. Schwartz. "The Case for Convertibles." *Journal of Applied Corporate Finance,* Summer 1988, 55–64.

Brennan, M. J., and E. S. Schwartz. "Convertible Bonds: Valuation and Optimal Policy for Call and Conversion." *Journal of Finance,* December 1977, 1699–1715.

Constantinides, G. "Warrant Exercise and Bond Conversion in Competitive Markets." *Journal of Financial Economics,* September 1984, 371–398.

Ingersoll, J. "A Contingent-Claims Valuation of Convertible Securities." *Journal of Financial Economics,* May 1977, 289–322.

Jensen, M. C., and W. H. Meckling. "Theory of the Firm: Managerial Behavior, Agency Costs, and Capital Structure." *Journal of Financial Economics,* October 1976, 305–360.

Merton, R. C. "An Analytical Derivation of the Cost of Deposit Insurance Loan Guarantees: An Application of Modern Option Pricing Theory." *Journal of Banking and Finance,* June 1977, 3–11.

Merton, R. C. "Theory of Rational Option Pricing." *Bell Journal of Economics and Management Science,* Spring 1973, 141–183.

Smith, C. W., and J. E. Warner. "On Financial Contracting: An Analysis of Bond Covenants." *Journal of Financial Economics,* June 1979, 117–161.

Evaluation of Investment Projects

There is a tide in the affairs of men,
Which, taken at the flood, leads to fortune:
Omitted, all the voyages of their life
Are bound in shallows and miseries.
Shakespeare, Julius Caesar

KEY TERMS

accounting rate of
  return (ARR)
contingent projects
cost-reduction
  project
equivalent annual
  cost (EAC)
expansion project

independent projects
internal rate of return
  (IRR)
mandated projects
multiple internal rates of
  return
mutually exclusive
  projects

net present value (NPV)
net present value (NPV)
  profile
new product introduction
payback period
project post-audit
replacement chain
value-additivity principle

CHAPTER LEARNING OBJECTIVES

Upon completion of this chapter, students should be able to:

■ Describe capital budgeting as a management process and its integration into a company's strategic plans.
■ List ways in which projects can be categorized.
■ Explain the similarities and differences between the net present value (NPV) and the internal rate of return (IRR) method for evaluating projects and discuss why NPV is the preferred criterion for making investment decisions.
■ Calculate a project's NPV and IRR and use these measures to make investment decisions.

■ Indicate the problems in using nondiscounted cash flow techniques such as payback and accounting rate of return to make capital budgeting decisions.
■ Describe the use of capital-budgeting techniques in practice and explain why managers use other methods than NPV to make investment decisions.
■ Indicate how the equivalent annual cost method can be used to evaluate projects with different economic lives.

Of the many decisions that senior managers make, none is likely to have more impact than the decision to invest capital, which often involves large, extended commitments of money and management time. In 1997 alone, capital expenditures of U.S. companies totaled nearly $770 billion. More important, the sum of these decisions determines the company's future course and, therefore, its market value. For example, an electric utility's choice between going nuclear or remaining with coal is of the utmost importance to owners and customers alike. Similarly, the decision by General Motors (GM) in the early 1980s to launch the Saturn represented a belief that a small automobile designed and built in the United States could successfully compete with the Japanese in terms of reliability and customer satisfaction. GM backed its vision with a multibillion-dollar investment in product and facility development.

Simply put, the *capital-budgeting decision,* the allocation of funds among alternative investment opportunities, is crucial to corporate success. It's not surprising, therefore, that firms devote so much effort to planning capital expenditures. The nature and consequences of the capital-budgeting process are so broad that top-level executives in all vital areas of the company must participate; investment decisions are just too important to be left to the chief financial officer.

> The ultimate goal of the capital budgeting process is to identify and implement those projects that will enhance shareholder value.

From a stockholder's standpoint, the ultimate objective of the process is for managers to identify and implement projects that will enhance shareholder wealth. Based on what we've learned up to this point, we know that for the investment analysis to do this, it must meet the following criteria:

1. It should place higher weight on earlier cash flows than on later cash flows.
2. It should focus on cash flows rather than accounting earnings.
3. It should penalize the expected cash flows from riskier projects more heavily.

In this chapter, we'll explore the basic principles of capital budgeting. Before looking at specific techniques, we will discuss, in turn, capital budgeting as a management process as well as ways in which to classify different investment projects. This background will allow us to examine and compare alternative techniques for evaluating prospective investments. The chapter concludes with a look at the methods actually used by companies in making their capital-budgeting decisions. In Chapter 9, we'll show how to apply the recommended procedures and describe in more detail some of the problems that often arise in practice.

8.1   CAPITAL BUDGETING AS A MANAGEMENT PROCESS

Unlike stock and bond investments, the projects that enter the corporate capital-budgeting process are not just sitting around waiting to be selected. *Someone has to think them up.* Sometimes these projects arise naturally, as when a machine tool wears out or when a more efficient production process appears. Other opportunities come out of the blue. A salesperson may propose the development of a more efficient blood-analysis unit when customers complain that existing products are slow and error prone. Or an engineer in research and development may come up with a novel color laser printer/copier/fax/scanner machine.

All of these situations require a capital-budgeting decision. As a general rule, a company will want to gather additional information before making a decision. However, before looking at the financial dimension, it is important to understand capital budgeting as an integral part of the strategic management process. The steps in the *capital-budgeting process* are as follows:

Development of a Strategic Plan

In a well-managed company, the capital-budgeting process begins at the strategic level with the senior managers developing a vision of the firm and communicating it to lower-level managers. This vision should consist of a clear definition of the businesses the firm wishes to pursue and the way that it is going to compete in these businesses. An integral part of this vision is the development of specific strategic goals. A strategic plan allows operating managers to translate goals into concrete action plans that may involve specific investment proposals.

Generation of Potential Investment Opportunities

Potential investment opportunities should be consistent with the firm's strategic plan.

Once a strategic plan has been developed, the generation of ideas for investment projects should begin with a search for market opportunities that build on the firm's core competencies or address competitive weaknesses. To be effective, this should be an ongoing process whose intent is to identify growth opportunities. For a company's strategy to be successful, there must be a direct connection between the search for and generation of ideas and the firm's overall strategic objectives. Too often, companies spend a great deal of time and energy gathering and evaluating financial data without first asking whether the project does anything to build and exploit the type of competitive advantage needed to achieve their strategic goals.

Estimate the Project's Cash Flows

Once investment opportunities have been identified, the next step is to estimate the magnitude, timing, and riskiness of the cash flows associated with each project. This is often the most difficult part of the process. In some cases, the project under consideration may be the first step in a series of investments needed to fully exploit a particular market or technology. Therefore, capturing all of the relevant cash flows associated with a project requires an extensive knowledge of the competitive setting and how a particular investment may relate to existing or future projects. We'll examine the challenges in cash-flow estimation in some detail in Chapter 9.

Acceptance or Rejection

Once cash-flow estimates have been made, the firm can evaluate the project in financial terms and assess whether the decision to go forward is consistent with the strategic goal of maximizing shareholder wealth. The idea that a project may have "strategic value" even though it dissipates shareholder value is a contradiction in terms. The key corporate stakeholders are, so to speak, "joined at the hip": Investments that destroy stockholder wealth also hurt customers and employees in the long run.

Project Post-Audit

Evaluating the performance of ongoing projects is an important control mechanism for assessing the overall effectiveness of the process. The primary mechanism for such an evaluation is a **project post-audit** that compares the project's actual cash flows with the projected figures. A successful feedback system may suggest needed improvements in the process by which the firm evaluates projects or the techniques used in preparing estimates of cash flows and risks.

All steps in the process are vital to ensure that the firm meets its strategic goals. Historically, the finance function has focused on the estimation of a project's cash flow and the techniques for selecting projects. However, there has been a growing awareness on the part of executives that building and exploiting competitive advantage and shareholder wealth maximization are two sides of the same coin. This has forced many firms to examine all aspects of the capital-budgeting process to ensure internal consistency.

8.2   CLASSIFICATION OF INVESTMENT PROJECTS

From an organizational standpoint, capital-budgeting projects can be characterized in a number of ways in order to specify: (1) who can make the decision to go ahead with the project, (2) the type of benefit to be expected, and/or (3) the degree of interaction between a specific project and other projects under consideration.

Project Size

Classifying projects by size is a mechanism for establishing who makes the decision to proceed.

Many firms classify projects by size as a way of determining who makes the decision to proceed. For example, depending on the firm's profitability standards, a large manufacturing firm may allow a plant manager to approve all project proposals costing $25,000 or less, and division managers might be allowed to approve projects costing no more than $100,000. Any expenditure of more than $100,000 might require the board's approval. The idea here is to allocate scarce management time to those few proposals that can influence a firm's strategic direction and viability.

Type of Benefit Expected

Some firms classify projects in terms of the benefits expected. A **cost-reduction project,** for example, might consider a new piece of equipment to replace one that has become physically or technologically obsolete. These projects are typically motivated by cost reduction and/or quality improvement considerations. For example, the desire to reduce costs and increase product reliability has encouraged the widespread use of robotics by auto manufacturers such as GM, Ford, DaimlerChrysler, and Toyota.

Expansion projects are those investments needed to meet projected increases in demand for the company's products or services due to either growth in existing markets or expansion into a new domestic or foreign market. Firms may also increase demand through **new product introductions,** which may involve a simultaneous phasing-out of existing products.

Finally, firms may be faced with **mandated projects,** such as investments in pollution-control equipment to meet Environmental Protection Agency (EPA) guidelines or health and safety equipment to comply with Occupational Safety and Health Administration (OSHA) standards. In many cases, these projects provide no direct benefit; however, the failure to comply with regulatory guidelines may cause an existing facility to be shut down. Thus, the benefit from mandated projects comes from the returns generated by other investments that are allowed to continue to operate.

> **Projects differ greatly in terms of the amounts of data available and risk.**

Investments in these categories differ dramatically in the amounts of information available and the risks involved. Simple replacement projects, for example, are viewed by many firms as low-risk investments because the potential savings are engineering-based estimates. The risk of new product introductions, on the other hand, is inherently greater than for projects that simply expand capacity for an existing line. Moreover, new product introductions frequently involve large expenditures for R&D, market research, advertising and promotion. As project risk increases—from cost reduction projects to expansion of existing product lines to projects involving new products or technology—the analysis becomes more detailed and more costly. Within each category, the more expensive projects typically get more scrutiny. Common sense suggests that a project involving a $250-million facility to produce a new generation of personal computers should be examined more closely than a $5,000 remodeling of an office cafeteria.

By Degree of Dependence

> **Understanding how projects relate to one another has an important bearing on how they are evaluated.**

It's also useful to classify projects according to how they interact with existing investments or other projects under consideration because the category they fall into will determine how they are evaluated. **Independent projects** are stand-alone investments whose acceptance or rejection is not dependent on another project. **Mutually exclusive projects,** on the other hand, represent competing investments; the acceptance of one would preclude the acceptance of the other. For example, a firm may be considering two approaches to expanding production capacity. One has a lower fixed investment but higher variable costs, and the other method involves expensive state-of-the-art equipment but has very low operating costs. In making its decision, the firm must not only decide whether the expansion is worthwhile (an accept–reject decision) but must rank the two approaches.

It is also necessary to recognize investment opportunities that involve contingent projects. As the name suggests, **contingent projects** represent investments that cannot be accepted unless one or more other projects are also accepted. For example, a firm may not be able to acquire and install a new piece of equipment unless it also expands plant floor space. For proper evaluation, contingent projects should be lumped together as a single investment.

Often, contingent investments are subtle. Here is an example of a contingent investment decision that is linked to the overall corporate strategy.

Illustration

Investing in Memory Chips

Since 1984, the intense competition from Japanese firms has caused most U.S. semiconductor manufacturers to lose money in the memory chip business. The only profitable part of the chip business for them is in making microprocessors and other specialized chips. Why did U.S. companies continue investing in facilities to produce memory chips (DRAMs) despite their losses in this business?

Historically, U.S. companies invested so much in DRAMs because of these chips' importance in fine-tuning the manufacturing process. Memory chips are manufactured in huge quantities and are fairly simple to test for defects, which makes them ideal vehicles for refining new production processes. Having worked out the bugs by making memories, chip companies apply an improved process to hundreds of more complex products. Until recently, without manufacturing some sort of memory chip, it was very difficult to keep production technology competitive. Thus, making profitable investments elsewhere in the chip business was contingent on producing memory chips. As manufacturing technology has changed, diminishing the importance of memory chips as process technology drivers, U.S. chip manufacturers such as Intel have stopped producing DRAMs.

8.3   DISCOUNTED CASH FLOW TECHNIQUES

Once a firm has identified projects that are consistent with its strategic objectives, it should then select from among them that set of projects that maximizes shareholder value. The measure of project worth must allow managers to answer two questions:[1]

1. Given a particular independent project, should the firm accept or reject it?
2. Given a set of mutually exclusive projects, which one (if any) should the firm take on?

---

[1]Some firms with lots of acceptable projects but limited resources have to decide which group of projects to select. The classical works in the area of capital rationing are Lorie and Savage (1955) and Weingartner (1963).

Ideally, we'd like a technique that, used consistently, will lead a company to make the same investment decisions that shareholders would if they had the same information and opportunities that are available to corporate management. We know that (in theory) the value of the firm's common stock is the present value of an infinite stream of dividends. Since dividends are paid with *cash*, discounted cash flow (DCF) techniques, which focus on the magnitude, timing, and risk of the cash flows from a project, provide a direct link between the project-selection process and the value of the firm's common stock.

Capital budgeting criteria should allow a company to make decisions in the same way that shareholders would if they had the same information.

Net Present Value Decision Criterion

Investments with positive net present values add to shareholder wealth; those with negative net present values reduce shareholder wealth. Companies, therefore, should invest in positive net present value (NPV) projects and reject negative NPV projects. This is the net present value investment decision rule.

Projects with positive NPVs should be accepted; those with negative NPVs should be rejected.

The **net present value** rule is implemented as follows: *Calculate the present value of the expected net cash flows generated by the investment, using an appropriate discount rate, and subtract from this present value the initial net cash outlay for the project. If the resulting NPV is positive, accept the project; if it is negative, reject it. If two projects are mutually exclusive, accept the one with the higher net present value.*

In choosing between two mutually exclusive projects, pick the one with the highest NPV.

In other words, if an investment is worth more than it costs, accept it; if it costs more than it's worth, reject it. By taking into account all cash flows, only cash flows, and the time value of money, NPV evaluates projects in the same way that investors do. Therefore, it is consistent with the objective of shareholder wealth maximization.

Mathematically, the NPV is given by

$$NPV = \sum_{t=1}^{N} \frac{CF_t}{(1 + k)^t} - I_0 \qquad [8\text{-}1]$$

where CF_t is the cash flow in time period t; I_0, the initial investment outlay in time zero; k, the required rate of return on the project; and N, the project's economic life in periods.

As we indicated in Chapter 4, the NPV is a measure of how much *better off* stockholders would be if we took on the investment. The first term in Equation [8-1] is the present value of the cash flows expected from the project after making some initial investment (I_0) today. If an independent project's NPV is positive—the value of the investment exceeds its cost—then we should accept it; negative NPV projects should be rejected. If the firm is trying to choose between two mutually exclusive projects, both of which have positive NPVs, the one with the highest NPV should be selected. When the company faces resource constraints, the combination of projects with the highest NPV should be chosen.

Illustration

Consider the case of Quickie Enterprises, which is looking to aggressively market its microprocessors to game and computer manufacturers in the Pacific Rim. Its current facilities are committed to supporting domestic demand growth, so Quickie will have to build a new chip-making plant to meet the expected increase in foreign demand. The proposed facility will contain expensive state-of-the-art technology and is expected to have an installed cost of $400 million. The firm is optimistic about its ability to compete and estimates that project cash flows will rise by $10 million a year, from $100 million in the first year to $140 million in year 5. Because of rapid technological change within the microprocessor industry, Quickie estimates that the facility will become obsolete at the end of year 5 and will have to be scrapped at a zero salvage value.

The calculation of the project's NPV in millions of dollars, assuming a required rate of return of 12 percent is[2]

$$NPV = \frac{\$100}{(1.12)} + \frac{\$110}{(1.12)^2} + \frac{\$120}{(1.12)^3} + \frac{\$130}{(1.12)^4} + \frac{\$140}{(1.12)^5} - \$400$$

$$= \$89.29 + \$87.69 + \$85.41 + \$82.62 + \$79.44 - \$400$$

$$= \$24.45 \text{ million}$$

Given management's cash flow estimates, the $24.45 million NPV represents, in theory, the increase in the value of the firm. Why? All of the project's $400 million cost comes either directly from shareholders in terms of dividends forgone or indirectly by their guaranteeing the debt-financed portion. In exchange for giving up dividends today, management proposes to take on a project whose value—as measured by the present value of future cash flows—is $424.45 million. Knowledgeable stockholders should be delighted with this investment.

The NPV criterion follows the value-additivity principle.

In addition to evaluating projects in the same way that shareholders would, the NPV decision criterion also has the desirable property of following the **value-additivity principle.** This means that the NPV for a set of independent projects is simply the sum of the NPVs for the individual projects. This property is useful in evaluating contingent projects or if companies face capital rationing and wish to choose the combination of projects that yield the highest NPV.

The discount rate used to calculate project NPVs should reflect financial market returns on investments of comparable risk.

Finally, we should note that the discount rate used to calculate an investment's NPV, known as the *cost of capital* or required rate of return, is the minimum

---

[2]The easiest way to perform this calculation is by using a spreadsheet. You can also compute the NPV for Quickie's microprocessor facility using a financial calculator. Appendix A at the back of this book gives you the sequence of keystrokes needed to calculate the NPV of a project when the cash flows are different in each period.

acceptable rate of return on the project. It is determined by the required return in the financial markets for investments of comparable risk. As a corollary, those investments undertaken by the same company that have different risks will have different required returns. For now we take the cost of capital as given. In Chapter 10, we shall study its derivation in detail.

Internal Rate of Return Decision Criterion

The IRR is the interest rate that equates the present value of a project's cash flows with its initial investment.

According to management surveys of capital budgeting practices, the **internal rate of return (IRR)** is the most widely used technique for evaluating investment projects. A first cousin to the NPV criterion, the IRR is the discount (or interest) rate that equates the present value of the project's cash flows with the initial investment. In mathematical terms, the IRR may be represented by Equation [8-2]:

$$I_0 = \sum_{t=1}^{N} \frac{CF_t}{(1 + IRR)^t} \qquad [8\text{-}2]$$

Projects whose IRRs are greater than the required rate of return should be accepted; IRRs below the required return should be rejected.

A close look at Equation [8-2] indicates that the IRR is the interest rate that would make the NPV of a project zero. The IRR may also be interpreted as the maximum interest rate that you would be willing to pay on long-term funds in order to finance the project. For a project to be accepted under the IRR decision criterion, its IRR must exceed the required rate of return. If the company is interested in ranking two acceptable mutually exclusive projects, the IRR criterion tells us to accept the investment project with the highest IRR.

For the cash flows related to Quickie's microprocessor facility, Equation [8-2] can be expressed as

$$\$400 = \frac{\$100}{(1 + IRR)} + \frac{\$110}{(1 + IRR)^2} + \frac{\$120}{(1 + IRR)^3} + \frac{\$130}{(1 + IRR)^4} + \frac{\$140}{(1 + IRR)^5}$$

Using a calculator (see Appendix A), you can establish that the project's IRR is 14.30 percent. Since the IRR is greater than the assumed required return of 12 percent, Quickie should go ahead with the project.

NPV and IRR: A Comparison

In general, the NPV and IRR methods give the same accept–reject decisions for independent projects.

As summary measures of project worth, the NPV and IRR share a number of similarities. First, both are DCF techniques that focus on the magnitude and timing of the project's cash flows. Second, because greater project risk implies greater shareholder required returns, both methods can accommodate differences in project risk easily by simply adjusting the project's required rate of return. Finally, subject to some important exceptions that we'll talk about shortly, the NPV and IRR yield the same accept–reject decision for independent projects. Since the IRR is the discount rate that makes the project's NPV zero, any investment whose IRR is greater than the required rate of return will have a positive NPV. Conversely, projects with an IRR that is lower than the required rate of return must have a negative NPV. This consistency in decision making of the NPV and IRR criteria explains, in part, the widespread use of the internal rate of return in practice. In some organizational settings, it may be easier to relate to the idea that a project should be accepted if its rate of return exceeds some "hurdle rate" than it is to understand the concept of accepting or rejecting an investment based on NPV. Because both methods yield the same answer, it isn't difficult to see why some companies have opted for IRR based on ease of communication.

However, there are several important differences between the two decision criteria that cause problems with the use of the IRR in some circumstances. First, the NPV method is an absolute measure of project worth in dollar terms and represents (in theory) how much the market value of the firm will rise if the project is accepted. The IRR, on the other hand, is a relative measure and tells us something about the return per dollar invested. This can create conflicts between the NPV and IRR in ranking mutually exclusive projects if there are (1) large differences in the initial investments and/or (2) significant differences in the timing of project cash inflows.

For example, let's assume that rather than building a $400 million state-of-the-art facility, Quickie Enterprises can expand chip-making capacity by putting up a less technologically advanced plant costing half as much. Manufacturing costs are expected to be higher with this lower-cost facility; hence, subsequent cash inflows will be lower. In this instance, Quickie must not only decide whether this alternative production strategy is worthwhile but whether it is economically superior to the state-of-the-art facility.

The cash flows, NPV, and IRR for the two facilities are presented in Exhibit 8-1. If they were independent projects, both production strategies would be worthwhile because (1) the NPVs for both projects are positive, and (2) the IRRs exceed the assumed 12 percent required rate of return. However, the state-of-the-art facility is superior under the NPV decision criterion, and the lower-investment facility is superior under the IRR decision criterion. The reason for these differences

EXHIBIT 8-1
Quickie Enterprises
Cash Flows, NPVs, and IRRs of Alternative Production Strategies (in million $)

Year	State-of-the-Art Facility	Lower-Investment Facility
0	−$400	−$200
1	100	50
2	110	60
3	120	70
4	130	70
5	140	60
Net Present Value @ 12%	$ 24.45	$ 20.83
Internal Rate of Return	14.30%	15.95%

NPV is a superior method for ranking mutually exclusive projects.

is related to differing reinvestment rate assumptions in the NPV and IRR criteria. The IRR decision rule implicitly assumes that the cash inflows are reinvested at the IRR, and the NPV criterion explicitly assumes reinvestment at the required rate of return. Because a properly chosen required rate of return reflects the reinvestment rate for the firm's stockholders, the NPV decision criterion can best choose between mutually exclusive projects. Given our analysis in Exhibit 8-1, Quickie should go ahead with the state-of-the-art facility to expand microprocessor capacity because its NPV is $3.6 million higher than the lower-cost alternative.

Another potentially troublesome problem with the use of IRR is that when a project has an initial cash outflow, a series of positive cash inflows, and then at least one additional cash outflow, there may be more than one IRR; that is, more than one discount rate will produce a zero NPV. Theoretically, the number of solutions may be as great as the number of sign reversals in the stream of cash flows (i.e., a shift from a cash outflow to a cash inflow or vice versa). This would be the case, for example, with a nuclear reactor, a coal mine, a logging operation, or any other project that has shutdown and cleanup costs following termination of the project. In practice, however, unless the abandonment costs are very large relative to the scale of the investment, the problem of **multiple internal rates of return** seldom arises.

Under some circumstances, there may be multiple IRRs.

For example, consider a project with the following cash flows:

Year	0	1	2	3
Cash Flow	−$200	+1,200	−$2,200	+1,200

To calculate the IRR, we must find the discount rate that equates the present value of the cash flows with the project's cost of $200:

$$\$200 = \frac{\$1,200}{(1 + IRR)} + \frac{-\$2,200}{(1 + IRR)^2} + \frac{\$1,200}{(1 + IRR)^3}$$

Solving this equation, we find internal rates of return of 0 percent, 100 percent, and 200 percent.

The NPV profile relates a project's NPV and the discount rate used to calculate the NPV.

These multiple IRRs also show up in the project's **net present value (NPV) profile** depicted in Exhibit 8-2. A project's NPV profile is the relationship between the NPV of a project and the discount rate used to calculate that NPV. Because the IRR is the discount rate that makes the project's NPV = 0, the NPV profile would intersect the x-axis at a project's IRR. As you can see, these intersections occur at 0, 100, and 200 percent.

Trying to make a decision under these circumstances using the IRR decision criterion is impossible. The IRR decision rule says that we should accept any project whose internal rate of return exceeds the required rate of return. If the company has a required rate of return of 20 percent, which IRR is relevant? 0 percent? 100 percent? Or 200 percent? The answer is none of them because they all implicitly—and wrongly—assume that the cash flows are reinvested at the IRR.

EXHIBIT 8-2
An Example of Multiple IRRs

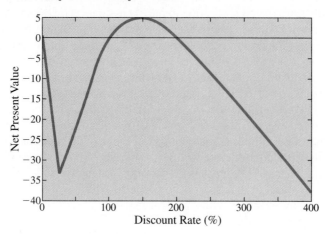

8.4   NONDISCOUNTED CASH FLOW TECHNIQUES

A number of alternatives to the NPV and IRR decision criteria do not rely on discounted cash flows. Two of the most widely used techniques are the **payback period** and the **accounting rate of return**.

Payback Period

> The payback period is the time necessary to recoup a project's initial investment from its future cash flows.

Companies frequently require that the cumulative expected cash flows from a project recover or "pay back" its investment cost within a maximum time period. Exhibit 8-3 illustrates how to calculate the payback period using the cash flow data from Quickie Enterprises' state-of-the-art microprocessor facility. The cumulative cash flows through year 3 are $330 million, leaving $70 million to be recouped in the fourth year. If the cash flows occur evenly over year 4, the payback of the initial investment will occur in another $70 million/$130 million = 0.54 years. The payback period is, therefore, 3.54 years.

As a decision rule, the payback period is easy to apply: Projects with a payback of less than some maximum cutoff period are accepted; those with longer paybacks are rejected. In ranking mutually exclusive projects, investments with shorter payback periods are preferred to those with longer paybacks. If Quickie had a maximum acceptable payback of three years, the state-of-the-art microprocessor facility would be turned down; with a four-year cutoff period it would be accepted. However, Quickie's lower-investment facility, having a shorter payback (3.29 years), would be seen as more desirable than the state-of-the-art facility even though it has a lower NPV.

The payback period was once the most popular method for making investment decisions. It's still widely used because it is simple to understand and easy

EXHIBIT 8-3
Quickie Enterprises
Calculation of Payback Period for State-of-the-Art Facility (in million $)

Year	Cash Flow	Cumulative Cash Flow
0	−$400	−$400
1	100	−300
2	110	−190
3	120	−70
4	130	+60
5	140	+200

Payback Period = 3.54 years

Payback has some value as a measure of project liquidity.

to apply. Further, the payback period has some value as a measure of project liquidity because it tells us how quickly a project's cash flows are recouped. This may be extremely important to firms that have limited access to the financial markets and, therefore, may have to rely heavily on the cash flows from accepted projects to internally finance future projects. In addition, the payback period provides us with a rough measure of project risk because in many investment settings cash flow estimates become more uncertain as time progresses. This is particularly true for industries in which the rate of technological change makes cash flow forecasting little more than a series of educated guesses.

Payback ignores the time value of money as well as cash flows beyond the payback period.

Despite these desirable features, the payback period has a number of serious drawbacks. First, as a summary measure of project worth, the payback period ignores the time value of money by focusing exclusively on the time it takes to recover the project's cost. The timing of cash flows is of critical importance because of the opportunity cost of money. Yet payback assigns the same value to a dollar received at the end of the payback period as it does to one received at the beginning.[3] Second, it ignores cash flows after the payback period and in doing so biases the capital-budgeting process against long-lived projects. Many strategically

---

[3]Payback's inability to deal with the time value of money can be overcome by looking at the *discounted payback period,* the time it takes a project to recoup both the initial investment *and* the project's required rate of return. The discounted payback period (DPB) is the shortest period of time that satisfies the following equation:

$$\sum_{t=1}^{DPB}\left[\frac{CF_t}{(1+k)^t}\right]=I_0$$

where DPB is the discounted payback period. The discounted payback period is, in essence, the length of time it will take to make the project's NPV zero. If the project's $NPV < 0$, then the $DPB = \infty$. However, the DPB suffers from some of the same drawbacks as simple payback. First, it also ignores cash flows beyond the payback period. Further, the maximum DPB used for project acceptance still reflects management's risk preferences rather than the shareholders'.

important projects, such as R&D or market development, would tend to be rejected because of long lags between initial outlays and cash returns.

Finally, although using the payback period tells us that quicker project paybacks are preferred to longer ones, management still has to decide on the maximum payback period in order to know whether to accept or reject a project. The financial markets are "calibrated" in terms of interest rates, so there's really no convenient way to directly link investors' required rates of return and maximum payback periods. As a result, firms using payback establish their cutoff periods on an ad-hoc basis, which in many cases reflects *management's*, rather than the *shareholders'*, preferences. With payback, the potential for conflicts of interest between owners and managers is high.

Accounting Rate of Return

As the name suggests, the **accounting rate of return (ARR)** is the ratio of the average after-tax profits to the average book value of the investment,[4] that is,

> **The accounting rate of return (ARR) is the ratio of the average after-tax profits to the average book investment.**

$$ARR = \frac{\text{Average Annual Profits}}{\text{Average Book Value of Investment}} \qquad [8\text{-}3]$$

The average book value of the investment includes both the cost of any fixed assets (less, of course, accumulated depreciation) as well as the project's working capital requirements. If profits vary over the life of the project, an average would be calculated and used in the numerator.

Like the payback period, the principal advantage of the ARR is its simplicity. Once the ARR is calculated, it is compared to some target return; investments yielding a greater return than this standard are accepted, and those falling below the target are rejected. As a ranking device, firms would choose between mutually exclusive projects by selecting the one with the highest ARR. The target rate of return is typically set in light of either the firm's past performance or the return on assets for the particular industry.

> **A serious weakness of the ARR is its focus on accounting profits rather than cash flows.**

However, the ARR has some serious weaknesses. First, by dealing with averages, the ARR ignores the time value of money by giving the same weight to all receipts regardless of when they are received. Second, it is based on accounting income rather than cash flow. Fundamentally, stockholders do not get accounting profits per se; the only direct benefits they get are dividends and any appreciation of share price. As we said repeatedly, shareholder well-being is directly related to the ability of the company to generate cash over time, and accounting profits and cash are not the same. Earnings not associated with cash flows cannot be spent and, therefore, are of no value to investors. In addition, the book value of assets and earnings—and, therefore, the average return on book value—depends on

---

[4]The accounting rate of return is also referred to as the *return on investment (ROI)* or the *return on funds employed*. Regardless of terminology, the ARR is conceptually identical to the return on assets we see in financial ratio analysis.

EXHIBIT 8-4
Cash Flow and Income

	Year 1	Year 2	Year 3
Project A			
Cash Flow*	$4,000	$3,000	$2,000
Income	2,000	1,000	-0-
Project B			
Cash Flow	$2,000	$3,000	$4,000
Income	-0-	1,000	2,000
Project C			
Cash Flow	$3,000	$3,000	$3,000
Income	1,000	1,000	1,000

*Annual cash flow equals net income plus $2,000 in depreciation.

which items are treated as capital expenditures and how quickly these assets are depreciated. Different depreciation methods will yield different book values and, therefore, different measured accounting rates of return for the same project.

To illustrate some of these points, consider the trio of projects A, B, and C in Exhibit 8-4. The investment in each case is $6,000, depreciated at a constant rate of $2,000 a year to an ending value of zero. With an initial investment of $6,000 and a final investment value of zero, the average book value over the three-year life is $3,000 [($6,000 + 0/2)]. The average annual income for each investment is $1,000. Therefore, the ARR is $1,000/$3,000 = 33 percent for all three projects. Yet A is clearly more desirable than either B or C because its cash flows are received in the early years, and C is more desirable than B when the time value of money is taken into account.

Finally, firms using the ARR have to establish target rates of return in order to judge whether a project should be accepted. This decision is fraught with problems. Using historical returns as a basis might cause a firm with high past returns on its existing business to reject good projects and a firm with low returns to accept poor ones. The same kinds of problems exist if "industry" standards are used. A firm with operating divisions in low-return industries should be considering divestiture of its divisions as an alternative to adding more low-yield projects.

8.5 CAPITAL BUDGETING IN PRACTICE

Surveys of business practice over the past 40 years show that DCF techniques have grown in popularity in American firms. In a survey of 100 of the largest U.S. firms in 1992, Bierman (1993) reports that (1) an overwhelming majority of companies use IRR and/or NPV, (2) IRR appears to be more popular than NPV, and (3) the payback period is used very heavily as a secondary method.

Business surveys of capital-budgeting methods indicate a strong preference for either NPV or IRR decision criteria.

According to the Bierman study, the profitability index, a measure related to NPV, is used infrequently for project evaluation.[5]

These results are similar to an earlier study by Kim, Crick, and Kim (1986), who examined the capital-budgeting practices of leading U.S. companies. Exhibit 8-5 summarizes the 367 responses received from a survey that was mailed to the chief financial officer of 1,000 large firms. Because the total number of responses to questions exceeds the number of respondents, it's clear that some companies use more than one quantitative capital-budgeting technique. The results indicate a strong preference for the IRR over NPV. Overall, techniques that explicitly consider the time value of money—like NPV and IRR—account for 70 percent of the primary evaluation techniques. The data also indicate that the most popular secondary or supplemental method of evaluation is the payback period.

Taken as a package, there's some good-news, bad-news in these results from the perspective of the finance academic. On the positive side, DCF techniques like NPV and IRR are not only the most widely used approaches but seem to be growing in popularity—at least in the large firms covered in these surveys. However, despite the claimed superiority of NPV as a decision-making tool, managers still use IRR more frequently. Let's explore some of the possible reasons.

As we suggested earlier, the basic weakness of NPV is that many corporate executives and nontechnical people have a tough time understanding the concept. The required rate of return and present value of future sums of money are not intuitively obvious to many people and are misunderstood concepts that are (unfortunately) either misused or not used at all. The IRR has none of these com-

EXHIBIT 8-5
Capital Budgeting Practices (circa 1985)

Technique	Primary Technique		Secondary Technique		Total Percentage Using the Technique
	Number	Percent	Number	Percent	
Net Present Value	123	21	113	24	45%
Internal Rate of Return	288	49	70	15	64
Payback Period	112	19	164	35	59
Accounting Rate of Return	47	8	89	19	27
Others	17	3	33	7	10
Total Responses	587	100	469	100	

Source: Suk H. Kim, Trevor Crick, and Seung H. Kim, "Do Executives Practice What Academics Preach?" *Management Accounting,* November 1986, 49–52.

[5]The *profitability index,* also called the *benefit-cost ratio,* of a project is the ratio of the present value of the cash inflows divided by the present value of the cash outflows. The profitability index tells us to accept projects with a ratio greater than 1.0. This method is consistent with the NPV method since profitability indexes greater than one imply an *NPV* > 0. As a ranking tool, the profitability index has many of the same drawbacks as the IRR.

plications. Also, to calculate a project's NPV, we must identify the correct discount rate. As we'll see in Chapter 10, coming up with a firm's or project's required rate of return is not an exact science. To take the results of an estimating process, use it to compute an NPV and then claim that this is a "solid" number makes many managers uncomfortable.

The frequent use of the payback period, even as a secondary method, is a bit more puzzling. True enough, payback is a measure of project risk of some value to companies that might have restricted access to the financial markets. In these instances, the cash inflows from one project can allow a company to take on future projects. Although this argument might be plausible for small firms, the companies represented in the two surveys reviewed here are among the largest in the United States and have no effective restrictions on their ability to finance positive NPV projects. Further, the financial staffs of these firms should be sophisticated enough to recognize the pitfalls of using the payback method.

> **Agency conflicts between owners and managers can explain the continued use of the payback method by businesses.**

Meir Statman (1982) points to the persistence of payback as another example of how conflicts between owners and managers influence the way firms make decisions. The following example will illustrate the nature of the agency problem: Suppose a company has two projects with the same NPV. One has a longer payback period. Shareholders would find it pointless to choose between the two projects because they can sell their stock in the marketplace at any time. In an efficient market, the NPV of either project should be reflected in the firm's stock price.

However, if a manager's tenure with the company was expected to be shorter than the economic life of the projects, the one with the shorter payback would be preferred. This preference would be reinforced if the manager's compensation were tied to something other than stock price, such as short-term cash flows or accounting earnings. In these cases, a manager will get no direct rewards for cash flows generated after he/she leaves; hence, cash flows beyond the payback period are ignored. Although this description of the capital-budgeting process may be difficult to verify, it provides a plausible explanation for the use of a flawed technique.

SUMMARY

The strategic direction of a company involves making judgments on the lines of business that it wishes to pursue and the way it intends to compete in these businesses. These decisions define the array of projects that a firm may wish to consider. Developing criteria to evaluate potential projects is an important dimension in designing strategies that will work to the shareholder's best interest.

In this chapter, we examined several different approaches that can be used by management to summarize the economic benefits from investments. Two approaches—net present value (NPV) and the internal rate of return (IRR)—are based on discounted cash flow (DCF) techniques and are consistent with shareholder wealth maximization. These DCF techniques were found to be superior to non-DCF approaches such as the payback period and the accounting rate of return. Comparing NPV and IRR, we found that:

1. For independent projects with conventional cash flow patterns (a cash outflow and subsequent cash inflows), both the NPV and IRR give the same answer. Unless one is more interested in the esoteric characteristics of a particular method, NPV and IRR are perfect substitutes for one another.
2. For independent projects with more than one cash outflow, use NPV since it eliminates the possibility of multiple IRRs.

3. For mutually exclusive projects in which the issue is one of project ranking, in addition to project acceptance, use the NPV method.

Generally, non-DCF approaches are not helpful as primary decision tools. Payback has some value as a measure of project risk, but ignores the time value of money as well as cash flows beyond the payback period. Further, the payback period systematically biases the selection process toward short-lived projects. The accounting rate of return has many of the same problems as payback (e.g., it ignores time value of money) and has the additional drawback of being based on accounting profits rather than cash flows.

APPENDIX 8A   MUTUALLY EXCLUSIVE PROJECTS WITH DIFFERENT ECONOMIC LIVES

Sometimes complications arise in evaluating mutually exclusive projects because of different economic lives. When the investment alternatives don't have equal lives, the asset with the highest NPV or the one with the lowest present value of cash outflows may not necessarily be the ideal choice. To properly choose, we have to come up with a common basis of comparing the investment alternatives.

For example, suppose a company is considering replacing its old Dole truck with either another new Dole or a new Daihatsu. Both trucks have the same capacity, but the Dole truck is sturdier than the Daihatsu. As a result, the Dole truck will last five years compared to four years for the Daihatsu. In addition, the Dole's annual cash operating costs of $3,000 a year are $1,000 less than the Daihatsu's annual cash operating costs of $4,000. However, the Daihatsu costs only $13,500, whereas the Dole costs $17,000. The data are summarized as follows:

	Dole Truck	**Daihatsu Truck**
Initial Cost	$17,000	$13,500
Salvage Value	-0-	-0-
Economic Life	5 years	4 years
Operating Cost	$3,000	$4,000

One way to choose between these two mutually exclusive investments is to compare the present value of their costs. Assuming a discount rate of 8 percent, the present values are as follows:

Year	**0**	**1**	**2**
Dole	$17,000	$3,000	$3,000
Daihatsu	13,500	4,000	4,000

3	**4**	**5**	**Present Value of Cost @ 8 Percent**
$3,000	$3,000	$3,000	$28,978.13
4,000	4,000		26,748.51

Is the Daihatsu preferable because it has a lower present value? Not necessarily. Because the Daihatsu will wear out in four years, it must be replaced a year before the Dole. Hence, the two investments aren't really directly comparable.

There are a couple of ways to resolve this problem. One solution would be to assume a cash salvage value for the Dole after four years of service. More frequently, the method of handling mutually exclusive projects with unequal lives is to assume that at the expiration of the economic life of each asset, the company will invest in a new asset with identical characteristics. This means if the company decides to buy a Daihatsu today, it will buy a new one every four years. Similarly, if it buys a Dole, it will replace it with a new Dole every five years. Thus, the firm will be buying replacement chains of Daihatsus or Doles into the indefinite future.

Given this replacement-chain assumption, we can calculate the equivalent annual cost of using mutually exclusive assets. The **equivalent annual cost (EAC)** of an asset is an annuity that has the same life as the asset and whose present value equals the cost of the asset. In the case of the Dole truck, it's a toss-up between paying $17,000 every five years or paying a five-year annuity of

$$EAC = \frac{\$17,000}{PVIFA_{8,5}} = \frac{\$17,000}{3.9927} = \$4,257.77$$

The equivalent annual cash cost of operating the Dole is the sum of its acquisition cost plus its operating expenses, or $4,257.77 + $3,000 = $7,257.77. Similarly, if a company buys the Daihatsu, it will be indifferent as to whether it pays out $13,500 every four years or an annuity of

$$EAC = \frac{\$13,500}{PVIFA_{8,4}} = \frac{\$13,500}{3.3121} = \$4,075.96$$

This gives a total equivalent cost of operation of $4,075.96 + $4,000 = $8,075.96. Because a chain of Doles is less expensive than a chain of Daihatsus, the Dole truck should be purchased.

The preceding suggests the following decision rule for comparing mutually exclusive projects with uneven lives: Compute the equivalent annual cost of each asset. Select the asset with the lowest equivalent annual operating cost. For revenue-generating projects, this rule becomes: Select the project with the highest equivalent annual net operating cash flow.

The validity of these decision rules rests on the idea that each asset will be replaced with an identical asset. When we're dealing with equipment that's not subject to much technological change, the equivalent annual cost approach is a sound practical way to deal with the problem of mutually exclusive projects having uneven lives because we are essentially looking at an optimal cycle for replacing worn-out parts. However, if we know in advance that the Dole might be replaced by a technologically superior Daihatsu, then the equivalent annual cost rule will be suboptimal relative to simply looking at the NPV for each mutually exclusive investment that (1) takes into account specific assumptions about reinvestment opportunities that may become available in the future and (2) selects the investment having the highest NPV (or lowest present value of costs).

 FINCOACH PRACTICE EXERCISES

To help you master the mathematics discussed in the chapter, open **FinCoach** on the *Prentice Hall Finance Center* CD-ROM and practice the exercises in the following categories: *1. Valuation of Multiple Cash Flows and 2. Project and Firm Valuation.*

QUESTIONS

1. Define and contrast accounting income and economic profit.
   a. What is the relationship between accounting income and economic profit?
   b. Construct an example to illustrate the two concepts.
2. Define and contrast accounting rate of return to economic rate of return.
   a. What is the relationship between accounting rate of return and economic rate of return?
   b. Construct an example to illustrate the two concepts.
3. Comment on the following statements.
   a. "The internal rate of return method is superior to the NPV method because we don't need to know the required rate of return in order to calculate it."
   b. "I don't know why academics keep knocking the payback method. Because money has time value, stockholders would prefer projects with

short payback periods over those with longer payback periods."
4. Under what circumstances do the NPV and internal rate of return methods lead to the same investment decision?
5. Suppose that a project with conventional cash flow patterns has an NPV of zero when all cash flows are discounted at 15 percent. What's the project's IRR?
6. What makes NPV a superior method for choosing between two mutually exclusive projects?
7. When might a company justify the use of payback as a decision-making tool?
8. What is the likely response by the stock market when a firm announces a positive NPV project? Is there any reason to believe that this response might sometimes be negative?
9. Suppose that the Regency Products Company used the accounting rate of return on assets to evaluate the performance of its division managers

and used NPV as a criterion for making investment decisions. Is this situation in the best interest of Regency's stockholders? How will this situation influence the projects that are proposed by division managers?

10. Surveys of business practices show a consistent preference for IRR over NPV. How would you explain these results?

11. In 1991, AT&T laid a transatlantic fiber-optic cable costing $400 million that can handle 80,000 calls simultaneously. What is the payback on this investment if AT&T uses just half its capacity while netting 1¢ per minute on calls?

12. A proposed project has the following properties: investment = $50,000; economic life = 5 years; straight-line depreciation; no salvage value; cash savings before taxes of $8,000; and tax rate = 40 percent. What are the relevant annual cash flows to be discounted and compared with the $50,000 initial investment?

13. Presently, the required rate of return on long-term government borrowing is 10 percent, but the central bank will allow the military governor of the District of New Amsterdam to borrow $50 million from the central bank at 5 percent if the funds are used to construct a new prison. Each year over the 20-year life of the loan, the district must make a loan payment of $4.013 million. Critics claim that, at $4.013 million a year for 20 years, the prison will cost the taxpayers over $80 million. Supporters urge the military governor to agree to build the prison because the borrowing of $50 million at 5

percent interest is a bargain. Evaluate the arguments of the two sides.

14. General Public Telephones had a cash inflow of $100 million last year. The company must decide whether to reinvest in an investment project or pay the cash out as dividends. The new project would cost $100 million but would reduce operating expenses by $12 million a year. The public utilities commission will allow GPT an 8 percent rate of return on the book value of investment. The new project has a positive NPV given a required rate of return of 10 percent for such riskless investment. What should GPT do? What are the implications of its decision?

15. During 1990, Dow Chemical generated the following returns on investment in its different business units:

Business Unit	Return on Investment
Plastics	16.6%
Chemicals/Performance Products	16.7%
Consumer Specialties	12.7%
Hydrocarbons/Energy	5.2%
Other	1.6%
Dow Chemical overall	11.8%

Given these returns, which of the business units should Dow invest additional capital in? What additional information would you need in order to make that decision?

PROBLEMS

—Excel templates may be downloaded from **www.prenhall.com/financecenter.**

1. A firm is considering investing in a project with the following cash flows:

Year	1	2	3
Net cash flow	$2,000	$3,000	$4,000

4	5	6	7	8
$3,500	$3,000	$2,000	$1,000	$1,000

The project requires an initial investment of $12,500, and the firm has a required rate of return

of 10 percent. Compute the payback, discounted payback, and net present value and determine whether the project should be accepted.

2. The satisfied owner of a new $15,000 car can be expected to buy another ten cars from the same company over the next 30 years (an average of one every three years) at an average price of $15,000 (ignore the effects of inflation). If the net profit margin on these cars is 20 percent, how much should an auto manufacturer be willing to spend to keep its customers satisfied? Assume a 9 percent discount rate.

3. Eastern Shallow, Ltd., is a gold mining company operating a single mine. The present price of gold is $300 an ounce and it costs the company $250

an ounce to produce the gold. Last year, 50,000 ounces were produced, and engineers estimate that at this rate of production the mine will be exhausted in seven years. The required rate of return on gold mines is 10 percent.

a. What is the value of the mine?

b. Suppose inflation is expected to increase the cost of producing gold by 10 percent a year, but the price of gold does not change because of large sales of stockpiled gold by foreign governments. Furthermore, imagine that the inflation raises the required rate of return to 21 percent. Now what is the value of the mine?

c. Suppose the company may shut, reopen, or abandon the mine in response to fluctuations in the price of gold. Can the NPV method be used to value the mine under these conditions?

4. A firm faces two investment projects that are mutually exclusive. Each would require an initial investment of $5 million. Management estimates that the first project will boost cash flow per share (CPS) immediately by 10 percent to a level of $2.20 a year, where it will stay for the next 20 years. The other project will not affect cash flow per share for five years. Thereafter, it will cause CPS to grow by 5 percent a year for 20 years. Given a required rate of return of 17 percent and three million shares of stock outstanding, which—if any—project should the firm select? Can you calculate the value of a share of stock if the company selects this project?

5. The Lucky Star Mining Co. is considering reopening one of its old silver mines. New extraction techniques will allow the company to mine a one-year production of silver worth $3 million in after-tax profit. However, in the second year of operation, the cost of returning the mine to the natural condition mandated by law will cost $1 million. Opening and preparing the mine will cost $1 million in the present year. The cost of capital is 8 percent.

a. What is the NPV of the reopened mine?

b. What is the IRR?

c. Should Lucky Star reopen the mine? Explain.

6. The Pennco Oil Co. must decide whether it is financially feasible to open an oil well off the coast of China. The drilling and rigging cost for the well is $5,000,000. The well is expected to yield 585,000 barrels of oil a year at a net profit to Pennco of $5 a barrel for four years. The well will then be effectively depleted but must be capped and secured at a cost of $4,000,000. Pennco re-

quires an annual rate of return of 14 percent on its investment projects. Should Pennco open the well? (Assume all of a year's production occurs at the end of the year.)

7. Jack Nicklaus, the golfing pro and real estate developer, is thinking of acquiring an 800-acre property outside Atlanta that he intends to turn into an exclusive community for 600 families. The cost of this property and the necessary improvements is $30 million. After setting aside a mandatory 25 percent of the property as green space, he figures he can sell the remaining lots for an average of $90,000 an acre. By putting in a golf course on the 200 acres of green space, Nicklaus believes he can instead sell the lots for an average of $140,000 an acre. The golf course, including clubhouse, has a projected price tag of $6 million. In either event, the project is expected to take eight years to sell out at a rate of 75 lots per year. Jack Nicklaus faces a marginal tax rate of 40 percent and can write off his land and development costs by prorating these costs against each lot sold.

a. If his required return is 14 percent, should Jack Nicklaus go ahead with the initial project (i.e., a community with no golf course)?

b. Should he put in the golf course?

8. The Coin Coalition is trying to get the U.S. government to replace the dollar bill with a gold-colored dollar coin. One argument is cost savings. A dollar bill costs 2.6 cents to produce and lasts only about 17 months. A dollar coin, on the other hand, although costing 6 cents to produce, lasts for 30 years. About 1.8 billion dollar bills must be replaced each year. The start-up costs of switching to a dollar coin are likely to be quite high, however. These costs have not been estimated.

a. What are the projected average annual cost savings associated with switching from the dollar bill to a dollar coin?

b. Taking into account only the cost savings estimated in (a), how high can the start-up costs for this replacement project be and still yield a positive NPV for the U.S. government? Use an 8 percent discount rate.

9. Recent Census Bureau data show that the average income of a college-educated person was $34,391 versus $24,701 for those without college. At the same time, the annual tuition at public universities was $1,566 versus $7,693 for private colleges. In the following questions, assume there is no

difference in income between public and private university graduates. 🖾

a. Based on these figures, what is the payback period for a college education, taking into account the four years of lost earnings while being in college? Do these calculations for both public and private colleges.

b. Assuming college graduation at age 22 and retirement at age 65, what is the internal rate of return on a college degree from a public university? From a private university?

c. Assuming a 7 percent discount rate and the same working life as in (b), what is the net present value of a college degree from a public university? From a private university?

10. Bensonhurst Breweries, Inc., plans to open a new brewery in southern Florida. The plant is expected to produce 500,000 six-packs of beer a year. The beer sold for $2.00 a pack last year and is expected to increase by 2 percent a year. Production costs last year would have been $500,000 in total. These costs are expected to grow at 3 percent a year. The plant will cost $800,000 to build and will be depreciated straight-line over its 10-year life. Given a required rate of return of 10 percent and tax rate of 40 percent, what is the NPV of the brewery? 🖾

11. The Fun Foods Corporation must decide on what new product lines to introduce next year. After-tax cash flows are listed below along with initial investments. The firm's cost of capital is 12 percent, and its target accounting rate of return is 20 percent. Assume straight-line depreciation and an asset life of five years. The corporate tax rate is 35 percent. All projects are independent. 🖾

Project	Investment	Year 1	2
A	$5,000	$ 800	$1,000
B	7,500	1,250	3,000
C	4,000	600	1,200

3	4	5
$ 350	$1,250	$3,000
2,500	5,000	5,000
1,200	2,400	3,000

a. Calculate the accounting rate of return on the project. Which projects are acceptable according to this criterion? (*Note:* Assume net income is equal to after-tax cash flow less depreciation.)

b. Calculate the payback period. All projects with a payback of fewer than four years are acceptable. Which are acceptable according to this criterion?

c. Calculate the projects' NPVs. Which are acceptable according to this criterion?

d. Calculate the projects' IRRs. Which are acceptable according to this criterion?

e. Which project(s) should be chosen?

12. Aptec, Inc., is negotiating with the U.S. Department of Housing and Urban Development (HUD) to open a manufacturing plant in South Central L.A., the scene of much of the rioting in April 1992. The proposed plant will cost $3.6 million and is projected to generate annual after-tax profits of $550,000 over its estimated four-year life. Depreciation is straight-line over the four-year period, and Aptec's tax rate is 35 percent. However, given the risks involved, Aptec is looking for a tax-exempt government subsidy. According to Aptec, the subsidy must be able to achieve any of the following four objectives: (1) Provide a 2-year payback. (2) Provide an accounting rate of return of 35 percent. (3) Raise the plant's IRR to 25 percent. (4) Provide an NPV of $1 million when cash flows are discounted at 18 percent. 🖾

a. For each alternative suggested by Aptec, develop a subsidy plan that minimizes the costs to HUD of achieving Aptec's objective. You can schedule the subsidy payments at any time over the four-year period.

b. Which of the four subsidy plans would you recommend to HUD if it uses a 15 percent discount rate?

13. Radio Hut, a discount consumer electronics retail chain, is considering two different strategies for expanding into the eastern United States. One strategy (plan A) is to open stores in the center of three major cities (New York, Boston, Philadelphia); the other strategy (plan B) is to open several stores in suburban shopping malls. The projected cash flows (000 omitted) are listed below: 🖾

Plan	Investment	Year 1	2	3	4	5
A	$2,000	$550	$550	$600	$650	$700
B	1,000	250	300	400	350	300

a. With a cost of capital of 12 percent, which plan, A or B, should Radio Hut adopt under the NPV method?

b. Which plan should be adopted under the IRR method?

c. An executive argues that B should be chosen because it gives more return for its smaller investment. How would you answer?

14. The Fast Food chain is trying to introduce its new Hot and Spicy line of hamburgers. One plan (S) will include a big media campaign but less in-house production capability. The other plan (L) will concentrate on a more gradual roll-out of the project but will involve more investment in personnel training and so forth. The cost of capital is 15 percent. The cash flows (000 omitted) are listed below. The initial investment for each is $400,000.

Plan	Year 1	2	3	4	5
S	$250	$250	$150	$100	$ 50
L	100	125	200	250	125

a. Construct the NPV profiles for plans S and L. Which has the higher IRR?

b. Which plan should Fast Food choose using the NPV method?

c. Which plan (S or L) should Fast Food choose? Why?

d. At what cost of capital will the NPV and the IRR rankings conflict?

15. Consider four new product ideas presented to the board of directors of Compufun. Only one of the lines will be chosen as the new major product line for the firm to present to analysts in December. The product lines' cash flows (000 omitted) are as follows: ✂

Product Line	Investment	Year 1	2
Hill	$500	$ 65	$ 75
Geometry	500	50	50
Plane	500	100	100
The Slope	500	125	135

3	4	5	6	7	8
$100	$125	$ 75	$ 65	$ 65	$ 50
100	150	150	150	150	200
100	100	100	100	100	—
125	75	65	65	65	50

a. Using a payback period of six years, which product line would be the best one to choose under the payback method?

b. Assume that each product line is depreciated using the straight-line method and that net income is equal to after-tax cash flow less depreciation. Which product line should be chosen under the accounting rate of return? The target rate of return is 12 percent.

c. Under the IRR method, which product line should be adopted?

d. Using NPV, which product line should be adopted if the cost of capital is 12 percent?

e. Which product line will maximize shareholder wealth if the cost of capital is 12 percent?

16. A project requiring an initial investment of $100,000 is expected to produce a cash inflow before tax of $26,000 per year for 5 years. Company A has accumulated substantial losses and is unlikely to pay tax in the foreseeable future. Company B pays corporate tax at a rate of 35 percent and can depreciate the equipment on a straight-line basis over the next 5 years. A purchaser of new equipment will receive a 10 percent investment tax credit (ITC) as well in the first year. The ITC reduces the purchaser's taxes by an amount equal to 10 percent of the equipment's purchase price. If the relevant cost of capital is 8 percent, which company finds the project more attractive?

17. Grand Trunk Railway, Ltd., wishes to acquire ten new diesel locomotives at a cost of $1 million each. The engines have a useful life of ten years and no scrap value. A purchaser of new equipment can deduct straight-line depreciation for the engine and receive a 10 percent investment tax credit (ITC) as well in the first year. The ITC reduces Grand Trunk's taxes by an amount equal to 10 percent of the equipment's purchase price. An alternative procedure is to deduct the full cost of the engines in the first year.

a. Suppose Grand Trunk's tax rate is 40 percent. Given an interest rate of 5 percent, which opportunity is the more attractive?

b. Suppose Grand Trunk is bankrupt and cannot take advantage of the depreciation tax shields: It has no income against which to deduct depreciation. However, Imperial Bank has offered to buy the engines and lease them to Grand Trunk. If Imperial's marginal tax rate is 40 percent and its cost of capital is 8 percent, what is the minimum yearly lease payment Grand Trunk can negotiate?

18. Owen Corporation plans to purchase a new machine that costs $120,000, has six years of economic life, and generates a net annual cash flow of $40,000 at the end of years 1–6 (all cash flows have taken into account depreciation and taxes). The firm also has the option to sell the machine at the end of years 1–6. The following are the net cash flows Owen will receive from the sale of the machine at the end of each year. ✍

End of Year	Net Cash Flow from Sale
1	$100,000
2	85,000
3	75,000
4	60,000
5	30,000
6	0

The manager wants to determine an optimal replacement policy for the machine. Once a policy has been adopted, it will be implemented perpetually because it is assumed that the cost of the machine, the cash inflows, and the net cash flow from selling the old machines will be the same over time. Determine the optimal policy, assuming a 12 percent discount rate.

19. Charter Manufacturing, a steelmaker, has invested $1.5 million in a more energy-efficient melting system. This new system will cut its energy-costs by $10 a ton. ✍

a. If Charter produces 25,000 tons of steel annually, what is its payback period? Assume these savings will continue indefinitely.

b. What is the IRR on this investment?

c. What is the net present value of the new system using an 8 percent discount rate?

20. Polaroid recently installed new equipment that recycles the solvent, CFC-113, through a closed-loop system. By recycling the CFC-113, which has been implicated in stratospheric ozone depletion, Polaroid realizes a net savings of $90,000 annually from lower disposal costs and reduced purchases of new solvents.

a. If the equipment costs $500,000 and will be depreciated straight-line over its 8-year life, what is Polaroid's NPV on this investment? Assume a 40 percent corporate tax rate and a 9 percent discount rate.

b. Are there any other factors that might influence this investment decision?

REFERENCES

Bierman, H., Jr. "Capital Budgeting in 1992: A Survey." *Financial Management,* Autumn 1993, 20–28.

Gordon, M. J. "The Pay-Off Period and Rate of Profit." *Journal of Business,* October 1955, 253–260.

Kim, S. H., T. Crick, and S. H. Kim, "Do Executives Practice What Academics Preach?" *Management Accounting,* November 1986, 49–52.

Levary, R., and N. Seitz. *Quantitative Analysis for Capital Expenditure Analysis.* Cincinnati, OH: Southwestern Publishing Company, 1989.

Lorie, J. H., and L. J. Savage. "Three Problems in Rationing Capital." *Journal of Business,* October 1955, 229–239.

Pettway, R. H. "Integer Programming in Capital Budgeting: A Note on Computational Experiences." *Journal of Financial and Quantitative Analysis,* September 1973, 665–672.

Plath, A. D., and W. F. Kennedy. "Teaching Return-Based Measures of Project Evaluation." *Financial Practice and Education,* Spring/Summer 1994, 77–86.

Statman, M. "The Persistence of the Payback Method: A Principal-Agent Perspective." *The Engineering Economist,* Summer 1982, 95–100.

Weingartner, M. H. *Mathematical Programming and the Analysis of Capital Budgeting Problems.* Englewood Cliffs, NJ: Prentice Hall, 1963.

The Art and Science of Estimating Project Cash Flows

If you can look into the seeds of time,
And say which grain will grow and which will not,
Speak.
Shakespeare, Macbeth

KEY TERMS

base case
best-cost provider strategy
decision trees
economies of scale
economies of scope
embedded options
learning curve

low-cost provider strategy
opportunity cost
product differentiation
product line
  cannibalization
purchasing power parity
  (PPP)

sensitivity analysis
simulation analysis
sunk-cost fallacy
terminal values
transfer prices

CHAPTER LEARNING OBJECTIVES

Upon completion of this chapter, students should be able to:

- Explain the importance of using incremental reasoning in identifying a project's cash flows.
- Identify a project's initial investment, incremental operating cash flows, and terminal value and use these estimates to calculate the project's NPV.
- Describe how the failure to deal with inflation and other biases in capital budgeting can lead to inappropriate investment decisions.
- Discuss the importance of properly assessing the effects of product-line cannibalization in a new product introduction.
- Use the principle of purchasing power parity to properly evaluate an overseas project.
- Describe how a failure to identify managerial options can systematically undervalue an investment project.
- Explain the importance of creating barriers to entry by potential competitors and why it is important to the generation of positive-NPV projects.
- Indicate how an option-valuation approach can be used to evaluate R&D projects.
- Describe how techniques such as sensitivity analysis, simulation, and decision trees can help managers understand the sources of project risk.

In Chapter 8, we looked at various criteria for making investment decisions and concluded that net present value was superior to other approaches in making accept–reject decisions. However, the fact that we use NPV for evaluating projects doesn't mean that we're going to automatically end up with "winners." This technique relies on good estimates of project cash flows; without reliable forecasts, capital-budgeting techniques have the same weakness as other sophisticated management information systems—"garbage in, garbage out."

This chapter looks at the process of estimating project cash flows. We begin by examining some guidelines for estimating cash flows. We will consider two important classes of investments: replacement projects and new product introductions. Many new products have sales (and cash flows) beyond some initial evaluation period. To avoid undervaluing these projects, we'll look at how to capture these later cash flows in the analysis. A discussion of inflation biases in capital budgeting and the evaluation of overseas projects is included in our consideration of mechanics.

We'll also spend some time talking about the strategic aspects of capital budgeting. In many instances, embedded managerial options can allow a company to alter the cash flows from a project once it's under way. Because options are always worth something, failure to account for them can seriously undervalue a project. The chapter concludes with a discussion of how a clearly defined strategy can help a company find positive-NPV projects.

9.1   SOME GUIDELINES FOR ESTIMATING PROJECT CASH FLOWS

A basic tenet in finance is that "cash is king." Like most slogans, the devil is in the details. A thoughtful analyst will routinely encounter subtle and sophisticated challenges to the basic focus on cash flows. Here are some do's and don'ts to help us focus on a project's cash flows.

Managers should focus on those cash flows that will change as a direct *result of accepting a project.*

Apply Incremental Reasoning. Shareholders are only interested in how many additional dollars they'll receive in the future in exchange for the dollars that are laid out today. Therefore, we should only be interested in those cash flows that will change as a direct result of the project being accepted.

Ignore Fictional Accrual Accounting Flows. As we indicated in Chapter 2, the basis for accounting statements is historical cost. The capital budgeting decision, on the other hand, is forward-looking and focuses on cash flows. It is important not to mix the two perspectives. We do not discount accounting profits; further, analysts should be suspicious of any item called an "accounting charge" or "fixed-cost allocation."

Be suspicious of any items labeled "accounting charges" or "fixed-cost allocation."

Be Careful about Transfer Prices. Companies pursuing a strategy of related diversification often have divisions that do business with one another. The prices at which goods and services are traded with one another, known as **transfer prices,** can significantly distort the profitability of a proposed investment if not selected carefully. For example, if General Motors raised the price at which its auto divisions buy radios from its Delco Electronics division, Delco's new car radio plant would show an increase in profitability, and the auto divisions' profits would decline. Where possible, the transfer prices used to evaluate project inputs and outputs should be based on market prices and not some administratively derived price.

<aside>Past expenditures should have no influence on whether to continue with or terminate a project.</aside>

Ignore Sunk Costs. Our perspective on investment projects should be incremental and forward-looking. Therefore, past expenditures should be ignored since they can't be recouped even if we decide not to go ahead with the project. This logic, however, is not always obeyed. For instance, consumer products companies frequently conduct test marketing to determine whether to introduce a new product on a national basis. Some companies then turn around and include these test-market expenses as part of the project's cost. The argument is that if you've just spent $1 million, you've got to assign these costs someplace.

This faulty logic illustrates the **sunk-cost fallacy,** the idea that past expenditures should somehow influence the decision on whether to continue or terminate the project. That decision should be based on *future* costs and benefits alone. Including sunk costs in the analysis could result in the rejection of a potentially good investment. Preoccupation with sunk costs can also result in going forward with projects that should be abandoned. The "logic" here is that a firm would lose the money already spent on the project. Somehow, the fact that a company could be throwing good money after bad gets lost as managers try to avoid a public admission that the project hasn't worked out as anticipated (perhaps because such an admission could hurt their career prospects).

<aside>Some projects may involve opportunity costs that should not be ignored.</aside>

Don't Ignore Opportunity Costs. Sometimes, the relevant cash flows take the form of **opportunity costs.** Suppose a firm owns some raw land that was bought and paid for 20 years ago. If the company now decides to build a facility on that piece of property, the value of the land becomes a relevant opportunity cost for the project even though the cash for its acquisition was spent years ago. Why? Because by proceeding with the new facility, the firm forgoes the opportunity to sell the land at today's market price.

<aside>Working capital needs are an important component of a project's cash flow and should not be overlooked.</aside>

Don't Forget Working Capital Requirements. Many projects, particularly those involving new product introductions, require working capital to support expected increased sales. Some managers believe that because a project's working-capital needs are recovered after the end of its economic life, changes in these current asset/liability accounts can be ignored. This is simply not true! Working-capital outflows are typically high at the beginning of a project's life. Even if the firm recovers all of the working capital invested in the project at the end, the present value of these cash inflows will be lower than the present value of the cash outflows at the start of the project.

Don't Forget Abandonment Costs or Terminal Values. These values and costs may represent significant inflows or outflows of cash. With increasing attention to environmental issues, project abandonment costs may be huge (e.g., in nuclear power or pesticide production) for certain industries. Beyond the recovery of working capital, the fixed assets typically have some salvage value even as scrap; even if the equipment has no value, there may be tax shields from writing off the remaining book value. Finally, the project may be able to generate cash flows beyond some initial evaluation period. In the case of new product introductions, the present value of these flows can be significant.

9.2 MECHANICS OF ESTIMATING CASH FLOWS

Although some facets of capital budgeting require insight and judgment, others simply represent the execution of good technique. In this section, we'll apply the guidelines for identifying relevant projects cash flows by looking at the two most frequently encountered issues in capital budgeting: the replacement problem and new product introduction.

The Replacement Problem

As the name suggests, this class of investments represents a situation in which a firm wants to replace an existing piece of equipment with a new piece of equipment. The motivation for these projects is typically either cost reduction or quality improvement (or both). To illustrate the cash flow patterns for equipment replacement, consider the following example. The Spectrum Manufacturing Company is currently using a semiautomated bench lathe that was purchased five years ago at an installed cost of $120,000. At the time of purchase, Spectrum thought that this piece of equipment would have an economic life of 10 years and began depreciating it at $12,000 a year to a zero salvage value. Despite its book value of $60,000 (its original cost of $120,000 less five years of depreciation at $12,000 a year), the market value of the semiautomated lathe is only $10,000; advances in robotics have now made the semiautomated lathe "old technology." If Spectrum continues to use it, future technological changes will make it totally worthless in five years or less.

Spectrum can purchase a new computerized lathe at a cost of $100,000. The new machine would be depreciated over its five-year economic life to a zero salvage value. Expected annual pre-tax cash savings for the computerized lathe are $24,000—the current salary of the machine operator who could be assigned to other duties if the new machine is purchased. For simplicity, it is assumed that the savings will be the same each year over the five-year life of the new lathe.[1] Spectrum has a 40 percent tax rate and requires a return of 10 percent on projects of similar risk. Management must decide whether to sell the existing lathe and purchase the new one.

The first order of business is to calculate the project's initial investment. For replacement projects, in general, the initial investment typically consists of three components: (1) the cost of acquiring and placing the necessary fixed assets into

> The initial outlay for replacement projects includes the cost of acquisition, proceeds from the sale of existing assets, and possible tax consequences from asset sales.

---

[1]The assumption that the savings will remain the same at $24,000 over the project's five-year life is unrealistic in an inflationary environment. What is being saved is the salary of one person whose *current* wages are $24,000. We'll discuss how to deal with inflation shortly.

service, (2) the net proceeds from the sale of existing assets (i.e., the old machine's salvage value), and (3) any tax consequences that may arise from the sale of the existing asset at a book gain or loss.[2] Given the facts in our example, the initial investment for the computerized lathe is presented in Exhibit 9-1.

The installed cost of the new computerized lathe is given at $100,000. In practice, this figure is not "handed" to an analyst on a silver platter; instead, it may be necessary to pull together the machine's purchase price, estimated freight costs (if not included in the equipment's invoice price), and all estimated installation expenses. The sum of these items generally becomes the depreciation basis for the asset. The salvage value of the existing lathe is also given as $10,000 and is handled as a cash inflow.

Estimating the tax effects from selling the existing machine involves a bit more work. The old lathe has an existing book value of $60,000. If the new lathe is purchased, it will be sold for $10,000, creating an accounting loss of $50,000. This isn't a cash loss because the only cash exchanges up to this point are the $100,000 cash outflow required to put the new computerized lathe into service and the cash inflow when the old lathe is sold. However, the accounting loss may be used by Spectrum to offset other accounting income generated by the firm and thus reduce its overall tax bill. If Spectrum can utilize this book loss, the cash benefit should be $20,000—the $50,000 book loss times Spectrum's tax rate of 40 percent.

> **The operating cash flows must be computed on an incremental basis.**

The operating cash flows for any project are the incremental revenues, costs, depreciation, and working capital that will result from the acceptance of the project compared to doing nothing. For each period, the incremental operating cash flows (ΔOCF) can be expressed as

$$\Delta OCF = (\Delta REV - \Delta COST - \Delta DEP)(1 - TAX) + \Delta DEP - \Delta WC \qquad [9\text{-}1]$$

where ΔREV is the change in revenues; $\Delta COST$ is the change in operating costs; ΔDEP is the change in depreciation; ΔWC is the change in working capital; and

EXHIBIT 9-1
Spectrum Manufacturing Company
Initial Investment Cost of Computerized Lathe

Installed Cost of Computerized Lathe	−$100,000
Salvage Value of Old Lathe	10,000
Tax Effects from Selling Old Lathe	20,000
Initial Investment Outflow	−$70,000

---

[2]An additional tax factor that may influence the size of the initial investment is the presence of an *investment tax credit (ITC)*. The ITC allows a company to reduce its taxes by an amount equal to some specified percentage of the cost of the new asset. In some years, this percentage had been as high as 10 percent of the cost of an asset with a life of over five years. Although the ITC was eliminated with the Tax Reform Act of 1986, there is always the possibility that it will be resurrected at a later date.

TAX is the marginal tax rate faced by the firm. Equation [9-1] is virtually identical to the concept of operating cash flows that we saw in Chapter 2 when we talked about a firm's cash flow statement. The major difference is that Equation [9-1] ignores the effects of financing costs such as interest on borrowed money. This isn't an oversight; as you'll see in Chapter 10, we can adjust the required rate of return to accommodate a firm's financing mix. Thus, it is unnecessary to take these costs into account in calculating the project's operating cash flows.

Equation [9-1] can also be written as

$$\Delta OCF = (\Delta REV - \Delta COST)(1 - TAX) + TAX\Delta DEP - \Delta WC \qquad [9\text{-}2]$$

For many projects, depreciation can play an important role as a tax shield.

Written in this form, the equation highlights depreciation's role as a tax shield. Recall that depreciation is just an accounting allocation of a project's cost over time. Although depreciation is a cost for tax purposes, it involves no expenditure of cash. Equation [9-2] is also a convenient format for examining project cash flows if changes in the tax law relating to tax rates or depreciation schedules are an important source of project uncertainty.

Let's get back to our example. For the Spectrum Manufacturing Company, we've assumed that (1) savings will be the same each year and (2) that Spectrum will depreciate the asset on a straight-line basis. Thus, cash flows will be the same for each year over the project's five-year economic life. Given the facts in our example, the operating cash flows are given in Exhibit 9-2.

Like most replacement projects whose focus is cost reduction, both ΔREV and ΔWC in Equation [9-1] are zero. Since reductions in cash outflows are, in essence, cash inflows, the $24,000 estimated annual savings carries a positive sign. The change in depreciation is $8,000. Why? The annual depreciation for the new computerized lathe is $20,000 (the $100,000 purchase cost divided by the project's life of five years). However, if the new lathe is bought, Spectrum will sell

EXHIBIT 9-2
Spectrum Manufacturing Company
Summary of Operating Cash Flows

	Year 1	Year 2	Year 3	Year 4	Year 5
Annual Cash Savings	$24,000	$24,000	$24,000	$24,000	$24,000
Change in Depreciation	(8,000)	(8,000)	(8,000)	(8,000)	(8,000)
Incremental Taxable Income	$16,000	$16,000	$16,000	$16,000	$16,000
Taxes @ 40%	(6,400)	(6,400)	(6,400)	(6,400)	(6,400)
Incremental After-Tax Income	$ 9,600	$ 9,600	$ 9,600	$ 9,600	$ 9,600
Plus: Change in Depreciation	8,000	8,000	8,000	8,000	8,000
Annual Operating Cash Flow	$17,600	$17,600	$17,600	$17,600	$17,600

the existing lathe and lose its depreciation of $12,000 a year. The change in depreciation from acquiring the new lathe is $8,000—the difference between the depreciation on the new lathe and the existing lathe.

If all goes as expected and the annual savings of $24,000 materialize, Spectrum's taxable income should increase by $16,000. After paying taxes at a 40 percent rate, after-tax income will rise by $9,600. Adding back incremental depreciation of $8,000 yields an operating cash flow of $17,600 per year over the project's five-year expected economic life. Given the initial investment of $70,000, the project's NPV is

$$NPV = \$17,600 \, [PVIFA_{5,10}] - \$70,000$$
$$= \$17,600 \, (3.7908) - \$70,000 = -\$3,282$$

Since the *NPV* < 0, Spectrum should not buy the new lathe but keep the existing one.

A final observation: our example assumed that the market value of both the existing and the new machine would be zero in five years. Because the project also had no incremental working capital requirements, its terminal value was zero. This may not be true in all cases. For example, suppose that the computerized lathe under consideration by Spectrum was expected to have a market value of $20,000 at the end of five years, and the existing lathe (if retained) would have a market value of $2,000 at the end of its five-year economic life. Spectrum is depreciating the computerized lathe to a zero salvage value, making the $20,000 fully taxable. The cash proceeds from the sale of the proposed lathe would be $12,000—the $20,000 received less $8,000 in taxes ($20,000 taxable gain times Spectrum's tax rate of 40 percent).

However, if Spectrum buys the new computerized lathe, it intends to sell the existing lathe. There are opportunity costs here; by selling the existing lathe at time zero (and getting the cash then), Spectrum gives up the opportunity to sell the asset later and receive $1,200 after taxes ($2,000 in estimated market value less $800 in taxes). The terminal value for the new computerized lathe would therefore be $10,800—the $12,000 in after-tax cash flows from the sale of the proposed lathe less the $1,200 in after-tax cash flows forgone from the sale of the existing lathe.

> **Terminal values are typically not equal to zero.**

Inflation Biases in Capital Budgeting

When evaluating projects, there's often a tendency to estimate future cash flows on the basis of current price levels. We did this in the case of Spectrum's purchase of a new lathe by assuming that the anticipated annual savings of $24,000—the payroll cost of one machine operator—would not change over the project's five-year life. With these assumptions, the NPV turned out to be negative, leading to our rejection of the project. However, assuming that the savings would be the same each year is equivalent to saying that the machine operator's salary and

Failure to properly account for inflation can result in rejecting projects that might otherwise be accepted.	benefits will not increase for five years. This assumption is clearly unrealistic in most real-world settings. It also biases the selection process because required rates of return for projects should be based on current capital costs, which, in turn, should embody inflationary expectations. Not properly adjusting for inflation puts firms in a position of discounting *real* cash flows with *nominal* (current) interest rates. This systematically understates NPVs and often leads to rejecting projects that might otherwise be accepted.[3]

Exhibit 9-3 illustrates the importance of adjusting cash flows for inflation by assuming that payroll costs beyond year 1 will increase at a compound annual rate of 4 percent. Because the project will eliminate the payroll cost of one machine operator, annual pre-tax cash savings will increase by 4 percent annually. Although these savings increase taxable income and, therefore, taxes, annual after-tax cash flows increase to the point where the project's NPV is greater than zero and should be accepted. In the earlier example, failure to adjust for inflation led to the project's rejection.

Other Biases in Capital Budgeting

Frequently, the realized return from a project can be quite different from its expected return. In many cases, pure chance has a good bit to do with these differences. Suppose that projected cash flows are estimated without any biases such as not properly adjusting for inflation. This means that the average error associ-

EXHIBIT 9-3
Spectrum Manufacturing Company
Summary of Operating Cash Flows Adjusted for Inflation

	Year 1	Year 2	Year 3	Year 4	Year 5
Annual Cash Savings	$24,000	$24,960	$25,958	$26,997	$28,077
Change in Depreciation	(8,000)	(8,000)	(8,000)	(8,000)	(8,000)
Incremental Taxable Income	$16,000	$16,960	$17,958	$18,997	$20,077
Taxes @ 40%	(6,400)	(6,784)	(7,183)	(7,599)	(8,031)
Incremental After-Tax Income	$ 9,600	$10,176	$10,775	$11,398	$12,046
Plus: Change in Depreciation	8,000	8,000	8,000	8,000	8,000
Annual Operating Cash Flow	$17,600	$18,176	$18,775	$19,398	$20,046
Present Value @ 10%	$16,000	$15,021	$14,106	$13,249	$12,447

NPV = $70,824 – $70,000 = $824

---

[3]Inflation creates another bias by lowering the present value of the depreciation tax shield.

The project selection process tends to be biased toward accepting projects with overestimated cash flows.

ated with the cash flow forecasts should be zero. Some of these cash flow estimates will be too high and some will be too low. In a world of uncertainty, it's impossible to determine in advance which is which. Because of their higher NPVs, projects with overestimated cash flows are more likely to be chosen than those whose cash flows have been underestimated. Given the nature of the selection process, the actual NPVs of the projects undertaken will be lower than their predicted values even though the underlying cash flow estimates are unbiased.

The more projects we evaluate, the more likely it is that this random error in estimating cash flows will lead to projects that should have, with 20-20 hindsight, been rejected. What can we do about this? Not a great deal except to be aware that the problem of natural bias exists and to try and anticipate future events that can produce after-the-fact negative NPV projects. The techniques of project risk analysis presented in Appendix 9B can be helpful in getting a better understanding of a project's characteristics and sensitivities to errors.

Although chance can turn a "good" project into a "bad" one quickly, other biases are more systematic. Managers are generally optimistic about the projects they sponsor. In addition, a manager who has spent a great deal of time and effort in developing and pushing an investment is generally emotionally involved in its acceptance. Also, project proposals are likely to reflect any tendency by senior management to pay more attention to optimistic, rather that realistic, investment forecasts.

For all these reasons, cash flow estimates are likely to reflect *overoptimism,* resulting in overstated project NPVs. Moreover, executives whose compensation is closely tied to the volume of assets, sales, or earnings they manage have a vested interest in empire building even if it means taking on substandard investments. Such a situation may lead to a deliberate overstatement of a project's benefits. The most effective way to deal with this problem is to establish a compensation system that ties executive rewards to shareholder returns. We'll deal with some of these approaches in Chapter 11.

It's also possible to get overly *pessimistic* forecasts from managers who are highly risk averse, especially if they feel that they'll be penalized as losers. If you are aware of these biases, it may be possible to correct for them by revising project estimates upward. However, in many instances, the estimator's biases are unknown. In such cases, the best defense against over-pessimism (or over-optimism for that matter) is to evaluate the underlying economic basis for the project.

New Product Introduction

The process of estimating cash flows for replacement projects can be technically intricate given the complexities of tax law relating to depreciation schedules and the like. However, the critical elements of the analysis—the project's cost and estimated savings—can often be determined accurately by a capable manufacturing engineer. Not so with a new product introduction. Depending on whether the "new product" is a simple extension of an existing product or a true product innovation, estimates of cash flows are subject to high degrees of uncertainty.

Illustration

The Smith Corporation is considering a major new product introduction. The project will require capital equipment with an installed cost of $6 million. During year 7, the plant will be dismantled and sold for $1 million. For tax purposes, Smith will depreciate the investment on a straight-line basis to a zero salvage value. If Smith has a required return of 20 percent, should the new product be introduced?

The key element in the analysis of new product introductions is the sales forecast.

The starting point for the financial projections shown in Exhibit 9-4 is the sales forecast. This is an extremely difficult task: The marketing staff must not only estimate the number of units of the product Smith expects to sell but also its selling price. Where there's a possibility of a competitive response, these sales projections may be little more than educated guesses. The sales pattern in Exhibit 9-4 indicates a product life cycle in which demand rises rapidly through year 4 and then declines until the product is eventually phased out by the end of the sixth year.

Once the sales forecast is developed, Smith can proceed with the task of identifying (1) the capital investment needed to satisfy projected demand, (2) operating costs, and (3) the project's working capital needs. This accounting-based financial forecast can then be used to identify relevant cash flows and calculate the project's NPV as shown in Exhibit 9-5.

Exhibit 9-5 displays the components of the cash flows to focus attention on the proper handling of the project's working capital requirements. The project's capital equipment needs are relatively straightforward. At time zero, Smith puts the equipment in place with an installed cost of $6 million. During year 7, after it is no longer needed to manufacture the new product, the equipment is expected to be dismantled and sold for $1,000,000. Since the equipment has been depreciated to a book value of zero, Smith

EXHIBIT 9-4
Smith Corporation
New Product Financial Forecasts
(in thousand $)

Period	0	1	2	3	4	5	6
Sales		500	5,500	8,000	14,000	7,000	4,000
Operating Expenses		800	3,410	4,960	8,680	4,340	2,480
Product Promotion	3,000	1,000					
Depreciation		1,000	1,000	1,000	1,000	1,000	1,000
Profit before Taxes	−3,000	−2,300	1,090	2,040	4,320	1,660	520
Taxes @ 34%	−1,020	−782	371	694	1,469	564	177
Profit after Taxes	−1,980	−1,518	719	1,346	2,851	1,096	343
Level of Working Capital		250	660	960	1,680	840	480

EXHIBIT 9-5
Smith Corporation
Summary of Cash Flows for New Product Introduction
(in thousand $)

Year	Capital Equipment	Profit after Tax + Depreciation	Working Capital	Total Cash Flow	Present Value @ 20%
0	−$6,000	−$1,980	—	−$7,980	−$7,980
1	—	−518	−250	−768	−640
2	—	1,719	−410	1,309	909
3	—	2,346	−300	2,046	1,184
4	—	3,851	−720	3,131	1,510
5	—	2,096	840	2,936	1,180
6	—	1,343	360	1,703	570
7	$ 660	—	480	1,140	318
					NPV = −$2,948

will have a taxable gain of $1 million. If Smith's tax rate is 34 percent, taxes on that gain will be $340,000. The $660,000 cash inflow in year 7 is the difference between the $1,000,000 cash proceeds from the equipment sale and taxes of $340,000 on the book gain.

The second column takes into account the fact that although depreciation may be an expense for accounting purposes, it does not represent an expenditure of cash. Adding back depreciation to profit after taxes allows us to adjust the accounting data in Exhibit 9-4 to ultimately arrive at cash flow from operations.

The third column highlights working capital flows. The last line in Exhibit 9-4 indicates the level of working capital (i.e., accounts receivable plus inventories less accounts payable) to support the projected level of sales. In year 1, once Smith begins generating sales, working capital needs rise to $250,000. Because an increase in working capital is a use of cash, this is represented in Exhibit 9-5 as a cash outflow. Subsequent figures in this column represent the changes in working capital and reflect the fact that increases in working capital are a use of cash; decreases in working capital are sources of cash. After the product's economic life, we assume (for simplicity) that the working capital of $480,000 remaining at the end of year 6 can be recovered in year 7 with no losses.

> Changes in a project's working capital requirements are directly related to changes in projected sales.

Once the components for each year are estimated, they are summed to give the total cash flows and multiplied by the appropriate present-value factor to arrive at the present value of the cash flows in that year. The NPV can then be calculated by adding the present value of the cash inflows and outflows over the project's economic life. In the case of Smith's new product introduction, the negative NPV indicates that the project should be rejected.

Estimating Terminal Values for New Product Introductions

The project being considered by Smith Corporation was assumed to have a six-year product life cycle, after which the new product will be phased out. **Terminal values** in this example were simply (1) the salvage value of the equipment (after taxes), and (2) recovery of the project's working capital. However, many new products may have sales (and cash flows) beyond the initial evaluation period. In these cases, limiting the analysis to a set time period may seriously underestimate a project's NPV. The challenge for the financial analyst is to capture these postevaluation cash flows without engaging in computational overkill.

The following variation of the constant dividend growth model can be used to conveniently estimate a project's terminal value (TV_n):

$$TV_n = \frac{CF_{n+1}}{(k - g)} \qquad [9\text{-}3]$$

where CF_{n+1} is the project's cash flow one year beyond the initial evaluation period; k, the required rate of return for the project; and g, the projected growth rate in the project's cash flows. Equation [9-3] is a flexible tool that allows us to value: (1) growing cash flow streams ($g > 0$), (2) declining cash flow streams ($g < 0$), as well as (3) no-growth situations ($g = 0$). We can also use Equation [9-3] to perform a **sensitivity analysis** to determine the impact of different cash flow growth rate assumptions on the project's NPV. By calculating a project's NPV for a range of values of g, the analyst can determine the *minimum* cash flow growth rate that will make the NPV positive. If this "threshold" value is below management's most pessimistic estimate, the project will produce a positive NPV.

To illustrate how Equation [9-3] can be used to evaluate cash flows beyond the initial evaluation period, let's suppose that Smith Corporation is considering introducing a second new product in a market that already has several competitors. Smith believes that its manufacturing expertise, coupled with a well-developed global distribution system for related products, will allow it to gain a foothold in this market. Capital equipment costs are modest at $3,000,000. Even though the equipment is expected to have a 20-year economic life, Smith intends to depreciate this equipment over four years to a zero salvage value. Financial forecasts for the six-year initial evaluation period are presented in Exhibit 9-6.

This new product differs in four important respects from the one described earlier: first, sales are expected to rise steadily over time, rather than rising for several years and then declining. It appears that Smith expects that this new product will have staying power in the marketplace beyond the sixth year. Second, selling and administrative expenses will continue to be high. This should come as no surprise. Breaking into a market with entrenched competitors typically requires heavy (and continuous) promotion and advertising expenses. Third, working capital requirements are high, at 30 percent of sales. This reflects Smith's belief that ample inventories of finished goods must be available throughout its distribution system to provide high levels of customer service. Finally, the project's required return has been set at 24 percent.

EXHIBIT 9-6
Smith Corporation
New Product #2 Financial Forecasts
(in thousand $)

Period	0	1	2	3	4	5	6
Sales		2,500	10,000	16,500	21,000	23,000	25,000
Cost of Goods Sold		1,625	6,500	10,725	13,650	14,950	16,250
Selling/Administration Expense	3,000	3,000	3,000	3,000	3,000	3,000	3,000
Depreciation		750	750	750	750	-0-	-0-
Profit before Taxes	−3,000	−2,875	−250	2,025	3,600	5,050	5,750
Taxes @ 34%	−1,020	−978	−85	689	1,224	1,717	1,955
Profit after Taxes	−1,980	−1,898	−165	1,337	2,376	3,333	3,795
Level of Working Capital		750	3,000	4,950	6,300	6,900	7,500

The cash flow estimates for this new product as well as the calculation of the project's NPV for the six-year initial evaluation period is presented in Exhibit 9-7. The NPV for this period is –$4,960,000. Even if Smith were to recover all of the $7.5 million in working capital with no losses (a heroic assumption) and sell the equipment in year 7 at its original cost of $3 million (an even more heroic assumption), the present value of these cash flows, discounted at 24 percent, would only be $2,329,365—not enough to make the project attractive. Clearly, the acceptance of this project will turn on its terminal value, the value Smith assigns to the cash flows beyond year 6. The terminal value, in turn, is dependent on how rapidly Smith believes the cash flows will increase over time. Performing a sensitivity analysis on cash flow growth rates can give Smith an indication of the minimum growth that will make the project's NPV positive.

EXHIBIT 9-7
Smith Corporation
Summary of Cash Flows for New Product #2 Introduction
(in thousand $)

Year	Capital Equipment	Profit After Tax + Depreciation	Working Capital	Total Cash Flow	Present Value @ 24%
0	−$3,000	−$1,980	—	−$4,980	−$4,980
1	—	−1,148	−750	−1,898	−1,531
2	—	585	−2,250	−1,665	−1,083
3	—	2,087	−1,950	137	72
4	—	3,126	−1,350	1,776	751
5	—	3,333	−600	2,733	932
6	—	3,795	−600	3,195	879
					NPV = −$4,960

To illustrate the mechanics of computing terminal values, suppose that Smith wants to look at the case in which the projected cash flow of $3,195,000 in year 6 will grow at 5 percent indefinitely. Using Equation [9-3], the terminal value (TV_6) as of the end of year 6 will be

$$TV_6 = \frac{\$3,195,000(1.05)}{(0.24 - 0.05)} = \$17,657,000$$

Discounting this terminal value back to the present at Smith's 24 percent required rate of return yields a present value of $4,857,000. Adding this to the NPV of −$4,960,000 obtained in the initial evaluation period makes the project's NPV −$103,000—still not enough to make the project acceptable.

Terminal values and project NPV's for other growth rates are presented in Exhibit 9-8. The results of this sensitivity analysis indicate that it will take a cash flow growth rate of slightly more than 5 percent to make the project's NPV positive. Because both terminal values and project NPV's are highly sensitive to growth-rate assumptions, Smith should go ahead with the project only if it is confident that growth will exceed 5 percent.

A final note: Equation [9-3] is a convenient way to generate terminal values. It also makes a number of simplifying assumptions. For instance, in our example it overstates terminal values by ignoring capital equipment costs beyond year 20. Although the present value of a dollar spent 20 years from now, discounted at 20 percent, is only $.0261, we might not be able to sweep this little "detail" under the rug if there are large amounts involved. It is just as important to note that a new product introduction often creates strategic options in the form of follow-on products. As we'll see in Section 9.4, failure to consider these growth options can seriously understate a project's value.

Analysts evaluating new product introductions must be sensitive to the possibility of product line cannibalization.

Product Line Cannibalization in New Product Introductions

Companies that rely heavily on new product introductions must deal with the possibility of **product line cannibalization,** a phenomenon by which the new product takes sales away from one or more of the firm's existing products. For ex-

EXHIBIT 9-8
Smith Corporation
Terminal Value Sensitivity Analysis
(in thousand $)

Growth Rate %	Terminal Value	Present Value of Terminal Value	Project NPV
3	$15,671	$4,311	−$649
4	16,614	4,570	−390
5	17,657	4,857	−103
6	18,815	5,176	216
7	20,110	5,532	572

ample, the introduction of a new combination of fruits, flakes, and nuts by Kellogg is likely to take sales away from its old standards such as Corn Flakes and Rice Krispies. Similarly, every time Intel comes out with a faster microprocessor, it essentially makes many of its products obsolete.

Exhibit 9-9 shows the profit consequences of a firm that introduces a new product. This company has an existing product, A, which is expected to generate sales of 800,000 units annually. Marketing and administrative costs are expected to be $700,000 annually. With a $5.00 unit price, and a $3.00 variable cost, forecasted sales are $4 million with an annual profit of $900,000. (Assume that there are no other costs besides the variable costs and marketing and administrative costs.)

The company produces a new product, B, that will satisfy some but not all buyer requirements met by the existing product. However, the product can serve other customer needs. Product B is priced at $4.00 per unit with a $2.50/unit variable cost. Marketing and administrative expenses for product B are projected to be $1 million. The lower price and modified features are expected to result in annual sales of 1.2 million units. Based on these forecasts, B's profits are projected to be $800,000 a year. But the launch of Product B is really much less profitable than it appears because it cannibalizes 300,000 units of product A. The lost profits on these lost sales is $600,000—the 300,000 units lost times their contribution margin of $2.00 a unit. The incremental analysis appears in the last column and reveals that the *incremental profit* from B is $200,000—only 25 percent of what it would be without the effects of cannibalization.

EXHIBIT 9-9
Example of Product Line Cannibalization

		After Introduction of Product B			
	Product A Alone	Product A	+ Product B	Products A + B	Incremental Amount
Forecasted Annual Unit Sales	800,000	500,000	1,200,000	1,700,000	900,000
Source of Volume:					
New Customers			700,000	700,000	700,000
Competitor's Customers			200,000	200,000	200,000
Cannibalized Customers			300,000	300,000	300,000
Repeat Customers	800,000	500,000		500,000	−300,000
Total	800,000	500,000	1,200,000	1,700,000	900,000
Unit Price	$5.00	$5.00	$4.00		
Total Revenue	$4,000,000	$2,500,000	$4,800,000	$7,300,000	$3,300,000
Unit Cost	$3.00	$3.00	$2.50		
Total Variable Cost	$2,400,000	$1,500,000	$3,000,000	$4,500,000	$2,100,000
Marketing and Administrative Costs	$700,000	$700,000	$1,000,000	$1,700,000	$1,000,000
Profit before Tax	$900,000	$300,000	$800,000	$1,100,000	$200,000

Assessing the effects of cannibalization is an exercise in incremental reasoning. The trick is to properly gauge what would happen to sales in the absence of
the new product. A critical error made by some companies is to ignore competitor behavior and assume that the **base case**—the firm's cash flow without the
investment—is the status quo. But in a competitive world economy, the least-
likely future scenario is the status quo. A company that opts not to come out with
a new product because it is afraid that the product will cannibalize its existing
product line is most likely leaving a profitable niche for some other company to
exploit. Sales will be lost anyway, but now they will be lost to a competitor. To
come up with a realistic base case and, thus, a reasonable estimate of incremental cash flows, the key question that managers must ask is, "What will happen if
we *don't* make this investment or introduce this new product?" Failure to heed the
answer could lead to the erosion of a firm's competitive position.

For example, suppose that Kellogg wants to come out with a new concentrated
oat-bran cereal, one serving of which is as healthy as three bunches of broccoli. The
new product will certainly take sales away from Kellogg's existing brands. However, what matters is the *incremental effect* of cannibalization—that is, the sales that
might not otherwise have been lost had the new product not been introduced. In
coming up with this estimate, Kellogg must consider the fact that failing to develop
its own entry in the healthy cereal category will open the door to the introduction
of new oat-bran products by rivals like Post and General Mills that could also erode
sales of Kellogg's products. Thus, instead of losing sales to its own entry, Kellogg
would have lost sales to a competitor. Here, the impact of cannibalization is likely
to be zero. In a competitive market, the lesson is simple: *If you must be a victim of
a cannibal, make sure the cannibal is a member of your own family.*

Illustration

General Electric Cannibalizes Its CAT Scanner

General Electric initially ignored the emerging magnetic resonance imaging
(MRI) technology for medical diagnosis, largely because MRI would have
cannibalized the market for GE's existing CAT scanners. Indeed, projected
cannibalization was sufficiently extensive that a DCF analysis showed a negative NPV for the introduction of MRI. However, senior management over-
ruled the DCF analysis because it realized that if GE didn't cannibalize its
CAT scanners, someone else would.

9.3   THE EVALUATION OF FOREIGN PROJECTS

Up to this point, we've implicitly assumed that the projects under consideration
are in the United States. For the U.S. multinational corporation, this is becoming
less true as firms like General Electric, Procter & Gamble, and Coca-Cola look to

foreign markets as a means of maintaining their earnings growth. An important question that these firms must answer is whether the risk in foreign projects is so different from that of domestic projects that they require a higher or lower required return.

In terms of project risk, it's not at all clear that foreign projects are inherently riskier than their domestic counterparts. Recall from the CAPM that the relevant component of risk is *systematic risk*. Much of this systematic risk is caused by the cyclical nature of the national economy in which a firm operates. For this reason, multinationals with operations in countries where the economic cycles are not highly correlated with the United States can reduce their earnings variability through global diversification.[4]

Although foreign projects may not be inherently riskier, such investments require an evaluation of inflation rates in the host country and the impact that this inflation has on (1) currency exchange rates and (2) project returns. Consider the following example: ACS Enterprises is thinking about putting in a plant to produce widgets in Carolonia, where the local currency is the puff. The plant would have an economic life of five years, after which time ACS would either close the facility or make an additional investment to upgrade the plant. Cash flow forecasts, assuming an environment of zero inflation and no change in exchange rates between the dollar and the puff, are presented in Exhibit 9-10. Under these very restrictive conditions, the project's IRR would be 12.8 percent. If ACS Enterprises' required rate of return on domestic projects of similar risk is 10 percent, the firm should go ahead and put in the widget plant in Carolonia.

A more interesting set of questions is what happens to project returns if ACS believes annual inflation rates in Carolonia will be 10 percent, and the U.S. inflation rate is expected to remain at approximately zero. In general, countries with high rates of inflation will find their currencies declining in value relative to currencies of countries with lower inflation rates. This relationship is known as **purchasing power parity (PPP)** and may be expressed formally as

> **PPP says that exchange rates should change to offset differences in inflation rates.**

$$\frac{e_1}{e_0} = \frac{1 + i_h}{1 + i_f} \qquad [9\text{-}4]$$

where i_h and i_f are the price level increases (rates of inflation) over some time period for the home and foreign country; e_0 is the current dollar value of one unit of the foreign currency; and e_1 is the end-of-period exchange rate.

With this background, we can now go back to our example of the widget plant in Carolonia. Our original cash flow projections assumed no inflation. Adjusting

---

[4]Surprisingly, the less-developed countries (LDCs), which have the greatest political risks, may also offer the greatest diversification benefits. This is because the economies of LDCs are less closely tied to that of the United States or any of the other industrialized economies. This reduced correlation may lower the ratio of systematic to total risk dramatically. However, because of the high total risk of investing in most LDCs, the systematic risk is unlikely to be significantly less than that of projects located in developed countries.

EXHIBIT 9-10
ACS Enterprises' Carolonia Project
(in thousand puffs unless otherwise noted)

Assumptions:
Zero Inflation Environment
Exchange Rate: 1 puff/dollar

				Years			
	0	1	2	3	4	5	6
Sales		200	200	200	200	200	0
Variable Costs @ 60% of Sales		120	120	120	120	120	0
Depreciation Expense		40	40	40	40	40	0
Profit before Taxes		40	40	40	40	40	0
Taxes @ 50%		20	20	20	20	20	0
Profit after Taxes		20	20	20	20	20	0
Net Working Capital @ 15% of Sales		30	30	30	30	30	0
Cash Flow Analysis							
Investment in Equipment	(200)	0	0	0	0	0	0
Investment in Working Capital	0	(30)	0	0	0	0	30
Cash Flow from Operations*	0	60	60	60	60	60	0
Period Cash Flows	(200)	30	60	60	60	60	30

Internal Rate of Return = 12.8%

*Profit after tax plus depreciation.

| **Failure to account for exchange rate changes can bias the project selection process.** |

the project's cash flows for the 10 percent forecasted annual inflation will tend to increase sales, working capital to support these higher sales, and profit after taxes. As Exhibit 9-11 indicates, the project's IRR in puffs increases to 16.9 percent.[5] However, PPP says that the puff will depreciate by 10 percent a year relative to the dollar. Therefore, when we convert puffs to dollars, we would wind up with an IRR in dollars of only 6.2 percent. This 6.2 percent IRR differs from the previously computed dollar IRR of 12.8% even though the effects of inflation and devaluation appear to offset each other owing to: (1) a lower value (in dollars) of the depreciation tax shield and (2) the opportunity costs associated with the higher working capital investment required. Given a dollar-denominated required rate of return of 10 percent, the widget project should be rejected.

---

[5]The inflation-adjusted IRR of 16.8 percent exceeds the unadjusted IRR of 12.8 percent. This is no fluke; as we saw in the Spectrum Manufacturing replacement example, failure to incorporate the effects of inflation tends to understate a project's return.

EXHIBIT 9-11
ACS Enterprises' Carolonia Project
(in thousand puffs unless otherwise noted)

Assumptions:
10 Percent Annual Inflation
Exchange Rate: Puff Declines by 10% a Year against Dollar

				Years			
	0	1	2	3	4	5	6
Sales		200	220	242	266	293	0
Variable Costs @ 60% of Sales		120	132	145	160	176	0
Depreciation Expense		40	40	40	40	40	0
Profit before Taxes		40	48	57	66	77	0
Taxes @ 50%		20	24	28	33	39	0
Profit after Taxes		20	24	28	33	39	0
Net Working Capital		30	33	36	40	44	0
Cash Flow Analysis							
Investment in Equipment	(200)	0	0	0	0	0	0
Investment in Working Capital	0	(30)	(3)	(3)	(4)	(4)	44
Cash Flow from Operations	0	60	64	68	73	79	0
Period Cash Flows (in puffs)	(200)	30	61	65	69	75	44
Period Cash Flows (in dollars)	(200)	27	50	49	48	46	25

Internal Rate of Return (in puffs) = 16.9%
Internal Rate of Return (in dollars) = 6.2%

9.4 MANAGERIAL OPTIONS AND CAPITAL BUDGETING

The discounted cash flow (DCF) procedures considered up to this point assumed that the cash flows from projects cannot be altered once the firm makes the decision to go ahead with the investment. This may be a reasonable assumption for simple cost reduction projects, such as the new lathe being considered by Spectrum Manufacturing Company, that involve the straightforward application of known technology. Such projects rarely involve future investment opportunities and can be evaluated on a stand-alone basis.

DCF techniques are incomplete indicators of value if managers can alter cash flows after a project has been accepted.

However, DCF techniques may distort the value of a project if management has the ability to alter the project's operating decisions *after* the project has been implemented. For example, the new product introduction by Smith Corporation assumed a six-year project life based on its current forecast of expected sales. By valuing the project based on what is known today, Smith ignored opportunities for (1) add-on projects if the new product turned out to be more successful than originally anticipated or (2) abandoning the product before its expected six-year life if sales forecasts turned out to be overly optimistic.

Operating a Gold Mine for Fun and Profit

To see how managers can respond to new information, let's look at the decision of whether to open a gold mine at a cost of $1 million. Suppose there are an estimated 40,000 ounces of gold remaining in the mine that can be removed in one year at a variable cost of $390 an ounce. Assuming an expected gold price of $400 an ounce in one year, the expected profit per ounce of gold mined is $10. Clearly, the expected cash flows (ignoring taxes) of $400,000 next year ($10 an ounce times the 40,000 ounces) are far below that necessary to recoup the $1 million cost of reopening the mine, much less delivering a 15 percent required return. However, the highly negative NPV based on expected values would be wrong in this case. The reason is that the cash flow projections underlying the classical DCF analysis ignore the option *not* to produce gold if it is unprofitable to do so!

The following example demonstrates the fallacy of always using expected cash flows to judge an investment's merits. Suppose there are only two possible gold prices next year: $300 an ounce and $500 an ounce, each with a probability of 0.5—hence, the expected price of $400 an ounce. However, this expected price is irrelevant to the optimal mining decision rule: Mine gold if, and only if, the price of gold at year's end is $500 an ounce. With a price of $500/ounce and variable costs of $390/ounce, the profit per ounce is $110. Exhibit 9-12 shows the cash flow consequences of that decision rule. As we can see, incorporating the mine owner's option *not* to produce when the price falls below the cost of extraction reveals a positive net present value of $913,043 for the decision to reopen the gold mine.

> The ability to produce or not to produce a product based on its selling price is a call option.

The case of the gold mine investment demonstrates that the ability of managers to alter decisions in response to new information can contribute significantly to the value of a project. Such investments share the characteristics of options on securities and should be valued accordingly. Just as a call option gives the holder

EXHIBIT 9-12
The Gold Mine Operating Decision

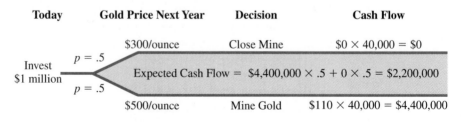

Today	Gold Price Next Year	Decision	Cash Flow
	$300/ounce	Close Mine	$0 × 40,000 = $0
Invest $1 million $p = .5$	Expected Cash Flow = $4,400,000 × .5 + 0 × .5 = $2,200,000		
$p = .5$	$500/ounce	Mine Gold	$110 × 40,000 = $4,400,000

NPV of Gold Mine Investment = −$1,000,000 + $2,200,000/1.15 = $913,043

the right but not the obligation to acquire shares at a fixed exercise price, opening the gold mine gives the mine owner the right to "acquire" the mine's output at the variable cost of production. In addition, the mine owner has the option to abandon the project at whatever the costs of shutdown. The traditional approach to investment analysis cannot really handle management's ability to respond to changes in the operating environment and hence tends to understate project values.

Strategic Options: An Example

Failure to consider strategic options can seriously undervalue a project.

The valuation of managerial options is far less precise than the valuation of stock options, but ignoring them can systematically undervalue a project. This problem of undervaluation is particularly acute for strategic investments.[6] Many strategic investments, such as R&D expenditures, plant automation, advertising to create and enhance brand image, or the development of a distribution network are often one step in a series of subsequent investments. Viewing these projects in isolation ignores their ability to create options on future products, markets, and production technologies.

To illustrate the nature of these strategic options, consider the case of Bubbly Beverage Co., a soft-drink manufacturer thinking about entering the fruit-drink segment with its Delightfully Delicious line. The firm is already a world leader in carbonated beverages and believes that its soft-drink marketing expertise, coupled with its global distribution network, will provide it with a long-term competitive advantage. Entering the fruited beverage segment wouldn't be costless because Bubbly would face formidable competition from a number of entrenched smaller firms who have been in this market for a number of years. However, not entering the fruited-beverage market at this time might preclude entry at a later date if one of the existing fruit-beverage firms were acquired by Kampy Kola, Bubbly's major competitor in the carbonated-beverage market. This would not only foreclose future product extensions but might make Bubbly vulnerable if soft-drink demand shifted dramatically from carbonated to noncarbonated beverages. Using standard DCF techniques, Bubbly develops its initial cash flow estimates, which are presented in Exhibit 9-13.

As Exhibit 9-13 indicates, traditional techniques show that, contrary to management's gut feel, the fruited-beverage line should not be introduced because the project doesn't meet Bubbly's required rate of return of 20 percent and has a negative NPV of $15.5 million. However, this analysis doesn't come close to capturing the project's strategic value. For example, if the Delightfully Delicious line is successful, Bubbly could follow up with a low-calorie version. A product extension such as this would, in all likelihood, require lower market-development costs because the brand name is already established. With two lines in place, vertical integration into the fruit-juice business and/or related diversification into wine coolers becomes a possibility. While these future investments may be risky,

---

[6]For a detailed discussion of this point, see Hayes and Garvin (1982).

EXHIBIT 9-13
Bubbly Beverage Company
Summary of Cash Flows for Delightfully Delicious Line
(in million $)

Year	1998	1999	2000	2001	2002
After-Tax Operating Cash Flow*	−140	−120	50	100	100
Capital Investment	−80	—	—	—	—
Working Capital Changes	−20	−30	−30	−20	—
Terminal Value†	—	—	—	—	500
Net Cash Flow	−240	−150	20	80	600

NPV @ 20 Percent = −$15.5 Million

*Equal to net profit after-taxes plus depreciation. After-tax operating cash flow is negative in 1998 and 1999 because of heavy promotion and advertising expenses.
†Cash flows beyond 2002 are assumed to be $100 million per year into the indefinite future. Discounting this by 20 percent yields the $500 million terminal value.

Bubbly doesn't have to commit additional resources today until it sees how the initial investment turns out. Moreover, because option values increase with risk, the speculative nature of these future ventures enhances the value of the option to invest in these potential new products. For a large firm like Bubbly, the $15 million negative NPV associated with the initial offering of Delightfully Delicious may be a small price to pay for a set of options to enter new markets if conditions are favorable.

Options Here, Options There, Options, Options, Everywhere

The preceding section suggests that the existence of strategic options increases the value of a project. In general, the value of a project (V_{PROJ}) can be viewed as follows:

$$V_{PROJ} = V_{DCF} + V_{STRAT} \qquad [9\text{-}5]$$

where V_{DCF} is the project's value using traditional DCF techniques, and V_{STRAT} is the value of the strategic options. The value of the strategic options may be difficult (if not impossible) to assess, but their presence can be treated as qualitative factors in making decisions. Further, remember from Chapter 7 that the value of an option increases with uncertainty. An option represents a *right,* but not the *obligation,* to buy or sell an asset, so there is no commitment to future investments unless conditions are favorable. In this way, a company can exploit a project's upside potential without incurring significant downside risks.

Many investments contain embedded options.

There are many classes of investment decisions containing **embedded options.** The potential for product-line extensions for Bubbly Beverage's Delightfully Delicious fruit drink is an example of a growth option, which is essentially an option to change output in response to changes in product demand. A variation on this theme is the decision to build a pilot plant to manufacture a new product. Although pilot plant operations, in general, do not exploit economies of scale, they do mitigate losses if sales are disappointing. On the other hand, if sales take off, the firm can invest in a higher-capacity and more efficient plant.

In some cases, the firm has the option to abandon a project after it is undertaken. This may consist of simply selling the assets for cash or redeploying the assets in some other area of the business, thereby eliminating the requirements for additional cash outlays. Effectively, the ability to abandon a project represents a put option for the firm. Whether we are dealing with a single piece of equipment or considering a divestiture of an entire product line or division, the decision rule is the same: A project should be abandoned if the abandonment value exceeds the present value of subsequent cash flows.

Project flexibility helps create a set of valuable operating options.

Although we don't usually think about it this way, the flexibility of a project represents a set of options available to management if the project is accepted. Baldwin, Mason, and Ruback (1983) refer to such options as "operating options," which may be inherent in some large-scale production projects. For example, the management of an electric utility may face the choice of building a power plant that burns only oil or one that is capable of burning both oil and coal. While the latter facility would cost more to build, it also provides greater flexibility because management now has the option to switch back and forth between fuel sources based on prices in the energy markets. Operating options also exist in such production facilities as oil refineries and chemical plants in which the firm can use different raw material mixes to produce the same final product or use the same inputs (e.g., crude oil) to produce a variety of outputs (e.g., gasoline, heating oil). In an environment characterized by highly variable commodity prices, such operating options can be extremely valuable.

These examples represent a "short list" of situations in which options are embedded in an investment project. As a practical matter, valuing these options may be extremely difficult; however, ignoring their existence can lead to the rejection of strategically valuable—and value-adding—projects. Thus, although DCF analysis represents a useful starting point for determining a project's value, its results should be tempered by the existence of real options.

9.5   WHERE DO WE FIND POSITIVE NPV PROJECTS?[7]

Traditional capital budgeting presumes that positive NPV projects exist and focuses, for the most part, on (1) estimating project cash flows, (2) determining the appropriate required rate of return, and (3) valuing the project based on some DCF criteria. Projects with positive NPVs are accepted; those with negative NPVs are rejected. In applying quantitative techniques, it's easy to get caught up in mechanics and lose sight of the fact that identifying the projects that are likely to

---

[7]This section builds heavily on Porter (1979) and Shapiro (1985, 1995).

yield positive NPV is probably the most important step in the process. In this section, we'll try to identify the areas in which such projects might be found.

Basic microeconomic theory is of value here. Specifically, if a firm operates in a perfectly competitive industry, it cannot generate excess returns in the long run. In such a market, as every student of microeconomics knows, each firm produces at the point at which price equals marginal cost. At this point, total revenues equal total cost for each firm individually and for the industry as a whole. This cost includes the required return on capital used by each firm. Thus, in the long run, the actual return on capital in a competitive industry must equal the required return.

Any excess return quickly attracts new entrants to the market. Their additional capacity and attempts to gain market share lead to a reduction in the industry price and the lowering of returns for all market participants. For example, in the early 1980s, the high returns in the video-game market, combined with the ease of entry into that business, attracted a host of competitors. This led to a red-ink bath for the industry in 1983, followed by the exit of many firms. Of course, should the actual returns for an industry fall below the required return, just the opposite happens. The weakest competitors exit the industry, resulting in a loss of capacity, an increase in prices within the industry, and a boost in the overall return on capital until average returns are once again equal to required returns.

The message is clear: The run-of-the-mill firm operating in a highly competitive commodity-type industry is doomed from the start in its search for positive NPV projects. Only firms that can bring to bear on new projects competitive advantages that are difficult to replicate have any assurance of earning excess returns in the long run. These advantages can take the form of either being the low-cost producer in the industry or being able to add value to a product or service—value for which customers are willing to pay a high (relative to cost) price. The latter advantage requires the ability to create products or services that are differentiated on the basis of quality and/or service. By creating such competitive advantages, a company can impose barriers to entry by potential competitors, resulting in a less-than-perfectly competitive market and the possibility of positive NPV projects.

> Finding positive NPV projects in a highly competitive commodity-type business is very difficult.

> Identifying projects that create or exploit competitive advantages is the key to finding positive NPV projects.

> Investments that are structured to exploit economies of scale and scope are more likely to be successful than those that are not.

Economies of Scale and Scope

Economies of scale exist whenever a given increase in production, marketing, or distribution activity results in a less-than-proportional increase in cost. The existence of scale economies means that there are inherent cost advantages to being large.[8] The more significant these scale economies are, the greater will be the cost

---

[8]Size in itself is not always a source of competitive advantage. In the steel industry, for example, minimills compete quite nicely with much larger producers. Unlike the major steel producers (both domestic and foreign), the minimill makes steel quickly from scrap, thereby avoiding the complex, capital-intensive operation needed to produce steel from iron ore and coke. Not having to deal with the restrictive work rules imposed by the United Steel Workers also helps the minimill's cost structure.

disadvantage to a potential new entrant into a market. For example, Intel's huge market share in microprocessors is a major deterrent to a potential new entrant. Because it can spread costs over millions of chips, Intel can spend more money on R&D, marketing, service, and new plants than other chip makers and still earn its cost of capital. Similarly, large integrated oil companies such as Exxon and Shell are able to fend off new market entrants by exploiting economies of scale in exploration, production, and distribution.

High capital requirements go hand in hand with economies of scale. To take advantage of scale economies in production, marketing, or new product development, firms must often make enormous up-front investments in plant and equipment, research and development, and advertising. These capital requirements themselves serve as a barrier to entry; the more capital that is required, the higher will be the barrier to entry. This is particularly true for capital-intensive industries such as petroleum refining, mineral extraction, and mainframe computer production as well as for the pharmaceutical and biotechnology industries in which heavy R&D spending may precede commercial success by as much as 10 years.

A potential entrant to a market characterized by scale economies in production may be reluctant to enter unless the market is growing at a sufficient rate to permit construction and profitable utilization of an economically sized plant. Otherwise, the new entrant will have to cut price to gain market share, thereby destroying the possibility of adequate returns for everyone. By expanding production capacity in line with market growth, entrenched competitors can pre-empt profitable market entry by new competitors.

The existence of **economies of scope** means that some efficiencies arise from variety and not from volume. There are numerous examples of the cost advantages of producing and selling multiple products related by a particular core technology, set of production facilities, or channel of distribution. For example, 3M has taken its basic adhesive and coating technology and applied it across a broad range of products and markets—bandages and dental appliances in health care, Post-it notes and Scotch tape in the office supplies market, and optical disks for computer products. Similarly, Honda has leveraged its investment in small-engine technology in the automobile, motorcycle, lawn mower, generator, marine engine, snowblower, and chain-saw businesses.

Matsushita has leveraged its investment in advertising and distribution of Panasonic-brand products in a number of consumer and industrial markets, ranging from personal computers to VCRs. Each dollar invested in the Panasonic brand name or distribution system aids sales of dozens of different products. Similarly, U.S. pharmaceutical companies typically have developed large sales forces to promote their products. The incremental cost of adding one more drug through the distribution system represented by this sales force essentially consists of adding another page to the sales catalogue.

Production economies of scope are becoming more prevalent as flexible manufacturing systems allow the same equipment to produce a variety of products more cheaply in combination than separately. The ability to manufacture a wide variety of products with little cost penalty as compared to the large-scale manufacture of a single product opens up new markets, customers, and channels of distribution along with new routes to competitive advantage. Related to this is the acquisition of another firm whose products complement those of the acquirer so that the firm can now provide a "full line" of products. This will expand sales to customers looking for one-stop shopping. At the same time, the acquirer can take advantage of economies of scope in distribution by combining overlapping portions of the distribution networks.

Cost Advantages

Entrenched companies often have cost advantages that aren't related to economies of scale or scope. These advantages may not be available to new entrants. For example, some firms may be in a position to take advantage of the **learning curve** to reduce costs and drive out existing and potential competitors. This concept is based on the idea that we all improve with practice. As production and distribution experience accumulates, costs should decrease as a result of more efficient use of labor, improved plant layout and production methods, product redesign, and efficient product distribution. This cost decline creates a barrier to entry because new entrants simply do not have the experience of established firms. By establishing market leadership, usually by aggressive pricing, and thereby accumulating experience faster, this entry barrier can be maximized.

Some firms can exploit the learning curve to gain competitive advantage.

Proprietary technology, protected by legally enforceable patents, provides another cost advantage to established firms. This is the route taken by pharmaceutical firms in developing prescription drugs. In the absence of patent protection, it would be difficult to justify the enormous R&D costs associated with the development of prescription drugs. Control of low-cost raw materials represents yet another advantage to entrenched firms. This advantage was held for many years by multinational oil companies that had access to low-cost crude oil.

Sometimes, however, new entrants can enjoy a cost advantage over existing competitors. This is particularly true of industries undergoing deregulation, such as airlines and trucking. In both of these industries, regulation insulated firms from the rigors of competition and fare wars. Deregulation has exposed these companies to new competitors not saddled with outmoded work rules and high-cost employees. For example, new low-cost competitors in the airlines industry, such as Southwest Airlines, pay lower wages and have more flexible work rules.[9]

Cost advantages can allow firms to successfully execute a low-cost or best-cost provider strategy.

Cost advantages allow a company to effectively execute either a **low-cost provider strategy**, where price is the primary competitive weapon, or a **best-cost provider strategy**, built around the idea of giving customers more value for their money by combining an emphasis on low cost in combination with some upscale product differentiation. The Toyota Motor Company is a good example of a firm pursuing a best-cost provider strategy. The company is known for making high-quality automobiles and trucks, but the Toyota production system has one of the lowest cost structures in the industry. This makes Toyota a formidable global competitor over a wide range of price categories.

---

[9]At Southwest, for example, flight attendants serve at reservation phones and check-in counters, thereby allowing the company to utilize their time more efficiently.

Product Differentiation

Investments devoted to differentiating products or services are more likely to be profitable.

Instead of a cost-based advantage, some firms invest in the ability to differentiate their products or services from the competition. This *product or service differentiation* may stem from the firm's investment in advertising, R&D, or the development of an organizational structure which is service- and quality-oriented. A firm may seek to differentiate its product offerings to serve a broad market, or it may offer highly customized products to serve a specific *market niche.* Regardless of the range of customers served, the idea is to have products sufficiently different from those of the competition so that direct price competition is avoided. These products, supported by heavy investment in advertising, can provide barriers to entry in the form of *brand-name recognition,* which allows the successful firm to charge a premium price for the product or service. Coca-Cola and Procter & Gamble have taken advantage of huge advertising expenditures and marketing skills to develop brands that are recognized globally.

Similarly, technologically innovative products can also lead to high profits. 3M, Motorola, and Intel have a long history of producing technologically advanced products and appear to understand that customers will pay for the value added by technology, not the technology per se. To a great extent, the risks in R&D are commercial, not technical, and firms that make technology pay are those that can link their R&D efforts with market realities. Unless the product serves customer needs and lowers costs, innovations will not be successful.

Firms can also differentiate through superior service. For example, Caterpillar Tractor has combined high quality with outstanding distribution and after-sales support to differentiate its line of construction equipment and gain a commanding share of the global market for earth-moving equipment. Quality and consistency can also be used to differentiate products or services that many people would consider commodities. McDonalds, for example, prides itself on cleanliness and consistency of service and, in this way, has become a global leader in the cluttered fast-food industry. Similarly, Mars candy factories have a reputation for being so clean that you can "eat off the factory floor."

Other firms have made their owners wealthy by understanding that they too are *selling solutions to their customers' problems,* not hardware or consumables.

Illustration

Nalco Chemical Manages Molecules from Cradle to Grave

Faced with a proliferation of environmental laws, Nalco Chemical introduced a delivery and storage system for hazardous chemicals called Porta-Feed. It eliminates the use of 55-gallon metal drums, those unsightly vessels that often end up discarded in landfills, leaking dregs into the soil and exposing their owners to potentially huge liability under federal environmental law. Porta-Feed consists of a refillable 400-gallon stainless steel container installed at a customer's plant. When the tank is nearly empty, an electronic sensor hooked to a telephone sends a signal to Nalco saying, in effect, "Fill me!" Soon a Nalco delivery truck shows up to refill the tank. The empty transport container is returned to Nalco for cleaning. Nalco charges premium prices for chemicals it delivers this way. But plant managers say Porta-Feed saves money by curbing pollution and simplifying the handling of dangerous chemicals.

Channels of Distribution

Investments devoted to gaining better product distribution often lead to higher firm profitability.

Gaining access to shelf space and channels of distribution for their products represents a major hurdle for newcomers to an industry. Most retailers of personal computers, for example, limit their inventory to about five product lines. Currently, over 200 manufacturers are competing for this limited shelf space. Moreover, the concentration of retail outlets among chains means that new computer manufacturers have even fewer avenues to the consumer. This presents the new manufacturer with a dilemma: You can't get shelf space unless you are a proven winner, but you may not be able to sell unless you get the shelf space. Some firms, such as Dell Computer, have resolved this dilemma by setting up their own distribution channels: selling over the telephone and the Internet.

Foreign drug manufacturers have a different challenge in attempting to expand their presence in the United States. Marketing drugs in the United States requires a good deal of political skill to get through the FDA regulatory process as well as great rapport with hospitals and doctors. This latter requirement means that pharmaceutical firms must have a large sales staff to maintain close contact with those individuals who are critical to the ultimate sale of their product. As noted earlier, there are significant economies of scope for the entrenched firm that already has a sales force in place to market dozens of existing products. Thus, only a firm with an extensive product line can afford such a large sales force, raising a major barrier to entry for firms with limited product lines.

Firms have gotten around these barriers in different ways. Avon and Tupperware market their products directly to the consumer on a house-to-house basis (or a "Tupperware party-by-party" basis), thereby reducing advertising expenditures. A number of firms have developed their own distribution outlets. The Tandy Company markets its audio and electronic products through its own retail outlet—Radio Shack—and Disney stores are springing up in virtually every major shopping mall in the United States. Alternatively, foreign drug manufacturers often license U.S. firms to sell their products.

Government Policy

In the past, government regulation has limited competition in many industries such as trucking, airlines, telephone communications, and gas and electric utili-

Projects protected from competition by government can be very profitable; however, this profitability erodes when the protection stops.

ties. Other government policies that raise partial or absolute barriers to entry include import restrictions, environmental controls, and licensing requirements. The effects of licensing restrictions on the taxi business in New York City, for example, are reflected in the high price of a medallion (the right to operate a taxi there), which, in turn, is reflected in high cab fares.

A change in government policy can greatly affect the value of current and prospective investments within an industry. For many years, airlines and trucking were insulated from competition and fare wars by regulation. Protected as they were, there was little incentive to control costs, since higher costs could be passed on to consumers in the form of higher fares or tariffs. The regulatory barriers created profits that were divided between the firms and their unionized employees. Deregulation has exposed these firms to competitors that are not saddled with outmoded work rules and high-cost union employees. The effect on profitability has been devastating, which, in turn, has forced drastic restructuring of regulated industries.

Building Competitive Advantage

The preceding discussion suggests that the search for investment projects should begin with the firm's strategy and should focus on building competitive advantages. This strategy could be geared to building volume if economies of scale are important or broadening its line of products or services where economies of scope are critical to success. Identifying the factors that are critical to success requires an understanding of customers, their current needs, and what their needs may be in the future. Companies that are tuned in to customer needs can create competitive advantage. More important, such firms are also very good at creating shareholder value in the process.

A company's ability to exploit an investment in one area may require supporting investments in other areas.

A strategy designed to build competitive advantage is likely to encompass a sequence of tactical projects. As our discussion on managerial options has suggested, projects that have negative NPVs in isolation may be desirable if they create additional future investment opportunities or allow the firm to continue earning excess returns on existing investments. To evaluate a sequence of tactical projects designed to achieve competitive advantage, the projects must be looked at collectively rather than individually.

For example, if the key to competitive advantage is high volume, the initial entry into a market should be assessed on the basis of its ability to create future opportunities to build market share and the associated benefits thereof. Alternatively, market entry overseas may be judged according to its ability to deter a foreign competitor from launching a market share battle by posing a credible retaliatory threat to the competitor's profit base. By reducing the likelihood of a competitive intrusion, foreign market entry may lead to higher future profits in the home market. Conversely, firms with high domestic market share and minimal sales overseas are especially vulnerable to the strategic dilemma illustrated by the example of Fiat.

Illustration

Fiat's Strategic Dilemma

Suppose Toyota, the Japanese auto company, cuts price in order to gain market share in Italy. If Fiat, the dominant Italian producer with minimal foreign sales, responds with its own price cuts, it will lose profit on most of its sales. In contrast, only a small fraction of Toyota's sales and profits are exposed. Fiat is effectively boxed in: If it responds to the competitive intrusion with a price cut of its own, the response will damage Fiat more than Toyota.

The correct competitive response is for the local firm (Fiat) to cut its price in the intruder's domestic market (Japan). Having such a capability will deter foreign competitors from using high home-country prices to subsidize marginal cost pricing overseas. But this necessitates investing in the domestic markets of potential competitors. The level of market share needed to pose a credible retaliatory threat depends on access to distribution networks and the criticality of the market to the competitor's profitability. The easier distribution access is and the more critical the market is to competitor profitability, the smaller the necessary market share.

In designing and valuing a strategic investment program, a company must be alert to the ways in which projects interact. For example, if scale economies exist, investment in a large-scale manufacturing facility may only be justified if the firm has made supporting investments in its distribution system. Investments in a global distribution system and a global brand franchise, in turn, are often only economical if a firm has a range of products (and the manufacturing facilities to supply them) that can exploit the distribution system and brand name. Developing a broad product line to exploit economies of scope usually requires investment in different technologies that cut across product lines. At the same time, global distribution capacity may be critical to exploiting new technology.

Individually or in pairs, investments in large-scale production facilities, worldwide distribution, a global brand franchise, and new technology are likely to be negative NPV projects. Together, however, they may yield a highly positive NPV by forming a mutually supportive framework for achieving global competitive advantage.

By linking strategic planning and capital allocation, companies gain two major advantages. First, the true economics of investments can be assessed more accurately for strategies than for projects. Second, the quality of the capital budgeting process typically improves greatly when capital expenditures are tied directly to the development and approval of business strategies designed to build or exploit competitive advantages.

Designing an Investment Policy

Let's see if we can summarize some of the critical relationships among corporate strategy, competitive advantage, and a firm's investment policy. First, firms that create value are those that develop business strategies geared to achieving one or both of the following competitive positions within their respective industries:

1. Becoming the lowest-total-delivered-cost producer in the industry while maintaining an acceptable service/quality combination relative to the competition.
2. Developing the highest product/service/quality differentiated position within the industry while maintaining an acceptable cost structure.

There are, to be sure, variations on these basic themes. Firms can become low-cost providers by combining low costs with some differentiation (e.g., quality). Or they can choose to differentiate with a broad-based product line or to be a niche player. Once a company decides on how it's going to compete within its industry, it must single-mindedly tailor its investments to attain this position.

A company also has to be prepared to change its strategies in response to changes in its markets. The computer market provides a case in point. Historically, IBM and other mainframe manufacturers enjoyed gross margins of over 70 percent. However, the personal computer (PC) and the microprocessor changed all that. The painful fact is that computers are now commodities that customers want to buy as cheaply as possible. Moreover, the rapid change in technology has made PCs so powerful that they are now encroaching on the turf once reserved for mainframes.

The PC has become a commodity because Intel, which makes its microprocessors, and Microsoft, which makes the operating system software, sell their technology to all comers. The companies that assemble PCs from these components press suppliers of all other parts—screens, power supplies, disk drives, and memory chips—to slash prices and push technology. At the same time, such firms as Sun Microsystems have developed powerful commodity-like workstations using interchangeable software that target users of minicomputers and mainframes. These developments made it clear that IBM, even though it helped create the PC, could not demand a premium price just because it was "IBM" when literally dozens of companies could assemble high-quality components from suppliers at a low cost. It took "Big Blue" most of the 1980s to figure out this simple truth.

Firms responded to the conversion of the PC into a commodity in different ways. In some cases, firms (e.g., Compaq Computer) pushed to reduce expenses in order to become the industry's low-cost provider. Other firms (e.g., Dell Computer and Gateway) turned to telecommunications as a way of developing non-traditional (and low-cost) channels of distribution. There are no cases in which a company simply did nothing and survived.

Finally, we should note that gaining competitive advantage is not an end in itself; it must be tied to value creation. For many companies, the investment in

Firms must be prepared to change their strategies in response to changes in market conditions.

advertising, R&D, or plant and equipment needed to sustain competitive advantage may far exceed the gains. Success breeds imitation, and many managers consistently underestimate how efficient the forces of competition are in erasing the advantages that their strategies are designed to create.

SUMMARY

This chapter presented some of the rules and techniques for estimating project cash flows. The most important principle is to include in the analysis only incremental cash flows—the difference between overall cash flows with and without the investment. Moreover, all of these cash flows must be calculated on an after-tax basis because shareholders only get their returns from after-tax dollars.

Project cash flows were divided into the initial cost of the investment, operating cash flows, and the terminal or ending value. We examined each of these components separately, taking into account the effect of taxation at each stage of the analysis. Particular attention was directed at estimating the terminal value of new product introductions: The assumption of cash flow growth beyond some initial evaluation period was shown to be critical to project acceptance or rejection.

Another important lesson demonstrated in this chapter was the need to be consistent in the treatment of inflation. The nominal discount rate already incorporates inflationary expectations. To be consistent, the projected cash flows being discounted must also take into account expected inflation. Ignoring the possibility that nominal revenues and/or costs rise at (approximately) the rate of inflation can systematically undervalue many projects. In a variation on a theme, we saw that differences in inflation rates between a home and host country complicate the analysis of overseas projects. To be consistent, project cash flows must be adjusted to reflect depreciation or appreciation in currencies in response to inflationary expectations.

The chapter also pointed out that failing to take into account the options available to managers can seriously undervalue many investment projects. These options include (but are not limited to) the possibility of product extensions, abandonment of a project, or the chance to utilize new skills developed from implementing a project.

Finally, we examined the question of where positive NPV projects come from and found that the answer to this question is intimately tied to the challenge of how a firm creates competitive advantage. We established the need to:

1. Invest in projects that take advantage of your competitive edge. The corollary is to stick to doing the one or two things that you do best and don't get involved in businesses with which you are unfamiliar.
2. Invest in developing, maintaining, and enhancing your competitive advantage. In markets in which being the low-cost provider is important, projects that exploit economies of scale or scope are more likely to be successful than those that do not. Where differentiation is possible, projects that create a market position based on quality and service have a good chance of being successful.
3. Pick markets or market niches in which there is little competition. Be prepared to abandon markets when competitors catch up unless you're willing to continuously invest to maintain your initial advantage.
4. Be careful of investing in businesses because of government protection and/or favorable tax treatment. These sources of profitability can evaporate quickly: What government gives, it can take away.

APPENDIX 9A   EVALUATING R&D PROJECTS: AN OPTION-VALUATION APPROACH

As noted in Chapter 9, traditional discounted cash flow (DCF) techniques tend to undervalue projects if managers have the ability to significantly alter their decisions in response to new information. Such investments resemble options on securities and should be valued accordingly. For example, investing in research and development (an option premium) gives a company the right to acquire the outcomes of these efforts at the costs of commercialization (the exercise price). However, management is under no obligation to bring the results of R&D to market if conditions are unfavorable. Management can abandon unsuccessful R&D (a put option) at some shutdown cost. These operating options should be captured in any evaluation of an R&D project.

Suppose that the Kolt Micropower Company is developing a new transmission and receiving system that allows communications companies to send phone messages without either lines or satellites. The product development phase is expected to cost $5 million a year from 1999 through 2001. At that time, Kolt will build a state-of-the-art plant costing $100 million to produce the new product. Assuming that the new transmitter actually performs up to expectations, the annual cash flows over the next ten years will be $13 million. The project's terminal value (including work-

ing capital recovery) is forecast to be $105 million. Exhibit 9A-1 summarizes these data.

Assuming a required rate of return of 14 percent, the present values of these cash flows as of January 1, 1999, and January 1, 2002, are shown in Exhibit 9A-2. They show a highly negative NPV. According to standard DCF techniques based on expected cash flows, Kolt would be wasting its shareholders' money by even starting the R&D phase. As in the case of the gold mine, these numbers are highly misleading.

The problem with the conventional analysis is that it assumes that the plant will be built regardless of how the product development effort turns out and what market conditions will prevail in 2002. For example, a leap in technology by a competitor in the next three years could make the new transmitter virtually obsolete. By ignoring the option not to build the plant, standard DCF projects a negative NPV of $15.7 million at the point of decision (2002). Option valuation allows for the decision not to build and values only

EXHIBIT 9A-1
Kolt Micropower Company
Expected Cash Flows from New Product Development
(in million $)

R&D Expense			Cost of New Plant*	Operating Cash Flows						Terminal Value
1999	2000	2001	2002	2003	2004	2005	2006	. . .	2012	2012
−5.0	−5.0	−5.0	−100	13	13	13	13		13	105

*Plant cost is incurred at the beginning of 2002.

EXHIBIT 9A-2
Kolt Micropower Company
Expected Cash Flows from New Product Development
(in million $)

	Present Value as of January 1	
Cash Flow Item	1999	2002
Research and Development Expense	−11.6	0
Plant Cost	−67.5	−100.0
Post-2002 Operating Cash Flows (2003–2012)*	40.1	59.5
Terminal Value	16.8	24.8
Net Present Value	−22.2	−15.7

*Present value of $13 million/year discounted @ 14%.

EXHIBIT 9A-3
Kolt Micropower Company
Expected Cash Flows from New Product Development
(in million $)

Present Value on January 1		1999 R&D Expense	2002 Plant Cost	2002 Possible Payoff	1999 Project NPV
DCF Analysis Assumes a single outcome as an expected value of possible outcomes		−11.6	−100.0	84.3	−22.2
Option Analysis	I	−11.6	−100.0	197.0	53.9
Assumes many scenarios and then	II	−11.6	−100.0	104.1	−8.8
values each one separately	III	−11.6		29.9	−11.6
	IV	−11.6		7.6	−11.6

those alternatives that will follow if the plant is built. Clearly, if the R&D efforts don't pan out or if the product market conditions aren't favorable, the plant won't be built. That is, the option valuation approach properly values only the *positive* NPV outcomes, whereas traditional DCF analysis values *all* outcomes, negative as well as positive.

Exhibit 9A-3 shows how the different assumptions underlying the two approaches affect their estimates of expected cash flows. The analysis considers only four possible scenarios, each with probability .25 of occurring. Let's look at some of the details of a standard DCF analysis first. We start out in 1999 with some estimates of R&D expenses and plant cost as well as forecasts of *expected* operating cash flows and terminal values through the year 2012. These projected cash flows were summarized in Exhibit 9A-1.

Kolt proceeds with the R&D phase, which costs $5 million a year. The present value of these cash outflows—as of 1999—is −$11.6 million. It's now 2002. The present value of the operating cash flows, plus the terminal value—as of 2002—is $84.3 million. If Kolt goes forward and puts in the plant at a cost of $100 million, the project's NPV—as of 2002—will be −$15.7 million. Discounting this −$15.7 million back to 1999 at 14 percent, and adding it to the present value of R&D costs gives us the negative NPV of $22.2 million in Exhibit 9A-3. As we've noted, this "arithmetic" assumes that Kolt has learned nothing during the 1999–2001 R&D phase and goes ahead in 2002

based on cash flow estimates derived in 1999. This is not particularly realistic.

In contrast, the option-valuation approach considers the four different and equally likely scenarios at the end of 2002 separately. Although the expected payoff from undertaking the project remains at $84.3 million as of 2002, the figures in Exhibit 9A-3 indicate that the payoff can range from $197.0 million down to $7.6 million. The high variability of the payoff means that the plant is worth building under some scenarios but not others. Under Scenarios III and IV, the option-valuation approach assumes the plant will not be built because the present value of the possible payoffs is negative. In these cases, the project's NPV is −$11.6 million—the cost of the R&D investment.

Unlike the DCF analysis, in which the NPV is calculated as −$22.2, the option valuation approach recognizes that the expected NPV of the new product development project cannot fall below −$11.6 million. The expected payoff in 2002 of $84.3 million used in the DCF analysis is a weighted average of the four possible outcomes. However, this number is totally irrelevant to the investment decision because the company will not build the plant unless the future payoff is at least equal to the $100 million cost. Hence, the outcomes of $29.9 million and $7.6 million can be disregarded.

To conclude this example, Exhibit 9A-4 shows that the expected project NPV in 2002, valuing only the favorable outcomes, is $25.3 million. This yields a present value in 1999 of $17.1 million. Subtract the $11.6

EXHIBIT 9A-4
Kolt Micropower Company
Expected NPV of R&D Investment in 2002
(in million $)

Scenario	Decision	Cost	Payoff	NPV	× Probability	= Value
I	Build Plant	−100.0	197.0	97.0	0.25	24.3
II	Build Plant	−100.0	104.1	4.1	0.25	1.0
III	Don't Build	-0-	-0-	-0-	0.25	0.0
IV	Don't Build	-0-	-0-	-0-	0.25	0.0
						Expected NPV = 25.3

million present value of the R&D investment, and the result is a highly acceptable project with a $5.5 million net present value. By contrast, the traditional DCF analysis tells Kolt to reject the project. The option approach indicates that Kolt should begin its developmental efforts on the transmission and receiving system and exercise the option of proceeding if the outcome looks favorable. Moreover, beyond the initial efforts, the R&D project may provide Kolt with a series of future—but as yet undefined—growth opportunities into other product lines and/or new markets.

The investment in R&D frequently provides growth opportunities because R&D is often but the first link in a chain of investment decisions that can create competitive advantage. For example, Robert Kaplan[10] pointed out that companies that invested in automatic and electronically controlled machine tools in the 1970s were ideally positioned to exploit the microprocessor-based revolution and capabilities (higher performance at a much lower cost) that hit during the 1980s. Machine operators, maintenance personnel, and process engineers were already comfortable with electronic technology, so it was relatively easy to retrofit existing machines with the new technology. Companies that had earlier deferred investment in the latest technology fell behind.

APPENDIX 9B   RISK ANALYSIS IN CAPITAL BUDGETING

This chapter, coupled with Chapter 8, showed us how to conduct a capital budgeting analysis once we had a good bit of information about a project and were comfortable with using a single-point estimate of the project's cash flows. We dealt with investment risk by assuming that we could choose an appropriate required rate of return and then went merrily on our way to calculate the project's NPV. However, in a global economy where events halfway around the world can affect the survival of companies and where the stakes may involve billion-dollar investments in plant and equipment or R&D, a single number—the project's NPV—often hides information about its riskiness. In this kind of world, managers responsible for evaluating high-impact strategic investments often "pray for the best, but prepare for the worst." For this reason, we need a set of tools that will help us understand the sources of project risk and how they might influence

the value of projects. The techniques of *project risk analysis*—sensitivity analysis, simulation, and decision trees—discussed in this appendix can help in this task.

Sensitivity Analysis

Sometimes referred to as "what if" analysis, sensitivity analysis is a procedure to study the effect of key variables—including sales, production costs, R&D expenses, and operating expenses—on a project's NPV. The first step is to identify key variables and have the engineering, marketing, and production people assign their pessimistic (most likely) and optimistic values for each of the variables. Then, a series of project NPVs is calculated based on setting each variable at its most pessimistic, most likely, and optimistic values while

---

[10]Robert S. Kaplan, "Must CIM Be Justified by Faith Alone?" *Harvard Business Review,* March–April 1986, 92.

holding all other variables to their most likely value. The goal is to see how sensitive the project returns are to different assumptions.

An Example

Suppose that the Crystal Glass Company is thinking about building a plate-glass plant in eastern Michigan. The plant, with an annual capacity of 100,000 tons, will cost $100 million to construct. The $100 million plant cost is considered pretty definite because it's guaranteed by fixed-price contracts with the equipment manufacturer and the construction company. Profits on the plant will be taxed at a rate of 50 percent.

The glass plant is designed to capitalize on the rapidly growing market for high-quality plate glass in the area. Total demand for plate glass within Crystal's market area is currently running at 800,000 tons annually. This figure is expected to grow to 832,000 tons by next year, a 4 percent annual growth rate. Crystal expects its plant to produce about 90,000 tons annually, an average of 90 percent of rated capacity. This would give it an approximately 11 percent market share in the first year of operation and annual revenues of $59.4 million based on an anticipated selling price of $660 a ton. Depending on market conditions, however, yearly production could rise to 100,000 tons or fall to 80,000 tons. Similarly, the price of plate glass could climb as high as $700 per ton or sink to as low as $600 a ton.

Operating costs are divided into fixed and variable components. Fixed costs include payroll cost, maintenance, repairs, supplies, and overhead expenses such as general selling and administrative costs. These costs are expected to average $12 million annually. Depending on current labor negotiations and other factors, these costs could be as low as $10 million or as high as $15 million. Payroll costs are treated as a fixed cost because labor inputs don't vary with output.

Variable production costs—which include the costs of raw materials and power—are expected to average $140 per ton. Possible fluctuations in energy and raw material costs could reduce these costs to $110 a ton or raise them to as much as $170 a ton. For simplicity, the $100 million cost of the plant is assumed to be depreciated on a straight-line basis over ten years for an annual depreciation charge of $10 million.

From these data, we put together Exhibit 9B-1, which calculates the project's yearly cash flows along with its NPV. The required rate of return on the project is taken as 15 percent because of the high degree of systematic risk associated with a cyclical product like plate glass. To simplify the analysis, we've assumed that the cash flows over the project's ten-year economic life will be the same. As shown in Exhibit 9B-1, the project's NPV is $12.4 million. The term $PVIFA_{15,10}$ refers to the present value of an annuity of $1 a year for ten years discounted at 15 percent. This value is 5.0188.

Exhibit 9B-2 shows what will happen to the NPV of Crystal Glass's proposed new plant when each variable is set, in turn, to its pessimistic and optimistic values, while simultaneously holding all other variables at their most likely values. For example, if fixed costs rise to $15 million annually (a jump of $3 million from their most likely estimate), then the plant's annual operating cash flow will drop by $1.5 million—the after-tax increase in cost—to $20.9 million. The project's NPV, using the same 15 percent required rate of return as before drops to

$$NPV = -\$100,000,000 + \$20,900,000(PVIFA_{15,10})$$
$$= -\$100,000,000 + \$20,900,000(5.0188)$$
$$= \$4,892,920$$

The value of $5 million shown for this scenario in Exhibit 9B-2 is the value calculated here, rounded to the nearest million.

The numbers from the sensitivity analysis indicate that the project is likely to be successful even though the NPV is sensitive to changes in the key variables. Only if the price drops to $600 a ton will the project have a negative NPV, and even then it will just be $-\$1$ million.

Using Sensitivity Analysis: Some Cautions

The virtue of sensitivity analysis is its simplicity. Once you set up the base-case model on a personal computer, alternative scenarios can be generated quickly. As a matter of fact, the major spreadsheet packages such as Excel and Lotus 1-2-3 already have built-in "what if?" functions.

However, sensitivity analysis has a serious drawback in that it assumes that the variables are unrelated to one another. For instance, the sensitivity analysis for Crystal Glass's new plant assumed that price and demand are independent of one another—a highly unlikely scenario. Typically, high demand and high price go hand in hand in those industries in which product demand begins to push available capacity. Similarly, low demand generally results in price cutting as firms

EXHIBIT 9B-1
Projected Cash Flows for Crystal Glass Company's New Plate-Glass Plant

	Year 0	Years 1–10
Initial Investment	−$100,000,000	
Sales		
Tons Sold		90,000
Price/Ton		× $660
Revenue		$59,400,000
Cost		
Variable Cost (90,000 tons @ $140 a ton)		12,600,000
Fixed Costs		12,000,000
Depreciation		10,000,000
Total Costs		34,600,000
Income before Taxes		$24,800,000
Taxes @ 50%		12,400,000
After-Tax Income		$12,400,000
Plus: Depreciation		10,000,000
Operating Cash Flow		$22,400,000
Net Cash Flow	−$100,000,000	$22,400,000

NPV @ 15% = −$100,000,000 + $22,400,000 (PVIFA$_{15,10}$)
    = $12.4 million

EXHIBIT 9B-2
Sensitivity Analysis for Crystal Glass Company's Proposed Plate-Glass Plant

Variable	Value for Each Variable under Alternative Scenarios			Project NPV under Each Scenario*	
	Pessimistic	Most Likely	Optimistic	Pessimistic	Optimistic
Demand (Tons)	80,000	90,000	100,000	$0	$25
Price per Ton ($)	600	660	700	−1	21
Fixed Cost (million $)	15	12	10	5	17
Variable Cost/Ton ($)	170	140	110	6	19

*Assumes a 15 percent required rate of return. Rounded to the nearest million dollars.

try to generate enough volume to cover their fixed costs. To see the effect of a low-demand, low-price scenario, rework the calculations incorporating both a $600-per-ton price and sales of 80,000 tons. This will produce a yearly operating cash flow of $17.4 million and a project NPV of −$12.7 million. Thus, the project turns out to be riskier than the simple sensitivity analysis indicates.

Simulation Analysis

Sensitivity analysis is a valuable technique for project risk analysis and, as such, is widely used by business. Despite this, sensitivity analysis does have its limitations. As we have indicated, the technique ignores variable interaction by focusing on one factor at a time while holding others constant. Further, even if a project is very sensitive to a change in a particular variable, sensitivity analysis tells us nothing about the likelihood of such a change because no probabilities are assigned to any of the pessimistic, most likely, or optimistic estimates.

By contrast, a computer simulation represents a project's NPV as a probability distribution rather than a single number. In order to conduct a **simulation analysis,** you must first estimate the probability distributions for each variable that will affect the project's cash inflows and outflows. For a new product introduction, these variables would include the initial investment, size of the market, market growth, price, market share, variable costs, fixed costs, product life cycle, and the project's terminal value. Some of these probability distributions, such as initial investment and production costs, can be estimated with greater confidence than can such others as the probability distributions for variables of price or market share. Determining the probability distribution for product revenues is particularly difficult because of the interaction of variables like market size, market growth rates, price, and market share.

The next step is to program a computer to select at random one value apiece from each of the probability distributions. These values—for market size, market share, production costs, and the like—are then used to calculate the net cash flows in each period. As each scenario is generated—a scenario being a particular set of values for the relevant project variables—the NPV is calculated and stored in the computer. This process is repeated, say, 1,000 times. The stored values are then printed out in the form of a probability distribution of NPVs along with the expected NPV and its standard deviation.[11]

In computing the project's NPV, we should discount the project's cash flows at a risk-free rate. After all, one of the reasons that we're performing the simulation is to evaluate the project's risk, and if we knew that, we wouldn't need to perform the simulation in the first place. Thus, assuming that we're trying to assess the project's risk, we use the risk-free rate solely as a mechanism for taking into account the time value of money.

Despite its appeal as a highly sophisticated, technologically advanced tool for evaluating project risk, simulation analysis has a number of practical and theoretical drawbacks. One major stumbling block is that realistic models tend to be highly complex. For example, a simple sensitivity analysis like the one we did for Crystal Glass's plate-glass plant assumed that the cash flows in one period were independent of what happens in other periods. This was clearly unrealistic: A higher market share in one period is likely to mean greater consumer acceptance and (relatively) higher market shares in the next period. Similarly, lower-than-expected costs in one period will likely imply lower costs in the future.

In theory, a well-constructed simulation model should be able to capture these time-related interdependencies. However, there's a high cost in getting the data needed to satisfy the model's information needs because the market share in, say, year four, would depend on the entire sequence of market shares in periods 1 through 3. That's a lot of probability distributions to estimate. However, ignoring these interdependencies would make the resulting probability distribution of NPVs less useful.

The second problem with simulation is both practical and theoretical. After conducting a simulation analysis, you are left staring at a probability distribution of NPVs or IRRs. True enough, we sense the likelihood that the project's NPV will be less than zero and the magnitude of losses if all of our worst fears materialize. However, we really don't know whether to accept or reject the project. Simulation, for all its technical sophistication, provides no guidance in resolving what's ultimately the only important capital budgeting issue—specifying an acceptable tradeoff between project risk and return.

Finally, the description of risk specified by a simulation model ignores the opportunities available to both the firm and its investors to diversify away unsystematic risk. As we indicated in Chapter 6, investments that are risky on a stand-alone basis may be quite "tame" as part of the portfolio of assets that makes up the firm. Similarly, the less correlated the project's returns are with stock market returns, the less risky the project will be to highly diversified investors.

Decision Trees

Investment decisions are not quite as cut and dried as the examples used would seem to indicate. Instead,

---

[11]At each iteration, we could compute the project's IRR instead of its NPV. The result would be a probability distribution for the project's internal rate of return rather than its NPV. Many managers find this distribution more informative than a distribution of NPVs.

many investment opportunities require a sequence of decisions over time, with each subsequent action depending on earlier decisions as well as on the outcomes of those decisions. Consequently, what you plan to do today will often depend on what you intend to do in the future.

A useful tool in solving sequential-decision problems is to diagram the alternatives and their possible decisions. The resulting chart is known as a **decision tree,** so called because it has the appearance of a tree with branches. The decision tree enables managers to visualize quickly the possible future events, their probabilities, and their financial consequences. It also helps in selecting the optimal sequence of decisions by facilitating the calculation of NPVs associated with the alternative decision paths.

To illustrate the process, suppose that Bubbly Beverage Inc. (BBI) has developed a new high-caffeine, high-sugar soft drink to compete with Zap—a similar beverage that its archrival Kampy Kola has had on the market for years. Demand for the product is uncertain. BBI estimates that there's a 60 percent chance that demand will be high in the first year. High initial demand is a good omen; it raises the probability of high demand in the second and subsequent years to 80 percent. On the other hand, if initial demand is low (there's a 40 percent probability of this), then there's a 70 percent chance that demand after the first year will also be low.

BBI has decided to bypass the test-market stage. Test marketing would only alert Kampy Kola to the product's introduction and invite a sharp competitive response. Instead, BBI has decided to build a plant to manufacture the product; its only decision is whether the plant should be large or small. If BBI builds a large plant at a cost of $15 million, it is stuck with that level of capacity regardless of subsequent demand. Alternatively, BBI could build a small plant at a cost of $10 million today (time 0) and then expand it next year at a cost of $7 million if demand is high. Building the smaller facility enhances flexibility because it gives BBI the *option* of minimizing its investment in the product if demand is low. However, if demand is strong, building a large plant is $2 million cheaper than building a smaller one initially and having to expand it later.

The decision tree in Exhibit 9B-3 displays the choices available to BBI with their potential consequences. The squares represent decision points, and the circles, chance events. After each decision has been made, "fate" selects the actual level of demand. This is represented by the branches of the tree. Each branch has the probability written on it, along with the payoffs associated with that combination of plant size and demand.

The sequence of events depicted by the tree is as follows: BBI builds a plant at time 0, after which fate (and BBI's competitor, Kampy Kola) "selects" either a high or low demand. Each of the four possible combinations of plant size and demand level during the first year generates a different cash flow. At time 1 (the end of year 1), the small plant can be expanded (if that were the year 0 choice). Unfortunately, we don't know exactly what the longer-term demand will be at this point although there's somewhat less uncertainty than there was a year ago. Thus, in year 2, fate once more selects a high or low demand level with the resulting payoff depending on the particular demand–plant size combination involved. The decision tree makes it clear that the demand probabilities in year 2 depend on the actual demand in year 1. For example, the probability of a high demand in year 2 given a high demand in year 1 is 0.80, but only 0.30 if year 1 demand was low. The likelihood of BBI seeing high demand in both years is $(0.60)(0.80) = 0.48$.

Note that there are two points in time at which BBI can make decisions—now (time 0) and next year (time 1). The first decision is whether to build a large or small plant. If the large plant is built, then BBI's course is set—it can only hope that demand is high. If the decision at time 0 is to build the small plant, then BBI has another decision to make at time 1: Should it expand or just sit tight? This depends on what the first-year demand turns out to be.

One solution to the problem is to make the more distant decision first—whether or not BBI should expand its small plant next year—and then work backward to the present. This requires that we determine the expected NPV of expansion, depending on whether the first year demand turns out to be high or low. According to the numbers in Exhibit 9B-3, expansion when demand is low has an expected NPV of −$3,601,000. This is clearly dominated by the expected NPV of $1,780,000 for the no-expansion choice.

Expansion subsequent to the high demand in year 1 has an expected NPV of $6,858,000. Alternately, the no-expansion decision has an expected NPV of $4,979,000. Therefore, if you choose to build a small plant, the decision rule at time 1 is clear: If demand in year 1 is high, expand; if not, don't expand. Now that

EXHIBIT 9B-3
Decision Tree for Bubbly Beverage's New Soft Drink

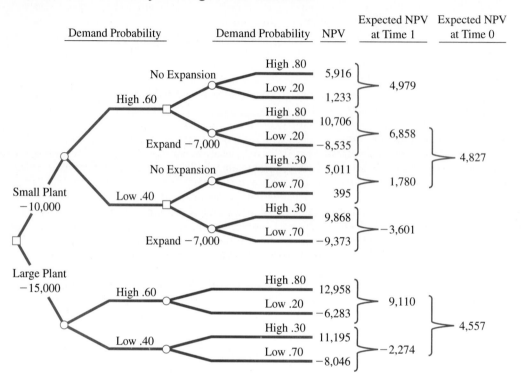

we know the optimal decisions at time 1 based on the observed demand, we can now go ahead and determine BBI's optimal decision at time 0.

The expected NPV at time zero for the small plant, given that the time 1 decisions are made optimally, is $4,827,000. If year 1 demand is low, we use the expected NPV associated with maintaining the small plant. If year 1 demand is high, we use the expected NPV associated with expansion at time 1. By contrast, the expected NPV associated with building the large plant is $4,557,000.

Thus, the expected NPV for building a small plant initially exceeds that for building the large plant by $270,000. But, if there were no option to expand, the expected NPV of the small plant would only be $3,699,000, and it would be optimal to build the large plant. This means that the option to expand, once the small plant is built, is worth $1,128,000 ($4,827,000 − $3,699,000). Before any investment, the option to expand has an expected NPV of $270,000, the difference between the expected NPVs of the optimal decisions with and without the expansion option ($4,827,000 − $4,557,000).

Decision trees are ideally suited to deal with investment projects containing imbedded options where decisions made today can have an impact on the strategic choices we have in the future. Structurally, we "solve" decision tree problems through a *folding-back process* in which we evaluate future decisions before working our way back to the present. This process forces managers to think carefully about the connections between choices over time and how they might dynamically respond to changes in their operating environment.

FINCOACH PRACTICE EXERCISES

To help you master the mathematics discussed in the chapter, open **FinCoach** on the *Prentice Hall Finance Center* CD-ROM and practice the exercises in the following categories: *1. Valuation of Multiple Cash Flows, and 2. Project and Firm Valuation.*

QUESTIONS

1. A new investment project is to demolish an existing gas station and construct a small shopping mall. Which of the items should be treated as incremental cash flows relevant to the investment decision? Explain.
   a. The current value of the land.
   b. The current value of the gasoline-retailing business.
   c. The cost of wrecking the gas station, digging up the tanks, and cleaning the land.
   d. The cost of new antipollution devices installed by order of the local government six months ago.
   e. Lost earnings on other real estate projects owing to staff time that will be spent if the mall is built.
   f. An allocated portion of the depreciation from the company's headquarters building.
   g. The fee that has already been paid to an architect for designing the mall.
   h. Future noncash expenses such as depreciation that will result if the mall is built.
   i. Allocation of corporate overhead to the project.
2. Wholesome Natural Products, Ltd., is considering an expansion of its pistachio plantation in Imperial County. Company managers are pondering how to figure overhead into the decision whether to add 500 acres to their present plantation of 1,000 acres.
   a. Presently, the company's pistachio division has operating overhead of $300,000 or $300 per acre. If the extra 500 acres are added, division overhead per acre will be reduced to $200. Should this be considered in making the decision?
   b. Additional overhead of about $50,000 will be required because of added equipment and labor needs if the extra 500 acres are added.

Should these overhead costs be considered in making the decision?
3. William Daley has just completed his doctorate in finance and wants to compute the present value of all the costs associated with his education. William spent four years obtaining a B.A. at Old Ivy University. Each year at Old Ivy cost $14,000. Two years were then spent abroad taking a master's degree at l'Université de Westmount. The cost per year was $7,000. Finally, William spent four years at Beverly Hills State University getting his Ph.D. at a cost of $9,000 per year. Given a discount rate of 10 percent, can you calculate the present value, from the point of view of William's first day in college ten years ago, of the cost of this education?
4. A soft-drink bottler is trying to determine the present value of its business in an area where it forecasts no growth in unit sales. Sales this year will be $10 million, and expenses will be $9 million. The present rate of return required is 20 percent, and inflation is expected to be 10 percent indefinitely. The company president believes that the present value of the business is $5 million, that is, $1 million per year discounted at 20 percent. His assistant argues that the present value is $1 million divided by 10 percent, the expected real interest rate. This yields an NPV of $10 million. What is the correct solution to the valuation problem?
5. In late 1985, Donald Trump, the New York real estate developer, unveiled a plan to build the tallest building in the world on Manhattan's West Side as the centerpiece of a commercial and residential complex to be known as Television City. He bought the land in 1981 for only $81 million. By 1985, its estimated value was $2 billion. "I can do things that no one else can do because I got the land so cheap," said Trump. The Donald is (was?) very rich, but is he correct?

6. Analysis of a proposed advertising campaign for an existing brand showed that the projected increase in profits (relative to that brand's current profits) will yield only a 4 percent return on investment. If the cost of capital is 12 percent, does this investment make sense? Explain.

7. Early results on the Lexus, Toyota's upscale car, showed it was taking the most business from customers changing from either BMW (15%), Mercedes (14%), Toyota (14%), General Motors' Cadillac (12%), and Ford's Lincoln (6%). With what in the auto industry is considered a high percentage of sales coming from its own customers, how badly is Toyota hurting itself with the Lexus?

8. In May 1992, IBM announced plans to resell the ultra-powerful PCs of Parallan Computer. However, according to one analyst, "In pushing into increasingly powerful and expensive PCs, IBM runs the risk of cannibalizing its own sales of mini-computers." How should this possibility be factored into IBM's investment decision?

9. Flexible manufacturing systems enable companies to respond quickly to emerging market trends and to easily accommodate product redesigns as technology changes. What is there in these advantages that sometimes leads companies applying the traditional discounted cash flow analysis to underinvest in such systems? That is, why do companies sometimes underestimate the value of flexible manufacturing systems in the sense of assigning negative NPVs to positive NPV projects?

10. Many companies are now installing marketing and sales productivity (MSP) systems that automate routine tasks and gather, update, and interpret data that were either scattered or uncollected before. These data include information about every sales lead generated, every sales task performed, and every customer prospect closed or terminated. Describe some of the direct costs and benefits that might be associated with an MSP system. What are some intangible benefits of an MSP system as well as some hidden costs of implementing such a system?

11. Comment on the following statement: "Bluntly stated, the willingness of managers to view the future through the reversed telescope of discounted cash flow analysis is seriously shortchanging the futures of their companies. . . . Beyond all else, capital investment represents an act of faith, a belief that the future will be as promising as the present, together with a commitment to making the future happen."

12. Comment on the following statement that appeared in *The Economist* (August 20, 1988, p. 60): "Those oil producers that have snapped up overseas refineries—Kuwait, Venezuela, Libya and, most recently, Saudi Arabia—can feed the flabbiest of them with dollar-a-barrel crude and make a profit. . . . The majority of OPEC's existing overseas refineries would be scrapped without its own cheap oil to feed them. Both Western European refineries fed by Libyan oil (in West Germany and Italy) and Kuwait's two overseas refineries (in Holland and Denmark) would almost certainly be idle without it."

13. Accrued pension benefits represent an obligation of a company for the past service of its employees. No current or future action can affect this obligation. The amortization of accrued pension benefits must be recognized, however, as a current expense in the company's financial statements. Many companies turn around and allocate these costs to divisions. One company allocated these costs in proportion to pension benefits accrued by its workers. A plant with an older work force received almost all of its division's accrued pension costs, adding $4 per hour to the plant's labor cost relative to the cost of several newer plants with much younger workers.

    a. How is this allocation of accrued pension benefits likely to affect future investment decisions? The competitiveness of products manufactured by the plant?

    b. Suppose that because of its high labor costs, the company decided to shut down the older plant and shift work to the newer ones. How will this decision affect the company's competitiveness?

    c. How should the company treat accrued pension benefits for investment, product sourcing, and pricing purposes?

14. Starshine Products is considering the launch of a new line of dolls on an assembly line that currently has some spare capacity. Some Starshine executives argued that because the assembly line was already paid for, its cost was sunk and should not be included in the project evaluation. Others argued that the assembly line was a scarce resource and should be priced accordingly. What cost should Starshine assign to use of the excess assembly line capacity?

15. In order to produce its new line of canned foods, Hammond Foods must purchase a specialized piece of equipment that has the capacity to fill a million cans annually. Suppose Hammond plans to initially produce 150,000 cans annually. Some executives argued that the new product line should be charged for only 15 percent of the cost of the new equipment. Others argued that it should bear the full cost of the special-purpose machinery. Who is right? Explain.

16. Some economists have stated that too many companies aren't calculating the cost of *not* investing in new technology, world-class manufacturing facilities, or market position overseas. What are some of these costs? How do these costs relate to the notion of growth options discussed in the chapter?

17. In December 1989, General Electric spent $150 million to buy a controlling interest in Tungsram, the Hungarian state-owned light bulb maker. Even in its best year, Tungsram earned less than a 4% return on equity (based on the price GE paid). What might account for GE's decision to spend so much money to acquire such a dilapidated, inefficient manufacturer?

18. Borden, already the world's largest dairy company, has made over 40 acquisitions in recent years to become the world's largest producer of pasta and the second-largest snack seller in the United States. Its basic strategy is to string together a network of regional pasta, dairy, and snack-food companies to try to take advantage of various operating and marketing efficiencies.
    a. What operating and marketing efficiencies might Borden be able to take advantage of through its acquisition strategy?
    b. What valuable options does Borden's acquisition strategy create?
    c. Borden's brand of processed lemon juice, ReaLemon, was the first in the market. What advantages might Borden be able to realize by being the pioneer in this business?

19. Historically, auto companies faced high equipment and tooling costs to develop new models. In addition, they had to shut down the production line for one to two weeks to switch over from one model to another. In order to be profitable, therefore, companies had to sell millions of copies of the same model and have long production runs, with the excess going into inventory. But consumers are no longer purchasing millions of copies of the same model; instead, they are looking for a wide—and unpredictable—variety of cars, trucks, and vans, and looking for bargains besides. In such a world, what business strategy might make sense for car companies and what investments would be consistent with this strategy?

20. Jim Toreson, chairman and CEO of Xebec Corporation, a Sunnyvale, California, manufacturer of disk-drive controllers, is trying to decide whether to switch to offshore production. Given Xebec's well-developed engineering and marketing capabilities, Toreson could use offshore manufacturing to ramp up production, taking full advantage of both low-wage labor and a grab bag of tax holidays, low-interest loans, and other government largess. Most of his competitors seemed to be doing it: The faster he followed suit, the better off Xebec would be, according to the conventional discounted cash flow analysis, which showed that switching production offshore was clearly a positive NPV investment. However, Toreson is concerned that such a move would entail the loss of certain intangible strategic benefits associated with domestic production.
    a. What might be some strategic benefits of domestic manufacturing for Xebec? Consider the fact that all its customers are American firms and that manufacturing technology—particularly automation skills—is the key to survival in this business.
    b. What analytic framework can be used to factor these intangible strategic benefits of domestic manufacturing (which are intangible *costs* of offshore production) into the factory location decision?
    c. How would the possibility of radical shifts in manufacturing technology affect the production location decision?
    d. Xebec is considering producing more sophisticated drives, which require substantial customization. How does this possibility affect its production decision?
    e. An alternative sourcing option is to shut down all domestic production and contract to have Xebec's products built for it by a foreign supplier in a country like Japan. What might be some potential advantages and disadvantages of foreign contracting vis-à-vis manufacturing in a wholly owned foreign subsidiary?

PROBLEMS

⚡ —Excel templates may be downloaded from **www. prenhall.com/financecenter.**

1. Purchase of a copying machine by a law office is expected to save the office $1,000 a year for five years. The machine will cost $5,000 and can be depreciated straight line for five years and then sold for $500. Given the law firm's tax rate of 40 percent, what are the annual cash flows arising from the purchase and what is its net present value? Assume a 10 percent discount rate.

2. What is the value of writing off a $200,000 machine immediately instead of over five years using straight-line depreciation if the appropriate discount rate is 12 percent? Assume a 35 percent tax rate.

3. TelCo must decide whether to replace a computer system with a new model. TelCo forecasts net before-tax cost savings from the new computer over five years as given below (in $000). It has a 12 percent cost of capital, a 35 percent tax rate, and uses straight-line depreciation. ⚡

Year	1	2	3	4	5
	$350	$350	$300	$300	$300

a. The new computer costs $1 million, but TelCo is eligible for a 15 percent investment tax credit (ITC) in the first year. The ITC reduces Telco's taxes by an amount equal to 15 percent of the equipment's purchase price. In addition, the old computer can be sold for $450,000. If the old computer originally cost $1.25 million and is three years old (depreciable, not economic, life is five years), what is the *net* investment required in the new system? Assume that there was no ITC on the old computer and that both computers are being depreciated to a zero salvage value.

b. Estimate the incremental operating cash flows associated with the new system.

c. If the new computer's salvage value at the end of five years is projected to be $100,000, should TelCo purchase it?

4. New diesel locomotives will cost a railroad $600,000 each and can be depreciated straight line over their five-year life. Using a diesel instead of a coal-fired steam locomotive will save $12,000 annually in operating expenses. Railroads have a required rate of return of 10 percent and a tax rate of 40 percent.

a. What is the maximum price a railroad would be willing to pay for a coal-fired steam locomotive? (*Hint:* Set up the cash flows for a coal-fired locomotive at a price of P, including depreciation, and then compare them to the incremental cash flows associated with a diesel costing $600,000.)

b. Will your answer to (a) change if the railroad has enormous tax-loss carryforwards that put it in a zero taxpaying position for the foreseeable future?

5. GTX sells 100,000 inexpensive telephones per year. Currently, GTX supplies its own components for the inside of the phone but buys the plastic phone body from outside suppliers for $1 a unit. GTX estimates that it could reduce the cost of the plastic body to $.75 a unit by producing it in-house. This would require buying a machine costing $75,000. The new machine would be eligible for a 10 percent investment tax credit and could be depreciated straight line over its eight-year life. If GTX begins to manufacture its own plastic phone bodies, additional working capital will be required. Management has not yet estimated how much extra working capital will be needed. Given a tax rate of 34 percent and discount rate of 9 percent, calculate the *maximum amount* of working capital GTX could commit before additions to working capital make the project undesirable. ⚡

6. Varico produces HO-scale trains, including a diesel locomotive that sells 100,000 units annually. Each unit requires an electric motor. Presently these are purchased once a week from a local manufacturer for $10 apiece. However, a foreign firm has offered to sell Varico a container of 100,000 motors of like quality for only $9.50 apiece. Given a discount rate of 15 percent, what should Varico do?

7. In building a new facility for producing trucks, International Truck (IT) must estimate the total investment required. In the current year, IT estimates it will acquire land for the plant at $1,000,000 and modify existing plant equipment

for $123,000. Next year, construction will begin and require $866,000, and further plant modifications will require $344,000. In addition, new equipment worth $140,000 will be purchased (with a 10 percent investment tax credit). The new equipment will require $250,000 of installation expense. Finally, in the next year, construction will be completed at a cost of $750,000; installation charges will total $229,000; and building modifications will require $350,000. Lastly, more new equipment will be purchased for $230,000 (with a 10 percent ITC). With a cost of capital of 10 percent, what is the present value of the initial investment required for the plant? ✖

8. Yankee Atomic Electric Co. announced in 1992 that it would decommission its Yankee Rowe nuclear plant at an estimated cost of $247 million. The cost includes: (1) $32 million to maintain the plant until 2000, when dismantling will begin. These expenses will accrue at the rate of $4 million a year. (2) $56.5 million for the cost of building a facility to store its spent fuel until it is shipped in 2000 to a permanent repository. This storage facility will be depreciated straight line over its eight-year estimated life. (3) $158.5 million for the cost of dismantling the plant in 2000 and disposing of its nuclear wastes.

At the same time, Yankee Atomic estimated that decommissioning the plant in 1992, eight years earlier than its planned retirement in 2000, will save it $116 million ($14.5 million a year) before tax by enabling the utility to purchase cheaper electricity than Yankee Rowe could provide. In addition, Yankee Atomic said it had accumulated $72 million in a decommissioning fund required by the Nuclear Regulatory Commission. ✖

a. What is the present value of Yankee's $247 million decommissioning cost? Assume a cost of capital equal to 12 percent and a 35 percent tax rate.

b. Taking into account the savings on the purchase of cheaper electricity, and the $72 million already set aside, how much additional money does Yankee Atomic have to set aside in 1992 to have enough money to pay for the decommissioning expense?

c. What other factors might you consider in calculating the cost of decommissioning?

9. Specialty Steel Products (SSP) is considering replacing some of its machinery with a new flexible machining center (FMC) that will permit it to respond more quickly to changes in the marketplace. The price of the new equipment is $1.2 million. Base your analysis on the following data contained in SSP's capital authorization request: (1) Because the new system will boost output quality significantly, it is estimated that SSP's annual sales will rise somewhat from its current level of $1.7 million to $1.8 million annually for the next five years. The before-tax and before-depreciation profit margin on SSP's sales, old and new, is estimated at 40 percent. (2) Working capital requirements are estimated to remain at 25 percent of sales. (3) The FMC will also cut overhead costs by $90,000 per year for the next five years. (4) The old machinery was purchased for $1 million three years ago and is being depreciated on a straight-line basis over its 5-year life. Its economic life as of today, however, is estimated to be five years. It can be sold for $300,000 today. (5) The FMC will be depreciated on a straight-line basis over its 5-year life. (6) SSP faces a 34 percent corporate tax rate. (7) Given the relatively low risk of the revenue enhancement and cost savings, SSP estimates that the incremental cash flows generated by the FMC will have a cost of capital of only 10.7 percent as compared to 14 percent for a typical company project. The risk-free interest rate is currently 8 percent. (8) SSP will receive an investment tax credit equal to 10 percent of the purchase price of the FMC. (9) The working capital will be recaptured at the end of five years.

a. What is SSP's *net* investment required in the FMC? Assume that both pieces of equipment are being depreciated to a zero salvage value.

b. What are the operating cash flows for each of the next five years?

c. Based on the information supplied, should SSP replace its current equipment with the new system?

d. What questions might you raise about some of the assumptions implicit in SSP's capital authorization request?

10. Molecugen has developed a new kind of cardiac diagnostic unit. Owing to the highly competitive nature of the market, the sales department forecasts demand of 5,000 units in the first year and a decrease in demand of 10 percent a year after that. After five years, the project will be discontinued with no salvage value aside from the recovery of

remaining working capital. The marketing department forecasts a sales price of $15,000 a unit. Production estimates manufacturing cost of $5,000 a unit, and the finance department estimates general and administrative expenses of $15 million a year. The initial investment is estimated at $60 million. Working capital requirements are estimated at 30 percent of sales.

a. Is the new project acceptable at a cost of capital of 10 percent? (*Note:* Use straight-line depreciation over the life of the project and a tax rate of 35 percent.)

b. If the marketing department had forecast a decline of 15 percent a year in demand, would the project be acceptable?

c. If the marketing department had forecast a decline in sales price of 10 percent a year, along with the 15 percent annual decline in demand predicted in (b), would the project be acceptable?

d. If prices decline by 10 percent a year, the marketing department estimates that demand will be a constant 5,000 units a year. Is the project acceptable?

11. Salterell Textiles is considering replacing the looming equipment in its North Carolina mill. The original purchase price was $79,300 two years ago. The machine has a useful life of ten years and is being depreciated using the straight-line method. The old equipment can be sold today for $10,800. The new equipment costs $80,500 and has an eight-year life. Its salvage value is expected to be $8,000. The new equipment is expected to increase output and sales revenue by $9,000 a year (after tax) and reduce costs by $7,500 (after tax).

a. With a tax rate of 35 percent and a 14 percent cost of capital, what should Salterell's decision be?

b. Would a 10 percent ITC change the analysis?

c. If an inflation rate of 7 percent a year must be incorporated into the decision, is the project acceptable? Assume that all costs and revenues increase at the rate of inflation.

12. Ross Designs is thinking of replacing its seven-year-old knitting machine with a new one that can also emboss designs on cloth. This will allow Ross to sell its textiles, which currently wholesale for $1.20 a yard, for $.07 a yard more. The embossing should also raise sales 15 percent, to 2.07

million yards annually. The new machine costs $320,000, has annual operating costs of $27,000, and is expected to last for eight years. Labor, materials, and other expenses are estimated to rise by $.02, to $1.10 per yard. Working-capital requirements should remain at 30 percent of sales. All working-capital investments will be recaptured in eight years. The current machine was purchased for $190,000 and is being depreciated on a straight-line basis assuming a 10-year life. Its economic life as of today, however, is estimated to be eight years, the same as that of the new machine. It can be sold for $70,000 today or for an estimated salvage value of $5,000 in eight years. The new machine will be depreciated straight line over a five-year period and has an estimated salvage value of $20,000 in eight years. The appropriate discount rate is estimated at 12 percent.

a. What is the NPV of the acquisition of the new knitting machine? Should Ross buy it?

b. Suppose that all prices and costs are in nominal terms and will increase at the rate of inflation, which is projected at 4 percent. How does the analysis in parts (a) through (d) change? The 12 percent discount rate is expressed in nominal terms as well.

13. KleenCote uses a 20 percent discount rate in assessing capital investments. One of KleenCote's capital authorization requests contains the following data:

Alternative 1: Rebuild present machines

Year	1	2
Sales	$2,240	$2,240
Cost of sales		
Labor	59	59
Material	109	109
Overhead	545	545

3	4	5	... 10
$2,240	$2,240	$2,240	$2,240
59	59	59	59
109	109	109	109
545	545	545	545

Alternative 2: Purchase new machines

Year	1	2
Sales	$2,240	$2,352
Cost of sales		
Labor	58	54
Material	109	114
Overhead	545	504

3	4	5	... 10
$2,470	$2,593	$2,723	$2,723
52	53	53	53
120	126	132	132
487	498	498	498

The figures for alternative 2 assume somewhat higher sales in anticipation of a small increase in market share owing to higher-quality output from the new machines. Because of its tax-loss carry-forwards, KleenCote is able to ignore depreciation and taxes. ✎

a. Suppose that alternative 1 costs $8,000 and alternative 2 costs $10,000. Based on the numbers above and assuming a 20 percent discount rate, which investment is preferable?
b. Suppose that the 20 percent discount rate contains an implicit forecast of 10 percent inflation. Reevaluate the project. (*Hint:* Reconsider the sales and cost projections.)
c. What other implicit assumptions contained in KleenCote's capital authorization request might be challenged?

14. G. D. Sorrell is developing an anticancer drug. The project is in its preliminary stage. G.D.S. must decide whether to initiate a large-scale drug test costing $1.5 million a year for two years. If the test results are positive, a $17.5 million plant to produce the drug for commercial trials will be built at the end of the testing period. If commercial sales of the drug meet the company's forecast for the next two years, the plant will be expanded at a cost of $50 million to produce the drug in quantity. The cash flows resulting from this larger plant are expected to be $18 million a year for eight years after it is built. The following are the relevant cash flows associated with the three possible scenarios. Assume these cash flows

take taxes, depreciation, and working capital into account. ✎

Year	0	1	2
Scenario 1	($1,500)*	($1,500)	Unsuccessful
Scenario 2	(1,500)	(1,500)	(17,500)
Scenario 3	(1,500)	(1,500)	(17,500)

3	4	5–12
$3,000	$2,000	Unsuccessful
5,000	7,500	9,500
	(50,000)	

*Cash flows in $000.

a. With a cost of capital of 10 percent, value the research project using DCF analysis. Is the project acceptable? (Assume the two plants are built.)
b. Assuming that the three possible scenarios have equal probability, is the project acceptable? (*Hint:* Value this project as a growth option.)

15. An oil company has paid $100,000 for the right to pump oil on a plot of land during the next three years. A well has already been sunk, and all other necessary facilities are in place. The land has known reserves of 60,000 barrels. The company wishes to know the market value of this operation. The interest rate is 8 percent, and the marginal cost of pumping is $8 per barrel. Both of these costs are expected to remain unchanged over the three-year period. The current price of oil is $10 per barrel. Company economists have estimated the following: (1) Oil will increase in price by 10 percent with a probability of 40 percent, or decrease in price by 12 percent with a probability of 60 percent during each of the next three years. (2) The cost of storing oil in aboveground tanks is $.50 per year. (3) The company can pump a maximum of 20,000 barrels per year at the site. (4) The site may be shut down for a year and then reopened at a cost of $2,000.

Determine the market value of the operation ignoring taxes. Assume that all cash flows occur at the end of each year and that all oil pumped during the year is sold at the price prevailing at the end of the year. (*Hint:* Chart all possible sequences of oil prices, and calculate the optimal production decisions and payoffs associated with each sequence.)

REFERENCES

Baldwin, C. Y., S. P. Mason, and R. S. Ruback. "Evaluation of Government Subsidies to Large Scale Energy Projects: A Contingent Claims Approach." Harvard Business School Working Paper, 1983.

Hayes, R. H., and D. A. Garvin. "Managing as If Tomorrow Mattered." *Harvard Business Review,* May–June 1982, 70–79.

Nelson, C. R. "Inflation and Capital Budgeting." *Journal of Finance,* June 1976, 923–931.

Porter, M. E. "How Competitive Forces Shape Strategy." *Harvard Business Review,* March–April 1979, 137–145.

Robichek, A. A., and J. C. Van Horne. "Abandonment Value and Capital Budgeting." *Journal of Finance,* December 1967, 557–589.

Shapiro, A. C. "Corporate Strategy and the Capital Budgeting Decision." *Midland Corporate Finance Journal,* Spring 1985, 22–36.

Shapiro, A. C. "Corporate Strategy and the Capital Budgeting Decision." Working Paper, School of Business Administration, University of Southern California, August 1995.

Van Horne, J. C. "A Note on the Biases in Capital Budgeting Introduced by Inflation." *Journal of Financial and Quantitative Analysis,* March 1971, 653–658.

Establishing Required Rates of Return

If a man will begin with certainties, he shall end in doubts, but if he will be content to begin with doubts, he shall end in certainties.
Francis Bacon

KEY TERMS

adjusted net present value (APV)
cost of debt capital
cost of equity capital
cost of preferred stock
equity beta

equity residual (ER) method
flotation cost
hurdle rate
leveraged buyout (LBO)
marginal cost

pure-play technique
target capital structure
unlevered or asset beta
weighted average cost of capital (WACC)

CHAPTER LEARNING OBJECTIVES

Upon completion of this chapter, students should be able to:

- Describe the relationship between risk and the cost of capital for a project.
- Explain the relationship among the weighted average cost of capital (WACC), the expected return on a project, and the expected return on the equity-financed portion of the project.
- Calculate the WACC for a company.
- Calculate the risk-adjusted required rate of return for a project or a division of a firm using the pure-play technique.
- Identify and avoid the common errors made in using the CAPM to estimate risk-adjusted costs of capital.

- Value a leveraged buyout (LBO) using the adjusted present value (APV) approach.
- Compare and contrast the WACC, APV, and equity residual approaches to capital budgeting.
- Identify the circumstances under which the cost of capital for foreign investments should be higher, lower, or the same as comparable domestic projects.

As we indicated in Chapters 8 and 9, the NPV of a project is dependent on both its expected cash flows and the rate at which those future cash flows are discounted. Up to this point, we have assumed that we know the discount rate and have focused our attention on the challenges of estimating project cash flows. In this chapter, we'll address the question of how to estimate the discount rate, also known as the *cost of capital* for an investment. Without this required rate of return as a financial standard, we can't make the informed investment decisions that will enhance shareholder value.

The cost of capital for a project is the minimum risk-adjusted return required by shareholders of the firm for undertaking that project. As such, it is the basic measure of financial performance. Unless the investment generates sufficient funds to repay the suppliers of capital, the firm's value will suffer. This return requirement can be met only if the net present value of future project cash flows, using the project's cost of capital as the discount rate, is positive. Thus, the emphasis here is on estimating the required rate of return for a specific project rather than for the firm as a whole.

This rate must take account of both the time value of money, measured by the risk-free rate of return, and the riskiness of the project's cash flows. As we will see, the key to measuring project risk is the capital asset pricing model and its focus on systematic or beta risk. In particular, when the systematic risk of a project is the same as the systematic risk of the firm, the firm's cost of capital is the correct discount rate. When systematic risk is similar for projects within each division but is different across divisions, a divisional cost of capital is appropriate. A project with risk characteristics that differ from the corporate or divisional norm will have its own unique cost of capital.

We'll begin with a discussion of the relationship between a project's riskiness and its cost of capital before moving on to the mechanics of estimating a company's overall cost of capital. As you will see, calculating the costs of various sources of long-term funds builds heavily on the valuation principles developed in Chapters 5 and 6. We then examine the pure-play technique as a way of developing required rates of return for divisions of firms or individual projects with a risk that is different from that of the firm as a whole. With this background, we can explore some issues associated with project valuation and financing side effects. The chapter concludes with a discussion of the international dimensions of cost of capital.

10.1   RISK AND THE COST OF CAPITAL FOR A PROJECT

A project's required return should reflect the real interest rate, an inflation premium, and a premium for risk.

Each project has its own required return, reflecting three basic elements: (1) the *real* or inflation-adjusted risk-free interest rate, (2) an inflation premium equal to the amount of expected inflation, and (3) a premium for risk. The first two elements are shared by all projects and reflect the time value of money, but the third element varies according to the risks borne by investors in the different projects. For a project to be acceptable to a company's shareholders, its returns must compensate them for all three components. This *minimum* or *required return* is the project's *cost of capital* and is sometimes referred to as the project's **hurdle rate.**

The preceding paragraph bears a crucial message: *The cost of capital for a project depends on the riskiness of the assets being financed, not on the identity of the firm undertaking the project.* As we saw in Chapter 6, the risk-return tradeoff is set in the financial markets and depends on yields available on other investments with similar risk characteristics. Therefore, the required rate of return on a project (the project's cost of capital) is an opportunity cost that depends on the alternative market investments of similar risk that investors must forgo. In short, the required rates of return on corporate investments are set not by management but in the financial markets.

> A project's cost of capital is a weighted average of the after-tax costs for different sources of financing.

One way of looking at a project's cost of capital is as a weighted average after-tax cost of the different sources of permanent (long-term) capital that the firm will use to finance the project. The logic behind this **weighted average cost of capital (WACC)** is that for a project to be acceptable to the firm's shareholders, it must generate a stream of returns sufficient to compensate its suppliers of capital in proportion to the amount and cost of capital supplied by each. As long as this criterion is satisfied—that is, the expected rate of return on a project (its IRR) exceeds its WACC—then the expected return on the equity-financed portion of the project will exceed the required rate of return on equity, and shareholder value will be created. Therefore, accepting projects with a positive NPV when the WACC is used as the discount rate will also ensure that expected returns to equity will exceed shareholders' required returns.

> If a project's IRR exceeds its WACC, then the expected return on the equity-financed portion will exceed the shareholder's required rate of return.

To explore the WACC concept in numerical terms, let's examine a $1 million expansion project being considered by the Wingler Iron Works. The company wants to finance future projects with half long-term debt and half common stock. The after-tax cost of newly-issued debt is estimated at 6 percent, and Wingler's shareholders are assumed to require a return of at least 15 percent on projects of similar risk. This 15 percent shareholder required rate of return is Wingler's cost of equity capital.

In general, the WACC is

$$\begin{array}{l}(\text{After-Tax Cost of Debt}) \times (\text{Proportion of Debt}) \\ + (\text{Cost of Preferred Stock}) \times (\text{Proportion of Preferred Stock}) \\ \underline{+ (\text{Cost of Common Stock}) \times (\text{Proportion of Common Stock})} \\ = \text{Weighted Average Cost of Capital (WACC)}\end{array}$$

Mathematically, the WACC for any firm, division, or project can be expressed as:

$$WACC = k_d^* w_d + k_p w_p + k_e w_e \qquad [10\text{-}1]$$

where k_d^* is the after-tax cost of debt; k_p, the cost of preferred stock; k_e, the cost of equity capital; and w_d, w_p, and w_e are the proportions of debt, preferred, and common stock that will be used to finance accepted projects. In the case of Wingler Iron Works, the WACC would be

$$WACC = 6\%\,(0.50) + 15\%\,(0.50) = 10.5\% \qquad [10\text{-}1a]$$

Using the WACC as a target rate of return indicates that Wingler should go ahead with the expansion if the expected return on the project exceeds 10.5 percent.

Why? Because if the project's expected return exceeds 10.5 percent, then the expected return on the equity-financed portion will exceed 15 percent—the required return on equity.

To see how all of this plays out from the common stockholders' standpoint, let's simplify our world by assuming that project returns are perpetuities.[1] Exhibit 10-1 illustrates the connection between project returns, the WACC, and the return on the equity-financed portion of the project for a range of expected rates of return. Because the cash flows from the project were assumed to be perpetuities, the annual after-tax cash flows are just the expected return on the project times the investment's cost of $1 million. The expected annual cash flow estimates ignore financing costs such as the interest on borrowed money and, therefore, represent cash that would be available to compensate all sources of capital. Since the $1 million project will be financed with half debt and half common stock, the $30,000 interest expense reflects the cost of borrowing $500,000 at a 6 percent after-tax rate. This interest must be paid regardless of how the project turns out.

Exhibit 10-1 shows that if Wingler expects a return that is exactly equal to the 10.5 percent WACC calculated using Equation [10-1], then its shareholders should earn exactly their 15 percent required return. With an expected return of 10.5 percent, cash flows generated by the project will be $105,000 (0.105 times the $1 million initial investment). Subtracting the $30,000 annual interest expense from the expected project cash flow leaves a "residual" return of $75,000 to common stockholders. Because shareholders "kicked in" $500,000 to finance the project, the return on the equity-financed portion is 15 percent ($75,000/ $500,000). Under these circumstances, the shareholders would be no better or no worse off if the project were accepted because expected and required returns to equity are identical. When the project's return is below its WACC, at 5 percent or even at 9.0 percent, expected returns to equity are lower than the required return of 15 percent. This contrasts to the case in which a 13 percent return on the project results in a return on the equity-financed portion of the project that far exceeds the return required by common stockholders. Exhibit 10-1 also indicates some of the costs and benefits of leverage, a topic to which we'll return in Chapter 14.

> The cash flows to be discounted by the WACC should ignore financing costs.

EXHIBIT 10-1
Wingler Iron Works Expansion Project
Project Returns and Returns to Equity

Expected Project Returns	5.0%	9.0%	10.5%	13.0%
Expected Annual Cash Flows	$50,000	$90,000	$105,000	$130,000
Annual Interest Expense	(30,000)	(30,000)	(30,000)	(30,000)
Equity Cash Flows	$20,000	$60,000	$75,000	$100,000
Return on Equity-Financed Portion	4.0%	12.0%	15.0%	20.0%

---

[1]Recall from our discussion of the time value of money that a perpetuity is just a series of cash flows of a constant amount that goes on forever.

Exhibit 10-1 demonstrates that companies can make investment decisions by comparing either (1) the project's return to the WACC or (2) the expected returns to equity with the cost of equity capital. Either way, you arrive at the same accept-reject decision. As a practical matter, it is generally more convenient to use the WACC approach, which embodies the firm or project's financing mix, as the required rate of return for making investment decisions.

10.2   ESTIMATING THE FIRM'S WEIGHTED AVERAGE COST OF CAPITAL

Suppose a new project involves an across-the-board expansion of a firm's existing product lines. The risk of the investment is identical to that of the company, so a corporatewide weighted average cost of capital can serve as a proxy for the project's required return. This required return is the *cost of capital for the firm*. Calculating the firm's cost of capital using Equation [10-1] is mathematically simple. The trick is to develop reasonable estimates for the costs of various sources of permanent financing and then to weight these in a way that reflects the firm's future financing mix. In this section, we will develop some approaches to calculating these component costs. When combined with the firm's target capital structure, the WACC so obtained can be used to value projects whose risk is similar to that of the firm as a whole.

The Cost of Equity Capital

Using the share-holders' required return as the cost of equity allows managers to make decisions in the same way as common stockholders.

The **cost of equity capital** is the required rate of return on common stock and, as such, represents the minimum acceptable rate of return on the equity-financed portion of new projects. Defining the cost of equity in this way is consistent with the idea of establishing a financial standard that would lead the company to the same decisions that common stockholders would make if they had the same information and the same investment opportunities.

One can estimate the cost of equity (k_e) with the constant dividend growth model:

$$P_0 = \frac{D_1}{(k_e - g)} \qquad [10\text{-}2]$$

where P_0 is the current stock price; D_1, the expected dividend in year 1; and g, the expected compound annual dividend growth rate. Rearranging Equation [10-2], we get

$$k_e = \frac{D_1}{P_0} + g \qquad [10\text{-}2a]$$

The reason for using Equation [10-2a] is to get at something that we can't measure directly—the common stockholders' required rate of return—by using current stock prices (which can be directly observed) and investor expectations of dividend growth rates, which we can try to estimate using historical information.

Illustration

Suppose that you are on the financial staff of DuPont (DD), and your boss has asked you to calculate the firm's cost of equity capital as the company goes into its 1998 capital budgeting year. One approach is to use the dividend growth model. The most critical input to this model is the dividend growth rate. You decide to base your forecast of future dividend growth on DuPont's recent dividend payment history.

A look at the historical record indicates that DuPont's dividends grew at a compound annual rate of 14.5 percent over the 15-year period from 1982 through 1997. The company paid dividends of $1.23 a share in 1997 ($D_0 = \$1.23$), and the stock price was $60.06 a share on December 31,1997. If future dividends are expected to grow at their historical rate, then the dividends *expected* for 1998 would be $D_1 = D_0(1 + g) = \$1.23(1.145) = \$1.41$. With these inputs, you would calculate DD's cost of equity as 16.8 percent:

$$k_e = \frac{\$1.41}{\$60.06} + 0.145 = 0.168 = 16.8 \text{ Percent}$$

Using the constant dividend growth model to estimate the cost of equity capital assumes that investors believe that dividends will grow forever at a fixed rate.

Using the constant dividend growth model to estimate the cost of equity capital has some clear limitations. Most important, it assumes that investors believe that the firm's dividends will grow at a constant rate into the indefinite future. This is probably a reasonable assumption for a company like DD, which has a long history of nondecreasing dividends. However, Equation [10-2a] is inappropriate for companies that pay no dividends or for firms in which dividend payments have been unstable. Aside from these considerations, some companies' historical growth rates are clearly not sustainable. For example, a firm's dividends may have grown more rapidly than its earnings. This can't continue indefinitely because dividend payouts will eventually reach and exceed 100 percent of earnings. In these instances, the past growth rate of earnings may provide a more reasonable estimate of future dividend growth.

The capital asset pricing model can be used to estimate a firm's cost of equity.

As an alternative to the constant dividend growth model, the financial staff at DD might want to use the capital asset pricing model (CAPM). Recall from our discussion of risk and value, that the CAPM specifies the following relationship between risk and required returns for individual securities:

$$k_e = r_f + \beta_i(r_m - r_f) \qquad [10\text{-}3]$$

where r_f is the risk-free rate; β_i, the beta for the firm's common stock, and $(r_m - r_f)$, a market risk premium that is the difference between the expected return on the market as a whole (r_m) and the expected risk-free rate.

In terms of generating input data for Equation [10-3], there is rather broad agreement that returns on U.S. Treasury securities should be used as the risk-free rate. Because investment projects tend to be long term in nature, the interest rate on 10- or 30-year U.S. Treasury bonds would be preferred.[2] The 30-year Treasury bond rate in January 1998 was about 6.0 percent.

Beta (β) is the common stock's systematic risk with respect to the market. A company can certainly calculate the beta for its common stock, but this is unnecessary. Investment advisory services, such as the *Value Line Investment Survey* and Standard & Poor's as well as brokerage firms such as Merrill Lynch, publish betas for virtually all publicly-traded firms. Value Line's estimate of DD's beta was 1.10.

The market risk premium ($r_m - r_f$) is most often estimated using historical data. Although the CAPM is an expectational model, the basic assumption in using realized returns is that, on average, investors get what they expect. Therefore, observing realized risk premiums over a long enough period of time can provide a "reasonable" estimate of expected risk premiums. For example, the data in Chapter 6 indicated that the average rate of return for large-firm stocks from 1926–1997 was 13.0 percent,[3] and returns on Treasury bonds over the same period were 5.6 percent. Therefore, a large company such as DD might set a market risk premium relative to Treasury bonds of 7.4 percent.

Using these inputs, the cost of capital for DD using the SML is

$$k_e = 6.00\% + 1.1(7.4\%) = 14.14\%$$

Different procedures for calculating the cost of equity can produce different estimates.

This number differs from the 16.8 percent cost of common stock estimated earlier with the constant dividend growth model. The discrepancies between the two values reflect the potential errors inherent in any estimating process. As a practical matter, DD's financial staff would recognize that neither figure represents the "true" cost of common stock and might use 15.5 percent—a simple average of the two numbers rounded up to the nearest half percent—as its estimate of the cost of equity capital.[4]

---

[2]A good argument for using the Treasury bond rather than the Treasury bill rate can be found in Seitz and Ellison (1995).

[3]See Ibbotson Associates (1998).

[4]As an alternative to the constant dividend growth model and the CAPM, some managers use their firm's earnings yield (earnings per share divided by the market price per share) as an estimate of the cost of equity capital. The rationale is that the price per share is the amount that will be received from selling new shares, and the earnings per share is the amount that must be earned on the new equity raised in order to avoid dilution of earnings per share.

The earnings yield is a dreadful way of estimating the cost of equity capital. First, it's based on accounting income rather than cash flows. Making investment decisions by comparing a project's rate of return based on cash flows with a financial standard based (in part) on accounting income makes no sense. Further, the measure is based on earnings per share for a past period, but the stock price is influenced by investors' growth expectations. In times of rapidly rising stock prices, the earnings yield for "growth" stocks may be on the order of 2–3 percent. Does this mean that these companies should issue new common stock to finance projects which earn no more than 2 or 3 percent? Clearly not, because shareholders can do better, with far less risk, by investing in short-term Treasury securities.

The Cost of Debt Capital

The basis for esti-
mating the cost of
debt is the interest
rate on *new* debt.

Estimating the cost of debt capital is relatively straightforward because interest rates are directly observable. Because the firm is trying to determine the required return on new projects, the basis for estimating the cost of debt is the interest rate on any new debt. The fact that a company could issue long-term debt 30 years ago at an interest rate of 6.0 percent is not relevant; what matters is the rate it will have to pay on newly issued debt.

Because interest expense on borrowed money is tax deductible, the cost of debt must be adjusted for taxes to reflect the true cost to the issuer. In general, the cost of debt capital (k_d^*) is

$$k_d^* = k_d(1 - \tau) \qquad [10\text{-}4]$$

The cost of debt is
the yield to matu-
rity on new debt,
adjusted for the
tax deductibility
of interest
payments.

where k_d is the yield to maturity on new debt sold, and τ is the firm's tax rate. Equation [10-4] indicates that as long as the firm is profitable, the after-tax cost of debt will be less than two-thirds of its pre-tax cost.[5] On the other hand, firms with large losses, which will be in a no-tax situation into the foreseeable future, will have a relatively high after-tax cost of debt.

A company can estimate the yield to maturity on new debt in a variety of ways. If the firm already has publicly-traded bonds with characteristics (e.g., maturity, callability, etc.) that are similar to the new debt envisioned, then the yield to maturity for these existing issues can serve as an estimate for the coupon rate the firm would have to offer on new debt. For example, DD has a callable bond issue maturing in 2022 with a coupon rate of 8.25 percent. On December 31, 1997, the bond was selling at $108.375 per $100 face, making its yield to maturity 7.49 percent. This tells us that if DD wanted to issue new callable long-term bonds (i.e., bonds with a 20–40 year maturity), it would have to offer a coupon rate of about 7.50 percent in order for the bonds to sell at par value. If the company had a 35 percent tax rate, its cost of debt would be

$$k_d^* = 7.50(1 - 0.35) = 4.88 \text{ percent}$$

If a firm had no publicly traded debt, it would have to use the yields on other firms with comparable credit quality. In the case of DD, it might look at the bond yields of other large chemical companies for guidance.

The Cost of Preferred Stock

The cost of pre-
ferred stock is its
dividend yield.

The **cost of preferred stock** (k_p) is equal to its dividend yield or

$$k_p = \frac{D_p}{P_p} \qquad [10\text{-}5]$$

where D_p is the preferred stock dividend (per share), and P_p is the price per share of the proposed stock issue. Equation [10-5] assumes that the preferred stock

---

[5]This assumes a 34 percent tax rate.

dividend is a perpetuity. Unlike debt, no tax adjustment is necessary since preferred stock dividends are paid from after-tax dollars.

Like the cost of debt, companies can determine their cost of preferred stock by looking at the market yields on existing issues. For instance, DD has a preferred stock issue paying a dividend of $4.50 a share. The issue was selling at $83.50 a share on December 31, 1997, making its yield

$$k_p = \frac{\$4.50}{\$83.50} = 5.39 \text{ percent}$$

This is DD's cost of preferred, and it tells the company that if it wants to incorporate preferred stock as part of its target capital structure, the combination of dividend payment and offering price must provide investors with a return of at least 5.39 percent.

Putting It Together

> The WACC should be a marginal cost reflecting the cost of raising new capital.

> The target capital structure is the mix of funds that a firm intends to use to finance accepted projects.

The WACC for DuPont (or any other company for that matter) should be a **marginal cost**, reflecting the cost of raising new capital to finance new investments. This means that the component cost of financing for each source of capital must equal the required return on new capital, not the past cost of raising capital from that source. It also means that the proportions used in calculating the WACC must reflect the firm's **target capital structure**—the mix of funds based on market values that it intends to use in financing accepted projects—not its historical debt-equity mix. As we'll see in Chapter 14, the choice of a firm's target capital structure is an important policy decision and should be selected with an eye toward maximizing shareholder value.

Using the target capital structure as a basis for computing the WACC doesn't mean that the firm should finance all projects in every year with the same financing mix. The target capital structure is, after all, a target—a set of policy guidelines around which annual tactical decisions are made. As a practical matter, companies raise capital in "chunks" and use either debt, preferred stock, or common stock in any given capital budgeting period. Therefore, the proportions called for in the target capital structure may not hold in a given year. However, over time, most firms can (and should) adhere to the guidelines developed.

Let's assume that DD's current financing mix is considered optimal. The book values for the company's long-term borrowings, preferred stock, and common stock are presented in Exhibit 10-2.

To serve as an estimate for DD's target capital structure, these balance sheet amounts must be converted into market values wherever possible. Exhibit 10-3 illustrates this process. The proportions in the right-hand column are calculated by simply dividing the market values of each source by the total market value. As we can see, DD's capital structure is dominated by common stock once we convert book into market values.

As shown in Exhibit 10-4, combining the proportions in Exhibit 10-3 with the component costs calculated earlier leads to an estimated WACC of 14.639

EXHIBIT 10-2
DuPont Company
Book Value of Long-Term Capital
December 31, 1997
(in million $)

Long-Term Borrowing	$ 5,929
Preferred Stock	
$4.50 Series; 1,672,294 shares	167
$3.50 Series; 700,000 shares	70
Common Stock	
1,152,762,128 shares	11,033

Source: DuPont's 1997 balance sheet as presented on its Web site.

EXHIBIT 10-3
DuPont Company
Market Values and Proportions of Long-Term Capital

	Market Value (in millions $)	Proportions
Long-Term Borrowings*	$ 5,929	0.079
Preferred Stock[†]	187	0.002
Common Stock[‡]	69,235	0.919
	$75,351	1.000

*DuPont's long-term borrowings include a number of publicly-traded bond issues, bonds placed with financial institutions, plus the value of capital lease obligations. For simplicity, book values and market values were assumed to be the same.
[†]On December 31, 1997, the $3.50 and $4.50 series preferred stock issues sold for $66.50 and $83.50 a share, respectively. The market value for the $3.50 series was, therefore, $47 million (700,000 shares @ $66.50 a share), and the market value for the $4.50 series was $140 million (1,672,294 shares @ $83.50 a share).
[‡]1,152,762,128 common shares outstanding on December 31, 1997, and a price per share of $60.06.

EXHIBIT 10-4
Calculating DuPont's Cost of Capital

	(1)	×	(2)	=	(3)
Source	Component Cost		Proportion		Weighted Cost*
Debt	4.88%		0.079		0.384%
Preferred Stock	5.40		0.002		0.013
Common Stock	15.50		0.919		14.242
					WACC = 14.639%

*These are exact figures, without the rounding in columns 1 and 2.

percent. DD can use this estimate as a financial standard for any project that has risk characteristics that are similar to those of the firm as a whole.

Flotation Costs

> Flotation costs can raise the effective costs of raising capital.

Up to this point, we have ignored the costs of selling new debt, preferred stock, and common stock issues. These **flotation costs** involve the various legal, administrative, and selling expenses associated with bringing a new issue to market and can range from less than 1 percent of gross proceeds for debt issues to over 20 percent for common stock issues of lesser-known firms.

One way to deal with flotation costs is to adjust component costs (k') using the following formula:

$$k' = \frac{k}{(1 - F)} \qquad [10\text{-}6]$$

where k is the component cost without considering flotation costs, and F, the flotation cost as a proportion of gross proceeds. For example, if the firm's estimate of its cost of equity is 15 percent and flotation costs are 10 percent of gross proceeds, the cost of equity, adjusted for issue costs, would be 16.67 percent [$15\%/(1 - .1)$]. An alternative approach is to simply include the flotation costs as part of the project's initial outlay. Although there are some sound theoretical arguments for handling flotation costs this way,[6] it may be difficult to assign specific flotation costs to specific projects, particularly if the company raises capital today in anticipation of some future (and perhaps undefined) set of projects.

Using the WACC: Some Cautions

> The WACC for the firm should be used only when a project's systematic risk is the same as that of the firm as a whole.

The firm's overall cost of capital should be used with care when making investment decisions. First, as a financial standard, the WACC can only be applied to projects for which the systematic risk is the same as that of the firm as a whole. When projects differ in their risk characteristics, applying the firm's cost of capital to all projects can bias the selection process. Since the required return will increase with risk, use of its overall cost of capital may cause a firm to (1) reject low-risk, low-return projects that it might otherwise accept and/or (2) accept high-risk, high-return projects that it might want to reject. If a company uses its WACC on an across-the-board basis for all projects regardless of risk, overall risk may increase because the high-risk projects typically have the higher expected returns.

Second, the WACC should be updated periodically to reflect changes in the financial markets and/or shifts in the target capital structure. The WACC should reflect the cost of *new* funds; a WACC that was calculated last year will probably not reflect current market conditions.

---

[6]See Ezzell and Porter (1976).

Managers should remember that the WACC is just an estimate and may require some judgment in using it as a benchmark.

Finally, a company must keep in mind that a number of assumptions are made in computing component costs. Any calculated WACC is no more than an estimate of the "true" cost of capital for the firm. Like any other estimate, a certain amount of judgment is required in its use. For instance, many firms calculate the WACC and then round up to the nearest percent. In doing this, the company is really saying that they're willing to reject a few projects that perhaps should be accepted rather than accept a project that should be rejected. There's nothing really wrong with this practice provided that a company recognizes the systematic biases being introduced.

10.3   RISK-ADJUSTED REQUIRED RETURNS: THE PURE-PLAY TECHNIQUE

Applying the firm's overall cost of capital to all projects works reasonably well for single-product/service-line companies in mature markets. However, for a diversified firm operating in many markets, the idea that all projects are of equivalent risk is rarely, if ever, met. Philip Morris, for example, operates in three distinctly different markets—beer (Miller Brewing), tobacco, and packaged foods (Kraft-General Foods). All of these markets involve consumer products, but the competitive and regulatory environments faced by each business segment results in different risks. For Philip Morris, the requirement that projects will have the same risk is more likely to hold within each business segment than for the firm as a whole. Therefore, the idea of division-specific required returns makes more sense than does a companywide cost of capital.

Some Theoretical Underpinnings

Diversified firms can use the pure-play technique to establish risk-adjusted required returns for their divisions.

The most widely used method for determining the required return of a project or division with risk characteristics that differ from those of the firm as a whole, is the **pure-play technique.** This approach identifies publicly traded firms that are in the same line of business as the project or division in question. Once the pure-play firms are identified, their market data are used as a basis for calculating required returns. To estimate the risk-adjusted required returns, a company should proceed as follows:

The steps in the pure-play technique are designed to yield a WACC for a division that reflects its business risk and target capital structure.

Step 1. Identify Pure-Play Firms: The basic idea here is to identify publicly traded firms having a line of business similar to the project or division. Rarely do perfect pure-plays exist, because no two firms or divisions have exactly the same operating characteristics. However, reasonable matches are possible if (1) the project (or division) has a clearly identified product line and (2) the product mixes of the project and pure-play are roughly equivalent. Where geographical features are important to the business line, pure-plays should be selected that operate in the same geographic area. Sample selection is as much an art as a science. Where good matches can be found, a sample of one or two pure-plays will be sufficient. If good matches are not available, broader samples may be necessary to diversify away differences among firms.

Step 2. Determine Betas for Pure-Plays: The betas for the pure-plays can be determined in one of two ways. First, betas can be computed from return data by regressing the returns of the pure-plays against some broad market index like the S&P 500. A second approach is to utilize betas that have already been computed by some investment advisory service such as Value Line or Standard & Poor's.[7] These betas observed in the market place are the betas for a firm's common stock—its **equity beta.**

Step 3. Adjust for Leverage: The betas calculated for pure-plays are equity betas, which depend on both the operating (business) and financial risk of the underlying companies. Thus, the betas for pure-plays reflect the debt ratios for the individual firms in the sample as well as their business risk. These debt ratios (and the betas associated with them) may differ from the firm's target capital structure. Therefore, the pure-play technique calls for converting the levered equity beta of each proxy firm into its unlevered or *all-equity* value. This so-called unlevering can be done in accordance with the following formula:

$$\beta_U = \beta_L / [1 + (1 - \tau)D/E] \qquad\qquad [10\text{-}7]$$

where β_U is the beta for the pure-play firm in the absence of leverage; β_L, the observed beta that incorporates the pure-play's leverage; τ, the tax rate for the pure-play, and D/E is the pure-play's debt-to-equity ratio in market terms. The **unlevered** or all-equity **beta** is often referred to as the *asset beta* because it reflects only the business risks of the firm's assets without regard to any financial risks associated with debt financing. Given some sample of pure-plays, we can calculate an average asset beta for the sample.

Step 4. Relever the Asset Beta: The average asset beta calculated in Step 3 represents the beta of a hypothetical firm that is financed entirely with common stock and whose business risk matches that of the project/division under consideration. We now *relever* this asset beta to reflect the firm's financing mix using the following equation:[8]

$$\beta_L^* = \beta_U [1 + (1 - \tau^*)(D/E)^*] \qquad\qquad [10\text{-}8]$$

where $(D/E)^*$ is the target debt-to-equity ratio for the firm, and τ^* is the firm's tax rate. This levered beta (β_L^*) represents the beta that would (in theory) be observed in the market for a firm whose business risk matches that of the project/division, but its target financing mix is identical to that of the evaluating firm.

---

[7]Care should be taken in using published betas since each service calculates betas somewhat differently; thus, using a mixture of betas from more than one source for a given sample of pure-plays is simply bad technique.

[8]Both Equations [10-7] and [10-8] assume that the firm issues "safe" debt. Because no corporate debt is completely risk free, the equations represent a simplification of reality that works well in practice for most large firms.

Step 5. Calculate the Project's or Division's Cost of Equity: Using the relationship between risk and required return specified by the CAPM, we can now calculate the cost of equity (k_e) for the project or division as follows:

$$k_e = r_f + \beta_L{}^*(r_m - r_f) \qquad [10\text{-}9]$$

where r_f is the risk-free rate, and ($r_m - r_f$) is the market-risk premium.

Step 6. Calculate the Project's or Division's Required Rate of Return: The project's or division's required rate of return is a weighted average of the costs of various sources of financing with the weights applied to each component being determined by the target capital structure. Many firms use their overall target leverage ratio to calculate the division's cost of capital.[9] The required return is then calculated using the following formula:

$$\text{Required Return} = w_d(1 - \tau^*)k_d + w_e k_e \qquad [10\text{-}10]$$

where w_d and w_e are the proportions of debt and equity in the target capital structure, and k_d and k_e are the required returns on debt and equity. As before, k_d is the yield to maturity that the firm would have to offer on newly issued debt. This yield is adjusted by a factor of ($1 - \tau^*$) to reflect the tax deductibility of interest at the corporate level.

Using the firm's target capital structure in applying the pure-play technique ignores differences in debt capacity across divisions.

The procedure outlined here does not take into account two important real-world considerations. First, by applying the firm's target capital structure, we ignore differences in debt capacity across divisions. After all, if a low-risk division were a stand-alone firm, its target capital structure might contain more leverage than the firm as a whole. One way in which a firm could accommodate these differences when calculating a risk-adjusted cost of capital is to bypass Steps 3 and 4 and base each division's target capital structure on its contribution to the debt capacity of the firm as a whole.

Another potential limitation of the pure-play technique is that it implicitly assumes no interactions between the divisions, that is, that the divisions operate as if they were independent firms. For some firms, such as a multinational oil company, this assumption does not hold. An integrated oil company represents a continuous pipeline of production, transportation, refining, and retailing. Balancing the flow of oil through all stages of the production-distribution process reduces the risk of idle capacity from wellhead to pump. These opportunities are not available to an independent firm that works in only one part of the production chain. Thus, the risk-adjusted required returns calculated using the pure-play technique may overstate the "true" risk-adjusted cost of capital of these divisions.

Financial theory has no particularly good answers to situations like that of the vertically integrated company. However, we'd argue that a risk-adjusted required return that perhaps somewhat overstates risk creates fewer problems in the capital allocation process than a single target rate of return. In practice, managers can

---

[9]This procedure forces a company to think clearly about what its target capital structure ought to be.

subjectively adjust the calculated rates downward to reflect the fact that their firms may possess sources of risk reduction that are not available to investors.

Implementing a risk-adjusted hurdle rate system can create organizational stress.

Finally, we should note that firms moving from a single-rate to a risk-adjusted hurdle rate system may face some organizational challenges. Low-risk, low-return units will welcome a change to a risk-adjusted system; after all, the likelihood of getting more projects accepted goes up. The high-risk, high-return divisions, however, won't be pleased if some of their high-return projects get turned down. The problems of getting people to accept change in a setting like this are non-trivial and could get ugly if improperly handled. Financial managers have to be aware that there's a human side to the organization and that good communication is essential if things are to get done.

Illustration

Applying the Pure-Play Technique to Time Warner Communications

Time Warner Communications (TWX[10]), is the result of combination of Time, Inc., and Warner Communications in 1989 and the 1996 acquisition of Turner Broadcasting. The company operates a number of divisions, which include (among others) Time Warner Cable, Time, Inc., and Warner Brothers.

Suppose that TWX wants to estimate the required rate of return for its cable division. As a first step in the process, the financial staff would identify a sample of companies that are (for the most part) cable operators. The leveraged (equity) betas and capital structures for this sample are presented in Exhibit 10-5.

Assuming a corporate tax rate of 35 percent, the betas for the pure-plays are unlevered using Equation [10-7] and presented in Exhibit 10-6.

Exhibit 10-5 indicates that the average asset beta for the pure-plays that correspond to TWX's cable unit is 0.586. Although it would be nice to see only small differences in the unlevered (asset) betas of cable firms, significant differences across these pure-plays may still occur because each operator covers a different geographic area.

Let's assume that TWX has a target capital structure of 40 percent debt and 60 percent common stock and wants to use this mix as a basis for calculating divisional required returns. Given a 35 percent corporate tax rate, the relevered beta using Equation [10-8] is

$$\beta_L{}^* = \beta_U[1 + (1 - \tau^*)(D/E)^*]$$

$$= 0.586[1 + (0.65)(0.40/0.60)]$$

$$= 0.840$$

The next step in the process is to calculate the cost of equity for the cable division using the CAPM. Because investments in cable infrastructure tend

---

[10]Time Warner trades on the New York Stock Exchange under the ticker symbol TWX.

EXHIBIT 10-5
Time Warner Communications
Unleveraged Betas of Cable Firms

Pure-Play Firm	Equity or Market Beta	Debt to Market Value of Capital	Debt to Market Value of Equity	Asset or Unlevered Beta
Cablevision Systems	1.20	68.2%	214.5%	0.501
Century	1.01	64.8	184.1	0.460
Comcast	1.18	48.5	94.8	0.730
Jones Intercable	1.07	60.7	154.5	0.534
TCI Group	1.17	50.0	100.0	0.705

Average Asset Beta = 0.586

Source: Value Line Investment Survey.

to be long-term projects, the current (late October 1998) 30-year Treasury bond rate of 5.1 percent will serve nicely as an estimate of the risk-free rate. If we assume that the long-term market risk premium of 7.4 percent for large firms is appropriate for Time Warner, then the cost of equity for the cable division using Equation [10-9] would be

$$k_e = r_f + \beta_L{}^*(r_m - r_f)$$

$$= 5.10\% + 0.84(7.4\%) = 11.32\%$$

At this stage, estimating the required rate of return for TWX's cable unit is relatively straightforward. TWX's bonds carry a Standard & Poor's rating of BBB–. In October 1998, the company's existing 20-year bonds were priced to yield close to 7.0 percent.[11] Assuming that TWX would have to offer 7.0 percent on any newly-issued long-term debt, the cable unit's required return (k_{TWC}) would be

$$k_{TWC} = (1 - \tau)k_d w_d + k_e w_e$$

$$= (0.65)(7\ \%)(0.4) + (11.32\ \%)(0.6)$$

$$= 8.61 \text{ percent}$$

As a practical matter, TWX would probably recognize the large number of assumptions needed to arrive at this estimate and round up to 9.0 percent.

---

[11]Standard & Poor's *Bond Guide,* October 1998.

Calculating the WACC Using the CAPM: Some Common Errors

There are a number of common errors in using the CAPM to calculating the risk-adjusted cost of capital for either a division or an individual project. We've alluded to some of these earlier; here's a more complete list of errors we've run across in our teaching and consulting:

1. Computing the betas of individual divisions by beginning with the equity beta for the company overall and then unlevering and relevering this equity beta based on the individual divisions' capital structures. Instead, the divisional betas should be based on the pure-plays.
2. Using different capital structure assumptions in computing the cost of equity than are used in calculating the WACC. No mixing and matching.
3. Using a risk-free rate of one maturity in the CAPM but then estimating the market risk premium based on a risk-free rate having a different maturity. You must match the risk premium with the maturity of the security used to compute the risk-free rate.
4. Using a market risk premium based on the most recent returns rather than using a long time series. As we indicated in Chapter 6, using a long time series will reduce the standard deviation of your estimate.
5. Using a negative market risk premium. The market risk premium, that is, the difference between the expected return on the market portfolio and the risk-free rate, is always positive. If you get a negative premium, you've made a mistake somewhere.
6. Using the historical average Treasury bond or Treasury bill return as the risk-free rate in the CAPM instead of using the actual (current) rate. You must use the current risk-free rate in the CAPM.
7. Using the unlevered beta in the computation of the cost of equity capital for individual divisions and then using this cost of equity capital to compute the WACC for the individual divisions based on their target debt ratios. You must relever the asset beta to come up with a new equity beta that matches the target capital structure of the individual divisions.
8. Using only one or two comparables to estimate the unlevered betas for the individual divisions. Unless you come up with a perfect match, you'll want a bigger sample to reduce the error involved in any such estimation.
9. Failing to include the effect of taxes when levering and unlevering beta.
10. Using the historical market return as the market risk premium instead of measuring it as the *difference* between the historical market return and the corresponding risk-free rate.
11. Computing the average asset beta of comparables by taking the average equity beta and delevering it using the average D/E ratio for the comparables instead of unlevering the beta for each individual comparable.

These errors are easy to avoid. Doing so will not guarantee a correct cost-of-capital estimate, but failing to avoid them will guarantee an incorrect one.

10.4   PROJECT VALUATION AND FINANCING SIDE EFFECTS

In our discussion up to this point, we have valued projects by discounting their cash flows (exclusive of financing costs) at a cost of capital that reflects the project's risk and its target capital structure. Implicit in using the WACC as a discount rate is the assumption that the debt ratio remains constant over time. Such a requirement is virtually impossible to meet in practice. Despite this gap between theory and practice, many companies find that they can live with the constant debt ratio assumption because it's easier than trying to estimate year-to-year variations from the target capital structure.

However, at times the assumption of a constant financing mix, even as an approximation, breaks down completely. For example, if a project has a financial package with debt to be repaid periodically, the project's capital structure will change over time. In these instances, an alternative and more flexible procedure is to value the project as if it were financed entirely with equity and then add the present value of the tax shields provided by debt financing. The net present value arrived at by using this approach, often referred to as the **adjusted net present value (APV)**, is given by

$$APV = \begin{array}{c} -\text{Initial} \\ \text{Investment} \end{array} + \begin{array}{c} \text{Present Value If Project} \\ \text{Is All-Equity Financed} \end{array} + \begin{array}{c} \text{Present Value of} \\ \text{Debt Tax Shields} \end{array} \qquad [10\text{-}11]$$

The APV Approach: An Example

The adjusted net present value (APV) of a project is the value of the project if all-equity financed plus the present value of financing side effects.

To see how the APV approach might work, suppose that the managers of Trifecta Products have the opportunity to purchase the company from its owner, who is going to retire. The firm makes private-label personal care products (toothpaste, mouthwash, and shampoo) that it has been selling for years to a number of large supermarket chains. Trifecta is a highly profitable debt-free operation with a current cash flow of $5 million a year that is expected to grow at a 3 percent rate into the indefinite future. The firm's owner wants $30 million for the business. The price is not negotiable; the owner feels he can get his asking price by selling the company in the open market. By pooling their savings, the managers can raise $2 million. The additional $28 million needed to buy the firm could be borrowed from a life insurance company. The loan would carry a 10 percent interest rate, with the principal being amortized in equal installments over the next 10 years.

The first step in applying the APV method is to value the business as if it were going to be financed entirely with equity. Let's assume that the all-equity cost of capital (k^*) for Trifecta Products is 17 percent. The NPV of the firm on an all-equity financed basis (NPV_e) would be

$$NPV_e = -\$30,000,000 + \frac{\$5,000,000(1.03)}{(0.17 - 0.03)} =$$

$$= -\$30,000,000 + \$36,785,714 = \$6,785,714$$

The $6,785,714 positive NPV indicates that Trifecta is a valuable enterprise. Moreover, the heavy use of debt to finance the purchase creates additional value. How? The interest paid on borrowed money is tax deductible. For a highly profitable company like Trifecta, this deductability reduces the tax bill by shielding the firm's operating income from taxation. The interest tax shield created in any year i is equal to the tax rate times the interest paid, or tk_dD_i, where t is the corporate tax rate, k_d is the before-tax interest rate, and D_i is the debt associated with the project in year i. Discounting these annual tax shields over the life of the debt gives us the total value of the tax savings. In valuing the interest tax shields, the pre-tax cost of debt is used as a discount rate to reflect the relatively certain value of the cash flows.

The process of valuing the tax shields on the debt used to buy Trifecta Products is illustrated in Exhibit 10-6. Adding the present value of the interest tax shield to the all-equity NPV yields an APV of $10.56 million:

$$APV = \$6{,}785{,}714 + \$3{,}779{,}000 = \$10{,}564{,}714$$

Clearly, the managers of Trifecta should go ahead with the purchase of the company. The procedure outlined here covers an important class of investments in which the debt used to finance a project is repaid over time. The purchase of Trifecta is an example of a **leveraged buyout (LBO)** in which a group of investors—typically including management—buys a company from its owners using mostly

EXHIBIT 10-6
Trifecta Products
Calculating the Present Value of Interest Tax Shields
(in thousand $)

Beginning of Year	Debt Outstanding	Interest	Interest Tax Shield*	Present Value of Tax Shields @ 10%
1	$28,000	$2,800	$980	$ 891
2	25,200	2,520	882	729
3	22,400	2,240	784	589
4	19,600	1,960	686	469
5	16,800	1,680	588	365
6	14,000	1,400	490	277
7	11,200	1,120	392	201
8	8,400	840	294	137
9	5,600	560	196	83
10	2,800	280	98	38
				$3,779

*Equal to interest times an assumed tax rate of 35 percent.

borrowed money secured by the firm's assets. We'll talk more about LBOs and other forms of leveraged recapitalizations when we get to Chapter 14.

Calculating the Value of Low-Cost Financing

The APV framework can be used to value the benefits of subsidized financing.

Many governments offer a variety of investment incentives designed to achieve goals other than economic efficiency. Fortunately, the APV framework is flexible enough to calculate the value of subsidized financing. In this case, the APV can be expanded to incorporate the value of low-cost financing as follows:

$$APV = \begin{array}{c} -\text{Initial} \\ \text{Investment} \end{array} + \begin{array}{c} \text{Present Value If Project} \\ \text{Is All-Equity Financed} \end{array} + \begin{array}{c} \text{Present Value of} \\ \text{Debt Tax Shields} \end{array} + \begin{array}{c} \text{Present Value of} \\ \text{Interest Subsidies} \end{array}$$

[10-12]

The application of Equation [10-12] to value the benefits of arranging low-cost financing can be illustrated by examining the case of Xebec, a California manufacturer of disk-drive controllers.

Illustration

Suppose that one of the inducements provided by Taiwan to woo Xebec into setting up a local production facility is a 10-year, $12.5 million loan at 8 percent interest. The principal is to be repaid at the end of the tenth year. The market interest rate on such a loan is about 15 percent. With a marginal tax rate of 40 percent, how much is this loan worth to Xebec? That is, what is its net present value?

At 8 percent interest, Xebec must pay $1 million in interest annually for the next 10 years and then repay the $12.5 million principal at the end of 10 years. In return, Xebec receives $12.5 million today. Given these cash inflows and outflows, we can calculate the loan's NPV just as we would for any project analysis. Note, however, that, unlike the typical capital-budgeting problem we looked at, the cash inflow occurs immediately and the cash outflows later. But the principle is the same.

Given a marginal tax rate of 40 percent, the annual after-tax interest payments on the loan will be $600,000 ($.6 \times .08 \times \$12,500,000$). Now we can calculate the NPV of Xebec's financing bargain:

$$NPV = \$12,500,000 - \sum_{t=1}^{10} \frac{\$600,000}{(1.15)^t} - \frac{\$12,500,000}{(1.15)^{10}}$$

$$= \$12,500,000 - \$6,101,070 = \$6,398,930$$

You don't need a degree in financial economics to realize that borrowing money at 8 percent when the market rate is 15 percent is a good deal. But what the NPV calculations tell you is just how much a particular below-market financing option is worth. Note that this analysis captures both the tax benefits *and* the interest subsidies.

The annual interest subsidy alone, ignoring tax effects, equals $875,000, the difference between the interest payment of $1,875,000 required on a 15 percent loan and the interest payment of $1 million on the 8 percent loan. The present value of this interest subsidy is

$$PV(\text{Interest Subsidy}) = \sum_{t=1}^{10} \frac{\$875,000}{(1.15)^t} = \$4,391,423$$

Similarly, the annual tax benefit associated with this loan is $.4 \times .08 \times \$12,500,000 = \$400,000$, the annual tax write-off associated with the interest payment. The present value of this tax benefit is

$$PV(\text{Interest Subsidy}) = \sum_{t=1}^{10} \frac{\$400,000}{(1.15)^t} = \$2,007,507$$

Adding these two figures yields a total benefit of $6,398,930, the same as the net present value for the loan that we calculated previously. This figure would be added to the NPV of the production facility in Taiwan, assuming it were financed on an all-equity basis. The resulting figure would the overall NPV to Xebec of the investment and subsidized financing package.

Equity Residual Method

> The equity residual approach to valuation discounts the project's cash flows, net of debt payments, by the cost of equity capital.

A third capital budgeting approach is the **equity residual (ER) method**. This approach discounts the levered cash flows—that is, the project's cash flows net of debt payments—at the levered cost of equity capital, k_e. This cost of equity capital with leverage is estimated using the levered equity beta, β_L, and is the same one that appears in the weighted average cost of capital. Ignoring preferred stock financing, which is rarely used by companies, there is a simple relation between the levered cost of equity capital, k_e, and the all-equity cost of capital k^*. Without proof, and using the same notation as before, this relation is as follows:

$$k_e = k^* + \frac{D}{E}(1-t)(k^* - k_d) \qquad [10\text{-}13]$$

The cash flows discounted with the equity residual method are those that flow to the shareholders of the company sponsoring the project. These cash flows are the unlevered cash flows used in the WACC and APV methods less the after-tax debt charges associated with the project's financing. To be consistent, the initial investment used in the ER method is the equity portion of the initial out-of-pocket investment expenses; that is, it equals I_0, less the amount borrowed to finance the project.

Comparing the WACC, APV, and ER Methods

Exhibit 10-7 summarizes the three different approaches to capital budgeting and cost of capital. This summary includes only debt and equity financing; it ignores preferred stock financing. As shown, the cash flows discounted and the discount rates vary depending on the method selected. The following simplified example illustrates the application of these alternative methods.

Giant Manufacturing Company has an opportunity to invest $30 million in a new solar power source. Once completed, the new solar energy project is expected to yield annual free cash flows of $4,880,000 in perpetuity. Assuming that $k*$ equals 16 percent, then this project has a net present value of $500,000:

$$NPV = -\$30,000,000 + \frac{\$4,880,000}{0.16} = \$500,000$$

EXHIBIT 10-7
Discount Rates and Cash Flows Used in Three Capital Budgeting Methods

Weighted Average Cost of Capital (WACC) Approach

WACC Formula: $NPV = -I_0 + \sum\limits_{t=1}^{n} \dfrac{CF_t}{(1+k_0)^t}$

where WACC discount rate $(k_0) = k_d^* w_d + k_p w_p + k_e w_e$
        WACC cash flows (CF_t) = Project cash flows ignoring debt servicing charges

Adjusted Present Value (APV) Method

APV Formula: $APV = -I_0 + \sum\limits_{t=1}^{n} \dfrac{CF_t}{(1+k^*)^t}$ + Financing side effects

where APV discount rate (k^*) = All-equity cost of capital

Equity Residual (ER) Method

ER Formula: $NPV = -(I_0 - D) + \sum\limits_{t=1}^{n} \dfrac{LCF_t}{(1+k_e)^t}$

where ER discount rate (k_e) = Levered cost of equity capital
        ER cash flows (LCF_t) = CF_t − debt servicing charges
        ER initial investment = I_0 − debt (D) used to finance the project

Given the initial investment, this project is just marginally profitable. However, suppose the project can support a permanent addition to debt equal to $6.5 million. If the interest rate on this debt is 10 percent and the company's marginal tax rate is 30 percent, we can calculate the value of the project using the three different approaches.

APV Method.   In this case, the only financing side effect is the tax saving provided by the tax deductibility of interest payments. As we saw previously, the annual tax savings equals the tax rate times the annual interest expense. For Giant, this works out to $195,000 (.30 × .10 × $6,500,000). Based on this interest tax shield, the APV of the solar energy project is $2.5 million:

$$APV = \$500,000 + \frac{\$195,000}{0.10} = \$2,450,000$$

The tax benefits of debt financing have turned this project from being marginally acceptable to one that is reasonably profitable.

Using market values, the debt ratio for this project is 6.5/32.45, or 20 percent. That is, the amount of debt selected for this project has been set equal to 20 percent of the project's $32.45 million present value.

WACC Method.   With a debt ratio of .20, we can now calculate the weighted average cost of capital. To begin, we use Equation [10-13] to estimate the project's levered cost of equity capital:

$$k_e = k^* + \frac{D}{E}(1 - t)(k^* - k_d) = 0.16 + \frac{6.5}{26}(1 - 0.30)(0.16 - 0.10)$$

$$= 0.1705$$

With a 17.05 percent cost of equity capital, the project's weighted average cost of capital equals 15.04 percent:

$$k_0 = 0.80(0.1705) + 0.20(0.10)(1 - 0.30) = 0.1504$$

At this discount rate, the net present value of Giant's project is $2.5 million, the same value we got using the APV method:

$$NPV = -\$30,000,000 + \frac{\$4,880,000}{0.1504} = \$2,450,000$$

ER Method.   To employ this method, we need to combine the levered cost of equity, which we have already calculated to be 17.05 percent, with the cash flows to equity. With permanent debt of $6.5 million, the annual after-tax interest expense is .7 × .1 × $6.5 million = $455,000. Subtracting this figure from the $4.88 million in free cash flow yields an annual cash flow to equity of $4,425,000. Lastly, Giant's initial equity investment in the project is $23.5 million ($30 million – $6.5 million). Using these figures, together with the ER method, we can now estimate the NPV value of Giant's project:

$$NPV = -\$23,500,000 + \frac{\$4,425,000}{0.1705} = \$2,450,000$$

The adjusted net present value, equity residual, and WACC approaches to valuation should give similar answers.

We see that, under this set of simplified assumptions, all three capital budgeting methods provide the same answer. Although these assumptions are commonly violated—after all, when do you see a project yielding a perpetuity and financed with an amount of debt that stays level over its lifetime?—the formulas usually yield answers that are off by only a few percent from the true present value.[12]

10.5   INTERNATIONAL DIMENSIONS OF COST OF CAPITAL

Up to now, we have implicitly assumed that the projects under consideration are located in the United States, but this is becoming less true all the time. According to the U.S. Department of Commerce, foreign investment by U.S. corporations was over $100 billion in 1997. The enormity of this stake and the fact that many U.S. corporations that are household names—IBM, General Electric, and Ford—earn over 40 percent of their profits abroad means that for many of these multinational corporations (MNCs), there is no turning back; foreign operations and successful foreign investments are crucial to success.

As the MNC becomes the norm rather than the exception, the issue of cost of capital for foreign projects is raised more frequently. A central question that must be addressed by the MNC is whether the required rate of return on foreign projects should be higher, lower, or the same as comparable domestic projects. Although a definitive answer is not possible, both the CAPM and APT supply some useful insights.

The importance of the CAPM and APT for the MNC is that the relevant component of risk in pricing the firm's stock is its systematic risk.[13] Much of the sys-

---

[12]For a further discussion, see Stewart C. Myers, "Interactions of Corporate Financing and Investment Decisions—Implications for Capital Budgeting," *Journal of Finance*, March 1974, 1–25.

International diversification can reduce the variability of corporate earnings.

tematic risk or general market risk affecting a company, at least as measured using a domestic stock index such as the S&P 500 or the NYSE index, is caused by the cyclical nature of the economy in which the firm is operating. For this reason, it is highly possible that MNCs, by having operations in a number of countries in which economic cycles are not perfectly in phase, may reduce the variability of their earnings through international diversification.

A number of studies suggest that this is, in fact, the case.[14] Studies find little correlation among the earnings of various national components of MNCs. Thus, to the extent that foreign cash flows are not perfectly correlated with those of domestic investments, the total risk of cash flows appears to be *reduced,* not increased, by international investment. Of greater importance, most of the economic and political risks faced by the MNC appear to be unsystematic and can, therefore, be eliminated by shareholder diversification.

Projects in LDCs can provide the greatest diversification benefits.

Rather surprisingly, it is the less-developed countries (LDCs), in which political risks are the greatest, that are likely to provide the greatest diversification benefits. This is because the economies of LDCs are less closely tied to the U.S. or any other Western industrialized economy. By contrast, the correlation among economic cycles of developed countries is considerably stronger; the diversification benefits from investing in industrialized countries from the standpoint of a U.S. or Western European MNC are proportionately less.

However, the systematic risk of projects even in relatively isolated LDCs is unlikely to be far below that of the average of all projects, because these countries and their project returns are still tied to the world economy. The important point about LDCs, then, is that while their ratio of systematic to total risk is generally quite low; their systematic risk, although perhaps slightly lower, is probably not significantly less than that of industrialized countries.

A foreign project's systematic risk, and hence its cost of capital, is unlikely to be greater than that of a comparable domestic project.

The implication of the preceding paragraphs is that the systematic risk of foreign projects is unlikely to be higher and, in fact, might well be lower, than that of comparable domestic projects. This means that the required returns on such projects will probably be lower, not higher, than the required returns on their domestic counterparts. At the very least, therefore, executives of MNCs should seriously question the use of a risk *premium* to account for the additional political and economic risks of overseas projects. The automatic inclusion of such a risk

---

[13]Systematic risk is measured relative to a particular market portfolio. The relevant portfolio is the portfolio held by the marginal investor in the company. If the marginal investor is holding a domestically diversified portfolio, then the systematic risk must be measured against that portfolio. However, if the marginal portfolio is diversified internationally, then the systematic risk must be measured relative to the world market portfolio. It is not clear whether the marginal investor in U.S. stocks is diversified domestically or internationally, but more and more investors are investing overseas.

[14]See, for example, Benjamin I. Cohen, *Multinational Firms and Asian Exports* (New Haven, CT: Yale University Press, 1975); and Alan Rugman, "Risk Reduction by International Diversification," *Journal of International Business Studies,* Fall 1976, 75–80.

premium may, in fact, penalize the firm's shareholders by causing management to reject positive-NPV foreign investments.

Based on these factors, the recommended approach is to use the same cost of capital to evaluate foreign projects as in domestic projects. In this way, the firm is likely to err on the side of conservatism in the calculation of project worth.

SUMMARY

In this chapter, we took a look at how a company should go about setting the required rates of return for investment projects. We began by looking at the idea of a weighted average cost of capital (WACC) for the firm as a whole. As the name suggests, WACC is just an average of the after-tax cost of different sources of permanent (long-term) capital, weighted by the proportions that the firm will use in financing accepted projects. As a financial standard, the WACC should be used only for projects whose systematic risk is similar to that of the firm as a whole. Where projects differ in terms of their systematic risk, applying the firm's cost of capital to all projects can bias the selection process.

When systematic risk is relatively homogeneous within a division, but heterogeneous across divisions, establishing divisional costs of capital using the pure-play technique is appropriate. The key to developing these risk-adjusted divisional costs of capital is to use financial data from publicly traded proxy firms whose business risk is comparable to that of the division. Use of the pure-play technique can also be extended to individual projects if it is possible to find a firm (or sample of firms) whose business risk is comparable to that of the project at hand. We also examined the use of the adjusted present value (APV) and equity residual (ER) methods to account for financing side effects.

FINCOACH PRACTICE EXERCISES

To help you master the mathematics discussed in the chapter, open **FinCoach** on the *Prentice Hall Finance Center* CD-ROM and practice the exercises in the following categories: *1. Bond Valuation, 2. Stock Valuation, 3. CAPM, 4. Cost of Capital I,* and *5. Cost of Capital II.*

QUESTIONS

1. Show how the following events change the discount rate applicable to an expansion of an existing restaurant chain.
   a. The covariance between restaurant sales and the market rate of return increases.
   b. The riskless rate decreases.
   c. Several other companies are planning to expand their chains.

2. How should a division manager adjust the divisional return on investment for risk? What measures of risk are available to her?

3. A large manufacturer is evaluating the purchase of a smaller firm. The firm has the same required return as the manufacturer, estimated at 10 percent, yet its actual rate of return is about 8 percent. Although the project appears to have a negative NPV,

company executives have considered the low cost of debt financing. Because the manufacturer has no existing debt outstanding, it may borrow at only 7 percent. Furthermore, interest deductibility and a tax rate of 50 percent lower the effective cost of debt to 3.5 percent. Because the cost of financing the acquisition with debt is much lower than the 8 percent expected return, the executives are considering going ahead with the acquisition. Comment.

4. Give an explanation of each of the following points:
   a. The cost of preferred stock is greater than the cost of debt.
   b. The cost of equity raised by a new share issue is greater than the cost of retained earnings.

5. Which of the following companies is likely to have a higher beta and, thus, a higher cost of capital?
   a. An auto manufacturer who runs an assembly line with union workers.
   b. A high-tech auto manufacturer with a fully automated line requiring only a handful of nonunion workers.

6. What impact will each of the following events have on a firm's weighted average cost of capital?
   a. The corporate tax rate is lowered.
   b. The firm increases its leverage.
   c. The firm's stock price falls dramatically.
   d. New York City imposes a stamp tax on share issues floated there.
   e. The government allows private investors to exclude up to $1,000 in dividends from taxable income.
   f. The firm sells a division and replaces it with a less risky project.

7. A corporation has the following balance sheet (liabilities side):

Current liabilities	$ 2,000
Long-term debt	5,000
Preferred stock	2,000
Common stock	8,000
Retained earnings	3,000
	$20,000

Currently, the riskless interest rate is 8 percent; the corporate tax rate is 50 percent; the current price of a share of common stock is $20 (200 shares are outstanding); and dividends have been level at $1 per share per year for many years.

Company executives are considering expanding the existing business by acquiring a competitor. To do so, they must estimate the NPV of the acquisition. Because the acquisition has the same degree of risk as the firm, the firm's WACC can be used.

A financial executive has used the following procedure to calculate the WACC. Debt and preferred stock are fixed claims offering a fairly secure constant return, and so their before-tax cost is assumed to equal the riskless rate. The dividend yield has held constant at about 5 percent, so this is used as the cost of new equity capital. Finally, the balance sheet shows the firm to be composed of 25 percent debt, 10 percent preferred stock, 55 percent equity (common stock plus retained earnings), and 10 percent current liabilities. Current liabilities and retained earnings are assumed to be costless; therefore the WACC is 3.8 percent.
   a. Comment on this procedure.
   b. How is this procedure likely to affect investment decisions?

8. "Our conglomerate recognizes that foreign investments have a very low covariance with our domestic operations and thus are a good source of diversification. We do not 'penalize' potential foreign investments with a high discount rate but, rather, use a discount rate just 3 percent above the prevailing riskless rate." Comment.

9. A large food processor and distributor is considering expansion into a chain of privately owned sports-shoe outlets. The food company wishes to estimate the discount rate for such investments so as to negotiate a fair price for the acquisition. Unfortunately, there are no stock exchange-listed sports-shoe companies with a price history with which a "sports-shoe outlet beta" can be estimated. However, executives are considering using the price history of another company to estimate the beta. Which of the following companies would be the most appropriate? Explain.
   a. Another large food company.
   b. A holding company for a football team.
   c. A company that manufactures shoes.
   d. A chain of swimwear and surfboard stores in California.

10. Which investment is likely to have a higher degree of systematic risk, a copper-mining project in Chile or an investment in a Brazilian auto plant whose output would be sold locally? Explain.

PROBLEMS

☒ —Excel templates may be downloaded from **www. prenhall.com/financecenter.**

1. A company is deciding whether to issue stock to raise money for an investment project that has a beta of 1.0 and an expected return of 20 percent. Suppose the risk-free rate is 10 percent, the company's stock price beta is 2.5, and the expected return on the market is 15 percent. Should the company go ahead with the project? Explain.

2. Calvin Inc. earned $2.00 per share during the past year and has just paid a dividend of $.40 per share. Investors forecast that Calvin will continue to retain 80 percent of its earnings for the next 4 years and that earnings will grow at 25 percent per year through year 5. The dividend payout ratio is expected to be raised in year 5 to 50 percent, reducing the dividend growth rate to 8 percent thereafter. If Calvin's equity beta is 0.9, the risk-free rate is 8.5 percent, and the market risk premium is 8 percent, what should its price be today?   ☒

3. An electric utility has an 80 percent debt-to-value ratio and an equity beta of .75, the riskless rate is 10 percent, and the expected return on the market is 14 percent. What is the expected rate of return on equity? On the unlevered assets of the firm? Assume corporate taxes of 40 percent.   ☒

4. The equity of an unlevered firm has a beta of 1.5. If the firm's tax rate is 35 percent, how much leverage must it take on to achieve a beta of 3?

5. If we define $(k_e - r_f)$ as a measure of risk compensation, then for the *unlevered* firm, this risk compensation will be a business risk premium. On the other hand, for the *levered* firm, this risk compensation $(k_e - r_f)$ will combine a business *and* a financial risk premium. Suppose the required return for a levered firm's stock is 15 percent; the risk-free rate is 6 percent; and the market risk premium is 5 percent. If the company were not levered, the stock's beta would be 1.2. Estimate the business risk premium and the financial risk premium for the levered firm.

6. Amalgamated Properties, Ltd., has a beta of 0.8, whereas a potential takeover target, Consolidated Industries, has a beta of 1.4. Both firms are unlevered and Amalgamated's market value is twice that of Consolidated. Currently, the riskless rate is 5 percent, and the risk premium on the market is 10

percent. Amalgamated plans to pay a $2 dividend this year. This dividend is expected to grow at the rate of 3 percent if there is no takeover. If there is a takeover, the dividend will grow at 4 percent. Given the above information, calculate the value of an Amalgamated share before and after the takeover. Should Amalgamated carry out its takeover plan? Ignore taxes.   ☒

7. As a financial analyst for National Engineering, you are required to estimate the cost of capital the firm should use in evaluating its heavy construction projects. The firm's balance sheet data and other information are listed below. Assume a 35 percent corporate tax rate.   ☒
   a. What is your estimate? What assumptions must you make to calculate this estimate?
   b. What qualifications to this estimate should you mention in your report when National applies this rate to its various projects?

Selected Balance Sheet Items	
Bonds	(see market data)
Preferred stock	$400,000
Common stock	$800,000
Retained earnings	$2,000,000

Market Data		
	Market Value	Yield
Bonds:		
8%, 10-year	$250,000	12%
12%, 15-year	$1,000,000	15%
21%, 1-year	$250,000	11%

Common stock:
   Average dividend growth (5 years) = 10%
   Current dividend yield = 7%
   Price = $47.25
   Shares = 100,000
Preferred stock:
   $4.50 preferred dividend
   Price = $22.50
   Shares = 20,000

8. A corporation's securities have the following betas and market values: ✍

	Beta	Market Value
Debt	.1	$100,000
Preferred	.4	200,000
Common	1.5	100,000

Calculate the following figures given a riskless interest rate of 10 percent, a corporate tax rate of 35%, and a market risk premium of 5 percent:
a. discount rates for each security.
b. the asset beta for the corporation.
c. the weighted average cost of capital.
d. the discount rate for the unlevered assets.

9. Multi-Foods has four divisions: pet foods, canned goods, frozen entrees, and instant foods. These contribute 10 percent, 25 percent, 50 percent, and 15 percent, respectively, to the firm's value. Multi-Foods has found what it feels are good proxies for its divisions in the following competitors: ✍

Company	Equity Beta	Debt/Total Assets
Pet Products	.50	.33
Candlelight	1.50	.50
Freezies	1.75	.20
RedyEeet	2.25	.25

a. Assuming the firms are accurate proxies, estimate the asset betas for Multi-Foods divisions. (Assume the debt betas are zero.) The corporate tax rate is 35%.
b. With a risk-free rate of 8 percent and an average market rate of return of 16 percent, what is the cost of capital for each of the divisions?
c. With a debt/total assets (D/TA) of .50, what is Multi-Foods' equity beta?

10. As part of its efforts at diversification, the Sherbert theater organization, producer of Broadway plays, is considering acquiring a movie theater chain. A prime acquisition candidate is Consolidated Cinemas, currently owned by a conglomerate, Tryon. Although Tryon has given Sherbert what it feels is an accurate forecast of expected cash flows from the cinema chain, Sherbert would like to have its own estimate of the required rate of return to apply to these cash flows. The chief financial officer has acquired the following information on independently owned movie house chains: ✍

Movie House	Equity Beta	Debt/Total Assets
NCO Theater, Inc.	1.70	0.40
Worldwide/Global	0.50	0.10
Screen Rocks	2.50	0.50
Ultimate Theater	0.40	0.75

a. Using a risk-free rate of 7.5 percent, a corporate tax rate of 40%, and a market risk premium of 8.5 percent, what is your estimate of the cost of equity capital for Consolidated? The debt/total assets ratio for Consolidated is 0.25.
b. What qualifications would you include with your estimate?

11. Equinox, a maker of sports equipment, is attempting to estimate its cost of capital. Equinox could issue additional debt at a cost of 15 percent; its ratio of debt to total assets is .50, and Equinox is subject to a 35 percent tax rate. Equinox estimates its cost of equity capital at 20 percent.
a. What is Equinox's weighted average cost of capital?
b. If Equinox reassessed its capital structure and decided its target debt/total assets (D/TA) ratio would be 75 percent, what would its cost of capital be? What conclusions could you draw about the amount of debt financing Equinox should have? What critical assumption is involved in this conclusion?
c. Equinox reassessed the required rate of return on its securities when it changed its capital structure. Here are the revised figures:

Debt/ Total Assets	.20	.30	.40	.50	.75
Debt	7.5%	8%	10%	15%	20.5%
Equity	14.5%	15%	17.5%	20%	24.5%

What capital structure would you recommend? Why?

12. C&W, a conglomerate, is seeking to acquire one or more independently owned companies. It has the following market value information concerning the firms: ✳

Company	Equity Beta	Total Assets ($ millions)	Debt/ Total Assets
1	1.15	400	0.50
2	2.00	250	0.70
3	0.85	125	0.30
4	0.10	100	0.25

The acquisitions would be financed in part by the acquired firm's taking on an additional debt of $50 million and selling off assets worth $25 million. Current Treasury rates are 8 percent; the market risk premium is expected to remain at 7 percent; and the corporate tax rate is 40 percent.

a. What are the firms' preacquisition costs of equity capital?

b. What are the firms' asset betas?

c. After the acquisition, what would the cost of equity capital be for each of the recapitalized companies?

13. Tom Swift Company has a target capital structure of 40 percent debt and 60 percent equity. Its estimated beta is 0.9. Tom Swift is evaluating a new project that is unrelated to its existing lines of business. However, it has identified three proxy firms exclusively engaged in this line of business. The average beta for these firms is 1.2, and their debt ratios (debt/assets) average 50 percent. Tom Swift's new project has a projected return of 10.5 percent. The risk-free return is 6 percent, and the market risk premium is 5 percent. All firms have a marginal tax rate of 39 percent. Tom Swift's before-tax cost of debt is 9 percent.

a. What is the unlevered project beta?

b. What is the beta of the project if undertaken by Tom Swift, assuming the company maintains its target capital structure?

c. Should Tom Swift accept the project?

14. The following are the beta estimates from Value Line for several computer firms as well as the D/TA for the firms. Suppose the risk-free rate of return is 8 percent; the expected market return is 17 percent; and the tax rate is 40 percent. ✳

a. What risk premium must these companies pay as a result of leverage?

b. What proportion of their total equity cost is a result of financing?

Company	Beta	Debt/Total Assets
Apple	1.70	0
Amdahl	1.55	.31
Burroughs	1.00	.24
Commodore	1.50	.14
Cray	1.45	.05
Sperry	1.25	.23
Tandem	1.60	.03

15. Compute the cost of capital for each of the following sources of funds. The tax rate is 40 percent. ✳

a. A 30-year, 9 percent coupon, $1,000 par bond sold at $1,070 less 3 percent underwriting commission.

b. A share of preferred stock sold at $80 with a $100 par value and a dividend of 6 percent. Flotation costs are $3.50.

c. A share of common stock with a market price of $25, earnings per share of $3, a payout of 55 percent, and an expected growth rate of 4 percent annually. Flotation costs are $5.

REFERENCES

Chambers, D. E., R. S. Harris, and J. J. Pringle. "Treatment of Financing Mix in Analyzing Investment Opportunities," *Financial Management*, Summer 1982, 24–41.

Ezzell, J. R., and R. B. Porter. "Flotation Costs and the Weighted Average Cost of Capital." *Journal of Financial and Quantitative Analysis*, September 1976, 403–413.

Harris, R. S., and F. C. Marston. "Estimating Share-holder Premia Using Analysts' Growth Forecasts," *Financial Management,* Summer 1992, 63–70.

Ibbotson Associates. *Stocks, Bonds, Bills and Inflation 1998 Yearbook.* Chicago: Ibbotson Associates, 1998.

Seitz, N., and M. Ellison. *Capital Budgeting and Long-term Financing Decisions.* Fort Worth, TX: Dryden Press, 1995.

Creating Value for Shareholders

[S]tockholders aren't dumb. Many companies . . . have a good stock price, sometimes without having any profit. Their stockholders believe in its future.
T. Boone Pickens

Management doesn't get paid to make the shareholders comfortable. We get paid to make the shareholders rich.
Roberto Goizueta
Chairman, Coca-Cola

KEY TERMS

acquisition
cross-subsidization
disciplinary acquisitions
economic value added
   (EVA)
focus

golden parachute
horizontal integration
market value added
   (MVA)
market-to-book ratio
merger

partial spinoff
strategic fit
synergistic acquisitons
trade loading
value-based analysis

CHAPTER LEARNING OBJECTIVES

Upon completion of this chapter, students should be able to:

- Calculate a firm's market-to-book ratio and indicate why it is a good measure of the value management creates for its shareholders.
- Discuss the nature of cross-subsidies within a multidivisional firm and how value-based analysis can eliminate these value-destroying activities.
- Discuss the nature of strategic fit and focus and their role in creating shareholder value.

- Indicate the degree to which the market is capable of recognizing management's ability to implement long-term value-creating strategies.
- Discuss the tradeoffs between short- and long-term profits and describe the methods that can be used to encourage long-term profit-maximizing behavior.
- Explain how the proper design of executive compensation contracts can improve organizational performance.

- Discuss the challenges in measuring economic profits and to indicate how approaches such as market value added (MVA) and economic value added (EVA) can be used to assess the wealth created by a firm's managers.

- List the synergies that can be generated by acquisitions that are designed to exploit strategic fit.
- Capture the effects of potential synergies in valuing an acquisition candidate.

This chapter takes another look at the question that should be foremost in the minds of executives: How can management increase the value of the firm's shares and thereby create value for shareholders? Our intuition tells us that a firm's economic value depends on (1) the expected long-run profitability of existing operations, (2) its future long-run investment opportunities and their likely returns, (3) the riskiness of its current and future investments, and (4) the market's required return on these investments. A company's future profitability, in turn, depends on the quality of its management, the competitive positions of its products, and its ability to adapt quickly to changing product–market conditions.

We shall now take a more systematic look at how these factors—investment prospects, expected returns, and required returns—combine to affect the value management creates for its shareholders. An important message is that it is not sufficient for the company as a whole to create value for its shareholders; each business segment within the company must also contribute to value creation. We'll also examine how the evaluation of managerial performance and executive compensation can influence the value-creation process. The chapter concludes with a discussion of how the concepts of market value added (MVA) and economic value added (EVA) can be used to measure economic profits. Appendix 11A discusses mergers and acquisitions from the standpoint of value creation and destruction.

11.1   INVESTMENT PROSPECTS AND VALUE CREATION

A firm's future profitability is largely determined by the future investment opportunities available to it and the returns that it expects to earn on those investments. When does the firm add to shareholder wealth by retaining earnings to invest in new investment projects each year instead of paying them out as dividends? When it earns true profit.

True profit is the amount of profit in excess of the cost of the capital employed. However, net income as reported includes a mixture of the required return on equity capital and true profit. Only if it earns a return on equity in excess of that required by shareholders—called the *cost of equity capital*—can the firm be said to be truly benefitting its owners. The point is that retaining earnings in the firm does not automatically benefit shareholders, even though the investments they finance will lead to higher earnings and dividends in the future.

> A company earns true profit when it earns a return on equity in excess of the cost of equity capital.

Shareholder wealth increases when managers find projects whose return is greater than the required rate of return.

If all this appears to be quite logical, the specific lessons should by now be self-evident: *Projects yielding a return greater than the required return increase the shareholders' wealth.* Conversely, any time the firm's cost of capital exceeds the return on its investments, the shareholders suffer. As with new equity financing, the required return or cost of retained earnings is an opportunity cost, the return that shareholders could have earned in the financial marketplace on other investments of similar riskiness. This return is the cost of equity capital.

This discussion suggests a key distinction between accounting and economic profitability. From an accounting perspective, a firm is profitable any time its earnings are positive, but from an economic perspective, a business is profitable (i.e., is creating shareholder wealth) only if the return on equity exceeds its cost of equity capital.

Illustration

Walt Disney's Not So Happy Time

In 1983, Thomas J. Peters and Robert Waterman celebrated Walt Disney in their best-selling book, *In Search of Excellence,* as one of the best-managed companies in America. Less than one year later, however, beginning in June 1984, Walt Disney was visited by several corporate raiders. How could this be? Were takeover artists willing to wreck one of America's—and the world's—most respected and best-loved companies in order to make a fast buck? Exhibit 11-1 suggests otherwise. It compares Disney's ROE to its cost of equity capital for the period 1965 through 1994. Note that through 1984, even as Disney was generating positive accounting profits, it was destroying shareholder value by consistently earning less than its cost of equity capital. The resulting value gap was what tempted the corporate raiders. In other words, despite the accolades of Peters and Waterman, Disney's managers were dissipating its unique collection of assets. For example, by 1984, more than 25 years had passed since Disney had adapted a classic fairy tale into an animated feature.

In response to these takeover threats, the board of directors instituted changes in management personnel and corporate policy that many shareholders felt were long overdue—in particular, enhancing and extending Disney's franchise and reemphasizing the creation of entertainment software and intellectual capital. The new CEO, Michael Eisner, used a blend of imagination, fierce cost control, and management incentives to revitalize the company. Among other things, Eisner increased the number of movies made annually, including a series of animated hits (*Roger Rabbit, The Little Mermaid, Beauty and the Beast,* and *Aladdin*); exploited Disney's rich film library; refurbished and expanded its theme parks while developing new ones in Europe, Japan, Florida, and California; launched Disney Stores; built additional hotels and free-standing resorts; restructured the Disney channel; and set up a Disney record label and Disney book and magazine publishing units. Raymond Watson, Disney's chairman during this period, said that the challenge to management and its policies "woke us up, though I hate to give credit to something like that. I think the company is stronger."[1] In response to these improvements, Disney's profitability jumped, its ROE rose above its cost of capital, and the price of Disney stock soared. Exhibit 11-2(A and B) shows Disney's cumulative stock returns relative to the S&P 500 from 1972 through 1984 and from 1985 through 1994. To give some idea of the magnitude of these returns, in June 1984, after the first raider was rebuffed, Disney's stock price was at $49 per share. By the end of 1994, taking into account several stock splits, its stock had risen to $736 per share—an increase in Disney's market value during this 10-year period of over $24 billion.

EXHIBIT 11-1
Walt Disney Return on Equity versus Its Cost of Equity Capital: 1965–1994

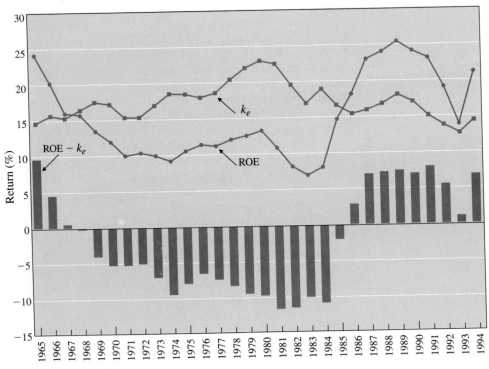

---

[1]*Business Week*, March 4, 1985, 82.

EXHIBIT 11-2A
Walt Disney versus the S&P 500: 1973–1984

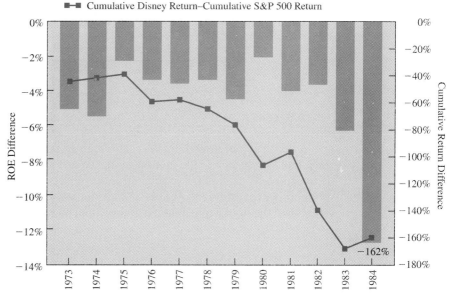

EXHIBIT 11-2B
Walt Disney versus the S&P 500: 1985–1994

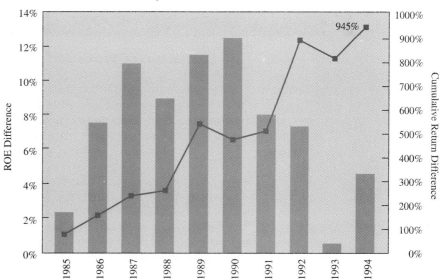

The **ratio of the market-to-book value** will be a good measure of the value created by the firm for its shareholders because it equals the present value of the dollars that stockholders receive for each dollar they invest in the business. This ratio turns out to equal

$$\frac{\text{Market Value}}{\text{Book Value}} = \frac{P_0}{B_0} = \frac{R - g}{k_e - g} \qquad [11\text{-}1]$$

where P_0 is the market value; B_0 is the book value; R is the return on equity; g the dividend growth rate; and k_e, the cost of equity capital.

A derivation of Equation [11-1] is presented on our Web site. At this point, we'd like to side-step mathematical formality and focus directly on what this relationship tells us about the value-creation process. To do this, we'll subtract 1 from both sides of Equation [11-1]. This operation yields the excess of market value over the book value relative to the initial equity investment:

$$\frac{\text{Market Value} - \text{Book Value}}{\text{Book Value}} = \frac{(P_0 - B_0)}{B_0} = \frac{R - k}{k_e - g} \qquad [11\text{-}2]$$

Another way to interpret Equation [11-2] is that it equals the value created per dollar of initial investment.

Illustration

Estimating the Market/Book Ratio

Ten investors have each contributed $10,000 for a share in a new company. Earnings at the end of the year are expected to be $30,000, of which 40 percent will be retained. Future retained earnings are also expected to average 40 percent of earnings. The required rate of return for the firm is 25 percent.

a. If the return on equity remains at 30 percent on both current and future investments, what should the current value of one share be? What is the ratio of market-to-book value?

Solution. Because there are 10 shares of stock, earnings per share are $3,000. With a payout of 60 percent, the first-year dividend is expected to be $1,800. The dividend growth rate, shown in Chapter 5 to be $(1 - b)R$, equals $(1 - .60) \times .30 = 12$ percent. Hence, the current value of one share is

$$P_0 = DIV_1/(k_e - g)$$
$$= \$1,800/(0.25 - 0.12) = \$13,846$$

With a price per share of $13,846 and an initial investment per share of $10,000, the market-to-book ratio is 1.38. Therefore, the excess of market value as a percentage of the initial investment is 38 percent.

b. If earnings are expected to be $20,000, how does this change the answers to part (a)? Assume a constant 20 percent ROE.

Solution. If earnings are now $20,000, the earnings per share will be $2,000 and the dividend per share will be $1,200. The dividend growth rate will be $(1 - .60) \times .20 = 8$ percent. Then, the price per share will be

$$P_0 = DIV_1/(k_e - g) = \$1,200/(0.25 - 0.08) = \$7,059$$

and the ratio of market-to-book value will be .71; that is, investors will get back only $.71 in value for each dollar they invest. Value is being destroyed here because the firm is earning just 20 percent on its investments, 5 percentage points less than the 25 percent return required by its shareholders.

The more positive the spread between a firm's return on equity and its cost of equity capital, and the more investments that are available yielding that spread, the more wealth the firm will be generating for its shareholders.

Equation [11-2] shows that the value created for shareholders, measured as the excess of the market value over the book value, depends on the size of the spread between the firm's return on equity and its cost of equity capital. The more positive the spread is and the more investments that can be undertaken at that positive spread, the greater the market-to-book ratio will be, and the more wealth the firm will be generating for its shareholders.

The converse also holds: Shareholder value is destroyed when firms invest in projects, including the acquisition of other firms, that yield a return less than that required by their shareholders. The loss in the value of the firm's stock will be directly proportional to the gap between the required and actual returns and the volume of investment undertaken at the below-market return.

One implication of this analysis is that the focus on growth in many businesses may be misplaced. Growth will add value only if it is profitable growth, that is, if $R > k$ on new investment. Indeed, growth will destroy value if new equity investments yield less than the cost of equity capital. This is apparent in Exhibit 11-3.

For example, a firm with shareholder equity of $10 million and a 15 percent cost of equity capital must earn at least $1.5 million annually to leave

EXHIBIT 11-3
Profitability Principles

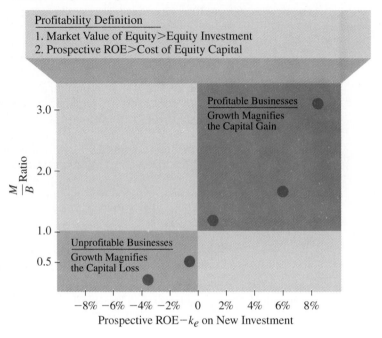

Profitability Definition
1. Market Value of Equity>Equity Investment
2. Prospective ROE>Cost of Equity Capital

Profitable Businesses
Growth Magnifies
the Capital Gain

Unprofitable Businesses
Growth Magnifies
the Capital Loss

$\frac{M}{B}$ Ratio

Prospective ROE$-k_e$ on New Investment

Corporate managers who emphasize growth at any cost may actually destroy rather than create shareholder value.

shareholders as well off at the end of a year as they were at the beginning. If it earns only $1 million in profit during the year (an ROE of 10 percent), the firm will have cost its shareholders $500,000. Companies that ignore this fact are vulnerable to hostile takeover: Such companies are more likely to treat retained earnings as free capital, giving them an added incentive to grow—even if their investments in new projects and corporate acquisitions are earning below-market returns and thereby destroying shareholder wealth. By reversing these "growth at any price" policies, raiders can afford to pay a premium price for such companies and still earn a profit for themselves.

Even Japanese companies are not immune to this economic logic. As a result of their relentless pursuit of market share, Japanese companies have historically had extremely low ROEs. Not surprisingly, as of 1998, many of the largest Japanese companies—for example, Sony, Nissan Motors, Hitachi, and Matsushita—were selling at below book value. Although hostile takeovers are very rare in Japan, most Japanese companies have become more conscious of their cost of capital and so are now emphasizing profit over market share, perhaps to ensure that they will not become the exceptions to this rule.

Illustration

Oil Companies Destroy Shareholder Value

Oil companies, which compiled a record of dismal and inefficient reinvestment of profits from their oil and gas reserves during the late 1970s and early 1980s, provide a striking illustration of the destruction of shareholder value. Atlantic Richfield, for example, took a $785 million write-down in 1984 on its investment in Anaconda, a minerals and metals company. Similarly, Mobil Oil's acquisition of the Montgomery Ward retail chain cost it in excess of $500 million, and Exxon is estimated to have lost over a billion dollars on its purchases of Reliance Electric and a host of office products firms. Neither has Phillips Petroleum's foray into plastics paid off for its shareholders.

Moreover, Michael C. Jensen argues that the oil industry has had surplus refining, distribution, and production capacity since the late 1970s, yet most major oil companies continued to spend heavily on exploration and development activities and added operating capacity.[2] The result is that the average returns on these oil investments fell below their required returns.

Given investors' skepticism that the major integrated oil companies would earn a market rate of return on the cash flow generated by their reserves, stock prices were well below the present value of these cash flows. In October 1983, the market value of all the outstanding stock of companies such as Gulf, Mobil, and Shell ranged from 37 percent to 43 percent of the market value (net of liabilities) of their oil and gas reserves alone, ignoring the value of their investments in pipelines, tankers, gas stations, refineries, and all the other assets that go to make up an integrated oil company. Given the substantial gap between the potential value of oil company assets and the market value of the financial claims issued against them, there was a struggle for corporate control, and raiders such as T. Boone Pickens tried to acquire oil companies and restructure them. In response to these threats, oil companies restructured their operations, changed their investment policies, and merged. The result was a more efficient industry, able to survive the severe slumps in oil prices in the mid-1980s and again in the late 1990s.

The preceding analysis assumes that a firm will be able to earn a return on equity in excess of its cost of equity in perpetuity. In reality, competitive pressures are likely to assert themselves eventually and drive returns to the level of the firm's cost of equity capital. The greater the projected number of years *n* that the firm will earn a positive spread over its cost of equity capital, the more value it will create.

---

[2]Michael C. Jensen, "Agency Costs of Free Cash Flow, Corporate Finance, and Takeovers," *American Economic Review,* May 1986, 323–329.

11.2   VALUE-BASED MANAGEMENT AND CORPORATE RESTRUCTURING

The era of restructuring began in the mid-1980s. Onto the scene rode the four horsemen of the corporate apocalypse: global competition, deregulation, accelerating technological change, and the threat of takeover. In response, company after company, including over half the Fortune 500, restructured—shedding businesses, cutting costs, laying off employees. The work of restructuring is not over, but it has now become part of the corporate routine. Underlying this restructuring is value-based analysis.

Value-based analysis stems from the recognition that you can calculate the value of each business in a company's portfolio with the valuation techniques discussed earlier. Add these up and you should arrive at the market value of the company as a whole.

> If the sum of the value of each line of business exceeds the market value of the company as a whole, some business units are destroying value.

When companies first applied this kind of analysis to themselves, many got a nasty surprise. Some of their businesses were actually destroying value and driving down the companies' stock prices, because the anticipated returns were less than the required returns. Such businesses were prime candidates for divestiture to someone else who could earn higher returns from them. As shown in Exhibit 11-4, selling off losing business units C and E will boost the company's value by $110 by ending **cross-subsidies** from the profitable units. If management is unwilling to weed its garden, a hostile takeover may be forthcoming.

> Value-based analysis can identify cross-subsidization.

Warren Buffett, legendary investor and Chairman of Berkshire Hathaway, stated the problem of cross-subsidies simply and eloquently in his 1984 Annual Report:

> Many corporations that show consistently good returns have, indeed, employed a large portion of their retained earnings on an economically unattractive, even disastrous, basis. Their marvelous core businesses camouflage repeated failures in capital

EXHIBIT 11-4
Value Analysis for Corporate Restructuring

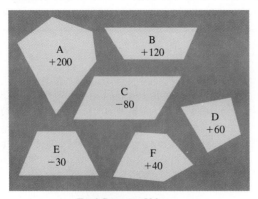

Total Corporate Value
No Restructuring=310
Losers Weeded Out=420

allocation elsewhere (usually involving high-priced acquisitions). The managers at fault periodically report on the lessons they have learned from the latest disappointment. They then usually seek out future lessons. (Failure seems to go to their heads.)

In such cases, shareholders would be far better off if the earnings were retained to expand only the high-return business, with the balance paid in dividends or used to repurchase stock (an action that increases the owners' interest in the exceptional business while sparing them participation in the sub-par businesses). Managers of high-return businesses who consistently employ much of the cash thrown off by those businesses in other ventures with low returns should be held to account for those allocation decisions, regardless of how profitable the overall enterprise is.

Illustration

Trans World Corporation Spins off TWA

Trans World Corporation (TWC), consisting of Trans World Airline (TWA), Hilton International, Century 21, Canteen, and Spartan Food Systems, was consistently profitable. But TWA had lost substantial amounts of money each year since airlines were deregulated in 1978, largely because of uneconomic wage and benefit levels for employees. With a strong parent for support, TWA's employees had no incentive to make necessary wage concessions. In effect, TWC's shareholders were subsidizing TWA's employees. Because of this large cross-subsidy, TWA had a negative value. The "breakup" value of TWC, therefore, exceeded its actual market value by a substantial amount.

Recognizing the potential for value creation, Odyssey Partners, a New York investment group, acquired a stake in TWC and launched a proxy battle to restructure the company. Although Odyssey lost the battle, it won the war. In February 1983, TWC sold a 19 percent stake in TWA to the public. On September 23, 1983, TWC spun off the remaining shares in TWA to its shareholders, creating a separate, publicly traded corporation. Upon the announcement, TWA's stock price fell nearly 4 percent, and TWC's stock price rose more than 11 percent. These reactions reflected the economic effects of ending TWC's subsidy to TWA employees. Overall, value was created because as an independent company, TWA could no longer have a negative value.

Cross-subsidies often arise when a company in a mature or declining business uses the free cash flow released by its core business to enter new lines of business in which it has no competitive advantage. The tobacco industry provides a striking illustration of the process of value destruction discussed by Warren Buffett. Exhibit 11-5 shows the return on assets (before taxes and interest expense) for Philip Morris and UST (the former U.S. Tobacco company) for 1988. These look like two successful companies, with an ROA of 20 percent overall for Philip Morris and 34.5 percent for UST. A closer look, however, shows a striking divergence in performance among the different business units. In both cases, tobacco's extraordinary returns are being dissipated by the low returns in the other units.

EXHIBIT 11-5
Value-Based Analysis: Opening Up
the Black Box

	ROA (1988)
Philip Morris	20.0%
Tobacco	64.1
Beer	11.7
Financial Services	5.1
Food	1.6
UST	34.5%
Tobacco	95.2
Wine	1.1
Pipes and Cleaners	Loss

Source: 10-K Statements.

Why do the tobacco companies continue to fund such low-return businesses? The answer is simple. Philip Morris and UST are operating in a tobacco market that is literally dying. Rather than slowly fade away, they have decided to redefine themselves as experts in making and selling small, frequently purchased, branded, packaged, consumer goods distributed by supermarkets and similar retail outlets. Philip Morris decided to enter the food business and acquired General Foods in 1985 for $5.6 billion. Despite its dismal performance in that business as revealed by Exhibit 11-5, Philip Morris decided to acquire Kraft in late 1988 for $13.9 billion. This was a 76 percent premium over Kraft's preacquisition market value of $7.9 billion. Exhibit 11-6 reveals that the relative disparity in performance among Philip Morris' major business segments has persisted over time, with the overall ROA falling through the early 1990s even as the tobacco business became increasingly profitable. The declining ROA is explained by Philip Morris's increasing investment in its low-return food and financial services businesses—a total of $36 billion by 1997.

Contrast Philip Morris' strategy to that of General Dynamics. In response to the dramatic cuts in defense spending following the collapse of the Soviet Union, the chairman of General Dynamics, William Anders, said:

> Given the shrinking defense marketplace, General Dynamics cannot effectively use all of the cash we are generating. The most effective and efficient way to apply our excess cash to the commercial economy is through distribution to our shareholders.[3]

In the 1991 General Dynamics annual report, Anders explains why he decided to return cash to shareholders rather than use it to fund a move into non-defense markets:

> Studies by outside consultants and by us clearly show that diversification by defense companies into commercial enterprises historically has had unacceptably high failure

---

[3]Reported in the *Wall Street Journal,* May 7, 1992, A3.

EXHIBIT 11-6
Philip Morris Segment Analysis: 1980–1997

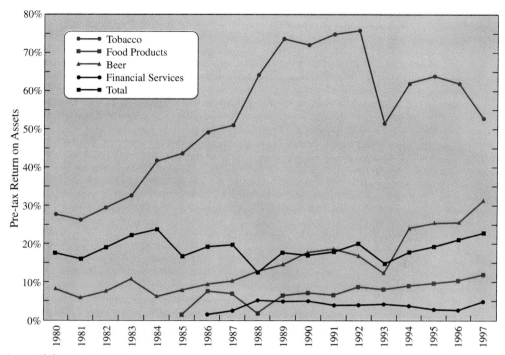

Source: Philip Morris's 10-K statements

rates, and for good reasons. Defense firms produce weapons systems for rugged environments at relatively low production rates and market to a customer whose primary emphasis is product performance. In contrast, commercial enterprises serve high volume markets with customers whose primary emphasis is product cost. Efforts by defense firms to develop new commercial products, to implement new marketing programs and distribution systems, and to then take market share from entrenched commercial competitors usually bring high risks and low rewards to investors, customers, and employees alike. . . . We believe that the process of widespread conversion of defense resources to commercial use at General Dynamics, while an alluring concept, is generally not practical. Instead, we are sticking to what we know best and are therefore focusing more sharply on our core defense competencies.

By distinguishing between the desirable and the possible, General Dynamics pruned its ambitions to fit its resources and reality. The result was a strategy under which General Dynamics sold off its nondefense businesses and used the money to buy back shares and boost its dividend. In the first year and a half of this strategy, General Dynamics' stock quintupled in price.

After eliminating value-destroying business units, the next step in value-based management is restructuring at the business unit level to end any hidden cross-subsidies. This means breaking down your business into the activities involved—purchasing, manufacturing, sales, distribution, research and development—and figuring out how much each costs and how much value each adds. It also means applying value-based analysis to every aspect of the business—product lines, customers, organizational structure—to identify those aspects that create value and those that destroy it.

Illustration

General Motors' Labor Cost Disadvantage Destroys Value

Historically, one of General Motors' strengths was that it made virtually everything it used—from bearings and radios to stampings and radiators. Now, however, Japanese companies, Ford, and Chrysler have shown that independent suppliers can produce parts at lower cost and with higher quality. As a result, GM's highly integrated approach to the auto business has turned into a great weakness. A 1992 study by Harbour and Associates shows that between its high-cost parts operation and lower assembly productivity, GM has a labor-cost disadvantage to Ford of $795 per car or $4 billion a year overall.[4] In effect, GM's parts and assembly operations are destroying billions of dollars of value annually in its auto business. GM has responded by attempting to transfer work outside and has shed tens of thousands of jobs. GM Chairman Robert Stempel was ousted in late 1992 when he didn't move fast enough to satisfy the board of directors. In 1998, GM took a strike that cost it over $2 billion in an attempt to outsource more of its parts and production processes and stanch the bleeding in these operations.

The obvious response is to weed out unprofitable products, customers, production facilities, or activities. For example, after a searching self-examination in 1980, Marriott Corporation decided that it added value as a developer and operator of hotels but not as an owner of hotels. As a public corporation, it could not benefit from the tax advantages available to private owners. So it sold most of its hotels but retained 75-year management contracts. The capital was then recycled into new hotels which were also sold under long-term contracts, enabling Marriott to grow faster while focusing on its true value-adding skills—in site selection, design, construction, and management.

Managers who don't divest value-destroying activities and assets may be subject to hostile takeover by those who have a greater emotional commitment to making money than to the old way of doing business. Conversely, by selling off underperforming and unrelated businesses and assets, companies reap the dual benefits of "fit" and "focus."[5]

---

[4]This study is discussed in Joseph B. White, "GM'S Labor Cost Disadvantage to Ford Is Placed at $4 Billion a Year by Study," *Wall Street Journal,* October 6, 1992, A2.

[5]The following discussion of fit and focus is based on the article by G. Bennett Stewart III and David M. Glassman, "Motives and Methods of Corporate Restructuring: Part II," *Journal of Applied Corporate Finance,* Summer 1988, 79–88.

Fit

Strategic fit exists when there are synergies across a firm's business units.

In deciding which businesses and assets to keep and which to divest, what counts is relative value: Is the business or asset worth more in someone else's hands? For example, value may be created if there are synergies between parts of the company and units of other companies. Recall from Chapter 9 that synergies exist when it's possible to generate economies of scale or scope through combining entities. These synergies arise through: (1) serving similar markets or using common channels of distribution, (2) employing similar production technologies, or (3) exploiting other skills. A key issue in divestiture, therefore, is whether another company or management team possesses a distinct competitive advantage or potential for synergies that enables it to further increase value. If so, the business or asset will be worth more to the buyer, and it can be sold for a price that exceeds its value to the seller. This is a tangible reward for finding a better "fit."

Illustration

Black and Decker Finds a Better Fit

In 1984, Black and Decker (BDK[6]) bought General Electric's (GE[7]) housewares business for $300 million. GE's brands had about a 25 percent share of the small-appliance market at the time of sale. The strategic fits with BDK's core power tools business were significant. First, small appliances could be sold through the same channels of distribution (e.g., Wal-Mart, Home Depot) as power tools. With both power tools *and* small appliances, BDK could increase its retail shelf space and, hence, its presence in stores. Second, housewares and power tools shared many common manufacturing elements such as the use of small motors. Finally, there was a "cultural fit" in that both BDK and GE had reputations for excellent product quality and value.

The divestiture of its housewares unit also made sense from GE's perspective. Despite its $500 million in sales and #1 market share, the small-appliance division wasn't making the kind of return GE wanted. At first blush, this may seem odd because GE also made large appliances. However, the synergies between small appliances, such as food mixers, can openers, and waffle irons, and large appliances, such as refrigerators and ranges, are minimal in terms of both channels of distribution and production technologies. By asking (and answering) tough questions, GE was able to get a fair price for a marginally profitable unit by selling it to someone like BDK, where the strategic fits were much better.

---

[6]Black and Decker trades on the New York Stock Exchange under the ticker symbol BDK.
[7]General Electric trades on the New York Stock Exchange under the ticker symbol GE.

Illustration

Quaker Doesn't Feel Its Oats

In November 1994, Quaker Oats Company (OAT[8]) acquired Snapple Beverage Company—the fruit drink and iced tea company—for $1.7 billion. Wall Street was unenthusiastic about the deal. OAT's stock price plummeted from $74.50 to $67.125 on the day of the announcement. The sharp drop in stock price was attributable to a poor earnings report from Snapple a day earlier and the market's sense that OAT had paid too much for Snapple.

Despite the poor market reaction, the acquisition seemed to make sense in terms of strategic fit. In 1983, OAT had acquired Gatorade from Stokely-Van Camp. Spurred by an aggressive marketing program, OAT increased sales from $100 million in 1983 to about $1.2 billion in 1994. With the addition of Snapple, OAT would become the market leader in beverage substitutes for soft drinks. The potential for marketing and production synergies appeared to be significant, particularly in the areas of: (1) purchasing raw materials, (2) new flavor development, (3) packaging design, (4) sales force consolidation, and (5) global distribution as well as (6) the transfer of promotional and advertising skills.

However, lurking just below the surface were some knotty problems. For instance, the channels of distribution for Gatorade and Snapple were fundamentally different. Gatorade is produced in-house and distributed to retailers through normal grocery products distributors as well as through direct sales to supermarket chains. Snapple, on the other hand, outsourced its production through an independent net of dealer–bottlers, who in turn accessed retailers of all types. One of the virtues of Snapple's distribution system was that the dealer–bottlers were able to get the product to retail outlets that were not easily reached through traditional grocery products distributors. Capturing the marketing-distribution synergies with these operating differences would be a challenge.

OAT never seemed to understand the differences in the modes of operations for the two products and began distributing Snapple through their grocery distribution channels. This angered Snapple's dealer–bottlers, and sales through this outlet dropped. At the same time, the alternative beverage segment was drawing intense competition from large companies such as Coca-Cola, Pepsi, and Procter & Gamble. As if OAT didn't have enough troubles, smaller firms such as Arizona Iced Tea also entered the market. The cumulative result of these internal blunders and external threats was disaster for OAT shareholders. Snapple was ultimately sold to Triarc (makers of the Mystic line of fruit beverages) in 1997 for $300 million—a loss of $1.4 billion!

---

[8]Quaker Oats trades on the New York Stock Exchange under the ticker symbol OAT.

These examples demonstrate that there can be significant rewards if a company understands the nature of **strategic fit** in operational terms, and big penalties when it doesn't. GE recognized that its housewares unit didn't fit with existing operating units and would be worth more to someone like BDK. That's a tough decision when the division is a market leader in sales. However, from the stockholders' perspective it was the right call and resulted in a "win-win" transaction. OAT, on the other hand, seemed unaware of the problems in capturing the synergies between the Snapple and Gatorade lines.

Focus

> Focus involves concentrating management's time and effort on its core business.

After divesting itself of unrelated business activities, a management team can focus on solving problems and finding attractive investment opportunities in the core business. A related benefit of pursuing a **focus** strategy is that by simplifying the company, superfluous management layers can often be stripped away, reducing expenses, speeding decision making, and promoting initiative.

A good example of a company that has created wealth by focusing its energies is Coca-Cola (KO). At various points over the past two decades, KO got into entertainment (Columbia Pictures, Merv Griffin Enterprises), pasta (Ronco Foods), and wine (Taylor Wine Company) as well as coffee and citrus groves. To say that the synergies are minimal among these operations and KO's core business is to belabor the obvious. Just because people drink Coke when they watch a movie doesn't mean that there are any advantages to owning a motion picture studio. During the 1980s, all of these unrelated businesses were sold, and the proceeds were used to support the penetration of global markets by purchasing interests in dealer–bottlers around the world.

The cumulative effect of KO's focus strategy can be seen in Exhibit 11-7, which looks at the company's market-to-book ratio in isolation as well as its market-to-book ratio relative to the market. Coke's results were nothing short of spectacular. In terms of raw numbers, the firm's market-to-book ratio increased from 2.94 in 1984 to 22.01 in 1997—almost an eight-fold increase. More significantly, KO's market-to-book ratio relative to the market (as measured by the S&P 500) continuously increased. Until his death in 1997, Roberto Goizueta and his management team lived up to the statement made by Goizueta at the beginning of this chapter.

The histories of Coke (KO) and Philip Morris (MO) from 1984 to 1997 are dramatic examples of how the design and execution of corporate strategy is central to creating shareholder value. KO's management recognized that it could enhance shareholder value by paying attention to the activities it knew best—the marketing of soft drinks. Management did this with a vengeance and made KO's stockholders rich. In contrast, MO's strategy of diversification, subsidized by huge cash flows from its tobacco business, didn't serve its shareholders well. MO's stockholders would have been better off if the firm: (1) had not invested over $36 billion in its low-return food and financial services businesses, (2) invested more

EXHIBIT 11-7
Coca-Cola Company Value Creation—1984 through 1997

December-Year	Market-to-Book Ratio	Market-to-Book Ratio Relative to Market-to-Book Ratio for S&P 500
1984	2.91	1.54
1985	3.65	1.92
1986	4.14	2.24
1987	4.40	2.38
1988	5.20	2.65
1989	8.17	3.45
1990	8.23	3.81
1991	12.05	4.59
1992	14.07	4.80
1993	12.63	4.02
1994	12.55	4.32
1995	17.24	4.89
1996	21.21	4.92
1997	22.61	5.26

Source: PC Compusat Files.

heavily in its overseas tobacco business, which could utilize its core skills in branded tobacco products, and (3) paid out higher dividends, which would have allowed shareholders to buy more KO stock.

Decentralization

Decentralization attempts to expose individual business units to competitive forces.

In many cases, the best way to improve the performance of a business unit—indeed, just to measure it—is to expose it more fully to market forces. That's clearly the motive behind the growing trend by companies to force their separate business units to operate as independent profit centers. Underlying decentralization is the view that with markets composed of an increasingly varied and rapidly changing array of products and services, managers at the top of the corporate pyramid don't have the kind of insight into these businesses that unit managers have. By giving unit managers responsibility for controlling costs and developing strategies for their own businesses, the company can tap their specialized knowledge and entrepreneurial instincts. In theory, such decentralized units would be leaner and quicker to respond to their customers. At the same time, the focus on individual unit performance keeps each unit on its toes; it helps to identify underperforming business units; it enables companies to reward managers and employees of value-creating units; it reduces the likelihood of hanging on to divisions that are sacred cows; and it reduces the possibility of cross-subsidization.

11.3   IS THE STOCK MARKET MYOPIC?

Does the market fully recognize management's ability to implement a sustainable, long-term value-creating strategy? This is a controversial question. Proponents of the efficient-market hypothesis would instinctively answer in the affirmative. This view is not widely shared among managers, however, who frequently believe that the stock market has a very short horizon. This belief has led many managers to become preoccupied with short-term financial results, usually the latest quarter's reported earnings per share, often at the expense of investments in research and development and plant modernization with longer-term payoffs.

Empirical evidence supports the idea that investors have the ability to assess the long-term economic consequences of current management actions.

Fortunately for the advocates of the EMH, the evidence overwhelmingly supports the ability of investors to peer far into the future and discern the effect of current management actions on the firm's true economic status over time. A good indication of the stock market's long-term focus and its willingness to pay cold cash for a promising future is provided by the biotechnology industry. Exhibit 11-8 shows the market valuations for the top 10 biotechnology companies as of December 31, 1991, along with their earnings for that fiscal year. Despite an aggregate loss of $342 million for 1991, these companies had an aggregate market value of almost $24 billion. Investors are clearly willing to pay huge amounts of money for companies that can credibly promise to provide large payoffs down the road.

EXHIBIT 11-8
Biotech's 10 Top Companies (in million $)

Company (1991)	Net Profit (loss)	Market Value*
Genentech	$ 34.9	$ 3,609.9
Amgen	40.4	9,885.4
Chiron	−28.7	2,063.5
Biogen	4.9	1,212.5
Genzyme	−45.5	1,219.5
Genetics Institute	−18.9	915.8
Immunex	−9.2	875.4
Centocor	−283.7	1,936.6
Synergen	−7.9	1,687.8
Xoma	−28.2	449.6
TOTALS	−$341.9	$23,856.0

*Market value as of 12/31/91.

This evidence goes against the grain of current thinking by many American business leaders. The best way to boost the stock price, or so it is said, is to boost short-term earnings by cutting back on capital spending and research and development. According to this view, companies that undertake long-term investments that boost their longer-term prospects but hurt short-term profits are penalized by the stock market. By contrast, Japanese companies, it is said, have more patient investors and are therefore better able to take a long-run view and make the expensive investments in R&D and factory automation that will improve their long-term competitive position.

But the notion that the way to lift a company's stock price is to pump up short-term earnings by skipping attractive long-term investments is inconsistent with the overwhelming evidence that the stock market takes a long-run view of capital expenditures and investments in R&D. For example, John McConnell and Chris Muscarella studied the stock market's responses to public announcements of changes in corporate capital budgets from 1975 through 1981.[9] They found that stock prices rose by 1.2 percent when companies increased their capital budgets and dropped by 1.5 percent when companies cut their capital budgets. Similarly, Gregg Jarrell, Kenneth Lehn, and Wayne Marr examined the stock market's reaction to public announcements between 1973 and 1983 that companies were embarking on new R&D projects. They found that stock prices increased by an average of 1 to 2 percent when companies increased their R&D expenditures.[10]

> In general, stock prices react positively to increases in capital budgets and R&D expenditures.

A major exception to McConnell and Muscarella's findings were oil companies. Their stocks dropped when they announced increased outlays for exploration and development and rose when they cut back investment. This result is consistent with Jensen's view (1986) that most major oil companies had been wasting money on too much exploration and too many refineries.

Clearly, the market cares most about firms' long-term prospects. Why then do stock prices sometimes react so strongly to short-term financial results? Largely because investors often see longer-term implications in new information, like the latest quarterly earnings report, and revise their expectations of future prospects accordingly. Thus a drop in quarterly earnings may cast a dark shadow over the company's longer-term outlook.[11] This is particularly true for a company that has been performing below expectations. After all, poor results today are likely to signal poor results in the future—unless the poor results today stem from a unique and one-time event. For example, the profits of Coca-Cola, McDonald's, and IBM depend heavily on market share, profit margins, and growth. If the bad news sug-

---

[9]John J. McConnell and Chris J. Muscarella, "Corporate Capital Expenditure Decisions and the Market Value of the Firm," *Journal of Financial Economics,* September 1985, 399–422.

[10]See Gregg A. Jarrell, Kenneth Lehn, and Wayne Marr, "Institutional Ownership, Tender Offers and Long-Term Investments," The Office of the Chief Economist, Securities and Exchange Commission, U.S. Government Printing Office: Washington, D.C., April 19, 1985. Additional evidence of the market's positive response to value—creating capital investments is provided by Woolridge (1988).

[11]This is the cockroach theory: When one bad earnings report shows up, there's usually another one right behind it.

gests a basic weakness in market share or margins or a slowdown in growth, analysts revise their profit forecasts—not only for the next quarter but perhaps for years. The results can be devastating, sending a stock down as much as 50 percent in a day.

Illustration

The Market Reacts to IBM's Earnings Announcements

The case of IBM illustrates the market's ability to discern long-term business implications from quarterly earnings announcements. On March 28, 1991, IBM announced that it would record a $2.3 billion charge to cover its adoption of FASB 106, which mandated that companies recognize their accrued liability for retiree health benefits. Despite this huge hit to earnings, IBM's stock price rose about 1 percent on that day even as the stock market overall fell. Why did IBM's stock price rise? Because IBM also announced on that day that it would reduce its worldwide employment by 10,000 people during the year, expanding cost-cutting efforts that had previously focused on its U.S. operations. In other words, the market ignored a nonevent—the adoption of FASB 106—and responded to an event that had positive implications for IBM's future profitability.

Two weeks later, however, when IBM announced its quarterly earnings and reported its first-ever quarterly loss, its stock price fell almost 2 percent. The quarterly loss of $1.73 billion stemmed largely from the adoption of FASB 106. Was this just a delayed reaction to the earlier earnings write-down? A closer examination shows that the market was not reacting to this write-down or to the loss at all. Rather, investors were reacting to IBM's revelation that sales of its computer hardware fell more than 17 percent during the quarter from the prior year, far more than analysts had anticipated. IBM had repeatedly blamed its business slowdown on the ongoing global recession and the effects of the Persian Gulf War—not on any internal company problems. But the quarterly earnings announcement revealed for the first time that IBM was losing market share across most of its product line. Although lower sales could be blamed on the recession, a loss in market share could not. Most importantly, these sales figures showed that IBM's share of the PC market, one of the better-performing segments of the lackluster computer industry, had declined. According to one respected analyst, "They are losing market share in the most vibrant sectors of the computer industry. This is a very bad omen."[12] Simply put, IBM's stock price fell because investors had lost confidence in the company's ability to maintain a competitive product line.

---

[12]Quoted in the *Los Angeles Times,* April 13, 1991, D3.

EXHIBIT 11-9
Effect of Write-Off Announcements on Earnings and Stock Prices

Company Announcing Write-Off	Date	Write-Off (millions)	Change in Stock Price Relative to Stock Market
Monsanto	1-Jul-91	($492)	3.22%
AT&T	18-Jul-91	($4,000)	4.00%
Digital Equipment	25-Jul-91	($1,100)	4.29%
Digital Equipment	24-Apr-92	($1,000)	1.27%
DuPont	25-Jul-91	($350)	2.94%
Allied-Signal	9-Oct-91	($880)	12.60%
Dial	29-Oct-91	($105)	6.41%
Allergan	4-Dec-91	($152)	1.67%
TRW	11-Dec-91	($250)	7.74%
Wells Fargo	13-Dec-91	($700)	5.68%
McDonnell Douglas	28-Oct-92	($291)	11.97%
Monsanto	20-Nov-92	($644)	2.26%
Westinghouse	23-Nov-92	($2,650)	24.49%
Chevron	27-May-93	($917)	4.63%
IBM	27-Jul-93	($8,900)	7.67%
U.S. WEST	19-Sep-93	($5,400)	4.68%

*Measured as the change in share price on the day of announcement minus the percentage return on the S&P 500 index.

> Accounting changes that affect reported earnings but not expected cash flow do not appear to affect stock prices.

In contrast to the impact of quarterly earnings announcements, research has shown that accounting changes that affect reported earnings but not expected cash flows do not affect stock prices.[13] A further example of the stock market's ability to see through accounting earnings to the underlying economic reality is provided by its reaction to announcements of corporate restructurings that disclose management's decision to cut its losses and exit a value-destroying business. Such announcements are invariably accompanied by large write-offs and increases in stock prices. Exhibit 11-9 shows some examples of this phenomenon.

The stock market is clearly not responding to the reduction in quarterly earnings associated with these large write-offs. Rather, its positive reaction stems from four different sources:

1. The problems that led to such large write-offs are unlikely to have escaped the notice of analysts. Thus, although the timing of these write-offs may be a surprise, their magnitude is not.

---

[13]The classic studies providing evidence of the ability of investors to see through accounting numbers to the underlying cash flow effects are R. Ball and P. Brown, "An Empirical Evaluation of Accounting Income Numbers," *Journal of Accounting Research,* Autumn 1968, 159–178; and Robert Kaplan and Richard Roll, "Investor Evaluation of Accounting Information: Some Empirical Evidence," *Journal of Business,* April 1972, 225–227.

2. These write-offs, which often involve non-cash charges, reduce taxes and thereby boost cash flow.
3. The firm is redeploying resources to higher-valued uses.
4. Management is signaling to the market that it recognizes its past mistakes and will not continue to throw good money after bad.

The final factor is perhaps the most important of all. In an uncertain world, companies will invariably make mistakes. The key to dealing with mistakes is to not persist in them but to recognize and correct them quickly. As Warren Buffett put it, "The most important thing to do when you find yourself in a hole is to stop digging." It is not surprising, therefore, that investors place such a high value on managerial pragmatism.

11.4 EVALUATING AND MOTIVATING MANAGERIAL PERFORMANCE

Implicit in our discussion up to this point is the notion that the separation of ownership and control in the modern corporation often leads managers to pursue goals other than shareholder wealth maximization. Ideally, therefore, companies should have an evaluation and reward system that motivates executives to achieve those business goals designed to create shareholder value. For the system to work as expected, management must be clear about what sort of performance it will reward, and it must be able to measure that performance. Then it must structure incentives to elicit that performance.

An important, though often-neglected point, is that a manager's performance should be judged on the basis of results in those areas over which he or she has control. It is unreasonable, as well as dysfunctional, to reward or penalize a manager for the impact of economic events beyond his or her control. Corporate headquarters must distinguish between the manager's performance and the business' performance: A business can be doing quite well despite the poor performance of its management and vice versa.

Illustration

Oil Company Management Rewards Itself

During the dramatic increase in oil prices during the 1970s, most oil companies were making enormous profits; and managers were rewarding themselves with high salaries and big bonuses. Yet, in an environment in which oil prices went from under $5 a barrel in 1970 to over $40 a barrel in 1980, it took no management skill at all to show big profits. Similarly, the steep drop in oil prices during the 1980s, down to under $10 a barrel in 1987, led to a sharp decline in oil industry profits, independently of any management actions. In either case, management was not responsible for and should not have been rewarded or penalized for price-related profit fluctuations.

The Tradeoff between Short-Term Profits and Long-Term Profits

Creating share-holder value often requires actions that can adversely affect short-run profits.

Maximizing shareholder wealth often requires resource commitments that may adversely affect short-run profits, even though these investments have highly positive net present values. Creating and maintaining an organizational environment in which the firm can earn excess returns may require adherence to a specific strategy—such as a product, market, or labor relations strategy—that in the short run leads to higher expenses. As short-term profit commitments become more difficult to achieve—because of a change in the external environment or overly optimistic forecasts—management may be tempted to cut these expenses. The immediate effect of such reductions is to boost current profits—but at the risk of sacrificing competitive position and longer-term profitability. The following are some short-run/long-run tradeoffs that managers can make.

Actions that make short-run profits look good often increase long-term costs.

Postponing Capital Outlays.   With the returns on most capital projects more than a year off, the costs of implementing the programs and the depreciation of project assets will ordinarily reduce near-term profits. Therefore projects are highly vulnerable to delay. By postponing projects, managers can reduce current expenses and report higher operating profits, even though postponement could significantly increase long-run costs to the firm.

Deferring Operating Expenses.   Many operating expenses for the current period can be postponed but at a significant cost. The cost of deferral is especially great for those discretionary operating expenses that, because their consequences extend beyond the current period, bear the characteristics of investments. This includes items such as advertising, research and development, maintenance of plant and equipment, marketing research, and personnel development.

Reducing Operating Expenses.   Managers under pressure to make their current profit target may choose to eliminate some operating expenses rather than merely defer them by cutting corners on product quality and customer service, laying off workers, or dropping some new product development work. These cuts can destroy some of the firm's intangible capital by adversely affecting its reputation for quality and fairness among customers and employees.

Making Other Operating Changes.   Firms can boost current profits at the expense of future profits in other ways as well. A common technique among consumer-goods companies is to launch various price promotions before the end of the current operating period. This action transfers sales from the coming period to the present period and at a lower profit margin. Moreover, customers begin waiting for the sales rather than buying at the higher regular price. Alternatively, raising prices can raise short-run profits if demand is inelastic but at the expense of longer-run profitability if the tactic draws additional competitors into the market or causes customers to search for substitutes.

Illustration

RJR Nabisco Loads the Trade

In September 1989, RJR Nabisco announced that it was going to stop "trade loading" and, as a result, would have to reduce its reported pre-tax earnings for the year by $360 million. In **trade loading,** manufacturers induce wholesalers—usually through price discounts—to buy more product than they can promptly resell. The manufacturer then books higher profits on the extra sales. However, RJR found trade loading an expensive habit. First, RJR was not paid until the wholesaler actually sold the cigarettes. Second, cigarette manufacturers must pay federal excise tax of 16 cents a pack on the goods they ship to the wholesalers—which means RJR was making an interest-free loan to the U.S. government until the cigarettes were actually sold. Third, RJR has a full-return policy for stale cigarettes, typically those that are six months old. When the stale cigarettes came back, RJR would receive an excise-tax credit, but it needlessly incurred the costs of producing the cigarettes that had to be destroyed and financing its excise taxes. And by managing this exercise well enough to show bogus profits, RJR had to pay income taxes it would otherwise not have owed.

Unfortunately, this practice was an economic treadmill. Suppose RJR loads the trade in the first quarter and thereby inflates first-quarter sales and profits. It will be powerfully tempted to repeat the exercise the next quarter since it has already stolen sales and profits from that quarter. Moreover, if some cigarettes come back from the wholesalers, RJR has to write down the profits it booked on those sales in the first quarter. Now it must load the trade still more to compensate for returns and to boost reported sales and profits again—all this in the face of declining U.S. cigarette sales. Like Alice in Wonderland, RJR has to run faster and faster just to stay in one place.

The net result of continual trade loading is that wholesalers start waiting until the end of the quarter to order so as to qualify for the predictable discounts, which have to be increasingly generous. Binge buying, in turn, distorts plant scheduling, with huge production peaks toward the end of the quarter and valleys in between. RJR wound up paying large amounts of cash—about $50 million a year—in order to boost short-term earnings. Why did RJR decide to go cold turkey on trade loading? Because it had just undergone a massive leveraged buyout—taking on an additional $25 billion in debt—and needed cash, not reported earnings, to service that debt.

> The budgeting process can be used to discourage short-run policies that can hurt the company's long-term interests.

Controlling Tradeoffs

One way to control such tradeoffs is to include in the budget allowances that encourage long-term profit-maximizing behavior or that at least discourage short-run-oriented policies that may provide immediate benefits for the manager (such as higher profits) but hurt the company's long-run interests. Such allowances include those for training programs, R&D, advertising, maintenance, and other vital functions that may be neglected if there are problems in meeting the budgeted profit figures.

In conjunction with locking managers into certain budget expenditures, companies can restrain harmful short-run profit-maximizing behavior by eliminating one of its main causes—unrealistic goals. Flexible budgets can account for unforeseen changes in the external environment, and senior management can make adjustments if they decide that certain projections are unduly optimistic.

Another way of decreasing the emphasis on short-run goals is to emphasize long-run goals when measuring performance. Most companies tend to rely too heavily on quantitative measures of performance because they are more easily measured, and they often slight more qualitative measures that may be crucial to long-term success—such as the quality of relationships with stakeholders or the degree of innovativeness—but are difficult to measure. Short-term profits are not a valid measure of a company's economic health because they ignore how today's policies affect the firm's stock of intangible assets, and these intangible assets—satisfied customers, loyal employees, reliable suppliers, and an efficient distribution network—largely drive future performance. A firm can raise its reported profits today by depleting its stock of intangible assets, but that will lower its future income and, thus, its current market value.

Linking Performance with Pay

A well-designed compensation system that aligns management and shareholder interests can mitigate owner-manager agency problems.

The basic premise underlying the design of a compensation system is that executives, being only human, will take actions that enhance their own welfare even if these actions reduce shareholder wealth. For most companies this will mean stressing the short term, because annual bonuses based on the current year's results tend to be more lucrative—and to be received more quickly—than are rewards based on the long-run consequences of decisions made today. Similarly, managers, whose fortunes are largely tied to the fate of the company, will tend to be more risk averse than well-diversified shareholders. Therefore, managers may pass up certain projects with positive net present values because they are highly risky.

Managers may also use corporate resources to further their own interests even if stockholders derive few, if any, benefits from these expenditures. This includes spending money on corporate jets, club memberships, luxurious offices, and other frills. Of more serious consequence to shareholders, executives may decide to build a corporate empire by acquiring other companies at costly premiums. The motivation underlying empire building is simple: Along with size go the four P's—power, prestige, perks, and pay.

Then, too, managers with little stake in the results of their actions may shirk their responsibilities and put less effort into their work. They may lack the entrepreneurial zeal that seems necessary to cope with a rapidly changing environment.

To the extent that the conflict between management and shareholders is serious, a well-designed compensation system can add to shareholder wealth by more closely aligning management and shareholder interests. But whether or not it is properly designed, the reward system influences the risk-taking behavior, decision-making horizon, work ethic, and expenditure decisions of management. What matters, in other words, is not how *much* managers are paid but *how* they are paid. For example, on February 26, 1992, ITT's stock price jumped 8.9 percent when its chairman, Rand Araskog, hinted that the company was now more willing to consider spinning off or selling some divisions. According to the *Wall Street Journal* (February 27, 1992, C2):

> Wall Street observers say a recent change in ITT's compensation system for executives helped spark the move. Top executives will be rewarded if the company achieves profits of 15% of stockholders equity or better and if the stock trades above 70. Last year, return on equity was under 11%. "It would be difficult for ITT in its present form to achieve that level of profitability," says Jack L. Kelly, an analyst with Goldman Sachs.

Illustration

Lincoln Electric's Incentive System

Lincoln Electric, a Cleveland-based manufacturer of welding machines and motors seems an unlikely candidate for survival, let alone success. But, despite taking some licks, Lincoln Electric has thrived. The key reason is Lincoln's approach to managing and rewarding people.

Lincoln's basic philosophy since its inception in 1895 has been to give nonmanagement employees direct and powerful incentives to manage their own work as efficiently as possible and to be on the lookout for opportunity. Lincoln pays people on the basis of what they produce. The more they produce, the more they get, with one caveat: Quality problems get corrected on the employees' own time. Second, everyone participates in Lincoln's bonus plan, with payments based on the performance of both the individual and the company. Unlike many bonus plans, these bonus checks are significant enough to make a difference. Since 1983, for example, bonuses have averaged 66 percent of other earnings. And lest employees worry about working themselves out of a job, Lincoln has a long-standing policy of no layoffs.

The combination of pay by output, large bonuses, and job security has worked liked a charm: Lincoln's employees produce an average of two to three times what their counterparts produce at competitors' plants, including those in Japan. Hard workers who don't mind overtime have been known to gross more than $80,000 in a good year.

To be sure, Lincoln's work environment would not be mistaken for a company picnic. People are producing all day long and competing with their peers for bonus money. Turnover rates are quite high—around 25 percent—during the first three months or so of employment, as people learn that nothing is given away. But, after that, most employees stay more than 30 years.

Designing Executive Compensation Contracts.   If organizations respond to incentives, it is because executives' compensation is linked to how well their organizations perform. Most firms reward people based partly on their contribution to profits. However, there's no necessary relationship between accounting measures of profit, like EPS, and shareholder wealth creation. Shareholder wealth is created when a company's economic value, not its earnings per share, is increased. As Section 11.1 showed, this occurs when a firm consistently finds investments that achieve returns on equity that exceed the cost of equity capital. What matters, therefore, is the spread between the return on equity and the cost of equity capital multiplied by the volume of investment opportunities yielding that return differential. Stressing current period profits in the reward system exacerbates the problems associated with purely accounting-based measures of performance and increases the clear disconnect between executive pay and economic reality.

The principal problem is that accounting measures of performance are not designed to promote the creation of dominant positions in the marketplace, positions that will provide sustained high cash flow and create shareholder wealth. An alternative to using accounting measures of performance is to tie executive compensation directly to value creation—as measured by the total return to shareholders. Executives get bonuses when shareholders fare well over the long term, but they get nothing when shareholders fare poorly. The problem with this approach is that stock prices are affected by many factors—such as interest rates, inflation rates, and exchange rates—beyond management's influence. Tying compensation very closely to stock returns will greatly increase executives' exposure to risk, and forcing executives to bear more risk can actually reduce shareholder wealth.

> Accounting measures of performance are not designed to promote marketplace power, which is the key to creating shareholder value.

Imposing large personal risks on managers will increase their incentive to forgo profitable but risky investments. More importantly, it will destroy a major advantage of the corporate form of organization, the fact that it permits specialization in risk bearing. It allows investors to bear most of the risk, while managers run the company. The advantage of this specialization is that well-diversified investors are willing to bear risk at a lower price than undiversified managers would charge.

> Compensation packages containing stock options can help to offset management's natural risk aversion.

Stock options can help offset management's risk aversion because their value rises in line with the riskiness of the return on assets. The proportion of option-like items in the compensation package should depend on the degree of discretionary decisions that managers make. The more discretion managers have, the more stock options are needed to counter their risk aversion. For example, managers in a regulated industry are less likely to be given stock options because they have minimal control over investment policy or the total return realized by shareholders. By contrast, stock options comprise a large fraction of the potential compensation received by managers of firms—such as high-technology companies—with substantial amounts of growth options. Stock options should also—but usually don't—comprise a large share of the potential compensation received by managers of companies with substantial amounts of free cash flow.

A compensation system should allow risk to be borne at a low cost while ensuring a close harmony of interest between management and shareholders. Although this goal cannot be completely realized, it is clearly desirable to insulate management from the effects of exogenous factors. One way to do this is to filter out the effects of random events on shareholder returns by using a relative measure of performance. Executive compensation is set according to some measure of how the firm's shareholders fare *relative* to the shareholders of a selected group of other firms.

Some companies supplement stock returns with specific benchmarks critical to the business' strategic success. These include market share, sales growth, cost position, and the maintenance of an acceptable level of new product development. To be truly effective, however, these indicators must reflect the contribution of management to shareholder wealth creation more clearly than do stock prices.

Another way to more closely align the interests of managers with those of outside shareholders is to force senior managers to buy significant amounts of company stock, the amount increasing with the level of the managers. For example, Eastman Kodak announced in early 1993 that its 40 top executives will be required to invest over the next five years the equivalent of one to four times their base salary in Kodak shares, depending on their seniority. Its stock price responded very positively to the news. Executives at other big companies, such as CSX and American Express are also encouraged to own stock.

Golden parachutes are agreements by a company to reward key executives if there is a change in control.	**Golden Parachutes.** In response to the merger and acquisition activity of the last decade, it is not unusual for a company to reward key executives with contracts that provide substantial (often millions of dollars) payments if they elect to (or are forced to) leave the company when a change of control takes place. Such an agreement is called a **golden parachute.**

Although often maligned as harmful to shareholder interests and the result of self-serving behavior by managers, the golden parachute is another example of the use of compensation packages to motivate some desired managerial behavior. For example, without a golden parachute contract, managers may block a takeover bid for fear of losing their jobs. Thus, by insulating a target firm's management from harm, even in the case of a hostile takeover, golden parachutes may offer managers the incentive—or at least less of a disincentive—to do what shareholders want them to do: Sacrifice position and wealth to negotiate the best deal for them.[14]

Like anything else, golden parachutes may be abused. For example, a rich golden parachute may tempt management to sell the company at a low price to the first bidder. In addition, because golden parachutes typically pay off only when a manager leaves the firm, they may create a conflict of interest between shareholders and executives. Current shareholders and the acquiring firm will want to retain executives with valuable knowledge and skills. But by paying off only when the manager leaves, the contract rewards him or her for taking an action that may hurt the business. These, however, are problems in the details of the contract's provisions and not with the existence of the golden parachute itself.

---

[14]A discussion of this point is contained in Jensen (1984).

Empirical evidence on whether golden parachutes are harmful or beneficial to shareholders is mixed. An early study by Lambert and Larker (1985) found that the adoption of golden parachutes by firms between 1975 and 1982 was viewed as "good news" by the financial markets. This result is consistent with the idea that golden parachutes help to reduce shareholder-manager agency problems. More recently, Mogavero and Toyne (1995) found that golden parachute announcements between 1982 and 1985 had no effect on share prices, but a sample of 23 announcements between 1986 and 1990 resulted in stock declines. These results tend to support the idea that golden parachutes may benefit managers at the expense of shareholders.

Partial spinoffs allow subsidiary managers to own a stake in their own operations.

Partial Spinoffs.   Evaluating managers of wholly owned subsidiaries is difficult because there is no independent measure of the market value they are creating for shareholders of the parent company. By the same token, managers cannot be compensated with shares or stock options in their units, making it difficult to attract and retain entrepreneurial managers. Giving managers shares or stock options in the parent company bases too much of their compensation on factors that they have no control over. One solution to these problems is being increasingly used by companies—a partial offering of shares in subsidiary units. A **partial spinoff** allows subsidiary managers to own a stake in their own operation, enabling the parent to more closely tie managerial compensation to managerial performance. At the same time, managers of each subsidiary know that what they do gets scrutinized not only by corporate management but also by their own stockholders.

Illustration

McKesson Sells a Partial Interest in Armour All

In 1987, McKesson Corp., a $6 billion distributor of drugs, beverages, and chemicals, sold to the public a 16.7 percent stake in its rapidly growing and highly profitable Armour All consumer-product subsidiary. Although Armour All accounted for less than 2 percent of McKesson's sales revenue, McKesson's stock price jumped by 10 percent upon announcement of the intended offering. One explanation for the stock market's reaction is that a public market for Armour All stock helps establish a separate identity for employees and enables the unit to attract and retain key executives through stock options, a key consideration in a marketing-oriented business with substantial growth options. A public market for the stock also allows Armour All to access the capital market directly (rather than by appealing to McKesson management) and increases the likelihood that it will be able to fully capitalize on its substantial growth opportunities.[15]

---

[15]These reasons were suggested by Stewart and Glassman (1988).

11.5   MEASURING ECONOMIC PROFITS

As we've noted in the last section, part of the challenge in designing executive compensation packages is that accounting measures of a firm's profitability may be a poor measure of the economic profit in a particular year. Therefore, rewarding managers on accounting returns may do little to establish the desired link between executive compensation and shareholder returns.

In recent years, many American companies have embraced **market value added (MVA)** and **economic value added (EVA)** as a means of assessing the wealth created by its managers. While the concepts underlying MVA and EVA are not new, these ideas were popularized by the consulting firm of Stern Stewart & Company.[16] Not to be outdone, other consulting companies such as McKinsey and Company have developed their own economic profit models that are conceptually very similar to MVA and EVA.[17]

Market Value Added (MVA)

> Market value added (MVA) is the difference between the market value of the firm's common stock and the amount of capital supplied by shareholders.

Market value added (MVA) can be used to measure shareholder wealth creation by looking at the difference between the market value of a firm's common stock, and the capital supplied by shareholders.[18] The difference is MVA;

$$\text{MVA} = \text{Market Value of the Common Stock} - \text{Equity Capital} \qquad [11\text{-}3]$$

A firm's MVA is directly related to its market-to-book ratio (M/B), the only difference being that MVA measures value creation in dollar terms and M/B reduces this to a ratio. Both measures are, in turn, related to NPV; after all, we'd expect firms that are generating lots of positive NPV projects to have high stock prices, high market-to-book ratios, and, hence high, MVAs.

To illustrate, let's take a look at the Occidental Petroleum Company (OXY[19]). At the end of 1997, the market value of OXY's common stock was $29.25 a share. With 341.126 million shares outstanding, OXY's common stock had an aggregate market value of $9.978 billion. On December 31, 1997, the book value of OXY's common stock was $3.109 billion.[20] Thus, OXY's MVA was $9.978 − 3.109 = $6.869 billion. This number represents the difference between what the firm's

---

[16]Stern Stewart & Company actually have a copyright on the term *Economic Value Added*. Details on Stern Stewart's approach to measuring economic profits may be found in Stewart (1991), and Stern, Stewart, and Chew (1995).

[17]For more information on McKinsey's approach to MVA and EVA, see Copeland, Koller, and Murrin (1996).

[18]MVA can also be defined in terms of the market value of the entire firm. In this case MVA is the market value of a company's debt, preferred stock, and common stock less the book value of these sources of capital.

[19]Occidental Petroleum trades on the New York Stock Exchange under the ticker symbol OXY.

[20]*Source:* Occidental Petroleum's 1997 Annual Report.

stockholders have put into the business since its inception and what they could get if they liquidated their investment.

Economic Value Added (EVA)

MVA measures the cumulative effect of the firm's economic profitability since it started in business. A way of looking at economic profits within a given year is economic value added (EVA). EVA is given by

$$EVA = EBIT(1 - T)$$
$$- \text{(Weighted Average Cost of Capital)(Amount of Capital Employed)}$$

[11-4]

Economic value added (EVA) is the after-tax operat-ing profits after the firm has been charged for *all of the capital* needed to generate these profits.

Essentially, EVA represents the after-tax operating profits of a company after we've charged it for the capital used to generate those profits.

Let's see how we might go about calculating the EVA for OXY. In 1997, OXY had operating income from continuing operations of $962 million; taxes for the year were $311 million or 32.3 percent of operating earnings. Invested capital at the end of the year was $6.761 billion.[21] With an estimated WACC of 10.1 percent,[22] OXY's EVA for 1997 was

$$EVA = \$962 \text{ million}(0.677) - 0.101 \, [\$6,761 \text{ million}]$$
$$= \$651 \text{ million} - \$683 \text{ million} = -\$32 \text{ million}$$

Based on these estimates, it would appear that OXY's managers destroyed value during 1997.

Using EVA: Some Cautions

The attraction of EVA to corporate managers is its theoretical simplicity. There are, to be sure, computational challenges in estimating a firm's cost of capital and in deciding what items should be included in "capital used." However, the major dif-ference between EVA and accounting profits is that EVA charges the firm for all sources of capital, not just interest on borrowed money. That's not much of a con-ceptual stretch from the systems already in place.

EVA can provide a basis for compen-sating managers of multidivisional firms.

In addition to its relative ease of use, EVA also provides us with a good way to measure performance of divisional managers because we can adjust for risk by

---

[21]For the purpose of the EVA calculation, capital used should be the assets associated with gen-erating the income stream less noninterest-bearing current liabilities.

[22]OXY's cost of capital was estimated as follows; first, the company's existing financing mix of 33.2 percent debt and 66.8 percent common stock was assumed to be its target capital struc-ture. The firm's bonds were rated A by Moody's Investment Service. Newly issued long-term bonds of similar credit quality carried yields of 8.75 percent at the end of 1997. With a 32.3 percent tax rate, OXY's after-tax cost of debt in 1997 was 5.9 percent. The company's beta, as reported by Value Line Investment Survey, was 0.90. A 5.90 percent Treasury bond rate and an assumed market risk premium of 7.0 percent produced a cost of equity capital of 12.2 percent.

using the pure-play technique to calculate costs of capital that are unique to a business unit. Divisional managers' compensation can then be tied to a measure of operating effectiveness that captures their ability to generate the highest operating profits (EBIT) using the lowest amount of capital possible.

> **Firms whose market values are related to future growth should be cautious about using EVA to reward their managers.**

Despite these benefits, companies need to be very careful about designing executive performance appraisal and compensation systems around EVA. The first term in Equation [11-4]—*EBIT*(1 − *T*)—measures the returns from a firm's existing assets. Therefore, EVA makes the most sense when market value is tied to a company's assets in place. However, for companies whose market values are related to their future growth opportunities, designing executive compensation around a single-period measure such as EVA may create incentives to sacrifice future benefits for current returns. This would be a disaster for technology-driven firms in which products from current R&D efforts might not show up for 5 to 10 years.

A company may also have negative economic profits (EVA) within a given year while still creating shareholder value. The OXY example discussed earlier is a case in point. In 1996, OXY's MVA was $3.923 billion. A year later, the firm's MVA rose to $6.869 billion, propelled mainly by a 25 percent increase in stock price. However, during 1997, OXY's EVA was negative.

To explain these seemingly contradictory results, we have to get behind the numbers to see what's been happening to OXY as a firm. During 1997, the company took a number of steps to transform itself into a more focused entity by (1) paying $3.5 billion to acquire additional oil and gas properties in the United States and (2) selling its natural gas transmission and marketing division. It also announced plans to sell off $1.6 billion in business units that were unrelated to either oil and gas exploration and production or chemicals. In short, the company was simplifying its operations to focus on those segments that management believed had the greatest growth potential.

The strategic repositioning of a company is often expensive and can result in weak short-term performance; OXY's negative EVA in 1997 is testimony to that. However, it's not unusual to see a corporate restructuring such as the one undertaken by OXY accompanied by rising stock prices as the market responds to the prospects of improved future performance. Penalizing OXY's executives for the company's weak performance in 1997 just because EVA happened to be negative does not reflect the fact that the firm's shareholders are far better off than they were at the beginning of the year.

SUMMARY

This chapter emphasized the fact that corporate management creates value for shareholders by finding investment opportunities that yield more than the required rate of return. The extent of value creation—the excess of the market value of the stock over the equity investment per share—is determined by three factors: (1) the spread between a project's actual and required rates of return on the equity-financed portion; (2) the volume of investment opportunities expected to earn higher than required returns; and (3) the number of years the higher yield is expected to persist.

By examining segmented financial statements, we saw that looking at companywide results in a multidivisional company can mask the effects of cross-subsidization. By asking the tough questions about strategic fit, companies can create value by divesting units that have no potential for synergies and focusing resources in their core businesses.

We also saw that one of the principal techniques used to manage an organization's performance is the evaluation and reward system. To maximize effectiveness, the data generated by the system must serve as inputs for compensation decisions. More companies are trying to explicitly link pay and performance in order to motivate executives to carry out strategies that serve the interests of shareholders. Central to this process is a focus on the firm's economic profits. Yet only a minority of firms use return to shareholders or even return on equity as one of the measures of financial performance. Thus, although some managers are underpaid and others overpaid, most are mispaid—with pay and bonus tied to accounting profits instead of the value they create for shareholders. This state of affairs is changing, however. Many companies are getting away from accounting-based performance appraisal measure in favor of such tools as market value added and economic value added that focus on economic profits.

APPENDIX 11A   CREATING VALUE: GROWING THROUGH MERGERS AND ACQUISITIONS

Companies can expand by either growing internally or by combining with another firm. Internal growth has the virtue of preserving a company's unique corporate culture, image, and reputation. To the extent that these qualities are a source of competitive advantage, internal growth makes sense from the standpoint of all corporate stakeholders—employees, customers, and stockholders. McDonalds, for example, has never purchased another fast-food company but instead relies on the symbol of the "Golden Arches" to propel its global growth. However, sometimes a company might not be able to develop the resources it needs to grow within a reasonable time frame. In these circumstances, some form of combination is critical to its corporate strategy.

Business combinations come in different forms. Although there's the tendency to use the terms mergers and acquisitions synonymously, there are some distinctions. **Mergers** involve the combination of two entities through an exchange of stock. Typically, mergers take place between firms of approximately the same size and are often friendly. **Acquisitions**, on the other hand, involve the purchase of one firm by another. Often the acquired company—referred to as the *target*—is integrated into the operations of the buyer.[23]

This appendix examines mergers and acquisitions from the perspective of their contribution to shareholder value. We'll begin with a look at the reasons for mergers and acquisitions before moving on to the critical issue of how to value a particular acquisition candidate. The appendix concludes with a look at the historical record of mergers and acquisitions and the reasons that many mergers fail.

Reasons for Mergers and Acquisitions

Most takeovers fall into two broad categories as defined by their motives. **Disciplinary acquisitions** are intended to correct nonvalue-maximizing behavior by the target's management. Such behavior might be some combination of excessive growth or unrelated diversification, lavish consumption of perquisites, and excessive employee compensation as well as the failure to manage the firm's assets efficiently. The purpose of the disciplinary acquisition is to improve the target company's existing operations. Many of the takeovers in the 1980s, such as KKR's acquisition of both Beatrice in 1983 and RJR Nabisco in 1987, were disciplinary in nature. Because their intent is to correct the poor performance of existing managers, many disciplinary takeovers tend to be hostile in nature.

In contrast, **synergistic acquisitions** tend to be friendly. This type of combination exploits strategic fit so that the value of the combined entity is greater than the value of the individual parts. For example, suppose firm A is considering the acquisition of firm B in order to take advantage of synergies between the two com-

---

[23]Another way that firms can combine is through *joint ventures*. Joint ventures represent a partnership between two or more companies to cooperate on a specific project or line of business. Unlike the case with of a merger or acquisition, only a small portion of a firm's resources are typically committed to a joint venture.

panies. If V_A and V_B are the market values of A and B respectively, then the potential for a successful merger will exist if the value of the combined entity, V_{A+B}, exceeds the sum of their market values on a stand-alone basis. That is, the precondition for a successful merger between A and B is that the firms are expected to be worth more together than apart:

$$V_{A+B} > V_A + V_B \qquad [11A\text{-}1]$$

This inequality will hold only if the operating cash flows of the two firms when combined exceed the sum of their operating cash flows as separate companies. In other words, the merger must bring about synergies that lead to an increase in revenue or a reduction in cost. Otherwise, there is no economic rationale for merging.

Synergies can be generated in a number of ways. Among the more important ones are the following.

1. ***To Exploit Economies of Scale or Scope:*** By acquiring firms dealing in similar products or markets, the buyer may reduce costs by combining production, purchasing, administrative services, and research and development, and eliminating some duplicate facilities, projects, and operations. The announced combination of Nationsbank and BankAmerica in 1998 was motivated, in part, by the desire to deliver financial services at a lower cost. It may also be possible to reduce costs by combining firms that deal in complementary products and can use similar R&D, production facilities, or distribution channels. For example, P&G's belief that it could use its powerful distribution network to market the Tampax brand tampon globally motivated its 1997 acquisition of Tambrands. Economies of scale and scope were also important factors in a number of pharmaceutical industry combinations (e.g., Glaxo Holdings and Burroughs-Wellcome, Ciba-Geigy and Sandoz) where R&D and marketing costs tend to be very high. Expanding a drug company's product line tends to lower these costs.

2. ***To Enter New Markets:*** Certain acquisitions may be justified because they enable the company to

   ■ obtain proprietary processes like patent, copyright, or trademark rights unavailable through conventional licensing arrangements.

   ■ obtain new selling and distribution channels in current and new markets.
   ■ acquire new products that complement or supplement its existing product line.

   For instance, when Pillsbury wanted to enter the frozen-pizza business, one of the fastest-growing sectors of the food industry, it acquired Totino's Finer Foods, which makes these pizzas. According to its chairman, "In the frozen-food business, we had to acquire because the sales and distribution in the field are different from what we have. It would take us years to build this."[24]

   Similarly, the Swiss pharmaceutical giant F. Hoffman-La Roche attempted to acquire Sterling Drug in order to expand its presence in the vital American market. Sterling's over-the-counter products, including Bayer Aspirin and Phillips' Milk of Magnesia, would complement Roche's strength in prescription drugs. Its aggressive sales force was also expected to broaden sales of Roche's vitamins, cold remedies, and skin-care products. As it turned out, Sterling was acquired by Kodak, which had entered the pharmaceutical business just a few years earlier. The acquisition gave Kodak a strong presence in the worldwide pharmaceutical industry as well as a distribution channel for its own products.

3. ***To Supplement Managerial Skills:*** When the buyer's management team is unable to address the challenges and opportunities in fields in which the buyer is now active or in which it intends to operate in the future, it may decide to acquire a company that does have the requisite management skills. Philip Morris' (MO) acquisition of Kraft in November 1988 for $13.9 billion is a case in point. Three years earlier, MO bought General Foods, the maker of such well-known brands as Maxwell House coffee, Jell-O, and Bird's Eye frozen foods. In July 1988, General Food's CEO, Philip Smith, left the firm to become chairman at Pillsbury. From MO's perspective, the purchase of Kraft was not only consistent with its strategy of diversifying out of tobacco, but it also filled a needed management gap at General Foods. Of

---

[24]Roger Ricklefs, "Mergers, Acquisitions Come Back into Style—But the Style Is New," *Wall Street Journal,* April 28, 1976, 1.

course, it may be possible to acquire managers by hiring them rather than spending $13 billion to buy their company.

4. ***To Gain Market Power:*** Mergers can also consolidate market power and limit competition. Buying one of your competitors is a way to do this; however, such activities may run afoul of antitrust laws. A more subtle form of market power is possible when a firm engages in **horizontal integration** by acquiring firms in the same broad line of business. By increasing its market share, a company's bargaining power with its suppliers and customers can be strengthened. This is particularly important to a consumer-products firm such as Nestlé, which may be able to increase shelf space at the retail level based on the breadth of the company's product line.

5. ***To Acquire Technical Skills in Industries in Which Technical Know-How or Rapid Obsolescence of Existing Technology Is the Rule:*** For example, General Motors acquired both Hughes Aircraft and Electronic Data Systems (EDS) in the hope that their technical skills in software and systems engineering, microelectronics, artificial intelligence, and other defense-related technology would enable GM to design and build higher-quality cars at a lower cost. However, although a few diversified firms have successfully interchanged military and commercial technology, a history of glaring failures attests to the difficulty of the undertaking. As it turned out, GM was not an exception to the rule, and it later divested these acquisitions.

This list is not intended to exhaust the possible sources of synergies. We've deliberately ignored diversification as a source of value. As we've indicated a number of times throughout this text, conglomerate mergers that divert resources from a company's core business simply to reduce risk are not a source of value because they don't do anything for shareholders that shareholders can't do through their own portfolio-building activities. At best, unrelated diversification will leave the shareholders' position unchanged. At worst, such activities can destroy vast amounts of shareholder wealth.

Valuing Acquisition Candidates

To create value for a firm's shareholders, a proposed acquisition must make sense from a strategic standpoint, i.e., there must be the potential for synergies. Once is-

sues of strategic fit are addressed, a perspective buyer must determine how much to pay for the candidate. What we want to avoid is situation in which an acquisition might be a sound business proposition but ends up costing too much.

The WACC Method

The WACC method is a convenient way to value the firm. Under this method, the firm's future cash flows are discounted at its weighted average cost of capital. The process of estimating the cash flows to be discounted is identical to that used in the capital budgeting evaluation of an individual project. We begin with forecasts of the target's operating earnings (*EBIT*) for each year of some initial evaluation period and then adjust these for taxes [$EBIT(1 - T)$]. Adding depreciation (a noncash charge against operating income) gives us the annual operating cash flows. The operating cash flows are then adjusted to reflect changes in working capital as well as any capital expenditures needed to support the projected level of sales. As in any capital budgeting exercise, the terminal value in the last year should reflect the present value of cash flows beyond the initial evaluation period. Because we are interested in the target's value to the acquiring firm, the cash flow estimates must incorporate the consequences of any changes that the acquirer expects to make to the target's current method of operation.

The annual cash flows calculated in this way ignore financing flows such as interest on debt, debt repayment, and preferred stock dividends. These *free cash flows* represent the cash flows that would be available to compensate *all* sources of capital used to finance the acquisition. Discounting these free cash flows at the "appropriate" weighted average cost of capital gives us the value of the assets.

The procedure outlined above establishes the *maximum amount* that should be paid for the assets of the target. Subtracting from the target's estimated value those liabilities that were not included in the forecast of working capital needs gives us the *value of the target's equity*. Dividing this equity value by the number of the target's common shares outstanding gives us an estimate of the *maximum price per share* that could be offered.

Applying the WACC Method: An Example

Like any valuation procedure based on DCF techniques, the WACC method is only as good as the acquirer's ability to estimate the target's cash flows *as part of the combined entity.* If there are significant economies of scale or scope, these cash flows may be quite different from those of the target. To illustrate the mechanics of the WACC method as well as the kind of strategic thinking that should go into developing cash flow estimates, let's suppose that Mosten Industries, a leading manufacturer of consumer and industrial power tools, wishes to buy Sower Electric, which specializes in producing small electric motors.

Strategically, both firms see this as a "match made in heaven," which should have the following benefits.

1. Mosten currently buys a significant number of electric motors for both its consumer and industrial power tool lines. The acquisition, as a major step in the direction of vertical integration, should (a) increase Sower's sales of small motors to Mosten and (b) produce some cost savings for both firms.
2. Mosten is financially strong with ample reserve borrowing capacity. Sower's ability to raise capital has been restricted in recent years by weak operating performance. As a result, Sower hasn't been able to modernize its facilities rapidly in order to meet growing cost competition from firms manufacturing in the Pacific Rim. With Mosten's financial assistance, Sower could acquire state-of-the-art production equipment that would allow it to lower manufacturing costs.
3. Because both firms serve the industrial market, a consolidation of the two sales forces would lower marketing costs. Sower's marketing expenses are currently among the highest in the industry.
4. The engineering staffs of both firms have successfully collaborated on the development of a new line of power tools targeted for the consumer market. Although future joint product development is speculative, opportunities would be enhanced with a combined entity.

Both firms have agreed to the acquisition, in principle. Sower's common stock is currently trading at $40 a share; it is assumed that some premium above this price will be offered. In structuring its bid, Mosten wants to ensure that its offer is seen as fair by Sower. This is, after all, a friendly acquisition in which the cooperation of Sower's management will be critical to achieving the projected synergies. On the other hand, an overly generous offer would make Sower management (and stockholders) deliriously happy at the expense of Mosten's stockholders.

To apply the WACC method to the valuation of Sower's common stock, Mosten begins by estimating an appropriate risk-adjusted cost of capital for Sower's cash flows as a part of the combined entity. Mosten will be acquiring the 1.25 million shares of Sower's outstanding common stock, assuming the responsibility for $10 million of Sower's outstanding long-term debt, and eventually integrating the operations of the two firms. Therefore, the cost of capital should reflect the riskiness of Sower's cash flows coupled with Mosten's capital structure. Let's assume that Mosten estimates this cost of capital at 14 percent using the pure-play technique.

The next step is to develop a set of forecasted cash flows for Sower that reflects the anticipated synergies. Exhibit 11A-1 presents Sower's current (1999) and forecasted performance (2000–2004). The estimates assume that: (1) Sower's sales will increase by 8 percent annually, in contrast to the the firm's current growth rate of 4 percent; (2) gross profit margins will increase from 35 percent in 1999 to 39 percent by the year 2004; and (3) operating expenses, as a percentage of sales, will decline from 25 percent in 1999 to 20 percent by 2004. Given these projected synergies, operating cash flows are expected to grow from $9.7 million in 1999 to $22.2 million by 2004.

Arriving at a terminal value for Sower (or any other acquisition candidate for that matter) is a bit of an adventure. Mosten arrived at the $128.0 million estimate in Exhibit 11A-1 by using a variation on the constant dividend growth model. Free cash flows of $12.8 million in the year 2004 ($22.2 million in operating cash flows less $9.4 million in working capital and capital expenditure additions) were assumed to grow at a 4 percent rate indefinitely. Given the 14 percent cost of capital, the terminal value (TV) would be:

$$TV = \frac{\$12.8 \text{ million} \times 1.04}{(0.14 - 0.04)}$$

$$= \frac{\$13.3 \text{ million}}{0.10}$$

$$= \$133 \text{ million}$$

The DCF analysis in Exhibit 11A-1 gives us a value of $95.44 million. Because we are discounting free cash flows, the $95.44 million is the estimated value of Sower's assets—not the value of the equity. To get the

EXHIBIT 11A-1
Cash Flows Forecasts for Sower Electric 2000–2004 (all figures in million $)

	Actual	Projected				
	1999	2000	2001	2002	2003	2004
Sales	$110.0	$118.8	$128.3	$138.6	$149.6	$161.6
Cost of Goods Sold*	71.5	77.2	82.1	87.3	89.8	98.6
Operating Expenses (including S,G & A)	27.5	28.5	29.5	30.5	31.4	32.3
Operating Profits (*EBIT*)	$ 11.0	$ 13.1	$ 16.7	$ 20.8	$ 28.4	$ 30.7
Taxes @ 40%	4.4	5.2	6.7	8.3	11.4	12.3
EBIT(1 − T)	$ 6.6	$ 7.9	$ 10.0	$ 12.5	$ 17.0	$ 18.4
+ Depreciation	3.1	3.3	3.5	3.6	3.7	3.8
Operating Cash Flow	$ 9.7	$ 11.2	$ 13.5	$ 16.1	$ 20.7	$ 22.2
+/− Working Capital Changes†		(3.5)	(3.8)	(4.1)	(4.4)	(4.8)
− Capital Expenditures Additions		(4.0)	(4.2)	(4.3)	(4.4)	(4.6)
+ Terminal Value		-0-	-0-	-0-	-0-	133.0
Free Cash Flow		$ 3.7	$ 5.5	$ 7.7	$ 11.9	$145.8
Present Value of Cash Flows @ 14%		$ 3.25	$ 4.23	$ 5.20	$ 7.05	$ 75.72
Total Present Value of the Cash Flows = $95.44						

*Depreciation expense is included as part of cost of goods sold.
†Estimated at 40 percent of the increase in sales. Working capital includes operating cash, accounts receivable, and inventories less accounts payable.

per-share value of the equity, we must subtract Sower's $10 million in outstanding debt and divide by the shares outstanding as follows:

Value per Share

$$= \frac{\text{Value of the Assets} - \text{Value of the Liabilities}}{\text{Number of Shares Outstanding}}$$

$$= \frac{\$95.44 \text{ million} - \$10 \text{ million}}{1.25 \text{ million shares}} = \$68.36/\text{share}$$

The $68.36 per share value is significantly higher than Sower's current market price of $40 a share. This is not unusual in strategic acquisitions because there may be numerous economies of scale and/or scope. Whether Mosten should offer $68.36 a share is another matter. The $28.36 premium over the current market price represents Mosten's best estimate of the synergies that may be possible by combining the two entities. This estimate is based on numerous assumptions about future operations, some of which may never materialize. If Mosten offers $68.36 per share for Sower's common stock, *all* of the projected benefits from the acquisition will flow to Sower's shareholders. Mosten will have essentially taken on a zero NPV project and assumed all of the risk that some, or all, of the projected synergies may never materialize. Mosten's management should be careful about giving too much away in its negotiations with Sower. Many strategically sound acquisitions fail to provide benefits to the stockholders of buying firms because their managers simply overpay.

Do Acquisitions Create Value?
A Look at the Record
Considering the volume of M&A transactions, we'd like to think that growth through acquisition would be a powerful tool for creating shareholder value. Unfortunately, the historical record indicates that the big winners are the stockholders of the target firms, who receive large premiums for their shares. Shareholders of acquiring firms don't seem to be as lucky. Research results are mixed: Some studies indicate small increases

in share price; others find no effect, and still others actually show a decline in value. All in all, there's little evidence that acquisitions do much for the stockholders of acquiring companies.[25]

There are a number of reasons for these disappointing results. First, conglomerate mergers that produce no synergies are unlikely to create value. Further, when an acquiring company lacks knowledge of the target's industry, it's impossible to objectively determine what a candidate is really worth. Therefore, when the buyer pays a 20 percent to 40 percent premium over the pre-bid market price—the "typical" premium for an acquisition candidate—we'd expect to see a decline in the acquiring company's market price.

Over-optimism has been the downfall of many acquisitions. Some executives tend to overestimate either their ability to improve the operating performance of the target firm or the synergies that may be inherent in the combination. Many acquisitions that get high marks in terms of strategic fit don't create value because the acquiring firm simply paid too much. Therefore, the economic benefits from any synergies produced by the combination flow to the shareholders of the target firm.

Over-optimism as a possible motive for takeovers is best expressed by Warren Buffett, chairman of Berkshire Hathaway, in the company's 1981 annual report:

> Many managements apparently were over-exposed in impressionable childhood years to the story in which the imprisoned, handsome prince is released from the toad's body by a kiss from the beautiful princess. Consequently, they are certain that the managerial kiss will do wonders for the profitability of the target company. Such optimism is essential. Absent that rosy view, why else should

the shareholders of company A want to own an interest in B at a takeover cost that is two times the market price they'd pay if they made direct purchases on their own? In other words, investors can always buy toads at the going price for toads. If investors instead bankroll princesses who wish to pay double for the right to kiss the toad, those kisses better pack some real dynamite. We've observed many kisses, but very few miracles. Nevertheless, many managerial princesses remain serenely confident about the future potency of their kisses, even after their corporate backyards are knee-deep in unresponsive toads.

A related problem to overoptimism in the merger game stems from the fact that even if the "average" bidding firm accurately estimates the value of the target, some bidders will overestimate the target's value, and other potential acquirers will underestimate its value. Unless the winner can exploit some strong synergies that are not available to other bidders, the winning bidder is likely to be the one who most overestimates the value. Known as the *winner's curse,* this phenomenon means that successful bidders tend to pay more for the target than it's worth.

If all bidders accounted properly for the winner's curse, there would be no particular bias associated with bidding above the market price. However, empirical evidence from auctions indicates that bidders do not fully incorporate the winner's curse. According to Richard Roll (1986), the winner's curse in takeovers is most likely to stem from *hubris;* the overbearing presumption of bidders that their above-average valuations are correct and that the market is wrong. Implied in this behavior is that these executives are somehow smarter than everyone else and can see value where others cannot. Even if there were no synergies from a merger, managerial hubris would still lead to higher-than-market bids and a transfer of wealth from the acquirer's shareholders to the target's shareholders. The empirical evidence is consistent with Roll's hubris hypothesis.

---

[25]Well over a dozen studies have examined the effects of acquisition announcements on the stock price of both target and acquiring firms. Some of the more comprehensive studies are Jarrell, Brickley, and Netter (1988), Jarrell and Poulson (1989), and Schwert (1996).

Illustration

Kodak Acquires Sterling Drug

In 1988, Kodak outbid Hoffman-La Roche for Sterling Drug. The purchase, for $5.1 billion, culminated Kodak's long-standing effort to build a life-sciences business based on its chemical expertise. Although Sterling was a minor player in its market, the acquisition gave Kodak managers experience in getting products approved by the federal Food and Drug Administration and into doctors' offices around the world. Sterling's highly regarded sales force could also help sell Kodak's blood analyzers, and Kodak could use its international operations to sell such popular household products as Lysol in overseas markets. At the same time, Kodak expected to use its background and financial resources to make Sterling a major player in the pharmaceutical market. Although few quibbled with Kodak's rationale for the merger, most analysts believed that the company overpaid by spending 23 times earnings to buy a lackluster drug company. Critics of the merger were also concerned because Kodak had been unable to conceive, develop, and profitably market new products that weren't closely related to its office-copier and photography businesses. They noted that there is a difference between competing in a mature market (film) in which you are dominant and competing in a leading-edge technology area. Kodak had already struck out with its acquisition of Verbatim, a maker of floppy disks; it struck out in the information-storage system business; and it struck out in the battery business. In line with these concerns, Kodak's stock dropped $2.2 billion in value following the announcement of the Sterling acquisition, which just approximated the $2.1 billion premium paid by Kodak relative to Sterling's $3.0 billion market value 30 days prior to the announcement of the bid. The market's reaction indicates that investors expected no synergies from the deal. Exhibit 11A-2 shows the contrasting fortunes of Sterling Drug and Kodak before and after the acquisition.

The critics were right. Kodak's attempt to diversify failed once again. In 1994, Kodak's new chairman sold off its pharmaceutical, household products, and clinical diagnostic units in order to refocus on its photography and digital-imaging products.

Finally, many acquisitions don't create value because of the failure of all parties to address issues of strategic fit before the deal is consummated. In its haste to make the seller feel better about the loss of autonomy, a buyer may tell a target that it will leave it alone after the purchase. Unfortunately, it's tough to deliver on such rhetoric and still create value. The simple fact is that it is impossible to capture synergies without integrating the buyer and seller in some way. Otherwise, it's like trying to make an omelette without breaking some eggs. At the same time, trying to combine operations without the seller's full cooperation is rarely productive. This problem is particularly critical for a target whose value is tied to its human assets.

Although the evidence is mixed, the final impression is that any gains to the acquiring firm are small at best and highly questionable. Gains to the acquirer's shareholders—especially in large, highly publicized contests—are likely to be negative. By contrast, stockholders of acquired firms earn large and statistically significant gains. The question of whether shareholders benefit or lose overall from a merger has been studied by examining the effect of the takeover on the combined value of the bidder and the target around the date of the takeover. The total gain has been positive in some studies and negative in others but statistically significant in none. The lack of demonstrable gains to the combined firms in mergers supports the view that many takeover bids result from valuation mistakes by the acquiring companies' managers.

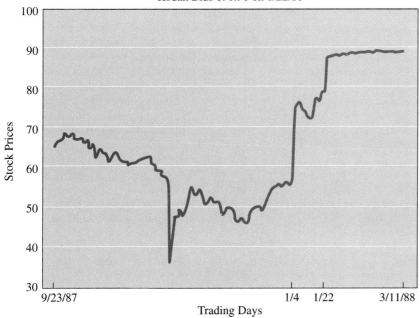

STERLING DRUG'S DAILY STOCK PRICE
Hoffman Bids $72 on 1/4/88
Kodak Bids $90.90 on 1/22/88

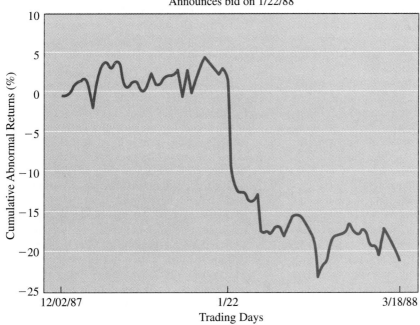

KODAK'S STOCK PRICE REACTION
Announces bid on 1/22/88

385

QUESTIONS

1. Explain to a skeptic why it makes sense to focus on shareholder value. When might boosting shareholder value be in conflict with ethical considerations?

2. Comment on the following statement: "Our shareholders benefit from the fact that we are reinvesting most of our earnings, instead of paying dividends, because this increases the value of their investment in the firm."

3. Why might managers focus on growth, even if the return on new assets was less than shareholders require?

4. It has been said that firms that sell for less than book value are prime candidates for a takeover, because the acquirer can purchase assets for less than their cost. Comment on this statement. Are there any other reasons why companies with low market-to-book ratios might be more subject to attack by corporate raiders?

5. What is the general stock price reaction to news that a company is increasing its spending on research and development? What implications does this reaction have for investment decision making?

6. The chief financial officer of a large grocery store chain was complaining that the market failed to recognize the value of its real estate assets: "Where does the value of our real estate appear in the market value of this company? Why, we could liquidate our real estate and realize far more than our current stock price." In view of this fact, is the stock market behaving irrationally?

7. In late 1988, Texas Air Corp. sold its Eastern Airlines shuttle to developer Donald Trump. The East Coast shuttle was the only profitable part of Eastern Airlines, a money-losing carrier with a history of troubled labor relations. Why might Texas Air have sold the shuttle? How do you think Eastern's unions reacted to the sale?

8. Comment on the following statement: "The creation of a more efficient market in corporate assets means that corporate executives will find it impossible to take a longer-term view of their business prospects. Large capital investments, in plant or new technology or research, are always risky; if they don't work out, the value of those corporate assets will depreciate. So corporate executives will be disinclined to take risks. Instead, they will concentrate on realizing, as much as possible, the current value of their assets as reflected in the price of their stock."

9. Classical "value analysis" of a corporation looked at corporate assets in its pursuit of "undervalued situations." But investors who did find such situations either purchased and held stock, in the belief that management would eventually realize the latent values, or brought in new management to do the job. Those who used value analysis did not envisage breaking up the corporation to sell off the parts. Today, that is a common occurrence. Explain why dismemberment is often likely to be more profitable than the old buy-and-hold strategy.

10. On May 19, 1988, Citicorp's chairman, John Reed, announced that Citicorp was adding a staggering $3 billion to its reserves against losses on Third World loans. Reed's decision created a $2.5 billion loss for the quarter and resulted in a loss for the year. Nonetheless, Citicorp's stock rose from $50.625 to $55.375 in the week following the announcement. Why did the market respond so positively to this disastrous earnings report?

11. Many manufacturing concerns have attempted to tie the wages of their work force to some measure of productivity or profitability.
    a. What advantages do such compensation plans have to the workers? To the stockholders?
    b. How might such plans affect corporate performance during a business downturn?
    c. Unions have generally been against this type of link with the "health of the company." Why do you think they oppose this form of compensation? Are such methods "fair"?

12. DaimlerBenz, maker of the Mercedes Benz, recently decided to set up a unit to produce semiconductor chips to provide an in-house source of supply. However, Daimler decided that the new unit must sell at least 80 percent of its output to third-party customers. What possible motivation could Daimler have for this rule?

13. In December 1992, Michael Eisner, Walt Disney's CEO exercised stock options on Disney stock that yielded him a pre-tax profit of $127 million. These options (to buy Disney stock at a price of $57 when it was selling for $45) were part of the employment contract designed to lure Mr. Eisner to Disney in 1984. A number of people thought it

was wrong that one person should be paid so much money for running a company. Comment.

14. According to General Dynamics' chairman: "At least half of each bonus paid as a direct result of increasing shareholder value *must* remain in a General Dynamics account, the value of which we intend to link directly to the company's long-term performance until the individual participant reaches age 65. In fact, all of my bonus and our president's bonus have been held back and placed in that company account."

   a. How are shareholders likely to respond to a compensation plan such as that of General Dynamics?

   b. Why might General Dynamics have inserted the requirement that bonus money cannot be removed from the account until the participant reaches 65?

15. Tridex Corporation generates revenues from three relatively unrelated business units serving three distinct markets. One of its businesses accounted for over 50 percent of revenues and more than 65 percent of operating profits, enjoyed a dominant market position, and generated large excess cash flows. The operating performance of the other two businesses, however, was marginal, and they required large infusions of cash.

Returns to shareholders had been excellent in the past, and the stock traded at 140 percent of book value. Overall, the company earned 17 percent on invested capital in contrast with a cost of capital estimated at about 13 percent. However, the strong performing business earned 22 percent on its invested capital (relative to an estimated cost of capital of 11 percent), whereas the other two businesses earned about 12 percent on invested capital (relative to their average estimated cost of capital of 15 percent).

The company was financially very strong: A modest amount of debt was offset more than twofold by excess cash and an overfunded pension plan. Management itself owned less than 2 percent of the company and compensation was heavily skewed toward cash.

   a. How successful has Tridex been? Is the market-to-book ratio a good indicator of Tridex's performance?

   b. Suggest opportunities to boost Tridex's share price through restructuring.

   c. For each of your suggestions in (b), explain how the restructuring can boost market value.

16. As the result of a recent audit, McKesson, the drug, beverage, and pharmaceutical distributor, has discovered that it has over 600 real estate properties around the United States, many of them warehouses located in the central business districts of major American cities.

   a. What opportunities might these properties present to McKesson? What problems?

   b. What would you recommend that McKesson do with its properties? How should it go about making its decision?

17. In early 1980, Westinghouse launched an ambitious program to boost shareholder value. Among other requirements, each business unit was pushed to do better than the corporate goal of 8.5 percent annual growth in sales and 10 percent annual increase in pre-tax earnings. It also emphasized nonfinancial measures of performance, such as quality, that will eventually affect the bottom line. Its primary focus, though, was on achieving a 20 percent return on equity. Business units that didn't measure up quickly were dumped. Even well-performing businesses were sold off if they were worth more to another company. The chairman claimed that despite his personal dislike of emphasizing annual corporate results, he was boxed in by the rules of American capitalism, which demand high returns and quickly.

   a. Why did Westinghouse focus on these measures of financial performance? How were these measures likely to drive its new business strategy? Is Westinghouse "boxed in by the rules of U.S. capitalism"?

   b. What techniques has Westinghouse used to improve its financial performance? Are these techniques usable at other companies?

   c. How might managers at Westinghouse or elsewhere raise the return on equity for their divisions at the expense of corporate health?

   d. What dangers might exist in Westinghouse's business strategy? For example, consider the possible responses of competitors to this strategy.

18. Comment on the following statements by John Smale, chairman of Procter & Gamble.

   a. "Over time, how well a company does depends importantly on how vigorously it prepares for the future. That preparation often involves decisions and investments that have short-term adverse consequences. And that's one of the things that should concern us about hostile takeovers: managers making expedient decisions to run up the price of their stock in order to try to prevent the takeover of their company."

b. "It's clear that opportunity exists for manipulation [of corporate structure] to produce profits for speculators without consideration of the real interests of the corporation's long-term investors, its employees, or the communities in which it operates."

c. "Until recently, putting a significant part of a company's profits into investments for future growth was considered essential—the driving force of future profit growth. Now, it is argued that companies should cut investments to provide shareholders quick returns. For example, oil companies have been attacked for using profits to search for new oil reserves."

d. "There can be little argument about the obligation that those who manage and govern corporations have to the shareholder. But what about the shareholder's obligation? In fact, doesn't ownership itself imply some responsibility if our economy and our society are to be healthy?"

19. If a corporate raider can acquire a company for $1 billion but sell its separate pieces for a total of $1.5 billion, should the raider do it?

   a. What does this value disparity say about the value of the firm as a going concern?

   b. What other reasons can you give for the disparity between the value of the firm's divisions sold separately versus the value of the firm as a whole?

20. Upon announcement of its takeover bid for Kraft, Philip Morris's stock sank 5 7/8, to 94 1/8. When RJR CEO Ross Johnson announced his LBO that same week, RJR stock jumped 21 3/8, to 77 1/4.

   a. Why had the stock market so undervalued Philip Morris and RJR?

   b. What can explain the gap between the pre- and post-LBO prices of RJR? Describe four sources of potential value creation by the LBO.

   c. What explains the drop in the price of Philip Morris following its announced offer for Kraft?

PROBLEMS

✒—Excel templates may be downloaded from **www. prenhall.com/financecenter.**

1. Standfast Company has an ROE of 40 percent, a P/E ratio of 8, and is not expected to grow. With a book value of $32, what should its stock price be?

2. XYZ has earnings per share of $2.50. ✒

   a. With a payout ratio of .75, what is the expected increase in net worth per share?

   b. If the company reduces its payout ratio to .25, what increase is expected in net worth per share?

   c. Given a net worth per share equal to $1 at present, what is the growth rate in net worth in (b)?

   d. Given the growth rate in (c), what is the rate of return on equity?

3. Here are five alternative growth and profitability scenarios. What are the value creation implications of investing under each of these scenarios?

Scenario		R (%)	k (%)	g (%)
1. Medium-growth:	$R = k$	12	12	4
2. Slow growth:	$R > k$	14	12	2
3. Slow growth:	$R < k$	10	12	2
4. High growth:	$R > k$	14	12	8
5. High growth:	$R < k$	10	12	8

4. The book value of New Company stock is $35. The rate of return on investments is currently 10 percent, and the growth rate of dividends is expected to continue at 5 percent. ✒

   a. With a required rate of return on equity of 12 percent, what is the current price of a share of New Co. stock?

   b. What rate of return does New Co. need before its stock will sell for more than book value?

   c. If the growth rate of dividends is expected to fall to 2 percent, what happens to the current price of a share?

d. If the required rate of return on equity rises to 15 percent, what will happen to the current price of a share?

5. Two engineers have incorporated themselves as a new medical engineering firm, each contributing $25,000 in equity capital. They have projected earnings for the first year of the company as $5,000, of which 75 percent is retained. The rate of return required for the company is 45 percent. ⬛
   a. What dividend is expected to be paid to each engineer?
   b. What is the expected growth rate of dividends?
   c. What is the current value of each engineer's stock?
   d. What is the market-to-book value?
   e. If the earnings are only $3,500, what will be the equilibrium value of equity?

6. Suppose that Digitronics, a small manufacturer of computer peripherals, has a 16 percent cost of equity capital. If Digitronics' actual return on equity is 22 percent and it has sufficient investment opportunities at that return to absorb 60 percent of its earnings, what will be its market-to-book ratio?

7. Coldberg and Cravatz, an investment firm specializing in leveraged buyouts, is considering a tender offer for Toolex, a maker of machine tools. Currently, Toolex pays 75 cents in dividends on every dollar of net income. CC estimates that the company is generating a 15 percent rate of return on its investments. Stocks of companies similar to Toolex are trading at a required rate of return of 12 percent. ⬛
   a. If Toolex has a book value of $25, what is Toolex's current stock price?
   b. What is the maximum over book value that CC should offer, assuming that it could reinvest as much as 50 percent of its earnings at a 15 percent rate of return? (Any additional investment would earn just 12 percent.)
   c. Compute the fair market value for Toolex if the company's ability to earn an excess rate of return on its investments is expected to last for only five years.

8. Fun-Time Food, a "concept" restaurant chain, is expected to earn an average rate of return of 17 percent on the 65 percent of its earnings that it reinvests. Similar stocks are priced to earn a 13 percent rate of return for investors.
   a. By how much will Fun-Time's earnings grow each year?
   b. What is an appropriate P/E multiple for Fun-Time?
   c. What portion of Fun-Time's rate of return is expected to come from dividends? From capital gains?

9. Kathryn Lee owns Microdisk, Inc. She expects after-tax profit of $4 million in the forthcoming year. During years 2 through 7, Lee forecasts that profits will grow by 20 percent annually, but she anticipates that all profits will need to be reinvested in the business to support its growth. Thereafter, she forecasts that growth will fall to 8 percent a year and that the company will need to reinvest only 60 percent of profits. Macrodisk has recently offered Lee $60 million for her company. Is this a fair offer for Microdisk if the appropriate cost of capital is 15 percent?

10. Rainbow Industries has a book value of $17.93 per share. Current earnings per share are $3.00, and the firm has just paid a dividend of $.60 per share. The investors forecast that Rainbow will continue to plow back 80 percent of its earnings for the next four years and that earnings will grow at 25 percent per year during this period. The dividend payout rate is expected to be raised in year 5 to 50 percent, reducing the subsequent dividend growth rate to 8 percent. If the required return for Rainbow Industries' stock is 15 percent, what is its current market-to-book ratio? ⬛

11. Two companies are competing for market share. Company A has a 30 percent share of market and has been averaging a stable 40 percent ROI. Company B has a 20 percent market share and a 15 percent ROI. Both firms have a 10 percent cost of capital and are projected to grow at the same rate of 7 percent annually.
    a. What is the value to A of a one percentage point increase in sustainable growth relative to its value to B, assuming no change in their ROIs?
    b. To gain one percentage point in sustainable growth, by how much could A afford to see its ROI shrink? How much of an ROI reduction could B afford for a 1 percentage point increase in its sustainable growth?

12. In planning the company's goals for the next year, management has decided to use a 10 percent return on book equity as an overall firm standard. The firm's goal for net income is $300,000. In

the past five years, variable cost has averaged 75 percent of sales; the sales force currently receives a commission of 25 percent on gross profit (sales less variable costs). Management estimates that fixed costs will be $2 million. 🐝

a. Calculate the level of sales required to achieve this net income goal. Use a tax rate of 40 percent.

b. Management has calculated that reducing the commission to 20 percent would lower the sales required to earn $300,000 to a more achievable level. What is this level?

c. What is wrong with management's assumption in (b)?

d. What criticism can you make concerning management's budget- and goal-setting process in general?

13. Firm A is planning to acquire firm B for $140 million in cash. The values of the two companies as separate entities are $200 million and $100 million, respectively. Firm A estimates that by combining the two companies it will increase operating cash flows by $5 million annually in perpetuity. If the relevant cost of capital is 20 percent, what is the NPV of the merger to firm A's stockholders?

14. The Alpha Company is selling for $15/share, and the Omega Company is selling for $10/share. Alpha has 100,000 shares outstanding, and Omega has 150,000 shares. Estimates of the value of a merged company range from $4 million to $5 million. 🐝

a. What is the maximum number of shares Alpha can offer to Omega in a takeover?

b. What is the maximum number of shares Omega can offer to Alpha in a takeover?

15. As the president of Toledo Boat Builders, Inc., you are considering the acquisition of one of your suppliers, Fiberglass R Us. Below are the relevant data for your analysis: 🐝

	A	**B**	**AB**
Pre-merger share price	$50	$40	—
Shares outstanding (millions)	1	.5	—
Total equity value (millions)	$50	$20	$80

a. If you were going to pay cash, what is the maximum you would pay B's stockholders?

b. Instead of paying 100 percent cash, you offer $15 million cash and the balance in stock. What is the maximum number of shares you can offer?

c. Give some possible explanations for the synergy expected with the combination of the two companies.

REFERENCES

Chambers, D. E., R. S. Harris, and J. J. Pringle. "Treatment of Financing Mix in Analyzing Investment Opportunities." *Financial Management,* Summer 1982, 24–41.

Copeland, T., T. Koller, and J. Murrin. *Valuation: Measuring and Managing the Value of Companies.* New York: John Wiley & Sons, 1996.

Cusatis, P. J., J. A. Miles, and J. R. Woolridge. "Restructuring Through Spinoffs." *Journal of Financial Economics,* 33, 1993, 293–311.

Dearden, J. "Measuring Profit Center Managers." *Harvard Business Review,* September–October 1987, 83–88.

Jarrell, G. A., J. A. Brickley, and J. M. Netter. "The Market for Corporate Control: The Evidence Since 1980." *Journal of Economic Perspectives,* Winter 1988, 49–68.

Jarrell, G. A., and A. B. Poulson. "The Returns to Acquiring Firms in Tender Offers: Evidence from Three Decades." *Financial Management,* Autumn 1989, 12–19.

Jensen, M. C. "Agency Costs of Free Cash Flow, Corporate Finance, and Takeovers." *American Economic Review,* May 1986, 323–329.

Jensen, M. C. "Takeovers: Folklore and Science." *Harvard Business Review,* November/December 1984, 109–121.

Lambert, R., and D. Larker. "Golden Parachutes, Executive Decision-Making and Shareholder Wealth." *Journal of Accounting and Economics,* April 1985, 179–204.

Michaely, R., and W. H. Shaw. "The Choice of Going Public: Spin-offs vs. Equity Carveouts." *Financial Management,* Autumn 1995, 5–21.

Mogavero, D. J., and M. F. Toyne. "The Impact of Golden Parachutes on Fortune 500 Stock Returns: A Reexamination of the Evidence." *Quarterly Journal of Business and Economics,* 22, 1995, 30–38.

Myers, S. "Interactions of Corporate Financing and Investment Decisions: Implications for Capital Budgeting," *Journal of Finance,* May 1974, 1–25.

Rappaport, A. *Creating Shareholder Wealth.* New York: Free Press, 1998.

Roll, R. "The Hubris Hypothesis of Corporate Takeovers." *Journal of Business,* April 1986, 197–216.

Schwert, G. W. "Markup Pricing in Mergers and Acquisitions." *Journal of Financial Economics,* June 1996, 153–192.

Stern, J. M., G. B. Stewart, and D. H. Chew. "The EVA Financial Management System." *Journal of Applied Corporate Finance,* Summer 1995, 32–46.

Stewart, G. B. *The Quest for Value.* New York: Harper-Collins Publishers, 1991.

Stewart, G. B., III, and Glassman, D. M. "The Motives and Methods of Restructuring." Stern Stewart & Co., New York, 1988.

Woolridge, J. R. "Competitive Decline: Is a Myopic Stock Market to Blame?" *Journal of Applied Corporate Finance,* Spring 1988, 26–36.

Global Financial Markets and Long-Term Corporate Financing

12

Property has its duties as well as its rights.
Benjamin Disraeli

KEY TERMS

ask price
bid price
brokered market
capital markets
corporate governance
dealer market
Eurobond
Eurocurrency
Eurodollar CDs
financial assets
financial deregulation
foreign bank market

foreign bond market
foreign equity markets
forward market
international financial
  markets
London interbank offer
  rate (LIBOR)
money markets
note issuance facility (NIF)
options contracts
organized exchange

over-the-counter (OTC)
  markets
primary claims
primary market
real assets
regulatory arbitrage
secondary claims
secondary market
securitization
spot or cash market
universal banking

CHAPTER LEARNING OBJECTIVES

Upon completion of this chapter, students should be able to:

■ Identify the functions and consequences of well-functioning financial
markets.

■ Describe how financial markets are
organized.

■ Define and explain the forces that underlie securitization and indicate how
it has affected the financing policies of
corporations.

■ Discuss the differences among financial systems and how they influence
corporate governance.

■ Explain the advantages and disadvantages of various sources of corporate
financing.

■ Describe the links between national
and international financial markets.

■ Explain why firms choose to raise capital overseas.

■ Describe the Eurocurrency and Eurobond markets and explain why they
exist.

When a firm decides to acquire long-term assets, it must also decide how to finance them. The firm can raise this money either internally or externally. Internal funds are primarily in the form of cash flow from operations (basically, net income plus depreciation) plus the liquidation of marketable securities. In addition, as part of its long-term business strategy, the firm may also decide to sell off some of its existing assets. After making any additions to working capital, the remainder of its internally generated funds is available for investment in long-term assets.

Because firms typically pay some portion of net income to shareholders in the form of dividends, this limits the amount of operating cash flow available for reinvestment purposes to retained earnings plus depreciation. Of course, the fraction of earnings retained in the business is usually linked to the size of the firm's capital budget; many growing companies pay no dividends and retain all of their earnings.

At times, internally generated funds will be insufficient to finance all of the firm's positive net present value investment opportunities. When this happens, the firm must either abandon some profitable projects, possibly putting its corporate strategy at risk, or else turn to external sources of long-term financing in what is known collectively as the *financial markets*. Most firms choose the latter course. Hence, senior managers must understand the nature of financial markets and how these markets operate. Given the globalization of business activities, this understanding should not be limited to domestic financial markets but should encompass the international financial markets as well.

This chapter provides a brief overview of the global financial markets and how companies use them to finance their operations. It begins by examining the nature and role of financial markets and how they are organized. Next, we survey the patterns of long-term financing employed by U.S. and foreign corporations. We then examine the advantages and disadvantages of the four principal forms of external corporate financing—common stock, preferred stock, debt, and convertible securities—as well as the prime source of internal financing, retained earnings. The final section discusses the international financial markets.

12.1   FLOW OF FUNDS AND THE FINANCIAL MARKETS

A market is any place where goods and services are traded. Given advances in telecommunications and information technology, a market doesn't need to be in a specific place; it can simply be a telephone network between market makers who assist in transferring ownership of some asset from one party to another.

> The value of real assets is tied to their physical characteristics; in contrast, the value of financial assets is derived from their claim on certain future cash flows of issuers.

The financial markets are really no different from any other market. What makes them unique is that the commodities being traded are **financial assets.** In contrast to **real assets** (e.g., inventory or plant and equipment) whose value is tied to their physical characteristics, financial assets have value through their claim on certain future cash flows of issuers. For instance, the value of a corporate bond depends on the firm's promise to pay periodic interest and principal at maturity.

The Role of Financial Markets

The principal role of the financial markets is to mobilize savings and allocate these savings to users on the basis of expected risk-adjusted returns.

The principal functions of a financial market and its intermediaries are to mobilize savings (which involves gathering current purchasing power in the form of money from savers and transferring it to borrowers in exchange for the promise of greater future purchasing power) and to allocate those funds among the potential users on the basis of expected risk-adjusted returns. As Exhibit 12-1 suggests, the financial markets can serve the needs of both investors and borrowers by facilitating the flow of cash between them. Borrowers are not necessarily spendthrifts who are unable to plan their financial affairs. Instead, they include firms whose growth opportunities in a particular year exceed their ability to generate cash internally. Rather than pass up strategically important projects, these companies issue financial assets to creditors and investors in exchange for cash today.

The financial markets mobilize and allocate savings, facilitate risk transfer, allow investors to reduce risk, and provide investors with liquidity.

Financial markets also facilitate both the transfer of risk (from companies to investors) and the reduction of risk (by investors holding a diversified portfolio of financial assets). Subsequent to the investment of savings, financial markets help to monitor managers (by gathering information on their performance) and exert corporate control (through the threat of hostile takeovers for underperforming firms and bankruptcy for insolvent ones). Financial markets also supply *liquidity* to investors by enabling them to sell their investments prior to maturity.

Financial markets play a crucial role in valuing financial assets.

The markets play a critical role in valuing financial assets as well. When a corporation issues a financial asset, it gives the holder a series of promises. If a debt instrument is issued, the firm promises to make a series of contractual interest and principal payments. The amount of cash that lenders are willing to give up represents the price of the instrument. If the financial asset is an equity security, the investor becomes a part owner and gets a share of any distributed profits. However, there is no contractual obligation regarding the timing or size of the payments.[1] Therefore, buyers of equity claims base their prices on a set of expected future cash flows. In a competitive market, the pricing mechanism allows the channeling of funds to those who can credibly promise the highest risk-adjusted returns.

The process of valuing the financial assets issued by corporations also allows investors to express their opinions about the decisions made by executives. These

EXHIBIT 12-1
Exchanges in the Financial Markets

---

[1]Some financial assets, such as preferred stock, have the characteristics of both debt and equity. We'll say more about preferred stock later in this chapter.

judgments influence the prices of a firm's bonds and common stock, thereby giving guidance to senior managers on whether their behavior is consistent with maximizing shareholder value.

Flow of Funds through Financial Intermediaries

The way funds are transferred from savers to spenders depends heavily on the amounts needed and their intended use. In some instances, the exchange is direct, and in other cases the parties supplying the funds never meet the ultimate borrowers. Instead, there's an indirect transfer of funds through financial intermediaries such as banks, insurance companies, and pension funds. Why do we need these intermediaries? Let's look at the following example.

Suppose that you want to buy a new Volkswagen (VW) Beetle costing $23,000. You can come up with a down payment of $2,000 but will have to finance the remaining $21,000 over the next four years. Putting an ad in the local paper isn't going to get you very far. If you're extraordinarily lucky, there might be someone out there with $21,000 who'd be willing to accept payment over the next four years at some mutually agreeable rate. However, the odds of finding someone who can accommodate you is extremely small. Rather than spending a lot of time searching for a willing lender, it is easier (and probably less expensive) to just go to a bank or finance company to arrange for an auto loan.

The bank or finance company gets the money to lend you from savers—those parties who have money left over after making their spending decisions. As Exhibit 12-2 indicates, these folks place their funds with some financial intermediary and receive a **secondary claim** in return. These secondary claims are little more than IOUs issued by the intermediary. In the case of banks, the IOU might take the form of a checking or savings account, but a life insurance company would give savers a contract that promises to pay big bucks to their survivors in the event of death. Intermediaries pool the cash from savers and then invest these funds directly, getting **primary claims** in return.

> Financial intermediaries can reduce the cost of bringing borrowers and lenders together.

In transforming savers' cash into direct investments, financial intermediaries provide several important functions. First, intermediaries reduce the cost of bringing borrower and saver together—particularly if the amounts involved are

EXHIBIT 12-2
Flows of Funds through Financial Intermediaries

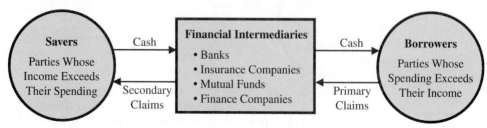

small. If there were no intermediaries, it would take us a lot of time and effort to find someone who was willing to lend us $21,000 to buy the VW Beetle. Even if we were lucky enough to find a willing lender quickly, we would have to draw up a loan agreement. Unless we were familiar with writing contracts, we'd have to get a lawyer. Going to a bank reduces the cost of looking for a lender. Further, bank loan officers are trained to make auto loans and have standardized contracts available. Therefore, using an intermediary reduces *search, processing, and contracting costs* and can result in lower borrowing rates.

> **Intermediaries can bridge maturity preference differences between borrowers and lenders.**

Second, intermediaries can often bridge a borrower and lender's maturity preferences. The classic example is the bank that does mortgage lending. Bank deposits, whether they are in the form of demand deposits (checking accounts) or time deposits (savings accounts), are typically short term in nature. In contrast, mortgage loans have maturities of up to 30 years. By serving as a *maturity intermediary,* the bank can meet a saver's preference for short-term, highly liquid investments, while at the same time meeting the borrower's need for long-term credit accommodation.

Third, intermediaries also help *reduce investment risk through diversification.* For example, a mutual fund pools the cash of a group of relatively small individual savers and invests this money in a large number of financial assets. By creating portfolios, mutual funds can reduce investment risk. Although individuals can also reduce risk by building portfolios, those savers with limited resources can't really diversify in a cost-effective way.

Finally, for some intermediaries, the process of converting secondary into primary claims provides us with a payments mechanism. For instance, most of us have checking accounts. From the bank's perspective, these are secondary claims that it issues against itself in exchange for money that we place on deposit. Checking accounts are substitutes for cash and can be used to pay bills. Payments can also be made using credit cards and debit cards as well as a wide range of electronic funds transfer systems such as on-line banking.

The Consequences of Well-Functioning Financial Markets

> **Well-functioning markets lead to more and better projects getting funded, bring about better managed firms, and enable investors to select their preferred risk–return trade-off and pattern of consumption.**

The consequences of well-functioning financial markets (and intermediaries) are that (1) more and better projects get financed (owing to higher savings, a more realistic scrutiny of investment opportunities, and the lower cost of capital associated with risk diversification and increased liquidity); (2) managers are compelled to run companies in accordance with the interests of investors (through active monitoring and the threat of bankruptcy or a hostile takeover for underperformers and by linking managerial compensation to stock prices); (3) the rate of innovation is higher (by identifying and funding those entrepreneurs with the best chances of successfully initiating new goods and production processes); and (4) individuals are able to select their preferred time pattern of consumption (saving consists of individuals deferring consumption in some periods so as to increase their consumption in later periods) and their preferred risk-return trade-off. The result is stronger economic growth and greater consumer satisfaction. These factors are summarized in Exhibit 12-3.

EXHIBIT 12-3
Factors, Functions, and Consequences of Well-Functioning Financial Markets

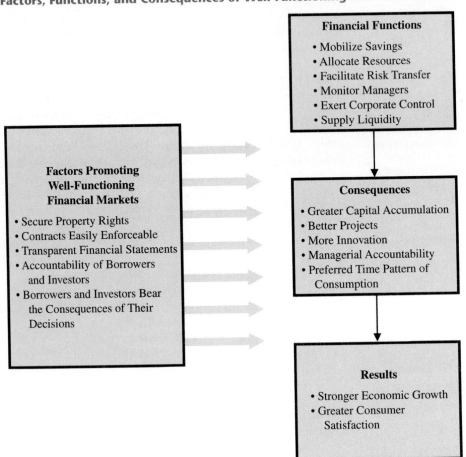

Financial markets work best when property rights are secure, contracts are easily enforceable, meaningful accounting information is available, and borrowers and investors are accountable for their decisions and bear the economic consequences of their behavior. Absent these conditions, markets cannot allocate capital efficiently and economic growth suffers.

The financial disaster in Asia points out the dangers of allocating capital by cronyism and bureaucratic dictate rather than through a rational process governed by realistic estimates of prospective risks and rewards. This "command-and-control" capitalism produced dysfunctional financial sectors that squandered hundreds of billions of dollars of hard-earned savings on unproductive investments and grandiose projects and begat corruption without end.

Conversely, a healthy dose of market discipline and the stringent credit standards it enforces can work wonders for an economy. A recent study by the

Efficient financial markets lead to higher capital productivity and stronger economic growth.

McKinsey Global Institute examined *capital productivity*—the ratio of output (goods and services) to the input of physical capital (plant and equipment)—in Germany, Japan, and the United States.[2] Overall, U.S. capital productivity exceeded that of Japan and Germany by about 50 percent. As a result, the United States can simultaneously save less, consume more, and grow faster. This economic hat trick can be traced directly to (1) activist shareholders demanding management accountability and paying for performance, (2) tough disclosure rules and financial transparency in corporate accounts that allow investors to make informed decisions, (3) rigorous credit analysis that helps screen out bad risks, and (4) a willingness to inflict pain on imprudent lenders, cut off capital to less competitive companies, and allow inefficient companies to fail. Although many politicians and others claim that U.S. financial markets have hindered productivity by forcing American companies to be short-term oriented, the McKinsey report suggests exactly the opposite—that the focus of U.S. financial markets on financial performance, reinforced by strong corporate governance, leads directly to improved business performance. In the process of rewarding success and penalizing failure, financial virtue creates its own reward.

12.2   THE ORGANIZATION OF FINANCIAL MARKETS

The money markets are markets for financial instruments that mature within a year.

There are many ways to describe the financial markets. One way is to distinguish between the money and capital markets. As the name suggests, the **money markets** are markets for financial assets that are close substitutes for cash and mature in one year or less. The principal U.S. money market instruments in order of increasing risk are presented in Exhibit 12-4. Conventional wisdom says that these markets are a source of short-term funds for borrowers. From an investor's perspective, the markets represent a temporary outlet for excess cash. However, because borrowers can refinance or *rollover* existing debt on a continuous basis, the markets provide ongoing investment and financing opportunities.

The capital markets are the markets for long-term financial instruments.

In contrast, the **capital markets** deal with relatively longer-term instruments. As Exhibit 12-5 indicates, capital market instruments include all of the "usual suspects"—bonds issued by a wide range of borrowers, mortgages, and equity securities such as preferred and common stock. Investors with different risk preferences can choose from default-free U.S. Treasury notes and bonds to the common stock of an emerging company.

The primary market is the market for new issues; these issues are subsequently traded in the secondary markets.

A primary market and a secondary market exist within each of the money and capital markets. The **primary market** is a "new-issues" market in which funds flow to the issuers from creditors and investors through the sale of financial assets. In the **secondary market**, already-issued financial assets are bought and sold. For example, the trading of equity securities on the London and New

---

[2]McKinsey Global Institute, *Capital Productivity*, Washington, D.C., June 1996. This report is summarized in Raj Agrawal, Stephen Findley, Sean Greene, Kathryn Huang, Aly Jeddy, William W. Lewis, and Markus Petry, "Capital Productivity: Why the U.S. Leads and Why It Matters," *The McKinsey Quarterly*, 1996, No. 3, 38–55.

EXHIBIT 12-4
Summary of Domestic Money Market Instruments

Instrument/Issuer	Maturities
Treasury Bills: Issued by the U.S. government to finance federal expenditures	91- and 182-day bills are sold weekly; 1-year bills sold on a monthly basis
Tax-Exempt Paper: Issued by states, local governments, agencies, and housing authorities	Up to 1 year
Negotiable Certificates of Deposit (CDs): Issued by money-center depository institutions	14 days and over
Bankers Acceptances: A firm's promise to pay that is also guaranteed by a bank	Up to 6 months
Commercial Paper: Unsecured promissory notes issued by large corporations	Up to 270 days

EXHIBIT 12-5
Summary of Domestic Capital Market Instruments

Instrument/Issuer	Maturities
Treasury Notes and Bonds: Issued by the U.S. government	2 to 30 years
Mortgages: Loans secured by real estate	Up to 30 years
Municipal Bonds: Issued by states, local governments, agencies, and housing authorities	Up to 30 years
Corporate Notes and Bonds: Long-term debt issued by firms	5 to 40 years
Preferred Stock: An equity-type security that pays a fixed or variable dividend	No set maturity
Common Stock: A pure equity representing the ownership interest in the firm. Common stockholders are last in line in terms of their claim on income and assets in liquidation.	None

York Stock Exchanges represents secondary-market transactions. A smoothly-functioning secondary market provides investors with liquidity and, therefore, improves the receptivity of new issues in the primary markets.

Segments of the financial markets can also be described in terms of their market makers. In a **dealer market,** individuals or firms facilitate trades by buying financial assets for their own account and selling to buyers out of their inventory. The market for most money-market instruments, including U.S. Treasury securities, is a dealer market. The price at which the dealer is willing to buy is the **bid price,** and the price at which the dealer is willing to sell is the **ask price.** As with most lines of business, the dealer's objective is to "buy low, sell high" and make a profit on the *spread* or difference.

Unlike dealers, who trade securities for their own account, brokers serve as agents to bring buyers and sellers together.

Transactions can also take place in **brokered markets.** Unlike the dealers who actually purchase and own securities, brokers simply serve as agents by bringing buyers and sellers together. Thus, they are never exposed to the potential losses in the value of their inventories if prices drop unexpectedly. Most trades on the New York Stock Exchange are brokered transactions.

Securities can be traded on either organized exchanges or over the counter. An **organized exchange** is an actual physical place that has members and a set of rules governing trading. In the United States, there are two national exchanges—the New York and American Stock Exchange—as well as a number of regional exchanges such as the Chicago, Philadelphia, and Boston Exchanges. Globally, there are organized exchanges in such important financial centers as Paris, Frankfurt, and Hong Kong.

Unlike organized exchanges, the **over-the-counter markets (OTC)** have no physical locations. They are a set of dealers tied together by sophisticated telecommunications networks that allow market makers to continuously post their bid and ask prices. While most secondary trading of common stock takes place on organized exchanges, bond trades—including trades of U.S. Treasuries—take place in the OTC market. A large and growing OTC stock market is called the National Association of Security Dealers Automated Quotation System, better known as NASDAQ.

We can also classify markets according to whether the financial assets in question are to be exchanged now or at some point in the future. When we have immediate transfer of ownership, we are dealing in the **spot** or **cash market.** In contrast, some contracts give the holder a future claim or choice to buy or sell some financial asset. These contracts derive their value from some underlying financial asset and are known as (surprise!) *derivative securities.*

Two classes of derivatives are **forward** and **options contracts.**[3] With a forward contract, two parties agree to transfer the ownership of a financial asset at a set price at some specified future date. There are no choices here; both buyer and seller must perform. On the other hand, as we have seen in Chapter 7, an options contract gives the owner the right *but not the obligation* to buy (or sell) a financial asset at a set price from (or to) another party.

The globalization of the financial markets has created choices for borrowers and investors outside their national markets.

Finally, we need to recognize that the globalization of the financial markets means that borrowers and investors have choices outside their national markets. For instance, U.S. savers seeking somewhat higher returns could put some money in **Eurodollar CDs,** which are dollar-denominated bank deposits outside the United States. Eurodollars are only part of a growing pool of deposits known as **Eurocurrencies.** A Eurocurrency is any currency that's deposited outside the country of origin. Besides the dollar, other important Eurocurrencies are Euromarks (Germany), Eurosterling (U.K.), and Euroyen (Japan). Eurocurrencies allow a Japanese investor to place money in a deutsche mark–denominated deposit in London. Similarly, a U.S.-based corporation might issue dollar-denominated

---

[3]Another type of derivative is a *futures contract,* which is essentially a standardized forward contract.

debt in the form of Eurobonds. These "offshore" markets allow issuers to offer securities to investors in a number of countries simultaneously with a minimum of government interference.[4]

12.3 TRENDS IN CORPORATE FINANCING PATTERNS

Firms that must raise funds externally can turn to investors or lenders. Investors give a company money by buying the securities it issues. These securities, which are generally *negotiable* (tradable), usually take the form of publicly issued debt or equity or some combination of the two such as convertibles.

The main alternative to issuing public debt securities directly in the open market is obtaining a loan from a specialized financial intermediary that issues its own securities (or deposits) in the market. These alternative debt instruments usually are commercial bank loans—for short-term and medium-term credit—or privately placed bonds—for longer-term credit. Unlike *publicly issued bonds, privately placed bonds* are sold directly to only a limited number of sophisticated investors, usually life insurance companies and pension funds.[5] Moreover, privately placed bonds are generally nonnegotiable and have complex, customized loan agreements—called *covenants*. The restrictions in the covenants range from limits on dividend payments to prohibitions on asset sales and new debt issues. They provide a series of checkpoints that permit the lender to review actions by the borrower that might impair the lender's position. These agreements have to be regularly renegotiated prior to maturity. As a result, privately placed bonds are much more like loans than publicly issued and traded securities.

> Privately placed bonds are sold directly to a limited number of individuals or financial institutions, such as pension funds or insurance companies.

Internal versus External Sources of Funds

Regardless of whether it is derived from securities markets or financial intermediaries, external financing has been diminishing in importance for American companies in the aggregate in recent years. Exhibit 12-4 shows that gross internal cash flow—retained earnings plus depreciation—typically supplies over 60 percent of the financing requirements of U.S. nonfinancial corporations. During the early 1970s, this percentage dropped when capital consumption allowances and profits did not keep pace with inflation. Basing depreciation expenses on historical cost during a period of high inflation severely understates true capital consumption, because assets must be replaced at current, inflated prices. A sharp reversal of this downtrend began in 1981 with the more generous depreciation allowances and investment tax credits provided by the Economic Recovery Tax Act of 1981.

> Internal cash flow—retained earnings plus depreciation—supplies more than 60 percent of the financing needs of U.S. nonfinancial corporations.

---

[4]The globalization of the financial markets has also led to some wonderful nicknames for debt instruments. For instance, Yankee bonds (and Yankee CDs) are issues of foreign-based companies in the U.S., while Samurai bonds are issued in Japan by foreign companies.

[5]The Securities Act of 1933 (see Chapter 13) exempts privately placed bonds from the normal registration process that the Securities and Exchange Commission enforces on public securities offerings. All else being equal, this lowers the cost of privately placed bonds as compared to publicly placed bonds.

This reversal was reinforced by the rapid increase in corporate profits beginning in the fourth quarter of 1982 (the end of the 1981–1982 recession). By 1985, U.S. companies were getting less than 20 percent of their funds from external sources. In recent years, however, companies have once again begun to rely more heavily on external sources of capital.

> Corporate financing needs vary with the level of economic activity.

Exhibit 12-6 reveals a pattern of corporate financing that varies systematically over the business cycle. The most noteworthy feature of this pattern is that the corporate need for external funds varies directly with the health of the economy:[6]

1. The demand for external financing is greatest just after economic activity peaks and starts turning down. The decline in sales reduces profits available for retained earnings, whereas capital spending and investment in inventory continue apace. Firms use external funds to finance the growing gap between investment and internal funds until they adjust their spending to the upcoming recession.
2. Most of the external financing is in the form of debt. Although not shown here, short-term debt accounts for the bulk of the increased debt financing during such periods.

EXHIBIT 12-6
Financing Decisions by U.S. Nonfinancial Corporations

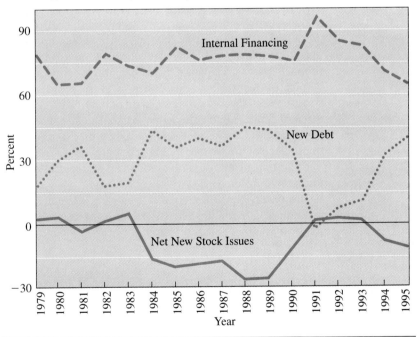

Source: Board of Governors of the Federal Reserve System, *Flow of Funds Accounts.*

---

[6]This discussion is based on Taggart (1986).

3. The need for external funds is at its lowest level when the economy is just starting to pull out of a recession. At this point, a small gain in sales generally results in a large jump in profits and retained earnings. But the corporate need for funds does not rise as sharply. Firms hold off on additional investment spending until sales grow enough to absorb the existing spare capacity. Internal funds, as well as long-term debt, are then used to reduce the corporate reliance on short-term debt.

4. From 1984 through 1990, net new equity issues—stock sold minus stock repurchased—were negative. The reason was the unprecedented extent of stock buybacks, including those associated with corporate takeovers and leveraged buyouts. Beginning in 1991, net new equity issues turned positive as corporate America began deleveraging its balance sheet. By 1994, however, it had turned negative again.

National Financing Patterns

Financing patterns differ across national boundries.

Companies in different countries have different financial appetites. British companies get an average of about 97 percent of their funds from internal sources in comparison to about 91 percent for U.S. companies and 81 percent for German companies. In Japan, where profitability has been low, companies have relied more heavily on external finance, getting more than 30% of their money from outside sources, primarily from banks.[7] The shortfall of funds reflects the Japanese strategy of making huge industrial investments and pursuing market share at the expense of profit margins. As Japanese firms emphasize profits over sales growth, they will probably rely more heavily on internal sources of funds. In the meantime, however, the combination of substantial bank borrowing and low profits means that Japanese firms have high debt/equity ratios.

In contrast to Japan, in Europe and the United States, internal finance has consistently supplied the lion's share of financial requirements. The percentage of external finance fluctuates more or less in line with the business cycle: When profits are high, firms are even less reliant on external finance. Moreover, the predominance of internal financing is not accidental. After all, companies could pay out internal cash flow as dividends and issue additional securities to cover their investment needs.

Another empirical regularity regarding financing behavior relates to the composition of external finance. Regardless of the country studied, debt accounts for the overwhelming share of external funds. By contrast, new stock issues play a relatively small role in financing investment.

In contrast to U.S. and British firms, who use the financial markets to raise external capital, German and French companies rely heavily on bank borrowing.

Financial Markets versus Financial Intermediaries

Industry's sources of external finance also differ widely from country to country. German and French companies rely heavily on bank borrowing (as have Japanese

---

[7]These figures represent the net sources of finance during the period 1970–1989 and appear in Bert Scholtens, "Bank- and Market-Oriented Financial Systems: Fact or Fiction?" *BNL Quarterly Review,* September 1997, 304.

companies, until recently) whereas U.S. and British industry raise much more money directly from financial markets by the sale of securities. In all these countries, however, bank borrowing is on the decline. There is a growing tendency for corporate borrowing to take the form of negotiable securities issued in the public capital markets rather than in the form of nonmarketable loans provided by financial intermediaries.

Securitization is the process of matching up borrowers and lenders by way of the financial markets.

This process, termed **securitization,** is depicted in Exhibit 12-7. An investor with surplus funds can deposit money with FirstBank, which lends the money to Company A. Alternatively, Company A can raise the funds it needs by issuing additional securities and selling them directly to the investor. The choice between financial intermediation and securitization depends on the relative costs and risks of the two processes.

Securitization largely reflects a reduction in the cost of using financial markets at the same time that the cost of bank borrowing has risen. Until recently, various regulatory restrictions enabled banks to attract low-cost funds from depositors. With *financial deregulation,* which began in the United States in 1981 and in Japan in 1986, banks must now compete for funds with a wide range of institutions at market rates. In addition, regulatory demands for a stronger capital base have forced U.S. banks to use more equity financing, raising their cost of funds. Inevitably, these changes have pushed up the price of bank loans. Any top-flight company can now get money more cheaply by issuing commercial paper than from its banks. As a result, banks now have a smaller share of the short-term business credit market. Japanese companies are also finding that issuing bonds or leasing equipment is a cheaper source of medium-term and long-term money as well.

EXHIBIT 12-7
Securitization versus Intermediation

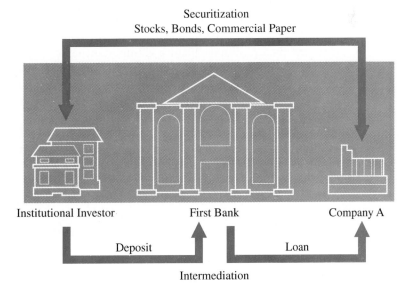

At the same time, the cost of accessing the public markets is coming down, especially for smaller and less-well-known companies. Historically, these companies found it more economical simply to obtain a loan from a bank or to place a private bond issue with a life insurance company. These *private placements* proved cheaper because banks and life insurance companies specialize in credit analysis and assume a large amount of a borrower's debt. Consequently, they could realize important cost savings in several functions, such as gathering information about the condition of debtor firms, monitoring their actions, and renegotiating loan agreements.

Recent technological improvements in such areas as data manipulation and telecommunications have greatly reduced the costs of obtaining and processing information about the conditions that affect the creditworthiness of potential borrowers. Any analyst now has computerized access to a wealth of economic and financial information at a relatively low cost along with programs to store and manipulate this information. Thus, investors are now more likely to find it cost-effective to lend directly to companies rather than through *financial intermediaries,* such as commercial banks. This borrowing often takes the form of high-yield or "junk" bonds.

Financial Systems and Corporate Governance

> Corporate governance, which refers to the means by which companies are controlled, is heavily influenced by the nature of the financial system.

Despite the apparent convergence of financial systems, there are still some notable differences among countries in terms of **corporate governance,** which refers to the means whereby companies are controlled. The United States and United Kingdom are often viewed as prototypes of a market-oriented financial system (frequently referred to as the Anglo-Saxon or AS model), whereas Germany, France, and Japan are generally regarded as typical representatives of bank-centered finance (the Continental European and Japanese or CEJ type of financial system). In AS countries institutional investors (pension funds, mutual funds, university and other nonprofit endowments, and insurance companies) make up an important part of the financial system, whereas in CEJ countries banks dominate the picture. Equity finance is important in AS countries and institutional shareholders exert a great deal of corporate control. The accepted objective is to maximize shareholder value and boosting the return on capital employed is stressed. The stress on shareholder value has recently been endorsed by an international advisory panel to the Organization for Economic Cooperation and Development (OECD). According to the head of the panel, the Asian economic crisis can be traced to weak corporate governance: "Nobody was watching [Asian] management; they were growing for the sake of growth with no concern for shareholder value."[8] The crisis could most likely have been avoided, he said, had American-style corporate governance been in place.

The board of directors of a typical firm in this AS system reflects its market orientation. For instance, only 5 out of the 16 members of General Electric's (GE)

---

[8]Quoted in Robert L. Simison, "Firms Worldwide Should Adopt Ideas of U.S. Management, Panel Tells OECD," *Wall Street Journal,* April 2, 1998, A4.

1998 board of directors are insiders, that is, part of GE management. The balance of the board includes: (1) current or retired executives from other firms, (2) university professors, and (3) individuals, such as former U.S. Senator Sam Nunn of Georgia, who bring valuable perspectives to the group. Conspicuously absent from the GE board are bankers.

In CEJ countries, in contrast, banks play a dominant role. Bank finance is prominent, share ownership and control are concentrated in banks and other firms, and corporate decision making is heavily influenced by close personal relationships between corporate leaders who sit on each other's boards of directors; individual shareholders have little voice, resulting in much less concern for shareholder value and relatively low returns on capital. However, in all countries, competitive pressures and the threat of hostile takeovers of underperforming companies are forcing greater managerial accountability and an increased focus on shareholder value.

Differences in financial systems have real consequences for financial structures. For example, as noted, large Japanese companies employ a high degree of leverage, particularly as compared to U.S. companies. The ability to take on such large amounts of debt stems in part from the vast mutual-aid networks that most large Japanese firms can tap into. These are the fabled *keiretsu*, the large industrial groupings—often with a major bank at the center—that form the backbone of corporate Japan. Keiretsu ties constitute a complex web of tradition, cross-shareholdings, trading relationships, management, cooperative projects, and information swapping. The keiretsu provide financial backing, management advice, and favorable contracts to their members and provide a safety net when corporate relatives get in trouble.

> Unlike U.S. firms, banks play a dominant role in the governance of European and Japanese companies.

Partly because of the difference in industrial structures in the two countries, U.S. and Japanese firms relate to the banking system in a different way. Almost all big Japanese companies have one main bank—usually the bank around which the keiretsu is formed—as their primary source of long-term loans. The main bank will have access to information about the company and have a say in its management that in most other countries would be unacceptable. Moreover, Japanese banks, unlike their U.S. counterparts, can hold industrial shares. So, the main bank often holds a sizable amount of the equity of its borrowers. For example, until recently, Japanese banks owned nearly 40 percent of the outstanding stock of Japanese manufacturing companies. Thus, for Japanese companies, the strong relation with one main bank—along with close ties to the other members of their keiretsu—is their main method of minimizing the risk of financial distress.[9]

> With universal banking, a commercial bank not only performs investment banking services but also takes major equity positions in client firms.

The same is true of Germany, where **universal banking** is practiced; German commercial banks perform not only investment-banking activities but also take major equity positions in companies. As both stockholder and creditor, German

---

[9]For a detailed analysis of the governance structure of the keiretsu, see Steven N. Kaplan and Bernadette A. Minton, "Appointments of Outsiders to Japanese Boards: Determinants and Implications for Managers," *Journal of Financial Economics,* October 1994, 225–258; and Erik Berglöf and Enrico Perotti, "The Governance Structure of the Japanese Financial Keiretsu," *Journal of Financial Economics,* October 1994, 259–284.

banks can reduce the conflicts between the two classes of investors, leading to lower costs and speedier action in "workouts" of financial problems. The resulting increase in organizational efficiency should mean less risk for German companies in taking on large amounts of debt. In the United States, where corporate bank relations are less intimate, companies rely primarily on equity as a shock absorber.

Illustration

Toyo Kogyo and Chrysler Experience Financial Distress

The contrasting experiences of Toyo Kogyo (producer of Mazda cars) and Chrysler during recent periods of financial distress illustrate the unusual features of the Japanese financial system. In 1973, Toyo Kogyo (TK) was a successful producer of light and medium-sized cars. The energy crisis of 1974 precipitated a crisis at TK because of the high energy consumption of its rotary-engine, Wankel-powered Mazda models. Worldwide sales plunged 19 percent. To weather the storm, TK required a massive infusion of funds to develop new product offerings. Sumitomo Bank, its main bank, had the resources to rescue TK. On the basis of its thorough knowledge of TK's operations, Sumitomo decided that the company could be profitable with new product offerings and massive cost-cutting. But because it lacked confidence in TK's senior management, Sumitomo replaced them. With its own hand-picked executives in place, Sumitomo then financed the simultaneous development of three new models and the overhaul of TK's production system, extended credit to suppliers, and had the vast group of related Sumitomo companies buy Mazda vehicles. The new models were highly successful and labor productivity grew by 118 percent over the next seven years.

In contrast to the situation at TK, Chrysler was able to persist with poor performance for over two decades because its investors had no effective remedies. Chrysler could ignore the need to restructure its operations because of its continued ability to borrow money (it still had a substantial, though dwindling, amount of shareholders' equity to support these loans). Despite the activities of some dissident shareholders, Chrysler continued under a self-perpetuating management until the crisis of 1979. Although Chrysler faced bankruptcy, its banks refused to lend it more money. In contrast to TK's Japanese banks, Chrysler's banks had an incomplete understanding of its plight and no way to obtain all the essential information. Even if they had, they could not have sent in the same type of rescue team that Sumitomo sent into TK. In the end, Chrysler was rescued by the U.S. government, which offered loan guarantees sufficient for the company's survival at about half its former size.

In a man-bites-dog turn of events, however, Chrysler eventually restructured to become the most profitable auto company in the world, and Mazda Motor Company once again got into deep trouble. Hurt by the strong yen and by a high-risk expansion strategy that backfired when global recession struck, by 1994 Mazda was stuck with $8 billion in debt and a main bank (still Sumitomo) that refused to bail it out. Instead, Sumitomo invited Ford Motor Company to take effective management control of Mazda, thereby entrusting Ford with the role that the bank itself played in the 1970s.

Japanese and German companies pay for their heavy reliance on bank debt with less freedom of action. As the cost of accessing the capital markets directly has dropped, the main-bank relationship has gradually eroded in Japan and Germany, and Japanese and German companies have looked more to the equity market as their cushion against financial distress. The pace of change was accelerated in Japan when a law forced Japanese banks to reduce their shareholdings in individual companies to 5 percent or less by December 1987. In addition, in the wake of the Japanese stock market collapse and eroding corporate profits, some companies have begun to raise money by selling major chunks of their cross-shareholdings in the less-important members of their keiretsu. Although relations between main banks and associated corporations remain intimate, companies are looking more carefully at second- and third-tier banks. Even main banks, however, are plagued with bad debts, declining bank capital, and a much higher cost of capital, forcing them to pay more attention to profitability and making them less reliable sources of capital for their corporate customers. In response, Japanese companies are increasingly turning to the corporate bond market to raise new capital.

Globalization of Financial Markets

Technological change and deregulation are blurring the distinctions between domestic and foreign financial markets.

The same advances in communications and technology that have lowered the cost of accessing financial markets directly, together with **financial deregulation** abroad—the lifting of regulatory structures that inhibit competition and protect domestic markets—have blurred the distinction between domestic and foreign financial markets. As the necessary electronic technology has been developed and transaction costs have plummeted, the world has become one vast, interconnected market. Enormous markets for U.S. government securities and certain stocks, foreign exchange trading, interbank borrowing and lending—to cite a few examples—operate continuously around the clock and around the world. The *globalization of financial markets* has brought about an unprecedented degree of competition among key financial centers and financial institutions that has further reduced the costs of issuing new securities.

Growing competition has also led to increasing deregulation of financial markets worldwide. Deregulation is hastened by **regulatory arbitrage**, whereby the users of capital markets issue and trade securities in financial centers with the lowest regulatory standards and, hence, the lowest costs. In order to win back business, financial centers around the world are throwing off obsolete and costly regulations. For example, concerned that Tokyo had fallen behind London and New York as a global finance center, the Japanese government has developed a "Big Bang" financial reform program. This program seeks to break down regulatory barriers between Japanese banks, insurance companies, and brokerage houses and create opportunities in Japan for foreign financial companies by cutting red tape and barriers to the market. Deregulation—in Japan and elsewhere—is little more than an acknowledgment that the rules do not—and cannot—work. For example, in mid-1989, Germany abolished its 10 percent withholding tax on interest income less than six months after it took effect. The tax led to record capital flight from Germany, putting downward pressure on the deutsche mark. Upon announcement of the repeal, German bonds jumped in value.

> **Bank-centered financial systems have been inadequate in meeting the needs of small and medium-sized firms.**

Financial deregulation has also been motivated by the growing recognition in nations with bank-centered financial systems that such systems are not providing adequately for the credit needs of the small and medium-sized firms that are the engines of growth and innovation. It has not escaped the notice of governments worldwide that corporate success stories of the past 20 years—companies like Microsoft, Dell, Cisco Systems, Amazon.com, 3Com, Yahoo!, Oracle, and Amgen—have come predominantly from the United States. Germany and Japan can boast of few Netscapes, AOLs, Iomegas, Suns, Compaqs, or Genentechs. By deregulating their financial markets, policymakers hope that their countries will emulate the results of the U.S. system of corporate finance.

The combination of freer markets with widely available information has laid the foundation for global growth. Cross-border trading in financial assets was estimated in 1992 to be $35 trillion, up from $5 trillion in 1980.[10] Fund-raising is global now as well. According to OECD figures, the amount of money raised on the international capital markets has grown rapidly, rising to nearly $1.8 trillion in 1997 (see Exhibit 12-8). Treasurers are no longer confined to domestic markets as their source of funding and are now quick to exploit any attractive opportunity that occurs anywhere in the world.

Competition drives the international financial system, and innovation is its fuel. *Financial innovation* segments, transfers, and diversifies risk. It also enables companies to tap previously inaccessible markets and permits investors and issuers alike to take advantage of tax loopholes. More generally, financial innovation presents opportunities for value creation. To the extent that a firm can design a security that appeals to a special niche in the capital market, it can attract funds at a lower cost than the market's required return on securities of comparable risk. But such a rewarding situation is likely to be temporary, because the demand for a security that fits a particular niche in the market is not unlimited. In addition, the supply of securities designed to tap that niche is likely to increase dramatically once the niche is recognized. Even though financial innovation may not be a sustainable form of value creation, it can, nonetheless, enable the initial issuers to raise money at a below-market rate.

---

[10]These figures appear in "The Global Capital Market: Supply, Demand, Pricing and Allocation," McKinsey Global Institute, November 1994.

EXHIBIT 12-8
Funds Raised on the International Capital Markets by Instrument

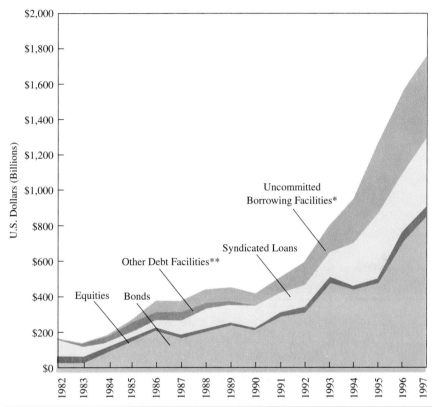

Source: Financial Market Trends, Organization for Economic Cooperation and Development, various issues.
*Euro-commercial paper and medium-term Euronote programs.
**Note issuance facilities and other backup facilities.

Illustration

The Swedish Export Credit Corporation Innovates

The Swedish Export Credit Corporation (SEK) borrows about $2 billion annually. To reduce its funding costs, SEK relies heavily on financial innovation. For example, SEK issued a straight bond, stripped it down to its two components—an annuity consisting of the interest payments and a zero-coupon bond consisting of the principal repayment at maturity—and sold the pieces to different investors. The annuity cash flow was tailored to meet the demands of a Japanese insurance company that was looking for an interest-

> only security, and the zero-coupon portion appealed to European investors who desired earnings taxed as capital gains rather than interest income. By unbundling the bond issue into separate parts that appealed to distinct groups of investors, SEK created a financial transaction in which the parts were worth more than the whole.

Financial innovation has dramatically increased international capital mobility. As in the domestic case, cross-border financial transfers can take place through securitization or financial intermediation. Whether international fund flows take place through one or the other depends on the relative costs and risks of the two mechanisms. The key determinant here is the cost of gathering information on foreign firms. As these costs continue to come down, international securitization should become increasingly cost-effective.

The wide variety of funding opportunities today presents companies with the pleasant dilemma of having to choose from among them. We shall now examine the pros and cons of five generic financing sources.

12.4   RETAINED EARNINGS

If depreciation charges are used—as intended—to replace worn-out assets (assuming that these assets have positive NPVs), the firm's major internal source of incremental financing will be retained earnings. These are the profits remaining in the firm after dividends are paid. As with all uses of funds, if earnings are retained for investment purposes, the firm must ensure that the projects financed have positive net present values; that is, the use of retained earnings must be justified by a rigorous capital-budgeting analysis, which requires that the projects they finance earn the cost of equity capital.

Advantages and Disadvantages of Financing with Retained Earnings

As an ongoing source of funds, retained earnings are limited by a firm's profitability over time.

The amount of retained earnings is limited by the firm's profits, but, unlike external equity or debt, this source does not require bringing in outsiders (e.g., additional lenders or new stockholders). A possible disadvantage is that retained earnings come at the expense of dividends or share repurchases. Moreover, firms usually try to avoid reducing the level of dividend payments even if earnings have declined temporarily, making retained earnings an unreliable source of financing unless the firm's earnings are very stable.

Although using retained earnings for expansion reduces current dividends, it increases the future amount of money available to shareholders as either dividends or share repurchases. Note that aside from tax considerations, shareholders care only about receiving cash from the firm and not about its form. If the firm decides to repurchase shares instead of paying dividends, shareholders can make their own dividends by selling shares.

If external financing is used instead, some portion of future cash flows must pay interest on new debt, preferred dividends on new preferred shares, or dividends on additional shares of common stock, depending on the source of external financing. This, of course, is the same tradeoff we have seen before between current dollars and future dollars. The terms of this tradeoff will be spelled out in greater detail in Chapter 15 when we talk about how a company should design its dividend policy. One potentially important consideration here is that shareholders are taxed on corporate profits only when these profits are paid as dividends. Hence, shareholders may prefer to see earnings retained in the firm.

Retained earnings are a direct substitute for common stock financing because both provide an infusion of equity capital; that is, both represent funds contributed by the firm's owners (old or new). However, the use of retained earnings avoids the flotation costs associated with a new stock issue. It also avoids the dilution of control that may occur when common stock is sold to new owners.

> **Retained earnings provide for an infusion of equity capital while avoiding the flotation costs associated with new common stock issues.**

Perhaps the most serious problem associated with retained earnings is that many firms do not recognize the opportunity costs associated with these funds and treat them as essentially free capital. This gives such firms an added incentive to grow—to expand their business beyond a profitable size, to diversify into new areas, and to acquire other firms. Often these are negative net present value investments. In contrast, forcing companies to raise funds externally subjects them to the periodic scrutiny of hard-nosed investors and lenders. Debt financing is particularly valuable in dealing with the problem of investing in low-return projects. By requiring managers to write out a check to creditors every six months, debt financing makes it clear to them what the cost of that capital is.

> **Some firms erroneously view retained earnings as free capital.**

12.5 COMMON STOCK

> **Because common stock has no maturity date, the issuance of new shares provides a permanent source of financing; however, its use divides control between new and existing owners.**

The sale of common stock provides permanent financing because common stock has no maturity date. The absence of a maturity date also means that stockholders can liquidate their investment in an ongoing firm only by selling their shares to another investor. Selling additional common stock divides the ownership and control of the firm between the new and the old owners, leading to potential problems.

Advantages and Disadvantages of Common Stock Financing

There are several advantages and disadvantages of common stock financing as compared to financing with debt or preferred stock. The advantages include the following:

1. The firm is not required to pay dividends. Thus, in the event of a cash flow squeeze, the firm can skip the payment of dividends without suffering any legal consequences. A skipped interest payment, on the other hand, could force the firm into bankruptcy. Equity thus acts as a shock absorber.
2. Similarly, because common stock has no maturity date, the firm has no obligation to redeem it. Principal repayments on debt are legally mandated.

3. Because the firm's equity provides a cushion against losses by creditors, the sale of common stock lowers the cost of issuing additional debt or preferred.
4. Dividends received from domestic corporations are 70 percent tax free to corporate investors, whereas interest income is fully taxed. This lowers the required return on stock by corporate investors relative to their required return on debt investments.

Disadvantages of issuing additional common stock include the following:

1. The sale of common stock usually brings in new owners to the firm, diluting the control of existing owners. Manager–owners who are unwilling to share control of their firms will often try to avoid equity financing for this reason.
2. Dividends are paid out of after-tax earnings, whereas interest payments are tax deductible. This affects the relative costs to the firm of debt and equity financing. Offsetting this disadvantage is the fact that shareholders are not taxed on the appreciation in the value of their shares until they sell these shares.
3. The cost of issuing common stock is usually higher than the cost of raising the same amount of money by selling additional debt.
4. A frequent complaint about selling additional common stock is that earnings will be diluted and cause the stock price to fall. But if the new issue is fairly priced and the proceeds are invested in projects that earn at least the cost of equity capital, the stock price should rise (or stay the same, if they were anticipated). If the investments don't pan out, both old and new stockholders will lose. But their loss is due to bad investments, not to the stock issue.

12.6   CORPORATE DEBT

Use of debt obligates the firm to mandatory interest and principal payments; failure to meet these obligations is an act of default.

If interest and principal payments are not made on time and in the amounts specified in the debt contract, the creditors can take a variety of actions to collect their due. This includes, but is not limited to, forcing the firm into bankruptcy and eventually liquidation. The stockholders, for their part, can exercise their option not to repay the firm's debts and turn over the firm and its assets to the creditors. They will do this only if the value of the firm's assets is less than the value of the claims against it. Because this turn of events sometimes occurs, the option to default on debt is valuable. If default and liquidation are opted for, lenders will have a priority claim on the firm's assets. This means that common and preferred stockholders receive a portion of the liquidation proceeds only after all creditors are paid in full.

Lenders are not owners; therefore, regardless of how profitable the firm is, their returns are limited.

The fact that lenders are not considered owners of the firm has three important consequences. First, lenders ordinarily have no voting power. Second, their returns are limited to interest plus principal repayments, no matter how profitable the firm's investments turn out to be. Third, interest payments are considered a cost of business and so are tax deductible; by contrast, dividends are not considered a necessary cost of doing business and must be paid out of after-tax income. The net effect is that the government penalizes equity financing relative to debt financing.

Advantages and Disadvantages of Debt Financing

Debt has several advantages and disadvantages from the perspective of the issuing firm. The advantages relative to equity financing include the following:

1. Interest payments are tax deductible, whereas common and preferred stock dividends are paid out of after-tax earnings.
2. Debtholders do not share in the value created by growth opportunities; their payments are limited to interest and principal.
3. Bondholders do not vote, enabling the owners to maintain greater control over the firm.
4. If the value of the firm drops precipitously, the common stockholders will have the option of defaulting on their debts and turning over the firm to the debtholders.
5. Issue costs on bonds are generally lower than those on common or preferred stock.
6. Debt provides protection against unexpectedly high inflation because its real cost varies inversely with the rate of inflation.

Disadvantages of debt financing include the following:

1. Greater use of debt financing increases the firm's financial risk, possibly leading to bankruptcy and eventual liquidation.
2. According to the CAPM (Chapter 10, Equation [10-8]), the increase in financial leverage raises the firm's cost of equity capital.
3. Bonds typically contain restrictive covenants that limit the firm's financial and operating flexibility. These restrictions may reduce the firm's ability to engage in value-maximizing behavior.
4. The real cost of debt will be greater than expected if the rate of inflation turns out to be unexpectedly low.

12.7   PREFERRED STOCK

Preferred stock is a hybrid security; like common stock it is viewed as equity even though it is considered a fixed income security.

Preferred stock is an infrequently used form of financing, and so we will not devote much time to it. One of the principal drawbacks to its use is that preferred dividends are not tax deductible. However, preferred financing is useful in certain circumstances, so it is worthwhile to understand its salient features.

We saw in Chapter 5 that preferred stock has attributes of both bonds and stock. Like common stock, preferred stock is a source of equity capital for the firm. On the other hand, it is considered a fixed-income security like long-term debt, although preferred stockholders receive dividends instead of interest and the preferred dividend payments are discretionary. The absence of a legal

obligation to pay preferred dividends means that the added capital supplied by
preferred stock reduces the probability of bankruptcy. It also means that these
payments are not tax deductible.

The claim of preferred stock to the firm's income and assets is between that
of common stock and debt. Preferred dividends take precedence over common
dividends but are subordinate to debt claims. Similarly, in the event of bankruptcy, preferred stock is senior to common stock but subordinate to all debt.

Advantages and Disadvantages of Preferred Stock Financing

The hybrid nature of preferred stock offers the firm a mixture of the advantages
and disadvantages of debt and common equity. The principal advantages include
the following:

1. In contrast to bonds, preferred stock provides the firm with favorable financial leverage without increasing the risk of bankruptcy.
2. The lack of a maturity date and the firm's ability to omit preferred dividends
   give the firm some flexibility in managing its cash flow.
3. Preferred stock does not carry voting rights unless the firm fails to meet its
   stated provisions.
4. Common stockholders do not have to share control of the firm with the preferred investors except in the case of financial distress.
5. As with common stock dividends, corporate holders can exclude from taxable income 70 percent of the preferred dividends they receive. Because of
   the tax advantage to corporate investors, preferred stock often carries a lower
   yield than bonds do despite the greater riskiness.

The main disadvantages are as follows:

1. Preferred dividends are not tax deductible, in contrast to interest expenses
   that are tax deductible. This is not a disadvantage if the firm is not paying
   taxes.
2. The claims of preferred stock on the firm's earnings and assets take priority
   over the common stockholders' claims.
3. The fixed dividend payments on preferred add to financial leverage, which
   is unfavorable if earnings decline.
4. The failure to meet preferred dividends could force the company to grant voting rights to preferred shareholders.

Uses of Preferred Stock Financing

Financial managers have traditionally been averse to using preferred stock financing because of its high after-tax cost relative to that of debt. Utilities, how-

The regulatory rate-making process makes preferred stock an attractive source of financing for public utilities.

ever, are permitted by regulatory agencies to treat preferred dividends as an expense for rate-making purposes. As a result, they can pass along the tax disadvantages of preferred stock to their customers while benefiting from the financial leverage provided by preferred stock. Thus, utilities are the most frequent users of preferred stock financing.

Preferred stock financing is also used often in mergers and acquisitions, also because of tax laws. If the owners of the acquired firm exchange their shares for cash or bonds, they must pay capital gains tax at the time of sale on the difference between the sale price and their original cost basis. Using preferred (or common) stock, however, renders the exchange tax free. The capital gains tax is deferred until the preferred (or common) is sold.

Although the tax advantages of using preferred and common stock to finance mergers and acquisitions are the same, preferred stock financing allows the acquiring firm to gain additional financial leverage without exposing it to greater risk of financial distress.

12.8 CONVERTIBLE SECURITIES

Convertible bonds and convertible preferred stock are combinations of the underlying security and a call option on the firm's common stock.

Convertible bonds and *convertible preferred stock* combine the characteristics of the underlying bond or preferred stock and common stock. As we indicated in Chapter 7, investors in convertibles have the option of exchanging these securities for a fixed number of common shares at a set price per share.

Advantages and Disadvantages of Convertible Financing

Companies raising money often favor convertibles because of several advantages:

1. They carry lower interest rates than straight bonds. Buyers will settle for less in return for the chance to participate in a run-up in the stock. They also find it comforting that the downside risk is limited because a convertible's price won't likely drop below what it would sell for as a straight bond.
2. The fact that investors can share in the upside also makes them willing to impose fewer restrictive covenants, thereby giving the firm more operating and financial flexibility.
3. Convertibles may also be a good choice for a firm that believes it is less risky than investors do. In this case, investors will overvalue the conversion option, offsetting the higher interest rate they will demand on the debt portion.

The main disadvantage is that the firm is giving convertible buyers the right to participate in an unexpected appreciation in the value of the firm. However, competition among potential investors should ensure that this option is fairly priced, meaning that the eventual purchaser should not expect to earn excess returns.

12.9   THE INTERNATIONALIZATION OF CAPITAL MARKETS

The growing internationalization of capital markets and the increased sophistication of companies means that the search for capital no longer stops at the water's edge. Instead of tapping a narrow base of investors, issuers can now raise capital from a worldwide pool. This is particularly true for multinational corporations (MNCs). A distinctive feature of the financial strategy of MNCs is the wide range of external sources of funds that they use on an ongoing basis.[11] For example, General Motors packages car loans as securities and sells them in Europe and Japan. British Telecommunications offers stock in London, New York, and Tokyo, and Beneficial Corporation issues Euroyen notes that may not be sold in either the United States or Japan. Swiss Bank Corporation, aided by Italian, Belgian, Canadian, and German banks, helps RJR Nabisco sell Swiss franc bonds in Europe and then convert the proceeds back into U.S. dollars. Although many of these sources are located in the countries in which the multinationals operate, a growing portion of their funds comes from offshore markets, particularly the Eurocurrency and Eurobond markets.

National Capital Markets as International Financial Centers

Most of the major financial markets attract both investors and fund raisers from abroad. That is, these markets are also **international financial markets,** in which foreigners can both borrow and lend money. International financial markets can develop anywhere, provided that local regulations permit the market and that the potential users are attracted to it. The most important international financial centers are London, Tokyo, and New York. All the other major industrial countries have important domestic financial markets as well, but only some, such as Germany and—recently—France, are also important international financial centers. On the other hand, some countries that have relatively unimportant domestic financial markets are important world financial centers. The markets of those countries—which include Switzerland, Luxembourg, Singapore, Hong Kong, the Bahamas, and Bahrain—serve as financial *entrepôts* or channels through which foreign funds pass. That is, these markets serve as financial intermediaries between nonresident suppliers of funds and nonresident users of funds.

The Foreign Bond Market.   The **foreign bond market** is an important part of the international financial markets. It is simply that portion of the domestic bond market that represents issues floated by foreign companies or governments. As such, foreign bonds are subject to local laws and must be denominated in the local currency. At times, these issues face additional restrictions as well. For example, foreign bonds floated in Switzerland, Germany, and the Netherlands are subject to a queuing system; they must wait for their turn in line.

The United States and Switzerland contain the most important foreign bond markets (dollar-denominated foreign bonds sold in the United States are called

> The foreign bond market is that portion of the domestic market that represents issues floated by foreigners.

---

[11]This section is based on Chapter 15 of Alan C. Shapiro, *Multinational Financial Management,* 6th ed. (New York: Wiley, 1999).

Yankee bonds). Major foreign bond markets are also located in Japan and Luxembourg (yen bonds sold in Japan by a non-Japanese borrower are called *Samurai bonds* in contrast to *Shogun bonds*, which are foreign currency bonds issued within Japan by Japanese corporations).

The Foreign Bank Market.   The **foreign bank market** represents that portion of domestic bank loans supplied to foreigners for use abroad. As in the case of foreign bond issues, governments often restrict the amounts of bank funds destined for foreign purposes. One indication of the importance of foreign banks, and particularly Japanese banks, is the fact that 6 out of the world's 10 largest banks (ranked by assets as of December 1996) are Japanese, including 4 of the top 5. The highest ranked U.S. bank, Chase, was 16th in size. (Of the world's 25 largest banks, only 1 is American: 10 are Japanese; 4 are French; 4 are German; 3 are British, with the Swiss, Dutch, and Chinese having one top-25 bank apiece.) The minimal representation by American banks among the world's largest owes primarily to prohibitions on interstate banking in the United States. Other factors include the high Japanese savings rate and relatively low U.S. savings rate.

The Foreign Equity Market.   The idea of placing stock in foreign markets has long attracted corporate finance managers. One attraction of the **foreign equity market** is the diversification of equity funding risk: A pool of funds from a diversified shareholder base insulates a company from the vagaries of a single national market. Some issues are too large to be taken up only by investors in the national stock market. For large companies located in small countries, foreign sales may be a necessity. When KLM, the Dutch airline, issued 15 million shares in 1986 to raise $304 million, it placed 7 million shares in Europe, 7 million in the United States, and 1 million in Japan. According to a spokesman for the company, "The domestic market is too small for such an operation."[12]

> Equity issues are increasingly being sold abroad.

Selling stock overseas can also increase the potential demand for the company's shares, and hence its price, by attracting new shareholders. For a firm that wants to project an international presence, an international stock offering can spread the firm's name in local markets. In the words of a London investment banker, "If you are a company with a brand name, it's a way of making your product known and your presence known in the financial markets, which can have a knock-off effect on your overall business. A marketing exercise is done; it's just like selling soap."[13] According to Apple Computer's investor relations manager, Apple listed its shares on the Tokyo exchange and the Frankfurt exchange "to raise the profile of Apple in those countries to help us sell computers. In Japan, being listed there gets us more interest from the business press."[14]

---

[12]"International Equities: The New Game in Town," *Business International Money Report,* September 29, 1987, 306.

[13]Ibid.

[14]Quoted in Kathleen Doler, "More U.S. Firms See Foreign Shareholdings as a Plus," *Investors Business Daily,* February 17, 1994, A4.

Illustration

Waste Management Lists Its Stock in Australia

Chicago-based Waste Management has been operating in Australia since 1984 and has gained a leading share of the garbage-collection market through expansion and acquisition. In 1986, the firm issued shares in Australia and then listed those shares on the Australian exchanges. A principal reason for the listing was to enhance its corporate profile. According to a Waste Management spokesman, "We view Australia as a growth market, and what we really wanted was to increase our visibility."[15]

Listing gets Waste Management better known in the financial community as well. This visibility, in turn, aids the expansion program, which hinges largely on mergers and acquisitions, by increasing contacts with potential joint venture or acquisition candidates. Listing also facilitates stock-for-stock swaps.

An Australian listing also enhances the local profit-sharing package. Waste Management uses an employee stock program as an integral feature of its compensation. By listing locally, the firm increases the prominence of its shares, and the program becomes more attractive to employees.

To capture some of these potential benefits, more companies are selling stock issues overseas. For example, Deutsche Telekom's global equity offering included a $1.9 billion piece to be sold in the United States because the company thought that its long-term capital needs required access to a larger and more liquid market than that provided by its German home market. Similarly, in October 1992, Roche Holding Ltd., the Swiss pharmaceutical giant, announced that it had completed a U.S. private placement of $275 million worth of stock. The move reflected Roche's desire to tap into the world's largest capital market because its rapid growth had "left Roche simply too big for the Swiss market."[16] Indeed, more foreign companies are selling their initial public offerings, or IPOs, in the United States because they "get a better price, a shareholder base that understands their business, and they can get publicity in a major market for their products."[17]

In 1993, Daimler-Benz, the industrial conglomerate that makes the Mercedes-Benz, became the first German company to list its shares on the New

---

[15]"Waste Management Who? Why One U.S. Giant Is Now Listed Down Under," *Business International Money Report,* December 22, 1986, 403.

[16]Quoted in "Roche Sells 100,000 Shares in U.S. Market," *Wall Street Journal,* October 2, 1992, A7.

[17]Quoted in Michael R. Sesit, "Foreign Firms Flock to U.S. for IPOs," *Wall Street Journal,* June 23, 1995, C1.

York Stock Exchange. To qualify for the listing, Daimler-Benz had to provide an onerous, by German standards, level of financial disclosure and undertake a costly revision of its accounting practices to conform to U.S. Generally Accepted Accounting Principles (GAAP). The difference between GAAP and German accounting rules is apparent in the publishing of Daimler-Benz's results for fiscal 1994. While Daimler showed a profit of $636 million under German rules, it reported a loss of $748 million after conforming to GAAP and eliminating the impact of drawing down hidden reserves (which is allowed in Germany). Daimler-Benz undertook the arduous task of revising its financial statements because the company wanted access to the large and liquid pool of capital represented by the U.S. market. Daimler also felt that the positive image of its Mercedes cars would help it raise capital at a lower price from wealthy Americans. During the six weeks between the announcement of its plans for a New York Stock Exchange (NYSE) listing and actually receiving the listing, Daimler-Benz's shares rose more than 30 percent, in contrast to an 11 percent rise for the German stock market overall.

It's not just large foreign companies that are issuing stock in the United States these days. The existence of numerous U.S. investment analysts, entrepreneurs, and investors familiar with the nature and needs of emerging firms means that many medium-sized European firms are now finding it easier and quicker to do initial public offerings (IPOs) on the NASDAQ exchange in the United States than to raise capital in their underdeveloped domestic capital markets.

Rule 144A has improved foreign access to the U.S. capital markets.

An important new avenue for foreign equity (and debt) issuers, ranging from France's Rhone-Poulenc to Korea's Pohang Iron & Steel, to gain access to the U.S. market was opened up in 1990 when the Securities and Exchange Commission (SEC) adopted *Rule 144A,* which allows qualified institutional investors to trade in unregistered private placements, making them a closer substitute for public issues. This rule greatly increases the liquidity of the private placement market and makes it more attractive to foreign companies, which are frequently deterred from entering the U.S. market by the SEC's stringent disclosure and reporting requirements.

The desire to build a global shareholder base is also inducing many American companies—which until recently issued stock almost exclusively in the United States—to now sell part of their issues overseas. For example, in May 1992, General Motors raised $2.1 billion by selling 40 million shares in the United States, 6 million in Britain, 4.5 million in Europe, and 4.5 million in the Far East. Exhibit 12-9 shows the announcement of that issue. As usual, the benefits of expanded ownership must be traded off against the added costs of inducing more investors to become shareholders.

Most major stock exchanges permit sales of foreign issues provided the issue satisfies all the listing requirements of the local market. Some of the major stock markets list large numbers of foreign stocks. For example, Union Carbide, Black & Decker, Caterpillar, and General Motors are among the more than 200 foreign stocks listed on the German stock exchanges. Almost 500 foreign stocks—including ITT, Hoover, and Woolworth—are listed on the British exchanges.

EXHIBIT 12-9
General Motors' Global Equity Issue

All of these Securities have been sold. This announcement appears as a matter of record only.

$2,145,000,000

GM

General Motors Corporation
$1⅔ Par Value Common Stock

55,000,000 Shares

Global Coordinator
MORGAN STANLEY & CO.
Incorporated

40,000,000 Shares
This portion of the offering has been offered in the United States by the undersigned.

MORGAN STANLEY & CO.
Incorporated

THE FIRST BOSTON CORPORATION

LEHMAN BROTHERS

MERRILL LYNCH & CO.

J.P. MORGAN SECURITIES INC.

PAINEWEBBER INCORPORATED

SMITH BARNEY, HARRIS UPHAM & CO.
Incorporated

DEAN WITTER REYNOLDS INC.

6,000,000 Shares
This portion of the offering has been offered in the United Kingdom by the undersigned.

MORGAN STANLEY INTERNATIONAL

CAZENOVE & CO.

S. G. WARBURG SECURITIES

4,500,000 Shares
This portion of the offering has been offered in the Asia Pacific region by the undersigned.

MORGAN STANLEY INTERNATIONAL

DAIWA EUROPE LIMITED

NOMURA INTERNATIONAL

4,500,000 Shares
This portion of the offering has been offered elsewhere internationally by the undersigned.

MORGAN STANLEY INTERNATIONAL

DEUTSCHE BANK
Aktiengesellschaft

UBS PHILLIPS & DREW SECURITIES LIMITED

May 21, 1992

Source: Reprinted with permission from General Motors Corporation.

Globalization of Financial Markets Has Its Downside

> International financial markets reward countries following sound economic policies and punish those following questionable policies.

The army of investors searching worldwide for the highest risk-adjusted returns wields a two-edged sword: It is likely to reward sound economic policies and swift to abandon countries whose economic fundamentals are questionable. As a result, countries such as Italy, Spain, Sweden, Russia, Thailand, Malaysia, Indonesia, and Mexico with large public-sector or trade deficits or rapid money supply growth have at one time or another received harsh treatment in the financial markets. By demanding bigger premiums for the risk of holding these nations' currencies, the markets force de facto devaluations of their currencies, thereby serving to punish the profligate and reward the virtuous. In the eyes of many international economists, markets have replaced public organizations such as the International Monetary Fund as the disciplinary force for the global economy.

A devaluation raises the cost of imports for a country, boosts its interest rates (to lure investors back), and forces the government to take steps to address the monetary, budget, or trade problems that led to the capital flight and devaluation in the first place. Of course, changing the policies that created these problems can impose significant costs on favored political constituents, which is why these problems weren't addressed earlier.

But blaming financial markets for the political and economic disruptions caused by these policy changes misses the point. Financial markets are in the business of gathering and processing information from millions of savers and borrowers around the world in order to perform their real function, which is to price capital and allocate it to its most productive uses. In performing this function, markets reflect the perceptions of risk and reward of its participants. But they do not create the underlying reality that caused those perceptions.

The long-run risk to the global economy caused by the abrupt shifts in capital flows and attendant waves of devaluations is that some politicians will seek to reimpose controls on capital and trade flows, particularly if the politicians manage to convince themselves that the markets are behaving in an irresponsible fashion. Such controls—whatever their motivation—would reverse the trend toward freer trade and capital markets and make the world worse off.

The Eurocurrency Market

The Eurocurrency market consists of banks that accept deposits and make loans in a foreign currency.

A Eurocurrency is a dollar or other freely convertible currency deposited in a bank outside its country of origin. Thus, U.S. dollars on deposit in London or Montreal become Eurodollars. These dollars can be placed in a foreign bank or in the foreign branch of a domestic U.S. bank. The Eurocurrency market consists of those banks (Eurobanks) that accept deposits and make loans in foreign currencies.

The Eurobond and Eurocurrency markets are often confused with each other, but there is a fundamental distinction between the two. **Eurobonds** are issued directly by the final borrowers, whereas the Eurocurrency market enables investors to hold short-term claims on banks, which then act as intermediaries to transform these deposits into long-term claims on final borrowers. However, banks do play an important role in placing Eurobonds with the final investors.

The Eurocurrency (and Eurobond) markets have thrived for one reason: government regulation. By operating in Eurocurrencies, banks (and investors) can avoid certain regulatory and tax costs that would otherwise be imposed. This allows Eurobanks to set lower rates on loans, while simultaneously paying higher rates on deposits.

The most important characteristic of the Eurocurrency market is that loans are made on a floating-rate basis. Historically, interest rates on Eurocurrency loans have been set at a fixed margin above the **London interbank offer rate** (LIBOR) for the given period and currency chosen. At the end of each period, the interest for the next period is calculated at the same fixed margin over the new LIBOR. For example, if the margin is .60 percent and the current LIBOR is 11.1 percent, then the borrower is charged 11.7 percent for the coming period. The period normally chosen is six months, but shorter periods such as one month or three months are possible. The margin varies a good deal among borrowers and is based on the borrower's perceived riskiness.

Lenders in this market are almost exclusively banks. In any single loan, a number of participating banks usually form a *syndicate*. The bank originating the loan will usually manage the syndicate. This bank, in turn, may invite one or two other banks to co-manage the loan. The manager(s) charges the borrower a fee of .25 percent to 1 percent of the loan value, depending on the size and type of the loan. Part of this fee is kept by the manager(s), and the rest is divided up among all the participants according to the amount of funds each bank supplies.

Eurobonds

As we indicated in Chapter 5, Eurobonds are medium- to long-term interest-bearing debt instruments that are similar in many respects to the public debt sold in domestic capital markets. Unlike domestic bond markets, however, the Eurobond market is almost entirely free of official regulation but instead is self-regulated by the Association of International Bond Dealers. The prefix "Euro" indicates that the bonds are sold outside the countries in whose currencies they are denominated. For example, the AT&T issue shown in Exhibit 12-10 is a Eurobond. You can tell that because the notice—known as a *tombstone*—says, "These debentures have not been registered under the United States Securities Act of 1933 and may not be offered, sold or delivered in the United States of America or to nationals or residents thereof."

Borrowers in the Eurobond market must be well known and must have impeccable credit ratings (for example, developed countries, international institutions like the World Bank, and large multinational corporations). Even then the amounts raised in the Eurobond market have historically been far less than those in the Eurocurrency market. As can be seen in Exhibit 12-11, however, the Eurobond market has grown dramatically over the past decade, and its size now rivals that of the Eurocurrency market. But Exhibit 12-11 shows that the Eurobond market has had its ups and downs as well and that nondollar Eurobonds are gaining in importance, particularly yen and deutsche mark issues.

The Eurobond market survives and thrives because, unlike any other major capital market, it remains largely unregulated and untaxed. Thus, big borrowers such as GM and IBM can raise money more quickly and more flexibly than they can at home. And because the interest that investors receive is tax free (if they don't report it), these companies have historically been able to borrow at a rate below the rate at which the U.S. Treasury can borrow.

The tax-free aspect of Eurobonds relates to the fact that they are issued in *bearer* form, meaning they are unregistered, with no record to identify the owners. (Money can be considered to be a zero-coupon bearer bond.) This feature allows investors to collect interest on Eurobonds in complete anonymity and, thereby, evade taxes. Although U.S. law discourages the sale of unregistered bonds to U.S. citizens or residents, bonds issued in bearer form are common overseas. As expected, investors are willing to accept lower yields on bearer bonds than on registered bonds of similar risk.

Highly rated American firms have long taken advantage of this opportunity to reduce their cost of funds by selling overseas Eurobonds in bearer form. Of-

EXHIBIT 12-10
Tombstone for AT&T Eurobond

U.S. $300,000,000

9% Debentures Due 2016

Credit Suisse First Boston Limited	**Salomon Brothers International Limited**
Nomura International Limited	**Swiss Bank Corporation International Limited**

Union Bank of Switzerland (Securities) Limited

Julius Baer International Limited	**Banque Bruxelles Lambert S.A.**
Banque Nationale de Paris	**Deutsche Bank Capital Markets Limited**
Goldman Sachs International Corp.	**Lloyds Merchant Bank Limited**
LTCB International Limited	**Merrill Lynch Capital Markets**
Morgan Guaranty Ltd	**Morgan Stanley International**

Algemene Bank Nederland N.V.	**Banca Commerciale Italiana**	**Banca Nazionale del Lavoro**
Banca della Svizzera Italiana	**Bank Leu International Ltd.**	**Bank Leumi le Israel (Switzerland) AG**
Bank of Tokyo International Limited	**Bank J. Vontobel & Co. AG**	**Compagnie de Banque et d'Investissements, CBI**
Crédit Lyonnais	**Credito Italiano**	**Daiwa Europe** Limited **Generale Bank**
Hentsch & Cie	**IBJ International** Limited	**Lombard Odier International Underwriters S.A.**
Manufacturers Hanover Limited	**Mitsubishi Trust & Banking Corporation (Europe) S.A.**	**Mitsui Trust Bank (Europe) S.A.**
The Nikko Securities Co., (Europe) Ltd.	**Orion Royal Bank** Limited **Paine Webber International**	**Pictet International Ltd**
Sanwa International Limited	**J. Henry Schroder Wagg & Co.** Limited	**Shearson Lehman Brothers International**
Swiss Volksbank	**Westdeutsche Landesbank** Girozentrale	**Yamaichi International (Europe)** Limited

ten corporations could borrow abroad below the cost at which the U.S. government could borrow at home. Exxon's issue of zero-coupon Eurobonds shows how companies were able to exploit the arbitrage possibility inherent in such a situation.

EXHIBIT 12-11
Eurobond New Issues: 1979–1997

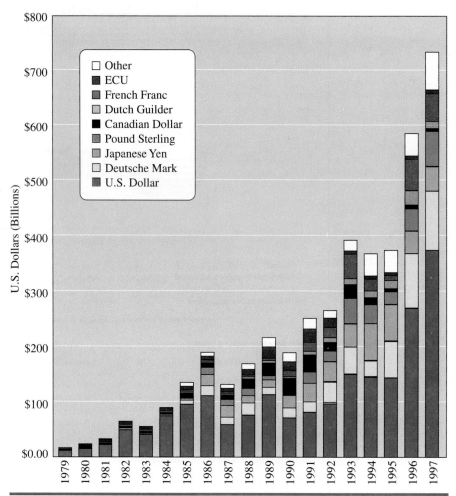

Source: Financial Market Trends, Organization for Economic Cooperation and Development, various issues.

Illustration

Exxon's Arbitrage Opportunity

In the fall of 1984, Exxon sold $1.8 billion principal amount of zero-coupon Eurobonds due November 2004 at an annual compounded yield of 11.65 percent, realizing net proceeds of about $199 million:

$$\text{Bond Value} = \$1,800,000,000/(1.1165)^{20}$$
$$= \$198,654,294$$

It then used part of the proceeds to buy $1.8 billion principal amount of U.S. Treasury bonds maturing in November 2004 from which the coupons had been removed and sold separately. The yield on these "stripped" Treasuries, which are effectively zero-coupon Treasury bonds, was around 12.20 percent.[18] At this yield, it would have cost Exxon $180 million to purchase the $1.8 billion in stripped Treasury bonds:

$$\text{Bond Value} = \$1,800,000,000/(1.1220)^{20}$$
$$= \$180,059,221$$

At this price, Exxon earned the difference of about $18.6 million.

A peculiar quirk in Japanese law is largely responsible for the big difference in yield between zero-coupon Eurobonds and stripped Treasuries: Japanese investors—who were the principal buyers of the Eurobonds—did not have to pay tax on a zero-coupon bond's accrued interest if they sold the bond prior to maturity. Because of this tax advantage, they were willing to pay a premium price for zeros (relative to coupon-bearing bonds). Although, in principle, the Japanese would have preferred to purchase the higher-yielding (and safer) stripped U.S. Treasury bonds, they are prohibited by Japanese law from doing so. The threatened taxation of the accrued interest on zeros in Japan has eliminated this arbitrage opportunity.

Despite several forecasts of imminent death, the Eurobond market has survived, largely because its participants are so fleet of foot. As demand for one type of bond declines, quick-witted investment bankers seem to find other opportunities to create value for their customers. The financial infrastructure in place in London should ensure the Eurobond market's survival. However, tax harmonization, financial deregulation, and the widespread loosening of capital controls mean that issuers have less incentive to borrow money offshore and so are returning to their domestic markets to raise capital. Whether these trends persist or not, the Eurobond market will still preserve its basic role—as the nimblest intermediary for international capital flows between domestic markets.

---

[18]This case is discussed at greater length in John D. Finnerty, "Zero Coupon Bond Arbitrage: An Illustration of the Regulatory Dialectic at Work," *Financial Management*, Winter 1985, 13–17.

Note Issuance Facilities and Euronotes

Eurobanks have responded to the competition from the Eurobond market by creating a new instrument: the **note issuance facility (NIF).** The NIF, a low-cost substitute for syndicated credits, allows borrowers to issue their own short-term *Euronotes,* which are then placed or distributed by the financial institutions providing the NIF. NIFs are more flexible than floating-rate notes and usually cheaper than syndicated loans.

Here's how the basic facility works (although alternate methods exist in abundance in the marketplace). A syndicate of banks underwrites an amount—usually about $50–$200 million—for a specified period, typically for five to seven years. A LIBOR-based underwriting margin is set based on the credit rating of the borrower, the size of the issue, and market conditions. When the borrower decides to draw on the facility, the borrower can choose to issue Euronotes with one-month, three-month, six-month, or twelve-month maturities. A panel of banks is then established, whose members submit competitive bids. Any bids above the agreed underwriting margin are automatically purchased by the underwriters at the agreed-upon margin over LIBOR. In effect, NIFs are put options. They give borrowers the right to sell their paper to the bank syndicate at a price that yields the prearranged spread over LIBOR. Borrowers will exercise this right only if they cannot place their notes at a better rate elsewhere.

SUMMARY

We began the chapter with an overview of the financial markets—how they are organized and how they facilitate the flow of funds between borowers and savers. As part of the funds transfer process, the financial markets also provide a mechanism for the transfer and reduction of risk in addition to playing a vital role in valuing financial assets. Through the pricing of corporate securities, investors express their opinions about whether executive decisions are consistent with maximizing shareholder value. The end result of well-functioning financial markets is greater capital productivity and more innovation.

We examined the four major sources of corporate financing. Common equity—in the form of retained earnings or newly issued shares—is the most important source of corporate funds. Next comes debt in all its many varieties. Preferred stock is another source of financing, combining some of the attributes of both common equity and debt. The fourth source of funds is convertible securities, either convertible debt or convertible preferred.

Historically, internally generated cash flow—retained earnings plus depreciation—has supplied over 60 percent of corporate fund requirements. The need for external finance is most pronounced during periods of economic growth; during recession or times of slow growth the demand for external funds falls. Most of the external financing comes in the form of debt; new equity issues account for a very small fraction of external finance. Indeed, net new equity issues have been negative in recent years.

Although there are significant differences among countries in their methods and sources of finance, corporate practice appears to be converging. Most significantly, more firms are bypassing financial intermediaries, mainly commercial banks, and going directly to the financial markets for funds. The convergence of corporate financing practice largely reflects the globalization of financial markets, the inextricable linkage—through arbitrage—of financial markets worldwide. In line with this trend, firms are finding that it pays to seek capital on a global basis, rather than restricting their search to any one nation or capital market.

We saw that the growth of the international capital markets, specifically the Eurocurrency and Eurobond markets, is largely a response to the various restrictions and regulations that governments impose on domestic financial transactions. At the same time, capital flows between the international capital markets and domestic markets have linked domestic markets in a manner that increasingly makes such government intervention irrelevant.

QUESTIONS

1. What are the differences between publicly issued debt and privately placed debt?
2. Why did internal funds account for a smaller fraction of the financing requirements of American companies in the 1970s? What changes in government policies and in the economic environment led to an increased reliance on internal funds in the 1980s?
3. How does economic growth affect corporate financing requirements? What accounts for this relation?
4. How has the recent wave of share repurchases and leveraged buyouts affected the pattern of American corporate financing?
5. What is securitization? What forces appear to be underlying the trend toward securitization and how has it affected corporate financing policies?
6. Why is bank lending on the decline worldwide? How have banks responded to their loss of market share?
7. What is meant by the globalization of financial markets? How has technology affected the process of globalization?
8. How has globalization affected government regulation of national capital markets?
9. What factors appear to underlie the increased leverage of U.S. companies? Discuss the role of taxes, inflation, and economic volatility in affecting corporate debt ratios.
10. Suppose banking rules were changed and U.S. banks were permitted to hold the equity of their corporate borrowers. How would such a rule change likely affect the degree of leverage employed by U.S. firms?
11. Give two reasons why it may be profitable for a firm to use retained earnings to finance new investment. Give at least one reason why this may be objectionable.
12. The concept of preemptive rights means that existing shareholders have first right to purchase an issue of new shares, each existing shareholder being entitled to purchase the exact number of shares necessary to maintain his or her fraction of ownership of the firm. Can you explain why shareholders might also insist on preemptive rights to new issues of convertible bonds?
13. What problems might a company face when it goes to raise equity by issuing new shares of common stock?
14. List some reasons that a U.S.-based corporation might issue debt denominated in a foreign currency.
15. Lenders typically are averse to a company's taking on highly risky new projects. By contrast, we have already seen that shareholders should be willing to take on even extremely risky projects as long as the projects appear to have positive net present values. What considerations might account for the difference in the perspectives on the part of lenders and shareholders?
16. It is said in the United States that the government encourages debt financing relative to equity financing. Comment on this viewpoint.
17. How might substantial amounts of debt constrain a company's operating flexibility? What type of company will be most affected by these constraints?
18. Comment on the following statement: "Preferred stock is a long-term fixed-income security, like debt. But because debt is a tax-deductible security and usually has lower rates (because the debt is safer than the preferred), the preferred is a poor choice."
19. Convertible debt carries a lower coupon rate than does straight debt. Does that make it the less expensive form of financing? Explain.
20. Why might issuing stock abroad lead to a higher stock price?
21. What is the difference between the Eurocurrency and the Eurobond markets?
22. What is the difference between a foreign bond and a Eurobond?
23. What factors account for the rise of the Eurobond market and its continuing survival?
24. There is a strong correlation between capital spending and corporate cash flow. A recent article

in *Forbes* explains this correlation as follows: Internal financing is cheaper than borrowing, so it is plausible that boardroom investment decisions are heavily influenced by corporate cash flow. Discuss the logic of this rationale.

25. Why are large multinational corporations located in small countries such as Sweden, Holland, and Switzerland interested in developing a global investor base?

PROBLEMS

⚙ —Excel templates may be downloaded from **www.prenhall.com/financecenter.**

1. At the beginning of 1999, General Electric was selling at $120 per share. At the same time, its book value per share was $38.
   a. What is the market-to-book value ratio for General Electric as of the beginning of 1999? What might account for the discrepancy between GE's market and book values?
   b. Suppose the debt-to-equity ratio for GE using book values is .25. What is the D/E ratio in terms of market values? (Assume market and book values of debt are the same.)

2. Suppose that the current 180-day interbank Eurodollar rate is 9 percent (all rates are stated on an annualized basis). If next period's rate is 9.5 percent, what will a Eurocurrency loan priced at LIBOR plus 1 percent cost?

3. Refer to the example of Exxon's zero-coupon Eurobond issue. ⚙
   a. How much would Exxon have earned if the yield on the stripped Treasuries had been 12.10 percent? 12.25 percent?
   b. Suppose that at maturity the Japanese government taxed the accretion in the value of zero-coupon bonds at a rate of 15 percent. Assuming the same 11.65 percent after-tax required yield, how would this tax have affected the price

Japanese investors were willing to pay for Exxon's Eurobond issue? What would the pretax yield be at this new price? Would any arbitrage incentive still exist for Exxon?
   c. Suppose Exxon had sold its zero-coupon Eurobonds to yield 11.5 percent and bought "stripped" Treasury bonds yielding 12.30 percent to meet the required payment of $1.8 billion. How much would Exxon have earned through its arbitrage transaction?

4. Given below are the annualized commercial paper and LIBOR (London interbank offer rate, the rate on Eurodollar borrowings) rates for a three-year period. Which would have been a better loan rate for a corporate borrower over the three-year period, assuming the borrower paid the new rate every six months? ⚙

	Commercial Paper	**LIBOR**
Year 1.1	8.15	8.63
Year 1.2	7.38	7.38
Year 2.1	7.80	7.00
Year 2.2	6.75	6.19
Year 3.1	6.10	6.93
Year 3.2	6.25	5.63

REFERENCES

Donaldson, Gordon. *Corporate Debt Capacity: A Study of Corporate Debt Policy and the Determination of Corporate Debt Capacity.* Boston: Division of Research, Harvard Graduate School of Business Administration, 1961, 67.

The Economist. "A Survey of Corporate Finance." June 7, 1986, 1–38.

Shapiro, Alan C. *Multinational Financial Management,* 6th ed. Upper Saddle River, NJ: Prentice Hall, 1999.

Taggart, Robert A., Jr. *Secular Patterns in the Financing of U.S. Corporations.* Cambridge, MA: National Bureau of Economic Research, 1985.

Taggart, Robert A., Jr. "Corporate Financing: Too Much Debt?" *Financial Analysts Journal,* May/June 1986, 35–42.

How Companies Raise Long-Term Capital

Money is the God of our times, and Rothschild is his prophet.
Heinrich Heine

KEY TERMS

adverse selection or
  lemons problem
after-market price
competitive bid
ex-rights
financing pecking order
Green Shoe option
initial public offering
  (IPO)
investment banker

mezzanine financing
negotiated offering
originating house
preemptive right
private placements
privileged subscription or
  rights offering
prospectus
public offering
red herring

registration statement
rights-on
selling concession
selling group
standby agreement
subscription price
syndicate
tombstone
underwriting
venture capitalist

CHAPTER LEARNING OBJECTIVES

Upon completion of this chapter, students should be able to:

- Describe how venture capitalists assist entrepreneurs in financing new businesses.
- Discuss the functions performed by an investment banker in helping a firm raise funds in the financial markets.
- Describe how the financial markets respond to new security offerings.
- Discuss the regulatory requirements that must be met before bringing a new security issue to market.

- Explain the mechanics of a rights offering and indicate when it may be superior to public offerings as a way of selling new common stock.
- Calculate the value of a right.
- Discuss the advantages and disadvantages of raising funds through a private placement rather than through a public offering.

We saw in Chapter 12 that firms can obtain long-term funds from the public markets or through **private placements.** The latter represent funds obtained directly from a limited number of individual investors or financial institutions such as commercial banks, pension funds, or insurance companies. Larger debt issues and almost all stock offerings are sold publicly and then traded in securities markets. Before offering new securities to the public, the firm must satisfy the Securities and Exchange Commission (SEC) that it has provided investors with full disclosure of relevant facts concerning the firm's legal, financial, and operational position. By contrast, privately placed issues are not traded, nor do they have to be registered with the SEC.

A public issue can be sold to the general public through a **public offering,** or it can be sold directly to existing stockholders through a **privileged subscription** or **rights offering.** Regardless of which of the three fund-raising methods the firm chooses—private placement, public offering, or rights offering—it will likely turn to a financing specialist—the **investment banker**—to assist in designing and marketing the issue. As the opening quotation implies, the legendary Rothschilds are probably the world's best-known investment bankers.

Investment bankers are used to dealing in large numbers. For example, in 1992, corporate America raised $851 billion in capital through the sale of new stock and bond issues. For their troubles, the investment bankers pocketed a record $6.76 billion in fees.

New firms usually must raise their equity capital from **venture capitalists,** so called because they invest in new business ventures. The investment often is a high-risk proposition promising tremendous returns—if the firm doesn't go belly up first. Individual venture capitalists generally use their own money, whereas venture capital firms serve as intermediaries, collecting funds from individuals and institutions—including insurance companies, pension funds, and large corporations—and pooling them into select companies. Instead of charging interest, they make their money by cashing in their equity holdings when a company sells shares to the public ("goes public") or by taking a predetermined share of the profits once the company begins selling its products.

> Venture capitalists invest money in new businesses.

This chapter describes how firms actually go about raising funds, from inception through maturity, and why they select the methods they do. In this way, you will be better able to decide on the most appropriate capital acquisition strategy.

13.1   VENTURE CAPITAL

In early 1999, Bobby Dayglo and two of his friends, Sunny Dude and Bunny Blonde, formed a new company, Rad Neato Enterprises, to design, produce, and market "Boomboards." These are surfboards with built-in 200-watt, waterproof boomboxes that will allow surfers to vibrate to the sound of the Beach Boys while hanging ten or waiting to catch a wave.

The founders contributed $250,000 from savings and mortgages on their homes and used the money to purchase 100,000 shares. At this initial stage, Rad Neato Enterprises had assets of $250,000 in cash plus an idea for an untried product, the "Boomboard." The money was quickly spent on legal fees, product design, prototype development, and testing.

In order to proceed, Rad Neato needed to raise more money. Yet banks rarely lend money to people whose only security is in their heads. The founders decided to approach several appropriate venture capital firms (venture capital firms tend to specialize by industry, such as biotechnology or computer-related products) for the necessary capital. (They found these firms listed in the indispensable reference tool for venture capitalists, *Pratt's Guide to Venture Capital Sources,* published by Venture Economics.) Typically, venture capitalists fund less than 1 percent of the deals that are brought to their attention. Fortunately, this was one of those times. One firm in particular, First Megadeal, was quite impressed with Rad Neato's business plan and the enormous profit potential of Boomboards that was carefully documented there. It was even more impressed with the fact that the founders had invested their savings and mortgaged their homes to fund the venture.

By putting its money where its mouth is, management signals its belief in the venture and its commitment to making the venture work. Managers who have invested heavily in the business, the venture capitalists figure, are managers who will devote themselves to their jobs.

Because there is a high probability of failure at this early stage of the company's life, First Megadeal sought significant ownership of the company in order to provide it with a high expected rate of return. Early-stage venture capitalists usually expect to receive one-third or more of the young firm's equity. But the ownership share demanded by the initial investors varies, depending on the track record of management, the stage of product development, and the negotiating ability of the parties.

The large ownership stake demanded translates into a high cost of capital for the entrepreneurs, ranging from 30 percent to 70 percent annually, depending on the company's stage of development and its track record. However, such high discount rates may have the unintended effect of leading the most competent entrepreneurs to seek alternative sources of risk capital—financial angels who were themselves successful entrepreneurs, corporate partners, or institutional investors such as pension funds—leaving the venture capitalists to finance only the second-rate.

This is the same **adverse selection** or **lemons problem** that confronts the buyer of a used car: If the car is such a good deal, why is the owner selling it? The potential buyer's fear is that the current owner wants to get rid of the car because he knows that it's a lemon. Fearing that she will get stuck with a lemon, the potential buyer will offer less than she would otherwise for the used car.

One way in which First Megadeal dealt with the adverse selection problem was to add sufficient value to its deals that the entrepreneurs expected to come out ahead, even with the high cost of capital. In this way, it attracted able entrepreneurs. It also carefully checked out the entrepreneurs' qualifications and their ideas before investing any money.

After being satisfied by the results of its examination, First Megadeal agreed to buy 50,000 new shares at a price of $10 apiece. This gave it one-third of Rad Neato's equity. By acquiring a certain ownership share in return for investing a

> By acquiring an ownership share at a specific price, the venture capitalist is implicitly setting a value on the firm's equity.

given amount of money, the venture capitalist is implicitly setting a value on the equity in the firm. In the case of Rad Neato, because First Megadeal receives a one-third share of the company for a $500,000 investment, the firm's equity is being valued at $1.5 million ($500,000 × 3). The founders' two-thirds share is worth $1 million.

Following this *first-stage* financing, Rad Neato's balance sheet showed a market value of $1.5 million:

Balance Sheet for Rad Neato Enterprises **First-Stage Financing** **(Market Values)**			
Cash from venture capital	$500,000	Equity from first-stage financing	$500,000
Growth option on Boomboard market	1,000,000	Equity held by founders	1,000,000
Total assets	$1,500,000	Total equity	$1,500,000

The founders now have a $750,000 capital gain based on the $1 million value that First Megadeal is implicitly placing on their idea and commitment to the company. In order to ensure that the founders remain committed to the business, venture capital firms try to structure the deal so that management benefits only if the firm succeeds.[1] This usually means minimal salaries for managers, with most compensation tied to profits and the appreciation in the value of the stock they own. Bobby Dayglo, Sunny Dude, and Bunny Blonde agreed to work for low wages and take their gains in the form of share appreciation. If Rad Neato failed to come up with a salable product, the founders would receive nothing because First Megadeal actually bought preferred stock convertible into 50,000 common shares when and if the company goes public. First Megadeal, therefore, has a prior claim on the assets of Rad Neato in liquidation, ensuring that Bobby Dayglo and his friends will not be able to liquidate the company at this point and hit the beach with their share of Rad Neato's $500,000 in cash. First Megadeal also has a prior claim on Rad Neato's earnings, because the preferred stock carries a 15 percent coupon, which entitles First Megadeal to receive up to $75,000 in dividends each year before the founders receive anything.

The obvious reason for using preferred stock instead of straight equity is to improve the venture capitalist's reward-to-risk ratio. However, this is probably not the primary reason because the founders are unlikely to give something away for nothing; if the founders have to bear more risk, they will raise the price to the venture capitalist of acquiring a given stake in the firm.

> In order to tie the founders to the business, venture capital firms structure deals so that management benefits only if the firm succeeds.

---

[1] For a good discussion of venture capital deal making, see Sahlman (1988).

The more likely reason for using a financial structure that shifts a major share of the risk to the founders is to accomplish two objectives:

1. The venture capitalist is trying to force the founders to signal whether they really believe the forecasts contained in their business plan. If they believe the Boomboard will be only marginally profitable, the founders will have little incentive to go ahead with the deal proposed by First Megadeal.
2. The venture capitalist wants to increase the founders' incentive to make the company succeed. By structuring the financing in this way, the founders will benefit greatly only if they meet their projections.

The financial structure of a deal has a critical impact on a project's success.

By their willingness to accept this deal, the founders increase First Megadeal's confidence in the numbers contained in the business plan. First Megadeal, therefore, is willing to pay a higher price for its equity stake. The financial structure also motivates management to work harder and thereby increases the probability that the outcome will be favorable. This example illustrates an important point about financing: *The value created by a project often depends critically on how the project's financing is structured.*

Unlike investors in publicly held companies, venture capitalists such as First Megadeal can't sell their stock. They are in for the duration. So they usually demand a great deal of control over the company. Venture capitalists frequently sit on the board of directors. And if the company flounders, these investors are quick to move in and, if necessary, move the entrepreneur out. Venture capitalists also demand either the right to sell their investment when they have the opportunity or the right to assume a senior position if the firm is sold or liquidated.

In addition to money, venture capitalists bring business skills and advice to a project.

Successful venture capitalists bring a lot more than money to the table. They also bring needed business skills and advice to the deals they do. They usually assist in the management of the company after investment, helping with policy decisions and financial problems, recruiting new management staff, defining new areas of activity, contributing knowledge of product markets, providing access to markets and other companies, and creating an incentive structure that harnesses entrepreneurial talent and energy. Such assistance is often as valuable as the money they bring.

Simply put, venture capitalists are participatory investors. Unlike commercial or investment bankers, whose job is to provide funds to ongoing firms, venture capitalists are building companies. Although the amount of venture capital available has historically been modest and variable (see Exhibit 13-1), averaging under $2.5 billion annually (compared to corporate capital spending of $770 billion in 1997), the industry has helped create some remarkable companies, including Apple Computer, Microsoft, Intel, Netscape, Yahoo!, Digital Equipment, Sun Microsystems, Lotus Development, Federal Express, Compaq Computer, and Genentech. The high returns associated with many of these companies has led in the past several years to an increase in the amounts of venture capital raised and disbursed (there is usually a lag between the time money is raised and when it is disbursed).

EXHIBIT 13-1
Capital Raised and Disbursed by Venture Capital Partnerships

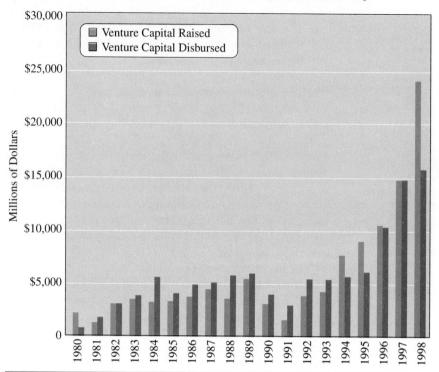

Source: Venture Economics Investors Services.

Even with the most careful preparation, history suggests that venture capitalists must be prepared to lose money. A general rule of thumb in the venture industry is that for every ten investments a financier makes, one will represent a total loss; one will represent a tremendous gain; and the other eight will be touch and go, with the venture firm realizing small profits from some and small losses from others.

The key in the words of one venture capitalist is to make sure that "if you're wrong, you're wrong half-a-million. But if you're right, you're right $20 million."[2] In other words, venture capitalists are investing in growth options, with enormous upside potential. But for the average return to justify the high risks being taken, the venture capitalist must limit the downside risk. Thus, there are two rules for the successful venture capitalist: (1) Identify losers early and cut your losses quickly, and (2) don't throw good money after bad.

Venture capitalists supply financing in stages in order to limit their downside risk.

To limit their downside risk, venture capitalists rarely give a start-up company all the money it needs at once. Typically, there are several stages of financing. At each stage, the venture capitalists give the firm enough money to get it to

---

[2]Quoted in "Going for Broke," *TWA Ambassador,* February 1982, 32.

the next product or market development milestone. By staging the commitment of capital, venture capitalists gain the option of abandoning the project or renegotiating a lower price for future purchases of equity in line with new information. In return for this option, venture capitalists are willing to accept a smaller ownership share for a given investment. The founders are amenable to this financing structure because it means giving up a smaller share of ownership for the needed funding. If the venture progresses according to plan, the founders will be able to bring in future capital with less dilution of their ownership share. Staged financing, therefore, gives the founders the option to raise capital in the future at a higher valuation.

Staged financing allows the founders to keep a larger share of their company

In the absence of staged financing, the deal would probably not get done. For example, suppose that to actually bring its Boomboard to market, Rad Neato estimates that it requires total outside funding of $4 million. Consider the problems if a venture capitalist had to put up all this money at once. Even if a venture capitalist were willing to consider such a deal—and there is little likelihood of that— the enormous risk means that the venture capitalist would have demanded such a large share of the firm that the founders would have had little incentive to proceed.

The knowledge that the company will run out of cash in the relatively near future also has a powerful motivating effect on management. Its energies are focused on getting the most out of limited resources. By treating cash as a scarce resource, management will behave in a way that redounds to the benefit of both it and the venture capitalist.

Subsequent capital needs are partly met by early-stage investors. Additional later-stage financing is supplied by venture capitalists who prefer to back more mature (and hence less risky) companies. These latter investors provide **mezzanine financing,** so called in recognition of their failure to get in on the "ground floor" with the venture capitalists who provided the seed capital.

Mezzanine financings are typically equity but may include some debt features; by this stage, a company generally produces enough cash flow to pay interest to investors. The need to pay interest is also a control mechanism because it forces companies to be honest in evaluating their prospects; a company that is unable to come up with the necessary cash could face very unwelcome consequences.

As the new venture achieves its objectives, the value of the founders' stock rises.

At each successive stage of financing, assuming the company meets its objectives, the price that venture capitalists will pay for a given equity stake rises and so does the implied valuation of the founders' stock. This reflects the lower risk associated with investing in a company that has a longer track record. Not surprisingly, mezzanine financing tends to be less profitable but also less risky than start-up financing. For the founders, the step up in valuation means receiving more capital yet giving up less of the company.

By late 1999, Rad Neato had designed and tested a successful prototype but needed another $1 million for pilot production and test marketing. By now, it was obvious that the product would work and that the trio of Southern Californians were not as laid back as their names suggested. The *resolution of uncertainty* made it easier for Rad Neato to raise the additional money and also improved the terms of this *second-stage* financing. The company issued 40,000 new shares, which it sold for $25 each. First Megadeal bought 16,000 shares for $400,000. The

balance of $600,000 came from another venture capitalist firm and a wealthy rock
star. Following the second-stage financing, here is what Rad Neato's balance sheet
looked like:

Balance Sheet for Rad Neato Enterprises
Second-Stage Financing
(Market Values)

Cash from venture capital	$1,000,000	Equity from second-stage financing	$1,000,000
Other tangible assets	500,000	Equity from first-stage financing	1,250,000
Growth option on Boomboard market	3,250,000	Equity held by founders	2,500,000
Total assets	$4,750,000	Total equity	$4,750,000

The value of the founders' equity stake in Rad Neato has now risen to $2.5
million, a 900 percent return on their original investment. Although this is starting to look like a money machine, it was not money in the bank for the founders
at the outset. The founders may not have been able to assemble a strong management team; the prototype might not have worked; new competition could have entered the market; or market research might have revealed a lack of customers. Who
could have predicted back in early 1999 that the Boomboard would catch a wave
and surf into the Product Hall of Fame? Or that the Boomboard concept could be
extended (with modifications) to the skateboard, wind-surfing, and snowboarding
markets?

The risks borne by the founders are magnified by the fact that most venture
capitalists are prepared to pull the plug and reorganize or liquidate a new venture
that doesn't reach the milestones set for it. If problems arise and the founders insist on going it alone, they will find it difficult to get second-stage financing. New
outside investors know that they have less information than the original investors
did and take it as a bad sign that the latter refused to provide further financing.

If all goes well, the firm will at a later date sell stock to the public in an **initial public offering (IPO),** and its founders and venture capital investors will be
able to convert into cash the paper gains on their company stock. In order to *cash
out,* as this process is called, they will require the services of an investment banker.

13.2   THE INVESTMENT BANKER AND THE PUBLIC OFFERING

Investment bankers serve as intermediaries between suppliers and demanders of
long-term capital. Their name is a misnomer, however, because investment
bankers are neither investors (they don't invest their own funds permanently) nor
bankers (they don't take deposits as do commercial or savings banks). Instead,
they help firms to design and then sell new issues of securities. The latter func-

When an investment bank underwrites a public offering, it buys the securities and then distributes them.

tion usually requires purchasing or **underwriting** the securities and then distributing them. Investment bankers are compensated by the *spread* between the price at which they buy the security and the price at which they can resell it to the public.

Their services are in demand because most firms do not raise long-term capital often enough to become expert at it. Investment bankers, who are constantly dealing with potential investors, are better able to match the key features of a new issue with what the market wants than a company trying to issue and sell securities on its own. By knowing who the potential buyers are and what they are looking for, investment bankers help firms get better prices for their securities and quicker, less costly distribution.

In serving as agents bringing together issuers and investors, investment bankers perform three principal functions: providing advice and counsel, underwriting, and distribution. This chapter considers each of these in turn. In doing so, it will chart the various steps in bringing a public offering to market, beginning with the selection of the firm's investment banker. First, however, we will examine the market's responses to announcements of security offerings, because these responses help provide some key insights into the capital acquisition process and the role of the investment banker. During the course of this examination, we will examine another function served by investment bankers: using their reputations to certify the information released by the issuer.

How the Market Responds to New Security Offerings

Depending on the type of security issued, the average stock market response to a new offering is either negative or zero.

If firms generally issue new securities for the purpose of financing positive net present value projects, then one might expect that the market would respond favorably to the announcement of a new issue. But this is not the case: The average stock market response to security offerings of all kinds—equity and debt, straight and convertible—is consistently either negative or approximately zero.[3] In addition, the market's reaction to a common stock offering is more negative than its reaction to preferred stock or debt offerings. It is also more negative to convertible offerings than to nonconvertibles and more negative to common stock offerings of industrial firms than utilities.

The pattern of responses to announcements of new security offerings can be explained in terms of informational asymmetries between managers and outside investors.

One possible explanation for this puzzling pattern of response is the *information asymmetry hypothesis*. Briefly put, this argument relies on the well-documented fact that managers, as insiders, have better information about the firm's prospects than do outside investors.[4] Rational behavior on the part of management would be to exploit this information asymmetry by issuing securities when management judges that the market price of the firm's securities exceeds their true value. Because sophisticated investors understand management's ability and incentives to exploit them by issuing overvalued securities, the mere act

---

[3]Most of these studies are cited in Smith (1986).

[4]See, for example, Jeffrey Jaffe's study of insider trading, "Special Information and Insider Trading," *Journal of Business,* July 1974, 410–420.

of announcing a new issue will lead them to revise downward their estimates of the firm's value. We already saw this problem arise when First Megadeal was unsure how credible the projections in Rad Neato's business plan were. Recall that the problem was so acute for Rad Neato—because it was a start-up with no history—that it could not issue straight equity at all.

With regard to security sales, the problem of potential insider information is most acute in the case of common stock offerings, because equity is the residual claimant (but less acute for utility offerings than industrials because the regulatory process reduces the potential for information disparity between management and outsiders). By contrast, because debt and preferred stock have more senior claims to a firm's cash flow, their values should be least sensitive to adverse information about the firm's future prospects. The values of equity-linked securities, such as convertible debt and convertible preferred, should be more sensitive to changes in anticipated firm value than straight debt or preferred but less sensitive than common stock.

Illustration

General Motors' Stock Offering

On April 24, 1992, General Motors announced plans to issue as much as $2.9 billion of new common stock in one of the largest common stock offerings ever. For GM, this was its first new issue of common stock since 1965 and a bold move to repair its battered balance sheet and finance its restructuring. Investors, however, took the equity issue as a sign that the company's financial hard times would likely continue and responded by knocking GM's stock price down 6.5 percent on the announcement day, a loss in market value of over $1.7 billion or 59 percent of the proposed offering. Investors' fears were subsequently borne out. General Motors lost further market share; its losses widened; and it kept burning cash at a rapid rate. By the end of 1992, GM's market value had fallen by an additional $5.4 billion.

The predictions of the information asymmetry hypothesis are consistent with the empirical evidence. More important to our purposes, this hypothesis helps explain certain characteristics of the capital acquisition process such as the overwhelming preference for underwritten versus rights offerings, despite the former's much higher cost, and the use of negotiated versus competitive bid contracts, which are discussed in the next section.

The Investment Banker as Guarantor of Issue Quality.   In explaining why capital is raised in the way it is, the information asymmetry hypothesis reveals a key role played by investment bankers in the capital acquisition process. This role, for which they are well paid in the form of high underwriting fees, is to monitor the issuer's activities in order to reduce the *credibility gap* between managers and outside investors and thereby implicitly guarantee the quality of the securities being sold. Investment bankers are particularly qualified to provide such guarantees because their reputation for probity is so valuable. An investment banker who abuses that reputation will lose the future rents that would otherwise accrue to it. As noted banker J. P. Morgan once said, "The client's belief in the integrity of our advice is our best possession." Note that investors as well as issuers are clients of the investment banker.

A Financing Pecking Order. For companies trying not to misrepresent the value of their assets, the credibility problem imposes a potentially large cost on the use of securities to raise funds. This cost is the added discount at which these securities must be sold because of investor fears that management *may* be misrepresenting important inside information.

The credibility problem helps explain the strong corporate preference for internal, as opposed to external, finance noted in Chapter 12. It also explains why firms that must raise external finance prefer to issue securities in ascending order of riskiness: first debt, then hybrids such as convertible bonds, with equity only as a last resort. Stewart Myers calls this set of preferences the **financing pecking order.**[5]

Myers' explanation for this pattern of financing preferences is that it reduces the security price discount imposed by investors when companies raise new capital. By using internal funds, the firm can bypass the capital markets altogether. If the company must issue new securities, the credibility problem is less severe for safer securities—those with more senior claims—and, hence, the smaller the discount applied to them by investors fearful of buying lemons.

This set of financing practices has two results: (1) it minimizes the amount of new equity that must be raised, and (2) it forces companies to issue equity only when necessary. By limiting management's discretion over when to issue new equity, adherence to the financing pecking order reduces investors' suspicion that management is simply trying to "time" the market and "unload" overpriced stock.

Competitive Bids versus Negotiated Offerings

The firm making a public offering must decide whether to select an investment banker on a **competitive bid** basis or a negotiated basis. Most firms will already have a long-standing working relationship with a particular investment banker. Over the years, the investment banker has gotten to know and understand the firm's business and financing requirements. Thus, when the firm decides to raise additional funds, it generally turns to its traditional financing agent at the planning stage. Together, they decide on the issue's features and other characteristics of the offering, including the underwriting fee. This is known as a **negotiated offering.**

Alternatively, the firm could decide on the various details of the issue in advance and then ask investment bankers to bid on the issue. The high bid wins the

---

[5]See Myers (1984).

offering. Most public utilities are mandated by law to solicit competitive bids for their securities. The trend in recent years, though, has been to reduce this as an absolute requirement, so as to give the issuer more flexibility in negotiating terms of the offering.

The relative desirability of the methods of selecting investment bankers is controversial. Competitive bidding does reduce the spread charged by underwriters.[6] Yet most firms that have the freedom to do so use negotiated offerings. One possible reason is that in gaining a lower cost on a competitive bid, the firm loses the advantage of the investment bank's expert advice. On its own, the firm may select issue features that are relatively unattractive to investors. In addition, a negotiated offering gives the investment banker more time to attract investors and market the issue. Investment bankers don't devote the same marketing effort to competitive offerings because, if they lose the bid, they will not be compensated for their time and effort. As a result, negotiated offerings may provide higher proceeds than do competitive bids. Thus, what the firm saves on underwriting expenses with a competitive bid may be offset by a less favorable price for its securities. Firms with valuable proprietary information will also prefer the confidentiality afforded by negotiated bids.

Another important consideration is that with a negotiated offering the firm has less control over the timing and terms of the issue, thereby reducing investors' fears that the offering was structured to exploit their informational disadvantage.[7] By being able to "certify" more effectively that the issue price is consistent with inside information, the investment banker selected via a negotiated contract should be able to sell the new offering at a higher price.

Advice and Counsel

Once a firm has selected its investment banker (assuming a negotiated offering is chosen), the two meet to decide on the terms and characteristics of the new issue. This includes the security type (e.g., debt, equity), size of the issue, price, issuing date, and nonprice features. The latter (primarily in the case of a debt issue) include maturity, call feature, coupon rate, and sinking fund provision as well as the investment banker's compensation.

Pricing the Issue.   Pricing the issue is one of the keys to a successful offering. Most firms prefer not to leave money on the table by pricing the issue too low. But too high a price will sink the issue. Investment bankers also have a vested interest in getting their clients a good price for their securities. After all, even if the firm prefers to use negotiated offerings, nothing can prevent it from shopping around among investment bankers the next time it goes to market.

---

[6]See Sanjai Bhagat and Peter Frost, "Issuing Costs to Existing Shareholders in Competitive and Negotiated Underwritten Public Utility Equity Offerings," *Journal of Financial Economics,* January–February 1986, 233–259.

[7]See Booth and Smith (1986).

Yet aggressively pricing an issue could cause it to fail, costing the investment bankers money and also reputation. Even if the issue succeeds, investors who get burned on an overpriced security may be reluctant to deal with the banker again. And investors are as much a part of the investment banker's clientele as are the issuers. Thus, both the issuer and the investment banker face a delicate balancing act in pricing a new issue.

Pricing is most difficult for *unseasoned* equity issues, those brought to market for the first time (e.g., Netscape and Amazon.com). On average, these initial public offerings (IPOs) are underpriced by about 15 percent relative to the **aftermarket price,** the price at which the issue trades immediately following its sale.[8] The main rationale for underpricing IPOs relates again to the information asymmetry hypothesis.[9] Because the stock in an IPO has no traded history, uncertainty about its true value is at a peak.

The problem is especially acute for uninformed investors. If the price is set too high, informed investors will submit fewer bids, and uninformed investors will wind up with more of the issue. If the issue is underpriced, however, informed investors will submit more bids, and the issue will be oversubscribed. The net result is that uninformed investors receive more of the overpriced issues and fewer of the underpriced issues.

Recognizing their informational disadvantage, uninformed investors will respond by bidding for IPOs only if the offer price is substantially below their estimate of the true market value. But don't expect to get rich by buying IPOs because, as mentioned, underpriced issues are typically oversubscribed; the available shares are rationed on a pro rata basis. Investors' suspicions that insiders are hiding unfavorable information are most likely to be aroused if company officers sell a sizable amount of their own stock in the IPO.

Venture capitalists also help alleviate investor uncertainty. By retaining most of their shares for at least one year following the IPO,[10] they signal their confidence in the firm's prospects. Further evidence of the weight given to reputations in capital markets is the finding that "IPOs with higher-quality venture capitalists are less underpriced."[11]

Another mechanism used to bond the investment banker's implicit guarantee of an issue's quality—and thereby reduce expected underpricing costs—is the **Green Shoe option** (so named because it originally was used in an offering by the Green Shoe Company). It gives the underwriter the right to buy at the offer

Initial public offerings are generally underpriced relative to the price at which they trade immediately after the sale.

To reduce underpricing, issuers can give underwriters an option to buy a specified number of additional shares at the offer price.

---

[8]Evidence on the underpricing of IPOs and additional references on this topic appear in Roger Ibbotson, "Price Performance of Common Stock New Issues," *Journal of Financial Economics,* September 1975, 235–272; and Jay R. Ritter, "The 'Hot Issue' Market of 1980," *Journal of Business,* September 1984, 215–240.

[9]Kevin Rock discusses the problems faced by uninformed investors in "Why New Issues Are Underpriced," *Journal of Financial Economics,* January–February 1986, 187–212.

[10]Evidence on post-IPO venture capital holdings is presented in Christopher B. Barry, Chris J. Muscarella, John W. Peavy III, and Michael R. Vetsuypens, "The Role of Venture Capital in the Creation of Public Companies," *Journal of Financial Economics,* 27, 447–471.

[11]Ibid., 469.

price a specified number of additional shares from the issuer. Because the option will be worthless if the offering is overpriced, investors can rely on the investment banker's self-interest to reduce this possibility. Thus, investors should be willing to pay a higher price for shares if the prospectus contains a Green Shoe option.

Features of the Offering.   Equally important to the success of an offering is the investment banker's ability to tailor the product to the market's changing appetite for different types of issues. For example, during periods of interest rate volatility, investors may prefer debt securities with floating interest rates and shorter maturities. More recently, as evidence of their high realized returns accumulated, investor demand spawned a spate of new junk bond issues.

Underwriting

Once the details of the new issue have been worked out, the issuer has two basic ways to sell the securities.

> When an issue is underwritten, the firm is relieved of the risk of price fluctuations between the time the issue price is set and when the issue is sold.

1. *Firm Commitment.* Under this method, which is the one typically used, the investment banker buys the entire issue and then resells it to the public. This is known as *underwriting.* The firm has been relieved of the risk of price fluctuations between the time that the issue price is set and the time that the issue is sold. If the issue doesn't sell well because it has been overpriced or because the market takes a turn for the worse, the underwriter will be stuck with the loss. On large issues ($20 million and up), the investment bank that handles the offering—known as the **originating house**—usually forms a **syndicate** to share the risks and assist in distributing the securities.

> The underwriter's spread—the difference between the buying and selling price—covers both underwriting risk and distribution costs.

   The underwriter's total compensation comes from the *spread* between the buying and the selling price. If the public offering price is $50 and the underwriter buys it for $48, there is a spread of $2 or 4 percent. This spread covers both the underwriting risk and the costs of distribution. The originating house acts as syndicate manager and receives about 15 to 20 percent of the spread. An additional 20 to 30 percent of the spread goes to the members of the syndicate in proportion to their underwriting participation. The remaining 50 to 60 percent, called a **selling concession,** is paid to the actual sellers of the issue, who aren't necessarily members of the underwriting syndicate.

   The data on the size and distribution of the underwriting spread on equity offerings indicate clearly that investment bankers are first and foremost salespeople. Of the total fees earned, about 60 percent is payment for selling the issues, with the other 40 percent almost equally divided between the underwriting and management fees. The spread is highest on IPOs, because these are the riskiest, and lowest on competitive offerings, probably because these were all made by utilities, which are the least subject to the information asymmetry problem.

Although the lead manager of an offering controls the distribution of the entire deal, its risk of loss is limited to the securities that it underwrites itself. Nevertheless, the large investment banking houses need enormous amounts of capital to be major players in the underwriting game.

2. *Best Efforts.* Some issues, particularly initial public offerings, are sold on a best-efforts basis. Under this arrangement, the investment bank does not buy the issue but only agrees to use its best efforts to sell as much of the issue as possible at the offering price. Because the investment bank is not performing an underwriting function, its compensation is reduced accordingly. Best-efforts arrangements are usually used in two situations: (1) A particularly strong firm is confident that its offering will be well received by the public and decides to save on the underwriting commission; or (2) the issue is so risky that investment bankers refuse to guarantee its sale. The best-efforts agreement usually specifies a minimum amount that must be sold within a given period of time; if this minimum is not met, the offering will be canceled.

> With a best-efforts offering, an investment bank doesn't buy the issue but only agrees to use its best efforts to sell as much of the issue as possible at the offer price.

Marketing

Once the syndicate has been formed, it then puts together a **selling group** to market the securities. This group usually comprises the sales organizations of the syndicate members and security dealers and brokers. The latter members of the selling group perform only a marketing function, using their customer contacts, and do not underwrite the issue.

> The process of registering a security prior to sale is designed to provide investors with relevant information concerning the firm's history, its operations, and its proposed financing.

SEC Regulation. The sales effort begins before the actual offering date. Prospective investors are alerted to the forthcoming offering, but under the *Securities Act of 1933,* most companies selling securities to the public must first register the issue with the *Securities and Exchange Commission* (SEC), a time-consuming and expensive process designed to protect investors against fraud. It includes preparing and filing a **registration statement** and a **prospectus** with the SEC. The registration statement sets forth detailed information concerning the firm's history, its operations, and its proposed financing. The prospectus summarizes this information and is intended for prospective investors. After reviewing the documents, the SEC may approve the registration. But if it feels the documents are misleading or incomplete, the SEC will send a *deficiency memorandum* requesting changes. When the SEC is satisfied that the amended documents are correct, the registration becomes *effective,* and the issue can be sold immediately.

The minimum waiting period between registration and approval is 20 days. But in practice, it usually winds up being twice that. The more complicated the issue is and the more active the new issues market is, the longer this "cooling-off" period will be. During this time, the firm may not sell or offer for sale any securities. Instead, interested investors are given a preliminary prospectus that sets forth the basic facts concerning the company and the proposed issue. The preliminary prospectus is known as a **red herring** because it contains a statement printed in red ink that a registration statement has been filed with the SEC but has not yet been approved.

Upon approval of the registration statement, the selling price to the public is established, and a final prospectus is printed. Members of the selling group then begin to solicit orders from investors. At the same time, the company publishes a "**tombstone**" advertisement, such as the one for Florida Power & Light Company shown in Exhibit 13-2, listing the names of the underwriters from whom the prospectus may be obtained. The selling group for this offering, as is true of

EXHIBIT 13-2
Tombstone for Florida Power and Light Company

This announcement is neither an offer to sell nor a solicitation of an offer to buy these securities.
The offer is made only by the Prospectus Supplement and the related Prospectus.

New Issue / April 25, 1986

$100,000,000

Florida Power & Light Company

First Mortgage Bonds, 9⅛% Series due May 1, 2016

Price 100% and accrued interest, if any, from May 1, 1986

Copies of the Prospectus Supplement and the related Prospectus may be obtained
In any State in which this announcement is circulated only from such of the
undersigned as may legally offer these securities in such State.

Salomon Brothers Inc

Goldman, Sachs & Co.

Merrill Lynch Capital Markets

The First Boston Corporation	Morgan Stanley & Co. Incorporated	Shearson Lehman Brothers Inc.
Bear, Stearns & Co. Inc.		Alex. Brown & Sons Incorporated
Daiwa Securities America Inc.	Deutsche Bank Capital Corporation	Dillon, Read & Co. Inc.
Donaldson, Lufkin & Jenrette Securities Corporation		Drexel Burnham Lambert Incorporated
E. F. Hutton & Company Inc.	Kidder, Peabody & Co. Incorporated	Lazard Frères & Co.
The Nikko Securities Co. International, Inc.	Nomura Securities International, Inc.	PaineWebber Incorporated
Prudential-Bache Securities		L. F. Rothschild, Unterberg, Towbin, Inc.
Smith Barney, Harris Upham & Co. Incorporated		Swiss Bank Corporation International Securities Inc.
UBS Securities Inc.		Wertheim & Co., Inc.
Dean Witter Reynolds Inc.		Yamaichi International (America), Inc.
First Equity Corporation of Florida		Raymond, James & Associates, Inc.

most large offerings, reads like a "Who's Who" of investment banking. Note that this "Who's Who" includes a number of foreign underwriters, who are becoming a growing force in the U.S. capital markets. For example, Deutsche Bank Capital is a German firm; Swiss Bank Corporation and UBS are Swiss firms; and Daiwa, Nikko, Nomura, and Yamaichi are Japanese firms.

Investment bankers take "bracketing" very seriously. Bracketing is Wall Street jargon for the order in which the tombstone lists the underwriters of a securities offering. It typically follows a strict pattern. First comes the lead manager, on the top left. Comanagers share the top line or follow in descending order if there is a clear differentiation in their roles. In the case of Florida P&L, Salomon Brothers is the lead underwriter, with Goldman Sachs and Merrill Lynch as comanagers. Immediately below the comanagers is the *major* bracket, occupied by First Boston, Morgan Stanley, and Shearson Lehman. Then comes the *mezzanine* bracket, followed by the *submajor* bracket and the *regional* brackets for the small fry. On this issue, that includes First Equity and Raymond James.

If the marketers have done their homework and the issue has been fairly priced, it will sell out quickly. A "hot" issue is sometimes fully subscribed before the end of the waiting period. The syndicate is broken once the issue is sold or—if an offering bombs—when discounting is needed to attract buyers. Although a firm may use the same originating house for a number of different issues, the syndicate usually differs from one issue to the next.

When the SEC passes on the registration statement, it is not certifying the quality of the securities; it is only making sure that there is full disclosure. Investors who believe otherwise could be lulled into a false sense of security when they purchase a new issue. Nonetheless, members of the selling group have a vested interest in ensuring not only that the facts are correct but also that the issue is fairly priced with respect to its risks and expected returns. The originating house needs to maintain the goodwill of the investors that buy the securities it underwrites. Overpricing an issue and then aggressively marketing it may earn the investment bank higher profits in the short run and the issuing company's gratitude, but it will hurt the investment bank's reputation and cost it business in the long run. Thus, the fact that a well-known investment bank has chosen to handle the issue should give investors more assurance about the issue's quality than the SEC registration process does.

> The registration process is not intended to guarantee investment quality; its only role is to make sure there is full disclosure of relevant information.

Flotation Costs on Public Offerings. The cost of selling an issue—its flotation cost—can be separated into two components. One set pertains to putting the issue together and readying it for the marketplace. These costs include the administrative, legal, and accounting expenses in preparing the registration statement and complying with various SEC requirements as well as the costs of printing and mailing out the different documents associated with the offering. The other cost component is the underwriting fee, the spread between the price at which the issue is sold to the public and the price paid by the underwriter.

Taken together, these costs are likely to be substantial. Indeed, average flotation costs on public offerings can exceed 15 percent of the total financing raised on small stock issues. In general, flotation costs as a percentage of the gross issue proceeds are greater for small issues than for larger ones. In addition, rights of-ferings (see Section 13.4) are substantially less expensive than are firm-commit-ment underwritten offerings. The rights offering without a standby arrangement is the least expensive of all.

Flotation costs re-flect the costs and risks of handling different kinds of issues.

Other data clearly indicate that flotation costs are lowest on bond issues, higher on preferred issues, and highest on common stock issues. These relation-ships can be explained by the costs and risks of handling the different issues. The greater volatility of common stocks relative to that of bonds and preferred stock means more underwriting risk and higher compensation for bearing this risk. In addition, the marketing expenses for bonds—which are typically sold in large blocks to relatively few institutional investors—are lower than for stocks, which are more likely to be bought by numerous individual investors. The lower cost of placing bonds helps hold down underwriting fees as well.

The inverse relationship between issue size and flotation costs can also be ex-plained on the basis of cost and risk. First, the large fixed costs associated with registering and selling an offering of any size result in economies of scale in issu-ing securities. For example, legal and other expenses of $120,000 translate into 12 percent of a $1 million issue, but only 1.2 percent of a $10 million offering. Second, smaller issues tend to be those of less-well-known firms, making them more of a risk to underwrite and more difficult to place.

13.3   THE METAMORPHOSIS OF INVESTMENT BANKING

Investment bankers, who have long considered themselves members of an elite and genteel fraternity, are adapting to a new state of affairs: wide-open price com-petition. Two factors account for the changing face of investment banking: the ad-vent of shelf registration and the entry of commercial banks into the business.

Shelf Registration

The time-consuming and costly requirements of obtaining SEC approval for each individual offering have long been seen by many as unnecessary (does General Motors really have to tell prospective investors who it is every time it comes to market?) and cumbersome and have led to many complaints over the years. In response to these complaints and to the pressures posed by the general trend to-ward deregulation of the financial services industry, the SEC has been experi-menting with a number of ways in which to simplify the process. The most important of these, *Rule 415* (issued in 1982), permits companies much greater flexibility in marketing their securities by means of the *shelf-registration* proce-dure. By filing a single prospectus outlining long-term financing plans and regis-tering the amount of debt or equity it reasonably expects to issue over a two-year period, a qualified company—one with more than $150 million in stock held by outside investors—can make continuous securities offerings without further SEC sign-off.

Shelf registration allows companies to make continu-ous security offer-ings without further SEC sign-off after the filing of a single prospectus.

At first glance, all that shelf registration does is make it easier for large corporations to issue new stock or debt. In practice, however, it is making the issuance of new securities more like a "block trade"—a huge trade involving a large block of shares of one stock—than a major underwriting activity. Large corporations now place expected financings on the "shelf" and then auction pieces—block by block—to the highest bidder. Therein lies the impact on investment banking: Spreads earned on underwriting are narrowing to those earned on large block trades. One consequence is that the trading arms of investment banking firms are rising to power as the profitability of underwriting declines.

Chief financial officers of large companies are benefitting from these changes. Under the old system, the high cost of raising external equity capital made the issuance of new stock an agonizing decision, carefully considered at the board level and implemented only after much delay. And because many of the issuing costs were fixed, it made sense to lump financings together into large, hard-to-place bundles. This made capital planning difficult and often completely unbalanced a company's capital structure. Shelf registration gives companies greater flexibility in placing issues at short notice and in smaller pieces without excessive transaction costs.

> **Shelf registration can give large companies great flexibility in placing small security issues on short notice without incurring high transaction costs.**

Despite the lower flotation costs on shelf registration, not all qualified companies use it. One reason is provided by the information asymmetry hypothesis. Because of the greater flexibility in timing issues under shelf registration, management has a greater opportunity to exploit its inside information and issue (temporarily) overvalued securities. Hence, shelf registration might be expected to exacerbate the problem of information disparity. Potential investors anticipating this problem will demand an even larger price discount to protect themselves. Thus, for many companies the savings on flotation costs might be more than offset by the necessity to discount the price more heavily on shelf offerings.

This suggests that shelf registration should appeal most to large, well-established companies that sell securities frequently, because these are the companies that are least likely to have a major problem. Using the same reasoning, shelf registration should be more cost effective for debt issues than for equity issues.

Commercial Banks on Wall Street

The changes facing investment bankers are of great interest to their would-be competitors: major U.S. commercial bankers who also are feeling the pressures associated with financial deregulation and are attempting to break into the lucrative investment-banking business. But commercial banks face a number of handicaps, the most important of which is the *Glass-Steagall Act of 1933,* which erects a now-crumbling wall between commercial and investment banking.

> **The barriers between commercial and investment banks are beginning to break down.**

Under Glass-Steagall, commercial banks can take deposits and make loans but they can't underwrite or trade corporate securities in the United States (although they can engage in such activities overseas). Investment banks can underwrite and trade securities but they can't take deposits. Commercial bank-holding companies have edged into the securities business through affiliates, and investment banks have edged into commercial banking through "nonbank" banks that fall just short of the legal description of commercial banks.

Neither industry is especially happy with this state of affairs, but there is no uniform view on deregulation in either industry. The big firms in each industry tend to be for it, and a good many small ones are against it. Because of these conflicting pressures, there has been little change in federal banking and securities law.

Opponents of Glass-Steagall argue that in a world of globalized financial services, American banks must be allowed to offer the new products and services that their foreign competitors do. Securitization—the widespread replacement of bank borrowing with the issuance of securities—has lost them a large chunk of what once was their mainstay business, lending to large corporations. Banks also face competition from large firms—including AT&T, General Electric, General Motors, Ford, Xerox, and American Express—that offer a wide range of financial products and services to individual consumers and corporate customers.

To a large extent, regulations separating commercial and investment banking have long been in conflict with economic forces. In the United States, for example, commercial banks underwrote almost 60 percent of new corporate security issues in the late 1920s. Even now, U.S. commercial banks are major providers of those investment-banking services they are allowed to offer on an unrestricted basis, such as underwriting municipal bonds and Eurobonds, trading foreign exchange, and engaging in interest rate and currency swaps.

In Great Britain, regulations separating commercial and investment banking have eroded, and it is now common for the large commercial banks to perform investment-banking functions through subsidiaries. Japanese banks are not allowed to engage in the securities business, but they own more than 22 percent of all corporate equity and often dispatch personnel to firms in financial distress. Then too, we saw in Chapter 12 that German *universal banks* combine the functions of commercial banks and investment banks in addition to taking major equity positions in companies.

Chapter 12 pointed out that as lenders and equityholders in a corporation, universal banks can reduce conflicts among the different classes of securityholders. For example, when the firm's various securities are held by separate investors, the only methods of control are for the debtholders to force the firm into bankruptcy or for the shareholders to remove incompetent management through proxy fights. These mechanisms are cumbersome, expensive, and subject to conflicts of interest between shareholders and creditors.

Universal banking can reduce agency conflicts between creditors and equityholders.

By owning the range of corporate securities, a universal bank could gain the control necessary to effect reorganization more economically. And because the debtholder is also an equityholder, there are fewer conflicts between holders of debt and equity to impede a needed reorganization. The result is fewer conflicts, lower costs in "workouts" of financial problems, and a resultant increase in organizational efficiency.

Critics of universal banking, however, argue that there is a fundamental conflict of interest when banks are permitted to own common stocks in their name and at the same time lend money to the companies they own—or perhaps deny loans to competitors or potential competitors of those companies. Others, wary of the costs of bailing out the excesses of the savings and loan industry, are concerned that universal banking could increase taxpayer costs by stretching the federal safety net protecting bank depositors to cover losses in bank security investments. Another major disadvantage of bank-dominated capitalist systems is their lack of robust venture capital markets. Because few small companies have gone public in Germany and Japan, it is difficult for start-up ventures to obtain risk capital from equity investors.

The tendency for commercial and investment-banking services to integrate when allowed, even where banks are not permitted to own equity in client firms, is partly due to the economies of scope in these activities. Virtually all capital-raising functions of investment banks have counterparts in commercial banking operations. In evaluating borrowers or in originating, certifying, syndicating, or selling loans, commercial banks perform the component activities in underwriting corporate securities and distributing them in the marketplace.

Large commercial banks are generating a growing portion of their revenues from investment banking activities.

By limiting the commercial banks' ability to underwrite or trade securities, Glass-Steagall restricts their contacts with potential investors and makes it difficult to gain an adequate understanding of public securities markets—an understanding that as investment bankers they need. Yet things are changing. Large commercial banks are generating a growing share of their income from investment-banking activities, such as arranging private placements, negotiating mergers and acquisitions, and providing corporate finance advice. Commercial banks are especially good at activities requiring enormous financial resources such as trading foreign exchange and government securities.

Commercial banks also excel in such areas of corporate finance as currency and interest rate swaps. Moreover, shelf registration has converted part of the underwriting business into block trading, and although commercial banks do not currently handle block trades, they are skillful at trading per se in foreign exchange and government securities.

Rule 415 means that billions of dollars in registered securities now sit on the shelf, waiting to be underwritten by investment bankers—or to be placed by commercial banks. Still and all, without as broad a range of relationships with institutional investors, commercial banks have a long way to go to be able to compete effectively with investment banks. Nevertheless, their presence in the marketplace is an added source of competitive pressure that is already benefiting companies that need to raise fresh capital.

The trend is for continuing erosion of Glass-Steagall. Currently, the Federal Reserve allows a bank affiliate to underwrite securities, including corporate debt and equity issues as long as they don't produce more than 10 percent of the affiliate's gross revenue. That slips under the legal bar against banks' affiliating with firms "principally engaged" in securities trading. The 10 percent ceiling is expected to be raised over time, permitting commercial banks to engage in relatively unfettered underwriting activities. The presence of commercial banks in securities markets will mean a further blurring of the distinction between investment and commercial banks; it will also add to the relentless pressure on investment banking fees.

13.4   RIGHTS OFFERING

With a rights of-
fering, firms offer
a new equity issue
to their current
shareholders on a
privileged sub-
scription basis.

Instead of selling a new equity issue through a public offering, some firms will offer the securities first to their current shareholders on a *privileged-subscription* basis. This is known as a *rights offering*. A rights offering is mandatory in those firms
in which shareholders have the **preemptive right**, or right of first refusal, to purchase new common stock issues in proportion to their current ownership position.

Mechanics of the Rights Offering

A rights offering
must go through
the same SEC reg-
istration process
as a public issue.

A company that decides to use a rights issue must go through the same SEC registration process previously described for a public offering. But the similarity
ends there. Marketing a rights issue is very different from marketing a public offering, and investment bankers play a very different role. Instead of underwriting
the entire issue, they underwrite only the unsold portion of the rights offering.
Under this **standby arrangement,** the underwriting syndicate is paid a *standby
fee,* in return for which it agrees to buy—at the offering price less a *take-up fee*—
those shares that remain unsold.

Shareholders receive one right for each share of common stock that they own.
The terms of the offering specify the number of rights required to buy a new
share, the **subscription price** per share, and the expiration date of the offering.
Shareholders have three choices: (1) to exercise the rights, (2) to sell them, or
(3) to let them expire unused. The third choice usually doesn't make sense because the rights have value. To purchase stock under a privileged subscription,
an investor sends the rights plus the subscription price to the company's agent.
Stockholders who choose not to exercise their rights can sell them.

At the time of the rights offering, the board of directors sets a date of record.
After that date, the stock is traded **ex-rights,** that is, without the rights attached.
Before the ex-rights date, the stock sells **rights-on,** meaning that the new owner
receives the rights.

Value of a Right

The value of a
right depends on
the rights-on
price, the sub-
scription price,
and the number
of rights needed
to buy one share.

The value of a right equals the difference between the rights-on price and the ex-
rights price. The ex-rights price, in turn, depends on the rights-on price, the subscription price, and the number of rights required to buy one new share. For
example, suppose a share of stock is currently selling rights-on for $50; the sub-
scription price is $45; and it takes four rights to subscribe to one share. This
means that there will be five shares ex-rights for every four rights-on shares. Exhibit 13-3 shows that the value of a right will be $1. Upon going ex-rights, there-
fore, the price of the stock should drop by $1 to $49 to reflect the loss of the right.

The general formula for the value of a right is

$$R = (P - S)/(N + 1) \qquad [13\text{-}1]$$

where R is the value of one right, P is the rights-on price, S is the subscription
price, and N is the number of rights required for one new share. Applying Equa-

EXHIBIT 13-3
Calculating the Value of a Right

	Subscription Price	
	$45	**$40**
Rights-on values		
Number of shares	4	4
Rights-on share price	$50	$50
Value of shares	$200	$200
Ex-rights values		
Number of new shares	1	1
New investment (equals subscription price)	$45	$40
Values of shares	$245	$240
Total number of shares	5	5
Ex-rights share price	$49	$48
Value of a right	$1	$2

tion [13-1] to the previous example yields the $1 theoretical value of the right calculated in Exhibit 13-3:

Changes in the subscription price should have no impact on shareholders as long as they exercise their rights.

What is the effect on shareholders of changing the subscription price? Suppose that in the preceding example the subscription price is lowered to $40. According to Equation [13-1], the value of a right should now be $2. This is shown in the second column of Exhibit 13-3. When the stock goes ex-rights, its price drops to $48. As before, the sum of the ex-rights price plus the value of the right remains constant. Changing the subscription price just changes the relative distribution of value between the stock selling ex-rights and the right. The value of the right is exactly offset by the decline in the stock's price when it goes ex-rights. This example illustrates a more general principle: *The rights offering is irrelevant to stockholders so long as they don't allow their rights to expire unused.*

Ensuring a Successful Rights Offering

Choosing the appropriate subscription price is the key to a successful rights offering.

The key to a successful rights offering—where the issue is fully subscribed to—is the subscription price. If the market price drops below the subscription price, the rights will not be exercised. Setting a low subscription price relative to the current market price reduces the risk that the market price will fall below it and increases the likelihood that the offering will sell out. Although many companies worry about the earnings dilution brought about by setting a low subscription price, their fears are unfounded: The lower earnings per share are exactly offset by the additional shares now held by each shareholder (or by the money received if the rights are sold).

Instead of setting a sufficiently low subscription price to ensure an offering's success, most firms arrange a standby agreement with an underwriting syndicate. But standby arrangements, which are put options, can be expensive. The firm can avoid these unnecessary expenses by setting the subscription price low enough to avoid the possibility of a failed issue.

Rights Offering versus Public Offering

A rights issue has a number of built-in advantages vis-à-vis a public offering:

1. If the subscription price is set low enough, the firm can do away entirely with the need for underwriters, saving a substantial expense. Flotation costs are up to 30 times lower for a rights offering than for a public offering.
2. The firm can tap an already existing market for its shares. If any of the current shareholders prefer not to increase their positions in the stock, they can sell their rights in the market.
3. In a public offering, there is always the danger of underpricing the new issue. But this is not a problem for a rights offering, because the lower the subscription price is, the more valuable the right is.
4. A rights offering allows current shareholders to maintain their present ownership and control positions.

> Compared to a rights offering, underwritten issues allow firms to raise capital easier and less expensively.

Despite these advantages, over 80 percent of equity offerings employ underwriters. One explanation for this is that raising capital is easier and less expensive with underwritten issues. In a normal underwritten issue, members of the syndicate attempt to sell shares to a select group of investors. In a rights offering, by contrast, the company must contact each and every one of its shareholders. Thus, the more shareholders there are, the higher the expense of a rights offering will be.

The high transaction costs for companies with many shareholders means that firms with concentrated ownership are the most likely candidates for a rights offering. These are primarily small firms, whose owners typically are unable to or prefer not to contribute more capital. This is one explanation of the rarity of voluntary rights offerings.[12]

In addition to the direct costs of a rights offering, there is an indirect cost. An increase in the size of the firm's investor base tends to reduce the firm's cost of capital and thereby increase its market value.[13] By issuing new shares through a negotiated underwriting, the firm can *both* raise new capital *and* increase its investor base. Indeed, if the latter is an important objective, then the firm should select an investment bank with broad distribution capabilities and choose the terms of the deal so as to maximize the number of new shareholders who buy the securities.

---

[12]This explanation is provided by Jurin (1988).

[13]See Robert C. Merton, "A Simple Model of Capital Market Equilibrium with Incomplete Information," *Journal of Finance,* July 1987, 483–510.

If, instead, the firm raises capital via a rights offering, it is unlikely to broaden its investor base, because the new securities will largely be held by the firm's current shareholders. An indirect or opportunity cost of a rights offering, therefore, is the forgone benefit of an expanded investor base. Thus, at least some of the underwriting costs associated with a negotiated offering can be viewed as an investment in expanding the firm's investor base.

Other possible explanations for why firms shun rights offerings are based on the information asymmetry hypothesis. One argument is that underwritten offerings lead to periodic monitoring of the firm by investment bankers, which should raise the price that investors are willing to pay for the firm's securities.[14] A related explanation is that a rights offering at a relatively high price allows higher-quality firms (in which management believes that the current price is lower than its true value) to distinguish themselves from other firms.[15] Lower-quality firms prefer the fully underwritten offer because of the costs associated with a failed rights offering in the form of forgone positive NPV investments or the costs of acquiring emergency interim financing. The alternative of using a rights offering and setting a low price to ensure its success is tantamount to signaling that such a firm believes its stock is overvalued.

Although these all are clever explanations, they have not been subject to empirical testing and so cannot be considered definitive. Thus, the preference for fully underwritten new equity offerings rather than the seemingly less costly rights offering remains an unresolved issue in finance.

Illustration

Time Warner's Controversial Rights Offering

On June 6, 1991, Time Warner, the world's biggest media and entertainment company, announced a rights offering designed to raise as much as $3.5 billion. The proceeds would be used to meet a $4.3 billion payment on the debt used to finance its 1989 value-destroying merger (see Appendix 5A). Under the plan, Time Warner would offer its shareholders rights to purchase 34.5 million shares, at prices ranging from $63 a share (if only 60 percent of shareholders participated) to $105 a share (if all holders participated). Time Warner's stock plummeted about 25 percent after the announcement as investors reacted negatively to the coercive

---

[14]See Smith (1986).
[15]On this point, see Heinkel and Schwartz (1986).

aspects of the offering: Shareholders who exercised their rights had to commit to buying stock without knowing the price they would pay. However, with the sliding scale, shareholders who failed to exercise their rights might be transferring wealth to those who did. Five weeks later, Time Warner was forced by a shareholders' revolt and pressure from the SEC to replace its variable-price rights issue with a straight rights offering that raised $2.8 billion.

Under the new offer, shareholders received 0.6 rights for each share of common stock. Each right (there were 34.5 million of them altogether) entitled the holder to buy one share at a fixed price of $80 per share. Since the stock was trading for about $90 a share at the time of the revised offer, the offer was oversubscribed. As is typical in rights offers, about 2 percent of the rights expired unexercised, so some shareholders did not protect their interests. The underwriters, led by Salomon Brothers, earned about $110 million for their services. Such a high fee—about 4 percent of the amount raised—on a deal this large is unusual and brought Time Warner further criticism from investors.

13.5   PRIVATE PLACEMENTS

Firms that raise money through the private placement market can avoid the lengthy and costly SEC registration process.

A *private placement* is a direct sale of securities to a limited number—sometimes only one—of knowledgeable investors, usually life insurance companies and pension funds. The offering's terms are negotiated directly with the purchaser, thereby eliminating the need for underwriting. Of equal importance, private placements are exempt from SEC registration. Although some equity issues are privately placed, debt offerings usually account for about 90 percent of all private placements. Private placements are an important source of money for many companies—particularly lower-rated companies that can't easily raise money with public sales of stocks and bonds or those that want to keep their financial data secret.

The most significant development in the private placement market in recent years occurred in 1990 when the SEC issued Rule 144A, which allows large institutions to trade private placements among themselves without going back to the registration and disclosure process. This allowance for secondary trading greatly increases the liquidity of the private placement market and makes it more attractive to foreign companies, who are frequently deterred from entering the U.S. market by the SEC's stringent disclosure and reporting requirements. Rule 144A has been an important avenue for such foreign issuers as France's Rhone-Poulenc and Korea's Pohang Iron & Steel to gain access to the U.S. market.

Advantages and Disadvantages of Private Placements

A major advantage of raising capital in the private placement market is that it avoids the lengthy and costly SEC registration process required of public offerings because the Securities Act of 1933 exempts from the normal registration process those offerings made to sophisticated investors. As a result, private placements are less expensive and can be placed more rapidly than can public offerings. The advantage of speed, however, is being eroded for those firms able to use shelf registrations.

A company may also turn to a private placement when it faces the following Catch-22: In order to convince investors to fund it, the company must reveal vital competitive information, but if it makes that information public, its business strategy may be compromised. A private placement allows the company to "tell a story" to investors with minimal public disclosure of confidential information. Companies contemplating takeovers also like the secrecy of the private market. Similarly, foreign companies, many of which aren't eager to comply with SEC disclosure requirements, use private placements.

Private placements can also be tailored more easily to fit the specific requirements of both the borrower and the lender. The terms of some issues may be so complex that they could be sold only to a sophisticated investor. Even then, it may be necessary to explain fully the financing terms to the investor, which would not be possible in a public offering. Furthermore, should the firm's prospects change or something unexpected occur, it is easier to renegotiate the terms of a private placement. In a public offering, the size of the investor base makes alterations of the original agreement difficult and uncertain. Not surprisingly, private placements are used most extensively by small and medium-sized firms, as they are likely to be the riskiest firms, thereby requiring more complex covenants as well as greater flexibility in enforcing those covenants.

> The flexibility afforded by private placements make them a useful financing vehicle for small and medium-sized firms.

Fees and other expenses for private placements tend to be lower than those for public issues. Many firms deal directly with the investor, thereby saving on investment-banking fees. But other firms prefer to use investment bankers to help locate potential investors and to help design the issue so as to meet the most favorable reception. Whether or not the firm uses investment bankers, it avoids paying underwriting fees.

But the advantages of a private placement are not free. Private investors typically demand tighter and more restrictive conditions on the issuer (e.g., limiting further debt issues) than do public issues. This, of course, relates to the fact that private placement issuers tend to be riskier firms or are involved in more complex deals. In addition, investors demand compensation for the illiquidity of a private placement—such an issue can't be resold in the public market—and for the higher investigation costs they must bear. This shows up in the form of a higher required yield on private issues relative to public issues with similar credit risks and/or equity "kickers" such as warrants (an option to buy stock). However, the increased liquidity of the private placement market following Rule 144A has narrowed the "illiquidity" spread.

SUMMARY

Firms seeking to raise funds in the capital market have several choices. Start-ups can turn to a venture capitalist for both money and advice. Later, they can sell securities to the public through a public offering or a rights offering. Alternatively, they can place their issues privately, thereby avoiding the costs and delays that publicly issued securities must bear in complying with SEC registration procedures. Regardless of the method selected, the firm usually turns to an investment banker for help in structuring and marketing the issue. Investment bankers also underwrite most public offerings by buying the securities from the issuing firm, thereby bearing the risk of price fluctuations and then distributing them to the public through a selling network. They also have the choice of raising money at home or abroad.

We saw that a critical consideration when selecting the method used to issue securities is the problem of information asymmetry, which arises because corporate management may have significant inside information about the company's prospects that it can use to exploit potential investors by issuing overpriced securities. Because of the potential for opportunistic behavior by insiders, underwriters can perform a valuable role in certifying to outside investors that the securities are fairly valued on the basis of management's inside information. They do this by repeatedly putting their reputation on the line with investors when pricing new

issues. To protect their reputation and the fees that accrue to it, investment bankers investigate and audit the activities of issuing firms, thereby certifying for investors the consistency of the issue price with insider information. Thus, the essential qualities of an investment banker are credibility, performance, integrity, and trust—the same valuable, though intangible, assets that any well-run company has.

We learn several lessons in this chapter. First, the way in which a company is financed can affect the value of the company by changing management incentives. Second, by reducing the credibility gap, companies can get better prices for their securities although underpricing is always a problem. Third, there are economies of scale in issuing securities because of the various fixed costs associated with any offering. Fourth, rights offerings are generally less expensive than public equity offerings, largely because underwriting expenses can be avoided. Fifth, absent any signaling costs, underpricing does not matter for a rights offering, because both the gains and the losses are borne by the current shareholders and thereby cancel out each other. Sixth, private placements are of greatest value for issues that are either small or complex. Seventh, shelf registration is a potentially valuable cost-reducing technique that can be used to best advantage by large, well-known firms with frequent financing needs.

QUESTIONS

1. How would you differentiate a venture capitalist from an investment banker?
2. What is the problem of information asymmetry? Why is it most severe for start-up firms? How does it affect the raising of capital?
3. How did Rad Neato's founders deal with the information asymmetry problem in structuring the firm's financing? What does this tell you about the likely debt-to-equity ratios of new ventures?
4. Consider two possible contracts between an entrepreneur and a venture capitalist. In the first, the entrepreneur demands 51 percent of the business up front. In the second, the entrepreneur gives 100 percent of the equity at the beginning to the

venture capitalist but is able to earn a 51 percent ownership stake based on performance.
   a. Which contract would the entrepreneur prefer? Explain.
   b. Which contract would the venture capitalist prefer? Explain.
   c. What does this example tell you about the role of contracts in affecting performance and the terms on which funds are supplied to new ventures?
5. Explain how staged capital commitment affects the terms on which capital is supplied to new ventures.
   a. What options does staged capital commitment provide to both the founders and venture capitalists?

b. Why are the options described in (a) valuable?

6. A firm plans an issue of 100,000 additional common shares to raise investment capital. The new issue will be sold with the help of an investment bank. What are the different types of costs that the new issue will incur?

7. Explain why flotation costs will be higher if
   a. the issuer is risky or unknown.
   b. the issue is small.
   c. stock is issued (instead of bonds).
   d. interest rates have been very volatile.
   e. the stock market has experienced recent sharp up-and-down movements.

8. What is the certification role of the investment banker? How does this role relate to the large fees investment bankers charge for their services?

9. What is the financing pecking order? How does the pecking order relate to the stock market's reaction to new security issues?

10. "Empirical research shows that competitive bidding reduces the spread charged by underwriters. This means that companies interested in reducing the cost of financing should always issue securities through competitive bidding. Thus, the fact that most companies use negotiated offerings is a sign of irrationality." Comment on this statement.

11. "The high average returns on initial public offerings mean that young companies overpay for their capital. These high returns also mean that investing in IPOs is a good way to earn excess risk-adjusted returns." Comment on this statement.

12. A recent headline in the *Wall Street Journal* was "Insiders Gobble IPOs to Reassure Investors." Explain what this headline might refer to.

13. a. Why might an issuer prefer a negotiated underwriting to competitive bidding?
    b. Under what circumstances might an issuer prefer a best-efforts offering over a firm commitment? Who bears the risks in these two types of offerings? Explain.

14. Pacific Columbia Corporation included a unique feature in its IPO: Before company officers and directors may sell any of their stock, the company must show net profits—the higher the profits are, the more stock they can sell. What purpose might be served by this feature?

15. The decision to "go public" should be made only after all opportunities for private placement have been exhausted. Comment.

16. A large microchip manufacturer is issuing debt for the first time: $1 million of 10 percent coupon, 20-year convertible debentures will be sold. The firm has not decided whether it will be a public or private issue. Outline the factors the firm should consider in deciding whether to issue publicly or by private placement.

17. The following entities are preparing to issue long-term debt:
    a. a local restaurant chain.
    b. a Fortune 500 automaker.
    c. a small Central American country.
    d. a company planning a hostile takeover.
    Explain which should consider a public offering and which should consider a private placement.

18. On May 18, 1988, Union Carbide announced that the company's combination of high leverage and high dividend payout was inappropriate to current business strategies. According to the chairman, Robert D. Kennedy, "To maintain that combination when financial strength and flexibility are required to capitalize on the best investment opportunities in years, especially in chemicals and plastics, would be shortchanging shareholder value." In order to reduce its heavy debt load and pump more cash into operations, Union Carbide said it planned to cut its dividend by 46 percent and offer 15 million new common shares. The new plan to trim Carbide's $3.2 billion debt seemed to contradict part of the corporate strategy that Kennedy had earlier disclosed. In an interview in the *Wall Street Journal* a month before, he said Carbide had decided to gamble on a rebuilding effort by boosting capital expenditures and "letting the debt float." Union Carbide stock closed at $18.75 on May 18, down $3.75.
    a. What might account for the stock market's negative response to Union Carbide's announcement?
    b. At the time, the company had about 132 million shares outstanding. How much did the announcement cost Union Carbide shareholders?

19. "Project" financing is a specialized type of lending where the proceeds are used for the construction of industrial power plants and specialized manufacturing facilities, and the development of large mines or oil fields. This financing is often done on a nonrecourse basis; that is, the lenders can look only to the project (not to its sponsors) for repayment of the

loan. Why do sponsors often turn to private placements for project financing?

20. Procter & Gamble needs to raise about $1 billion to finance an Employee Stock Ownership Plan.

ESOP financing is very complicated. What type of financing would you recommend as particularly suited for P&G? Explain.

PROBLEMS

🖎 —Excel templates may be downloaded from **www. prenhall.com/financecenter.**

1. Suppose that instead of selling newly issued shares to First Megadeal, Rad Neato's founders wanted half the shares being sold to come out of their holdings; that is, they planned to sell 25,000 of their shares plus 25,000 newly issued shares. 🖎
    a. If the price demanded remained at $10 a share, what would this imply for the valuation of Rad Neato?
    b. Given that Rad Neato's founders sold 25,000 of their shares and issued another 25,000 shares, what price per share would be necessary for the value of Rad Neato to remain at $1.5 million?
    c. How would First Megadeal respond to the desire by Rad Neato's founders to sell their shares? What would this do to the implicit valuation set by First Megadeal on the firm's equity? Explain.

2. Amalgamated Donut Ltd. (ADL) will float an issue of $120 million in long-term debt. The coupon rate will be set so that the issue sells for its face value of $1,000. Legal and administrative costs at $400,000 will be borne by ADL explicitly, and ADL's investment bank will handle the issue for a spread of $8 per bond. Calculate the
    a. total flotation costs.
    b. flotation costs per bond.
    c. net cash proceeds.
    d. flotation costs as a fraction of proceeds.

3. On October 15, 1987, an international syndicate agreed to underwrite the British government's sale of more than £12 billion in British Petroleum stock at £3.30 a share. Four days later, but before the underwriters could sell the issue, stock markets around the world crashed. The price of BP stock fell to £2.96 a share, but the British government refused to cancel the issue. In round numbers, how much did the underwriters lose on this deal?

4. The Ceres Fruit Co., distributor of organically grown fruit, has determined that it will require $100,000,000 in new, long-term funds this year to expand into vegetables. 🖎
    a. Ceres has been offered the following terms on its debt from Megan Sturly, the investment banker: The underwriting spread will be equal to 1.75 percent of the offering. In addition, administrative and legal expenses are estimated to be $200,000. How much total debt does Ceres need to issue to net its funding requirements?
    b. If the bonds are sold in $1,000 face value units, how many bonds will Ceres issue?

5. Empire Builders is trying to decide between the following two debt issues: (1) *A $100 million public issue of 15-year debt.* The bond would carry an 8 percent coupon and be sold at par. The underwriting commission would be 2 percent and other expenses would be $500,000. (2) *A $100 million private placement of 15-year debt.* The bond would carry an 8.3 percent coupon and be sold at par. Issuing expenses would total $700,000.
    a. What are the net proceeds to Empire Builders from each of the issues?
    b. Which bond carries the lowest effective cost?

6. Compute the cost of capital for each source of funds. The tax rate is 35 percent. 🖎
    a. A 20-year, 8.5 percent coupon, $1,000 par bond sold at $900 less a 5 percent underwriting commission.
    b. A 20-year, 8.75 percent coupon, $1,000 par bond sold through a private placement at $925 less issuing expenses of $35.
    c. A preferred stock offering sold at $75 per share with a $100 par value and a dividend of 7 percent. Flotation costs are $3 per share.
    d. A share of common stock with a market price of $20, earnings after taxes of $6, a payout of 60 percent, and an expected dividend growth rate of 3 percent. The price net of flotation costs is $16.

7. A firm's common equity currently sells for $25 a share, and 100,000 shares are outstanding. Rights

to subscribe to one new share at a price of $20 per four shares held have just been issued. ✕

a. What is the value of one right?

b. What will be the ex-rights value of a stock?

c. An investor has $15,000 and wishes to hold shares in the above firm. Show that she is indifferent as to whether she buys shares rights-on or ex-rights.

8. Suppose the firm in problem 7 used a public offering instead to raise funds. An investment bank will arrange to sell 25,000 additional shares at an issue price of $24 and an underwriting spread of $2 per share.

a. How much money will this raise?

b. What will be the total cost?

c. How does the public issue compare with the rights offering?

9. Owners of AgCorp shares selling at $16 are given the right to subscribe to new shares at $13. If it takes five rights to buy one new share, what is the theoretical value of a right?

10. A large corporation plans a rights issue. For every ten shares held, a new share may be purchased. Currently, there are 10 million shares outstanding. The company hopes to raise $20 million in new capital with the rights issue. ✕

a. What subscription price should the company set so that exactly $20 million is raised?

b. Suppose the shares currently trade at $23 per share. What is the value of a right? What is the ex-rights stock price?

c. Is there any chance the rights issue will fail? Explain.

11. Regent Software plans a rights issue to finance its new database program. For every two shares held, a new share may be purchased. Currently, there are 5 million shares outstanding. Regent hopes to raise $40 million in new capital with the rights issue. ✕

a. What subscription price should Regent set so that it raises exactly $40 million?

b. Suppose Regent's shares currently trade at $19 per share. Assuming that the software project has a zero NPV, what is the value of a right? What is the ex-rights stock price?

12. Peoplegenes, a genetic testing firm, has decided to raise $65 million in a rights issue. The current market price of Peoplegenes' 10 million shares is $75 per share. Peoplegenes is considering setting the subscription price at $65. ✕

a. Assuming the shares will be fully subscribed, how many rights will be required to purchase one share?

b. What is the value of each right? What is the ex-rights price of one share of stock?

c. What is the answer to (b) if the subscription price is $70?

13. Silver Saks, the investment banker, must fix its fee schedule for the rights offering in problem 12. Silver Saks feels there is a good chance that, with a subscription price of $65 a share, the rights issue will be only 95 percent subscribed. In this case, the investment banker must buy the unsold shares and resell them in the market at the ex-rights price. If Silver's take-up fee is $1 per share, at what level should the standby fee be set so that Silver will make $2 per share in total fees?

14. In the Time Warner rights offer discussed in Section 13.4, Salomon Brothers received a commitment fee of 3 percent plus a discount price of $77.60 on any rights they exercise. Suppose Time Warner stock was selling for $90 prior to expiration of the rights offer. How much could Salomon Brothers afford to pay for a right and still make money?

15. You are working for Zenith Machines as a financial consultant. The company is all-equity financed with 500,000 shares outstanding and fixed assets that are expected to generate a perpetual annual after-tax cash flow of $1 million. Zenith is contemplating a project to expand its market share. The project will cost $2 million and is expected to generate a perpetual annual after-tax cash flow of $300,000. The shareholders feel that a return of 10 percent is appropriate to use in discounting the cash flows of both the existing assets and the new project.

The financial manager has decided to finance the project with a rights issue. But he cannot decide whether he should propose a "1 for 5" or a "1 for 10" issue. He is afraid that the "1 for 5" issue many have a larger "dilution effect" on share prices, even though he admits that the whole issue is not at all clear to him. He wants your advice, including your rationale, on the following questions.

a. Should he propose that the board accept this new project?

b. What should be the issue prices for the two rights issues he is considering? What are the expected ex-rights share prices, assuming the rights offering is successful?

c. Does it matter which rights issue Zenith will use?

REFERENCES

Booth, James R., and Richard Smith. "Capital Raising, Underwriting and the Certification Hypothesis." *Journal of Financial Economics,* January–February 1986, 261–281.

Heinkel, Robert, and Eduardo S. Schwartz. "Rights Versus Underwritten Offerings: An Asymmetric Information Approach." *Journal of Finance,* March 1986, 1–18.

Jurin, Bruce. "Raising Equity in an Efficient Market." *Midland Corporate Finance Journal,* Winter 1988, 53–60.

Myers, Stewart. "The Capital Structure Puzzle." *Journal of Finance,* July 1984, 575–592.

Sahlman, William A. "Aspects of Financial Contracting in Venture Capital." *Journal of Applied Corporate Finance,* Summer 1988, 23–36.

Sahlman, William A. "The Structure and Governance of Venture-Capital Organizations." *Journal of Financial Economics,* 27, 1990, 473–521.

Smith, Clifford W., Jr. "Investment Banking and the Capital Acquisition Process." *Journal of Financial Economics,* January–February 1986, 3–29.

Establishing a Target Capital Structure

Debt is a gamble. If the economy is good, then you drew the right hand. If the economy goes bad on you, then you lose.
Merton Miller

KEY TERMS

agency conflicts
agency costs
bankruptcy costs
business risk
EBIT-EPS indifference point
   or break-even EBIT

financial distress
financial flexibility
financial leverage
financial risk
law of the conservation
   of value

leveraged buyout (LBO)
leveraged cashout (LCO)
leveraged recapitalization
organizational assets
postcontractual
   opportunism

CHAPTER LEARNING OBJECTIVES

Upon completion of this chapter, students should be able to:

- Describe the effects of financial leverage on equity risks and return.
- Use EBIT-EBS indifference analysis to evaluate financing alternatives.
- Explain why capital structure doesn't influence the value of the firm in a world without taxes, transaction costs, or other market imperfections.
- Explain the existence of an optimal capital structure in terms of the trade-offs between the tax advantages of debt and the expected costs of financial distress.
- Identify those elements of business risk that influence the probability of financial distress.

- Discuss how the possibility of financial distress may affect management behavior.
- Explain how agency costs can affect a firm's financing strategy.
- Explain how leveraged recapitalizations such as leveraged buyouts can mitigate the agency costs of equity.
- Discuss how financing flexibility and the need for financial reserves can influence the capital structure choice.

The collection of assets that a firm invests in generates a stream of cash flows. In an all-equity-financed firm, these cash flows belong to the shareholders alone. Alternatively, the firm can split these cash flows into two components: (1) a relatively safe stream that it sells to debtholders and (2) a riskier stream that it sells to shareholders.

From this perspective, choosing the firm's *capital structure*—the combination of debt and equity financing used—is a marketing problem. It involves deciding on the share of future cash flows to repackage as debt; the rights to the residual cash flows are sold as equity claims. Given the objective of maximizing shareholder wealth, the key issue in determining capital structure can be succinctly summarized: Can the firm create value by judiciously selecting its debt–equity combination?

There are two strands of thought. One says that capital structure is irrelevant: Firm value is determined by the yield on the company's real assets, and juggling the claims on those assets doesn't change their total value. The second strand of thought is that because of taxes and other factors, an optimal degree of financial leverage—the ratio of debt to equity—does exist, and firms can boost their market value by adding debt to the capital structure up to a certain point. These other factors include the adverse incentives that shareholders may have to undertake risky projects when financed primarily with debt (an agency problem), the harmful effects of financial distress on company sales and costs, and the potential loss of financial flexibility if heavily leveraged. On the other hand, the extraordinary performance of many leveraged buyouts indicates that there are also beneficial effects associated with the use of debt for certain types of firms. This chapter examines these costs and benefits of leverage and then presents guidelines for developing a corporate debt policy.

14.1   FINANCIAL LEVERAGE, RISK, AND RETURN

Financial leverage involves the substitution of fixed-charge financing for common stock.

Financial leverage refers to the substitution of fixed-charge financing—primarily debt (interest and principal payments) but also preferred stock (preferred dividend payments) and leases (lease payments)—for common stock with its variable dividend payments. These fixed financing charges magnify a given change in earnings before interest and taxes (EBIT) into a larger change in earnings per share (EPS). Financial leverage, therefore, adds to the risk faced by the firm's stockholders.

Business risk relates to the variability of a firm's operating earnings; financial risk is the added risk borne by shareholders from the use of financial leverage.

In the all-equity-financed firm, fluctuations in earnings per share are due solely to the firm's **business risk**—the inherent variability in its operating earnings. Substituting debt for equity concentrates this business risk onto a smaller number of equity shares, thereby increasing the risk that equityholders must bear. This added risk is **financial risk.** For example, suppose a firm with $1 million in assets starts with 100,000 shares valued at $10 apiece. If half this equity is replaced by riskless debt, the remaining 50,000 shares must bear all the firm's business risk. Hence, each share is now twice as risky as before. More generally, as debt replaces equity, the risk borne by the firm's shareholders rises because each dollar of equity capital must bear a correspondingly greater proportion of the business's risk.

Financial leverage also affects the expected level of EPS and return on equity (ROE). To see how financial leverage affects the expected ROE, we can represent a firm's return on equity (ROE) as follows:

$$ROE = ROA + (ROA - i)D/E \qquad [14\text{-}1]$$

If the return on assets exceeds the after-tax cost of debt, then financial leverage will increase the return on equity.

where *ROA* is the firm's after-tax return on assets before financing charges, *i* is the after-tax cost of borrowing, and *D/E* is the firm's debt-to-equity ratio.

Equation [14-1] reveals that if the return on assets exceeds the after-tax interest rate on debt, then financial leverage—measured here as *D/E*—will increase the return on equity and, therefore, the earnings per share of the firm's stock. On the other hand, if ROA falls below the after-tax cost of debt, then financial leverage will decrease both ROE and EPS.

Financial leverage has opposing effects on valuation: It increases the return on equity, while simultaneously increasing the variability of these returns.

Because the *expected* return on assets invariably exceeds the required yield on debt, this means that financial leverage has two opposing effects on equity valuation: It increases the expected return on equity while simultaneously raising the variability of those returns. It is the tradeoff between these two effects that largely determines whether financial leverage will increase, decrease, or leave unchanged the value of the firm.

The Consequences of Financial Leverage

To illustrate the consequences of financial leverage, suppose that Hi-Tech Running Shoes, Inc., requires $5 million in assets to support its sales efforts. It is considering two different financing plans: all-equity financing and equal proportions of debt and equity. The all-equity financing option is issuing 500,000 shares of common stock priced at $10 apiece. Hi-Tech could also issue 250,000 shares of equity at $10 per share and fund the remaining $2.5 million with debt bearing an interest rate of 10 percent.

Hi-Tech's earnings before interest and taxes are expected to be $1,000,000 annually. These earnings are not guaranteed; they could be as low as $200,000 or as high as $2.0 million in any given year. The effects of financial leverage on earnings per share and the return on equity under several alternative earnings scenarios are shown in Exhibit 14-1 for the two financing alternatives. Income is assumed to be taxed at a rate of 50 percent.

Exhibit 14-1 shows that financial leverage has a significant impact on EPS and ROE. For example, with 50 percent debt financing, if EBIT is $1,000,000, earnings per share and return on equity will be 50 percent greater than what they are with no leverage. Alternatively, in bad years, leverage causes EPS and ROE to be negative, but they are positive with all-equity financing. In general, when more leverage is used, EPS and ROE rise more in good years and fall more in bad years. When EBIT is increasing, added leverage causes EPS and ROE to increase more rapidly, and vice versa when EBIT is falling.

EXHIBIT 14-1
Effect of Leverage on Hi-Tech's Earnings per Share and Return on Equity

	States of the World			
	Bad	Mediocre	Normal	Good
A. No Leverage; 500,000 Shares @ $10/Share				
EBIT	$200,000	$500,000	$1,000,000	$2,000,000
Less: Interest @ 10%	0	0	0	0
Equity Income	200,000	$500,000	$1,000,000	$2,000,000
Less: Tax @ 50%	100,000	250,000	500,000	1,000,000
Equity Income after Tax	100,000	$250,000	$500,000	$1,000,000
EPS	$.20	$.50	$1.00	$2.00
ROE (%)	2	5	10	20
B. 50 Percent Debt; 250,000 Shares @ $10/Share; $2.5 Million in Debt @ 10% Interest				
EBIT	$200,000	$500,000	$1,000,000	$2,000,000
Less: Interest @ 10%	250,000	250,000	250,000	250,000
Equity Income	($50,000)	$250,000	$750,000	$1,750,000
Less: Tax @ 50%	(25,000)*	125,000	375,000	875,000
Equity Income	($25,000)	$125,000	$375,000	$875,000
EPS	($.10)	$.50	$1.50	$3.50
ROE (%)	−1	5	15	35

*It is assumed that losses can be carried forward or backward for tax purposes.

We can also see that the benefits of leverage depend on the return the firm earns on its assets and the cost of debt. If Hi-Tech can issue debt at 10 percent and earn 20 percent on its assets ($1 million on assets of $5 million), it should do so; the more it borrows, the higher its EPS and return on equity will be. But if EBIT is $500,000, yielding a return on assets of 10 percent, the same as Hi-Tech's cost of debt, there is no advantage to debt financing. In the worst-case scenario, in which Hi-Tech's ROA is less than its cost of debt, the effect of leverage is unfavorable; Hi-Tech is in a loss position, and its EPS and ROE are negative.

> Financial leverage magnifies the effect on EPS of fluctuations in EBIT.

These results are shown graphically in Exhibit 14-2, which displays the results of plotting EPS against EBIT for the two financing alternatives. The EBIT-EPS chart shows the EPS that would result from a given level of EBIT for the two financing plans. Line A, which represents the all-equity financing plan, shows that a given percentage change in EBIT will result in the *same* percentage change in EPS. Plan B, which uses 50-percent debt financing, is represented by line B. The slope of line B is steeper than that of line A. The practical import of this is that a given percentage change in EBIT will result in a more-than-proportionate percentage change

EXHIBIT 14-2
The EBIT-EPS Relationship and Financial Leverage

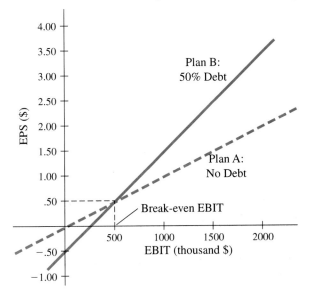

in EPS. Thus, financial leverage magnifies the effect on EPS of fluctuations in EBIT. This is beneficial in good times but harmful in bad times.

The EBIT-EPS indif-
ference point is
the level of EBIT at
which the earn-
ings per share for
alternative financ-
ing plans are
equal.

The level of EBIT at which earnings per share are equal under the two plans is called the **EBIT-EPS indifference point** or the **break-even EBIT,** and it occurs when the return on assets just equals the interest cost of debt. Graphically, break-even EBIT—$500,000 for Hi-Tech—is the point in Exhibit 14-2 at which the two lines intersect. If EBIT is below the indifference point, common stock financing will be preferred; above that point, the substitution of debt for equity financing will result in higher EPS. Although EBIT-EPS indifference analysis will not tell you how much debt to use, it can help you assess the risk–return tradeoff associated with adding more debt to the capital structure.

We can also find the EBIT-EPS indifference point ($EBIT^*$) algebraically be-tween two financing plans A and B by setting EPS for each plan equal to each other and solving for $EBIT^*$:

$$\frac{[(EBIT^* - I_A)(1 - t_c) - P_A]}{N_A} = \frac{[(EBIT^* - I_B)(1 - t_c) - P_B]}{N_B} \qquad [14\text{-}2]$$

where I_A and I_B are the interest expenses under financing plans A and B; P_A and P_B, the preferred stock dividends under plans A and B; N_A and N_B, the number of shares issued under plans A and B, and t_c, the corporate tax rate. If preferred stock is used, the dividends must be subtracted from after-tax income in computing EPS because they are not tax deductible.

We can use Equation [14-2] to determine the indifference point between financing plans A and B for Hi-Tech:

$$\frac{(EBIT^* - 0)(0.50)}{500,000} = \frac{(EBIT^* - \$250,000)(0.50)}{250,000}$$

or

$$EBIT^* = \$500,000$$

In this example's worst-case scenario, Hi-Tech's earnings will be insufficient to pay all the interest owed. Should this happen, Hi-Tech will not necessarily be forced into bankruptcy. It can draw down its cash and other liquid assets and even sell some of its fixed assets (note, too, that its earnings may understate its operating cash flow because of depreciation charges). Hi-Tech can also try to raise funds by selling more debt and equity securities or by borrowing more money from a bank. If all else fails and Hi-Tech has exhausted its ability to meet its debt payments, it will default and enter bankruptcy. In the extreme case, the firm will be *liquidated*, meaning that all its assets will be sold off and the proceeds given to its creditors. The shareholders will divide up anything that remains after the creditor claims are met in full. Usually, though, if it comes to a forced liquidation, debtholders are not paid in full, and, therefore, shareholders get nothing.

We can summarize our analysis as follows:

1. *When the return on assets exceeds the interest cost of debt, financial leverage raises both EPS and ROE.* Leverage reduces EPS and ROE when the return on assets is less than the cost of debt. Thus, in normal and good years, when the return on assets exceeds the cost of debt, financial leverage is beneficial. But when the bad times come, leverage multiplies the firm's problems.
2. *Financial leverage increases the variability of EPS and ROE.* This financial risk is caused by the fixed nature of creditor claims. No matter what happens to the firm's earnings, a fixed amount of interest must be paid. When EBIT falls, the entire earnings decline is subtracted from the amount going to equity. On the other hand, when EBIT rises, the entire increase in earnings goes to the shareholders.
3. *Financial leverage usually increases the expected levels of EPS and ROE.* Therefore, substituting debt for equity should increase expected EPS and ROE, but because financial leverage also increases the variability of EPS and ROE, a financing plan that maximizes expected EPS or ROE is also likely to maximize financial risk. Thus, financial leverage involves the familiar trade-off between risk and return. Focusing on expected EPS or ROE alone in selecting a financing plan is inappropriate because it ignores risk and the effect of that risk on the stock price.

14.2   ALTERNATIVE THEORIES OF CAPITAL STRUCTURE

We have seen that there are positive and negative aspects to financial leverage. Does this mean that an optimal capital structure exists, in which the benefits of added debt just offset its costs? Or is the value of the firm independent of its financing mix? We shall now examine some answers to that question. These answers are set forth in the form of alternative theories of capital structure.

The Traditional Approach

The traditional approach to capital structure states that the prudent use of leverage can lower a firm's overall cost of capital.

According to the *traditional approach* to capital structure, a moderate degree of financial leverage can lower the firm's weighted average cost of capital—as cheaper debt is substituted for more expensive equity—and thereby increase the total value of the firm; any initial increase in the cost of equity capital, k_e, is more than offset by the lower interest rate on debt capital, k_d. But as leverage is increased, shareholders begin exacting a higher and higher penalty—in the form of a more rapidly rising k_e—until a point is reached at which the advantage of lower-cost debt is more than offset by more expensive equity. Consequently, the weighted average cost of funds, k_0, declines at first and then rises. The rise in k_0 is reinforced after a while by an increasing cost of debt (as lenders become concerned about the firm's excessive borrowing).

The result of these opposing trends is an optimal degree of financial leverage at the point that k_0 attains its minimum value. This is the point—L^* in Exhibit 14-3—at which the lower cost of debt financing is just offset by the resulting higher cost of equity. Thus, the traditional position implies that the value of the firm *is not* independent of its financing mix and that there exists an optimal capital structure even in the absence of taxes.

The Modigliani–Miller Position

Modigliani and Miller proved that, in a world free of market imperfections, the value of a firm is independent of its capital structure.

The traditional position held until the classic article on capital structure by Franco Modigliani and Merton Miller.[1] In what may justly be considered the most important paper in modern finance, Modigliani and Miller (MM) demonstrated that capital structure doesn't matter in a world without taxes, transaction costs, or other market imperfections.[2] This is MM's proposition I: *The value of the firm is independent of its capital structure.*

---

[1]Franco Modigliani and Merton H. Miller (1958).

[2]In the words of Robert Merton ("In Honor of Nobel Laureate, Franco Modigliani," *Journal of Economic Perspectives,* Fall 1987, 150), "The Modigliani–Miller work stands as the watershed between 'old finance,' an essentially loose collection of beliefs based on accounting practices, rules of thumb and anecdotes, and modern financial economics, with its rigorous mathematical theories and carefully documented empirical studies." Both the authors have won the Nobel Prize in Economics partly in recognition of this seminal work.

EXHIBIT 14-3
Required Returns and Financial Leverage:
The Traditional Approach

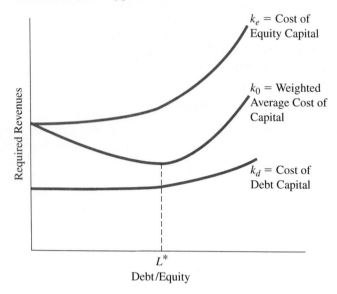

k_e = Cost of Equity Capital

k_0 = Weighted Average Cost of Capital

k_d = Cost of Debt Capital

Required Revenues

L^*

Debt/Equity

Proposition I

Proposition I is based on the assumption that the firm's operating cash flows are independent of its capital structure. Given this assumption, Proposition I follows from an arbitrage argument: In equilibrium, identical assets must sell for identical prices, regardless of the manner in which the assets are financed.[3] This is a straightforward application of the **law of the conservation of value.** It says that no matter how you package and repackage a set of cash flows, its value remains the same. We have already run across this idea in capital budgeting, where it is known as the *principle of value additivity.* The basic notion is that if there are two cash flow streams A and B, the present value of A + B will equal the present value of A plus the present value of B. Otherwise, an arbitrage profit can be earned.

The law of conservation of value states that the value of a set of cash flows is independent of how they are packaged.

To see the application of this principle in the context of capital structure, consider two firms that are identical in all respects except capital structure: Firm U is unlevered, and firm L has $1 million in 10 percent debt. Both firms have expected EBIT of $500,000 per annum forever and are in the same risk class. Under the traditional position, suppose that k_e is 15 percent for U and 16 percent for L.

[3]We have already seen the arbitrage argument applied twice: to the CAPM, which shows that two stocks that contribute the same risk to a portfolio of stocks must bear the same risk premium; and the Black–Scholes option pricing model, which depends on the ability of investors to replicate exactly the payoffs from a call option by holding an investment in the underlying asset that is financed in part with borrowed money.

Under these conditions, the valuation of both firms is

	Firm U	Firm L
EBIT	$ 500,000	$ 500,000
Interest	0	–100,000
Dividends	$ 500,000	$ 400,000
Cost of equity	.15	.16
Market value of equity	$3,333,333	$2,500,000
Market value of debt	0	1,000,000
Market value of firm	$3,333,333	$3,500,000

The market capitalization rate for the earnings of firm U is just its cost of equity capital, 15 percent, and the implied overall rate, or WACC, for firm L is 14.29 percent ($500,000/$3,500,000). Thus two identical firms are selling for different prices. The addition of $1 million in debt financing has increased shareholders' wealth by $166,667.

Modigliani and Miller argue that the possibility of arbitrage will not permit this situation to persist. By investing in firm U, shareholders in firm L can increase their expected investment income without increasing their financial risk. This will lead them to sell off their shares in L and buy shares in U. The result will be a decline in the price of firm L shares and a rise in the price of firm U shares. These arbitrage transactions will continue until the market values of both firms are equal. At this point, there will be no further arbitrage opportunities.

To see this, suppose you owned 10 percent of L's stock, with a market value of $250,000. According to MM, you should

1. Sell off your shares in L for $250,000.
2. Borrow an amount equal to 10 percent of L's debt ($100,000) at an interest rate of 10 percent.
3. Buy 10 percent of the shares of U for $333,333.

You would receive $350,000 from the sale of your stock in L plus your borrowing, whereas you would be spending only $333,333 to buy U's stock, leaving you with $16,667 in extra cash.

The effect of these financial transactions on your income will be:

	Old Income from Investment in L	New Income from Investment in U
10% of firm's equity income	$40,000	$50,000
10% interest on $100,000 loan	0	–10,000
Net income	$40,000	$40,000

Your net investment income from common stocks, $40,000, is the same in both cases, but now you would have $16,667 left over to spend as you please.

In perfect capital markets, the ability of investors to engage in arbitrage ensures that the values of an unlevered firm and an identical levered firm will be the same.

Therefore, the total return on your original investment position of $250,000 will rise. Moreover, your risk remains the same as before; you have substituted $100,000 in personal borrowing for your share of firm L's corporate debt. In effect, you have substituted "homemade" leverage for corporate leverage.

This argument can be generalized for any values of corporate debt, equity, or total market value. As long as the value of the unlevered firm, V_U, is less than the value of the levered firm, V_L, you can continue earning risk-free profits by selling stock in L and buying stock in U, financed in part with borrowed money. But the very process of taking advantage of this arbitrage opportunity would quickly eliminate it by driving up the price of the unlevered firm and driving down the price of the levered firm until $V_U = V_L$. The ability to arbitrage differences in value by these transactions, financed in part with personal borrowing, is the basis for MM's proposition I.

Proposition II

The cost of equity capital increases as leverage increases.

For financial leverage to be irrelevant, the weighted average cost of capital k_0 must remain constant, regardless of the amount of debt employed. This is MM's proposition II: *The cost of equity capital for a levered firm equals the constant overall cost of capital plus a risk premium that equals the spread between the overall cost of capital and the cost of debt multiplied by the firm's debt-equity ratio.* Equation [14-3], which shows that the cost of equity capital must rise in a deterministic manner as leverage increases, represents MM's Proposition II algebraically:

$$k_e = k_0 + (k_0 - k_d)D/E \qquad [14\text{-}3]$$

The contrast between MM's proposition II and the traditional view is shown graphically in Exhibit 14-4. Exhibit 14-4 implicitly assumes that at low levels of financial leverage, there is virtually no chance of default. Thus, k_d is independent of the debt-equity ratio, and the cost of equity capital increases linearly with the firm's debt-equity ratio. Once bankruptcy becomes a possibility, however, the cost of debt begins rising with leverage, and this slows down the rate of increase in k_e. Why does this happen? As the firm borrows more, debtholders bear a larger share of the firm's business risk, thereby offsetting some of the increased financial risk that shareholders must bear at higher debt levels. The source of this financial risk and how it affects the firm's cost of equity are now addressed.

Modigliani–Miller with Corporate Taxes

In the perfect capital markets environment posited by Modigliani and Miller, their argument that capital structure is irrelevant is unassailable. In the absence of market imperfections, no matter how corporate cash flows are divided up between debt and equity claims, their total amount remains fixed. The risk attached to these cash flows taken as a whole also remains fixed because it depends only on the firm's basic business risk. Thus, for capital structure to matter, there must be market imperfections that cause changes in financial leverage to change the amounts or riskiness of the firm's cash flows. Perhaps the most important market

EXHIBIT 14-4
Required Returns and Financial Leverage: Modigliani–Miller's
Proposition II versus the Traditional Approach

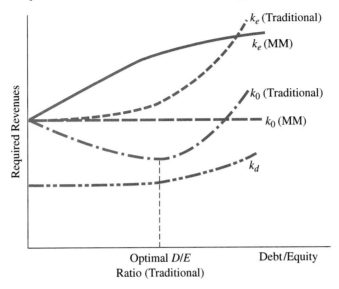

imperfection is the existence of corporate taxes and the asymmetric tax treatment of different forms of capital costs and income.

Under current tax law, debt has an important advantage over equity: Interest payments on debt are tax deductible, whereas dividend payments and retained earnings are not. The importance of this point can be seen by examining how capital structure affects the amount of money the firm has available after taxes to pay its investors.

Consider again the two firms that are identical in all respects except capital structure. Firm U is unlevered, whereas firm L has borrowed $1 million at an interest rate of 10 percent. Expected EBIT is $500,000 for both firms and is assumed to be independent of capital structure. If the marginal corporate tax rate (federal plus state) is 40 percent, the income statements for these firms will be:

	Firm U	**Firm L**
Earnings before interest and taxes	$500,000	$500,000
Interest paid to bondholders	0	–100,000
Pre-tax profit	$500,000	$400,000
Taxes @ 40%	–200,000	–160,000
Income to stockholders	$300,000	$240,000
Income to stockholders plus bondholders	300,000	340,000
Interest tax shield (interest × 0.40)	0	40,000
Present value of tax shield (interest tax shield/0.10)	0	400,000

We can see that annual cash flows to firm L's investors will exceed the annual cash flows to firm U's investors by $40,000, the value of the tax shield provided by L's borrowings. In other words, the combined cash flows available to investors increase with leverage by an amount equal to the value of the tax deduction on interest. The loser is the government, which collects less tax. The winner is L, whose market value rises. This changes the relative market values of U and L. In particular, assuming firm L maintains its capital structure permanently, the $40,000 interest tax shield becomes a perpetuity with a present value of $400,000 ($40,000/0.10). That is, the $1 million in debt financing has increased the value of firm L by $400,000. This increase in market value accrues directly to the firm's shareholders.

In general, in a world in which the only market imperfection is corporate taxes, Modigliani and Miller showed that the value of the levered firm (V_L) equals the value of the unlevered firm (V_U) plus the present value of the levered firm's interest tax shield:[4]

> **In a world where the only market imperfection is corporate taxes, the use of debt increases the value of the firm.**

$$V_L = V_U + t_c D \qquad [14\text{-}4]$$

where t_C is the marginal corporate tax rate, and D is the market value of the firm's debt. The second term in Equation [14-4] assumes that the firm will borrow an amount of debt D in perpetuity and will always be able to use the tax shield supplied by the debt. If either of these conditions is violated (e.g., the firm goes bankrupt and no longer has income to shield from taxes), the present value of the tax shield will be reduced. In computing the present value of the interest tax shield, the pre-tax interest rate on the firm's debt is used as the discount rate.

> **Not all firms can utilize the tax benefits of debt.**

To the extent that the firm has other tax shields such as depreciation and investment tax credits or has highly uncertain cash flows, the value of the interest tax shield for a given amount of debt is reduced. Similarly, as financial leverage increases, the firm becomes less likely to be able to utilize fully the resulting higher interest tax shield, decreasing the tax advantage of adding debt to the capital structure. These problems become more severe at high levels of financial leverage, moderating the firm's incentive to substitute debt for equity.

Beautiful Theory Meets Ugly Fact.   Taking the preceding material at face value, in the presence of corporate income taxes, we see that additional borrowing will always increase the value of the firm. Thus, the logical conclusion of the original MM argument, adjusted for corporate taxes, is that firms should be 100 percent debt financed. But this beautiful theory has no takers—except for those firms in bankruptcy. If adding value is as easy as the theory seems to indicate, why don't we see firms with virtually all debt in their capital structures? In reality, most successful firms—for example, Microsoft, Merck, and Coca-Cola—have very little debt in their capital structures. Moreover, corporate debt ratios are not much higher today than they were before World War II, when corporate taxes were virtually nonexistent.

---

[4]Modigliani and Miller (1963).

There is always the possibility that firms don't take full advantage of financial leverage because of management stupidity or cupidity. But because firms like Coca-Cola and Merck don't appear to be shortchanging their shareholders in other ways, we can probably rule out these explanations for the observed pattern of less than 100 percent debt financing. Instead, it is more likely that the advantages of borrowing are less compelling in practice than in theory.

The personal tax disadvantage of debt may offset part of the corporate tax advantage.

One possibility is that the personal tax disadvantage of debt negates its corporate tax advantage. According to Merton Miller, the value of the corporate tax shield will be entirely offset by personal taxes, making the value of the firm independent of its capital structure even with taxes.[5] Miller's argument assumes that the personal tax rate on equity income is effectively zero and that the personal tax rate on interest income equals the corporate tax rate. Although these assumptions are questionable, most financial economists concede that the tax advantage of debt is probably less than $t_c D$.

Even if personal taxes moderate the tax advantages of financial leverage, the evidence suggests that for many firms the value of the interest tax shield is significantly positive. Yet we have already seen that the most likely candidates for high degrees of financial leverage have very low debt ratios. Because these firms seem intent on maximizing shareholder wealth, there must be potential costs to debt financing that sooner or later come to outweigh its tax advantages.

Indeed, the evidence suggests that borrowers incur costs, such as bankruptcy and agency costs, that can offset the value of the interest tax shield. To the extent that financial distress and agency problems are related to financial leverage, the key assumption underlying Modigliani–Miller's Proposition I—that a firm's operating cash flows are independent of its financing mix—is violated, and capital structure matters for reasons other than taxes. We will now examine the effects of financial distress and agency conflicts on the choice of capital structure.

14.3   FINANCIAL LEVERAGE AND FINANCIAL DISTRESS

Financial distress occurs when a firm has difficulty in meeting its contractual obligations; bankruptcy is an extreme form of financial distress.

Financial distress occurs when a firm has difficulty in meeting its contractual obligations. In the extreme case, the firm defaults on its obligations and enters bankruptcy. **Bankruptcy** is a formal legal proceeding under which a company that has overextended itself is placed under the protection of the bankruptcy court, allowing it to keep operating while a plan is developed to pay off creditors in an equitable manner. More generally, the term financial distress refers to any weakening of a company's financial condition. As we will see, all forms of financial distress involve costs to the firm and, therefore, are reflected in a reduced price for the shares of leveraged firms. Because more highly leveraged firms have more financial commitments outstanding, they are more likely to encounter financial distress. Thus, the expected costs of financial distress—the probability of distress times the actual costs—will rise with financial leverage.

---

[5]Miller (1977).

The optimal debt ratio involves a tradeoff between the tax benefits of additional debt and the expected higher costs of financial distress.

Exhibit 14-5 shows that—ignoring other factors—the optimal debt ratio involves a tradeoff between the tax advantage of additional debt and the higher expected costs of financial distress. At low levels of debt, the probability—and hence the expected costs—of financial distress are minimal. But as more debt is added to the capital structure, both the probability and the expected costs of financial distress increase, eventually exceeding the present value of the interest tax shield. As we saw earlier in the chapter, as the debt ratio rises, the firm becomes less certain of being profitable enough to take advantage of the interest tax shield, so the tax shield's value may decline. The optimal debt ratio—L^* in Exhibit 14-5—is reached when the tax advantage of another dollar of debt just equals the added expected costs of financial distress.

The Probability of Financial Distress

The higher the business risk facing a firm, the higher will be the likelihood of financial distress.

All else being equal, the higher the business or operating risk facing a firm, the greater will be the probability—and hence the expected costs—of financial distress at any given level of debt financing. Determinants of business risk include the following:

1. *The firm's cost structure.* When a high proportion of the firm's operating costs are fixed, operating profits tend to fluctuate dramatically with changes

EXHIBIT 14-5
The Optimal Debt Ratio Trades Off the Interest Tax Shield against the Costs of Financial Distress

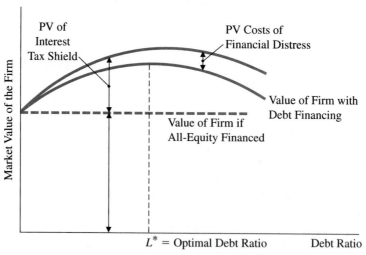

The value of the firm equals the value if it were all-equity financed plus the value of the interest tax shield minus the costs of financial distress. The value of the interest tax shield may decline if financial leverage becomes too great and the company's ability to take advantage of the tax shield becomes questionable.

in sales. Steel, auto, and petrochemical firms, which are very capital intensive, tend to have high fixed costs, making them very risky. Service firms are typically less capital intensive and so have less volatile earnings.

2. *Demand stability.* The sales of some products, including pharmaceuticals, groceries, fast foods, and other nondurables, such as cigarettes and alcohol, stay relatively constant over the business cycle. In contrast, changes in national income greatly affect the sales of such products as steel, automobiles, and capital equipment. Companies with stable demand for their products tend to be less risky than those selling products for which demand is cyclical.

3. *Competition.* Industries with high levels of competition, such as personal computers, consumer electronics, and commodity-type businesses, tend to have high business risk. On the other hand, regulated industries, such as utilities, and companies with strong brand franchises, such as Coca-Cola and Disney, have less competition and fairly stable earnings.

4. *Price fluctuations.* The prices of certain products, especially basic commodities such as copper and wheat, fluctuate greatly, increasing the business risks of companies dealing in those products. The prices of manufactured goods typically are more stable, lowering the business risk of their producers.

5. *Firm size and diversification.* Larger firms are typically better diversified and, hence, less risky, than smaller firms.

6. *Stage in the industry life cycle.* Products often go through a life cycle. In the early stages, when the industry is just getting underway and growing rapidly, there is a lot of sorting out and high failure rates. Similarly, when the industry begins its decline, competition is intense, and failure rates are again high—witness the steel industry. In between, during the mature phase, firms that have survived the growth phase probably face the least business risk.

Bankruptcy Costs

We saw in Chapter 7 that with limited liability, stockholders have a valuable option; they can default on the firm's obligations with no further responsibility to the creditors. They will exercise this option and throw the firm into bankruptcy if the value of the firm's liabilities exceeds the value of its assets. Bankruptcy is not costless, however. In the event of bankruptcy, the firm must bear certain direct costs in the form of various legal, accounting, and administrative expenses. The firm may also have to sell off some of its assets at "fire sale" prices to meet creditors' claims.

The possibility of bankruptcy lowers the value of creditor claims. Understanding this, lenders raise their required interest rate to compensate for the expected costs of bankruptcy. This reduces the market value of equity claims by a corresponding amount. Because the probability of bankruptcy rises with financial leverage, the more a firm borrows, the higher its expected costs of bankruptcy and the lower the market value of its equity will be.

The direct costs of bankruptcy, however, do not seem to be the reason for the minimal amounts of debt in many corporate capital structures. Studies indicate

The direct costs of bankruptcy appear to be small in relation to the tax benefits of debt.

that the legal and administrative expenses associated with bankruptcy, although not trivial in dollar terms, are small in relation to the firm's market value and appear trivial when measured against the estimated value of the interest tax shield they are supposed to offset.

Costs of Financial Distress

Far more important to an explanation of the observed pattern of capital structures are the indirect costs of financial distress. These costs, which increase with the probability of bankruptcy, arise from the deterioration in the firm's operating performance brought on by financial distress. Part of this deterioration is the result of management's focusing its attention and energy on keeping creditors at bay rather than on running the firm. More importantly, a company's prospects are not independent of the perceptions of its noninvestor stakeholders—its customers, suppliers, distributors, employees, and so on—regarding its longevity and viability. In particular, financial distress weakens the bonds between the firm and its stakeholders, reducing the expected cash flows that will be generated by the unique factor and product market franchises the firm has developed.

Financial distress creates management incentives that conflict with the best interests of individuals that do business with the firm.

The inverse relation between financial leverage and expected cash flows arises, in part, because financial distress creates management incentives that conflict with the best interests of the individuals that do business with such firms. The negative effect of these *adverse incentives* on sales and operating costs is compounded by the risk aversion of customers, managers, employees, suppliers, and other corporate stakeholders.[6]

The Adverse Incentive Problem.   Financial distress, or the threat of bankruptcy, affects management behavior in three fundamental ways. First, managers are more likely to select certain high-risk projects that benefit shareholders but at the expense of bondholders. Second, they may pass up projects with positive net present values because most payoffs will go to bondholders. Third, they may focus on short-term profits at the expense of the firm's longer-term viability. We shall examine each of these possibilities.

The possibility of bankruptcy leads firms to invest in high-risk projects, even if they have negative NPVs.

Selection of High-Risk Projects.   The possibility of bankruptcy leads firms to choose possibly suboptimal investment projects that expropriate wealth from their creditors. Specifically, if bankruptcy is likely, the firm's stockholders will have an incentive to invest in very risky projects even if they have negative net present values. The bondholders, not the stockholders, will bear most of the downside risk from these investments, but the stockholders will enjoy most of the gain from the upside potential.

To illustrate this point, suppose that the book value of IOU, Inc.'s assets and liabilities are as follows:

---

[6]These costs are elaborated in Shapiro and Titman (1985).

IOU, Inc., Balance Sheet (book values)			
Working capital	$2,000,000	$3,000,000	Bonds
Fixed assets	2,000,000	1,000,000	Equity
Total assets	$4,000,000	$4,000,000	Total liabilities plus equity

But when we have converted IOU's balance sheet to market values, we see that it is in financial distress, because the book value of its liabilities exceeds the market value of its assets:

IOU, Inc., Balance Sheet (market values)			
Working capital	$1,000,000	$1,500,000	Bonds
Fixed assets	1,000,000	500,000	Equity
Total assets	$2,000,000	$2,000,000	Total liabilities plus equity

The market value of its assets is only $2 million, but it has debts outstanding of $3 million. But suppose that IOU's bonds will not mature until next year. In the meantime, the firm has enough cash to pay the interest, thereby avoiding default this year. The one-year time to expiration of IOU's call option on the firm explains why its shares still have value. Something may happen in the interim that would allow the company to repay its debts and leave money left over for the shareholders. This "something" that would bail out the firm could be the following investment opportunity that IOU runs across:

Initial Investment	Possible Return (present value)	×	Probability	=	Expected Value
$1 million	$10 million		.05		$500,000
	0		.95		0
			Expected value 0		$500,000

Expected net present value = −$1,000,000 + $500,000 = −$500,000

With a project NPV of −$500,000, this is a lousy investment. But IOU's stockholders will be tempted to take it anyway because they are gambling with the bondholders' money. If they don't take the project, they are guaranteed to receive nothing, but if they take the project and it succeeds, they stand to make $8 million. If it fails, the bondholders will lose the full $1 million. For the stockholders, this is a "Heads I win, tails the bondholders lose" proposition.

Exhibit 14-6 shows how the payoffs on the project are divided. If the project turns out well, the stockholders will realize the lion's share of the $10 million in proceeds, $8 million versus $2 million for the bondholders; if it fails, the bondholders will bear the full $1 million loss. This is because the bondholders will

EXHIBIT 14-6
Possible Payoff to Investors from IOU's New Project

	Project Status		
	Successful	Unsuccessful	No Project
Available Funds			
Corporate Assets	$ 2,000,000	$ 2,000,000	$2,000,000
Cost of Project	(1,000,000)	(1,000,000)	—
Net Assets Available	$1,000,000	$ 1,000,000	$2,000,000
Project Return	10,000,000	0	—
Total Funds	$11,000,000	$ 1,000,000	$2,000,000
Division of Funds			
Bondholders			
Corporate Assets	$ 1,000,000	$ 1,000,000	$2,000,000
Project Proceeds	2,000,000	0	—
Total	$ 3,000,000	$ 1,000,000	$2,000,000
Stockholders	8,000,000	0	0

now receive only $1 million, whereas without the project, they would receive the $2 million in available corporate assets. Thus, the project's expected NPV from the stockholders' perspective is $400,000 ($8,000,000 × .05); from the bondholders' perspective it is −$900,000(−$1,000,000 + 0 × .95 + $2,000,000 × .05). The overall project NPV, as computed earlier, is −$500,000 (−$900,000 + $400,000).

Immediately following the investment, the total value of the firm drops to $1.5 million—the initial value of $2 million less the loss of $.5 million from undertaking the project. The shareholders' claim on the firm goes from 0 to $400,000, whereas the bondholders' claim drops from $2 million to $1.1 million. In effect, the stockholders have expropriated $900,000 from the bondholders by undertaking the project even though they get to keep only $400,000 of the expropriated wealth; the difference of $500,000 is a deadweight loss equal to the project's negative NPV.

The incentive for stockholders of highly leveraged companies to engage in high-risk projects is perhaps best illustrated by the behavior of the savings and loan industry. As we saw in Chapter 7, with their businesses effectively bankrupt and with the federal government guaranteeing deposits, the S&Ls took huge risks. In effect, the S&Ls' shareholders expected to pocket the higher returns while sticking the government with the increased downside risk.

Passing Up Positive Net Present Value Projects.   Suppose that IOU is unable to undertake the risky investment because it can't raise enough cash. However, it now finds a reasonably safe project that requires an initial investment of $1 million and has a net present value of $500,000.

Ordinarily, we would expect IOU to issue new shares worth $1 million to undertake the project. If it does, the new balance sheet of IOU, Inc., will look like this on a market value basis:

IOU, Inc., Balance Sheet (market values)			
Working capital	$1,000,000	$2,600,000	Bonds
Fixed assets	2,500,000	900,000	Equity
Total assets	$3,500,000	$3,500,000	Total liabilities plus equity

The total value of IOU rises by $1.5 million, the $1 million in new capital contributed by the shareholders plus the $500,000 NPV. Note, however, that most of this added value is captured by the bondholders. Their bonds are now worth $2.6 million—a capital gain of $1.1 million—because there are now more assets securing those bonds. The probability of default has declined, and the payoff to the bondholders if default occurs is larger.

By contrast, the shareholders will lose $600,000 by undertaking the project. They will receive only $400,000 in expected value on an investment of $1 million. The remaining $1.1 million of the project's value will go to the bondholders. Even though this project is worthwhile from the standpoint of the firm, the shareholders will not undertake it. The possibility of forgoing positive NPV projects is another cost of financial distress.

> The possibility of bankruptcy creates incentives for firms to pass up positive NPV projects in which the primary beneficiaries of accepting such projects are the creditors.

Myopic Decision Making.   Financial distress or the threat of bankruptcy also has an important impact on the firm's sales and costs. As the firm progresses through the various stages of financial distress toward bankruptcy, both stockholders and managers may do things under the threat of financial distress that they would not otherwise do. For example, a firm having difficulty raising cash may be tempted to lower its product and service quality as well as cut corners on employee safety. Other problems associated with financial distress also have their origin in the emphasis on maximizing short-run cash flow. A firm facing financial distress may be tempted to conserve cash by cutting back on research and development, plant maintenance, and advertising and promotional expenditures.

These are dangerous moves, however, because the firm will be gaining short-run profits at the expense of its reputation for providing quality products and reliable service and, ultimately, its longer-run ability to remain competitive and stay in business. A financially healthy firm, therefore, has a strong incentive to produce high-quality products and to take other actions to ensure its long-term viability.

If the firm is suffering financial distress, however, long-term profit considerations may be less important than generating enough cash to meet current debt-servicing charges. The cost savings associated with cutting quality levels may be particularly attractive to firms facing creditors threatening to take over and possibly liquidate the firm.

Potential customers, suppliers, and distributors, anticipating these incentive changes, will be reluctant to do business with firms in financial distress or with high-risk firms likely to face financial distress in the future. Similarly, valuable employees may leave to find jobs with companies where their futures are more secure. These effects of financial distress will adversely affect the firm's future sales and operating costs and reduce the market value of the firm's equity; that is, the costs of financial distress are borne by the firm's stockholders.

> Firms pursuing a strategy of differentiation are likely to have higher costs of financial distress than firms in commodity-oriented businesses.

Firms selling products that are highly differentiated are likely to have far higher costs of financial distress than those in commodity-oriented businesses because product differentiation requires a large investment in **organizational assets.**[7] These intangible assets take a variety of forms: managers and others with firm-specific knowledge and skills, a network of outside distributors and suppliers, strong brand names, and a reputation for quality and reliability.

An important attribute of the firm's stock of organizational capital is that it cannot be separated from the firm as an ongoing operation. It is this inseparability that differentiates organizational capital from other capital assets. If the firm gets into financial trouble, it can sell physical assets, but it cannot liquidate its organizational capital. These intangible assets disappear along with the firm. Because the value of a firm's intangible assets largely depends on its staying power, a strong financial posture is important to firms such as Microsoft or Amgen that have large amounts of these assets.

Characteristics of Firms with High Expected Costs of Financial Distress

> Industry-specific product characteristics can have an important impact on the cost of financial distress.

Based on the preceding discussion, it's possible to identify specific characteristics of firms for which financial distress is especially costly or highly likely. These firms should, therefore, choose to maintain low debt ratios. Some of these characteristics are industry specific, based on product type, yet others are firm specific, based on certain unique factors. Industry-specific product characteristics include the following:[8]

1. *Products that require repairs.* When Chrysler was flirting with bankruptcy in the later 1970s, Lee Iacocca, its chairman at the time, talked about the difficulties the company faced in selling its cars: "Our situation was unique. . . . It wasn't like the cereal business. If Kellogg's were known to be going out of business, nobody would say: 'Well, I won't buy their cornflakes today. What if I get stuck with a box of cereal and there's nobody around to service it?' "[9] Financial distress is costly here because demand drops as potential customers begin to worry about buying products that can't be serviced should the firm exit the business.

2. *Goods or services whose quality is an important attribute but is difficult to determine in advance.* An example is air transportation. In fact, airline com-

---

[7]The concept of organizational assets, also termed organizational capital, is discussed in more detail in Cornell and Shapiro (1987).

[8]These categories are from Shapiro and Titman (1985).

[9]*Fortune,* November 26, 1984, 224.

panies in financial difficulty have been hurt by the common belief that they are more likely to cut corners on safety, thereby increasing the risk of an accident. In general, customers become concerned that a company in financial distress will reduce product quality and so will prefer to stick with a healthier company unless given a substantial price discount.

3. *Products for which there are switching costs.* Such products—for which customers must bear large fixed costs to switch suppliers—include computers and office and factory automation equipment. Rather than be stuck with obsolete equipment if a financially distressed firm exits the business, customers will prefer to buy products from a financially strong firm. For example, many customers of Wang Laboratories, the pioneer of word processing computers, were frightened away by reports of its financial troubles. According to the *Wall Street Journal* (October 18, 1989, p. B1), "Wang's customers are data processing managers who want to be sure that their suppliers are stable, well-run companies that will be around to fix bugs and upgrade computers for years to come," and doing business with Wang was too risky for many of them. By the time Wang filed for bankruptcy in 1992, its stock market value had shrunk from $5.6 billion to $70 million.

4. *Products whose value to customers depends on the services and complementary products supplied by other companies.* Many firms, such as computer manufacturers and auto companies, require third parties to distribute, sell, service, upgrade, and otherwise add value to their products. Being a low-risk firm helps persuade others to enter these strategic alliances.

Firm-specific factors arguing for low debt ratios include the following:

1. *High growth opportunities.* Firms having more positive net present value projects available than they can finance with internally generated funds should not jeopardize their access to outside financing by the appearance of being risky. Otherwise, prospective investors could be scared off by the previously discussed management incentive problems, and the firm will be unable to capitalize on its growth options. Further, the problem of asymmetric information (see Chapter 13) is likely to be more severe for a firm in financial distress, as investors figure that the company is covering up even more severe financial troubles.

2. *Substantial organizational assets.* Firms whose principal assets are intangible—in the form of managers and employees with firm-specific human capital, outside distributors, suppliers, brand names, a reputation for quality and reliability—will have higher costs of financial distress than will firms with mostly physical assets. These intangible assets will rapidly depreciate in value if the firm experiences or seems likely to experience financial distress. As the firm's risk increases, the value of a reputation for quality products diminishes, and managers and other stakeholders are increasingly likely to sever their ties with the firm.

   Conversely, the fact of bankruptcy or other form of financial distress should not detract much from the value of assets like oil, factories, or hotel rooms. Therefore, firms whose principal assets are physical—for example, an oil company, a firm producing bulk steel, or a hotel—should be willing to carry higher debt ratios.

3. *Large excess tax deductions.* Companies that cannot take full advantage of their available tax losses, much less the interest on new debt, have less incentive to take on more debt.

14.4 AGENCY COSTS AND CAPITAL STRUCTURE

Potential conflicts of interest among corporate stakeholders—particularly among classes of securityholders—affect the firm's financial strategy.

The modern corporation has no "owners" in the traditional sense. Instead, it is an interrelated set of contracts among a variety of stakeholders: shareholders, lenders, employees, managers, suppliers, distributors, and consumers. These stakeholders share a common interest in the firm's success. But conflicts of interest may also arise among the stakeholders (e.g., in the case of financial distress). The emphasis here is on how these potential conflicts of interest—particularly among classes of securityholders—affect the firm's financial strategy.

Stockholder–Manager Conflicts

As we saw in Chapter 7, although management is legally bound to act as the shareholders' agent, the separation of ownership and control in the modern corporation may lead to conflicts between the two parties. The **agency conflict** between managers and outside shareholders derives from two principal sources.[10] The first is management's tendency to consume some of the firm's resources in the form of various perquisites such as fancy offices, corporate jets, and golf-club memberships.

The second important conflict arises because managers have a greater tendency to shirk their responsibilities as their equity interest falls. They are less willing to make the hard, though necessary, choices in managing employees. Most managers have little stomach for eliminating jobs, closing unprofitable operations, and slashing overhead spending. They also tend to shy away from the difficult task of measuring performance and disciplining those who fail to measure up. Managers—like most people—prefer to avoid the emotionally draining experience of constantly operating on the razor's edge of efficiency. This is especially true if the costs of underperforming employees and other operating inefficiencies are borne by others. Thus, as outside equity accounts for a larger share of corporate ownership, there is a corresponding decrease in managerial incentive, resulting in more shirking and higher costs to shareholders.

Stockholder–Bondholder Conflicts

Agency conflicts also exist between stockholders and bondholders. The market value of any firm equals the market value of its bonds plus the market value of its stock. This means that managers can create shareholder wealth either by in-

---

[10]These insights first appeared in Jensen and Meckling (1976).

creasing the value of the firm or by reducing the value of its bonds. The latter possibility is at the root of stockholder–bondholder conflicts.

An important characteristic of corporate debt is that bondholders have prior but fixed claims on a firm's assets, whereas stockholders have limited liability for the firm's debt and unlimited claims on its remaining assets. If the firm is heavily leveraged, the limited liability of shareholders—which gives them the choice of turning over the firm's assets to its creditors instead of repaying its debts—means that bondholders must bear most of the risk while shareholders gather most of the potential rewards. Increasing the risk of the firm transfers wealth from bondholders to shareholders. An intuitive explanation of this wealth transfer is that the risk of default has risen, but bondholders are not compensated for the added risk.

Of course, as pointed out in the previous section, raising the corporate risk profile could cause corporate cash flows to decline, but even if a risky action reduces the value of the firm, the value of equity claims could still rise. This would happen if the reduction in the value of corporate debt associated with the greater risk exceeded the reduction in the value of the firm.

Postcontractual Opportunism and the Issue Price of Securities

The net result of these agency problems is that the amounts and riskiness of future cash flows are not independent of the firm's ownership structure. However, as long as investors anticipate these agency problems, which they do in efficient markets, the firm and its managers, not outside investors, bear the effects of this divergence of interests. That is, outside investors will take into account expected agency costs by discounting the prices they are willing to pay for the firm's security issues.

Because the costs associated with agency problems are borne by management, either alone or in conjunction with shareholders, firms wishing to raise capital in an efficient market have clear-cut incentives to evolve mechanisms to assure the market that they will not engage in **postcontractual opportunism,** and to provide these assurances at the lowest possible cost. These mechanisms include providing managers with incentives, such as stock options, to act in accordance with shareholder wealth maximization; bearing monitoring costs in the form of audits and specific reporting procedures; and including various restrictive covenants in bond and bank loan agreements. If the firm violates any of these covenants, it can be declared in default on its debt, and the loan will become due and payable immediately. If it does not pay up or renegotiate the loan, the firm can be forced into bankruptcy and possible liquidation by its creditors. This possibility provides a strong incentive to obey the covenants.

> Firms wishing to raise capital in an efficient market have the incentive to find ways to assure the market that they will not engage in post-contractual opportunism.

Although the constraints imposed by lenders can avoid many of the potential agency problems associated with debt financing—by limiting management actions that may be harmful to bondholders—they can also prove costly to shareholders by greatly reducing the firm's operating and investment flexibility. For example, lenders may veto certain high-risk projects with positive net present values because of the added risk they would have to bear without a corresponding increase in their expected returns. The opportunity cost associated with the loss of operating flexibility is likely to be especially high for firms with substantial growth options.

The costs of these monitoring and control procedures and the loss of flexibility as well as the costs of any residual divergence from firm value maximization are known collectively as **agency costs.** As the percentage of outside equity or debt in the capital structure rises, so do the associated agency costs. Ignoring other factors, the optimal capital structure for a given amount of outside financing is achieved when total agency costs are minimized.

Agency Costs of Debt

> The agency cost of debt reduces the desirable amount of debt in a firm's capital structure.

The agency costs of debt include the monitoring and control expenditures to ensure that bondholders are not exploited by shareholders as well as the discount at which the bonds of more highly leveraged companies sell. They also include the costs arising from the restrictive loan covenants that are a consequence of the firm's reduced operating and investment flexibility. All else being equal, these agency costs reduce the desirable amount of debt in the firm's capital structure, because the conflicts and their costs increase with financial leverage.

Agency Costs of Equity

Because the agency costs of equity also rise as the proportion of outside equity increases, there is a tradeoff between the desire to reduce the agency costs of debt and the need to reduce the agency costs of outside equity. As noted earlier, the problem with adding more outside equity to the capital structure is that management's interest in the firm diminishes along with its stake in the firm. At one extreme, if management goes from owning 100 percent of the firm to having no ownership interest, its willingness to put forth the effort and to take the risks necessary to maximize shareholder welfare is likely to alter dramatically.

> Management's incentive to expand its firm beyond the point at which shareholder wealth is maximized is an important agency cost of equity.

Michael Jensen pointed out another agency cost of equity—the incentive managers have to expand their firms beyond the point at which shareholder wealth is maximized.[11] Growth increases managers' power and perquisites by increasing the resources at their command as well as their compensation, because changes in compensation are positively related to sales growth.

Given these considerations, managers have strong incentives to reduce the payout of cash to shareholders. By retaining funds internally, managers seeking to expand their domains can bypass the capital markets and avoid the monitoring costs associated with the capital acquisition process. Jensen observed that conflicts of interest between shareholders and managers over payout policy are especially severe in companies that generate substantial amounts of free cash flow. As defined in Chapter 2, *free cash flow* is cash flow in excess of that required to fund all positive NPV projects. Shareholder wealth maximization dictates that free cash flow be paid out to shareholders. The problem is how to get man-

---

[11]See Jensen (1986).

agers to return excess cash to the shareholders instead of reinvesting it in substandard projects and overpriced acquisitions or wasting it on organizational inefficiencies.

Debt as One Solution to the Agency Costs of Equity

Increasing leverage can reduce the agency cost of equity.

One answer is to greatly expand leverage. By issuing large amounts of debt and using the proceeds either to pay a big dividend or to buy back stock, management is committed to using corporate cash flows for principal and interest payments. Because the value of equity equals the value of the firm less the value of its debt, using excess cash to make debt payments effectively returns this cash to shareholders. Any expansion must henceforth be financed with new capital, subjecting management's investment plans to the exacting discipline of the market.

But why should managers take on such large amounts of debt and reduce their discretion over free cash flow when they were previously unwilling to return the cash directly to the shareholders? Because companies that waste large amounts of resources become subject to hostile takeovers. A raider can offer shareholders a price for their shares that exceeds the current market price and still make money by running the company more efficiently.

With a leveraged recapitalization, a company boosts its debt level either by paying a large one-time dividend to stockholders or by repurchasing large amounts of stock.

Leveraged Recapitalizations. Managers fearing a hostile takeover can promise to mend their spendthrift ways and pay out free cash flow to shareholders. But such promises will not be credible unless managers will incur a large penalty if they dishonor their promises. Announcing a dividend increase is not an adequate guarantee, because managers can always cut the dividend later without penalty. A **leveraged recapitalization,** by contrast, can effectively bond managers' promise to pay out free cash flow. In this transaction, a company boosts its debt and shrinks its equity, either by paying a huge one-time dividend to stockholders or by repurchasing a large amount of stock. The pressure to make debt payments is usually adequate to keep management honest; if the firm reverts to its old ways and is forced into bankruptcy, the managers will most likely lose their jobs. Lenders also have a strong incentive to scrutinize internal investments and ensure that resources are not wasted. Added leverage, therefore, reduces the scope of management discretion, changes the process by which management's actions are monitored, and thus changes the managers' motivation.

Illustration

Reining in the Oil Companies

The "reinvestment risk" that companies with substantial free cash flow impose on their shareholders is perhaps best illustrated by the behavior of the large oil companies since 1973. Between 1973 and 1980, oil prices increased tenfold, creating huge cash flows in the industry. At the same time, average returns on investments in exploration and development were below the cost of capital.[12] Rather than return these excess resources to shareholders to reinvest in more promising businesses, the oil companies continued to fund projects that yielded present values of only 60 to 90 cents for each dollar invested.[13] Further, they dissipated literally billions of dollars of shareholder funds in a series of ill-fated attempts to take their organizations into new products and new markets in which they had no competitive advantage. Acquisitions included companies in retailing (Montgomery Ward by Mobil), manufacturing (Reliance Electric by Exxon), office equipment (Vydec by Exxon), mining (Kennecott by Standard Oil, Anaconda Minerals by Atlantic Richfield, Cyprus Mines by Amoco), meat packing (Iowa Beef by Occidental), and insurance (Integon by Ashland).

It fell to T. Boone Pickens, Jr., to set a solution in motion. Pickens began by buying a stake in Gulf Oil and pressed management to restructure. Instead Chevron bought Gulf; Gulf shareholders received $13.3 billion; and Chevron's need to service the debt it incurred to pay for the deal prevented it from pouring its cash into unproductive holes in the ground. Next, Pickens turned to Phillips Petroleum and then Unocal. Both companies succeeded in fighting him off but only at the price of adopting much of his program. Phillips borrowed $4.5 billion to buy back 53 percent of its shares, and Unocal took on over $4 billion in debt to repurchase one-third of its stock. Both companies then made major asset sales, slashed their exploration and development budgets, and cut their work forces substantially.

Other oil companies ultimately took Pickens's point and restructured more or less along the same lines. They sold assets, slashed capital budgets, and cut operating outlays and overhead. In the process of shrinking their operations, the oil companies returned billions to their shareholders through share repurchases, often by taking on mountains of debt. The case of Atlantic Richfield is dramatic and representative enough to stand for them all. A regional refiner and marketer, Arco hit it big with the enormous Prudhoe Bay field in Alaska's North Slope, just when the price of oil surged from $12 to $30 a barrel. In 1977, management bought Anaconda, a major mining and metals concern, for more than $680 million. Arco's oil exploration budget also jumped.

In early 1985, a new management team, under Lodrick Cook, announced a major restructuring plan. The steps included

- Repurchase of $4 billion of its stock. This followed on the heels of a $1 billion stock buyback.
- An increase in long-term debt of $4 billion to finance the repurchase.
- Sale of all the company's refining and marketing operations east of the Mississippi River.

---

[12]B. Picchi, "Structure of the U.S. Oil Industry: Past and Future," Salomon Brothers internal publication, July 1985.
[13]See Jensen (1986).

- An $800 million reduction in annual capital outlays, equivalent to 22 percent of previous outlays.
- Reductions in operating expenditures of about $500 million annually.
- A 30 percent reduction in the exploration budget, an annual savings of about $400 million.
- The sale of all nonoil mineral operations other than coal.
- An increase in its quarterly dividend to $1 a share from 75 cents a share.

Following the announcement, Arco's shares closed at $58.25, up $5.25, representing a total gain for shareholders in excess of $1.3 billion. Over the next five years, profits at the leaner Arco more than tripled. Moreover, Cook declared that Arco would replace declining oil reserves only when it was clearly profitable to do so, cautioning that "people can get caught up in the romance and joys of looking for oil; the purpose of this business is to make money."[14]

Leveraged Cashouts and Leveraged Buyouts.   As the example of the oil industry indicates, a highly leveraged capital structure may promote efficiency by giving management a strong incentive to streamline operations, cut costs, divest underperforming assets, and otherwise generate cash to service the debt. This is especially true in the case of **leveraged cashouts (LCOs)** and **leveraged buyouts (LBOs)**. Both these techniques, which use deliberately use leverage to rearrange ownership claims and thereby change management incentives, were frequently employed during the 1980s to squeeze excess cash out of mature industries (such as tobacco, tires, chemicals, oil, food processing, forest products, retailing, and broadcasting) that had to consolidate and shrink to remain economically viable.

> A leveraged cashout (LCO) is a leveraged recapitalization in which management and employee stock plans receive new shares rather than cash for their existing shares.

An LCO is a leveraged recapitalization in which management and employee stock plans receive new shares of roughly equivalent value rather than cash for the old shares they own.[15] The resulting concentration of ownership in management's hands ties managerial rewards more closely to performance. Hence, LCOs strengthen management's incentive to operate efficiently and curtail unproductive reinvestment of free cash flow. The combination of the carrot and the stick has often led to remarkable shareholder gains from LCOs.

> With a leveraged buyout (LBO), a small group of investors—typically including management—buys the firm and takes it private using mostly borrowed funds.

A leveraged buyout carries this premise to its logical conclusion. In an LBO, a small group of investors—typically including management—buys the firm and takes it private, using mostly borrowed funds secured by the firm's assets to finance the transaction. What usually follows is an extraordinary transformation, marked by a single-minded focus on producing cash to reduce debt.

---

[14]Quoted in Frederick Rose, "Oil's Maverick: Atlantic Richfield Co. Is Winning the West by Breaking the Mold," *Wall Street Journal,* August 7, 1991, p. A6.
[15]For a good discussion of LCOs, see Kleiman (1988).

LBOs have taken three principal steps to boost their cash flow and thereby avoid insolvency: (1) Divest underperforming assets, such as businesses that don't fit their basic strategy and expensive real estate and corporate jets that are nice perks but unnecessary; (2) streamline operations by paring staff, slashing overhead, and reducing working capital items such as inventories and accounts receivable; and (3) improve investment performance by curtailing capital expenditures in low-return businesses and avoiding large, overpriced acquisitions.

Why don't executives employ these lean-and-mean tactics under public ownership? Probably because managers in public companies don't have the same stake in slimming down that their private company peers have. Although the top executives who run a newly private company typically hold no more than 20 percent of its stock, the stake may comprise an overwhelming share of their personal assets. Thus, what they save by cutting wasteful spending winds up in their pockets. Anecdotal evidence suggests also that owner–managers, from the top down, are far less tolerant of missed budgets or commitments. Peer-group pressure is a powerful force that makes everyone perform better and more effectively. It is reinforced by the fact that the outside investors who put up most of the equity capital are very active on the board of directors. Managers who don't shape up are often summarily fired. The active monitoring by interested investors, owing to the concentration of ownership, reduces the separation of ownership and control, further reducing agency costs. Hence, LBOs strengthen management's incentive to operate efficiently and improve investment decisions.

> **LBOs create powerful incentives for managers to operate more efficiently.**

Of course, leverage has its own costs. As we saw earlier, as leverage goes up, the agency costs of debt also rise as well as the costs of financial distress. Managers of a highly leveraged firm have to persuade suppliers to continue to sell on credit; suppliers may wonder (justifiably) whether the company will be able to pay its bills. Customers can also get the jitters. They tend to worry about continuity and quality of service. Employees are also concerned that companies will cut staff and sell or close facilities in order to pay back the large amount of debt they are now saddled with. The optimal debt-to-equity ratio is the point at which the marginal costs of debt just offset the marginal benefits. At this point the value of the firm is maximized.

Performance of Leveraged Buyouts.   The single undeniable fact is that LBOs create large gains for their stockholders. Public shareholders receive an average premium for their shares that ranges from 40 percent to 56 percent. Post-buyout investors appear to do even better. In a study of 25 buyouts from 1980–1986 that went public again or were otherwise sold (which occurred on average 2.7 years after the original LBO), Steven Kaplan found that the median market-adjusted return on buyout equity is 785 percent, or 125 percent annually.[16]

Despite the extraordinary stock price gains associated with LBOs, there are basic disagreements among economists about their overall costs and benefits. Proponents of LBOs claim that these gains arise because of dramatic increases in a

---

[16]Steven N. Kaplan, "The Effects of Management Buyouts on Operating Performance and Value," *Journal of Financial Economics,* 24 (1989), 581–618.

firm's productivity and profitability. Critics note, however, that rising stock prices benefit only stockholders directly and may come at the expense of other stakeholders such as employees and bondholders. Moreover, they fear that the collateral damage from high financial leverage—the increased risk of financial distress and a focus on the short-term that leads to a loss of long-term competitiveness—will more than offset any real efficiency gains.

The empirical evidence indicates that LBOs improve a firm's operating performance.

A number of researchers have responded to this controversy by trying to document the economic consequences of LBOs. Their basic conclusion is that LBOs have achieved dramatic post-buyout improvements in productivity, investment policy, sales, and operating performance:

1. LBOs achieve dramatic gains in operating efficiency and asset management in the years immediately following a buyout, and they do this without massive layoffs or big cuts in spending on research and development and maintenance.[17] Overall, the evidence suggests that the firm's new owners have acted like proprietors, not bureaucrats or quick-buck artists.

2. Pre-buyout bondholders suffer losses at the buyout, but these losses are small on average and account for a very small fraction of the gains to shareholders. In addition, convertible bondholders and preferred stockholders receive statistically significant gains.

3. The increased interest and depreciation tax shields associated with LBOs account for a significant fraction of the wealth gains from these transactions. However, the full tax effect of leveraged buyout activity is not only much more complex than a simple increase in the amount of deductible interest in the system would suggest but also appears to generate net additional tax revenues for the U.S. Treasury.[18] Tax revenue gains stem from four main sources: (1) capital gains paid by pre-buyout shareholders; (2) capital gains taxes paid by post-buyout shareholders; (3) taxes on increases in operating earnings generated by the buyouts; and (4) taxes on interest income received by LBO lenders.

4. Although LBOs have much greater financial risk, the associated changes in corporate strategy and structure appear to dramatically reduce their operating risk. The net result is that the total risk of the company goes down after it is taken private, and LBO investors bear much less risk than comparably leveraged investments in public companies.[19]

---

[17]These studies include Steven Kaplan, "The Effects of Management Buyouts on Operating Performance and Value," *Journal of Financial Economics,* 24 (1989), 217–254; Chris Muscarella and Michael R. Vetsuypens, "Efficiency and Organizational Structure: A Study of Reverse LBO's," *Journal of Finance,* 45 (1990), 1389–1413; and Abbie J. Smith, "Corporate Ownership Structure and Performance," *Journal of Financial Economics,* 27 (1990), 143–164.

[18]See Michael C. Jensen, Steven N. Kaplan, and Laura Stiglin, "Effects of LBOs on Tax Revenues of the U.S. Treasury," *Tax Notes,* 727–733.

[19]See Steven N. Kaplan and Jeremy C. Stein, "How Risky Is the Debt in Highly Leveraged Transactions?" *Journal of Financial Economics,* 27 (1990), 215–245.

Early versus Later Leveraged Buyouts.   Despite the impressive performance by LBOs described by most studies to date, the final verdict on LBOs is not yet in. For one thing, these studies have examined performance changes only over a relatively short period following the buyouts. More recent studies indicate that there may have been a change in the nature of LBO activity over time. In particular, LBOs in the late 1980s seem to have done much worse than the earlier ones. Many of them have experienced financial distress, and LBO activity declined sharply after 1989. These problems are partly attributable to the 1990–1991 recession. However, new evidence suggests that more recent LBOs differ from earlier ones in important ways. If so, then later LBOs may not follow the same pattern of improved post-LBO performance.

The performance improvement for LBOs occurring in the early 1980s appears to be greater than for those deals done in the latter part of the 1980s.

William Long and David Ravenscraft find that performance improvement was much more visible for LBOs occurring in the four years prior to 1985, than for LBOs occurring from 1985 to 1987.[20] At the same time, however, the premiums paid for taking companies private escalated dramatically, boosting debt service requirements. Moreover, in a study of 124 large management buyouts between 1980 and 1988, Kaplan and Jeremy Stein find that LBO deals grew shakier as the decade went on, especially between 1986 and 1988.[21] Taken together, the new data seem to indicate that many LBOs in the latter part of the 1980s should not have been done, because the buyout premiums and the resulting debt were not justified either by the existing cash flow or by potential post-buyout improvements in cash flow.

A convincing explanation for the failure of many later LBOs is that too much LBO money chasing too few good deals, combined with conflicts of interest between managers of LBO funds and investors, drove up prices and led to unsound deals. The mind-numbing returns earned by investors in the early deals enabled managers of LBO partnerships to raise a large amount of additional risk capital. At the same time, the growing tendency of LBO partnerships to take more of their compensation in front-end fees rather than in back-end profits earned through increased equity values increased the incentive to do deals rather than wait for good deals. The search for LBO candidates eventually swept up highly cyclical and vulnerable businesses such as airlines and defense contractors. At the same time, the competition to do deals enabled managements to get their equity stake, if not for free, then by simply rolling over their old stock options. This meant that the downside risk to management of doing an uneconomic deal was reduced. The failure of both management and the LBO dealmakers to put significant equity into the later deals increased the probability that many of these deals would be overpriced and, hence, overleveraged. In the early deals, in contrast, managers had to put significant amounts of their own money at risk, and they profited only when they made fundamental improvements in their businesses.

[20]William F. Long and David J. Ravenscraft, "The Aftermath of LBOs," unpublished manuscript, April 1991.

[21]Steven N. Kaplan and Jeremy C. Stein, "The Evolution of Buyout Pricing and Financial Structure," NBER Working Paper 3695, May 1991.

Characteristics of Successful LBO and LCO Candidates.   Clearly, not all companies are suited for LBOs or LCOs. According to Jensen's free cash flow theory, the best candidates for LBOs and LCOs have similar characteristics: (1) substantial and predictable amounts of free cash flow that can be used to service debt; (2) low-growth prospects in the core business, leading to low future capital expenditure requirements; (3) a strong market position in mundane product lines that are unlikely to become obsolete; (4) excess, and typically underperforming, assets that can be sold to retire debt; (5) a "clean" balance sheet with little debt; and (6) an experienced management team with a proven track record.

14.5   OTHER FACTORS INFLUENCING FINANCIAL STRUCTURES

Once the firm has completed the cash flow analysis and determined its capacity to bear fixed charges, it can turn its attention to several other factors that could have a significant, though nonquantifiable, effect on its capital structure decision. This emphasizes the point made in the introduction to this chapter that there is no set of quantitative or other techniques that can "solve" the capital structure problem. Rather, a series of factors—many of them qualitative and any one of which may be predominant at any point in time—acts in concert to determine the firm's actual and preferred capital structure.

Financial Flexibility and Corporate Strategy

Although a cash flow analysis might indicate that a firm is able to handle additional fixed charges without significantly increasing its probability of bankruptcy, this does not necessarily mean that more debt is optimal. Such a conclusion will be warranted only if the future were fairly certain and the scenarios considered in the analysis represent the true range of adverse possibilities. If this is not the case, it is the better part of wisdom to maintain some degree of **financial flexibility** to allow for error. Adverse economic events could severely damage a highly leveraged firm's competitive position and its stock of organizational assets.

> The need to preserve financial flexibility should limit the use of debt.

Moreover, the more highly leveraged the firm is, the more subject it will be to restrictive debt covenants that further constrain management's choice of operating, financial, and investment policies and reduce its capacity to respond to changes in the business environment. The reduction in operating and financial flexibility will prove especially costly to firms competing in continually changing product and factor markets. These include firms whose markets are undergoing deregulation, high-technology firms, and firms facing competitors scattered around the world. By contrast, firms operating in stable markets can afford more debt because their competitive stance will be less compromised by the restrictions and delays associated with high financial leverage.

> Financial flexibility is most valuable to firms with large amounts of organizational assets or firms that operate in unstable markets.

In recognition of these costs, many companies—especially those with large amounts of organizational capital or that operate in unstable markets—maintain substantial financial resources in the form of unused debt capacity, large quantities of liquid assets, excess lines of credit, and access to a broad range of fund sources. This financial flexibility helps preserve operating flexibility. A firm that has financial reserves for contingencies can respond to an adverse turn of events based on long-term considerations. A firm with a high debt-to-equity ratio, minimal liquid assets, and few other financial resources might have to alter its commercial strategy to meet adverse circumstances—with a detrimental effect on its future competitive position.

Firms with significant financial reserves are less likely to be seen as easy prey by their competitors.

The ability to marshal substantial financial resources also signals to competitors that the firm will not be an easy target. Consider the alternative, a firm that is highly leveraged, with no excess lines of credit, or cash reserves. A competitor can move into the firm's market and gain market share with less fear of retaliation. In order to retaliate—by cutting price, say, or by increasing advertising expenditures—the firm would need more money. Because it has no spare cash and can't issue additional debt at a reasonable price, it will have to go to the equity market. But we saw in Chapter 13 that firms issuing new equity are suspect because of the asymmetric information relationship between investors and management (is the firm selling equity now because it knows the stock is overpriced?). The credibility problem is particularly acute when the firm is trying to fend off a competitive attack. Thus, a firm that lacks financial reserves faces a Hobson's choice: Acquiesce in the competitive attack or raise funds on unattractive terms.

Similarly, when opportunity knocks, a firm with substantial financial resources will be better positioned to take advantage of it than a firm with few financial resources that faces tightly drawn debt covenants. Thus, firms with valuable growth options should also place a high priority on financial flexibility. To summarize, the opportunity cost of being highly leveraged can be considerable.

The desire for financing flexibility requires firms to perform a balancing act, which can be viewed in the context of the pecking-order framework suggested by Stewart Myers.[22] Consider the three major financing sources in Myers's pecking order: internal funds, issuing debt, and issuing equity. Assuming that information and transaction costs make it more expensive to use financing sources at the top of the pecking order (equity), a firm that needs to raise funds faces an intertemporal tradeoff. If sources low on the pecking order (internal funds and debt) are used in this period, current financing costs will appear to be low, but the firm will face the hidden opportunity cost of being pushed up the pecking order (by being forced to issue more expensive equity in the future). On the other hand, if new equity is issued in this period and the funds are held as cash, current costs will be high, but by moving down the pecking order (to internal funds and debt), the firm will have a cheaper source of funds in the future. For this reason, firms that have substantial organizational assets and growth options should be predominantly equity financed and hold relatively large cash balances.

The tradeoff from the standpoint of investors is that companies with substantial financial resources are more insulated from the discipline exerted by the financial marketplace. In well-run firms—and those with valuable organizational assets or growth options typically are—this isn't a problem. But for many com-

---

[22]See Myers (1984).

panies, particularly those with sizable amounts of free cash flow, the advantages of financial flexibility may be more than offset by the greater opportunity to indulge their spendthrift habits.

The Value of Financial Reserves

Financial reserves cannot save a failing company or protect it against permanent business setbacks.

Although financial reserves can prove beneficial, there are limits to these benefits. First, financial reserves cannot save a failing business; they can only tide a company over temporary adversity. Second, even in the case of temporary adversity, financial reserves are beneficial only to the extent that the firm cannot or will not issue new equity to restore its solvency. Corporate debt is reversible; a company in financial distress can rearrange its capital structure by issuing new stock to retire debt. Thus, as long as the business is basically healthy and the firm has access to the equity market on fair terms, a big debt load need not be a crippling burden.

The real danger for companies with a heavy debt load is that the market may undervalue their stock when they are forced to issue new equity. If a company could always issue new equity at a fair price, it would only need to hold minimal financial reserves. A *fair* price, it must be stressed, refers to a price that fully reflects the company's long-run prospects without placing undue emphasis on its short-term financial difficulties; it does not mean a *high* price. Financial reserves cannot protect a company against permanent business setbacks, nor can they prevent an inevitable bankruptcy due to a change in the business environment.

If markets were always efficient, undervaluation would not be a problem. But the problem of information asymmetry may lead the equity market to unduly discount a company's stock. Having financial slack in the form of reserve borrowing capacity allows the firm to finance its investments without being forced to sell common stock at a discount to a less-informed market. Thus, those companies most prone to a credibility gap in their dealings with the financial markets are the ones that should maintain the largest financial reserves.

The need for financial reserves is most valuable to firms that may have limited access to the financial markets.

The following company characteristics should affect the size of financial reserves:[23]

1. Credibility is less likely to be a problem for large, closely followed New York Stock Exchange companies than for smaller, younger companies that are unlisted. Hence, well-established firms can take fuller advantage of their available debt capacity.

2. Privately held companies that cannot raise equity financing quickly should use less debt in their capital structure, other things being equal. For these companies, the time-consuming nature of the equity-raising process—consider the protracted negotiations between existing and prospective shareholders as well as the creditors—can prove an expensive proposition, especially if noninvestor stakeholders are focusing on corporate staying power.

---

[23]These corporate characteristics are suggested in Amar Bhide, "Why Not Leverage Your Company to the Hilt?" *Harvard Business Review,* May–June 1988, 92–98.

3. Small companies with stock that is thinly traded are more susceptible to a credibility problem and, hence, should maintain more financial reserves.

4. Companies that the market has difficulty valuing are most prone to the credibility problem. These companies should, therefore, maintain more financial reserves. Here are some clues that the market may be having trouble valuing a company: There are large swings in the stock price in the absence of major changes in the business environment; the stock price fell much more than management believes was justified the last time the company faced business difficulties; and stock analysts have difficulty grasping the company's investment needs. The last-named situation may arise if the company cannot give outsiders the necessary information to analyze its investments properly, because to do so would jeopardize the company's competitive position.

5. The market is also likely to have difficulty valuing firms such as Genentech and eBay with substantial amounts of growth options. Unlike companies whose value depends primarily on familiar, straightforward projects, the value of a growth company depends on expectations about future profits from novel market niches (e.g., Federal Express at its inception) or yet-to-be-developed products whose potential applications have not been fully defined (e.g., Genentech and Microsoft). The lack of an objective basis for assessing the profitability of these companies ten years from now may make their stock prices more prone to extreme swings. The danger for a heavily leveraged growth company is that it might be forced to come to the equity market at a time when its stock is overly discounted. Again, competitive pressures may preclude the company's sharing inside information with investors.

The Financing Pecking Order and History

Thus far, we have discussed capital structure as if it were the end product of a series of conscious tradeoffs among tax factors, the desire for financial flexibility, agency costs, and the costs of financial distress. By contrast, the financing pecking-order story, which describes management's preference for internal versus external finance and debt versus external equity, suggests that observed corporate debt ratios at any one time may instead reflect the firm's cumulative requirements for external finance. Highly profitable firms will tend to use lots of internal equity—in the form of retained earnings—and have low debt ratios, whereas less profitable firms will tend to have high debt ratios.

Management's preference for internal finance stems from its desire to be insulated from the capital markets. Shareholders benefit from this state of affairs—because it reduces transaction costs and the problems associated with information asymmetry—as long as management performs as expected. At the same time, however, management's preferences are limited by the capital markets and their business strategies. We saw that the oil companies, which began with virtually no debt, are now awash in debt. Similarly, fast-growing companies that must raise external funds, while simultaneously trying to assure customers and other stakeholders of their staying power, tend to raise equity capital. It is only highly profitable companies, with few requirements for external finance, that seem to be able to stray far from what appears to be an optimal capital structure. Yet even these companies will be subject sooner or later to the discipline of the financial marketplace if they stray too far from a policy of shareholder wealth maximization.

SUMMARY

We began this chapter by examining the effects of financial leverage—the substitution of fixed-charge financing, primarily debt, for equity—on expected earnings per share and the riskiness of those earnings. To summarize our findings, financial leverage increases the expected level of earnings per share, but at the same time it increases the riskiness of those earnings.

We then investigated the consequences of capital structure for stock prices and the value of the firm. We found that the issue of capital structure is one of the most studied and debated in all of finance. It boils down to whether firms can increase their market value by repackaging their cash flows into different combinations of debt and equity securities. Traditionalists argue in the affirmative. Their position is that judicious use of debt financing can indeed increase the market value of the firm. In their seminal contribution to the logic of financial decision making, Modigliani and Miller showed that, in a world without taxes and other market imperfections, the value of the firm is independent of its capital structure.

Once taxes are taken into account, the picture becomes cloudy. In the presence of corporate taxes, the interest tax shield creates a substantial advantage to debt financing. However, most well-run firms have very low debt ratios, suggesting that there must be potential costs to debt financing that sooner or later come to outweigh its tax advantages. For example, using debt instead of equity financing may foreclose the option of using additional debt financing at a later date. Alternatively, equity financing leaves a firm in a more flexible financial position for later years. Thus, any decision should be part of a long-term financial plan that recognizes the probable requirement for a sequence of capital issues.

When borrowing reaches a point that financial distress becomes a real possibility, the self-interest of management and the shareholders will probably restrain the firm from adding more debt to the capital structure. Even if this proves not to be the case, the firm will find it difficult to lever itself to such a dangerous degree. When the leverage ratio increases to the point that there is a real danger of insolvency, banks will simply refuse further loan requests, and investment bankers will strongly suggest that the firm issue equity for its next round of financing.

There are other reasons that the firm might not want to push its debt ratio to the limit of its debt capacity. Prudence usually dictates that the firm maintain some reserve borrowing power in the event that a sudden need for funds arises when the time is not propitious for a new equity offering. The capital structure selected on the basis of these considerations is usually referred to as the target capital structure.

The target capital structure is a function of the agency costs associated with debt, the costs of financial distress, and taxes. We saw in this chapter that the costs of financial distress rise with the firm's organizational assets. These intangible assets are primarily in the form of a reputation for quality and service and skill at coordinating and communicating with corporate stakeholders. The distinguishing characteristic of these intangible assets is that they are inseparable from the firm as an ongoing operation. Thus, their value in liquidation is zero. Firms with substantial amounts of organizational capital will protect these assets by adopting a low-risk profile, as reflected in a low debt ratio.

Perhaps the best way to summarize these observations is to note that without agency costs, any opportunities to create value by modifying capital structure are likely to be arbitraged away. This suggests that in a well-run firm, in which agency costs are minimal, financial policy must emphasize supporting the commercial strategy of the firm, where shareholder wealth is created.

For many companies, however, the separation of ownership and control and the conflicts between bondholders and stockholders may influence the optimal amounts of debt and equity. As outside investors hold a larger fraction of equity, conflicts between owners and managers increase. Similarly, bondholder–stockholder conflicts rise with the degree of leverage. On the other hand, added leverage may mitigate some of the owner–manager conflicts by reducing management's discretion over the reinvestment of free cash flow. In the extreme cases of leveraged buyouts and leveraged cashouts, managerial incentives seem to be aligned in a way that enhances the firm's productive efficiency.

These are the complex factors that determine capital structure in practice. Putting them all together to come up with the "optimal" debt-to-equity ratio is beyond our current powers. The best we can do is to be aware of these considerations and try to balance them as well as possible in a particular set of circumstances.

QUESTIONS

1. Comment on the following statements:
   a. Because both bondholders and stockholders demand higher rates of return on more highly leveraged firms, a company that uses less financial leverage can reduce both its cost of debt and its cost of equity. Therefore, reducing a company's debt ratio is an easy way to boost its value.
   b. If IBM borrows an extra $500 million, it won't significantly affect IBM's probability of financial distress or bankruptcy. Hence, such borrowing won't increase the rate of return demanded by IBM's shareholders.
2. A financial manager has made some calculations and discovered that expected earnings per share will increase by 40 percent if the firm shifts from 100 percent equity to a one-to-one debt-equity ratio. Does this mean the manager should endorse a large increase in the firm's leverage? Explain.
3. Suppose a new U.S. tax law permits companies to expense capital investments in the first year in lieu of depreciating these assets. What effect will this change in the tax law likely have on the optimal debt ratio for the U.S. economy as a whole? For the optimal capital structure of individual U.S. companies? Explain.
4. Operating cash flow (cash revenue minus cash expenses) and EBIT do not include payments to bondholders. They represent the profitability of the firm's underlying line of business. Though we might therefore think of operating cash flows and EBIT as *independent* of capital structure, why may this be incorrect for a highly leveraged firm?
5. What types of costs owing to potential financial distress or agency problems might the following firms face if they take on a large amount of debt?
   a. a small biotechnology firm developing a patented cancer cure.
   b. a large Madison Avenue advertising agency.
   c. an automobile manufacturer.
   d. a bank, mutual fund, or investment company.

6. Although Kwalitee Home Products, a TV marketing firm, is experiencing difficulties, its managers have found a new product, basement astro turf for home gyms, that they feel has a positive present value of $50,000. Management would like to raise the $35,000 in additional capital for the project by issuing new shares to its current shareholders. An added benefit of the project, management feels, is that half of the project's present value will be reflected in a higher market price for the firm's bonds, because the new project will represent additional security. Will the shareholders be willing to contribute additional capital to finance this new project?
7. Two corporations have approached a bank to obtain debt financing for a business expansion. One firm is a real estate corporation that purchases and operates apartment complexes, and the other consists of a new chain of Cajun and sushi restaurants.
   a. To which firm will the bank be more reluctant to lend? Explain.
   b. Suppose the bank can request a firm to reorganize itself from a limited liability corporation into a personal proprietorship, with the partners personally liable for their company's debts. How might this affect the bank's lending decision?
8. In explaining his company's debt policy, the chief financial officer of Tandem Computers said, "We were a young company competing with the likes of IBM. Not taking on debt was a marketing decision because we might not get customers if we seemed financially shaky."
   a. What concerns might its customers have if Tandem had a high debt ratio?
   b. As Tandem matures, should it take on more debt? What factors might influence this decision?
9. Comment on the following statements.
   a. "The less a company needs to raise capital to finance expansion, the more money it should

borrow. Instead, it is those companies that need to raise new capital that should shun debt, preferring equity."

b. "A good reason to borrow money is to repay it!"

c. "The current wave of restructurings has much to do with the increasing sophistication of capital markets worldwide, and not the alleged lack of it."

d. "The high degree of leverage in LBOs has two consequences, both highly speculative. First, it bets the company on a combination of continued growth and lower interest rates, with no margin for error. Second, it substitutes debt for permanent capital, which is exactly the opposite of what our national investment objectives should be."

10. Chicago-based FMC Corp. evolved out of the old Food Machinery & Chemical Corp. and still makes food-processing equipment, but that is now a relatively small part of its total business. Industrial and agricultural chemicals are a major source of revenues and profits. It is also a big defense contractor, with contracts to produce armored troop carriers, rocket launchers, and other military equipment. In the spring of 1986, FMC Corp. decided to distribute a good deal of its capital to shareholders by means of a leveraged cashout. The CEO explained the LCO as follows:

> Basically we had fairly good market positions in most of the markets we are in. Most of them were not growing very rapidly. All of them with a few exceptions were generating more cash than we could internally use. We made a very aggressive effort to look for acquisitions as a way of intelligently using shareholder money and weren't very successful. We looked at a lot of them and the market was such that the greater fools would outbid us. We could have used our money that way. We could have closed some of those deals but I—and I think my associates—felt it was not in the shareholders' best interest to overpay. So therefore we bought very few. We had a few small acquisitions that have done very well, but we couldn't use the bulk of the cash we were generating. So I was casting around for some way of using this money effectively.

At the time of the LCO, FMC's shares were selling for about $70. As part of the recapitalization, public shareholders received $80 and a new share of stock valued at $17 for each old share. The cash could be treated as a capital gain for tax purposes. Management and FMC's employee thrift program, however, received in lieu of cash an equivalent amount of new stock. The upshot was a sharp rise in management and employee ownership, which now stands at 40 percent compared with 18 percent before the LCO. To finance the recapitalization, FMC borrowed an additional $2 billion (on top of $300 million of already existing debt) and took net worth down from $1 billion to −$500 million. The LCO increased FMC's total market value by $750 million, an increase in value that is net of $60 million in costs incurred and fees paid to professional advisors.

a. The CEO says the FMC board decided to do the recapitalization because the company was in mature industries but generating a lot of cash. What do you think motivated management to engage in the LCO?

b. To what would you attribute this remarkable appreciation in value? Consider the likely effects of the LCO on taxes, investment policy, and management and employee motivation.

c. What conflict of interest was avoided by the LCO that could not have been avoided by a management-led LBO?

d. Using a source such as *Value Line*, examine what happened to the beta of FMC stock following its LCO. Explain.

e. Gather financial data on FMC to see how it has performed since the LCO. What has happened to FMC's use of working capital, operating margins, return on equity, sales growth, and share price?

11. Not long ago, the Boston Consulting Group popularized the notion that the ideal corporation consisted of a portfolio of projects at various stages of development. According to this planning paradigm, the company's mature "cash cows" were supposed to fund the growth of promising businesses ("question marks") and highly performing "stars." Eventually, when the "cows" and "stars" became "dogs," they would be harvested, and the cash would be used to feed more "question marks" and "stars."

a. Explain how the BCG planning paradigm might be consistent with the implications of the information asymmetry hypothesis.

b. What might explain the appeal to corporate management of BCG's planning paradigm?

c. Despite its strong appeal to corporate management, BCG's planning paradigm has not stood the test of time. What was its fatal flaw?

12. According to Linda Wachner, the CEO of Warnaco, a maker of men's and women's apparel that underwent a leveraged buyout in 1986, "In a public company, everybody's looking at earnings per share. But in a private company, a leveraged buyout like ours, you're driven by cash. You've got to get your people to think about cash."

a. What might explain the difference in focus between a public corporation and an LBO?

b. What are some ways in which you could get managers to focus on cash flow instead of earnings? Can you use the same techniques in a public company?

13. According to one businessman, "The best news anyone can get is that his competition is in the process of undergoing a leveraged buyout." Do you agree with this statement? Explain.

14. Drexel Burnham Lambert, once the leading junk bond dealer, held huge positions (typically over $1 billion) in illiquid, highly risky securities.

a. What would be an appropriate capital structure for a company such as Drexel?

b. In fact, Drexel financed over $700 million of this portfolio with short-term loans that had to be refinanced over every six months or so. What problems might Drexel encounter with such a capital structure?

15. Concurrent Computer makes superminicomputers—ultra-fast machines that crunch loads of data from different sources. Concurrent's promising product line includes machines that tote up bets for horse racetracks and state lotteries, and run space shuttle flight simulators. With about $200 million in sales, its machines are used by the National Security Agency, Lockheed, Boeing, Toyota, and Wall Street firms. It specialized in proprietary, rather than open, systems—meaning that customers were locked into Concurrent hardware and software. But times were changing, and customers wanted equipment that would work on open systems. So in 1988, Concurrent—with $222 million in sales and earnings of about $10 million—decided to acquire MassComp, a real-time computer maker known for its Unix-based open systems technology with sales of $76 million and earnings of about $3 million. The agreed-upon price was $240 million,

a. Would you finance this deal with debt or equity? Explain.

b. What problems can you foresee if the acquisition were to be financed with debt?

PROBLEMS

1. These questions relate to the example of Hi-Tech in the chapter. ✄

a. Calculate earnings per share and return on equity for Hi-Tech if it uses 25 percent leverage. If it uses 75 percent leverage.

b. Recalculate Exhibit 14-1 for Hi-Tech, assuming its capital structure now contains 50 percent common stock, 25 percent debt ($1.25 million at 10 percent), and $1.25 million of $1.25 cumulative preferred at $10 a share. Does the issuance of preferred stock change EPS and return on equity?

2. A firm with $400,000 of debt in its capital structure and a corporate tax rate of 40 percent is currently worth $960,000. Calculate the value of the firm if it were financed with no debt or with 99 percent debt. Assume Modigliani–Miller with taxes holds. ✄

3. General Broadcasting Services is planning to finance its $30.5 million satellite project with either debt or preferred stock. The current yield on debt comparable to GBS is 12.5 percent, and the current preferred yield is 14.5 percent. GBS's tax rate is 35 percent. ✄

a. What would the annual interest expense be if GBS financed the project with debt? What would the annual preferred dividends be if GBS used preferred stock only?

b. What level of EBIT must GBS earn to meet its interest payments? To meet its preferred dividend payments?

4. A small retailer is considering the advantages of adding debt to the business' capital structure. Currently, $400,000 of assets have been financed entirely with 20,000 shares of common stock. The retailer is considering repurchase of 50 percent of the equity using proceeds from a bond issue that will require payment of 10 percent coupon interest. EBIT is projected to be $88,000 for next year, and the applicable corporate income tax rate is 40 percent.

   a. Calculate earnings per share under the current all-equity financing and under the bond issue alternative.

   b. Calculate EPS given an 80 percent repurchase. Should the retailer be encouraged to take on a higher debt-equity ratio?

5. American Presidential is currently financing its $250 million in assets with 10 million shares of common stock. American is thinking of replacing its all-equity capital structure with a new capital structure containing 10% preferred stock, 40% debt, and 50% equity. The preferred stock bears a 6% dividend rate and debt pays a coupon of 9%. Projected EBIT is $40 million and the corporate tax rate is 34%. ✎

   a. Calculate earnings per share under the current all-equity capital structure and under the alternative financing plan.

   b. At what EBIT will American be indifferent between the two capital structure alternatives?

6. MicroTech anticipates $12.5 million in earnings before interest and taxes. Currently it is all-equity financed. It is considering a plan to recapitalize the company by issuing $15 million in perpetual debt (the principal is never repaid) at 9% interest and using the proceeds of the debt issue to repurchase stock.

   a. With a corporate tax rate of 40%, what is the annual income to all security holders if MicroTech remains all-equity financed? If it is recapitalized? Ignore personal taxes.

   b. Assuming Modigliani–Miller holds with taxes, what is the present value of the interest tax shield for MicroTech?

   c. Suppose that the risk-free rate is 6.1% and the all-equity beta is 0.80. If the market risk premium is 8%, what is MicroTech's all-equity cost of capital?

   d. Based on your answer to part c, what is the market value of MicroTech as an all-equity financed company?

   e. What is the market value of MicroTech (both debt and equity) under its recapitalization plan?

   f. If MicroTech has one million shares outstanding before the recapitalization, what is the price per share as an all-equity financed company?

   g. If MicroTech buys back its shares at the prevailing price as an all-equity company, how many shares will it have following the leveraged recapitalization? What will be the price per share after the recapitalization?

   h. Calculate earnings per share under the current all-equity capital structure and under the leveraged recapitalization plan.

   i. At what EBIT will MicroTech be indifferent between the two capital structure alternatives?

   j. What is MicroTech's weighted average cost of capital following its leveraged recapitalization? (*Hint.* The weighted average cost of capital is the rate at which after-tax EBIT is capitalized.) What is MicroTech's cost of equity capital following the leveraged recap? (*Hint.* The cost of equity capital is the rate at which equity earnings are capitalized.)

7. Here are book and market values for Walker Co.:

Book		Market	
Assets $100	Debt $30	Assets $140	Debt $30
	Equity 70		Equity 110

   The interest rate on this debt is 9 percent, the corporate tax rate is 40 percent, there is no growth, and the $30 of debt is expected to be permanent.

   a. Suppose that Modigliani and Miller's theory holds with taxes. What will be the effect on shareholder wealth if Walker issues $25 of new debt at an interest rate of 11 percent and uses the proceeds to buy back some of its shares?

   b. Following issuance of the new debt, Congress passes a new law that eliminates the tax deductibility of interest payments. What will be the new value of Walker's equity if the law takes effect immediately? At the end of three years? Assume all else stays the same.

8. Excel Corporation is all-equity financed. It distributes all its earnings to shareholders as dividends each period. These earnings are expected to remain constant at $1,000 per period forever. ✎

   a. If Excel's cost of equity capital, k_e, is 10 percent, what will be its market value? If there are 1,000 shares of stock outstanding, what will be the market price per share?

b. Now suppose that Excel borrows $3,000 at 5 percent and uses the proceeds to repurchase some of its stock. What does this leveraged recapitalization do to the firm's debt-to-equity ratio? Suppose k_e rises to 11 percent. (Why is it likely that k_e will increase?) What is the new price per share? The new market value of Excel? The firm's new cost of capital?

c. Excel decides to alter its capital structure further. It issues $6,000 of new debt and uses the proceeds to repurchase the $3,000 of old 5 percent bonds at par and to buy up an additional $3,000 of its stock. However, the interest rate on the new debt is 6 percent (why are creditors likely to require a higher interest rate?), and the cost of equity capital rises to 14 percent. What is the market value of Excel's remaining equity? Excel's new market value? Excel's new cost of capital?

9. Reliance Filters has projected earnings per share for the coming year of $3.20. Investors foresee that Reliance will have a dividend payout rate of about 60 percent in the future, while its ROE on both current and future investments is expected to remain at 15.4 percent.

a. Suppose the current risk-free interest rate is 8 percent, the market risk premium is 5 percent, and the corporate tax rate is 35 percent. If Reliance's asset β is 0.6 and its debt/equity ratio is 1.2, what is its cost of equity capital? Assume Reliance's debt β is zero.

b. What is your best estimate of Reliance's current market-to-book ratio? Explain why this ratio is more or less than 1.

c. Suppose Reliance issues $400 million in debt, carrying an interest rate of 9.5 percent and uses the money to buy back stock. If Modigliani and Miller's theory holds with taxes, how will this leveraged recapitalization affect shareholder wealth? That is, by how much will shareholder value change with the leveraged recap?

10. A firm has outstanding long-term debt with a market value of $8 million and a required yield of 9.5 percent. The corporate income tax rate is 35 percent.

a. Calculate the value of the tax benefit of debt. Assume there are no personal taxes.

b. Now suppose investors are taxed on the income they receive from stocks and bonds. If the tax

rate on bond income is twice the rate on stock income, at what personal tax rate on interest income will the advantage to debt financing vanish? Suppose the maximum personal tax rate on interest income is 28 percent. Redo your calculation assuming a maximum personal tax rate of 40%. What do your calculations imply about the optimal debt ratio, ignoring all considerations other than taxes?

11. Lev Redge owns 1 percent of the total shares outstanding of Deter, Inc., and has a required rate of return on the stock of 8.5 percent. Deter's operating earnings are expected to remain at $750,000 a year. Currently, Deter pays 6 percent interest on its $3 million debt. This is also the rate on personal loans and risk-free debt in general. Ignore taxes and assume Lev's stock entitles him to a 1 percent share of the net income paid as a dividend.

a. What is the dollar value of Lev's shares?

b. What is the total value of Deter, Inc.?

c. Lev sees that there is a firm, Eckwity, that resembles Deter in all respects except that it has no debt. If Lev's required rate of return for Eckwity is also 8.5 percent, what will be Eckwity's value?

d. What should Lev do?

12. Whirlpool has projected earnings per share for the coming year of $2.85. These earnings are expected to grow at a rate of about 9.8 percent annually. Whirlpool's dividend payout rate is around 40 percent. 🐦

a. Suppose the current risk-free interest rate is 9 percent, the market risk premium is 4 percent, and the corporate tax rate is 34%. If Whirlpool's asset β is .69 and its debt/equity ratio is 1, what is the company's cost of equity capital? Assume Whirlpool's debt β is zero.

b. What is your best estimate of Whirlpool's current stock price?

c. Suppose Whirlpool issues $500 million in debt, carrying an interest rate of 9.5 percent and uses the money to buy back stock. If Modigliani and Miller's theory holds with taxes, what will be the impact of this leveraged recapitalization on shareholder wealth? If Whirlpool currently has 70 million shares outstanding, what will be the new price per share?

13. A firm consists of one share owned by the manager and debt maturing in one year with a face value of $100,000. After paying off this year's bond interest and liquidating the firm's assets,

$95,000 in cash remains. The manager must decide which of two projects to place the $95,000 in. Project A will return $102,000 with certainty. Project B will return $110,000 with a 60 percent chance and 0 with a 40 percent chance.

a. Which project will the manager select? What sort of problem does his choice illustrate?

b. Suppose the $100,000 bond is convertible into 54 shares of stock. How does this change your answer to (a)? What can you conclude about the function of convertible debt in a firm's capital structure?

14. Sunray Corp. is considering a leveraged recapitalization that would involve issuing $12 million in bonds and using the proceeds to repurchase an equivalent amount of common stock. The bonds can be issued at an interest rate of 8 percent. Currently, Sunray is an all-equity-financed firm with an expected annual EBIT of $10 million and one million shares outstanding. It faces a 40 percent corporate tax rate and a cost of equity capital of 14 percent. ✖

a. Suppose that the costs associated with leverage (e.g., agency costs and costs of financial distress) are zero. Compute for Sunray, following the recapitalization, (i) the value of the firm, (ii) the price per share of equity, (iii) the number of shares repurchased, and (iv) the after-tax required return on equity.

b. Now suppose that the expected costs associated with $12 million in leverage have a present value of $2 million. What is the required return on equity following the recapitalization?

15. Indigent Inc. makes proprietary equipment that requires extensive software investments on the part of owners to use properly. Although the book values of its debt and equity are $40 million and $20 million, respectively, it has the following market value balance sheet:

Indigent Inc. Balance Sheet (market values)			
Working capital	$11,000,000	$23,000,000	Bonds
Fixed assets	15,000,000	3,000,000	Equity
Total assets	$26,000,000	$26,000,000	Total liabilities plus equity

How do the following transactions affect the various investors and stakeholders of the company?

a. Indigent decides to pay a $3 million dividend to its shareholders.

b. Indigent decides that it is worth more dead than alive so it shuts down its operations and converts its working capital and fixed assets into $24 million dollars in cash. It invests the cash in junk bonds.

c. Indigent finds an investment opportunity with an NPV of +$100,000. However, given its current financial situation, pursuing this investment would require its shareholders to finance the entire investment of $10 million.

d. As part of an urban renewal project, Indigent has found a way to get the state government to finance the new investment described in part c with a $10 million bond issue guaranteed by the state. These bonds have the same seniority as the old bonds.

REFERENCES

Barnea, Amir, Robert A. Haugen, and Lemma W. Senbet. *Agency Problems and Financial Contracting.* Englewood Cliffs, NJ: Prentice-Hall, 1985.

Cornell, Bradford, and Alan C. Shapiro. "Corporate Stakeholders and Corporate Finance." *Financial Management,* April 1987, 5–14.

Cornell, Bradford, and Alan C. Shapiro. "Financing Corporate Growth." *Journal of Applied Corporate Finance,* Summer 1988, 6–22.

DeAngelo, Harry, and Ronald H. Masulis. "Optimal Capital Structure under Corporate and Personal Taxation." *Journal of Financial Economics,* March 1980, 3–29.

Donaldson, Gordon. *Corporate Debt Capacity.* Boston: Division of Research, Harvard Business School, 1961.

Donaldson, Gordon. *Strategy for Financial Mobility.* Homewood, IL: Irwin, 1971.

Jensen, Michael C. "Agency Costs of Free Cash Flow, Corporate Finance, and Takeovers." *American Economic Review,* May 1986, 323–329.

Jensen, Michael C., and William H. Meckling. "Theory of the Firm: Managerial Behavior, Agency Costs and Ownership Structure." *Journal of Financial Economics,* October 1976, 305–360.

Kensinger, John W., and John D. Martin "The Quiet Restructuring." *Journal of Applied Corporate Finance*, Spring 1988, 16–25.

Kleiman, Robert T. "The Shareholder Gains from Leveraged Cash-Outs: Some Preliminary Evidence." *Journal of Applied Corporate Finance,* Spring 1988, 46–53.

Masulis, Ronald H. "The Impact of Capital Structure Change on Firm Value." *Journal of Finance,* March 1983, 107–126.

Miller, Merton H. "Debt and Taxes." *Journal of Finance,* May 1977, 261–276.

Modigliani, Franco, and Merton H. Miller. "The Cost of Capital, Corporation Finance and the Theory of Investment." *American Economic Review,* June 1958, 261–297.

Modigliani, Franco, and Merton H. Miller. "Taxes and the Cost of Capital: A Correction." *American Economic Review,* June 1963, 433–443.

Myers, Stewart C. "Determinants of Corporate Borrowing." *Journal of Financial Economics,* November 1977, 138–147.

Myers, Stewart C. "The Capital Structure Puzzle." *Journal of Finance,* July 1984, 575–592.

Ross, Stephen A. "The Determination of Financial Structure: The Incentive-Signalling Approach." *Bell Journal of Economics,* Spring 1977, 23–40.

Shapiro, Alan C., and Sheridan Titman. "An Integrated Approach to Corporate Risk Management." *Midland Corporate Finance Journal,* Summer 1985, 41–56.

Stewart, G. Bennett, III, and David Glassman. "The Methods and Motives of Corporate Restructuring." *Journal of Applied Corporate Finance,* Spring 1988, 85–99.

Titman, Sheridan. "The Effect of Capital Structure on a Firm's Liquidation Decision." *Journal of Financial Economics,* vol. 13, 1984, 137–183.

Dividend Policy

If you took all the economists in the world and laid them end to end, they still wouldn't reach a conclusion.
George Bernard Shaw

What should the corporation do about dividend policy? We don't know.
Fischer Black

KEY TERMS

"bird-in-the-hand"
  argument
declaration date
dividend payout ratio
ex-dividend date
greenmail

holder-of-record date
insolvency rule
legal list
M&M dividend
  irrelevance proposition
payment date

residual dividend policy
share repurchase
stock dividend
stock split
tender offer

CHAPTER LEARNING OBJECTIVES

Upon completion of this chapter, students should be able to:

- Explain the procedures for cash dividends and discuss the legal and Internal Revenue Service constraints on dividend payments.
- Describe the differences and similarities between stock dividends and stock splits.
- Discuss the rationale for share repurchases.

- Explain why dividend policy is irrelevant in perfect capital markets.
- Explain how taxes and agency costs may make dividend policy relevant.
- List the factors that a firm should consider when setting its dividend policy.

Dividend policy is the division of profits between payments to shareholders and reinvestment in the firm. As such, it is an important component of the firm's long-run financing strategy. Earnings retained in the firm can fund additional investments or retire debt. Alternatively, a firm that pays higher dividends has less internally generated cash available for investment purposes. Here, and in the remainder of the chapter, we shall treat accounting earnings and cash flows as being synonymous, even though this is often not the case. This assumption is to aid exposition.

Assuming that a firm's investment decisions are independent of its dividend policy and that investment opportunities exceed operating cash flow, then paying out more dividends means that the firm must raise more external capital—debt, common stock, or preferred stock. Thus, a firm's choice of dividend policy, *holding its capital budget constant,* is really a choice of financing strategy. The firm can pay higher dividends and rely more heavily on external funds to finance its growth, or it can cut back on dividends and fund more of its growth with retained earnings.

The dividend decision will be more than just a choice of financing strategy, however, if the company's investment decision is influenced by the amount of dividends paid out. For example, if management insists on maintaining or raising the firm's dividends at the same time that outside funds are more costly than internal funds, the capital budget may have to be cut.

One thing is clear: The dividend decision is not just a by-product of the capital budgeting decision, with companies paying out in dividends only those internally generated funds that exceed its investment requirements. Otherwise, in 1997, American corporations would not have paid dividends in excess of $275 billion, at the same time that they raised over $178 billion in new common stock to fund more than $770 billion in capital expenditures. Yet practitioners and academics still disagree on the answers to two key questions regarding dividend policy. The first and more basic one is: Why do firms pay dividends? Although this is a seemingly curious question, as firms pay out an average of 45 to 55 percent of their earnings as dividends, it still is raised because none of the answers is fully satisfactory. Resolving the first question would help answer the second question, which is more important from the standpoint of financial management: Does dividend policy matter? That is, can dividend policy affect the value of a company? And, if so, how? But despite the considerable amount of intellectual effort that has been given to this second issue, it, too, remains unresolved.

This chapter deals with both issues and tries to summarize the current theories and available evidence. It discusses some of the institutional features of paying dividends and presents alternative dividend policies along with the empirical evidence of corporate practice. Most of the chapter, however, is devoted to the controversy over the effects of dividend policy.

15.1   INSTITUTIONAL FEATURES OF DIVIDEND PAYMENTS

Dividend payments must be declared by the company's board of directors. Most companies pay dividends on a quarterly basis. For example, Eastman Kodak paid quarterly dividends per share of $.44 in 1998 for an annual dividend of $1.76.

As we will see in the following pages, dividends are normally set at a level that management believes to be sustainable, even during years with below-average earnings. In making this judgment, management takes into account projected future earnings, anticipated investment opportunities, and the proportion of those opportunities that will be financed by internal funds. Kodak management, therefore, is conveying its belief to shareholders that the firm's profits will be sufficient over the foreseeable future to maintain an annual dividend of $1.76 per share while also providing enough retained earnings to satisfy its internal financing requirements.

Payment Procedures

The following payment procedure, summarized in Exhibit 15-1, is standard for most firms:

1. *Declaration date.* As the name suggests, the **declaration date** is the date that the payment of a dividend is declared by the board of directors. For example, on April 30, 1998, Kodak declared its regular quarterly dividend of $.44 per share, payable on July 1 to holders of record on June 1.
2. *Holder-of-record date.* The dividend will be paid to all those shareholders registered on the company's books on the **holder-of-record date** as owners of specific shares of stock. So, for example, if Kodak is notified before June 1 of the sale and transfer of ownership of some stock, the new owner will receive the dividend; otherwise, the old owner will receive it.
3. *Ex-dividend date.* The major stock exchanges require several days to process stock transactions. For this reason, the brokerage houses have established a convention that the right to the dividend remains with the stock until four

EXHIBIT 15-1
Chronology of Kodak's Dividend Payment Procedure

Thursday, April 30 Declaration date	Monday, May 26 Ex-dividend date	Monday June 1 Holder-of-record date	Friday, July 1 Payment date

1. *Declaration date:* Kodak's board of directors declares a quarterly dividend of $.44 on April 30, 1998.
2. *Record date:* The dividend is paid to shareholders of record on June 1, 1998.
3. *Ex-dividend date:* The dividend is attached to the stock until the ex-dividend date May 26, 1998 (four business days before the holder-of-record date), after which date it stays with the seller.
4. *Payment date:* On July 1, Kodak mails dividend checks to its shareholders.

business days prior to the holder-of-record date; on the fourth day before the record date, the dividend goes to the old owner. In the case of Kodak, the **ex-dividend date** is May 26 because June 1 is a Friday. Therefore, in order to receive the $.44 dividend, a new investor must purchase the stock before May 26. On May 26, the stock is said to sell *ex-dividend.*

The price of the stock will reflect the fact that it has gone ex-dividend. All else being equal, we would expect to see the stock drop by the amount of the dividend on the ex-dividend date, because buyers are no longer entitled to the dividend. For example, on May 26, Kodak stock dropped by $.25 a share.

4. *Payment date.* Once a dividend has been declared, it becomes a current liability of the corporation. With 327.4 million Kodak common shares outstanding, the accounting entries would be a $144 million credit (increase) in current liabilities and a $144 million debit (decrease) in retained earnings. On July 1, Kodak's **payment date,** the firm mails out the dividend checks. When this happens, the current liability is eliminated, and cash declines by $144 million.

Legal Constraints on Paying Dividends

A firm's ability to pay dividends is often restricted by legal constraints.

A firm's ability to pay dividends is often restricted by various legal constraints. Long-term debt contracts and preferred stock agreements contain covenants that limit the maximum amount of common stock dividends a firm can pay. Sometimes they prohibit the payment of any dividends at all until earnings or net asset values reach a specified level. For example, General Motors may not pay dividends on its common or preferred stock so long as current assets in excess of current liabilities are less than $75 per share of preferred stock. Such covenants are designed to protect the bondholders and preferred stockholders from excessive withdrawals by the common stockholders.

Creditors are also protected from stockholder abuse by state laws that regulate the amount of dividends a firm can pay. Most states have a *net profits rule* that prohibits dividend payments in excess of retained earnings. This rule is designed to preserve the firm's original capital contribution as a cushion for its creditors. Otherwise, management could sell the firm's assets and pay a huge liquidating dividend to its shareholders, leaving its creditors with an empty shell. The *capital impairment rule* is designed to achieve a similar aim. It prevents firms from paying dividends out of capital. The definition of capital varies by state; in some states it includes only the par value of common stock, whereas in others it also includes the contributed capital in excess of par value (capital surplus).[1] A third restriction, known as the **insolvency rule,** prevents an insolvent firm from paying dividends. This rule ensures that the firm's assets are set aside to meet its creditors' claims.

---

[1]The firm can pay liquidating dividends out of capital, but only if these dividends are clearly identified as such and are permitted by its debt covenants.

Penalty Taxes on Retained Earnings

Companies are also constrained from paying out too few dividends. The current taxation of dividends may strongly tempt stockholders, especially those of closely held firms, to retain most or all corporate earnings and, thereby, take their returns in the form of tax-deferred capital gains. A firm that does this, however, may run afoul of Sections 531–537 of the IRS Code, which will assess a penalty tax (the *accumulated earnings tax*) on an "unreasonable" accumulation of retained earnings for the purpose of avoiding income taxes on dividends.

What is unreasonable? Every corporation is allowed accumulated earnings of $250,000. Additional retained earnings can be justified if they were accumulated for reasonable business needs. Although the burden of proof is on the IRS to substantiate its allegation, the accumulated earnings tax discourages blatant tax avoidance by the owners of closely held companies.

Dividend Policies in Practice

Under a residual approach to dividend policy, only earnings in excess of those required to finance the equity portion of new investments are paid out in dividends.

Given a company's investment and capital structure policies, dividends can be treated as a pure residual: Any earnings in excess of those required to finance the equity portion of new investments are paid out as dividends. If investment requirements exceed the firm's earnings, no dividends will be paid, and new shares will be issued to meet the shortfall. This is the **residual dividend policy,** which companies can implement in three different ways.

Under the *pure* version of the residual dividend policy, dividends will fluctuate from year to year as the company's earnings and investment opportunities change. This policy can produce highly volatile dividends, especially if earnings and capital spending follow opposite paths. In general, though, rapidly growing companies with many investment opportunities would pay small or no dividends, whereas mature companies with few attractive investment prospects would tend to pay large dividends. Although the empirical evidence largely agrees with this implication of the pure residual dividend policy, it does not conform in one important respect: Rather than varying dividends from period to period, most companies try to maintain a relatively stable dollar dividend per share.

U.S. firms tend to increase dividends gradually over time in response to earnings changes.

In particular, most U.S. corporations tend to adjust their dividends gradually in response to changed earnings.[2] Firms set a specific dollar dividend and will increase it only if management believes that future earnings will be high enough to justify the higher dividends.

Similarly, dividend decreases are infrequent and occur only when the firm's earnings prospects are such that the current level of dividends is not sustainable. The reluctance to cut dividends is so great that even during the Great Depression, over half the firms listed on the New York Stock Exchange paid cash dividends, resulting in dividend payments that exceeded total corporate earnings.

---

[2]The classic study of dividend payment practices by U.S. companies is Lintner (1956). His results were later corroborated by Fama and Babiak (1968).

Under a smoothed residual policy, dividend payments are set equal to the *long-run* residual between *forecasted* earnings and investment needs.

This behavior is consistent with the *smoothed* version of the residual dividend policy: Dividends are set equal to the *long-run* residual between forecasted earnings and investment requirements. Dividend changes, in turn, are made only when this long-run residual is expected to change; earnings fluctuations believed to be temporary are ignored in setting dividend payments. The clear preference is for a stable, but increasing, dividend per share.

There are two basic consequences of such a dividend policy: (1) Dividend changes tend to lag behind earnings changes on both the upside and the downside, and (2) after-tax earnings are much more volatile than dividends. These effects are documented in Exhibit 15-2, which shows the general tendency of U.S. corporations to pay stable, but increasing, dividends over time.

A corollary of this policy is that in years when a company's earnings are unexpectedly good, the percentage of earnings paid out in dividends—the **dividend payout ratio**—will drop; conversely, the dividend payout rate will rise if earnings fall sharply. The result, as shown in Exhibit 15-3, is that the dividend payout rate may fluctuate dramatically over time.

Dividend payouts vary across national boundaries.

A similar pattern of time-varying payouts exists for foreign companies. The payout rate varies by country, with Britain showing the highest and Germany the lowest payout rate. Japanese firms pay, on average, only 40 percent of their after-tax profits as dividends, but this figure is currently rising. During the 1980s, soaring stock prices handed investors huge capital gains, reducing the demand for

EXHIBIT 15-2
Dividends versus Corporate Profits

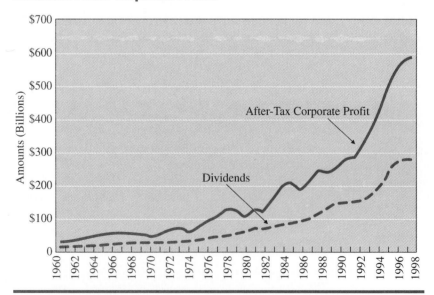

Source: Department of Commerce, Bureau of Economic Analysis.

EXHIBIT 15-3
Dividend Payout Ratio for U.S. Corporations

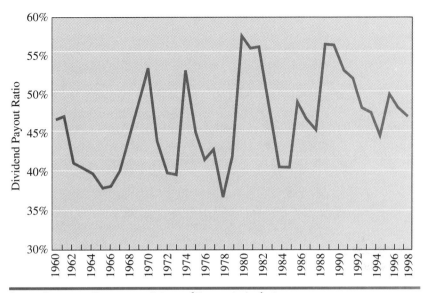

Source: Commerce Department, Bureau of Economic Analysis.

dividends. In 1990, however, these capital gains went into reverse, causing investors to demand higher dividends. This is especially the case in Japanese companies, which have overinvested in their businesses and destroyed shareholder value in the process. A striking feature of dividend policy is the growing divergence among the payout ratios of the countries shown. In 1992, Britain's payout ratio was 74 percent; the U.S. ratio was 56 percent; Japan's, 40 percent; and Germany's, 35 percent. In the mid-1970s, the ratios were closer, with all between 40 percent and 55 percent.

> **Smoothing dividends reduces the need to raise additional equity capital.**

In addition to providing some certainty to investors, a policy of smoothing dividend payments over time also reduces the chances—relative to those of companies with a pure residual dividend policy—that the firm will have to go to the external equity market. Under the latter policy, the firm will issue new equity whenever earnings fall below the desired level of equity investment.

A third version of the residual dividend policy features a constant dividend payout rate. A firm following this policy would set the payout rate so that over the long run, dividends equal the residual between earnings and investments. Under this policy, dividends will be as variable as earnings, which helps explain why it is almost never used. Instead, in line with the smoothed residual dividend policy, payout rates tend to increase when profits drop and to decrease when profits rise. Over time, however, the aggregate payout rate for American corporations has held fairly steady at about 40 to 50 percent of earnings.

Stock Dividends and Stock Splits

With a stock dividend, additional shares are distributed to common stockholders; a stock split is a proportionate increase in the number of common shares.

In addition to or in lieu of paying cash dividends, companies may pay stock dividends or split their stock. A **stock dividend** is the payment of additional shares of stock to common stockholders. So, for example, when Horizon Bank declared a 15 percent stock dividend in March 1993, it meant that for every 100 shares owned, a stockholder on the record date (May 4) would receive an additional 15 shares. A **stock split** is a proportionate increase in the number of common shares. On February 19, 1992, for example, Walt Disney split its stock four for one. On that date the stockholders received three additional shares for each one held on the record date (April 20). Although there is no real financial difference between stock dividends and stock splits—stockholders simply receive more paper—both the typical motives behind them and their accounting treatment differ.

The technical distinction between the two is that a stock dividend appears as a transfer of retained earnings to the capital stock account, whereas a stock split is shown as a reduction in the par value of each share. The New York Stock Exchange classifies any distribution of stock totaling 25 percent or more of outstanding stock as a stock split; if it is less than 25 percent, the NYSE classifies the distribution as a stock dividend.

Reasons for Stock Dividends and Splits.   The usual motive for a stock dividend is to conserve cash while maintaining a record of paying dividends. Stock dividends and stock splits are also used to keep the price of the stock within a popular trading range—say $20 to $60 per share. This is done by diluting the cash flow per share. For example, suppose a stock is selling for $140. By declaring a four-for-one stock split, the firm will create four shares of stock for each one currently existing. Because the cash flow for each preexisting share is now divided four ways, the price of each new share should be one-fourth its presplit value, or $35.

Despite the lack of supporting empirical evidence, many executives believe that by holding down the price of their stock they can broaden its appeal to small investors and, thereby, increase its value. A typical statement is that of Disney's Chairman and CEO Michael Eisner: "The price of our shares has recently moved higher after having been well above the $100 figure for most of the past three years. By taking this action, our board hopes to make Disney shares accessible to a broader segment of the investing public."[3]

Although stock prices often respond favorably to the announcement of a stock split, this appears to be an information effect rather than the result of a broader appeal. For example, Disney's stock jumped by $3.50 (2.4 percent) on the announcement of the split. According to one analyst, "It's a psychological boost and an indication that management has confidence in their performance and that the stock price can be sustained. These are all signals that things will be continuing on a positive path for the next few quarters, especially with prospects

---

[3]This quote appeared in David J. Jefferson, "Disney Splits Its Stock 4 for 1 and Shares Soar," *Wall Street Journal*, February 19, 1992, A4.

for a pickup in attendance at the theme parks."[4] Stock splits are usually used by firms, like Disney, whose shares have experienced recent run-ups in price. A stock split may be taken as confirmation that the firm's earning power and, hence, its dividend-paying capacity has indeed risen. (In the year following its stock split, Disney raised its quarterly dividend twice—a total of 42 percent altogether—and its stock price rose by over 26 percent.) A study by Eugene Fama, Lawrence Fisher, Michael Jensen, and Richard Roll found that price increases on stocks that split were transitory unless the cash dividend was subsequently raised.[5]

> Stock dividends and stock splits cannot increase shareholder wealth; only good investment decisions increase shareholder wealth.

In sum, despite their popularity, stock dividends and stock splits cannot increase shareholder wealth. Shareholder wealth is created by smart investment decisions, not by a lot of paper shuffling. The only beneficiaries of noncash dividends are the financial printing houses supplying the additional shares and the brokers because commission charges rise in the wake of a stock split. That is, most brokerage houses structure their commission schedules so that firms with low share prices will have relatively high commissions. An investor who buys 100 shares of Walt Disney at its presplit price of $146 would pay roughly $85 in commissions. After the stock splits four for one, however, the same dollar amount of Walt Disney stock—that is, 400 shares at $36.50 apiece—will cost about $190 in commissions.

Stock Repurchases

> For U.S. firms, stock repurchases are becoming an increasingly popular alternative to paying cash dividends.

An increasingly popular alternative to paying cash dividends is for a firm to distribute funds to its shareholders by repurchasing its own stock. As shown in Exhibit 15-4, U.S. companies returned $181 billion to their shareholders in 1997 in contrast to $251 billion in cash dividends. Not only are share buybacks increasing in size, they are also increasing as a percent of dividends, with many companies now returning almost as much cash to their shareholders through buybacks as dividends. Overall, during the twelve-year period 1986 through 1997, U.S. companies announced programs to buy back shares valued at almost $300 billion. The jump in 1987 buybacks is largely attributable to the October market crash. Following Black Monday, over 700 companies announced buybacks totaling $45 billion. These buybacks had a dual purpose: Executives wanted to indicate their confidence in the company, but they also viewed their stocks as undervalued. The list of repurchasers includes many large and well-known firms: Exxon, IBM, General Motors, Philip Morris, ITT, Boeing, Coca-Cola, Merck, and Tandy. Typically, the purchased stock is kept as treasury stock to be reissued at a later date. Shareholder approval is not required to resell treasury stock.

> Stock repurchases can be effected through tender offers, open market purchases, or private transactions.

Methods of Share Repurchase.   There are three principal methods of stock repurchases: (1) Under a **tender offer** the company announces that it will buy a stated number of shares at a price that is above the current market price. If the offer is oversubscribed, the company can buy all the shares offered or prorate its

---

[4]Quoted in "Disney Splits Its Stock 4 for 1."
[5]Fama, Fisher, Jensen, and Roll (1969).

EXHIBIT 15-4
Share Repurchases by U.S. Companies (billion $)

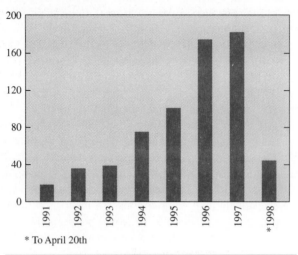

* To April 20th

Source: Securities Data Company.

purchases. (2) The firm can acquire treasury stock in the same way that an ordinary investor can, by an *open market purchase*. This is the method used in approximately two thirds of share repurchases. (3) In a *private transaction* the firm buys a block of stock directly from a major shareholder. This type of buyback has been linked in recent years with the controversial practice of **greenmail.** Greenmail—named after blackmail—is the repurchase of stock from an unwanted suitor at a higher-than-market price.

Reasons for Share Repurchases.   In theory it should make no difference whether a company returns cash to its shareholders through share buybacks or higher dividends. In practice, however, we saw that a company that raises its dividend generally feels compelled to maintain it at the new higher level or risk signaling investors that its future earnings prospects are dimmer than expected. A share repurchase imposes no such commitment. Returning shareholder funds via share repurchases instead of cash dividends provides a major tax advantage as well: Dividends are taxed as ordinary income at rates up to 39.6%, whereas investors who sell shares back to the firm are taxed at a maximum capital gains rate of 20% on their profits (if they owned the shares for at least a year). In effect, share repurchases convert investors' returns from ordinary income into less heavily taxed capital gains. Moreover, investors can avoid paying capital gains tax by retaining their appreciated shares; the capital gains tax is deferred until they sell their shares and actually realize the gains.

Executives with large stock options may also favor share repurchases to boost the value of their options. For example, suppose a company worth $100 with ten shares outstanding has $20 to distribute. If it pays a $2 dividend per share, its shares will fall to $8 afterwards. On the other hand, if it uses the $20 to buy back two shares, the remaining shares will be worth $10, or even more because shares tend to rise on the announcement of a buyback. Since stock options are not adjusted to reflect dividends, executives with options would clearly prefer to repurchase stock in lieu of paying dividends.

Restrictions on Share Repurchases.   The major drawback to substituting a regular program of share repurchase for the payment of dividends is that the IRS might regard such repurchases as an attempt to avoid paying taxes on the dividends. Indeed, if the IRS can establish that this is the case, it can assess penalty taxes on the firm. In addition, the IRS can treat the repurchases as ordinary dividends for tax purposes and tax the returns accordingly. But this is more of a hypothetical possibility for large publicly traded companies; despite the huge share buybacks in recent years, none seems to have triggered an IRS investigation.

15.2   THE DIVIDEND CONTROVERSY

The crucial question about dividend policy is whether it matters. As George Bernard Shaw noted in the opening quotation to this chapter, economists tend to disagree with one another. The issue of dividend policy relevancy is no exception to this rule. Some financial economists argue that dividend policy is irrelevant, others believe that all earnings should be paid in dividends, and a third group argues that no dividends should be paid. To examine this issue, we first study dividend policy in a perfect capital market.

Dividend Irrelevance in a Perfect Capital Market

In perfect capital markets, dividend policy is irrelevant in that it cannot affect shareholder value.

As we saw in Chapter 14, a perfect capital market is characterized by no taxes, no transaction or flotation costs, and no information costs. This is the highly abstract and simplified world described by Merton Miller and Franco Modigliani in another seminal article, this one on dividend policy.[6] In their world, dividend policy is irrelevant in the sense that it cannot affect shareholder wealth. To briefly summarize their argument, now known as the **M&M dividend irrelevance proposition,** the effect of any particular dividend policy can be offset without cost by managers adjusting the firm's sale of new shares and by investors adjusting their dividend streams through stock purchases or sales. In addition, the absence of taxes makes shareholders indifferent as to whether they receive their returns in the form of dividends or in the form of capital gains.

The assumption that a firm's investment policy is independent of dividend policy is crucial to the dividend irrelevance proposition.

Crucial to Miller and Modigliani's proof is the assumption that investment policy is *independent* of dividend policy; that is, the dividend irrelevance proposition will hold only if investment decisions are not influenced by the payment of dividends. Under these circumstances the firm's investment policy is all that matters, because this is what determines its earning power or stream of future cash flows. The value of the firm, in turn, equals the present value of these future cash

---

[6]See Miller and Modigliani (1961).

flows. How these cash flows are split between dividends and retained earnings is irrelevant. This can best be seen by isolating the effects of dividend policy from the firm's investment and capital structure decisions.

To begin, we assume that the firm is following a pure residual dividend policy: Any earnings not required for investment purposes are paid out as dividends. External equity financing is used whenever equity investment requirements exceed retained earnings.

Now suppose management decides to increase the dividend, while holding constant the firm's investment policy and the quantity of debt in its capital structure. Without changing the amount of money the firm is investing or borrowing, the only way to finance the higher dividend is to sell additional stock. Thus, each dollar in dividends requires that the firm issue one dollar in new shares. Assuming that the shares are fairly priced, the present value of the dividends paid to investors for each dollar of new shares they buy must equal exactly one dollar.

The bottom line is this: For each dollar they receive in current dividends, stockholders must sacrifice future dividends with a present value of one dollar, thus reducing share values by one dollar. Therefore, under the assumptions of a perfect capital market and the absence of interactions between investment and financing decisions, each additional dollar of dividends paid results in a one-dollar capital loss to old shareholders. As long as capital gains and dividends are untaxed or at least not subject to different tax treatment, dividend payments cannot create or destroy value.

By paying dividends and issuing additional stock to replace the cash spent, the old shareholders are indirectly converting into cash part of their claim on the firm. They can also do this directly by selling some of their shares to new investors. But whether the old stockholders "cash out" by receiving dividends or by selling some shares, their wealth—the sum of their cash plus the value of their remaining claim on the firm—remains constant.

This equivalence means that shareholders should be indifferent as to whether they convert their holdings into cash by having management pay higher dividends or by selling off some of their stock. Paying dividends dilutes share value because more shares must be issued, whereas selling stock reduces the number of shares owned by the old shareholders. In either case, the transfer of value from old to new shareholders is identical.

The example of MicroGeneral, Inc., illustrates the irrelevance of dividend policy in a perfect capital market. The balance sheet for MicroGeneral, expressed in market values, is shown in the following table:

Balance Sheet for MicroGeneral (market values)

Cash	$ 2,000	Debt	$ 4,000
Fixed assets	5,000		
Growth opportunities*	3,000	Equity (100 shares)	6,000
Total assets	$10,000	Value of firm	$10,000

*The value of future opportunities to invest in positive net present value projects.

MicroGeneral needs the $2,000 in cash to invest in its growth opportunities. At the moment, each share is worth $60, which is the market value of equity divided by the number of shares outstanding ($6,000/100). Suppose now that management decides to pay a dividend of $10 per share or $1,000 in total. Total assets drop to $9,000, giving the firm a new net worth (total assets minus debt) of $5,000. The new price per share is $50 ($5,000/100), a decline of $10.

Holding capital structure constant (no new debt can be sold) and assuming that MicroGeneral still intends to invest in its growth opportunities, the company must raise $1,000 in new equity to replace the dividend it paid. Because new shares must sell for the same price as old shares or $50, MicroGeneral must issue 20 more shares. MicroGeneral's new balance sheet will be identical to the old one except that the equity account, which still has a market value of $6,000, will now list 120 shares. Because MicroGeneral's old shareholders have sold off $1,000 of their equity position for $1,000 in cash, the value of their shares is now $5,000. Add in their dividend of $1,000 and we see that the wealth of the old shareholders remains unchanged at $6,000. This is shown in Exhibit 15-5.

Given their assumptions, Miller and Modigliani's arguments are compelling. However, the idea that dividend policy is irrelevant seems at odds with the empirical evidence. Many studies indicate that increases in dividends are viewed as good news by the market, whereas firms that cut or eliminate dividends suffer price declines.[7] If dividends are irrelevant, why would we see this reaction?

EXHIBIT 15-5
The Irrelevance of Dividend Policy

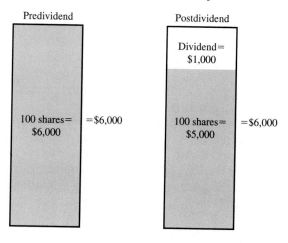

---

[7]For a small sampling of this literature, see Aharony and Swary (1980); Eades, Hess, and Kim (1985); Healey and Palepu (1988); and Michaely, Thaler, and Womack (1995).

Signaling via Dividends

The reaction of a firm's stock to the announcements of dividend increases or cuts can be explained in terms of the information content of dividends.

MM would argue that investors aren't responding to the dividends per se but to their information content. Much of the "hard" data available to investors is accounting based. At best accounting information tells us where a company is and how it got there. What investors are really interested in, however, is where the company is headed. To the extent that the company pursues a typical stable dividend policy, with dividends adjusted only when the firm's earnings prospects have altered fundamentally, then changing dividends will alert investors to these changed prospects. A dividend increase, for example, will signal investors that management is optimistic about future earnings and generally results in a higher stock price. However, it is the message—higher future earnings—that investors are reacting to and not the means of communication—the dividend.

Dividend policy can signal the firm's future prospects in ways that cannot otherwise be creditably communicated.

The idea that dividends have information content and can be used to signal the firm's future prospects is an important one. Signaling via dividends may prove costly to management, however, and so will make sense only if two conditions are fulfilled: (1) Investors value this information, and (2) dividends convey information about the firm's prospects that cannot be credibly communicated by some other means (e.g., annual reports, earnings forecasts, or presentations to security analysts).

The first issue is easy to address. To the extent that management, through dividend policy or some other means, helps ensure that the market draws correct inferences about the firm's profit potential, the stock is more likely to be correctly priced. This reduces investor uncertainty and may increase the stock's value.

With regard to the second point, dividend payments can provide information not convincingly conveyed by other means because they are backed by cold cash.[8] As the saying goes, "Talk is cheap." Thus, because paying dividends not backed by earnings is costly—as it requires the firm to raise external funds or otherwise reduces management's future financing flexibility—the announcement of a dividend increase may command greater credibility; it also implies greater management commitment and a higher degree of irreversibility than do other pronouncements. An increase in the dividend, therefore, signals a firm's optimism and usually leads to a rise in the stock price. Conversely, because of the historical reluctance to cut the dividend, the announcement of a dividend cut tells investors that management believes the firm's future earnings potential has dropped whether or not that is management's intention.

From a signaling standpoint, the most valuable dividend policy is one that provides information not available from other sources. In turn, the most informative dividend policies are likely to be those that most closely mirror the company's longer-term earnings prospects. An erratic dividend policy or one in which dividends rarely change does not provide such information and hence is less likely to compensate for the costs of processing dividend checks and the need to replace the funds distributed to shareholders with potentially more expensive external financing.

---

[8]The dividend-signaling hypothesis is discussed in Bhattacharya (1979) and Miller and Rock (1985).

Illustration

General Motors' Dividend Increase

On February 6, 1989, General Motors split its common stock for the first time in 34 years and raised its annual regular dividend 20 percent to $6.00 from $5.00 on a presplit basis. The moves were major planks in GM's campaign to convince investors that its turnaround effort was taking hold. Chairman Roger Smith said, "This sends a message to our stockholders that we've got a fundamental improvement in our earnings power."[9] The message was believed on Wall Street, where GM stock jumped almost 5 percent, a gain in market value of over $1.3 billion. As it turned out, this was a false signal, for which General Motors and its management paid dearly. In 1992, GM had to cut its dividend by more than 70 percent and issue over $7 billion in equity at a significant discount to its previous market price.

The issue of whether dividend policy is the most cost-effective means of communicating a firm's prospects to shareholders has not yet been resolved. It is most likely to be valuable when there is a large discrepancy between a firm's reported earnings and its actual cash flow. But the significance of dividend signaling for explaining the prevalence of the smoothed residual dividend policy is not known; the dividend-signaling hypothesis may just be a tribute to the creative minds of financial economists who strain their imaginations for ways to rationalize observed practices.

To the extent that dividends do provide signals, the value of these signals may be fading. Because companies are so anxious to maintain their dividends, these have ceased to be a real sign of optimism. Investors increasingly look beyond the dividend to the free cash flow available to pay the dividend. They are not fooled by a dividend not supported by cash flow. As a result, companies that are paying dividends in excess of their free cash flow tend to have high dividend yields. That is, their stock price adjusts to reflect the market's belief that the dividend is not sustainable. For example, in mid-1990, the dividend yields on the Big Three auto company stocks (GM, Ford, and Chrysler) were averaging about 9.7 percent in comparison to a 3.9 percent yield on the S&P 500 and a 9.1 percent yield on 30-year Treasury bonds. According to one analyst, "The market is telling you that the Big Three are likely to trim their dividends."[10] This belief stemmed from two related causes: (1) Most economists believed that the United States was in a recession (it was), and (2) in virtually every postwar recession, including the slumps

---

[9]*Wall Street Journal,* February 7, 1989, A3.

[10]Roger Lowenstein, "Is the Market Signaling Dividend Cut by Automakers?" *Wall Street Journal,* September 9, 1990, C1.

in the mid-1970s and the early 1980s, automakers cut or eliminated their dividends. As it turned out, every automaker slashed its dividend in 1991.

The signaling value of dividends is also being eroded by the desktop computers, low-cost databases, and powerful spreadsheets that are providing analysts with more reliable information about corporate operations and prospects. For example, in September 1992, Intel, the Silicon Valley company that dominates the PC microprocessor market, announced its first-ever dividend. According to its chairman, "We have sufficient cash flow and faith in the future to make us comfortable that we can afford to fund both a dividend program and a $2 billion per year capital spending and R&D effort."[11] Although this dividend declaration was unexpected and should, therefore, have been a powerful signal to Wall Street about Intel's prospects, its stock rose by just 1.2 percent. The minimal reaction was probably due to the fact that information about Intel, its products, and its market was already widely diffused among analysts.

Whether the signaling hypothesis is valid or not, investors clearly recognize the bad news associated with dividend cuts. In general, the stock market responds negatively to announcements of dividend reductions. The actual market reaction to a dividend change, however, depends on investor expectations. In many cases, the market discounts the change weeks in advance—so when it actually comes, it has little impact. For example, when IBM announced on January 26, 1993, that it was cutting its dividend by 55 percent, its stock price rose slightly, not because investors were happy about the dividend cut but because it had already been widely anticipated. The big drop in IBM's stock price occurred one month earlier, when IBM announced that it was thinking of cutting the dividend. Similarly, when BASF AG, the giant German chemical company, cut its dividend to 10 marks from 12 marks (on March 9, 1993), its stock price jumped 5.25 percent. According to the *Wall Street Journal* (March 10, 1993, A11), "Many European analysts had expected BASF to slash its 1992 dividend to nine marks a share. Because the market had been braced for a gloomier report, BASF shares surged on the news." By extension, an expected dividend increase that doesn't materialize will be taken by investors as a signal that management believes that the firm's future earnings potential is less than the market assumes it is. The result will be a fall in the stock price.

It is also important not to overlook the effects of a dividend cut on noninvestor stakeholders. Because a dividend cut will tend to signal suppliers, distributors, employees, and consumers of impending problems, dividend stability may be especially important to companies that rely on intangible assets, such as customer confidence, to earn high profits. Such companies should be particularly careful to set the dividend at a level that can be maintained. For example, computer manufacturers should set dividends at more conservative levels than electric utilities, which have few intangible assets.

---

[11]Stephen Yoder, "Intel Will Pay Company's First Cash Dividend," *Wall Street Journal,* September 18, 1992, C5.

The "Bird-in-the-Hand" Argument

A perennial argument for the relevance of dividend policy originates from the unscientific but enduring belief on Wall Street that investors want higher dividend payouts. The best expression of this orthodox view of dividends is by Benjamin Graham and David Dodd in their classic book *Security Analysis: Principles and Techniques:*

> The considered and continuous verdict of the stock market is overwhelmingly in favor of liberal dividends as opposed to niggardly ones. The common stock investor must take this judgment into account in the valuation of stock for purchase. It is now becoming a standard practice to evaluate common stock by applying one multiplier to that proportion of the earnings paid out in dividends and a much smaller multiplier to the undistributed balance.[12]

A more sophisticated version of this **"bird-in-the-hand" argument** is that because investors are risk averse, they prefer a stream of relatively certain dividends over the uncertain capital gains that arise from reinvested earnings.[13] Hence, they will discount the expected stream of future dividends at a lower rate (giving it a higher present value) than the stream of expected future capital gains. As a result, one dollar of expected dividends is worth more than one dollar of expected capital gains.

The argument that investors prefer certain dividends over risky capital gains confuses a firm's dividend decision with its investment decision.

This argument, however, confuses the firm's dividend decision with its investment decision. As long as the company's investment and capital structure decisions remain the same, the company's overall cash flows will be the same regardless of its dividend payout policy. Likewise, the risk assumed by the firm's shareholders is determined by the risk inherent in its investment and financing policies. With identical risks and cash flows, the value of the firm will be the same regardless of its dividend policy. Put another way, *given the firm's investment policy,* investors can't be any more certain of future dividends than they are of future earnings. Hence, the riskiness of—and thus the discount rate applied to—future expected dividends and future expected earnings must be the same. Therefore, the validity of M&M's dividend irrelevance proposition does not depend on the absence of risk. Regardless of risk, as long as retained earnings yield at least the required return, investors will feel the same about earnings that are retained in the firm and earnings that are distributed as dividends.

Behavioral Explanations for Dividend Preference

We have just seen that dividends and capital gains should be perfect substitutes for each other if taxes and transaction costs are ignored. However, Hersh Shefrin and Meir Statman argue that because of behavioral reasons, many investors will

---

[12]Benjamin Graham and David L. Dodd, *Security Analysis: Principles and Techniques,* 3rd ed. (New York: McGraw-Hill, 1951); 432.

[13]This argument appeared in Gordon (1959).

prefer dividends over capital gains.[14] Their arguments are based on theories involving self-control and regret aversion.

Shefrin and Statman's first explanation for paying dividends depends on the observation that many individuals lack self-control. To compensate for this lack of willpower, people often turn to rules or programs to constrain their opportunities to yield to temptation. Smoking clinics, diet programs, and alcohol and drug abuse programs all exist to limit the amount of damage done when individuals are weak willed. With regard to financial management, Shefrin and Statman note that an individual who wishes to safeguard long-run wealth against an obsession with immediate gratification might employ a rule that prohibits spending from capital. By financing consumption from dividends instead of capital, such a rule reduces the amount of willpower required by the planner, along with the potential damage resulting from weakness of will. It also leads to a preference for dividends among people who have difficulty practicing self-denial. Although this rule makes no sense in standard financial theory, it also doesn't make sense for a rational person to pay thousands of dollars to join a smoking clinic when he or she wants to quit smoking. It's much cheaper just to stop.

The regret aversion argument can be illustrated by comparing the following two choices:

1. You take $600 received as dividends and use it to buy a TV set.
2. You sell $600 worth of stock and use it to buy a TV set.

Subsequently, the price of the stock increases significantly. Would you feel more regret in case 1 or case 2? Although dividends and receipts from the sale of stock are perfect substitutes in the absence of taxes or transaction costs, there is evidence that for most people, the sale of stock would cause more regret because they can readily imagine not having taken that action. Thus Shefrin and Statman argue that consumption from dividends may be preferable to consumption from capital for people who are averse to regret. This, in turn, adds to the demand for dividend-paying stocks.

15.3   DIVIDEND POLICY AND MARKET IMPERFECTIONS

Miller and Modigliani's proof of dividend irrelevance follows logically from their assumption that capital markets are perfect. In reality, there are taxes on dividends and capital gains, financial frictions in trading and issuing securities, information asymmetry between corporate management and investors, and possible behavioral reasons for investors to prefer some dividends. Do these market imperfections render the dividend irrelevance proposition irrelevant? A number of researchers have argued in the affirmative. We now examine the validity of these arguments.

---

[14]See Shefrin and Statman (1984).

The Tax Case against Dividends

Most academic economists accept that investors in a mythical tax-free world should place equal value on capital gains and dividends. But in the real world, where dividends are taxed at substantially higher rates than capital gains are, it was natural for some academic researchers to speculate that investors might actually be averse to dividends.[15] This would be reflected in a lower price for companies that pay dividends relative to those that retain their earnings. To see why, consider two companies, A and B, that are identical in all respects except for dividend policy: Both companies earn X dollars after interest and taxes. But firm A pays no dividends and provides shareholders with capital gains, whereas firm B pays out all its earnings as dividends.

> Investors may be averse to dividends if these dividends are taxed at a higher rate than capital gains.

Given that capital gains are taxed less heavily than dividend income, investors in company B must receive a higher pre-tax return to achieve the same after-tax return available on stock in company A. How much more depends on the marginal investor's tax rate and when investors expect to realize their capital gains. Consider the following example, which corresponds to current tax rules. Under these rules, dividend income for the highest earning individuals is taxed at a 39.6% rate, whereas capital gains on assets held at least one year are only taxed at a 20% rate. Assume that the highest-bracket shareholders realize their capital gains at the end of each year and are taxed at a rate of 20%. Let DIV be the amount of pre-tax dividends that would be equal after taxes to the after-tax value of $1 in pre-tax capital gains. To solve for DIV, we set the after-tax value of the dividend equal to the after-tax value of the dollar in capital gains:

$$\text{AFTER-TAX DIVIDEND} = \text{VALUE OF CAPITAL GAIN}$$
$$0.604\ \text{DIV} = 0.80\ (\$1)$$
$$\text{DIV} = \$1.32$$

This means that an investor would have to receive $1.32 in dividends to get the same after-tax return as $1 in capital gains provides, because both yield $.80 after taxes ($1.32 × 0.604 and $1.00 × 0.8). In this case, assuming identical earnings for both firms, the market value of firm A's equity would be worth 1.32 times the market value of firm B's equity. This is shown in Exhibit 15-6.

The Case for Tax Neutrality of Dividends

According to the antidividend school, because of the asymmetrical tax treatment of dividends and capital gains, generous dividend payments must lead to a severe reduction in share price. Yet we observe that most American corporations regularly pay out 40 to 50 percent of their earnings as dividends. Can it be that

---

[15]See, for example, Brennan (1970). Controversial evidence that high-dividend-yield stocks may pay a higher before-tax return than low-dividend yield stocks do is provided by Litzenberger and Ramaswamy (1982).

EXHIBIT 15-6
The Effect of Capital Gains on Equity Values
(Capital Gains Taxed at 20 Percent)

	Company	
	A	B
Dividend Payout Rate	0%	100%
Income Available to Stockholders	E	E
Investors' After-Tax Return	0.80E	0.604E
After-Tax Required Return on Equity	r	r
Market Value of the Equity	0.80E/r	0.604E/r

corporate management has overlooked such an obvious opportunity to increase shareholder wealth? Fischer Black and Myron Scholes don't think so.

In another of their seminal articles, Black and Scholes addressed the issue of apparent management myopia by trying to find some justification for paying dividends despite the seemingly adverse tax consequences.[16] Underlying their approach was the basic notion that if corporations pay dividends, it must be because investors derive some benefits from such a policy.

Black and Scholes began by pointing out some of these benefits: Dividends can help investors who need current income to avoid having to sell some shares and incur costly brokerage fees, and they can signal investors about the level of corporate risk, allowing them to hold portfolios more in keeping with their risk preferences.

Then Black and Scholes went one step further, adding a subtle twist to their argument. They reasoned that each investor implicitly trades off the benefits of receiving dividends—primarily in the form of reduced transaction costs from not having to sell shares—against the tax disadvantages. On the basis of these calculations, investors sort themselves out into three different categories or "clienteles": (1) a clientele that prefers dividends, (2) a clientele that is indifferent to dividends, and (3) a clientele that is averse to dividends. Thus, high-dividend payout stocks tend to attract one clientele and low-dividend payout stocks another one.

> Different investor clienteles have different attitudes toward dividends; thus, high-payout stocks tend to attract one clientele and low-payout stocks another.

For example, individual investors in high-tax brackets might prefer capital gains to dividends. Tax-exempt institutions, on the other hand, are likely to feel the same about capital gains and dividends. Corporate investors actually prefer dividend income because they can exclude from their taxable earnings 70 percent of the dividend income they receive from another corporation. Individuals in lower tax brackets who need current income may also prefer dividends to save on transaction costs.

Black and Scholes then presented the crux of their argument, which can be summarized as follows: One dividend clientele is as good as another. The reason, they say, is that competition among companies ensures that the supply of divi-

---

[16]See Black and Scholes (1974).

dends will equal investors' demands for dividends, eliminating any possible gains from changing dividend policy. Although the Black–Scholes argument is a clever one, it seems to beg the question: If academic financial economists—working with the most sophisticated statistical techniques—disagree on the consequences of dividend policy, how are companies to determine whether changing their dividend payout will boost their stock price?

Whether or not the argument presented by Black and Scholes is correct can be determined only by empirical tests, and such tests are notorious for leaving issues unresolved. Although the debate continues, with most economists still believing that there are tax disadvantages to dividends, the research by Black and Scholes has had a major influence on the terms of the debate; they have demonstrated that the tax disadvantages commonly associated with dividends are likely to be less than they were thought at one time to be.

Agency Costs and the Case for Paying Dividends

Flotation costs on new securities and the agency costs of new equity issues can lead to a preference for low dividend payouts.

Flotation costs on new securities and the agency costs attendant on new equity issues—known collectively as financial frictions—lead to a preference for internal financing. Therefore, unless a firm can finance all new investments with retained earnings, higher dividend payouts mean larger external financing requirements and higher costs. These costs are especially high for smaller, riskier, and less established companies. Alternatively, a firm could forgo undertaking new investments rather than raise external funds. These potentially high opportunity costs accompanying a high dividend payout rate are another argument for retaining earnings and restricting dividends.

To summarize, taxes and financial frictions provide reasons for eliminating or at least restricting dividend payouts. What is lacking is a positive reason for paying dividends. We already saw two possible rationales for paying dividends—the information-signaling argument and conserving on transactions costs by investors who would otherwise be continually forced to sell off shares as a dividend substitute. Another rationale is provided by the agency costs that result from the potential conflict of interest between management and outside investors.

Several researchers believe that dividend payments lower agency costs by eliminating some of the asymmetry in information that underlies the shareholder–manager conflict.[17] The gist of the argument is that a higher dividend payout will force management to seek external financing rather than allow it to rely solely on internal financing. Although this process is costly, it provides important information for shareholders because they can observe the terms on which new financing is provided. The implicit assumption is that investment bankers and new lenders are in a better position than are individual shareholders to gather and assess new information concerning the firm's future prospects.

A consistent policy of paying dividends and, thereby, forcing the firm into the capital market on a regular basis can also reduce the problem of shirking and

---

[17]This hypothesis was first presented in Rozeff (1982). See also Easterbrook (1984).

> Dividend payments can reduce owner–manager conflicts by forcing the firm into the capital markets more frequently.

managerial risk aversion. New investors will discount the prices they pay for corporate securities by the amount of existing agency costs. Managers who must constantly raise new capital have an incentive to lower these agency costs in order to sell their securities at the highest possible price.

Perhaps the most important consequence of paying dividends is to reduce management's control over the deployment of free cash flow, reducing reinvestment risk and leading to better resource allocation. Management looking to fund expansion must then appeal to investors to vote for its investment plans by contributing new capital. Of course, there are other ways to force managers into the capital markets on a regular basis, such as issuing short-term debt that must be renewed periodically or issuing substantial amounts of debt that force the company to make regular debt payments. The agency cost explanation claims only that paying regular dividends is another way to impose a certain discipline on managers that may otherwise be lacking.

15.4   SETTING DIVIDEND POLICY

The totality of the available empirical evidence and theoretical considerations suggests that a company should ask itself the following questions when setting its dividend policy.

> Dividend payments should be set in relation to a firm's long-term growth opportunities.

1. **What Are Our Investment Opportunities?** Setting dividend payouts in relation to long-term growth opportunities maximizes financial flexibility and reduces the financial frictions associated with raising external capital. It also helps communicate more clearly to the market the nature of the firm and where it is headed. Hence, a rapidly growing firm, with an abundance of positive net present value projects, should retain a larger share of its operating cash flow than a firm with few profitable investment opportunities. Conversely, a firm holding a portfolio of low-growth, cash-cow type businesses should have generous payouts.

> All else being equal, firms with unstable or cyclical earnings should have lower dividend payouts than those firms whose earnings are stable.

2. **What Kind of Business Risk Do We Face?** Given the strong reluctance of managements to cut dividends and the adverse price reactions when they do, companies should set a dividend policy that can be maintained over time. Thus, a firm with unstable or cyclical earnings should set a low dividend payout rate to reduce the odds that it will be forced to cut its dividend. Conversely, firms with stable earnings should be more willing to pay a high dividend.

3. **Who Are Our Stockholders?** Dividend policy should match the needs of a firm's stockholders for dividends versus capital gains. Although there's no evidence that one dividend clientele is any better than another, it makes no sense for a company to pay generous dividends to a shareholder clientele consisting of high tax-bracket individuals who are primarily interested in capital gains.

4. **How's Our Liquidity Position?** Because dividends must be paid out of cash, companies with large amounts of liquid assets and good access to the finan-

All else being equal, firms with high liquidity and good access to the financial markets are in a better position to pay generous dividends than those firms with limited financial resources.

cial markets, are better able to pay dividends. Rapidly growing companies, even very profitable ones with lots of retained earnings, may not be liquid enough to pay a large dividend. Their funds are likely to be tied up in fixed assets and less-liquid working capital such as inventory and accounts receivable. A firm could, of course, borrow the money to pay dividends. But this would reduce its financial flexibility, perhaps forcing it at some later date to forgo a profitable investment opportunity for lack of funds. Thus, an illiquid company may elect not to pay large dividends because the opportunity cost of doing so, especially for a rapidly growing one, may simply be too great. Liquidity will be a less important determinant of the dividend decision if the firm has a large debt capacity relative to its investment requirements.

5. *Is Legal Listing Important to Us?* **Legal lists** are lists prepared by various government bodies of those securities in which pension funds, savings banks, insurance companies, and other financial institutions may invest. A typical requirement for legal listing is that a stock pay a minimum and *uninterrupted* dividend. Omitting or even cutting a dividend payment may lead to removal from these legal lists, reducing demand for the stock by institutional investors. According to MCI's CFO, this rationale explains why the long-distance carrier decided to declare its first-ever dividend (in May 1990): "Many institutional investors can't hold stock of a company that doesn't pay a dividend. This will help widen our base [of ownership]."[18]

6. *Is Control an Issue?* If a firm's current owners or managers are concerned about maintaining control, they may be reluctant to issue additional stock. This leaves retained earnings as the preferred source of equity capital for such firms, mandating a lower dividend payout rate if the present debt–equity ratio is considered to be at its upper limit.

SUMMARY

One of the major long-term financing decisions confronting a company is the choice between retaining earnings and paying them out as dividends. In the absence of any change in investment policy, we saw that this choice comes down to whether the firm should finance the equity portion of its investments with retained earnings or by selling new shares.

We began by exploring the various institutional characteristics and practices relevant to the dividend decision. Next, we addressed the all-important question of whether a firm can affect its market value by changing its dividend policy. In the absence of market imperfections and taxes, the answer is a resounding "no." But because such perfection hardly characterizes

actual markets, the debate over dividend policy continues. The conclusion to emerge from over 40 years of research and debate is that academic researchers have been unable to isolate clearly the effects of dividend policy on stock prices. Most academics believe that one or more of the following factors are likely to cause dividend policy to be relevant: the asymmetrical tax treatment of capital gains and dividends, flotation and transaction costs, and agency problems.

By contrast, another camp argues that competition among firms for various dividend clienteles as well as the ability of dividend recipients to shelter their income from taxes results in dividend neutrality; that is, one dividend policy is as good as any other. Although

---

[18]Julie Lopez, "MCI Decides to Offer Payout Semiannually," *Wall Street Journal,* May 8, 1990, C16.

this is an extreme view, it has caused academics to question apparent matters of fact and to rethink their positions on dividend policy. In the process of doing so, a new consensus appears to have emerged: Whether or not dividend policy can affect a firm's value, it is unlikely to matter much relative to the effect of the firm's investment policy—and the market-

ing, personnel, production, and R&D decisions that underlie it—on the firm's value. Most academics would also agree that to the extent that dividend policy can influence stock price, the most appropriate policy is likely to be the one that sends the strongest signal as to the company's economic prospects and strategic intentions.

QUESTIONS

1. a. What is dividend policy?
   b. What are the three main positions on the question "Does dividend policy matter?"
2. Explain how the following situations could affect a firm's dividend policy:
   a. The firm is about to go bankrupt.
   b. Losses have reduced cumulative retained earnings to zero.
   c. Years of research have finally paid off, with several new products ready for development.
   d. Nontaxable institutions have recently acquired 85 percent of the firm's shares.
3. Several empirical studies suggest that corporations are reluctant to lower dividends paid per share. How should this reluctance to cut dividends be reflected over the years in the pattern of dividends paid and the firm's payout ratio? Relate your answer to the dramatic rise in the dividend payout rates for the DJIA companies in the early 1980s and early 1990s.
4. Utilities tend to have very high dividend payout ratios. What reason can you give for this?
5. What issues arise when the firm is deciding how to partition profits between dividends and retained earnings?
6. How will each of the following changes probably affect corporate payout rates? Explain your answers.
   a. An increase in the personal income tax rate.
   b. An increase in the capital gains tax rate.
   c. A liberalization in depreciation policies for tax purposes.
   d. A rise in interest rates.
   e. An increase in corporate profits.
   f. A decline in investment opportunities.
   g. A tightening of rules on takeovers.
7. Suppose you studied a company's records and discovered that it has been much more costly for the

company to obtain new capital through new stock issues than through retention of earnings. How should this knowledge influence the company's dividend policy?
8. Rank the following investors in order of their tax preference for dividends over capital gains: pension funds, private individuals, corporations.
9. According to Miller and Modigliani, dividend policy is a mere detail. What assumptions underlie their view of dividend policy? Do these assumptions appear to hold?
10. Does dividend irrelevance contradict the stock price valuation model based on the present value of expected future dividends? Explain.
11. Comment on the following statements.
    a. If my Benghazi Orange Groves annual report is correct, the company has done very well during its recent expansion and is continuing to expand. If the report is correct, why haven't my dividends, which represent my share of the profits, increased in the past three years?
    b. Stocks with high dividend yields may look tempting, but a fat payout often is a warning flag.
    c. Share buybacks make good economic sense because by reducing the number of shares outstanding, they increase earnings per share.
12. When a company announces an increase in its dividend, its stock price typically rises. Conversely, dividend decreases usually lead to stock price declines. Does this constitute evidence against the dividend irrelevance proposition? Explain.
13. Suppose that equal numbers of investors prefer a zero dividend payout, a 30 percent payout ratio, and a 60 percent payout ratio. If all firms initially were paying out 30 percent of their earnings as dividends, what would you expect to see happen?
14. Suppose all investments offered the same expected return before tax. Consider two equally risky

shares, Hi and Lo. Hi shares pay a generous dividend and offer low expected capital gains. Lo shares pay low dividends and offer high expected capital gains. Which group(s) of investors would most likely prefer Hi shares?

15. Stock splits merely create more shares without altering the value of the firm or the wealth of any individual shareholder. Yet stock splits are often associated with a period of rising stock prices for splitting firms. Does this mean that stock splits do in fact increase stock returns and thus shareholder wealth?

16. The following questions relate to the impact of dividend policies on a firm's bonds.
    a. What does the Black–Scholes option pricing model predict will happen to the price of a company's bonds when it announces its intention to increase its cash dividend? To lower its dividend?
    b. What does the dividend-signaling hypothesis predict will happen to the price of a company's bonds when it announces its intention to increase the cash dividend? To lower its dividend?
    c. Can you reconcile the predictions in (a) and (b)?

17. The 1986 Tax Reform Act reduced individual and corporate tax rates and eliminated the distinction between dividend income and capital gains. Explain how each of these changes was likely to affect dividend policy by itself and in combination with the other changes.

18. President Carter in 1977 and President Reagan in 1984 attempted to eliminate double taxation of equity income by permitting dividends to be deducted from before-tax income, just like interest expense. Both attempts failed because of corporate opposition. What might explain big business' opposition to tax relief for equity income?

19. The finding that closely held companies, where the agency conflict is likely to be minimized, have low dividend-payout rates is consistent with the agency cost explanation. What other dividend hypothesis might this finding also be consistent with?

20. U.S. companies have long complained that the low dividend payout rates of Japanese corporations give them an unfair advantage by lowering their cost of capital. Discuss this argument.

21. Contrast the consequences for financing and investment decision making of an investment tax credit and a lower capital gains tax rate. Who will benefit from each of these tax policies?

22. How might the stock market react to a highly leveraged company that issues stock to pay down much of the debt while simultaneously boosting its dividend? Explain.

23. Suppose the government lowers the capital gains tax rate from 30 percent to 15 percent. What will happen to capital gains tax revenues? Explain.

24. In January 1989, Texaco reached a peace pact with corporate raider Carl Icahn that eliminated him as a bidder for the company. The accord involved Texaco paying a special dividend that would put $300 million in Mr. Icahn's pocket. According to the *Wall Street Journal* (January 30, 1989, A3), "If Mr. Icahn chooses to rid himself of his Texaco stake, it's hardly likely he'd sell before the special dividend is paid." Comment on this statement.

25. In May 1992, Philip Morris announced that it would buy back $3 billion of its common shares over the next two years, expanding on a $2 billion buyback program that it began in November 1991. What message(s) might the company be sending to the market?

26. Between 1991 and 1992, Delta Airlines had cumulative losses of over $1 billion. On December 17, 1992, Delta announced that it would slash its dividend by 83 percent, reduce wages by 5 percent, and postpone $400 million in aircraft orders. Its stock price jumped almost 6 percent. Why might the market have reacted so positively to this set of announcements?

27. According to the *Wall Street Journal* (January 30, 1992), "Westinghouse Electric Corp., as expected, moved to stabilize its shaky finances by cutting its quarterly dividend to 18 cents a share from 35 cents." How do you think the stock market responded to this 49 percent cut in Westinghouse's dividend?

28. In June 1994, the British Labour Party stated that a future Labour government would seek to discourage high dividend payments. According to a Labour Party spokesman, there is a strong connection between the fact that British companies' investment is low and the fact that British companies pay more of their profits to shareholders as dividends than do firms in Germany or Japan, which have relatively high investment rates. Comment.

29. In 1995, investor Kirk Kerkorian launched a hostile struggle for control of Chrysler. One of his

primary charges was that Chrysler, with approximately $7.5 billion in cash, was hoarding cash that should instead be distributed to shareholders through dividends or share buybacks. What are arguments for and against Chrysler's accumulating so much cash?

30. What was the likely reason for the drop in Colt Industries' bond prices and the jump in its stock price after management announced that it would borrow $1.4 billion to pay a huge dividend to shareholders?

PROBLEMS

✂ —Excel templates may be downloaded from **www. prenhall.com/financecenter.**

1. The current P/E for the fast-food industry is 15. With an average dividend payout of 25 percent, what is the average dividend yield in the industry?

2. The financial data for Newport Co. are as follows: ✂

EPS	$4.25
Dividend payout	45 percent
Market price	$75.00

a. Newport declares a three-for-one stock split. What is the effect on EPS, dividend per share, and market price? What is the effect on the firm's value? On your holding of 250 shares?

b. If Newport instead declared a 50 percent stock dividend, what would be the effect on EPS, dividend per share, market price, and the value of the firm?

c. If the value of the firm does not change, why do firms split their stocks or issue stock dividends?

3. Persistent Corp. has stable operating income of $15,000 annually. The firm is all-equity financed, and it pays out its full operating income as dividends every year. Assume that Persistent's cost of capital is 15 percent, that markets are perfect, and that there are no corporate or personal taxes. ✂

a. What is the market value of Persistent Corp.?

b. If there are 5,000 shares outstanding, what is the current price per share?

Persistent now decides on a one-time-only change in its dividend policy. During the coming year, it will sell $30,000 worth of new stock and pay $45,000 in dividends to its current shareholders. Thereafter, Persistent will issue no more new stock

and will pay $15,000 in dividends in all future years.

c. If the new shares are sold at the end of the year, how many shares must be sold and what will be their price?

d. Show that the current price per share and current market value of the firm are unaffected by this one-time-only change in dividend policy.

Suppose that shareholders want $45,000 in cash next year but Persistent refuses to pay more than $15,000 in dividends. To obtain the desired cash, the shareholders can sell some of their shares.

e. How many shares must be sold at the end of the year (ex-dividend) and what will be the price per share?

f. What will be the value of the shares still held by the original shareholders after the sales in (e)?

g. Are the final holdings of cash and shares by the original shareholders different if Persistent increases total dividends to $45,000 and sells $30,000 worth of new shares than if Persistent holds dividends constant at $15,000 and the shareholders sell $30,000 worth of their stock? [*Hint:* Compare the total cash receipts and value of remaining shares held in (c) and (d) above with the total cash receipts and the value of the remaining shares in (e) and (f).]

4. The Ritz Coney Island, Ltd., had earnings of $5 million in 1998. Earnings have grown at a steady 10 percent per year for 20 years, and dividends of $2 million were paid in 1998. Unusually high earnings of $6 million were recorded in 1999, along with investment of $4 million in new facilities. Calculate total 1999 dividends if:

a. Ritz follows a 40 percent payout policy.

b. Ritz follows a pure residual policy while financing 30 percent of new investment with debt.

c. Ritz follows a stable dollar dividend policy.

d. New investment is financed with 50 percent retained earnings and 50 percent debt.

5. As part of its overall strategic plan, Tobasco, Inc., has adopted three corporate policies. First, the dividend payout will be 50 percent of earnings. Second, the debt/total asset ratio will remain at .40. Third, the firm will undertake new capital investment of $72 million for each of the next two years. The company is paying a 10 percent interest rate on its debt. Tobasco's earnings forecast for the next 2 years is $88 million (year 1) and $125 million (year 2). Currently, Tobasco has debt of $200 million and equity of $300 million.
   a. Calculate the new financing required if Tobasco attempts to meet all three policy goals.
   b. Lizard Freres, Tobasco's investment banker, has informed the firm that market conditions preclude a new equity issue at this time. What are Tobasco's policy options?

6. Lancaster and York, Inc., a floral display company, is considering a 33 percent stock dividend or a four-for-three stock split. L&Y has the following current balance sheet accounts:

Common stock ($25 par value)	$1,350
Retained earnings	2,000

   a. If L&Y is currently selling at $30 a share, what will be the equity account changes resulting from the stock dividend? From the stock split?
   b. What will be the likely market price for L&Y shares after the stock split? After the stock dividend?

7. Myron Co. currently pays no dividends and has been using internal financing to fund its growth. Fred Sparrow, the new financial officer, believes that investors would react positively to a dividend of $.90 a share. The current market value of Myron's stock is $3.75 a share, and the current number of shares outstanding is 250.
   a. If Myron continues to grow at its present rate, it must finance the dividend by issuing new shares. At what price would the new shares sell?
   b. How many new shares would be required?
   c. Next year, Myron will have $99 available to its shareholders for dividends. If Myron did not pay dividends this year, what would the dividend per share be for each shareholder? If, on the other hand, the $.90 dividend is paid, as

Sparrow suggests, how much will each old shareholder receive in dividends next year?

8. A stock analyst preparing a report on USA Express stock must calculate the average growth in the price of its common shares for the last eight years. The year-end price is reported as follows:

Year	1	2	3	4	5	6	7	8
	$17	$20	$23	$27	$28	$30	$35	$40

In addition, Moody's reports that the firm split its stock two for one at the beginning of year 2, and three for one at the beginning of year 5. The firm also issued a 25 percent stock dividend at the beginning of year 6. What is the average growth rate of USA Express' stock price?

9. Calorific distributes diet beverages and diet frozen foods. Current earnings are $10,500,000 and earnings are forecast to grow at 10 percent a year. The five-year strategic plan calls for a capital budget as follows:

Year	1	2
	$5,750,000	$6,000,000

3	4	5
$8,000,000	$5,500,000	$6,500,000

Current dividends are $1 per share on the 5 million shares outstanding.
   a. If Calorific adopts a residual dividend policy, calculate the dividend per share for each of the next five years.
   b. If Calorific maintains a 60 percent dividend payout ratio and funds its capital budget exclusively through new equity, if needed, calculate the dividend per share for both old and new shareholders. Assume a market price of $5 a share throughout.
   c. Calculate the payout ratio to shareholders under (a).
   d. If Calorific instead decides to distribute the residual to shareholders through share repurchase, how many shares must Calorific buy back each year? Assume a market price of $5 a share and no changes in price *except* through share repurchase.

10. A company projects with great certainty the following levels of net income and capital expenditures ($000) over the next five years: ✖

Year	1	2	3	4	5
Net income	1000	750	1250	1150	900
Capital expenditures	500	750	1000	750	1000

Currently, a dividend of 50 cents per share is paid on 1 million outstanding common shares. Determine the amount of external financing required each year under the following dividend policies:
a. pure residual.
b. smoothed residual dividend based on the average of the current and previous year's residual (the residual last year was 500).
c. constant 50 percent payout rate.

11. The shares of No Dividend Corp. and Hi Dividend Corp. are equally risky. It is expected that the price per share of No Dividend will be $57.50 next year with no cash dividend, whereas the price of Hi Dividend will be $52.50 next year with a $5 cash dividend per share. Assume that the required after-tax rate of return on the stocks of these firms is 12 percent, that income is taxed at a 50 percent rate, and that capital gains (whether realized or not) are taxed at a 20 percent rate. What are the current prices of the shares of No Dividend and Hi Dividend?

12. A firm earns one dollar per share per year in perpetuity. Shareholders are taxed at the rate of 50 percent on cash dividends but pay no taxes on capital gains.
a. Show how the firm can increase its value by switching from paying cash dividends to repurchasing shares.
b. Why might this strategy fail in the real world?

13. In 1960, Uncle Jack bought $1,000 of stock. By 1992, Jack's stock was worth $10,000. During this 32-year period, however, inflation totaled 370 percent. Jack is in the 31 percent tax bracket. ✖
a. Suppose Jack sells his stock in 1992 for $10,000. What is his after-tax dollar return? What is his annualized percentage return?
b. What is Jack's *real* after-tax dollar return? What is his annualized percentage return? What is his

real capital gains tax rate (the fraction of his real gains paid in tax)?
c. How much tax would Jack owe if the IRS indexes capital gains for inflation? What would his real dollar return be? What would be his real annualized percentage return?
d. Suppose Jack died in 1992 and left the stock to his niece Jane. At the time of Jack's death the stock is worth $10,250. How much tax will Jane owe (she is also in the 31 percent bracket)? What would be the real after-tax total and annualized rates of return on this stock over the 32-year period?

14. The expected pre-tax returns on stocks A, B, and C are divided between dividends and capital gains as follows:

Stock	Expected Dividend	Expected Capital Gain
A	$0	$6
B	3	3
C	6	0

a. If each stock is currently priced at $40 and will be sold in one year, what is the highest return available to an individual who is taxed at 40 percent on ordinary income and 28 percent on capital gains?
b. Suppose that stocks were priced to yield a 10 percent after-tax return to investors facing the same tax rates as the ones described in part a. What would be the prices of stocks A, B, and C?

15. An investor in the 55 percent marginal tax bracket has just invested $4,000 in shares of a corporation expected to yield yearly dividends of 4 percent and yearly capital gains of 10 percent.
a. If the investor plans to sell the shares in one year, what will be the expected after-tax dollar return? Assume capital gains are taxed at half the rate for ordinary income.
b. Suppose the investor may borrow at 10 percent interest, and this interest can be written off against ordinary income. How much borrowing will negate the taxable dividend income, and what is the new expected after-tax dollar return? Compare percentage returns as well.
c. How will the borrowing affect the investor's exposure to market risk?

REFERENCES

Aharony, J., and I. Swary. "Quarterly Dividend and Earnings Announcements and Stockholders' Returns: An Empirical Analysis." *Journal of Finance,* March 1980, 1–12.

Bhattacharya, Sudipto. "Imperfect Information, Dividend Policy, and the 'Bird-in-the-Hand' Fallacy." *Bell Journal of Economics,* Spring 1979, 259–270.

Black, Fischer, and Myron Scholes. "The Effects of Dividend Yields and Dividend Policy on Common Stock Prices and Returns." *Journal of Financial Economics,* May 1974, 1–24.

Brennan, Michael J. "Taxes, Market Valuation, and Financial Policy." *National Tax Journal,* December 1970, 417–420.

Eades, Kenneth M., Patrick H. Hess, and E. Han Kim. "Market Rationality and Dividend Announcements." *Journal of Financial Economics,* December 1985, 581–604.

Easterbrook, Frank H. "Two Agency-Cost Explanations of Dividends." *American Economic Review,* September 1984, 650–659.

Fama, Eugene F., and Harvey Babiak. "Dividend Policy: An Empirical Analysis." *Journal of the American Statistical Association,* December 1968, 1132–1161.

Fama, Eugene F., Lawrence Fisher, Michael Jensen, and Richard Roll. "The Adjustment of Stock Prices to New Information." *International Economic Review,* February 1969, 1–21.

Gordon, Myron J. "Dividends, Earnings and Stock Prices." *Review of Economics and Statistics,* May 1959, 99–105.

Healey, Paul M., and Krishna Palepu. "Earnings Information Conveyed by Dividend Initiations and Omissions." *Journal of Financial Economics,* September 1988, 149–175.

Lewellen, G. Wilbur, K. L. Stanley, Ronald C. Lease, and Gary G. Schlarbaum. "Some Direct Evidence on the Dividend Clientele Phenomenon." *Journal of Finance,* December 1978, 1385–1399.

Lintner, John. "Distribution of Income of Corporations Among Dividends, Retained Earnings, and Taxes." *American Economic Review,* May 1956, 97–113.

Litzenberger, Robert H., and Krishna Ramaswamy. "The Effect of Dividends on Common Stock Prices: Tax Effects or Information Effects." *Journal of Finance,* May 1982, 469–482.

Long, John B., Jr. "The Market for Valuation of Cash Dividends: A Case to Consider." *Journal of Financial Economics,* June–September 1978, 235–264.

Michaely, Roni, Richard H. Thaler, and Kent Womack. "Price Reactions to Dividend Initiations and Omissions: Overreaction or Draft?" *Journal of Finance,* June 1995, 573–608.

Miller, Merton, and Franco Modigliani. "Dividend Policy, Growth and the Valuation of Shares." *Journal of Business,* October 1961, 411–433.

Miller, Merton, and Kevin Rock. "Dividend Policy Under Asymmetric Information." *Journal of Finance,* September 1985, 1031–1051.

Miller, Merton, and Myron Scholes. "Dividends and Taxes." *Journal of Financial Economics,* December 1978, 333–364.

Petit, Richardson. "Dividend Announcements, Security Performance, and Capital Market Efficiency." *Journal of Finance,* December 1972, 86–96.

Petit, Richardson. "Taxes, Transactions Costs and the Clientele Effect of Dividends." *Journal of Financial Economics,* December 1977, 419–436.

Rozeff, Michael S. "How Corporations Set Their Dividend Payout Ratios." *Chase Financial Quarterly,* Winter 1982, 68–83.

Shefrin, Hersh M., and Meir Statman. "Explaining Investor Preference for Cash Dividends." *Journal of Financial Economics,* June 1984, 253–282.

Woolridge, J. Randall, and Chinmoy Ghosh. "Dividend Cuts: Do They Always Signal Bad News?" *Midland Journal of Corporate Finance,* Summer 1985, 20–32.

Using a Business Calculator

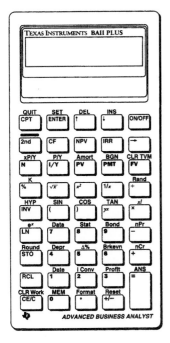

A business calculator is an absolute must in today's business environment, whether you are doing finance, accounting, marketing, production, strategy, or human resource management. You can easily learn to make the time-value-of-money calculations we illustrate here. However, with just a little more effort, you can also learn to do much more with your calculator, such as calculating averages, standard deviations, depreciation, linear regression coefficients, and breakdown amounts. The list is almost endless.

There are many different business calculators on the market today. The one you choose depends on your own personal preferences. We have chosen the Texas Instruments BAII PLUS to illustrate the use of a business calculator.

Key strokes are illustrated by boxes. An unshaded box indicates the function shown on the face of the key. For example, the four-key-stroke sequence 3 + 2 = adds the numbers 3 and 2 using the red keys with + and = on them. A shaded box preceded by a 2nd indicates the function shown in gray above the key. For example, 4 2nd x! computes 4 factorial (4 times 3 times 2 times 1) using the secondary function shown above the times key, which is the red key with × on it.

ASSUMED PAYMENTS PER PERIOD *(very important)*

Your calculator can assume any number of payments per period. For simplicity, our calculations here, and throughout the book, *always* assume the mode is set to 1.00. For example, if there are 12 monthly payments per year over 5 years, we make the conversion and use N = 60.

To set your calculator for use with our calculations:

2nd P/Y 1 ENTER CE/C CE/C

This setting continues indefinitely (even though the calculator is turned off and on), until it is changed.

Decimal Place Display

Your calculator always calculates with 9-digit accuracy. However, the numbers it displays depend on the number of decimal places to which you have it set. Our calculations generally display 2, 3, or 4 decimal places.

To set the number of decimal places displayed to three:

| 2nd | Format | 3 | ENTER | [the display will show: DEC = ⬚ 3.000] | CE/C | CE/C |

This setting also continues indefinitely (even though the calculator is turned off and on), until it is changed.

End-of-Period Annuity Cash Flows

Your calculator can assume that annuity cash flows occur either at the end of the period or at the beginning of the period. For simplicity, our calculations *always* assume the mode is set to end-of-period annuity cash flows. If a small BGN appears above the number display, the mode is set to beginning-of-period annuity cash flows. Otherwise, the mode is already set to end-of-period annuity cash flows.

To set the mode to end-of-period annuity cash flows:

| 2nd | BGN | [the display should show BGN; if it shows END, hit | CE/C |] | 2nd | SET | CE/C | CE/C |

This setting also continues indefinitely (even though the calculator is turned off and on), until it is changed.

EXAMPLES

Present Value of a Single Future Cash Flow

The present value of $5000 to be received in 4 years at 12% APY is $3,177.59:

| 4 | N | 1 | 2 | I/Y | 0 | PMT | 5 | 0 | 0 | 0 | FV | CPT | PV | = −3177.59

Future Value of a Current Amount

The future value of $2000 to be received in 7 years at 9% APY is $3,656.08:

| 7 | N | 9 | I/Y | 2 | 0 | 0 | 0 | PV | 0 | PMT | CPT | FV | = −3,656.08

Present Value of an Annuity

The present value of $200 per month for 5 years (60 months) at 9% APR (0.75% per month) is $ 9634.67:

| 6 | 0 | N | . | 7 | 5 | I/Y | 2 | 0 | 0 | PMT | 0 | FV | CPT | PV | = −9,634.67

Future Value of an Annuity

The future value of $50 per week for 3 years (156 weeks) at 6% APR (0.115% per week) is $8,540.70:

| 1 | 5 | 6 | N | . | 1 | 1 | 5 | I/Y | 0 | PV | 5 | 0 | PMT | CPT | FV | = −8,540.70

Annuity Cash Flows for a Present Value

The monthly payments for a $100,000 20-year (240-month) mortgage at 8.16% APR (0.68% per month) are $846.43:

| 2 | 4 | 0 | N | . | 6 | 8 | I/Y | 1 | 0 | 0 | 0 | 0 | 0 | PV | 0 | FV | CPT | PMT | = −846.43

Annuity Cash Flows for a Future Value

Suppose you are going to save some money from the paycheck you get every two weeks, and you will earn 4.42% APR (0.17% per 2-week period) on your savings. To save $10,000 over 2.5 years (65 pay periods), you will need to put aside $145.63 from each paycheck:

| 6 | 5 | N | . | 1 | 7 | I/Y | 0 | PV | 1 | 0 | 0 | 0 | 0 | FV | CPT | PMT | = −145.63

Interest Rate for a Present Value

A $15,000 10-year (120-month) loan requiring monthly payments of $209.96 has an APR of 11.04%:

`1` `2` `0` `N` `1` `5` `0` `0` `0` `PV` `2` `0` `9` `.` `9` `6` `+/-` `PMT` `0` `FV` `CPT` `I/Y` = 0.949 `×` `1` `2` `=` 11.39

Interest Rate for a Future Value

To save $1,000,000 by investing $155.50 per month for 35 years (420 months), your investments must earn an APR of 12.00%:

`4` `2` `0` `N` `0` `PV` `1` `5` `5` `.` `5` `0` `+/-` `PMT` `1` `0` `0` `0` `0` `0` `0` `FV` `CPT` `I/Y`

= 1.00 `×` `1` `2` `=` 12.00

Present Value of Annuity Cash Flows and a Future Value

The present value of a 10%-coupon ($50 semiannually) corporate bond that pays $1000 at maturity in 8 years (16 semiannual periods) and has a yield to maturity of 12% (6% semiannually) is $898.94:

`1` `6` `N` `6` `I/Y` `5` `0` `PMT` `1` `0` `0` `0` `FV` `CPT` `PV` = −898.94

Interest Rate for Annuity Cash Flows and a Future Value

The yield to maturity of a 6%-coupon ($30 semiannually) corporate bond that pays $1000 at maturity in 5.5 years (11 semiannual periods) and currently sells for $833.87 is 10%:

`1` `1` `N` `8` `3` `3` `.` `8` `7` `+/-` `PV` `3` `0` `PMT` `1` `0` `0` `0` `FV` `CPT` `I/Y` = 5.00 `×` `2` `=` 10.00

NPV and IRR for Uneven Cash Flows

CF0	CF1	CF2	CF3	CF4	CF5
−110,000	45,000	45,000	45,000	10,000	60,000

The NPV at a cost of capital of 12% and the IRR for the above cash flows from a capital budgeting project are $38,483.20 and 25.73%, respectively:

`CE/C` `CE/C` `CF` `2nd` `CLR Work` `1` `1` `0` `0` `0` `0` `+/-` `ENTER` `↓` `4` `5` `0` `0` `0`

`ENTER` `↓` `3` [3 is the number of times the cash flow repeats] `ENTER` `↓` `1` `0` `0` `0` `0`

`ENTER` `↓` `ENTER` `↓` `6` `0` `0` `0` `0` `ENTER` `↓` `ENTER` `2nd` `Quit`

[all the cash flows have been entered]

`NPV` `1` `2` [12 is the cost of capital (required return)] `ENTER` `↓` `CPT` = 38,483.20

IRR `CPT` = 25.73

at a 20% cost of capital, the NPV is $13,726.85:

`NPV` `2` `0` `ENTER` `↓` `CPT` = 13,726.85

Future Value of $1 at the End of N Periods

APPENDIX B

Period	1%	2%	3%	4%	5%	6%	7%	8%	9%	10%
1	1.0100	1.0200	1.0300	1.0400	1.0500	1.0500	1.0700	1.0800	1.0900	1.1000
2	1.0201	1.0404	1.0609	1.0816	1.1025	1.1236	1.1449	1.1664	1.1881	1.2100
3	1.0303	1.0612	1.0927	1.1249	1.1576	1.1910	1.2250	1.2597	1.2950	1.3310
4	1.0406	1.0824	1.1255	1.1699	1.2155	1.2625	1.3108	1.3605	1.4116	1.4641
5	1.0510	1.1041	1.1593	1.2167	1.2763	1.3382	1.4026	1.4693	1.5386	1.6105
6	1.0615	1.1262	1.1941	1.2653	1.3401	1.4185	1.5007	1.5869	1.6771	1.7716
7	1.0721	1.1487	1.2299	1.3159	1.4071	1.5036	1.6058	1.7138	1.8280	1.9487
8	1.0829	1.1717	1.2668	1.3686	1.4775	1.5938	1.7182	1.8509	1.9926	2.1436
9	1.0937	1.1951	1.3048	1.4233	1.5513	1.6895	1.8385	1.9990	2.1719	2.3579
10	1.1046	1.2190	1.3439	1.4802	1.6289	1.7905	1.9672	2.1589	2.3674	2.5937
11	1.1157	1.2434	1.3842	1.5395	1.7103	1.8983	2.1049	2.3316	2.5804	2.8531
12	1.1268	1.2682	1.4258	1.6010	1.7959	2.0122	2.2522	2.5182	2.8127	3.1384
13	1.1381	1.2936	1.4685	1.6651	1.8856	2.1329	2.4098	2.7196	3.0658	3.4523
14	1.1495	1.3195	1.5126	1.7317	1.9799	2.2609	2.5785	2.9372	3.3417	3.7975
15	1.1610	1.3459	1.5580	1.8009	2.0789	2.3966	2.7590	3.1772	3.6425	4.1772
16	1.1726	1.3728	1.6047	1.8730	2.1829	2.5404	2.9522	3.4259	3.9703	4.5950
17	1.1843	1.4002	1.6528	1.9479	2.2920	2.6928	3.1588	3.7000	4.3276	5.0545
18	1.1961	1.4282	1.7024	2.0258	2.4066	2.8543	3.3799	3.9960	4.7171	5.5599
19	1.2081	1.4568	1.7535	2.1068	2.5270	3.0256	3.6165	4.3157	5.1417	6.1159
20	1.2202	1.4859	1.8061	2.1911	2.6533	3.2071	3.8697	4.6610	5.6044	6.7275
21	1.2324	1.5157	1.8603	2.2788	2.7860	3.3996	4.1406	5.0338	6.1088	7.4002
22	1.2447	1.5460	1.9161	2.3699	2.9253	3.6035	4.4304	5.4365	6.6586	8.1403
23	1.2572	1.5769	1.9736	2.4647	3.0715	3.8197	4.7405	5.8715	7.2579	8.9543
24	1.2697	1.6084	2.0328	2.5633	3.2251	4.0489	5.0724	6.3412	7.9111	9.8497
25	1.2824	1.6406	2.0938	2.6658	3.3864	4.2919	5.4274	6.8485	8.6231	10.8350
26	1.2953	1.6734	2.1566	2.7725	3.5557	4.5494	5.8074	7.3964	9.3392	11.9180
27	1.3082	1.7069	2.2213	2.8834	3.7335	4.8223	6.2139	7.9881	10.2450	13.1100
28	1.3213	1.7410	2.2879	2.9987	3.9201	5.1170	6.6488	8.6271	11.1670	14.4210
29	1.3345	1.7758	2.3566	3.1187	4.1161	5.4184	7.1143	9.3173	12.1720	15.8630
30	1.3478	1.8114	2.4273	3.2434	4.3219	5.7435	7.6123	10.0630	13.2680	17.4490
40	1.4889	2.2080	3.2620	4.8010	7.0400	10.2850	14.9740	21.7250	31.4090	45.2590
50	1.6446	2.6916	4.3839	7.1067	11.4670	18.4200	29.4570	46.9020	74.3580	117.3900
60	1.8167	3.2810	5.8916	10.5190	18.6790	32.9870	57.9460	101.2600	176.0300	304.4800

*FVIF > 99,999.

12%	14%	15%	16%	18%	20%	24%	28%	32%
1.1200	1.1400	1.1500	1.1600	1.1800	1.2000	1.2400	1.2800	1.3200
1.2544	1.2996	1.3225	1.3456	1.3924	1.4400	1.5376	1.6384	1.7424
1.4049	1.4815	1.5209	1.5609	1.6430	1.7280	1.9066	2.0972	2.3000
1.5735	1.6890	1.7490	1.8106	1.9388	1.0736	2.3642	2.6844	3.0360
1.7623	1.9254	2.0114	2.1003	2.2878	2.4883	2.9316	3.4360	4.0075
1.9738	2.1950	2.3131	2.4364	2.6996	2.9860	3.6352	4.3980	5.2899
2.2107	2.5023	2.6600	2.8262	3.1855	3.5832	4.5077	5.6295	6.9826
2.4760	2.8526	3.0590	3.2784	3.7589	4.2998	5.5895	7.2058	9.2170
2.7731	3.2519	3.5179	3.8030	4.4355	5.1598	6.9310	9.2234	12.1660
3.1058	3.7072	4.0456	4.4114	5.2338	6.1917	8.5944	11.8060	16.0600
3.4785	4.2262	4.6524	5.1173	6.1759	7.4301	10.6570	15.1120	21.1990
3.8960	4.8179	5.3503	5.9360	7.2876	8.9161	13.2150	19.3430	27.9830
4.3635	5.4924	6.1528	6.8858	8.5994	10.6990	16.3860	24.7590	36.9370
4.8871	6.2613	7.0757	7.9875	10.1470	12.3190	20.3190	31.6910	48.7570
5.4736	7.1379	8.1371	9.2655	11.9740	15.4070	25.1960	40.5650	64.3590
6.1304	8.1372	9.3576	10.7480	14.1290	18.4880	31.2430	51.9230	84.9540
6.8660	9.2765	10.7610	12.4680	16.6720	22.1860	38.7410	66.4510	112.1400
7.6900	10.5750	12.3750	14.4630	19.6730	26.6230	48.0390	85.0710	148.0200
8.6128	12.0560	14.2320	16.7770	23.2140	31.9480	59.5680	108.8900	195.3900
9.6463	13.7430	16.3670	19.4610	27.3930	38.3380	73.8640	139.3800	257.9200
10.8040	15.6680	18.8220	22.5740	32.3240	46.0050	91.5920	178.4100	340.4500
12.1000	17.8610	21.6450	26.1860	38.1420	55.2060	113.5700	228.3600	449.3900
13.5520	20.3620	24.8910	30.3760	45.0080	66.2470	140.8300	292.3000	593.2000
15.1790	23.2120	28.6250	35.2360	53.1090	79.4970	174.6300	374.1400	783.0200
17.0000	26.4620	32.9190	40.8740	62.6690	93.3960	216.5400	478.9000	1033.6000
19.0400	30.1670	37.8570	47.4140	73.9490	114.4800	268.5100	613.0000	1364.3000
21.3250	34.3900	43.5350	55.0000	87.2600	137.3700	332.9500	784.6400	1800.9000
23.8840	39.2040	50.0660	63.8000	102.9700	164.8400	412.8600	1004.3000	2377.2000
26.7500	44.6930	57.5750	74.0090	121.5000	197.8100	511.9500	1285.6000	3137.9000
29.9600	50.9500	66.2120	85.8500	143.3700	237.3800	634.8200	1645.5000	4142.1000
93.0510	188.8800	267.8600	378.7200	750.3800	1469.8000	5455.9000	19427.0000	66521.0000
289.0000	700.2300	1083.7000	1670.7000	3927.4000	9100.4000	46890.0000	*	*
897.6000	2595.9000	4384.0000	7370.2000	20555.0000	56348.0000	*	*	*

Present Value of $1 at the End of N Periods

Period	1%	2%	3%	4%	5%	6%	7%	8%	9%
1	.9901	.9804	.9709	.9615	.9524	.9434	.9346	.9259	.9174
2	.9803	.9612	.9426	.9246	.9070	.8900	.8734	.8573	.8417
3	.9706	.9423	.9151	.8890	.8638	.8396	.8163	.7938	.7722
4	.9610	.9238	.8885	.8548	.8227	.7921	.7629	.7350	.7084
5	.9515	.9057	.8626	.8219	.7835	.7473	.7130	.6806	.6499
6	.9420	.8880	.8375	.7903	.7462	.7050	.6663	.6302	.5963
7	.9327	.8706	.8131	.7599	.7107	.6651	.6277	.5835	.5470
8	.9235	.8535	.7894	.7307	.6768	.6274	.5820	.5403	.5019
9	.9143	.8368	.7664	.7026	.6446	.5919	.5439	.5002	.4604
10	.9053	.8203	.7441	.6756	.6139	.5584	.5083	.4632	.4224
11	.8963	.8043	.7224	.6496	.5847	.5268	.4751	.4289	.3875
12	.8874	.7885	.7014	.6246	.5568	.4970	.4440	.3971	.3555
13	.8787	.7730	.6810	.6006	.5303	.4688	.4150	.3677	.3262
14	.8700	.7579	.6611	.5775	.5051	.4423	.3878	.3405	.2992
15	.8613	.7430	.6419	.5533	.4810	.4173	.3624	.3152	.2745
16	.8528	.7284	.6232	.5339	.4581	.3936	.3387	.2919	.2519
17	.8444	.7142	.6050	.5134	.4363	.3714	.3166	.2703	.2311
18	.8360	.7002	.5874	.4936	.4155	.3503	.2959	.2502	.2120
19	.8277	.6864	.5703	.4746	.3957	.3305	.2765	.2317	.1945
20	.8195	.6730	.5537	.4564	.3769	.3118	.2584	.2145	.1784
21	.8114	.6598	.5375	.4388	.3589	.2942	.2415	.1987	.1637
22	.8034	.6468	.5219	.4220	.3418	.2775	.2257	.1839	.1502
23	.7954	.6342	.5067	.4057	.3256	.2618	.2109	.1703	.1378
24	.7876	.6217	.4919	.3901	.3101	.2470	.1971	.1577	.1264
25	.7798	.6095	.4776	.3751	.2953	.2330	.1842	.1460	.1160
26	.7720	.5976	.4637	.3607	.2812	.2198	.1722	.1352	.1064
27	.7644	.5859	.4502	.3468	.2678	.2074	.1609	.1252	.0976
28	.7568	.5744	.4371	.3335	.2551	.1956	.1504	.1159	.0895
29	.7493	.5631	.4243	.3207	.2429	.1846	.1406	.1073	.0822
30	.7419	.5521	.4120	.3083	.2314	.1741	.1314	.0994	.0754
40	.6717	.4529	.3066	.2083	.1420	.0972	.0668	.0460	.0318
50	.6080	.3715	.2281	.1407	.0872	.0543	.0339	.0213	.0134
60	.5504	.3048	.1697	.0951	.0535	.0303	.0173	.0099	.0057

*This factor is zero to four decimal places.

10%	12%	14%	15%	16%	18%	20%	24%	28%	32%
.9091	.8929	.8772	.8696	.8621	.8475	.8333	.8065	.7813	.7576
.8264	.7972	.7695	.7561	.7432	.7182	.6944	.6504	.6104	.5739
.7513	.7118	.6750	.6575	.6407	.6086	.5787	.5245	.4768	.4348
.6830	.6355	.5921	.5718	.5523	.5158	.4823	.4230	.3725	.3294
.6209	.5674	.5194	.4972	.4761	.4371	.4019	.3411	.2910	.2495
.5645	.5066	.4556	.4323	.4104	.3704	.3349	.2751	.2274	.1890
.5132	.4523	.3996	.3759	.3538	.3139	.2791	.2218	.1776	.1432
.4665	.4039	.3506	.3269	.3050	.2660	.2326	.1789	.1388	.1085
.4241	.3606	.3075	.2843	.2630	.2255	.1938	.1443	.1084	.0822
.3855	.3220	.2697	.2472	.2267	.1911	.1615	.1164	.0847	.0623
.3505	.2875	.2366	.2149	.1954	.1619	.1346	.0938	.0662	.0472
.3186	.2567	.2076	.1869	.1685	.1372	.1122	.0757	.0517	.0357
.2897	.2292	.1821	.1625	.1452	.1163	.0935	.0610	.0404	.0271
.2633	.2046	.1597	.1413	.1252	.0985	.0779	.0492	.0316	.0205
.2394	.1827	.1401	.1229	.1079	.0835	.0649	.0397	.0247	.0155
.2176	.1631	.1229	.1069	.0930	.0708	.0541	.0320	.0193	.0118
.1978	.1456	.1078	.0929	.0802	.0600	.0451	.0258	.0150	.0089
.1779	.1300	.0946	.0808	.0691	.0508	.0376	.0208	.0118	.0068
.1635	.1161	.0829	.0703	.0596	.0431	.0313	.0168	.0092	.0051
.1486	.1037	.0728	.0611	.0514	.0365	.0261	.0135	.0072	.0039
.1351	.0926	.0638	.0531	.0443	.0309	.0217	.0109	.0056	.0029
.1228	.0826	.0560	.0462	.0382	.0262	.0181	.0088	.0044	.0022
.1117	.0738	.0491	.0402	.0329	.0222	.0151	.0071	.0034	.0017
.1015	.0659	.0431	.0349	.0284	.0188	.0126	.0057	.0027	.0013
.0923	.0588	.0378	.0304	.0245	.0160	.0105	.0046	.0021	.0010
.0839	.0525	.0331	.0264	.0211	.0135	.0087	.0037	.0016	.0007
.0763	.0469	.0291	.0230	.0182	.0115	.0073	.0030	.0013	.0006
.0693	.0419	.0255	.0200	.0157	.0097	.0061	.0024	.0010	.0004
.0630	.0374	.0224	.0174	.0135	.0082	.0051	.0020	.0008	.0003
.0573	.0334	.0196	.0151	.0116	.0070	.0042	.0016	.0006	.0002
.0221	.0107	.0053	.0037	.0026	.0013	.0007	.0002	.0001	*
.0085	.0035	.0014	.0009	.0006	.0003	.0001	*	*	*
.0033	.0011	.0004	.0002	.0001	*	*	*	*	*

Present Value of an Annuity of $1 per Period for N Periods

Period	1%	2%	3%	4%	5%	6%	7%	8%	9%
1	0.9091	0.9804	0.9709	0.9615	0.9524	0.9434	0.9346	0.9259	0.9174
2	1.9704	1.9416	1.9135	1.8861	1.8594	1.8334	1.8080	1.7833	1.7591
3	2.9410	2.8839	2.8286	2.7751	2.7232	2.6730	2.6243	2.5771	2.5313
4	3.9020	3.8077	3.7171	3.6299	3.5460	3.4651	3.3872	3.3121	3.2397
5	4.8534	4.7135	4.5797	4.4518	4.3295	4.2124	4.1002	3.9927	3.8897
6	5.7955	5.6014	5.4172	5.2421	5.0757	4.9173	4.7665	4.6229	4.4859
7	6.7282	6.4720	6.2303	6.0021	5.7864	5.5824	5.3893	5.2064	5.0330
8	7.6517	7.3255	7.0197	6.7327	6.4632	6.2098	5.9713	5.7466	5.5348
9	8.5660	8.1622	7.7861	7.4353	7.1078	6.8017	6.5152	6.2469	5.9952
10	9.4713	8.9826	8.5302	8.1109	7.7217	7.3601	7.0236	6.7101	6.4177
11	10.3676	9.7868	9.2526	8.7605	8.3064	7.8869	7.4987	7.1390	6.8052
12	11.2551	10.5753	9.9540	9.3851	8.8633	8.3838	7.9427	7.5361	7.1607
13	12.1337	11.3484	10.6350	9.9856	9.3936	8.8527	8.3577	7.9038	7.4869
14	13.0037	12.1062	11.2961	10.5631	9.8986	9.2950	8.7455	8.2442	7.7862
15	13.8651	12.8493	11.9379	11.1184	10.3797	9.7122	9.1079	8.5595	8.0607
16	14.7179	13.5777	12.5611	11.6523	10.8378	10.1059	9.4466	8.8514	8.3126
17	15.5623	14.2919	13.1661	12.1657	11.2741	10.4773	9.7632	9.1216	8.5436
18	16.3983	14.9920	13.7535	12.6593	11.6896	10.8276	10.0591	9.3719	8.7556
19	17.2260	15.6785	14.3238	13.1339	12.0853	11.1581	10.3356	9.6036	8.9501
20	18.0456	16.3514	14.8775	13.5903	12.4699	11.4699	10.5940	9.8181	9.1285
21	18.8570	17.0112	15.4150	14.0292	12.8212	11.7641	10.8355	10.0168	9.2922
22	19.6604	17.6580	15.9369	14.4511	13.1630	12.0416	11.0612	10.2007	9.4424
23	20.4558	18.2922	16.4436	14.8568	13.4886	12.3034	11.2722	10.3711	9.5802
24	21.2434	18.9139	16.9355	15.2470	13.7986	12.5504	11.4693	10.5288	9.7066
25	22.0232	19.5235	17.4131	15.6221	14.0939	12.7834	11.6536	10.6748	9.8226
26	22.7952	20.1210	17.8768	15.9828	14.3752	13.0032	11.8258	10.8100	9.9290
27	23.5596	20.7069	18.3270	16.3296	14.6430	13.2105	11.9867	10.9352	10.0266
28	24.3164	21.2813	18.7641	16.6631	14.8981	13.4062	12.1371	11.0511	10.1161
29	25.0658	21.8444	19.1885	16.9837	15.1411	13.5907	12.2777	11.1584	10.1983
30	25.8077	22.3965	19.6004	17.2920	15.3725	13.7648	12.4090	11.2578	10.2737
40	32.8347	27.3555	23.1148	19.7928	17.1591	15.0463	13.3317	11.9246	10.7574
50	39.1961	31.4236	25.7298	21.4822	18.2559	15.7619	13.8007	12.2335	10.9617
60	44.9550	34.7609	27.6756	22.6235	18.9293	16.1614	14.0392	12.3766	11.0480

10%	12%	14%	15%	16%	18%	20%	24%	28%	32%
0.9091	0.8929	0.8772	0.8696	0.8621	0.8475	0.8333	0.8065	0.7813	0.7576
1.7355	1.6901	1.6467	1.6257	1.6052	1.5656	1.5278	1.4568	1.3916	1.3315
2.4869	2.4018	2.3216	2.2832	2.2459	2.1743	2.1065	1.9813	1.8684	1.7663
3.1699	3.0373	2.9137	2.8550	2.7982	2.6901	2.5887	2.4043	2.2410	2.0957
3.7908	3.6048	3.4331	3.3522	3.2743	3.1272	2.9906	2.7454	2.5320	2.3452
4.3553	4.1114	3.8887	3.7845	3.6847	3.4976	3.3255	3.0205	2.7594	2.5342
4.8684	4.5638	4.2883	4.1604	4.0386	3.8115	3.6046	3.2423	2.9370	2.6775
5.3349	4.9676	4.6389	4.4873	4.3436	4.0776	3.8372	3.4212	3.0758	2.7860
5.7590	5.3282	4.9464	4.7716	4.6065	4.3030	4.0310	3.5655	3.1842	2.8681
6.1446	5.6502	5.2161	5.0188	4.8332	4.4941	4.1925	3.6819	3.2689	2.9304
6.4951	5.9377	5.4527	5.2337	5.0286	4.6560	4.3271	3.7757	3.3351	2.9776
6.8137	6.1944	5.6603	5.4206	5.1971	4.7932	4.4392	3.8514	3.3868	3.0133
7.1034	6.4235	5.8424	5.5831	5.3423	4.9095	4.5327	3.9124	3.4272	3.0404
7.3667	6.6282	6.0021	5.7245	5.4675	4.9675	5.0081	4.6106	3.4587	3.0609
7.6061	6.8109	6.1422	5.8474	5.5755	5.0916	4.6755	4.0013	3.4834	3.0764
7.8237	6.9740	6.2651	5.9542	5.6685	5.1624	4.7296	4.0333	3.5026	3.0882
8.0216	7.1196	6.3729	6.0472	5.7487	5.2223	4.7746	4.0591	3.5177	3.0971
8.2014	7.2497	6.4674	6.1280	5.8178	5.2732	4.8122	4.0799	3.5294	3.1039
8.3649	7.3658	6.5504	6.1982	5.8775	5.3162	4.8435	4.0967	3.5386	3.1090
8.5136	7.4694	6.6231	6.2593	5.9288	5.3527	4.8696	4.1103	3.5458	3.1129
8.6487	7.5620	6.6870	6.3125	5.9731	5.3837	4.8913	4.1212	3.5514	3.1158
8.7715	7.6446	6.7429	6.3587	6.0113	5.4099	4.9094	4.1300	3.5558	3.1180
8.8832	7.7184	6.7921	6.3988	6.0442	5.4321	4.9245	4.1371	3.5592	3.1197
8.9847	7.7843	6.8351	6.4338	6.0726	5.4509	4.9371	4.1428	3.5619	3.1210
9.0770	7.8431	6.8729	6.4641	6.0971	5.4669	4.9476	4.1474	3.5640	3.1220
9.1609	7.8957	6.9061	6.4906	6.1182	5.4804	4.9563	4.1511	5.5656	3.1227
9.2372	7.9426	6.9352	6.5135	6.1364	5.4919	4.9636	4.1542	3.5669	3.1233
9.3066	7.9844	6.9607	6.5335	6.1520	5.5016	4.9697	4.1566	3.5679	3.1237
9.3696	8.0218	6.9830	6.5509	6.1656	5.5098	4.9747	4.1585	3.5687	3.1240
9.4269	8.0552	7.0027	6.5560	6.1772	5.5168	4.9789	4.1601	3.5693	3.1242
9.7791	8.2438	7.1050	6.6418	6.2335	5.5482	4.9966	4.1659	3.5712	3.1250
9.9148	8.3045	7.1327	6.6605	6.2463	5.5541	4.9995	4.1666	3.5714	3.1250
9.9672	8.3240	7.1401	6.6651	6.2492	5.5533	4.9999	4.1667	3.5714	3.1250

Future Value of an Annuity of $1 per Period for N Periods

Period	1%	2%	3%	4%	5%	6%	7%	8%	9%	10%
1	1.0000	1.0000	1.0000	1.0000	1.0000	1.0000	1.0000	1.0000	1.0000	1.0000
2	2.0100	2.0200	2.0300	2.0400	2.0500	2.0600	2.0700	2.0800	2.0900	2.1000
3	3.0301	3.0604	3.0909	3.1216	3.1525	3.1836	3.2149	3.2464	3.2781	3.3100
4	4.0604	4.1216	4.1836	4.2465	4.3101	4.3746	4.4399	4.5061	4.5731	4.6410
5	5.1010	5.2040	5.3091	5.4163	5.5256	5.6371	5.7507	5.8666	5.9847	6.1051
6	6.1520	6.3081	6.4684	6.6330	6.8019	6.9753	7.1533	7.3359	7.5233	7.7156
7	7.2135	7.4343	7.6625	7.8983	8.1420	8.3938	8.6540	8.9228	9.2004	9.4872
8	8.2857	8.5830	8.8923	9.2142	9.5491	9.8975	10.2590	10.6360	11.0280	11.4350
9	9.3685	9.7546	10.1590	10.5820	11.0260	11.4910	11.9780	12.4870	13.0210	13.5790
10	10.4620	10.9490	11.4630	12.0060	12.5770	13.1800	13.8160	14.4860	15.1920	15.9370
11	11.5660	12.1680	12.8070	13.4860	14.2060	14.9710	15.7830	16.6450	17.5600	18.5310
12	12.6820	13.4120	14.1920	15.0250	15.9170	16.8690	17.8880	18.9770	20.1400	21.3840
13	13.8090	14.6800	15.6170	16.6260	17.7130	18.8820	20.1400	21.4950	22.9530	24.5220
14	14.9470	15.9730	17.0860	18.2910	19.5980	21.0150	22.5500	24.2140	26.0190	27.9750
15	16.0960	17.2930	18.5980	20.0230	21.5780	23.2760	25.1290	27.1520	29.3600	31.7720
16	17.2570	18.6390	20.1560	21.8240	23.6570	25.6720	27.8880	30.3240	33.0030	35.9490
17	18.4300	20.0120	21.7610	23.6970	25.8400	28.2120	30.8400	33.7500	36.9730	40.5440
18	19.6140	21.4120	23.4140	25.6450	28.1320	30.9050	33.9990	37.4500	41.3010	45.5990
19	20.8100	22.8400	25.1160	27.6710	30.5390	33.7600	37.3790	41.4460	46.0180	51.1590
20	22.0190	24.2970	26.8700	29.7780	33.0660	36.7850	40.9950	45.7620	51.1600	57.2750
21	23.2390	25.7830	28.6760	31.9690	35.7190	39.9920	44.8650	50.4220	56.7640	64.0020
22	24.4710	27.2990	30.5360	34.2480	38.5050	43.3920	49.0050	55.4560	62.8730	71.4020
23	25.7160	28.8450	32.4520	36.6170	41.4300	46.9950	53.4360	60.8930	69.5310	79.5430
24	26.9730	30.4210	34.4260	39.0820	44.5020	50.8150	58.1760	66.7640	76.7890	88.4970
25	28.2430	32.0300	36.4590	41.6450	47.7270	54.8640	63.2490	73.1050	84.7000	98.3470
30	34.7840	40.5680	47.5750	56.0840	66.4380	79.0580	94.4600	113.2800	136.3000	164.4900
40	48.8860	60.4020	75.4010	95.0250	120.7900	154.7600	199.6300	259.0500	337.8800	442.5900
50	64.4630	84.5790	112.7900	152.6600	209.3400	290.3300	406.5200	573.7600	815.0800	1163.9000
60	81.6690	114.050	163.0500	237.9900	353.5800	533.1200	813.5200	1253.2000	1944.7000	3034.8000

12%	14%	15%	16%	18%	20%	24%	28%	32%
1.0000	1.0000	1.0000	1.0000	1.0000	1.0000	1.0000	1.0000	1.0000
2.1200	2.1400	2.1500	2.1600	2.1800	2.2000	2.2400	2.2800	2.3200
3.3744	3.4396	3.4725	3.5056	3.5724	3.6400	3.7776	3.9184	4.0624
4.7793	4.9211	4.9934	5.0665	5.2154	5.3680	5.6842	6.0156	6.3624
6.3528	6.6101	6.7424	6.8771	7.1542	7.4416	8.0484	8.6999	9.3983
8.1152	8.5355	8.7537	8.9775	9.4420	9.9299	10.9800	12.1350	13.4050
10.0890	10.7300	11.0660	11.4130	12.1410	12.9150	14.6150	16.5330	18.6950
12.2990	13.2320	13.7260	14.2400	15.3270	16.4990	19.1220	22.1630	25.6780
14.7750	16.0850	16.7850	17.5180	19.0850	20.7980	24.7120	29.3690	34.8950
17.5480	19.3370	20.3030	21.3210	23.5210	25.9580	31.6430	38.5920	47.0610
20.6540	23.0440	24.3490	25.7320	28.7550	32.1500	40.2370	50.3980	63.1210
24.1330	27.2700	29.0010	30.8500	34.9310	39.5800	50.3980	65.5100	84.3200
28.0290	32.0880	34.3510	36.7860	42.2180	48.4960	64.1090	84.8520	112.3000
32.3920	73.5810	40.5040	43.6720	50.8180	59.1950	80.4960	109.6100	149.2300
37.2790	43.8420	47.5800	51.6590	60.9650	72.0350	100.8100	141.3000	197.9900
42.7530	50.9800	55.7170	60.9250	72.9390	87.4420	126.0100	181.8600	262.3500
48.8830	59.1170	65.0750	71.6730	87.0680	105.9300	157.2500	233.7900	347.3000
55.7490	68.3940	75.8360	84.1400	103.7400	128.1100	195.9900	300.2500	459.4400
63.4390	78.9690	88.2110	98.6030	123.4100	154.7400	244.0300	385.3200	607.4700
72.0520	91.0240	102.4400	115.3700	147.6200	186.6800	303.6000	494.2100	802.8600
81.6980	104.7600	118.8100	134.8400	174.0200	225.0200	377.4600	633.5900	1060.7000
92.5020	120.4300	137.6300	157.4100	206.3400	271.0300	469.0500	811.9900	1401.2000
104.6000	138.2900	159.2700	183.6000	244.4800	326.2300	582.6200	1040.3000	1850.6000
118.1500	158.6500	184.1600	213.9700	289.4900	392.4800	723.4600	1332.6000	2443.8000
133.3300	181.8700	212.7900	249.2100	342.6000	471.9800	898.0900	1706.8000	3226.8000
241.3300	356.7800	434.7400	530.3100	790.9400	1181.8000	2640.9000	5873.2000	12940.0000
767.0900	1342.0000	1779.0000	2360.7000	4163.2000	7343.8000	22728.0000	69377.0000	*
2400.0000	4994.5000	7217.7000	10435.0000	21813.0000	45497.0000	*	*	*
7471.6000	18535.0000	29219.0000	46057.0000	*	*	*	*	*

*FVIFA > 99,999.

Put A New Twist On Time-Value-of-Money, And $5 In Your Pocket.

You will learn a great deal in this book about the Time-Value-of-Money. TI wants to help you learn the "value of time and money" with a great offer on the BAII PLUS™ financial calculator.

Save time. The easy-to-use features of the BAII PLUS will speed you through calculations such as net present value, internal rate of return, time-value-of-money, and more. And because the BAII PLUS is available at most stores where calculators are sold, you won't spend time searching for it.

Save money. You don't have to spend a lot of money because the BAII PLUS is priced to fit your budget. Plus, for a limited time, TI will put an extra $5 in your pocket.

Take advantage of this offer on the BAII PLUS today, and get the most value out of your time and money.

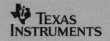

TEXAS INSTRUMENTS

TEXAS INSTRUMENTS

BAII PLUS Rebate Terms and Conditions

This offer is valid only for BAII PLUS purchases between January 1, 1999 and April 30, 2001. All claims must be postmarked by May 31, 2001. Allow 8 to 10 weeks for processing. All purchases must be made in the U.S. or Canada. Rebates will be sent only to addresses in the U.S. and Canada and paid in U.S. dollars. Not redeemable at any store. Send this completed form along with the cash register receipt (original or copy) and the UPC bar code to the address indicated. This original mail-in certificate must accompany your request and may not be duplicated or reproduced. Offer valid only as stated on this form. Offer void where prohibited, taxed, licensed, or restricted. Limit one rebate per household or address. Texas Instruments reserves the right to discontinue this program at any time and without notice.

Yes! I Want $5 Back On My Purchase of the BAII PLUS.

Glossary

Accelerated depreciation   A depreciation method that allows a firm to write off a greater percentage of an investment in the early years.

Acceleration clause   Covenant that permits the lender to demand immediate repayment of the loan balance in the event the borrower fails either to make the necessary payments or live up to the provisions of the agreement.

Acceptance   Time draft that is accepted by the drawee.

Accounting exposure   Change in the value of a firm's foreign currency-denominated accounts due to a change in exchange rates.

Accounting income   The difference between revenues and the costs associated with generating these revenues during the accounting period.

Accounting rate of return   The ratio of after-tax profit on an investment project and the average book investment.

Accounts receivable   The amounts owed to a company by its customers.

Accounts receivable financing   A method of secured borrowing in which a firm uses its accounts receivable as collateral for a loan.

Accounts receivable turnover   A measure of activity: net credit sales divided by accounts receivable.

Acid-test ratio   A measure of liquidity: current assets less inventory divided by current liabilities. Also known as the *quick ratio.*

Acquirer   In general, an individual or company that buys something. Used frequently in an acquisition setting to refer to the buyer of another firm.

Acquisition   The purchase of one firm by another.

Activity ratios   Ratios that measure the efficiency with which a company uses its resources.

Adjustable-rate mortgage   Mortgage whose interest rate is adjusted every month or so, in line with the changing short-term cost of funds.

Adjusted net present value   Net present value of a project if all-equity financed plus the value of financing side effects.

Adverse incentives   Management incentives that motivate management behavior that is not in the best interest of stockholders and other firm stakeholders.

Adverse selection, or lemons problem   A potential buyer's fear that the current owner wants to get rid of an asset he or she knows is a "lemon."

Affirmative covenant   A provision in a loan agreement that describes actions, such as supplying periodic financial statements, that a firm must do over the course of the agreement.

After-market price   The price at which an initial public offering trades immediately following its sale.

Agency costs   The sum of all costs associated with having managers make decisions on behalf of the owners. These costs include the costs of monitoring and control procedures, as well as the loss in value when managers do not make decisions in the best interest of the owners.

Agency problem or conflict   Conflicts of interest that arise when corporate decisions are delegated to agents (the managers) who work on behalf of the owners.

Agency securities Debt instruments sold by federally sponsored credit agencies.

Aggressive financing strategy A financing strategy in which a company uses short-term funds to finance its temporary assets plus part of its permanent assets.

Aggressive stock Stocks with betas greater than 1.0. These stocks tend to fluctuate more than the market.

Aging of accounts receivables Categorizing accounts receivable according to the length of time that they are outstanding.

All-equity beta Beta of a project or company financed with 100 percent equity.

All-equity rate Required return on a project or company financed with 100 percent equity.

American Depository Receipt (ADR) A certificate of ownership issued by a U.S. bank as a convenience to investors in lieu of the underlying foreign shares it holds in custody.

American option Option that can be exercised at any time prior to expiration.

American shares Security certificates issued in the United States by a transfer agent acting on behalf of a foreign issuer. The certificates represent claims to foreign equities.

American terms Number of U.S. dollars per unit of a foreign currency.

Amortization The repayment of a loan.

Annual percentage rate (APR) The rate that takes into account the effect of compounding within a year. Also known as the *effective interest rate*.

Annuity A series of equal cash payments per period for a specified number of periods.

Annuity due An annuity in which the payments begin at the beginning of each period.

Anti-takeover charter amendments Corporate charter amendments that are designed to make takeovers more difficult.

Arbitrage Profiting from differences in price when asset is traded in two or more markets by buying in the market with the low price and selling in the market with the high price.

Arbitrage pricing theory (APT) A model of asset valuation that attempts to relate required returns to a common set of risk factors. The prices for risk factors are set so that there's no potential for arbitrage profits in the market. The model is a competitor to the capital asset pricing model.

Asked price The price at which one can sell a security or currency.

Asset A property that someone owns and whose economic value is determined by its ability to generate future cash flows.

Asset-based financing A financial arrangement whereby a bank or a commercial finance company lends money secured by some asset, usually accounts receivable or inventories.

Asset beta Beta of the firm's assets.

Assets in place A firm's already existing investments.

At-the-money option Option whose exercise price just equals its asset price.

Authorized shares The number of shares that a firm's board of directors gives it permission to issue.

Automatic Clearinghouse (ACH) Organization that sorts and routes electronic transfers among financial institutions for payment.

Average collection period Measures the average amount of time it takes a firm's customers to pay their bills. Equals credit sales times 365, divided by accounts receivable.

Balance sheet A financial statement that presents the firms assets, liabilities, and equity at a specific point in time.

Balloon payment A large final payment that pays off the outstanding balance on some debt obligation.

Bank draft Draft addressed to a bank.

Bankers' acceptance (B/A) A draft accepted by a bank. Most bankers' acceptances arise in international transactions.

Bankruptcy Formal legal proceedings in which a company in financial difficulty is placed under the protection of the court. The court allows the company to keep operating until a plan is developed to pay off the creditors.

Bankruptcy costs   The direct legal, accounting, and administrative costs associated with bankruptcy plus the losses associated with the sale of assets at "fire sale" prices.

Barriers to entry   The costs that a new entrant to a market must overcome to do business.

Base case   An initial set of assumptions used to generate estimates of a project's cash flows.

Basis point   One-hundredth of a percentage point of interest.

Basis risk   Risk that there will be a divergence between the value of the risk being hedged and the value of the futures contract.

Bearer bonds   Bonds that are not registered with the issuer. Ownership of these bonds is evidenced by their physical possession.

Best-cost provider   A corporate strategy in which a firm tries to establish cost leadership coupled with some other feature (e.g., quality and service) to gain competitive advantage.

Best-efforts basis   Special arrangement to sell newly issued securities whereby an investment bank does not buy the issue but only agrees to use its best efforts to sell the securities.

Beta   Measure of the sensitivity of an asset's return to movements in the market as a whole.

Bid price   The price at which one can buy a security or currency.

Bill of exchange   See *Bank draft.*

Bird-in-the-hand argument   The notion that, because investors are risk averse, they prefer a stream of relatively certain dividends over the uncertain capital gains associated with reinvested earnings.

Black Monday   Day (October 19,1987) on which share prices on the New York Stock Exchange dropped 23 percent.

Black-Scholes option pricing model   Formula developed by Fisher Black and Myron Scholes to value European options.

Blank check   Anti-takeover device that permits management to give key voting rights to

friendly shareholders to help vote down hostile takeovers.

Blanket mortgage bond   Bond that is secured by substantially all of the issuing firm's assets.

Bond   Long-term debt security that promises to pay its owner periodic interest until the bond matures, at which time the bondholder will also receive a specified principal sum.

Book value per share   Balance sheet assets minus balance sheet liabilities. This represents the cost of the company's investments less the debt used to finance them. Dividing by the number of shares outstanding gives us the book value per share.

Brand-name capital   The value of a company's brands built up through years of advertising and promotion and the provision of quality goods and services. Often referred to as *brand equity.*

Break-even EBIT   See *EBIT-EPS indifference point.*

Broker   A person who facilitates financial market transactions by bringing buyers and sellers together. Brokers never own the securities and receive their compensation by charging commissions.

Brokered market   A market in which trades are primarily facilitated by brokers.

Business judgment rule   Generally accepted principle of common law that judges should not second-guess management's decisions.

Business risk   The variability of a firm's operating earnings due to the inherent risks of the markets in which it serves.

Buy-and-hold strategy   Risk-reducing strategy that consists of setting up a position and holding it over the length of the period when risk reduction is required.

Call option   Option to buy a specific asset at an agreed-upon price and terms within a specific time period.

Call premium   (1) The penalty for retiring an entire debt or preferred stock issue prior to maturity. (2) The price of a call option.

Call provision   A feature in a debt agreement that gives the issuer the right to retire an entire issue prior to maturity.

Capital asset pricing model (CAPM)   A model of asset pricing in which the premium for bearing risk is proportional to beta—the volatility of an asset's return with the market as a whole.

Capital budgeting decision The process of choosing long-term investment projects.

Capital expenditure An investment that is expected to generate cash flows beyond one year.

Capital gain The appreciation in the value of an asset.

Capital impairment rule Rule preventing corporations from paying dividends out of paid-in capital.

Capital lease See *Financial lease.*

Capital market The market where long-term securities are bought and sold.

Capital market line (CML) The relationship between risk and return for portfolios constructed from securities traded in competitive markets.

Capital rationing A situation in which a firm's capital budget is insufficient to fund all acceptable projects.

Capital structure The combination of debt and equity used by a company to finance the purchase of its assets.

Cash budget A forecast of a firm's cash receipts and disbursements.

Cash concentration service Moves funds from different bank accounts into a single account from which investments or payments can be made.

Cash conversion cycle The length of time, in days, between when goods or services purchased by a firm have to be paid for, and when the firm collects payment from its customers.

Cash discount The percentage that a customer can deduct from an invoice for paying before some *discount period.*

Cash flow Amount of money changing hands on a transaction or during a certain time period.

Cash flow coverage A leverage ratio that measures the ability of a company to service its debt. Equal to operating earnings plus lease payments plus depreciation, divided by the firm's tax-adjusted fixed financial charges.

Cash inadequacy Inability to fund all desired, but not absolutely essential, expenditures.

Cash in advance Payment must be received before shipment.

Cash insolvency Probability of a company running out of cash.

Cash matching Risk-reducing strategy that involves taking a position that, when through time, will exactly offset the risk.

Cash on delivery (COD) Payment must be received upon delivery.

Cash pool Centrally managed bank account.

Certificate of deposit (CDs) Receipt issued by a bank in exchange for a deposit of funds. The CDs of well-known banks are highly marketable.

Chapter 7 Provision in the U.S. Bankruptcy Code under which a firm's assets are assigned to a trustee who sells off the assets.

Chapter 11 Provision in the U.S. Bankruptcy Code under which a firm in financial difficulty can file for "protection" from its creditors in order to give the firm time to reorganize.

Characteristic line A line of best fit that relates the realized return on a stock with that of the market portfolio.

Chattel mortgage A lien on property other than real estate. Typically seen when equipment is used as security against a firm's borrowing.

Check-clearing float Time it takes to clear each check deposited.

CHIPS (Clearing House Interbank Payments System) Computerized network for transfer of international dollar payments.

Cleanup period A provision in a loan agreement requiring that the borrower reduce outstanding balances to zero for at least 30 to 90 days during the year. This is seen most frequently with loans taken out for seasonal needs.

Clearinghouse Organization that sorts and routes checks to the proper bank or savings institution for payment.

Closed-end mortgage   Mortgage whose indenture forbids the issuance of additional bonds against pledged property.

Collateral   Assets used to secure a loan.

Collatereralized bond   A bond secured by some of the firm's assets as collateral.

Collateral trust bond   A bond secured by financial assets such as stocks and bonds, rather than real property.

Collection float   Time that receivables spend in the process of being collected.

Commercial paper   Short-term unsecured promissory notes issued by large businesses.

Commitment fee   A fee paid to commercial banks in order to obtain their legal commitment to lend.

Commodity   An undifferentiated product sold exclusively on the basis of price.

Common stock   A security that represents the ownership interest in a company. Holders of common stock are entitled to a pro rata share of income and assets in liquidation after creditor and preferred stockholder needs have been accommodated.

Compensating balance   The minimum cash balance that a company is required to keep on deposit in order to "compensate" a bank for services provided.

Competitive bid   The process of selecting an underwriter on the basis of their bidding on an offer whose details already have been decided on by the issuer.

Competitive equilibrium   A situation in which competitors catch up with market leaders so that it becomes difficult for a firm to generate projects that earn more than the required return.

Competitive industry   An industry characterized by costless entry and exit, undifferentiated products or services, and increasing marginal costs of production.

Compound interest   Interest earned is added to the principal amount so that interest may be earned on interest.

Conditional sales contract   Sale in which the seller retains title to the equipment until the loan is repaid.

Conglomerate   Company consisting of units in unrelated businesses.

Conglomerate merger   Merger of two companies in unrelated businesses.

Consignment   Credit term under which the seller retains title to the goods until the buyer has sold the goods to a third party.

Conservative financing strategy   A financing strategy in which a firm uses long-term funds to finance both permanent and part of its temporary assets.

Consol   The name given to perpetual bonds issued by the British government.

Constant dividend growth model   A model of common stock valuation that assumes that a firm's dividends will grow at a constant rate into the indefinite future.

Contingent projects   A situation in which the adoption of one project is dependent, or contingent, on the acceptance of one or more other projects.

Contractual cash flows   Cash flows fixed in nominal dollar amounts.

Controlled foreign corporation (CFC)   Foreign corporation whose voting stock is more than 50 percent owned by U.S. stockholders, each owning at least 10 percent of the voting power.

Conversion premium   The difference between a convertible security's conversion price and the stock price at the time of issue.

Conversion price   The par value of the convertible security divided by the number of shares into which the security may be converted.

Conversion ratio   The number of shares for which a convertible security may be exchanged.

Convertible bond   Bond that can be exchanged at the option of the holder into a fixed number of shares of common stock.

Convertible preferred stock   A preferred stock issue that can be exchanged at the option of the holder into a fixed number of shares of common stock.

Core competency A skill or something a company does well that can be a source of competitive advantage.

Corporate culture Set of values, norms, and beliefs held by the employees of a company.

Corporation A form of business organization that is a legal being, separate and apart from its owners.

Correlation coefficient Measures the extent to which two quantities are related to one another. In finance, the correlation coefficient is used to indicate how two securities move with respect to one another. Can take on values ranging from +1 to −1.

Cost of capital Minimum acceptable rate of return on an investment as determined by investors.

Cost of debt capital The after-tax cost of raising new debt capital.

Cost of equity capital Minimum return common stockholders require on their equity capital.

Cost of preferred stock The required rate of return for preferred stockholders.

Cost reduction project A project whose primary benefits are in the form of reducing a firm's operating costs.

Cost-volume-profit (CVP) analysis Technique to determine the impact of changes in variable costs, overhead expenses, sales, sales prices, and sales volume on profits and financial requirements.

Countertrade The exchange of goods for other goods in lieu of cash. Often used in international transactions.

Coupon The periodic interest paid on a bond. Equals the face value of the bond times the coupon interest rate.

Coupon interest rate Annual coupon amount divided by the face value of the bond.

Covariance Statistical measure of the tendency of two variables to move together that is related to the correlation coefficient.

Covenants The provisions in a loan agreement that defines what the borrower must do (affirmative covenants) and the restrictions on a borrower's behavior (negative covenants).

Covered interest arbitrage Movement of short-term funds between two currencies to take advantage of interest differentials with the exchange rate risk eliminated by means of forward contracts.

Credit period The length of time for which trade credit is granted. Usually measured from the date of invoice.

Credit scoring Procedure for assigning scores to credit applicants to determine their risk of default.

Credit transfer basis Banking convention whereby the payer benefits from any disbursement float.

Cross-border lease Lease transaction in which the lessor and lessee are in different countries.

Cross-hedge Use of a futures contract on a related commodity to hedge a commodity for which a futures contract does not exist.

Cross-sectional analysis The comparison of a firm's ratios in a given year with other companies in the same industry.

Cross-subsidization A situation in which profits from a high-return business unit are used to subsidize units with low returns. Also used frequently by multinational firms as a means of penetrating foreign markets.

Crown jewel Particularly profitable or important business unit. Often sold to a friendly party to forestall a hostile takeover.

Cumulative provision Provision in a preferred stock issue that requires that unpaid dividends be carried forward from year-to-year. Until this obligation is cleared up, the firm cannot pay dividends to common stockholders.

Currency swap Simultaneous borrowing and lending operation whereby two parties exchange specific amounts of two currencies at the outset at the spot rate. They also exchange interest payments in the two currencies. The parties also undertake to reverse the exchange after a fixed term at a fixed exchange rate.

Current assets   Assets that are expected to be converted into cash within a year.

Current liabilities   Debts that mature within one year.

Current ratio   Measure of liquidity. Current assets divided by current liabilities.

Current yield   The annual coupon interest payment dividend by a bond's current market price.

Cyclical stock   Stocks whose returns move in line with the state of the economy.

Daylight overdraft   Intraday loan extended by the Federal Reserve when an institution has sent more funds over FedWire than it has reserves or clearing account, or has sent more funds over CHIPs than it has received.

Dealer   A person who facilitates market transactions by buying and selling securities out of his or her own inventory. Like any other investor who owns securities, dealers make money by buying low and selling high.

Dealer market   A market in which trades are primarily facilitated by dealers.

Debenture   An unsecured bond.

Debit transfer basis   Banking convention whereby the bank benefits from any disbursement float.

Debt capacity   The maximum amount of debt a company can add to its capital structure without incurring undue risks.

Debt-equity ratio   Leverage ratio; total liabilities divided by equity.

Debt ratio   Leverage ratio; total liabilities divided by total assets.

Decision trees   Aid in solving problems that involve a sequential decisions by diagramming the alternatives and their possible consequences,

Declaration date   The date the board of directors meets and announces its intention to pay a dividend.

Default risk   Chance that the debt will not be repaid.

Defensive stocks   Stocks with betas less than 1.0. These stocks are less volatile than the market.

Depreciation   An accountant's allocation of the cost of a fixed asset over its life. Although depreciation is an expense for tax purposes, it doesn't involve an expenditure of cash.

Derivative securities   A security that derives its value from some other asset.

Devaluation   Decrease in the spot value of a currency.

Differentiation   An attempt to build attributes into a product that distinguish it from others in the marketplace. Effective product differentiation lowers the total cost of use to the buyer.

Direct debiting   See *Preauthorized payment.*

Direct lease   Lease of an asset not previously owned by the lessee.

Disbursement float   Checks a firm has written but have not yet been cleared.

Disciplinary acquisitions   Acquisitions whose primary focus is to correct non-value-maximizing behavior on the part of the target's management.

Discounted payback   The length of time it takes for the present value of a project's cash inflows to recover its investment costs.

Discount rate   The interest rate used to convert future dollars to their present value.

Diversifiable risk   That portion of an asset's variability that can be eliminated by holding a well-diversified portfolio. Also known as *unsystematic risk.*

Dividend   Periodic payment made to either preferred or common stockholders.

Dividend irrelevance proposition   The idea that dividend policy is irrelevant in the sense that it cannot affect shareholder value.

Dividend payout ratio   The proportion of the earnings paid out as dividends.

Dividend yield   Expected annual dividend divided by the current stock price.

Documentary draft   Draft accompanied by shipping documents to be delivered to the drawee on payment or acceptance of the draft.

Double-dip lease   Cross-border lease in which the disparate rules of the lessor's and lessee's countries let both parties be treated as the owner of the leased equipment for tax purposes.

Draft   An unconditional written order signed by a person, usually the seller, and addressed to the buyer, ordering the buyer to pay on demand (a sight draft), or at some future date (a time draft), the amount on the face of the draft.

Drawee   The party to whom the draft is addressed.

DuPont analysis   A tool of financial analysis that relates return on equity to the net profit margin, asset utilization, and leverage.

Duration   Measures the average time that lapses until the "average" dollar of the present value of an asset's payment stream is received.

Dynamic strategy   Risk-reducing strategy that consists of setting up a position and periodically changing it through time.

Earnings   A measure of the increase in owner's wealth during a certain time period.

Earnings per share (EPS)   The earnings available to common stockholders (which is equal to net income less preferred stock dividends) divided by the number of common shares outstanding.

EBIT   Earnings before interest and taxes; also known as the firm's *operating earnings*.

EBIT-EPS indifference point   That level of EBIT at which the EPS for two financing alternatives are the same.

Economic depreciation   The decline in the economic value of an asset over some time period.

Economic exposure   The extent to which the value of the firm will change due to an exchange rate change.

Economic income   Change in the owner's wealth during the accounting period.

Economic order quantity (EOQ)   Amount of inventory to order that minimizes the total order costs plus carrying costs.

Economic value   The value of an asset (or liability) based on its ability to generate (or consume) cash over time.

Economic value added (EVA)   The after-tax operating profits for a firm in a given year less the dollar cost of the capital needed to generate these profits.

Economies of scale   Condition in which an increase in activity (e.g., production, sales) causes a less-than-proportional increase in costs.

Economies of scope   Condition in which there are cost advantages associated with producing and selling multiple products related through common technology, production facilities, or channels of distribution.

Effective interest rate   The interest rate on an investment that reflects the holder's ability to earn interest on interest within a year. Also known as *annual percentage rate*.

Efficient capital markets   A market in which asset prices adjust rapidly to reflect all relevant and available information.

Efficient frontier   Set of efficient portfolios.

Efficient markets hypothesis   Proposition stating that security prices tend to fully reflect everything known about the prospects of their issuers and the economies in which the issuers operate.

Efficient portfolio   Combination of assets that yields the smallest possible standard deviation for its level of expected return and also a maximum expected return for a given level of risk.

Embedded options   Options that are an integral part of some investment project or financing choice.

Employee stock ownership plan (ESOP)   Trust set up to buy stock on behalf of employees. Under current law, ESOPs receive substantial tax benefits.

Enhancing shareholder value   The financial goal of the firm focusing on making decisions that will make shareholders better off by increasing stock price.

Entrepôts   Markets that serve as financial intermediaries between nonresident suppliers of funds and nonresident users of funds.

Equipment financing loan　Loan used to finance a new piece of equipment that is secured by the equipment itself.

Equipment trust certificate　Bond secured by equipment.

Equity beta　Asset beta adjusted for leverage. The observed betas of stocks are equity betas because they reflect the firm's financing mix.

Equity multiplier　Total assets divided by shareholder's equity.

Equity residual (ER) method　Valuation method in which the cash flows to equity are discounted at the cost of equity capital.

Equivalent annual cost (EAC)　The annuity with the same life of the asset and whose present value equals the cost of the asset.

Eurobond　A bond sold outside the country in whose currency the bond is denominated.

Eurocommercial paper (Euro-CP)　Euronotes that are not underwritten.

Eurocurrency　Any currency deposited in a bank outside the country of its origin.

Eurodollar CDs　Dollar-denominated bank deposits outside the United States.

Euroequity issue　Syndicated equity offering placed throughout Europe and handled by one lead manager.

Euronote　Short-term note issued outside the country in which it is denominated.

European option　An option that can be exercised only at its expiration date.

European terms　Number of foreign currency units per U.S. dollar.

Exchange rate risk　The variability in a firm's value that is due to uncertain exchange rate changes.

Ex-dividend　Shares that are sold without the right to the forthcoming dividend.

Ex-dividend date　Prior to this date, which is four business days before the holder-of-record date, the right to the dividend remains with the stock.

Exercise price　Price at which an option can be exercised. Often referred to as the *strike price*.

Expansion project　A project needed to meet projected increases in demand for a firm's existing products or services.

Expectations hypothesis　Explanation for the term structure of interest rates that states that the current observed rate is a geometric average of future expected rates.

Expected rate of return　The weighted average of all possible returns in which the weights reflect the likelihood of each return occurring.

Expiration date　Date when an option expires.

Export-Import Bank (Eximbank)　U.S. government agency that facilitates U.S. exports through subsidized export financing.

Ex-rights　Stock that trades without the right to purchase additional shares attached.

Ex-rights date　After this date, the shares will trade ex-rights.

Face value　Specified principal sum a bondholder is scheduled to receive when the bond matures.

Factor　Specialized buyer, at a discount, of company receivables.

Factoring　The sale of a firm's receivables, at a discount, to a specialized buyer known as a factor.

Fair-price approach　Anti-takeover device that requires an equivalent price be paid for all shares of stock that a raider is attempting to purchase.

Federal funds　Uncommitted reserves of a bank available for sale to other banks.

FedWire　Electronic system operated by the Federal Reserve and used for domestic money transfers.

Field warehouse　A warehouse established on the buyer's premises by a field warehouse company that manages the inventory on behalf of a seller or creditor.

Field warehouse receipt　Receipt issued by a warehouse company that lists the inventory placed in a field warehouse.

financial assets　Assets whose value is derived from their claim on certain cash flows of issuers.

Financial distress   A situation that occurs when a company has difficulty in meeting its contractual obligations.

Financial economics   Discipline that emphasizes economic analysis to understand the basic workings of the financial markets.

Financial flexibility   Flexibility that comes from a firm having unused borrowing capacity, liquid assets, and access to a broad range of funding sources.

Financial intermediary   Financial institution, such as a bank or insurance company, that issues securities (or deposits) on its own, and then lends the proceeds to a third party.

Financial lease   Long-term, noncancelable lease.

Financial leverage   The substitution of fixed-charge financing—primarily debt, but also including preferred stock—for common stock that has no contractual payments.

Financial leverage ratios   Ratios that measure a firm's ability to handle its debt.

Financial pecking order   Corporate preference for internal, as opposed to external financing, and for issuing debt over common stock.

Financial risk   The additional risk borne by the shareholders due to the substitution of debt for common stock.

Financing function   The process of generating funds internally or from sources external to the firm at the lowest possible cost.

First-in, first-out (FIFO)   An accounting inventory valuation method under which cost of goods sold reflects the prices paid for the oldest—and usually the cheapest—items in inventory.

Fisher effect   The relationship that states that the nominal interest rate is equal to the real interest rate plus the expected rate of inflation.

Fixed charge coverage ratio   Leverage ratio: EBIT plus lease payments divided by the firm's tax-adjusted fixed financial charges.

Fixed exchange rate   Exchange rate whose value is fixed by the governments involved.

Float   The difference between the balance shown in a firm's checking account and the balance in the bank's books.

Floating exchange rate   Exchange rate whose value is determined in the foreign exchange market.

Floating lien   Borrowing arrangement that gives the lender a general claim against the borrower's entire inventory.

Floating-rate debt   Debt whose interest rate is adjusted periodically to be in line with the changing cost of funds.

Floor planning   A form of trust receipt financing in which pledged inventory is held on the borrower's premises for sale to customers. Used primarily with high-ticket items such as appliances and automobiles.

Flotation cost   The cost of bringing a security issue to market.

Focus   A corporate strategy in which management's time and energy are concentrated in its core business.

Foreign bank market   That portion of the domestic bank loans that is supplied to foreigners for use abroad.

Foreign bond market   That portion of the domestic bond market that represents issues by foreign companies or governments.

Foreign direct investment   Acquisition abroad of physical assets, such as plant and equipment, with operating control residing in the parent company.

Foreign equity market   That portion of a domestic equity market that represents shares issued by foreign firms.

Foreign exchange market   The market for the exchange of currencies.

Foreign exchange risk   The risk that the value of one currency may fluctuate in relation to another currency.

Foreign tax credit   Home country credit against domestic income tax for foreign taxes already paid on foreign source earnings.

Form 10-K   Detailed financial report filed each year with the Securities and Exchange Commission by all publicly traded firms.

Form 10-Q   Quarterly SEC filing that is less detailed, but more current, than the 10-K.

Forward contract Contractual obligation to buy or sell a specific amount of a given commodity or asset on a specified future date, at a price set at the time the contract is entered into.

Forward differential Annualized percentage differential between spot and forward rates.

Forward market The market in which contracts are made to buy or sell currencies or other commodities for future delivery.

Forward rate The rate quoted today for the delivery at some future date of a specified amount of one currency or commodity.

Free cash flow The cash flows available to all suppliers of long-term capital after accommodating a firm's investment needs.

Free float Exchange rate system characterized by the absence of government intervention. Also known as *clean float*.

Futures contract Standardized contract that entails a contractual obligation to buy or sell a specific amount of a given commodity or asset on a specified future date, at a price set at the time the contract is entered into. Futures contracts are similar to forward contracts except that they are traded on organized futures exchanges, and the gains and losses on each contract are settled each day.

Future value The amount of money to which an investment will growth over a specified time period.

Future value interest factor The amount to which a dollar will grow over a specified time period when invested at a particular interest rate.

Future value of an annuity The amount to which an annuity will grow to at the end of some annuity period.

Glass-Steagall Act of 1933 Law that separates commercial and investment banks in the United States.

Global efficient set The set of efficient portfolios that can be generated by combining both foreign and domestic securities.

Golden parachute An agreement by a company to reward its key executives with substantial payments should the company be taken over.

Greenmail Repurchase of stock from an unwanted suitor at a higher-than-market price.

Green shoe option Option to give the underwriters the right to buy at the offer price a specified number of additional shares from the issuer.

Gross profit margin Profitability ratio: gross profits divided by net sales.

Growth option The opportunity that a firm may have of increasing the profitability of its existing product lines or to benefit from expanding into new products or markets.

Hedge (1) To enter into a forward contract in order to protect the home currency value of foreign currency–denominated assets or liabilities; (2) managing risk by establishing an offsetting position such that whatever is lost or gained on the original exposure is exactly offset by a corresponding gain or loss on the hedge.

High-yield bond Bond rated BB or lower by Standard and Poors and Ba or lower by Moodys. Also known as *junk bonds*.

Holder-of-record date Dividend is paid to stockholders registered as owners of shares on the company's books as of this date.

Horizontal integration A strategy designed to gain control or acquire firms in the same line of business.

Hurdle rate See *cost of capital for a project*.

Immunization Neutralizing interest rate risk.

Income bond Unsecured bond on which interest is due only to the extent that it is covered by corporate earnings.

Income statement A financial statement reporting a firm's revenues, expenses, and profits (or losses) in a given year.

Incremental cash flow The additional revenue that will be generated or expenses that will be incurred by undertaking a particular action.

Incremental cash flow of an investment The difference between the cash flows with the investment and the cash flow without the investment.

Indenture The legal agreement between a bond issuer and the lender.

Independent projects Project whose cash flows are not dependent on the acceptance or rejection of some other project.

Indexed bonds Bonds whose interest payments are linked to an index, such as the consumer price index.

Individual retirement accounts (IRAs) IRS provision that permits individuals to establish tax-deferred pension plans.

Industrial development bonds (IDBs) Tax-exempt securities issued on behalf of private companies by states and municipalities.

Inflation risk Uncertainty about the future rate of inflation and their impact on the prices of securities.

Information asymmetry A reference to the fact that one party to a transaction often knows something relevant about a transaction that is not known to the other party.

Initial public offering (IPO) A common stock issue sold to the public for the first time.

Insolvency rule Rule that prohibits an insolvent firm from paying dividends.

Intangible assets Assets that do not have any physical presence but may nevertheless be valuable. Intangible assets include items such as patents, brand names, as well as the value of the firm's human assets.

Interbank market A wholesale market in which major banks trade currencies with one another.

Intercept point Central corporate point to which all collections within a country are forwarded.

Interest The cost of borrowing money. Typically expressed as a percent of the amount borrowed.

Interest coverage Leverage Ratio: EBIT divided by interest. Often referred to as *times interest earned*.

Interest only (IO) Package of coupons stripped from bonds and sold separately.

Interest rate cap Contract that puts an upper bound on the interest on a floating-rate debt.

Interest rate collar Contract that reduces the risk of floating-rate debt by putting both a floor and ceiling on the interest rate that can be charged.

Interest rate parity Condition that arises when the interest differential is (approximately) equal to the forward differential between the two currencies.

Interest rate swap An agreement between two parties to exchange interest rate payments for a specific maturity on an agreed-upon principal amount. The most common interest rate swap involves exchanging fixed-interest payments for floating-rate payments.

Interest tax shield The tax savings associated with debt financing.

Internal rate of return The discount rate that equates the present value of a project's cash inflows with the present value of the investment's cash outflows.

International financial market Any national financial market where foreigners can borrower and lend money.

International Fisher effect The theory that the interest rate differentials between two countries equal expected changes in the spot exchange rates.

In-the-money option An option that would be profitable to exercise at an asset's current price.

Intracorporate loan Loan made by one unit of a corporation to another unit of the same corporation.

Intracorporate transaction Transaction carried out by two units of the same corporation.

Inventory conversion period The number of days of inventory a firm has on hand.

Inventory turnover An activity ratio: cost of goods sold divided by inventory.

Investment banker A financing specialist who helps firms design and sell new issues of securities.

Investment-grade bonds Bonds rated Baa or better by Moody's or BBB or better by Standard and Poors.

Investment tax credit Provision in the tax code that allows a company to reduce its tax bill by an amount equal to a specified percentage of the cost of qualifying property. This provision has been eliminated.

Invoicing float Period from the issue and mailing of an invoice by a company to payment by a customer.

Issued stock Authorized shares of common stock that are sold.

Junk bond   Another name for a high-yield bond.

Just-in-time   An inventory management technique which requires that raw materials, and work in progress be delivered when needed. The Japanese refer to this as *kanban*.

Last-in, first-out (LIFO)   A method of valuing inventory that values cost of goods sold according to the most recently purchased items in stock.

Law of conservation of value   The principle that states that, regardless of how the cash flows from an asset (or a firm) are packaged and repackaged, the value remains the same.

Law of one price   Theory stating that the prices for identical goods must be the same in all markets after adjusting for the transactions cost to move them from one place to another.

Leading and lagging   Accelerating (leading) and delaying (lagging) international payments by modifying credit terms, normally in trade between affiliates of a multinational corporation.

Learning curve   The idea that as production experience accumulates, costs will be expected to decrease because of a more efficient use of labor, capital, and materials.

Lease   Rental agreement.

Legal list   Lists, prepared by various government bodies, of those securities in which pension funds, insurance companies, and other financial institutions may invest. A typical requirement for a legal listing is some minimum and uninterrupted dividend payment.

Lessee   User of the leased asset.

Lessor   Owner of the leased asset.

Letter of credit   Letter addressed to a seller, written and signed by a bank on behalf of a buyer, in which the bank promises to honor drafts drawn on itself if the seller conforms to specific conditions contained in the letter.

Leveraged buyout (LBO)   A transaction in which a small group of investors—usually including management—buys a firm and takes it private, using mostly borrowed funds to finance the transaction.

Leveraged cashout (LCO)   Leveraged recapitalization wherein management and employee stock plans receive new shares of roughly equivalent value rather than cash for the old shares they own.

Leveraged lease   Lease in which the lessor finances a large portion of the cost of the asset with borrowed money.

Leveraged recapitalization   In these transactions, a firm increases debt and shrinks equity either by paying a huge one-time dividend to stockholders or by issuing debt to repurchase a large amount of stock.

Leverage ratios   Ratios that measure a firm's ability to service its debt.

Limited liability   The statute that limits stockholders' liability to their money already invested in a company.

Line of credit   Informal agreement that permits a company to borrow up to a stated maximum amount from the bank.

Liquidation   Process whereby a firm's assets are sold off and the proceeds given to its creditors.

Liquidity   Ability to convert an asset quickly into cash at a low transaction cost.

Liquidity premium theory   Theory that the term structure of interest rates reflects both interest rate expectations and risk premiums.

Liquidity ratios   Financial ratios that measure the degree to which current assets can meet current liabilities as they come due.

Loan amortization schedule   A schedule that breaks down each loan payment into its principle and interest components.

Lock-box   Collection and processing service in which payments to a company are intercepted by a bank through the use of a postal box in a company's name or a unique zip code.

Lock-up option   An anti-takeover device that gives a friendly acquirer the right to buy valuable assets at an attractive price.

London Interbank Offer Rate (LIBOR)   Interest rate at which banks lend to one another in the

Eurocurrency market. Used as a basis for adjustable-rate loans outside of the United States.

Long-term debt Debt having a maturity of more than one year.

Low-cost provider A strategy designed to help a company achieve the lowest possible cost for a good or service.

Mail float Time taken by the postal service to deliver a customer's check.

Marginal cost The required return on new capital; not the past (historical) cost of raising capital from that source.

Marginal tax rate The tax rate at which additional income is taxed.

Market capitalization rate Overall capitalization, or discount, rate for a firm.

Market niche A segment of the market having specific needs for products or service.

Market portfolio Portfolio that contains all risky assets, with each asset being held in proportion to that asset's share of the total market value of all assets. In practice, a proxy portfolio that contains all shares listed on the New York Stock Exchange is often used.

Market price of risk The risk premium expected by investors per unit of market risk. Defined formally as the expected return on the market portfolio less the risk-free rate, divided by the standard deviation of returns on the market portfolio.

Market risk That element of an asset's risk that cannot be completely eliminated through diversification. For common stock, market risk is related to movements in the market. Also known as *systematic risk*.

Market risk premium The difference between the expected return on the market portfolio and the risk-free rate.

Market-to-book ratio Ratio of the market value of the equity to the book value of the equity. The ratio represents the value created for the shareholders relative to the cost of creating that value.

Market value added (MVA) Difference between the market value of a firm's common stock and the

capital supplied by shareholders. MVA is a measure of shareholder wealth creation.

Market value of the equity The value investors place on the ownership of the firm. Equal to the market price per share times the number of shares outstanding.

Marking to market Practice of settling futures contracts daily by paying out profits and losses on the contracts at the end of each trading day.

Matching financing strategy A financing strategy in which the maturity of the source of funds should match the maturity of the assets being financed.

Material requirements planning (MRP) Computerized control system that tells a company precisely what adjustments are necessary to bring raw material orders in line with production needs.

Maturity Date on which a security becomes due and payable.

Merger An agreement between the boards of directors of two companies to combine.

Mezzanine financing Later-stage financing provided by venture capitalists who prefer to back more mature (and less risky) companies.

Mission statement That element of the strategic plan that describes the scope of the firm's operations in terms of customers and markets served, and/or technologies utilized.

Mobilization points Central locations to which customers are instructed to remit their payments.

Modified duration Measures the sensitivity of an asset's value to changes in market interest rates.

Modified internal rate of return (MIRR) A variation of the internal rate of return. The method assumes that all project cash flows are reinvested at the required rate of return. Using the required rate of return as a reinvestment rate, the terminal value of the project's cash flow is calculated. The MIRR is the discount rate that equates the present value of this terminal value with the project's cost.

Money market The markets for credit instruments maturing in one year or less.

Money market hedge Financing technique involving the use of foreign currency debt and designed to reduce exchange risk.

Mortgage bond   A bond secured by a lien on real property (e.g., land, plant, and equipment.)

Multiple discriminate analysis (MDA)   Widely used statistical procedure for assigning the weights to different factors in such a way as to best discriminate between good and bad credit risks.

Mutually exclusive projects   Projects are mutually exclusive if the acceptance of one precludes the acceptance of any alternative projects.

Negative covenant   Covenant that prohibits certain actions by the borrower without prior written permission of the lender.

Negative pledge covenant   Covenant that prohibits a firm from pledging any of its assets as security for other debts.

Negotiable security   Security that is tradable.

Negotiated offering   Security offering in which the issue's features and other terms, including the underwriting fee, are determined by negotiation with a preselected investment bank. The issue is not put up for bid with other banks.

Net cash flow   A cash inflow or outflow from an investment during a given period, usually calculated as profit plus depreciation, less any required additions to working capital.

Net lease   Financial lease under which the lessee is responsible for maintenance and insurance of the leased asset in addition to property taxes.

Net-net lease   Financial lease under which the lessee must also return the asset to the lessor at the end of the lease with a prespecified value.

Net operating income   The firm's earnings before interest and taxes (EBIT).

Net present value (NPV)   Present value of a project's cash flows minus the initial investment.

Net present value profile   Graph showing the relationship between the NPV of a project and the discount rate used to compute the NPV.

Net profit margin   Profitability ratio: net income divided by sales.

Net profits rule   The rule that prohibits dividend payments in excess of retained earnings.

Net working capital   Current assets less current liabilities. Also known as *working capital.*

Net worth   The book value of the equity.

New product introduction   An investment associated with the introduction of a new product or service.

Next-in, first-out (NIFO)   Inventory valuation method that values goods taken out of inventory at their replacement value.

Nominal interest rate   The actual or current interest rate.

Nominal quantities   Quantities that are measured in money terms, not adjusted for inflation.

Noncash charge   A cost, such as depreciation, that does not involve an expenditure of cash.

Nonrecourse   A provision in a factoring arrangement in which the factor bears the credit risk on the receivable.

Note   An unsecured bond with a short maturity.

Note issuance facility   A facility provided by a syndicate of banks that allows a borrower to issue some maximum amount of short-term notes that are then placed by the group. Borrowers usually have the right to sell their notes to the bank syndicate at a price equal to some prearranged spread over LIBOR.

Notional principal   Reference amount against which interest on a swap is calculated.

One-for-one futures hedge   A hedge in which the risk being managed can be exactly matched by an available futures contract.

Open account   Payment method in which a seller ships the goods first and bills the customer later.

Open-end mortgage   Mortgage that permits the firm to issue additional bonds secured by the same property.

Operating cash flow   The sum of net income plus any noncash charges to income less changes in working capital.

Operating cycle   The length of time from the purchase of resources until the conversion of the finished product into cash.

Operating exposure   Degree to which an exchange rate change will alter a company's future operating cash flows.

Operating lease   Short-term lease that may be cancelled at the option of the lessee.

Operating profit margin   Profitability ratio: the ratio of EBIT to sales.

Opportunity cost   The cost of the road not taken. Any decision made involves a decision not to do something else. The lost profit on the next-best alternative is the opportunity cost.

Opportunity cost of capital   The return forgone on the best available investment alternative. This depends on the rate of interest at which money can be invested.

Option   The right—but not the obligation—to do something in the future.

Option premium   The value of the option in excess of the cash flow that would be received from immediate exercise.

Ordinary annuity   An annuity in which the payments occur at the end of each period.

Organizational assets   Intangible assets that cannot be separated from the firm as an ongoing operation. Such assets include managers and others with firm-specific knowledge and skills, a network of outside distributors and suppliers, strong brands, and a reputation for quality and reliability.

Organized exchanges   An actual physical place for the exchange of financial assets.

Originating house   The investment house that handles a security offering.

Out-of-the-money option   Option that would not be exercised at the asset's current market value.

Overdraft   Written order, directed to a bank, to pay a stated sum that is in excess of the funds available in the account for which the order is to be paid.

Overhanging issue   Convertible issue whose underlying stock value has not risen high enough to force conversion.

Over-the-counter (OTC) markets   A set of dealers tied together by a telecommunications network that allows market makers to facilitate the exchange of financial assets.

Partial spinoff   Partial offering of shares in a subsidiary. The spinoff allows subsidiary managers to own a stake in their own operation while ensuring that both corporate management and the market scrutinize their actions.

Partnership   A form of business organization involving shared ownership by two or more individuals. Unlike corporations, the partners (owners) do not usually have limited liability.

Par value   See *Face value.*

Payables period   The length of time, on average, it takes a company to pay its suppliers of goods and services.

Payback period   The length of time necessary to recoup an investment's cost.

Payment date   The date a firm mails out the dividend checks.

Payments netting   Reducing funds transfers between affiliates to only a netted amount. Netting can be done bilaterally (between pairs of affiliates) or multilaterally (taking all affiliates together).

Percent-of-sales method   A forecasting method that estimates the level of each expense, asset, and liability item as a percent of sales.

Perfectly competitive capital markets   A financial market in which buyers and sellers can (1) enter and leave freely, (2) buy and sell securities with no transactions costs, and (3) have costless access to economically relevant information.

Permanent current assets   The level of current assets needed at all times to support a given level of sales.

Perpetuity   A set of annuity payments that continue forever.

Pledging accounts receivable   An arrangement whereby a firm uses receivables as collateral against a loan.

Poison pill   Anti-takeover device that gives the shareholders the right to buy additional securities in the surviving company at very attractive prices if their company is the target of a hostile bid.

Political risk   Uncertain government action that affects the value of a firm.

Pooling   Transfer of excess affiliate cash into a central account (pool) usually located in a low-tax country, where all corporate funds are managed by corporate staff.

Pooling of interest method   Method of accounting for mergers whereby the assets and liabilities of the two merging firms are simply added together.

Portfolio risk   The variability associated with the return on a portfolio of assets.

Postcontractual opportunism   A situation in which one party to a contract subsequently takes advantage of the other party.

Preauthorized payment   System in which customers allow their accounts to be charged periodically by a supplier up to a maximum amount.

Preemptive right   Right of first refusal held by shareholders to purchase new common stock issues in order to maintain proportional ownership.

Preferred stock   A type of equity security whose dividends take preference over the payment of dividends on common stock.

Present value (PV)   The amount of cash today that is equivalent in value to the payment or stream of payments in the future.

Present value interest factor (PVIF)   The present value of $1 to be received at a specific date in the future, given a particular discount rate.

Present value of an annuity   The cash amount today that is the equivalent in value to a stream of annuity payments to be received in the future.

Present value of growth opportunities (PVGO)   The value created by the presence of profitable future investment opportunities.

Price-earnings multiple   Price per share divided by earnings per share.

Primary claim   The claims issued to financial intermediaries by borrowers.

Prime rate   The interest rate a bank charges its most creditworthy customers.

Principal   The amount invested on which interest is earned.

Principal only (PO)   Package of principal amounts stripped from bonds and sold separately.

Private placements   Securities that are sold directly to a limited number of individual investors or financial institutions, such as a pension fund or life insurance company.

Privileged subscription   New equity issue first offered to a firm's current stockholders instead of being sold through a public offering.

Processing float   Time it takes a check to pass through a company's accounting system on its way to be deposited.

Product cycle   The time it takes to bring a new or improved product to market.

Product line cannibalization   When a new product takes away sales from an existing product line.

Profitability index   Present value of the cash flows from a project divided by its initial cost.

Profitability ratios   Ratios that measure management effectiveness by examining returns on sales, assets, and shareholder's equity.

Pro forma financial statements   Forecasted financial statements.

Project post-audit   A comparison of a project's actual cash flows with the projected cash flows.

Promissory note   Unconditional promise to pay the face amount of a loan at a specified date in the future.

Prospectus   A brochure intended for prospective investors that summarizes the information in the registration statement.

Proxy   Transfer of a shareholder's right to vote to a second party.

Proxy fight   Battle between management and an outside group that involves both sides soliciting other shareholders for the right to cast their proxies.

Public offering   Security sold to the general public.

Purchase method   Method of accounting for a merger whereby the acquired firm is treated as an investment. Any excess of the amount paid over the book value of the assets is recorded as an asset called *goodwill* on the balance sheet of the combined firm.

Purchase of assets   Acquisition of another firm's assets.

Purchasing power   The quantity of goods and services that can be bought with a given amount of money.

Purchasing power parity   Theory stating that the ratio between domestic and foreign price levels should equal the equilibrium exchange rate between domestic and foreign currencies.

Pure-play technique   Method for determining the risk-adjusted cost of capital for a division of a multi-division firm by using data from publicly traded firms whose business risk matches that of the division.

Put option   An option permitting its holder to sell a certain asset at an agreed price and terms within a specified time.

Quick ratio   Measure of liquidity: current assets minus inventories divided by current liabilities. Also known as the *acid-test ratio*.

Real assets   Assets whose value is tied to their physical characteristics.

Real interest rate   The nominal (observed) interest rate adjusted for inflation.

Real quantities   Quantities that are measured in inflation-adjusted terms. For example, real cash flows are the flow that we would see in the absence of inflation.

Recourse   If pledged receivables cannot be collected, the lender can ask the firm to make good on the loan.

Red herring   A preliminary prospectus that sets forth the basic facts about a company and the proposed issue.

Refunding   Process of replacing high-interest debt with less expensive debt in the event of a decline in interest rates.

Registration statement   The statement that sets forth detailed information concerning a firm's history, its operations, and its proposed financing.

Regulatory arbitrage   The process whereby users of the capital markets issue and trade securities in financial markets with the lowest regulatory standards.

Related diversification   A business strategy in which a firm gets involved in other businesses that are related to its major businesses through either customers served or technologies utilized.

Remote disbursement   Technique that involves writing checks drawn on banks in relatively remote areas in an effort to increase the time it takes for the checks to be cashed and accounts debited.

Reorganization plan   Plan that describes how a company in Chapter 11 will be reorganized.

Replacement chain   Sequential replacement of an asset with an equivalent asset over some time period.

Repurchase agreements (RPs or "repos")   Borrowing transaction that involves selling government securities to an investor with the promise to repurchase them at a higher price on a specified future date.

Required rate of return   The minimum acceptable return on an investment project.

Required rate of return on equity   The minimum acceptable rate on the equity financed portion of a project. Also known as the *cost of equity capital*.

Residual dividend policy   An approach whereby earnings in excess of those needed to finance the equity portion of new projects is paid out in dividends.

Restrictive covenant   A provision in a debt agreement that limits a firm's ability to engage in certain actions.

Restructuring   A change in the firm's capital structure, incentive system, operations, ownership, or lines of business in order to increase shareholder value.

Retained earnings   Earnings leftover for reinvestment in the firm after dividends have been paid.

Return on assets (ROA)   Profitability ratio: net income divided by total assets. Also known as *return on investment*.

Return on equity (ROE) Profitability ratio: net income divided by equity capital.

Revaluation Increase in the spot value of a currency.

Revolving credit line An agreement under which a bank or group of banks is legally committed to extend credit up to a stated maximum.

Rights The option to buy a prespecified number of shares at a set price over a short period of time.

Rights offering New equity issue offered on a privileged subscription basis.

Rights-on When shares are sold, the new owner receives the right.

Risk The uncertainty associated with future cash flows. Uncertainty is typically measured by the variance or standard deviation of these future cash flows.

Risk-adjusted required rate of return A required return that reflects the risk characteristics of the cash flows being discounted.

Rule 415 Rule enacted in 1982 that allows companies to market their securities by means of the shelf registration procedure.

Safe harbor leases Leases that enable lessors to get tax benefits of ownership even though the economic ownership was held by the lessee.

Sale and leaseback Under this arrangement, a firm sells an asset it already owns and then leases the asset back from the buyer.

Scorched earth tactics Takeover defenses that imperil the defending firm itself.

Seasonal dating Credit terms under which a seller will ship goods in advance of a seasonal period but set the payment due date following that period.

Secondary claims The claims issued by financial intermediaries to savers.

Secondary market The market in which previously issued securities are traded.

Securities Act of 1933 Federal law regulating public offerings. Under this act, companies selling securities to the public must first register the issue with the Securities and Exchange Commission.

Securities and Exchange Commission (SEC) The federal government agency established under the Securities Act of 1933 to regulate publicly issued securities.

Securitization Matching up borrowers and lenders by way of the public financial markets rather than through financial intermediaries.

Security market line (SML) The relationship between risk and required returns for individual securities.

Segmented markets theory A theory of the term structure of interest rates that rests on the idea that the debt markets consist of a set of submarkets based on maturity preferences of buyers and sellers. Interest rates are determined by supply and demand conditions within each segment.

Selling concession The fee paid to the actual sellers of a security who are not members of the underwriting syndicate.

Selling group The group organized to market newly issued securities. This group usually comprises the sales organizations of the syndicate members and the security dealers and brokers.

Senior debt Bonds whose claims are paid off before the claims of subordinated creditors.

Sensitivity analysis Procedure to systematically study the effect of changes in the values of key parameters on the project's NPV.

Serial bond With this type of bond, a creditor will know in advance which bonds will be repurchased first and when.

Service lease See *Operating lease.*

Share repurchase The process whereby a firm buys back its own stock.

Shark repellant Defensive maneuvers by a target firm to ward off an acquirer in a hostile takeover attempt.

Shelf registration Procedure that allows companies to make continuous securities offerings without further SEC sign-off after filing a single prospectus.

Short-term debt Debt that must be paid back within a year.

Simple interest   Interest received only on the principal amount of the investment.

Simulation analysis   Procedure to analyze the risk of a project by representing its NPV by a probability distribution rather than as a single number, as in sensitivity analysis.

Sinking fund   Bond provision that requires the firm to pay a certain amount of money into a fund that is then used to repay the bonds. Some preferred stock issues also have sinking fund provisions.

Sole proprietorship   A form of business organization in which a single person owns the enterprise and is responsible for its debts.

Spontaneous sources of funds   Liabilities such as payables and accruals that increase spontaneously as a firm's sales increase.

Spot market   The market in which currencies and other commodities are traded for immediate delivery, which is actually within two business days after the transaction has been concluded. Also known as *cash market*.

Spot rate   Price at which foreign exchange can be bought or sold today with payment made within two business days.

Spread   The price differential at which investment bankers buy a security and the price at which they can resell it to the public.

Standard deviation   The square root of the variance of a probability distribution. In finance, the standard deviation of a probability distribution of investment returns is used as a measure of risk.

Standby agreement   An agreement in which an investment banker agrees to buy any unsold securities from a rights offering at a predetermined price.

Standby fee   The fee paid to underwriters in a rights offering.

Statement of cash flows   Financial statement that attempts to account for all sources and uses of cash during an accounting period.

Stock dividend   The payment of additional shares to common stockholders.

Stock repurchase   Corporate repurchase of its own common stock.

Stock split   Proportionate increase in the number of common shares.

Straight-line depreciation   With this method, a fixed asset is depreciated in equal yearly amounts over its life.

Strategic analysis   A look at a firm in terms of its internal strengths and weaknesses and its external opportunities and threats.

Strategic block investing   The purchase of enough stock to demand an important voice in the target company's affairs.

Strategic fit   A situation in which different businesses share common (1) production technologies, (2) distribution channels, or (3) skills. In these circumstances, management can create value through related diversification.

Subordinated debentures   Bonds ranking behind senior debt in terms of claim on assets. In the event of default, subordinated claims are paid only after all other creditor claims are fully satisfied.

Subscription price   The price per share that must be paid under a rights offering.

Subsidiary   An affiliate that is a separate incorporated entity. In a global context, a foreign-based affiliate is incorporated under the laws of the host country.

Sunk cost   An expenditure that has already been made and cannot be recovered regardless of what else is done.

Sunk cost fallacy   Mistaken idea that past expenditures on a project should influence the decision on whether to continue or terminate a project.

Sustainable growth rate   Maximum growth rate for a firm that chooses to maintain a specific debt ratio and refuses to issue more common stock.

Syndicate   A group of investment banks formed to share the risks and assist in the distribution of a new issue of securities.

Synergistic acquisition   An acquisition built on strategic fit in which the value of the surviving entity is greater than the sum of the two firms valued separately.

Take-up fee   The fee paid to the underwriters for each share they must buy in a standby agreement.

Target capital structure   The financing mix that a firm intends to use in the future to pay for new accepted projects.

Tax-oriented lease   Lease that qualifies as a true lease for tax purposes.

Tax shield   The value of the savings associated with a permissible tax deduction. Depreciation and interest expense are the two most important tax shields dealt with in corporate finance.

Temporary current assets   Those assets needed to support seasonal and other short-term needs.

Tender offer   Offer by the bidder to purchase a stated number of shares at a premium above the current market price.

Terminal value   The value of an investment project at its end. For longlived projects, the terminal value refers to the present value of a project's cash flows beyond some initial evaluation period.

Terminal warehouse   A public warehouse where goods are stored until released on the lender's orders.

Terminal warehouse receipt   Receipt issued by a warehouse company that lists the inventory placed in a public warehouse.

Term loan   A debt contract with a financial intermediary having a specified schedule of principal and interest payments.

Term structure of interest rates   The relationship between the interest rates on debt of the same credit quality and maturity.

Theoretical value   Value of the option if the holder were forced to exercise it immediately.

Times interest earned   Leverage ratio: EBIT divided by annual interest expense.

Time value of money   The idea that a dollar today is worth more than a dollar in the future.

Tombstone   Advertisement in the financial press listing the underwriters of a new security issue.

Total asset turnover   Activity ratio: net sales divided by total assets.

Trade acceptance   Draft accepted by a commercial enterprise.

Trade draft   Draft addressed to a commercial enterprise.

Trade loading   A practice whereby manufacturers induce wholesalers—usually through price discounts—to buy more product than they can promptly sell. The effect is to shift future sales and profits to the current accounting period.

Transaction exposure   Extent to which a given exchange rate change will alter the value of foreign currency–denominated transactions already entered into.

Transaction loan   A single loan that is negotiated and administered by itself.

Transfer price   Price at which one unit of a firm sells goods or services to an affiliated firm.

Treasury bill   Short-term debt issued by the central government of many countries.

Treasury stock   Issued common stock repurchased by the firm.

Trend analysis   The comparison of a company's ratios over time.

True lease   Lease recognized the tax authorities as providing the lessor with the benefits and risks of ownership.

Trustee   Person whose job it is to ensure that the terms of a bond indenture are meet.

Trust receipt   Financing arrangement under which a firm pledges to hold in trust for the lender proceeds from the sale of certain identified inventory.

Two-tiered price offer   Takeover bid in which the acquiring firm initially offers a large premium above market price for a controlling portion of the target firm's shares. Later, a lower price is offered for the remaining shares.

Underwriting   The process of buying the entire issue of a new security and then reselling it to the public.

Universal banking   A system of banking in which commercial banks not only perform investment banking services but also take major equity positions in their client firms.

Universal commercial paper (UCP)   Commercial paper issued by U.S. corporations that is both denominated and payable in specified foreign currencies, yet is settled in the United States.

Unlevered beta   The beta of a firm's assets. This would also be the beta we would observe on the stock of a firm that is entirely equity-financed. Also known as *asset beta.*

Unlevering   Converting a leveraged (equity) beta to its all-equity value.

Unrelated diversification   A situation in which a company gets involved in areas that are unrelated to its core businesses. Also known as *conglomerate diversification.*

Unsystematic risk   Risk that can be eliminated through diversification. For common stock, the risk that is unrelated to movements in the market.

Value-additivity principle   The principle that present values are additive; thus, the net present value of a set of independent projects is the sum of the NPVs of the individual projects.

Value-based analysis   Method of analyzing a company by calculating the value of each business unit in a company's portfolio. If the sum of these values exceeds the market value of the company as a whole, a restructuring opportunity exists.

Value compensation   Bank operating procedure whereby a firm does not give up domestic funds until foreign funds are provided.

Value dating   Refers to when value (credit) is given for funds transferred between banks.

Value gap   The difference between the value of a firm optimally managed and the actual value of the firm.

Variance   The sum of the squared deviations between the actual and expected returns, weighted by the associated probabilities.

Venture capitalists   An investor who puts money into new businesses.

Warrant   Security that gives the holder the right to purchase a prespecified number of common shares over the course of a prespecified time period.

Weighted average cost of capital   The after-tax cost of each source of capital weighted by the proportion of these capital sources that will be used to finance new projects. The weight should be based on market, not book, values.

White knight   Third party who steps in at the target's behest to rescue the target from a hostile takeover bid.

Winner's curse   A problem that occurs in an acquisition setting in which the buyer overvalues the target and therefore pays too much.

Working capital   Current assets less current liabilities. Also known as *net working capital.*

Yield curve   A graphical representation of the term structure of interest rates.

Yield to maturity   The interest or discount rate that equates a bond's price with present value of its coupon interest and principal payments.

Zero-balance account   Service that moves all excess cash balances from a firm's various bank accounts into a single account, from which all disbursements are funded. Transfers are made automatically and all individual accounts are maintained at a zero balance.

Zero-beta portfolio   A portfolio having no systematic risk.

Zero-sum game   A type of game wherein one player can gain only at the expense of some other player.

Z-score   Financial model that combines financial ratios to measure the likelihood of bankruptcy.

Index

SINGLE PC LICENSE AGREEMENT AND LIMITED WARRANTY

READ THIS LICENSE CAREFULLY BEFORE OPENING THIS PACKAGE. BY OPENING THIS PACKAGE, YOU ARE AGREEING TO THE TERMS AND CONDITIONS OF THIS LICENSE. IF YOU DO NOT AGREE, DO NOT OPEN THE PACKAGE. PROMPTLY RETURN THE UNOPENED PACKAGE AND ALL ACCOMPANYING ITEMS TO THE PLACE YOU OBTAINED THEM FOR A FULL REFUND OF ANY SUMS YOU HAVE PAID FOR THE SOFTWARE. THESE TERMS APPLY TO ALL LICENSED SOFTWARE ON THE DISK EXCEPT THAT THE TERMS FOR USE OF ANY SHAREWARE OR FREEWARE ON THE DISKETTES ARE AS SET FORTH IN THE ELECTRONIC LICENSE LOCATED ON THE DISK:

1. GRANT OF LICENSE and OWNERSHIP: The enclosed computer programs ("Software") are licensed, not sold, to you by Prentice-Hall, Inc. ("We" or the "Company") and in consideration of your purchase or adoption of the accompanying Company textbooks and/or other materials, and your agreement to these terms. We reserve any rights not granted to you. You own only the disk(s) but we and/or our licensors own the Software itself. This license allows you to use and display your copy of the Software on a single computer (i.e., with a single CPU) at a single location for academic use only, so long as you comply with the terms of this Agreement. You may make one copy for back up, or transfer your copy to another CPU, provided that the Software is usable on only one computer.

2. RESTRICTIONS: You may <u>not</u> transfer or distribute the Software or documentation to anyone else. Except for backup, you may <u>not</u> copy the documentation or the Software. You may <u>not</u> network the Software or otherwise use it on more than one computer or computer terminal at the same time. You may <u>not</u> reverse engineer, disassemble, de-compile, modify, adapt, translate, or create derivative works based on the Software or the Documentation. You may be held legally responsible for any copying or copyright infringement which is caused by your failure to abide by the terms of these restrictions.

3. TERMINATION: This license is effective until terminated. This license will terminate automatically without notice from the Company if you fail to comply with any provisions or limitations of this license. Upon termination, you shall destroy the Documentation and all copies of the Software. All provisions of this Agreement as to limitation and disclaimer of warranties, limitation of liability, remedies or damages, and our ownership rights shall survive termination.

4. LIMITED WARRANTY AND DISCLAIMER OF WARRANTY: Company warrants that for a period of 60 days from the date you purchase this SOFTWARE (or purchase or adopt the accompanying textbook), the Software, when properly installed and used in accordance with the Documentation, will operate in substantial conformity with the description of the Software set forth in the Documentation, and that for a period of 30 days the disk(s) on which the Software is delivered shall be free from defects in materials and workmanship under normal use. The Company does not warrant that the Software will meet your requirements or that the operation of the Software will be uninterrupted or error-free. Your only remedy and the Company's only obligation under these limited warranties is, at the Company's option, return of the disk for a refund of any amounts paid for it by you or replacement of the disk.

THIS LIMITED WARRANTY IS THE ONLY WARRANTY PROVIDED BY THE COMPANY AND ITS LICENSORS, AND THE COMPANY AND ITS LICENSORS DISCLAIM ALL OTHER WARRANTIES, EXPRESS OR IMPLIED, INCLUDING WITHOUT LIMITATION, THE IMPLIED WARRANTIES OF MERCHANTABILITY AND FITNESS FOR A PARTICULAR PURPOSE. THE COMPANY DOES NOT WARRANT, GUARANTEE OR MAKE ANY REPRESENTATION REGARDING THE ACCURACY, RELIABILITY, CURRENTNESS, USE, OR RESULTS OF USE, OF THE SOFTWARE.

5. LIMITATION OF REMEDIES AND DAMAGES: IN NO EVENT, SHALL THE COMPANY OR ITS EMPLOYEES, AGENTS, LICENSORS, OR CONTRACTORS BE LIABLE FOR ANY INCIDENTAL, INDIRECT, SPECIAL, OR CONSEQUENTIAL DAMAGES ARISING OUT OF OR IN CONNECTION WITH THIS LICENSE OR THE SOFTWARE, INCLUDING FOR LOSS OF USE, LOSS OF DATA, LOSS OF INCOME OR PROFIT, OR OTHER LOSSES, SUSTAINED AS A RESULT OF INJURY TO ANY PERSON, OR LOSS OF OR DAMAGE TO PROPERTY, OR CLAIMS OF THIRD PARTIES, EVEN IF THE COMPANY OR AN AUTHORIZED REPRESENTATIVE OF THE COMPANY HAS BEEN ADVISED OF THE POSSIBILITY OF SUCH DAMAGES. IN NO EVENT SHALL THE LIABILITY OF THE COMPANY FOR DAMAGES WITH RESPECT TO THE SOFTWARE EXCEED THE AMOUNTS ACTUALLY PAID BY YOU, IF ANY, FOR THE SOFTWARE OR THE ACCOMPANYING TEXTBOOK. BECAUSE SOME JURISDICTIONS DO NOT ALLOW THE LIMITATION OF LIABILITY IN CERTAIN CIRCUMSTANCES, THE ABOVE LIMITATIONS MAY NOT ALWAYS APPLY TO YOU.

6. GENERAL: THIS AGREEMENT SHALL BE CONSTRUED IN ACCORDANCE WITH THE LAWS OF THE UNITED STATES OF AMERICA AND THE STATE OF NEW YORK, APPLICABLE TO CONTRACTS MADE IN NEW YORK, AND SHALL BENEFIT THE COMPANY, ITS AFFILIATES AND ASSIGNEES. HIS AGREEMENT IS THE COMPLETE AND EXCLUSIVE STATEMENT OF THE AGREEMENT BETWEEN YOU AND THE COMPANY AND SUPERSEDES ALL PROPOSALS OR PRIOR AGREEMENTS, ORAL, OR WRITTEN, AND ANY OTHER COMMUNICATIONS BETWEEN YOU AND THE COMPANY OR ANY REPRESENTATIVE OF THE COMPANY RELATING TO THE SUBJECT MATTER OF THIS AGREEMENT. If you are a U.S. Government user, this Software is licensed with "restricted rights" as set forth in subparagraphs (a)-(d) of the Commercial Computer-Restricted Rights clause at FAR 52.227-19 or in subparagraphs (c)(1)(ii) of the Rights in Technical Data and Computer Software clause at DFARS 252.227-7013, and similar clauses, as applicable.

Should you have any questions concerning this agreement or if you wish to contact the Company for any reason, please contact in writing:

Director New Media
Higher Education Division
Business Publishing Group
Prentice-Hall, Inc.
One Lake Street
Upper Saddle River, NJ 07458